Fodor's First Edition

Naples and the Amalfi Coast

The complete guide, thoroughly up-to-date

Packed with details that will make your trip

The must-see sights, off and on the beaten path

What to see, what to skip

Mix-and-match vacation itineraries

City strolls, countryside adventures

Smart lodging and dining options

Essential local do's and taboos

Transportation tips, distances and directions

Key contacts, savvy travel tips

When to go, what to pack

Clear, accurate, easy-to-

D1056927

Fodor's Travel Publications • New York, Toronto, London, Sydney, Auckland
www.fodors.com

Fodor's Naples and the Amalfi Coast

EDITOR: Robert I. C. Fisher

Editorial Contributors: Gregory W. Bailey, Frank Gerard Godlewski, Lea Lane, Mark Walters

Editorial Production: Tom Holton

Maps: David Lindroth, *cartographer*; Rebecca Baer, *map editor*

Design: Fabrizio La Rocca, *creative director*; Guido Caroti, *art director*; Jolie Novak, *photo editor*

Cover Design: Pentagram

Production/Manufacturing: Mike Costa

Cover Photograph: Robert I. C. Fisher (view from terrace at Hotel San Pietro, Positano)

Copyright

First Edition

ISBN 0–679–00457–2

ISSN 1527–4837

Special Sales

Fodor's Travel Publications are available at special discounts for bulk purchases for sales promotions or premiums. Special editions, including personalized covers, excerpts of existing guides, and corporate imprints, can be created in large quantities for special needs. For more information, contact your local bookseller or write to Special Markets, Fodor's Travel Publications, 201 East 50th Street, New York, NY 10022. Inquiries from Canada should be directed to your local Canadian bookseller or sent to Random House of Canada, Ltd., Marketing Department, 2775 Matheson Boulevard East, Mississauga, Ontario L4W 4P7. Inquiries from the United Kingdom should be sent to Fodor's Travel Publications, 20 Vauxhall Bridge Road, London SW1V 2SA, England.

PRINTED IN THE UNITED STATES OF AMERICA

10 9 8 7 6 5 4 3 2 1

Important Tip

Although all prices, opening times, and other details in this book are based on information supplied to us at press time, changes occur all the time in the travel world, and Fodor's cannot accept responsibility for facts that become outdated or for inadvertent errors or omissions. So **always confirm information when it matters,** especially if you're making a detour to visit a specific place.

CONTENTS

ON THE ROAD WITH FODOR'S

THE TRIPS YOU TAKE THIS YEAR AND NEXT are going to be significant trips, if only because they'll be your first in the new millennium. Acutely aware of that fact, we've pulled out all stops in preparing *Naples and the Amalfi Coast.* To guide you in putting together your experience in southern Italy, we've created multiday itineraries and neighborhood walks. And to direct you to the places that are truly worth your time and money in these important years, we've rallied the team of endearingly picky know-it-alls we're pleased to call our writers. Having seen all corners of the regions they cover for us, they're real experts. If you knew them, you'd poll them for tips yourself.

Many months with his nose buried in art history books helped **Gregory W. Bailey** cast his Texas days aside and blossom as a full-fledged Italian after relocating to Rome in 1996. While recording the sights, sounds, smells, and tastes of the Roman countryside, he ventured down to the southern end of Italy and fell in love with Naples, quickly learning to remain *sempre tranquilla* (always calm) when riding in a taxi that never bothered to stop for red lights and speeding buses. Even so, Gregory has decided to remain in much more tranquilla Rome, where he contributes to various publications, including *Saveur* and the *International Herald Tribune.* For this guidebook, he wrote nearly the entire Naples chapter (except the Nightlife, Arts, and Outdoor Activities and Sports sections) and also the Chapter 1 essay, "Napoli Ever After."

Having earned his architecture degree at New York City's Cooper Union, **Frank Gerard Godlewski** landed a job in the Milan studio of famed designer Aldo Rossi in the early 1980s. Family connections—the Godlewskis were a leading family of 19th-century Naples and helped found the city's celebrated Aquarium—led him to set up base in the Vesuvian city. Realizing that a country's beauty lies not in its monuments, not even in its pasta, but in its people, he was soon giving some of Naples's most talked-about (and written-up) parties, along with helping to produce features for

Gente Viaggio and *Elle Decor Italia.* Frank has given the benefit of his knowledge to the Nightlife and the Arts and Outdoor Activities and Sports sections of the Naples chapter; in addition, he helped craft the Essential Information chapter. Today, he curates special programs for the National Italian American Foundation.

Language editor, travel consultant, and naturalist, British-born **Mark Walters** has been able to practice French, German, *napolitano,* and on occasion even Italian for many years now from his base in Naples. He settled in the city by the bay as an English instructor for the British Council, but soon realized that there was more to life than toiling at the blackboard and became a tour guide and naturalist specializing in Mediterranean wildlife. In between playing field hockey, hiking, and dodging Italian motorcycles, Mark has dusted down his graduate studies in classical art and archaeology and now leads expeditions in Italy and Greece for such groups as the American Association for the Advancement of Science, the Commonwealth Club, and Betchart Expeditions, besides handling a broad portfolio of activities back in Naples. For this book, he wrote the chapters on the Bay of Naples and its islands.

Lea Lane covers the world in varied guises: She was a columnist at Gannett newspapers, managing editor of the newsletter "Travel Smart," author of a cruise book and a guide to New England inns, and a talking head on The Travel Channel. Having been to more than one hundred countries, she has a special place in her heart for Italy—after all, she spent two honeymoons there. For this book, she spent many weeks exhaustively visiting Campania sights, but now knows a lazy visitor might come to know the country quite well without ever stirring from one spot. "Instead of sallying forth to see Sorrento," she chuckles, "why not take root on a convenient café terrace and let Sorrento come to you?" For this edition, she wrote and researched—kilometer by beautiful kilometer—the chapter on Sorrento and the Amalfi Coast.

All that studying of art and architecture paid off for editor **Robert I. C. Fisher** on his frequent trips to Naples, especially when he accurately guessed the date of the Palazzo Donn'Anna based solely on its architectural ornament, which he viewed as he fell from the palazzo's terrace into the Bay of Naples (it's much saltier than he had imagined). Having been to Lake Como in northern Italy, he thought he knew what beauty was—that is, until he visited Ravello and Positano. In 1999 he wrote the text and took the photographs for the first book in Fodor's new full-color Escape series, *Escape to the Amalfi Coast*; this title captures twenty of the most noted destinations in Campania, from Greta Garbo's Villa Cimbrone to the sky-kissing terrace of the Hotel Cappuccini Convento, and can serve as a handy travel aperitif to the region.

Don't Forget to Write

Keeping a travel guide fresh and up-to-date is a big job. So we love your feedback—positive and negative—and follow up on all suggestions. Contact the Naples and the Amalfi Coast editor at editors@fodors.com or c/o Fodor's, 201 East 50th Street, New York, New York 10022. And have a wonderful trip!

Karen Cure

Editorial Director

Italy

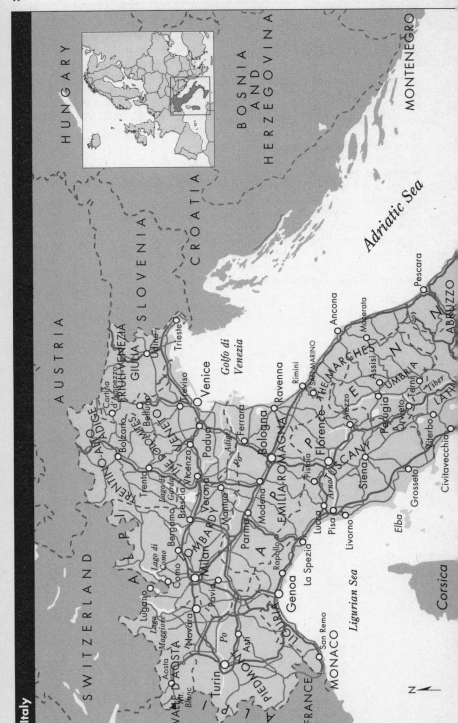

HUNGARY

AUSTRIA

SWITZERLAND

SLOVENIA

FRIULI-VENEZIA GIULIA

CROATIA

BOSNIA AND HERZEGOVINA

MONTENEGRO

Adriatic Sea

TRENTINO-ALTO ADIGE

VENETO

THE DOLOMITES

ALPS

LOMBARDY

VALLE D'AOSTA

PIEDMONT

LIGURIA

EMILIA-ROMAGNA

TUSCANY

THE MARCHES

UMBRIA

ABRUZZO

LATIUM

Corsica

Ligurian Sea

Elba

MONACO

FRANCE

Golfo di Venezia

Udine

Trieste

Cortina d'Ampezzo

Belluno

Bolzano

Trento

Treviso

Venice

Vicenza

Padua

Verona

Ferrara

Ravenna

Rimini

SAN MARINO

Ancona

Macerata

Pescara

Brescia

Bergamo

Lago di Garda

Adige

Po

Bologna

Modena

Florence

Arezzo

Assisi

Perugia

Orvieto

Terni

Viterbo

Tiber

Milan

Lago di Como

Pavia

Parma

Pistoia

Lucca

Pisa

Arno

Siena

Grosseto

Civitavecchia

Como

Lugano

Lago Maggiore

Novara

Po

Asti

Turin

Mt Blanc

Aosta

Rapallo

La Spezia

Livorno

Genoa

San Remo

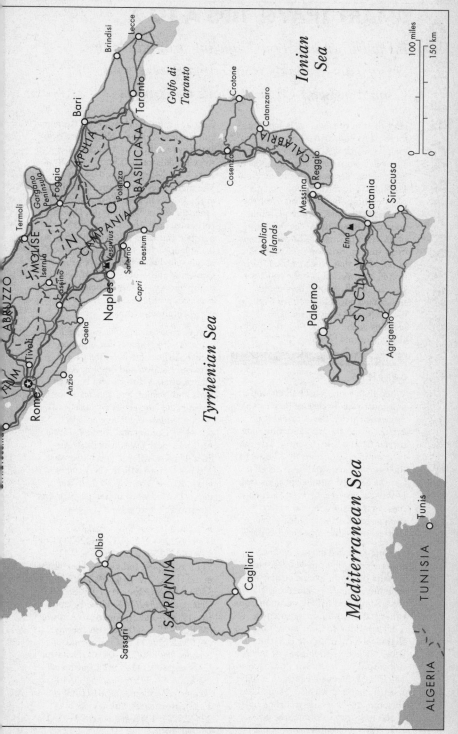

Ionian
Sea

100 miles
150 km

Lecce
Brindisi
Bari
Taranto
Golfo di
Taranto
Crotone
Catanzaro
APULIA
Foggia
Potenza
BASILICATA
CALABRIA
Cosenza
Termoli
Gargano
Peninsula
Reggio
Messina
Catania
Siracusa
MOLISE
Isernia
N
CAMPANIA
Vesuvius
Salerno
Paestum
Aeolian
Islands
Etna
SICILY
ABRUZZO
Cassino
Capri
Naples
Gaeta
Palermo
Agrigento
Tivoli
Anzio
Rome
Tyrrhenian Sea

Olbia
SARDINIA
Sassari
Cagliari

Mediterranean Sea
Tunis
TUNISIA
ALGERIA

SMART TRAVEL TIPS A TO Z

*Basic Information on Traveling around Naples,
Savvy Tips to Make Your Trip a Breeze, and
Companies and Organizations to Contact*

Half the fun of traveling is looking forward to your trip—but when you look forward, don't just daydream. There are plans to be made, things to learn about, serious work to be done. The following information will give you helpful pointers on many of the questions that arise when planning your trip. In addition, the organizations listed in this section will supplement the information in this guide book. Note that much of the information in this section is Italy-wide; for specific details about the various topics covered below *within* Campania itself, also consult the A to Z sections at the end of each regional chapter in this book.

AIR TRAVEL

CARRIERS

When flying internationally to Italy, you must usually choose between a domestic carrier, the national flag carrier of the country, and a foreign carrier from a third country. You may, for example, choose to fly Alitalia to Italy—as the national flag carrier it has the greatest number of nonstops. Domestic carriers, such as Meridiana, may have better connections to smaller destinations. Third-party carriers may have a price advantage.

No international carrier makes a transatlantic flight to Naples, but Alitalia offers an extensive and varied schedule of flights connecting Naples with Rome and Milan and numerous other Italian and European cities. They continue to offer more nonstop flights to Italy from the U.S. than any other airline, including, as of 1999, a nonstop flight from San Francisco to Milan's Malpensa Airport. Alitalia recently merged with KLM, making the company the largest airline outfit based in Europe. Among the cities that Alitalia connects with Naples (often with daily flights) are Amsterdam, Bologna, Cagliari, Florence,

Genoa, Milan, Palermo, Pisa, Rome, and Venice. Alitalia's North American gateways are Boston, Chicago, Los Angeles, Miami, San Francesco, New York City, Montreal, and Toronto. The main sales offices for the airline in the U.S. is in New York City, with other offices in Washington, D.C. and San Francisco; The main reservations number and sales office numbers are listed below. For further information about schedules, special fare promotions, and Italiatour—their tour-group agency—contact their web sites: www.alitalia.com or www.alitaliausa.com.

Many other carriers link European capitals with Naples—for instance, British Airlines offers a direct route between London and Naples, Air France offers a direct route between Paris and Naples, and Sabena offers a direct route connecting Brussels and Naples. Milan and Rome are also served by Continental Airlines, Delta Air Lines, and TWA. American Airlines, United Airlines, and Northwest Airlines fly into Milan. US Airways serves Rome. Lower-priced charter flights to a range of Italian destinations are available throughout the year.

➤ To AND FROM ITALY: **Alitalia** (☎ 800/223–5730; 0171/602–7111 or 0990/448–259 in Britain; 081/542–5111 in Naples; Individual sales offices in the U.S.: New York: ☎ 212/903–3300; Los Angeles: ☎ 310/568–5941; Chicago: ☎ 312/644–0404; Boston: ☎ 617/267–2882). **American Airlines** (☎ 800/433–7300). **British Airways** (☎ 0345/222–111). **Continental Airlines** (☎ 800/231–0856). **Delta Air Lines** (☎ 800/241–4141). **Lufthansa** (☎ 800/247–9297; 081/551–5440 in Naples). **Meridiana** (☎ 0171/839–2222). **Northwest Airlines** (☎ 800/225–2525). **TWA** (☎ 800/892–4141). **United Airlines** (☎ 800/538–2929). **US Airways** (☎ 800/428–4322).

➤ AROUND ITALY: **Air One** (☎ 06/488800). **Alitalia** (☎ 06/65621 or 06/65643 in Rome; 02/24991 in Milan; 1475/65640 within Italy). **Meridiana** (☎ 06/478041).

CHECK-IN & BOARDING

Assuming that not everyone with a ticket will show up, airlines routinely overbook planes. When that happens, airlines ask for volunteers to give up their seats. In return these volunteers usually get a certificate for a free flight and are rebooked on the next flight out. If there are not enough volunteers, the airline must choose who will be denied boarding. The first to get bumped are passengers who checked in late and those flying on discounted tickets, so **get to the gate and check in as early as possible,** especially during peak periods.

Always **bring a government-issued photo ID to the airport.** You may be asked to show it before you are allowed to check in.

CUTTING COSTS

The least-expensive airfares to Italy must usually be purchased in advance and are nonrefundable. It's smart to **call a number of airlines, and when you are quoted a good price, book it on the spot**—the same fare may not be available the next day. Always **check different routings** and look into using different airports. Travel agents, especially low-fare specialists (☞ Discounts & Deals, *below*), are helpful.

Consolidators are another good source. They buy tickets for scheduled international flights at reduced rates from the airlines, then sell them at prices that beat the best fare available directly from the airlines, usually without restrictions. Sometimes you can even get your money back if you need to return the ticket. Carefully read the fine print detailing penalties for changes and cancellations, and **confirm your consolidator reservation with the airline.**

When you **fly as a courier** you trade your checked-luggage space for a ticket deeply subsidized by a courier service. There are restrictions on when you can book and how long you can stay.

➤ CONSOLIDATORS: **Cheap Tickets** (☎ 800/377–1000). **Discount Airline Ticket Service** (☎ 800/576–1600). **Unitravel** (☎ 800/325–2222). **Up & Away Travel** (☎ 212/889–2345). **World Travel Network** (☎ 800/409–6753).

ENJOYING THE FLIGHT

All flights within Italy are smoke free. However, smoking is allowed on a limited number of international flights; **contact your carrier about its smoking policy.** For more legroom **request an emergency-aisle seat.** Don't sit in the row in front of the emergency aisle or in front of a bulkhead, where seats may not recline. If you have dietary concerns, **ask for special meals when booking.** These can be vegetarian, low-cholesterol, or kosher, for example. On long flights, try to maintain a normal routine, to help fight jet lag. At night **get some sleep.** By day **eat light meals, drink water** (not alcohol), and **move around the cabin** to stretch your legs.

FLYING TIMES

Flying time to Rome is 8½ hours from New York, 10–11 hours from Chicago, 11½ hours from Dallas (via New York), 11½ hours from Los Angeles, 2 hours from London (to Milan), and 12½ hours from Sydney.

HOW TO COMPLAIN

If your baggage goes astray or your flight goes awry, complain right away. Most carriers require that you **file a claim immediately.**

➤ AIRLINE COMPLAINTS: U.S. Department of Transportation Aviation Consumer Protection Division (✉ C-75, Room 4107, Washington, DC 20590, ☎ 202/366–2220). **Federal Aviation Administration Consumer Hotline** (☎ 800/322–7873).

AIRPORTS

Located just outside Naples, **Aeroporto Capodichino** serves the Campania region. It handles domestic and international flights, including several flights daily between Naples and Rome (flight time 45 minutes). From May to September there is direct **helicopter service** (☎ 081/584–1481) between Aeroporto Capodichino and Capri or Ischia. The major gateways to Italy include Rome's **Aeroporto Leonardo da Vinci,** better known as **Fiumicino,** and Milan's **Aeroporto Malpensa 2000** (MXP). Smaller, minor gateways are served by domestic and some international flights.

➤ AIRPORT INFORMATION: **Aeroporto Capodichino** (✉ Via Umberto Maddalena, 8 km/5 mi northwest of Naples, ☎ 081/789-6111). **Aeroporto Leonardo da Vinci** or **Fiumicino** (35 km/20 mi southeast of Rome, ☎ 06/65953640). **Aeroporto Malpensa 2000** (45 km/28 mi north of Milan, ☎ 02/74852200).

Bologna: Aeroporto Guglielmo Marconi (✉ Borgo Panigale, 7 km/4½ mi from Bologna, ☎ 051/6479615). **Florence: Aeroporto A. Vespucci,** called Perétola (✉ 6 km/4 mi northwest of Florence, ☎ 055/333498) and **Aeroporto Galileo Galilei** (✉ Pisa, 80 km/50 mi west of Florence, ☎ 050/500707). **Milan: Aeroporto Linate** (✉ 10 km/6 mi east of Milan, ☎ 02/74852200). **Palermo: Aeroporto Punta Raisi** (✉ 32 km/20 mi west of Palermo, ☎ 091/591698). **Venice: Aeroporto Marco Polo** (✉ Tessera, about 10 km/6 mi north of Venice, ☎ 041/2609260).

DUTY-FREE SHOPPING

As of July 1999 duty-free shopping in airports was eliminated in Italy (and Europe); you can still make in-flight duty-free purchases however.

BOAT & FERRY TRAVEL

As one of the great harbors of the world, Naples offers a wide array of boat, ferry (*traghetti*), hydrofoil (*aliscafo*), and steamer services between the city, the islands of the bay, and the Sorrentine peninsula. The main station is at the Molo Beverello—the port of Naples opposite the Castel Nuovo—along the waterfront of Piazza Municipio. Here, hydrofoils and ferries run by Caremar, Linee Laura, SNAV, and Alilauro connect Naples with Sorrento, Capri, Ischia, and Procida. Navigazione Libera del Golfo runs hydrofoils from the Molo Beverello to Amalfi and Positano. More hydrofoils depart for Sorrento, Capri, Ischia, and Procida from the Mergellina harbor (a short walk from the Mergellina train station) at the far western end of

the Riviera di Chiaia; the trip to Ischia and Procida is shorter and cheaper if you use the ferry that departs from Pozzuoli harbor. Next to the Molo Beverello is the Stazione Maritima (Molo Angioino), where larger ferries and steamers make trips to Ponza, the Aeolian Islands, Sicily, and Sardinia. *Il Mattino* features a *Per chi Parte* ("For Those Departing") section every day which lists schedules for Naples–Rome trains, flights from Capodichino Airport, and complete ferry and hydrofoil listings. *Qui Napoli,* the helpful monthly English-lanquage periodical for visitors to Naples, also lists ferry and hydrofoil schedules.

Hydrofoil service is generally twice as fast as ferries and double the price. Service is considerably more frequent during the summer months. For specific information about boat, ferry, and hydrofoil travel between Naples and other destinations on the Bay of Naples and the Amalfi Coast, *see* the A to Z sections at the end of each regional chapter. Car ferries operate to the islands of the Bay of Naples, but advance reservations are best.

➤ BOAT & FERRY INFORMATION: **Caremar** (☎ 081/551–3882). **FS** (☎ 0766/23273). **Lauro** (☎ 081/552–2838). **LMV/Linee Marittime Veloci** (☎ 081/552–7209). **Navigazione Laghi** (☎ 167/551801 toll-free or 0322/233200). **SNAV** (☎ 081/761–2348). **Siremar** (☎ 081/580–0340). **Tirrenia** (☎ 081/720–1111).

BUS TRAVEL

Campania's bus network is extensive and in some areas buses can be more direct (and therefore, faster) than local trains, so it's a good idea to **compare bus and train schedules.** Bus service outside cities is organized on a regional level, and often by private companies. Campania has two main bus companies, listed below. ANM handles buses within Naples, ACTP usually handles medium- and long-distance routes out of Naples, while SITA services the Amalfi Coast. For more specific information, *see* the A to Z sections at the end of each regional chapter.

➤ BUS INFORMATION: **ACTP** (✉ Via Arenaccia 29, Napoli, ☎ 081/700–1111). **ANM** (✉ Piazza Garibaldi, main Servizio CTP bus stop, Napoli, ☎ 081/763–1111). **SITA** (✉ Via Pisanelli 3, just south of Piazza Municipio, Napoli, ☎ 081/552–2176; 081/593–4644).

TICKETS

Tickets are not sold on board buses so you must purchase your tickets in advance by machine, at newsstands, or at tobacconists. Remember to time-stamp your ticket after you board as conductors often make spot-checks. Keep in mind that many ticket sellers close for several hours at midday, so it's always wise to stock up on bus tickets when you have the chance.

BUSINESS HOURS

BANKS & OFFICES

Banks are open weekdays 8:30 to 1:30 and 2:45 to 3:45. Most churches are open from early morning until noon or 12:30, when they close for three hours or more; they open again in the afternoon, closing about 7 PM or later.

Post offices are open Monday through Saturday 9 to 2; central and main district post offices stay open until 6 PM weekdays, 9 to 2 on Saturday.

MUSEUMS & SIGHTS

A few major sights, such as Naples's Museo Archeologico Nazionale, the Museo di Capodimente, and the Aquario, the famous excavations at Pompeii and Herculaneum, and the temples at Paestum, feature selected days with extended (day-long) opening hours during the summer months, but most attractions are only open from 9 AM to 1 or 2 PM. Museum hours vary and can change with the seasons: When this book refers to summer hours, it means approximately Easter to October; winter hours run from November to Easter. Many museums are closed one day a week, often on Monday. Always check locally.

SHOPS

Most shops are open from 9 to 1 and from 3:30 or 4 to 7:30, Monday through Saturday. In addition, clothing shops are generally closed on Monday mornings. Barbers and hairdressers, with some exceptions, are closed Sunday and Monday.

CAMERAS & PHOTOGRAPHY

The *Kodak Guide to Shooting Great Travel Pictures* is an excellent tool and is available in bookstores or from Fodor's Travel Publications.

➤ PHOTO HELP: **Kodak Information Center** (☎ 800/242–2424). *Kodak Guide to Shooting Great Travel Pictures* ($16.50 plus $4 shipping); contact Fodor's Travel Publications (☎ 800/533–6478).

EQUIPMENT PRECAUTIONS

Always **keep your film, tape, or computer disks out of the sun.** Carry an extra supply of batteries, and **be prepared to turn on your camera, camcorder, or laptop** to prove to security personnel that the device is real. Always **ask for hand inspection of film,** which becomes clouded after successive exposure to airport X-ray machines, and **keep videotapes and computer disks away from metal detectors.**

CAR RENTAL

Renting a car in Italy is helpful when exploring the off-the-beaten-track countryside, but not necessary, as the bus system throughout Campania is excellent and far-flung (indeed, it has to be, since many residents in Campania do not own their own vehicles). Signage on country roads is usually pretty good, but be prepared for fast and impatient fellow drivers. Major car-rental companies have boxy Ford-type cars (such as Astras) and Fiats in various sizes that are always in good condition.

➤ MAJOR AGENCIES: **Alamo** (☎ 800/ 522–9696; 0181/759–6200 in the U.K.). **Avis** (☎ 800/331–1084; 800/ 879–2847 in Canada; 02/9353–9000 in Australia; 09/525–1982 in New Zealand). **Budget** (☎ 800/527–0700; 0144/227–6266 in the U.K.). **Dollar** (☎ 800/800–6000; 0181/897–0811 in the U.K., where it is known as Eurodollar; 02/9223–1444 in Australia). **Hertz** (☎ 800/654–3001; 800/ 263–0600 in Canada; 0181/897– 2072 in the U.K.; 02/9669–2444 in Australia; 03/358–6777 in New Zealand). **National InterRent** (☎ 800/227–3876; 0345/222525 in the U.K., where it is known as Europcar InterRent). For specific information about car-rental agencies within Campania, *see* the A to Z sections in each regional chapter.

CUTTING COSTS

Most major American rental-car companies have offices or affiliates in Italy, but the rates are generally better if you make a reservation from abroad rather than from within Italy. To get the best deal **book through a travel agent who will shop around.** Do **look into wholesalers,** companies that do not own fleets but rent in bulk from those that do and often offer better rates than traditional car-rental operations. Payment must be made before you leave home. Note that in Italy no matter what your credit cards might refund you, Italian rental-car companies usually make it mandatory to purchase the collision-damage waiver (and do not allow your credit card to waive the fees).

➤ WHOLESALERS: **Auto Europe** (☎ 207/842–2000 or 800/223–5555, FAX 800–235–6321). **DER Travel Services** (✉ 9501 W. Devon Ave., Rosemont, IL 60018, ☎ 800/782–2424, FAX 800/282–7474 for information; 800/860–9944 for brochures). **Europe by Car** (☎ 212/581–3040 or 800/223–1516, FAX 212/246–1458). **Kemwel Holiday Autos** (☎ 914/835–3000 or 800/678–0678, FAX 914/835–5126).

INSURANCE

When driving a rented car you are generally responsible for any damage to or loss of the vehicle. Many companies impose mandatory theft insurance on all rentals; coverage costs $12–$18 a day or 25%.

Collision policies that car-rental companies sell for European rentals usually do not include stolen-vehicle coverage. Before you buy it, check your existing policies—you may already be covered. Note that in Italy, all car-rental companies make you buy theft-protection and collision-damage policies.

REQUIREMENTS & RESTRICTIONS

In Italy your own driver's license is acceptable. An International Driver's Permit is a good idea; it's available from the American or Canadian automobile association, and, in the United Kingdom, from the Automobile Association or Royal Automobile Club. These international permits are universally recognized, and having one in your wallet may save you a problem with the local authorities. In Italy you must be 21 years of age to rent an economy or subcompact car and at least 25 years of age to rent a bigger car.

SURCHARGES

Before you pick up a car in one city and leave it in another **ask about drop-off charges or one-way service fees,** which can be substantial. Note, too, that some rental agencies charge extra if you return the car before the time specified in your contract. To avoid a hefty refueling fee **fill the tank just before you turn in the car,** but be aware that gas stations near the rental outlet may overcharge.

CAR TRAVEL

There is an extensive network of *autostrade* (toll highways), complemented by equally well-maintained but free *superstrade* (expressways). The ticket you are issued upon entering an autostrada must be returned when you exit and pay the toll; on some shorter autostrade, mainly connecting highways, the toll is paid upon entering. Viacard cards, on sale at many autostrada locations, make paying tolls easier and faster. A *raccordo* is a ring road surrounding a city. *Strade statali* (state highways, denoted by *S* or *SS* numbers) may be single-lane roads, as are all secondary roads; directions and turnoffs are not always clearly marked.

AUTO CLUBS

➤ IN AUSTRALIA: **Australian Automobile Association** (☎ 02/6247–7311).

➤ IN CANADA: **Canadian Automobile Association** (CAA, ☎ 613/247–0117).

➤ IN NEW ZEALAND: **New Zealand Automobile Association** (☎ 09/377–4660).

➤ IN THE U.K.: **Automobile Association** (AA, ☎ 0990/500–600). **Royal Automobile Club** (RAC, ☎ 0990/722–722 for membership; 0345/121–345 for insurance).

➤ IN THE U.S.: **American Automobile Association** (☎ 800/564–6222).

EMERGENCIES

ACI Emergency Service offers 24-hour road service. Dial 116 from any phone, 24 hours a day, to reach the ACI dispatch operator.

GASOLINE

Gas stations are generally open Monday through Saturday from 7 AM to 7 PM with a break at lunchtime. Many stations have automatic self-service pumps which only accept bills of 10,000 lire and 50,000 lire. Gas stations on autostrade are open 24 hours. Gas costs about 1,900 lire per liter.

PARKING

Parking space is at a premium in Naples and most towns, but especially in the *centri storici* (historic centers), which are filled with narrow streets and restricted circulation zones. It is often a good idea (if not the only option) to park your car in a designated (preferably attended) lot. Parking in an area signposted ZONA DISCO (disk zone) is allowed for limited periods (from 30 minutes to two hours or more—the limit is posted); if you don't have the cardboard disk (inquire at the local tourist office) to show what time you parked, you can use a piece of paper. The *parcometro*, the Italian version of metered parking in which you put coins into a machine for a stamped ticket that you leave on the dashboard, has been introduced in some cities, including Naples. Within Naples, it is advisable to **leave your car only in designated parking areas.** A red sign with a horizontal white stripe through it means do not enter; a blue circular sign with a red slash or an X means no parking, as do the sings VIETATO SOSTARE, VIETATO DI SOSTA, and NON PARCHEGGIARE.

ROAD CONDITIONS

Autostrade are well maintained, as are most interregional highways. The condition of provincial (county) roads varies, but road maintenance at this level is generally good in Italy. Street and road signs are often challenging—a good map and patience are essential. Italians drive fast and are impatient with those who don't. Tailgaiting is the norm here—the only way to avoid it is to get out of the way.

RULES OF THE ROAD

Driving is on the right. Regulations are largely as in Britain and the United States, except that the police have the power to levy on-the-spot fines. In most Italian towns the use of the horn is forbidden in certain, if not all, areas; a large sign, ZONA DI SILENZIO, indicates where. Speed limits are 130 kph (80 mph) on autostrade and 110 kph (70 mph) on state and provincial roads, unless otherwise marked. Fines for driving after drinking are heavy, including the suspension of license and the additional possibility of six months' imprisonment.

CHILDREN IN ITALY

Although Italians love children and are generally very tolerant and patient with them, they provide few amenities for them. In restaurants and trattorias you may find a high chair or a cushion for the child to sit on, but rarely do they offer a children's menu. Order a *mezza porzione* (half-portion) of any dish, or ask the waiter for a *porzione da bambino* (child's portion).

Discounts do exist. Always ask about a *sconto bambino* (child's discount) before purchasing tickets. Children under a certain height ride free on municipal buses and trams. Children under 18 who are EU citizens are admitted free to state-run museums and galleries, and there are similar privileges in many municipal or private museums.

If you are renting a car don't forget to **arrange for a car seat** when you reserve.

FLYING

If your children are two or older **ask about children's airfares.** As a general rule, infants under two not occupying a seat fly at greatly reduced fares or even for free. When booking **confirm carry-on allowances** if you're traveling with infants. In general, for babies charged 10% of the adult fare, you are allowed one carry-on bag and a collapsible stroller; if the flight is full the stroller may have to be checked or you may be limited to less.

THE GOLD GUIDE / SMART TRAVEL TIPS

Experts agree that it's a good idea to use safety seats aloft for children weighing less than 40 pounds. Airlines set their own policies: U.S. carriers usually require that the child be ticketed, even if he or she is young enough to ride free, since the seats must be strapped into regular seats. Do **check your airline's policy about using safety seats during takeoff and landing.** And since safety seats are not allowed just everywhere in the plane, get your seat assignments early.

When reserving, **request children's meals or a freestanding bassinet** if you need them. But note that bulkhead seats, where you must sit to use the bassinet, may lack an overhead bin or storage space on the floor.

LODGING

Most hotels in Italy allow children under a certain age to stay in their parents' room at no extra charge, but others charge for them as extra adults; be sure to **find out the cutoff age for children's discounts.**

➤ CONTACTS: **ITT-Sheraton Hotels** (☎ 800/221–2340). **Club Med** (✉ 40 W. 57th St., New York, NY 10019, ☎ 800/258–2633). **Valtur** (✉ Piazza della Repubblica 59, Roma, ☎ 06/4821000, FAX 06/4870981).

CONSULATES

➤ AUSTRALIA: **Australian Consulate** (✉ Via Borgogna 2, Milan, ☎ 02/777041).

➤ CANADA: **Canadian Consulate** (✉ Via Zara 30, Rome, ☎ 06/445981).

➤ NEW ZEALAND: **New Zealand Consulate** (✉ Via Zara 28, Rome, ☎ 06/4417171).

➤ UNITED KINGDOM: **British Consulate** (✉ Via Francesco Crispi 122, off Piazza Amedeo, ☎ 081/583–8111).

➤ UNITED STATES: **U.S. Consulate** (✉ Piazza della Repubblica 2, at west end of Villa Comunale, ☎ 081/583–8111).

CONSUMER PROTECTION

Whenever shopping or buying travel services in Italy, **pay with a major credit card** so you can cancel payment or get reimbursed if there's a problem. If you're doing business with a particular company for the first time, **contact your local Better Business Bureau and the attorney general's offices** in your state and the company's home state, as well. Have any complaints been filed? Finally, if you're buying a package or tour, always **consider travel insurance** that includes default coverage (☞ Insurance, *below*).

➤ LOCAL BBBs: **Council of Better Business Bureaus** (✉ 4200 Wilson Blvd., Suite 800, Arlington, VA 22203, ☎ 703/276–0100, FAX 703/525–8277).

CUSTOMS & DUTIES

When shopping, **keep receipts** for all purchases. Upon reentering the country, **be ready to show customs officials what you've bought.** If you feel a duty is incorrect or object to the way your clearance was handled, note the inspector's badge number and ask to see a supervisor. If the problem isn't resolved, write to the appropriate authorities, beginning with the port director at your point of entry.

IN AUSTRALIA

Australia residents who are 18 or older may bring home $A400 worth of souvenirs and gifts (including jewelry), 250 cigarettes or 250 grams of tobacco, and 1,125 ml of alcohol (including wine, beer, and spirits). Residents under 18 may bring back $A200 worth of goods. Prohibited items include meat products. Seeds, plants, and fruits need to be declared upon arrival.

➤ INFORMATION: **Australian Customs Service** (Regional Director, ✉ Box 8, Sydney, NSW 2001, ☎ 02/9213–2000, FAX 02/9213–4000).

IN CANADA

Canadian residents who have been out of Canada for at least 7 days may bring home C$500 worth of goods duty-free. If you've been away less than 7 days but more than 48 hours, the duty-free allowance drops to C$200; if your trip lasts 24–48 hours, the allowance is C$50. You may not pool allowances with family members. Goods claimed under the C$500 exemption may follow you by mail; those claimed under the lesser exemptions must accompany you. Alcohol and tobacco products may be included in the 7-day and 48-hour exemptions but not in the 24-hour exemption. If you meet the age requirements of the province or territory through which you reenter Canada, you may bring in, duty-free, 1.14 liters (40 imperial ounces) of wine or liquor *or* 24 12-ounce cans or bottles of beer or ale. If you are 16 or older you may bring in, duty-free, 200 cigarettes and 50 cigars. Check ahead of time with Revenue Canada or the Department of Agriculture for policies regarding meat products, seeds, plants, and fruits.

You may send an unlimited number of gifts worth up to C$60 each duty-free to Canada. Label the package UNSOLICITED GIFT—VALUE UNDER $60. Alcohol and tobacco are excluded.

➤ INFORMATION: **Revenue Canada** (✉ 2265 St. Laurent Blvd. S, Ottawa, Ontario K1G 4K3, ☎ 613/993–0534; 800/461–9999 in Canada).

IN ITALY

Of goods obtained anywhere outside the EU or goods purchased in a duty-free shop within an EU country, the allowances are: (1) 200 cigarettes or 100 cigarillos or 50 cigars or 250 grams of tobacco; (2) 2 liters of still table wine or 1 liter of spirits over 22% volume or 2 liters of spirits under 22% volume or 2 liters of fortified and sparkling wines; and (3) 50 milliliters of perfume and 250 milliliters of toilet water.

Of goods obtained (duty and tax paid) within another EU country, the allowances are: (1) 800 cigarettes or 400 cigarillos or 400 cigars or 1 kilogram of tobacco; (2) 90 liters of still table wine plus (3) 10 liters of spirits over 22% volume plus 20 liters of spirits under 22% volume plus 60 liters of sparkling wines plus 110 liters of beer.

IN NEW ZEALAND

Homeward-bound residents 17 or older may bring back $700 worth of souvenirs and gifts. Your duty-free allowance also includes 4.5 liters of wine or beer; one 1,125-ml bottle of spirits; and either 200 cigarettes, 250 grams of tobacco, 50 cigars, or a combination of the three up to 250 grams. Prohibited items include meat products, seeds, plants, and fruits.

➤ INFORMATION: **New Zealand Customs** (Custom House, ✉ 50 Anzac Ave., Box 29, Auckland, New Zealand, ☎ 09/359–6655, FAX 09/359–6732).

IN THE U.K.

If you are a U.K. resident and your journey was wholly within the European Union (EU), you won't have to pass through customs when you return to the United Kingdom. If you plan to bring back large quantities of alcohol or tobacco, check EU limits beforehand. From countries outside the EU, including Italy, you may bring home, duty-free, 200 cigarettes or 50 cigars; 1 liter of spirits or 2 liters of fortified or sparkling wine or liqueurs; 2 liters of still table wine; 60 ml of perfume; 250 ml of toilet water; plus £136 worth of other goods, including gifts and souvenirs. If returning from outside the EU, prohibited items include meat products, seeds, plants, and fruits.

➤ INFORMATION: **HM Customs and Excise** (✉ Dorset House, Stamford St., Bromley Kent BR1 1XX, ☎ 0171/202–4227).

IN THE U.S.

U.S. residents who have been out of the country for at least 48 hours (and who have not used the $400 allowance or any part of it in the past 30 days) may bring home $400 worth of foreign goods duty-free.

U.S. residents 21 and older may bring back 1 liter of alcohol duty-free. In addition, regardless of your age, you are allowed 200 cigarettes and 100 non-Cuban cigars. Antiques, which the U.S. Customs Service defines as objects more than 100 years old, enter duty-free, as do original works of art done entirely by hand, including paintings, drawings, and sculptures.

You may also send packages home duty-free: up to $200 worth of goods for personal use, with a limit of one parcel per addressee per day (and no alcohol or tobacco products or perfume worth more than $5); label the

THE GOLD GUIDE / SMART TRAVEL TIPS

package PERSONAL USE and attach a list of its contents and their retail value. Do not label the package UNSOLICITED GIFT or your duty-free exemption will drop to $100. Mailed items do not affect your duty-free allowance on your return.

➤ INFORMATION: **U.S. Customs Service** (inquiries, ✉ 1300 Pennsylvania Ave. NW, Washington, DC 20229, ☎ 202/927–6724; complaints, ✉ Office of Regulations and Rulings, 1300 Pennsylvania Ave. NW, Washington, DC 20229; registration of equipment, ✉ Resource Management, 1300 Pennsylvania Ave. NW, Washington, DC 20229, ☎ 202/927–0540).

DINING

The restaurants we list are the cream of the crop in each price category. Properties indicated by a ✕🏠 are lodging establishments whose restaurant warrants a special trip. For price categories, see the price charts found under Pleasures and Pastimes in Chapters 2, 3, 4, and 5.

RESERVATIONS & DRESS

Reservations are always a good idea: we mention them only when they're essential or are not accepted. We mention dress only when men are required to wear a jacket or a jacket and tie.

DISABILITIES & ACCESSIBILITY

Italy has only recently begun to provide facilities such as ramps, telephones, and rest rooms for people with disabilities; such things are still the exception, not the rule. Travelers' wheelchairs must be transported free of charge, according to Italian law, but the logistics of getting a wheelchair on and off trains and buses can make this requirement irrelevant. Seats are reserved for people with disabilities on public transportation, but few buses have lifts for wheelchairs. High, narrow steps for boarding trains create additional problems. In many monuments and museums, even in some hotels and restaurants, architectural barriers make it difficult, if not impossible, for those with disabilities to gain access.

Contact the nearest Italian consulate about bringing a Seeing Eye dog into Italy; this requires an import license, a current certificate detailing the dog's inoculations, and a letter from your veterinarian certifying the dog's health.

➤ LOCAL RESOURCES: The **Italian Government Travel Office** (ENIT; ☞ Visitor Information, *below*) can give you a list of hotels that provide access and addresses of Italian associations for travelers with disabilities.

LODGING

When discussing accessibility with an operator or reservations agent **ask hard questions.** Are there any stairs, inside *or* out? Are there grab bars next to the toilet *and* in the shower/tub? How wide is the doorway to the room? To the bathroom? For the most extensive facilities meeting the latest legal specifications **opt for newer accommodations.**

TRAVEL AGENCIES

In the United States, although the Americans with Disabilities Act requires that travel firms serve the needs of all travelers, some agencies specialize in working with people with disabilities.

DISCOUNTS & DEALS

Be a smart shopper and **compare all your options** before making decisions. A plane ticket bought with a promotional coupon from travel clubs, coupon books, and direct-mail offers may not be cheaper than the least expensive fare from a discount ticket agency. And always keep in mind that what you get is just as important as what you save.

DISCOUNT RESERVATIONS

To save money **look into discount-reservations services** with toll-free numbers, which use their buying power to get a better price on hotels, airline tickets, even car rentals. When booking a room, always **call the hotel's local toll-free number** (if one is available) rather than the central reservations number—you'll often get a better price. Always ask about special packages or corporate rates.

When shopping for the best deal on hotels and car rentals **look for guar-**

anteed exchange rates, which protect you against a falling dollar. With your rate locked in, you won't pay more, even if the price goes up in the local currency.

➤ AIRLINE TICKETS: ☎ 800/FLY–4–LESS. ☎ 800/FLY–ASAP.

➤ HOTEL ROOMS: Hotel Reservations Network (☎ 800/964–6835). International Marketing & Travel Concepts (☎ 800/790–4682). Steigenberger Reservation Service (☎ 800/223–5652). Travel Interlink (☎ 800/888–5898).

PACKAGE DEALS

Don't confuse packages and guided tours. When you buy a package, you travel on your own, just as though you had planned the trip yourself. Fly/drive packages, which combine airfare and car rental, are often a good deal. If you **buy a rail/drive pass** you may save on train tickets and car rentals. All Eurail- and Europass holders get a discount on Eurostar fares through the Channel Tunnel. A German Rail Pass is also good for travel aboard some KD River Steamers and some Deutsche Touring/Europabus routes. Greek Flexipass options may include sightseeing, hotels, and plane tickets.

ELECTRICITY

To use your U.S.-purchased electric-powered equipment **bring a converter and adapter.** The electrical current in Italy is 220 volts, 50 cycles alternating current (AC); wall outlets take Continental-type plugs, with two round prongs.

If your appliances are dual-voltage you'll need only an adapter. Don't use 110-volt outlets, marked FOR SHAVERS ONLY, for high-wattage appliances such as blow-dryers. Most laptops operate equally well on 110 and 220 volts and so require only an adapter.

EMERGENCIES

General emergencies: ☎ 113. **Police:** ☎ 112. Naples's main police station (✉ Via Medina 75, ☎ 081/794–1111) has an *ufficio stranieri* (foreigners' office) that usually has an English speaker on staff and can help with passport problems.

Ambulance: ☎ 081/752–0696. **Medical emergency after 8 PM:** ☎ 081/761–3466 (ask for an English-speaking nurse). **Hospital:** Cardarelli (081/747–1111). If the *farmacia* (pharmacy) in Stazione Centrale is closed, it will post the address of one that's open; the newspaper *Il Mattino* also prints a list of pharmacies that are open nights and weekends. **Car breakdowns and emergencies:** ☎ 116. *Also see* Emergencies *in* the A to Z section in regional chapters.

ENGLISH-LANGUAGE AND ITALIAN MEDIA

The Azienda Autonoma di Soggiorno, Cura e Turismo publishes *Qui Napoli,* an English-language monthly periodical for visitors to Naples, which lists all the special events held in the city, along with complete listings of train, bus, subway, ferry, and hydrofoil routes and schedules. In addition, there are exhaustive listings of the city's libraries, theaters, cinemas, and sports facilities. A gratis publication, it is available at all visitor information centers in Naples and at many hotels.

BOOKS

For Naples's largest selection of books in English, head to **Universal Books** (✉ Via Rione Sirgnano 1, just off Riviera di Chiaia, ☎ 081/663217).

NEWSPAPERS & MAGAZINES

Il Mattino is the leading newspaper of Naples, while the national daily, *La Repubblica,* also offers a multipage Naples section in its editions. Other newspapers published for Campania include *Il Giornale di Napoli* and *La Città.*

TELEVISION & RADIO

One of the main regional papers, *Il Mattino,* lists the various local TV stations in its entertainment pages. Viewers are fed a fairly indigestible diet of television auctions, dubbed B movies from the U.S., soccer highlights, soft porn (after 10 PM), and the odd tidbit of news. If you have a smattering of Italian, watch the better-quality state-funded RAI TRE station with local news and weather coverage at 2, 7, and 10:40 PM (approximately)

SMART TRAVEL TIPS / THE GOLD GUIDE

every day. The main private radio station is the curiously named Kiss Kiss (103.0 MHz), which broadcasts late-night music directly from its own disco up on the Vomero Hill, but also does a fair amount of handy traffic news for those on the move. For a good blend of traffic news (a permanent topic of conversation), interviews, news, and music, the state-run ISO Radio broadcasts on 103.3 MHz and is designed for those using the Italian motorway network.

FURTHER READING AND VIDEOS

As one of the great centers of civilization in the Western World, Campania and its splendid history have been exhaustively covered by authors great and small. What follows is just a Whitman's Sampler of books that will enhance anyone's trip to the region. Back in the early 19th century, Goethe wrote his *Italian Journey* and Stendhal his *Rome, Naples, and Florence*, both setting the style for the flood of travel literature to come. The Grand Tour unleashed a stream of travelers, two of whom left written accounts: Lady Blessington's *Lady Blessington in Naples* and Sir William Gell's *Letters to the Society of Dilettanti, 1831–1835*. Among the most poetic and moving of all modern travel essays on southern Italy and Campania are Aubrey Menen's *Four Days in Naples*, Herbert Kubly's *An American in Italy*, and Sean O'Faolain's sublime *An Autumn in Italy*.

For art, architecture, and splendor, consult the array of books on Neapolitan art history. The 18th-century "golden age" of Neapolitan painting is best captured in *Painting in Naples 1606–1705 from Caravaggio to Giordano* by Clovis Whitfield, the catalogue for a show mounted by the National Gallery of Art; *The Golden Age of Naples* is another impressive catalogue, this one for a show mounted by the Detroit Institute of Arts. In addition, consult *Neapolitan Painting of the Seicento* by Aldo De Rinaldis. For architectural trends of the 17th and 18th century, see Sir Anthony Blunt's *Neapolitan Baroque and Rococo Architecture*. George L. Hersey, the

eminent Yale art historian, has written several books on the art of the region, including *The Aragonese Arch at Naples, 1443-1485,* and *Alfonso II and the Artistic Renewal of Naples*—both dealing with the Renaissance period—and *Architecture, Poetry, and Number in the Royal Palace at Caserta,* on the vast 18th-century palace outside the city. *The Angel Tree: The Loretta Hines Howard Collection of Eighteenth-Century Neapolitan Creche Figures at the Metropolitan Museum of Art,* by Linn Howard, treats the finest collection of these figures in America. On the vivid history of the Teatro San Carlo, Michael F. Robinson's *Naples and Neapolitan Opera* will be of interest to music lovers. For the early 19th-century Romantic era, read C. Powell's *Turner in the South: Rome, Naples, Florence,* while *Vases and Volcanoes: Sir William Hamilton and His Collection,* written by Ian Jenkins and Kim Sloan, studies the legendary antiquities collection formed by "Mr." Emma Hamilton through the optic of Grand Tour–era esthetics.

On Naples's complicated history, start with the famous Neapolitan author and philosopher, Benedetto Croce: two of his many works are *Between Naples and Europe,* and *History of the Kingdom of Naples*. On medieval history, consult B. Kreutz's *Before the Normans: Southern Italy in the Ninth and Tenth Centuries*. On the Renaissance era, check out A. Ryder's *The Kingdom of Naples and Alfonso the Magnanimous: The Making of a Modern State,* Jerry H. Bentley's *Politics and Culture in Renaissance Naples,* and Antonio Calabria's *The Cost of Empire: The Finances of the Kingdom of Naples in the Time of Spanish Rule*. For the Baroque and Empire eras, consult Sir Harold Acton's *The Bourbons of Naples (1734-1825)* and *The Last Bourbons of Naples (1825–1861)*. On the notorious Lady Hamilton, read K. McKay's *A Remarkable Relationship: The Story of Emma Hamilton and Sir Charles Greville, Sir William Hamilton, and Horatio Nelson,* Flora Fraser's magisterial *Emma Hamilton,* and Norah Lofts' *Emma Hamilton.*

That Hamilton woman was also dealt with in Susan Sontag's award-winning novel, *The Volcano Lover*. Much of the region was put on the map of the public imagination thanks to the old Victorian 1842 potboiler, *The Last Days of Pompeii*, by Sir Edwin Bulwer-Lytton. More recent fiction efforts have been Shirley Hazzard's *The Bay of Noon* and Patricia Highsmith's devilishly clever mystery, *The Talented Mr. Ripley*, made into a film in 1999 staring Gwyneth Paltrow and Matt Damon. Other fictional forays include *The Flame of Life* by Gabriele d'Annunzio and Gregory Dowling's murder mystery, *See Naples and Kill*.

Capri has been the subject of many books, the best of which have been written by Norman Douglas, including *Siren Land*; Edwin Cerio also dealt with the isle in numerous titles, including *That Capri Air* and *The Masque of Capri*. Dr. Axel Munthe's famous *Story of San Michele* was first published in 1929 and is still in print.

For Pompeii, start with the fine exhibition catalog, *Pompeii AD 79*, edited by J. B. Ward-Perkins, to accompany a major 1978 show at the Museum of Fine Arts, Boston. An accompanying luxurious art-book volume, with the same title, has a enthralling text by the eminent professor of archeology, Richard Brilliant. A noted title is *Cities of Vesuvius: Pompeii and Herculaneum,* by Michael Grant, while more recent entries are *Pompeii: The Day A City Died,* by Robert Etienne; *Rediscovering Antiquity: Karl Weber and the Excavation of Herculaneum, Pompeii, and Stabiae,* by C. Parslow; *Pompeii: An Architectural History,* by L. Richardson, Jr.; Paul Zanker's excellent *Pompeii: Public and Private Life*; and *Roman Pompeii: Space and Society,* by Ray Laurence. For the fascinating history of Vesuvius in the European imagination, see *Volcano: The Search for Vesuvius* by William Hoffer.

To get you to Positano before you arrive and to leave you in Ravello after you've left, there's nothing like a glossy photography book. Two recent entries to the field cover many of the most beautiful spots in the region, so can come in handy for planning your trip: *Gardens of Naples,* by Elisabeth

B. MacDougall, M. T. Train, and exquisite photographs by Prince Nicholas Sapieha, and *Escape to the Amalfi Coast* by Robert I. C. Fisher, which includes photographs of many of the celebrated hotels and sights covered in this guide book. For pictures of Ravello, consult the Franco Maria Ricci *edition de luxe, Ravello,* which includes an essay by part-time Ravello resident, Gore Vidal. Finally, to whip up some of the great Neapolitan specialities you enjoyed on your trip once back home, read Arthur Schwartz's delicious *Naples at Table: Cooking in Campania.*

As for videos, look for the wonderful series of comedic films directed by Vittoria di Sica and starring Sophia Loren, starting with the 1950s classic *The Gold of Naples* and ending in the 1960s with *Marriage, Italian Style* and *Yesterday, Today, and Tomorrow.* Two early films are difficult to find but reward efforts: Robert Hussein's bleak look at postwar Naples, *Paisan* (1951), and Roberto Rossellini's *The Miracle* (1948), in which Anna Magnani memorably plays a waif seduced by a blonde man she thinks is Christ (played by Federico Fellini, no less), filmed in glorious black-and-white around Atrani and Il Furore along the Amalfi Coast. For a more recent take on Campania, see the ravishing scenes set in Naples and on Ischia in the 1999 film of Patricia Highsmith's novel, *The Talented Mr. Ripley.*

GAY & LESBIAN TRAVEL

➤ LOCAL CONTACT: **Arci–GAY/Lesbica** (✉ Vico S. Geronimo 17/20, Napoli, ☎ 081/552–8815 and 081/551–8293); this is the main clearinghouse for information in Naples and the region.

➤ GAY- AND LESBIAN-FRIENDLY TRAVEL AGENCIES: **Kennedy Travel** (✉ 314 Jericho Turnpike, Floral Park, NY 11001, ☎ 516/352–4888 or 800/237–7433, FAX 516/354–8849). **Now Voyager** (✉ 4406 18th St., San Francisco, CA 94114, ☎ 415/626–1169 or 800/255–6951, FAX 415/626–8626). **Yellowbrick Road** (✉ 1500 W. Balmoral Ave., Chicago, IL 60640, ☎ 773/561–1800 or 800/642–2488, FAX 773/561–4497). **Skylink Travel and Tour** (✉ 1006 Mendocino Ave.,

Santa Rosa, CA 95401, ☎ 707/546–9888 or 800/225–5759, FAX 707/546–9891), serving lesbian travelers.

HEALTH

The Centers for Disease Control and Prevention (CDC) in Atlanta caution that most of Southern Europe is in the "intermediate" range for risk of contacting traveler's diarrhea. Part of this risk may be attributed to an increased consumption of olive oil and wine, which can have a laxative effect on stomachs used to a different diet. The CDC also advises all international travelers to swim only in chlorinated swimming pools, unless they are absolutely certain the local beaches and freshwater lakes are not contaminated.

➤ MEDICAL-ASSISTANCE COMPANIES: **International SOS Assistance** (✉ 8 Neshaminy Interplex, Suite 207, Trevose, PA 19053, ☎ 215/245–4707 or 800/523–6586, FAX 215/244–9617; ✉ 12 Chemin Riantbosson, 1217 Meyrin 1, Geneva, Switzerland, ☎ 4122/785–6464, FAX 4122/785–6424; ✉ 331 N. Bridge Rd., 17-00, Odeon Towers, Singapore 188720, ☎ 65/338–7800, FAX 65/338–7611).

HOLIDAYS

National holidays include January 1 (New Year's Day); January 6 (Epiphany); April 23 and 24 (Easter Sunday and Monday); April 25 (Liberation Day); May 1 (Labor Day or May Day); August 15 (Assumption of Mary, also known as Ferragosto); November 1 (All Saints' Day); December 8 (Immaculate Conception); December 25 and 26 (Christmas Day and Saint Stefano). During these holidays many shops, restaurants, and museums are closed.

The feast days of patron saints are observed locally in various towns and villages; some of the more famous festas are: San Costanzo, Capri, May 14; San Antonio, Anacapri, June 13; Sant'Andrea, Amalfi, June 25–30; San Pietro, Positano, June 29; Sant'Anna, Ischia, July 26; and San Pantaleone, Ravello, July 27. In Naples, two annual celebrations are held at the Duomo on the first Sunday in May and on September 19 to celebrate the Festa di San Gennaro, or the Lique-

faction of the Blood of San Gennaro. For information on these and other holidays, *see also* Festivals and Seasonal Events *in* Chapter 1.

INSURANCE

The most useful travel insurance plan is a comprehensive policy that includes coverage for trip cancellation and interruption, default, trip delay, and medical expenses (with a waiver for preexisting conditions).

If you're traveling internationally, a key component of travel insurance is coverage for medical bills incurred if you get sick on the road. Such expenses are not generally covered by Medicare or private policies. U.K. residents can buy a travel-insurance policy valid for most vacations taken during the year in which it's purchased (but check preexisting-condition coverage). British and Australian citizens need extra medical coverage when traveling overseas. Always **buy travel policies directly from the insurance company**; if you buy it from a cruise line, airline, or tour operator that goes out of business you probably will not be covered for the agency or operator's default, a major risk. Before you make any purchase **review your existing health and homeowner's policies** to find what they cover away from home.

➤ TRAVEL INSURERS: In the U.S. **Access America** (✉ 6600 W. Broad St., Richmond, VA 23230, ☎ 804/285–3300 or 800/284–8300), **Travel Guard International** (✉ 1145 Clark St., Stevens Point, WI 54481, ☎ 715/345–0505 or 800/826–1300). In Canada **Voyager Insurance** (✉ 44 Peel Center Dr., Brampton, Ontario L6T 4M8, ☎ 905/791–8700; 800/668–4342 in Canada).

➤ INSURANCE INFORMATION: In the U.K. the **Association of British Insurers** (✉ 51–55 Gresham St., London EC2V 7HQ, ☎ 0171/600–3333, FAX 0171/696–8999). In Australia the **Insurance Council of Australia** (☎ 03/9614–1077, FAX 03/9614–7924).

LANGUAGE

In Naples and the leading resorts, language is not a big problem. You can always find someone who speaks at least a little English; remember that the Italian language is pronounced exactly as it is written (many Italians try to speak English by enunciating every syllable, with disconcerting results). You may run into a language barrier in the countryside, but a phrase book and close attention to the Italians' use of expressive gestures will go a long way. Try to **master a few phrases for daily use** (☞ Italian Vocabulary, at the back of this book) and familiarize yourself with the terms you'll need to decipher signs and museum labels.

LANGUAGES FOR TRAVELERS

A phrase book and language-tape set can help get you started.

➤ PHRASE BOOKS & LANGUAGE-TAPE SETS: *Fodor's Italian for Travelers* (☎ 800/733–3000 in the U.S.; 800/668–4247 in Canada; $7 for phrase book, $16.95 for audio set).

LODGING

The lodgings we review in this book are the cream of the crop in each price category. We always list the facilities that are available—but we don't specify whether they cost extra: When pricing accommodations, always ask what's included and what costs extra. Extra fees can be charged for everything from breakfast to use of parking facilities to air-conditioning. For price categories, consult the price charts found under Pleasures and Pastimes in Chapters 2, 3, 4, and 5.

Assume that hotels operate on the Continental Plan, with a Continental breakfast daily. Unless arrangements are made with the hotel for half or full board—an arrangement which many hotels in Campania offer to their guests—all other meals would be extra. Properties indicated by a ✕⊞ are lodging establishments whose restaurants warrant a special trip.

APARTMENT & VILLA RENTALS

If you want a home base that's roomy enough for a family and comes with cooking facilities **consider a furnished rental**. These can save you money, especially if you're traveling with a group. Home-exchange directories list rentals (often second homes owned by prospective house swappers), and some services search for a house or apartment for you (even a castle if that's your fancy) and handle the paperwork. Some send an illustrated catalog; others send photographs only of specific properties, sometimes at a charge. Up-front registration fees may apply.

➤ INTERNATIONAL AGENTS: **At Home Abroad** (⊠ 405 E. 56th St., Suite 6H, New York, NY 10022, ☎ 212/421–9165, ℻ 212/752–1591). **Drawbridge to Europe** (⊠ 5456 Adams Rd., Talent, OR 97540, ☎ 541/512–8927 or 888/268–1148, ℻ 541/512–0978). **Europa-Let/Tropical Inn-Let** (⊠ 92 N. Main St., Ashland, OR 97520, ☎ 541/482–5806 or 800/462–4486, ℻ 541/482–0660). **Hometours International** (⊠ Box 11503, Knoxville, TN 37939, ☎ 423/690–8484 or 800/367–4668). **Interhome** (⊠ 1990 N.E. 163rd St., Suite 110, Miami Beach, FL 33162, ☎ 305/940–2299 or 800/882–6864, ℻ 305/940–2911). **Rental Directories International** (⊠ 2044 Rittenhouse Sq., Philadelphia, PA 19103, ☎ 215/985–4001, ℻ 215/985–0323). **Rent-a-Home International** (⊠ 7200 34th Ave. NW, Seattle, WA 98117, ☎ 206/789–9377, ℻ 206/789–9379). **Vacation Home Rentals Worldwide** (⊠ 235 Kensington Ave., Norwood, NJ 07648, ☎ 201/767–9393 or 800/633–3284, ℻ 201/767–5510). **Villas and Apartments Abroad** (⊠ 420 Madison Ave., Suite 1003, New York, NY 10017, ☎ 212/759–1025 or 800/433–3020, ℻ 212/755–8316). **Villas International** (⊠ 950 Northgate Dr., Suite 206, San Rafael, CA 94903, ☎ 415/499–9490 or 800/221–2260, ℻ 415/499–9491). **Hideaways International** (⊠ 767 Islington St., Portsmouth, NH 03801, ☎ 603/430–4433 or 800/843–4433, ℻ 603/430–4444; membership $99).

➤ ITALY-ONLY AGENTS: **Cuendet USA** (⊠ 165 Chestnut St., Allendale, NJ 07041, ☎ 201/327–2333; ⊠ Suzanne T. Pidduck, c/o Rentals in Italy, 1742 Calle Corva, Camarillo, CA 93010, ☎ 800/726–6702). **Vacanze in Italia** (⊠ 22 Railroad St., Great Barrington, MA 01230, ☎ 413/528–6610 or 800/533–5405).

➤ In the U.K.: **CV Travel** (⊠ 43 Cadogan St., London SW3 2PR, England, ☎ 0171/581–0851). **Magic of Italy** (⊠ 227 Shepherds Bush Rd., London W6 7AS, England, ☎ 0181/748–7575).

CAMPING

Camping is a good way to find accommodations in otherwise overcrowded resorts, and camper rental agencies operate throughout Italy; contact your travel agent for details. Make sure you **stay only on authorized campsites** (camping on private land is frowned upon), and get an international camping *carnet* (permit) from your local camping association before you leave home. The Touring Club Italiano publishes a multilingual *Guida Camping d'Italia* (Guide to Camping in Italy), available in bookstores in Italy for about 30,000 lire, with more detailed information on sites. Camp rates for two people, with car and tent, average about 50,000 lire a day.

➤ Directory of Campgrounds: Write to the **Federazione Italiana del Campeggio e del Caravanning** (⊠ Federcampeggio, Casella Postale 23, 50041 Calenzano, Firenze, FAX 055/8825918) and request *Campeggiare in Italia;* send three international reply coupons to cover mailing. It's also available through the ENIT office in the United States and at tourist information offices in Italy (☞ Visitor Information, *below* and *in* individual chapters).

FARM HOLIDAYS & AGRITOURISM

Rural accommodations in the *agriturismo* (agritourism) category are increasingly popular with both Italians and visitors to Italy.

➤ Agencies: **Italy Farm Holidays** (⊠ 547 Martling Ave., Tarrytown, NY 10591, ☎ 914/631–7880, FAX 914/631–8831). **Essentially Tuscany** (⊠ 30 York St., Nantucket, MA 02554, ☎ FAX 508/2282514). **Agriturist** (⊠ Corso Vittorio 101, 00186 Roma, ☎ 06/6852342). **Turismo Verde** (⊠ Via Flaminia 56, 00196 Roma, ☎ 06/3611051).

HOME EXCHANGES

If you would like to exchange your home for someone else's **join a home-**exchange organization, which will send you its updated listings of available exchanges for a year and will include your own listing in at least one of them. It's up to you to make specific arrangements.

➤ Exchange Clubs: **HomeLink International** (⊠ Box 650, Key West, FL 33041, ☎ 305/294–7766 or 800/638–3841, FAX 305/294–1448; $88 per year). **Intervac U.S.** (⊠ Box 590504, San Francisco, CA 94159, ☎ 800/756–4663, FAX 415/435–7440; $83 per year).

HOSTELS

No matter what your age you can **save on lodging costs by staying at hostels.** In some 5,000 locations in more than 70 countries around the world, Hostelling International (HI), the umbrella group for a number of national youth-hostel associations, offers single-sex, dorm-style beds and, at many hostels, couples rooms and family accommodations. Membership in any HI national hostel association, open to travelers of all ages, allows you to stay in HI-affiliated hostels at member rates (one-year membership is about $25 for adults; hostels run about $10–$25 per night). Members also have priority if the hostel is full; they're eligible for discounts around the world, even on rail and bus travel in some countries.

➤ Organizations: **Australian Youth Hostel Association** (⊠ 10 Mallett St., Camperdown, NSW 2050, ☎ 02/9565–1699, FAX 02/9565–1325). **Hostelling International—American Youth Hostels** (⊠ 733 15th St. NW, Suite 840, Washington, DC 20005, ☎ 202/783–6161, FAX 202/783–6171). **Hostelling International—Canada** (⊠ 400–205 Catherine St., Ottawa, Ontario K2P 1C3, ☎ 613/237–7884, FAX 613/237–7868). **Youth Hostel Association of England and Wales** (⊠ Trevelyan House, 8 St. Stephen's Hill, St. Albans, Hertfordshire AL1 2DY, ☎ 01727/855215 or 01727/845047, FAX 01727/844126). **Youth Hostels Association of New Zealand** (⊠ Box 436, Christchurch, New Zealand, ☎ 03/379–9970, FAX 03/365–4476). Membership in the U.S. $25, in Canada C$26.75, in the

U.K. £9.30, in Australia $44, in New Zealand $24.

HOTELS

Italian hotels are awarded stars (one to five) based on their facilities and services. Those with three or more stars feature bathrooms in all rooms. Keep in mind, however, that these are general indications, and that a charming three-star might make for a better stay than a more expensive four-star. During low seasons and whenever a hotel is not full, it is often possible to negotiate a discounted rate. In Naples, room rates can be on a par with other European capitals: Deluxe and four-star rates can be downright extravagant. In those categories, **ask for one of the better rooms,** since less desirable rooms—and there usually are some—don't give you what you're paying for. Except in deluxe and some four-star hotels, bathrooms usually have showers rather than bathtubs.

In all hotels there is a rate card inside the door of your room, or inside the closet door; it tells you exactly what you will pay for that particular room (rates in the same hotel may vary according to the location and type of room). On this card, breakfast and any other optionals must be listed separately. Any discrepancy between the basic room rate and that charged on your bill is cause for complaint to the manager and to the police.

Although, by law, breakfast is supposed to be optional, most hotels quote room rates including breakfast. When you book a room, specifically **ask whether the rate includes breakfast** (*colazione*). You are under no obligation to take breakfast at your hotel, but in practice most hotels expect you to do so. It is encouraging to note that many of the hotels we recommend are offering generous buffet breakfasts instead of simple, even skimpy "Continental breakfasts."

Hotels that we list as ($$) and ($)—moderate to inexpensively priced accommodations—may charge extra for optional air-conditioning; somewhat surprisingly, this is usually the case for luxury hotels in southern Italy. In older hotels the quality of the rooms may be very uneven; if you don't like the room you're given, request another. This applies to noise, too. Front rooms may be larger or have a view, but they also may have a lot of street noise—happily, many of Naples's finer hotels offer windows with double-pane glass to effectively silence the noise. If you're a light sleeper, **request a quiet room when making reservations.** Rooms in lodgings listed in this guide have a shower and/or bath, unless noted otherwise. Remember **to specify whether you care to have a bath or shower** since not all rooms, especially lodgings outside major cities, have both. It is always a good idea to **have your reservation, dates, and rate confirmed by fax.**

Naples has no official off-season as far as hotel rates go, though outside the city some hotels do offer substantial discounts during the slower parts of the year. Major cities have hotel-reservation service booths in train stations.

MAIL & SHIPPING

The Italian mail system can be slow, so allow up to 15 days for mail to and from the United States and Canada, about a week to and from the United Kingdom.

POSTAL RATES

Airmail letters and postcards (lightweight stationery) to the United States and Canada cost 1,300 lire for the first 20 grams; 2,700 lire up to 40 grams; and 3,100 lire up to 50 grams. Always stick the blue airmail tag on your mail, or write "airmail" in big, clear characters to the side of the address. Postcards and letters (for the first 20 grams) to the United Kingdom, as well as to any other EU country, including Italy, cost 800 lire. You can buy stamps at tobacconists.

RECEIVING MAIL

Correspondence can be addressed to you care of the Italian post office. Letters should be addressed to your name, "c/o Ufficio Postale Centrale," followed by "Fermo Posta" on the next line, and the name of the city (preceded by its postal code) on the next. You can **collect it at the central post office** by showing your passport or photo-bearing ID and paying a small fee. American Express also has a general-delivery service. There's no charge for cardholders, holders of American Express Traveler's checks, or anyone who booked a vacation with American Express.

MONEY MATTERS

The days when Italy's high-quality attractions came with a comparatively low Mediterranean price tag are long gone. Italy's prices are in line with those in the rest of Europe, with costs in its main cities comparable to those in other major capitals, such as Paris and Madrid. As in most countries, prices vary from region to region and are a bit lower in the countryside than in the cities. Good value for the money can still be had in many places in Campania, especially in Naples and the Amalfi Coast.

Here are some sample prices: Admission to the Museo Archeologico Nazionale is 12,000 lire; the cheapest seat at Naples's Teatro San Carlo runs 32,000 lire; a movie ticket is 12,000 lire. Going to a Naples nightclub might set you back about 15,000 to 25,000 lire. A daily English-language newspaper is 2,500 lire. A Naples taxi ride (1⅓ km, or 1 mi) costs 12,000 lire. An inexpensive hotel room for two, including breakfast, in Naples is about 100,000 to 150,000 lire; an inexpensive Naples dinner is 25,000 to 40,000 lire, and a ½ liter carafe of house wine, 8,000 lire. A simple pasta item on the menu runs about 13,000 lire, a cup of coffee 1,500 lire, and a rosticceria lunch, about 15,000 lire. A Coca-Cola (standing) at a café is 2,500 lire and a pint of beer is 7,000 lire.

Prices throughout this guide are given for adults. Substantially reduced fees are almost always available for children, students, and senior citizens. For information on taxes, see Taxes, below.

CREDIT CARDS

Throughout this guide, the following abbreviations are used: **AE,** American Express; **DC,** Diner's Club; **MC,** MasterCard; and **V,** Visa.

➤ REPORTING LOST CARDS: **American Express** (☎ 336/668–5110 international collect). **Diner's Club** (☎ 702/797–5532 collect). **Master Card** (☎ 1678/70866 toll-free). **Visa** (☎ 1678/177232).

CURRENCY

The unit of currency in Italy is the lira. There are bills of 500,000 (practically impossible to change outside of banks), 100,000, 50,000, 10,000, 5,000, 2,000, and 1,000 lire. Coins are 500, 200, 100 and 50 lire. At press time (fall 1999), the exchange rate was about 1,864 lire to the U.S. dollar; 1,271 lire to the Canadian dollar; 2,972 lire to the pound sterling; 1,233 to the Australian dollar; and 990 lire to the New Zealand dollar. Although prices are increasingly quoted in the Euro (European common currency), everyday business is still conducted in lire.

CURRENCY EXCHANGE

For the most favorable rates, **change money through banks.** Although fees charged for ATM transactions may be higher abroad than at home, Cirrus and Plus exchange rates are excellent because they are based on wholesale rates offered only by major banks. You won't do as well at exchange booths in airports or rail and bus stations, in hotels, in restaurants, or in stores, although you may find their hours more convenient. To avoid lines at airport exchange booths, **get a bit of local currency before you leave home.**

➤ EXCHANGE SERVICES: **International Currency Express** (☎ 888/842–0880 on East Coast; 888/278–6628 on West Coast). **Thomas Cook Currency Services** (☎ 800/287–7362 for telephone orders and retail locations).

TRAVELER'S CHECKS

Do you need traveler's checks? It depends on where you're headed. If you're going to rural areas and villages, go with cash; traveler's checks are best used in Naples, Capri, Ischia, Sorrento, and the more popular destinations along the Amalfi Coast. Lost or stolen checks can usually be replaced within 24 hours. To ensure a speedy refund, buy your own traveler's checks—don't let someone else pay for them: irregularities like this can cause delays. The person who bought the checks should make the call to request a refund.

PACKING

The weather is considerably milder in Italy than in the north and central United States or Great Britain. In summer, stick with clothing that is as light as possible, although a sweater may be necessary for cool evenings, especially in the Lattari mountains along the Amalfi Coast (even during the hot months). Sunglasses, a hat, and sunblock are essential. Contrary to myth, the sun does not shine 24 hours a day on Campania: Brief summer thunderstorms are common in Naples, while typhoonlike storms occasionally arrive along the Amalfi Coast, so an umbrella will definitely come in handy. In winter bring a medium-weight coat and a raincoat; winters in Naples can be both humid *and* cold. Even in Naples, central heating may not be up to your standards, and interiors can be chilly and damp; take wools or flannel rather than sheer fabrics. Bring sturdy shoes for winter, and comfortable walking shoes in any season.

In Campania, laid-back style is the way to go. Residents do not usually wear shorts. Men aren't required to wear ties or jackets anywhere, except in some of the grander hotel dining rooms and top-level restaurants, but are expected to look reasonably sharp—and they do. Formal wear is the exception rather than the rule at the opera nowadays, though people in expensive seats usually do get dressed up. A certain modesty of dress (no bare shoulders or knees) is expected in churches.

For sightseeing, **pack a pair of binoculars**; they will help you get a good look at Naples's wondrous painted ceilings and domes. If you stay in budget hotels, **take your own soap**; many such hotels do not provide it or give guests only one tiny bar per room.

PASSPORTS & VISAS

When traveling internationally **your passport** is essential even after you arrive in the country; without it no Italian hotel will let you have a room. It is a good idea to make **two photocopies of the data page** (one for someone at home and another for you, carried separately from your passport). If you lose your passport, promptly call the nearest embassy or consulate and the local police.

U.S. CITIZENS

All U.S. citizens, even infants, need only a valid passport to enter Italy for stays of up to 90 days.

CANADIAN CITIZENS

Canadian citizens need only a valid passport to enter Italy for stays of up to 90 days.

U.K. CITIZENS

Citizens of the United Kingdom need only a valid passport to enter Italy for stays of up to 90 days.

AUSTRALIAN CITIZENS

Citizens of Australia need only a valid passport to enter Italy for stays of up to 90 days.

NEW ZEALAND CITIZENS

Citizens of New Zealand need only a valid passport to enter Italy for stays of up to 90 days.

PASSPORT OFFICES

The best time to apply for a passport or to renew is during the fall and winter. Before any trip, check your passport's expiration date, and, if necessary, renew it as soon as possible.

➤ AUSTRALIAN CITIZENS: **Australian Passport Office** (☎ 131–232).

➤ CANADIAN CITIZENS: **Passport Office** (☎ 819/994–3500 or 800/567–6868).

➤ NEW ZEALAND CITIZENS: **New Zealand Passport Office** (☎ 04/494–0700 for information on how to apply; 04/474–8000 or 0800/225–050 in New Zealand for information on applications already submitted).

➤ U.K. CITIZENS: **London Passport Office** (☎ 0990/210–410) for fees and documentation requirements and to request an emergency passport.

➤ U.S. CITIZENS: **National Passport Information Center** (☎ 900/225–5674; calls are 35¢ per minute for automated service, $1.05 per minute for operator service).

SAFETY

Most of the destinations in this guide book are among the safest spots in Italy. Naples, like any modern metropolis, has had certain problems with crime, but great inroads have been made in the past decade and the city today is as safe as many other big urban centers in Europe. For special provisos, *see* Being Streetwise in Naples *in* the Getting Around section, Naples A to Z *in* Chapter 2.

SENIOR-CITIZEN TRAVEL

To qualify for age-related discounts **mention your senior-citizen status up front** when booking hotel reservations (not when checking out) and before you're seated in restaurants (not when paying the bill). When renting a car ask about promotional car-rental discounts, which can be cheaper than senior-citizen rates.

➤ EDUCATIONAL PROGRAMS: **Elderhostel** (✉ 75 Federal St., 3rd fl., Boston, MA 02110, ☎ 877/426–8056, FAX 877/426–2166). **Interhostel** (✉ University of New Hampshire, 6 Garrison Ave., Durham, NH 03824, ☎ 603/862–1147 or 800/733–9753, FAX 603/862–1113). **Folkways Institute** (✉ 14600 Southeast Aldridge Rd., Portland, OR 97236-6518, ☎ 503/658–6600 or 800/225–4666, FAX 503/658–8672).

SHOPPING

The notice PREZZI FISSI (fixed prices) means just that; in shops displaying this sign it's a waste of time to bargain unless you're buying a sizable quantity of goods or a particularly costly object. Always try to bargain, however, at outdoor markets (except food markets) and when buying from street vendors. For information on VAT refunds, *see* Taxes, *below.*

STUDENTS IN ITALY

Italy is a popular student destination, and in Naples there are plenty of facilities (information, lodging) geared to students' needs. Students with identification cards may obtain discounts at museums, galleries, exhibitions, entertainment venues, and on some transportation. The main division of the Università di Napoli can be found in buildings extending the length of Via Mezzocannone, off Corso Umberto I, near the district of Spaccanapoli.

LOCAL RESOURCES

The **Centro Turistico Studentesco** (CTS; ☞ Travel Agencies, *below*) is a student and youth travel agency with an office in Naples; CTS helps its clients find low-cost accommodations and bargain fares for travel in Italy and elsewhere but to avail yourself of CTS's student discount you need to purchase a membership card (about 50,000 lire). CTS is also the Rome representative for EuroTrain International. Dedicated to helping students, **Euro Study Travel** is a travel agency across from the central Naples university building near the heart of Spaccanapoli. The **Associazione Italiana Alberghi per la Gioventù** operates hostels for student members, including the famous Ostello Mergellina in Naples.

TRAVEL AGENCIES

To save money, **look into deals available through student-oriented travel agencies.** To qualify you'll need a bona fide student I.D. card. Members of international student groups are also eligible.

➤ STUDENT IDs & SERVICES: **Associazione Italiana Alberghi per la Gioventù** (✉ Salita della Grotta 23, Napoli, ☎ 081/761–2346). **Associazione Italo-Americana (American Studies Center)** (✉ Via D'Isernia 36, Napoli, ☎ 081/660562). **British Council** (✉ Via Crespi 92, Napoli, ☎ 081/667410). **Centro Turistico Studentesco (CTS)** (✉ Via Mezzocannone 25, Napoli, ☎ 081/552–7960). **Council on International Educational Exchange** (CIEE, ✉ 205 E. 42nd St., 14th fl., New York, NY 10017, ☎ 212/822–2600 or 888/268–6245, FAX 212/822–2699) for mail orders only, in the U.S. **Euro Study Travel** (✉ Via Mezzocannone 119, Napoli, ☎ 081/552–0947). **Travel Cuts** (✉ 187 College St., Toronto, Ontario M5T 1P7, ☎ 416/979–2406 or 800/667–2887) in Canada. **Università di Napoli** (✉ Via Mezzancannone, Napoli, ☎ 800/322020).

TAXES

HOTEL

The service charge and the 9% IVA, or VAT tax, are included in the rate except in five-star deluxe hotels, where the IVA (12% on luxury hotels) may be a separate item added to the bill at departure.

RESTAURANT

A service charge of approximately 15% is added to all restaurant bills; in some cases the menu may state that the service charge is already included in the menu prices.

VALUE-ADDED TAX (V.A.T.)

Value-added tax (IVA or VAT) is 19% on clothing, and luxury goods. On most consumer goods, it is already included in the amount shown on the price tag, whereas on services, it may not be.

To **get an IVA refund,** when you are leaving Italy take the goods and the invoice to the customs office at the airport or other point of departure and have the invoice stamped. (If you return to the United States or Canada directly from Italy, go through the procedure at Italian customs; if your return is, say, via Britain, take the Italian goods and invoice to British customs.) Under Italy's IVA-refund system, a non-EU resident can obtain a refund of tax paid after spending a total of 300,000 lire in one store (before tax—and note that price tags and prices quoted, unless otherwise stated, include IVA). Shop with your passport and ask the store for an invoice itemizing the article(s), price(s), and the amount of tax. Once back home—and within 90 days of the date of purchase—mail the stamped invoice to the store, which will send the IVA rebate to you. A growing number of stores in Italy (and Europe) are members of the Tax-Free Shopping System, which expedites things by providing an invoice that is actually a Tax-Free Cheque in the amount of the refund. Once stamped, it can be cashed at the Tax-Free Cash refund window at major airports and border crossings, you can also opt to have the refund credited to your credit card or bank account, or sent directly home. To save a step at the airport or border, you can send the Cheque to a Tax-Free Shopping address.

Europe Tax-Free Shopping is a V.A.T. refund service that makes getting your money back hassle-free. E.T.S. is Europe-wide and has 90,000 affiliated stores. In participating stores, **ask for the E.T.S. refund form** (called a Shopping Cheque). As is true for all customs forms, when leaving the European Union you get them stamped by the customs official. Then you take them to the E.T.S. counter and they will refund your money right there in cash, by check, or a refund to your credit card. All that convenience will cost you 20%—but then it's done.

➤ VAT REFUNDS: **Europe Tax-Free Shopping** (✉ 233 S. Wacker Dr., Suite 9700, Chicago, IL 60606-6502, ☎ 312/382–1101).

TELEPHONES

COUNTRY & AREA CODES

The country code for Italy is 39. Here are area codes for major cities: Bologna, 051; Brindisi, 0831; Florence, 055; Genoa, 010; Milan, 02; Naples, 081; Palermo, 091; Perugia, 075; Pisa, 050; Rome, 06; Siena, 0577; Turin, 011; Venice, 041; Verona, 045. Essentially, the region from Naples to the islands (Capri, Ischia, Procida) and around the Bay of Naples to Sorrento uses the area code 081; the region along the Amalfi Coast from Positano to Salerno uses the area code 089. For example, a call from New York City to Naples would be dialed as 011 + 39 + 81 + phone number. From the U.K., dial 00 + 39 + 81 + phone number. When dialing an Italian number from abroad, you no longer drop the initial 0 from the local area code. When dialing from Italy overseas, the country code is 1 for the U.S. and Canada, 61 for Australia, 64 for New Zealand, and 44 for the U.K.

DIRECTORY & OPERATOR INFORMATION

For general information in English, dial 176. To place international telephone calls via operator-assisted service, dial 170 or long-distance access numbers (☞ International Calls *below*).

INTERNATIONAL CALLS

Since hotels tend to overcharge, sometimes exorbitantly, for long-distance and international calls, it is best to make such calls from public phones, using telephone cards. At Telefoni offices, operators sell international telephone cards and will help you place your call. There are Telefoni offices, designated TELECOM, in all cities and towns, usually in major train stations and in the center business districts. You can **make collect calls from any phone by dialing 172–1011,** which will get you an English-speaking operator. Rates to the United States are lowest 'round the clock on Sunday and 10 PM–8 AM (Italian time) on weekdays.

From major Italian cities, you can place a direct call to the United States by reversing the charges or using your phone credit card number. When calling from pay telephones, insert a 200-lire coin that will be returned upon completion of your call. You automatically reach an operator in the country of destination and thereby avoid all language difficulties.

LOCAL CALLS

For all calls within Italy—local and long distance—you must dial the area code (*prefisso*), which begins with a 0, as 081 for Naples, 089 for Amalfi. If you are calling from a public phone you must deposit a coin or use a calling card to get a dial tone.

LONG-DISTANCE SERVICES

AT&T, MCI, and Sprint access codes make calling long distance relatively convenient, but you may find the local access number blocked in many hotel rooms. First ask the hotel operator to connect you. If the hotel operator balks ask for an international operator, or dial the international operator yourself. One way to improve your odds of getting connected to your long-distance carrier is to travel with more than one company's calling card (a hotel may block Sprint, for example, but not MCI). If all else fails call from a pay phone.

➤ ACCESS CODES: **AT&T USADirect** (☎ 172–1011). **MCI Call USA** (☎ 172–1022). **Sprint Express** (☎ 172–1877).

PUBLIC PHONES

Pay phones accept a 200-lire coin, two 100-lire coins, or a 500-lire coin, but **consider buying a *carta telefonica* (prepaid calling card).** Scheda phones are becoming common everywhere. You buy the card (values vary—5,000 lire, 10,000 lire, etc.) at Telefoni offices, post offices, and tobacconists. Tear off the corner of the card, and insert it in the slot. When you dial, its value appears in the window. After you hang up, the card is returned so you can use it until its value runs out.

TIME

Italy operates on a 24-hour clock. In other words, AM hours are listed as in the U.S. and Great Britain, but PM hours continue through the cycle (1 PM is 13, 2 PM is 14, etc.). Daylight-saving time begins on the last Sunday in March, when clocks are set forward one hour; on the last Sunday in September, clocks are set back one hour. When it's 3 PM in Naples, it is 2 PM in London, 9 AM in New York City, and 6 AM in Los Angeles.

TIPPING

The following guidelines apply in Naples, but Italians tip smaller amounts in smaller cities and towns. In restaurants a service charge of about 15% usually appears as a separate item on your check. A few restaurants state on the menu that cover and service charge are included. Either way, it's customary to leave an additional 5%–10% tip for the waiter, depending on the service. Tip checkroom attendants 500 lire per person, rest room attendants 200 lire (more in expensive hotels and restaurants). Tip 100 lire for whatever you drink standing up at a coffee bar, 500 lire or more for table service in cafés. At a hotel bar tip 1,000 lire and up for a round or two of cocktails.

Tip taxi drivers 5%–10% of the meter amount. Railway and airport porters charge a fixed rate per bag. Tip an additional 500 lire per person, but more if the porter is very helpful. Theater ushers expect 500 lire per person, and more for very expensive seats. Give a barber 2,000–3,000 lire and a hairdresser's assistant 3,000–8,000 lire for a shampoo or cut, depending on the type of establishment.

On sightseeing tours, tip guides about 2,000 lire per person for a half-day group tour, more if they are very good. In museums and other places of interest where admission is free, a contribution is expected (500–1,000 lire). Service station attendants are tipped only for special services, for example, 1,000 lire for checking your tires.

In hotels, give the *portiere* (concierge) about 15% of his bill for services, or 5,000–10,000 lire if he has been generally helpful. For two people in a double room, leave the chambermaid about 1,000 lire per day, or about 4,000–5,000 lire a week, in a moderately priced hotel; tip a minimum of 1,000 lire for valet or room service. Double amounts in a very expensive hotel. In very expensive hotels, tip doormen 1,000 lire for calling a cab and 2,000 lire for carrying bags to the check-in desk, bellhops 3,000–5,000 lire for carrying your bags to the room and 3,000–5,000 lire for room service.

TOURS & PACKAGES

On a prepackaged tour or independent vacation everything is prearranged so you'll spend less time planning—and often get it all at a good price.

BOOKING WITH AN AGENT

Travel agents are excellent resources. But it's a good idea to collect brochures from several agencies because some agents' suggestions may be influenced by relationships with tour and package firms that reward them for volume sales. If you have a special interest **find an agent with expertise in that area**; ASTA (☞ Travel Agencies, *below*) has a database of specialists worldwide.

Make sure your travel agent knows the accommodations and other services of the place they're recommending. Ask about the hotel's location, room size, beds, and whether it has a pool, room service, or programs for children, if you care about these. Has your agent been there in person or sent others whom you can contact?

BUYER BEWARE

Each year consumers are stranded or lose their money when tour operators—even large ones with excellent reputations—go out of business. So **check out the operator.** Ask several travel agents about its reputation, and try to **book with a company that has a consumer-protection program.** (Look for information in the company's brochure.) In the United States, members of the National Tour Association and United States Tour Operators Association are required to set aside funds to cover your payments and travel arrangements in case the company defaults. It's also a good idea to choose a company that participates in the American Society of Travel Agent's Tour Operator Program (TOP); ASTA will act as mediator in any disputes between you and your tour operator.

Remember that the more your package or tour includes the better you can predict the ultimate cost of your vacation. Make sure you know exactly what is covered, and **beware of hidden costs.** Are taxes, tips, and transfers included? Entertainment and excursions? These can add up.

➤ TOUR-OPERATOR RECOMMENDATIONS: **American Society of Travel Agents** (☞ Travel Agencies, *below*). **National Tour Association** (NTA, ✉ 546 E. Main St., Lexington, KY 40508, ☎ 606/226–4444 or 800/682–8886). **United States Tour Operators Association** (USTOA, ✉ 342 Madison Ave., Suite 1522, New York, NY 10173, ☎ 212/599–6599 or 800/468–7862, ℻ 212/599–6744).

TRAIN TRAVEL

All Italian trains have first and second classes. On local trains the higher first-class fare gets you little more than a clean doily on the headrest of your seat, but on long-distance trains you get wider seats and more legroom and better ventilation and lighting. At peak travel times, first-class train travel is worth the difference. Remember to **always make seat reservations in advance,** for either class.

The fastest trains on the Ferrovie dello Stato (FS), the Italian State Railways, are the Eurostar trains, operating on several main lines, including Rome–Milan, via Florence and Bologna; seat reservations and supplement are included in the fare. Some of these (the ETR 460 trains) have little aisle and luggage space (though there is a space near the door where you can put large bags). To avoid having to squeeze through narrow aisles, board only at your car (look for the number on the reservation ticket). Car numbers are displayed on their exterior. Next-fastest trains are the Intercity (IC) trains, for which you pay a supplement and for which seat reservations may be required and **are always advisable.** *Interregionale* trains usually make more stops and are a little slower. *Regionale* and *locale* trains are the slowest; many serve commuters.

Trains can be very crowded; it is always a good idea to make a reservation. To avoid long lines at station windows, **buy tickets and make seat reservations up to two months in advance** at travel agencies displaying the FS emblem. Tickets can be purchased at the last minute, but seat reservations can be made at agencies (or the train station) up until about five hours before the train departs from its city of origin. For trains that require a reservation (all Eurostar and some Intercity), you may be able to get a seat assignment just before boarding the train; look for the conductor on the platform.

All **tickets must be date-stamped in the small yellow or red machines near the tracks before you board.** Once stamped, your ticket is valid for six hours if your destination is within 200 km (124 mi), for 24 hours for destinations beyond that. You can get on and off at will at stops in between for the duration of the ticket's validity. If you forget to stamp your ticket in the machine, or you didn't make in time to buy the ticket, you must actively seek out a conductor and pay a 10,000 lire fine. Don't wait for the conductor to find out that you are without a valid ticket (unless the train is overcrowded and walking becomes impossible), as he might charge you a much heavier fine. You can buy train tickets for nearby destinations (within a 200-km [62-mi] range) at tobacconists and at ticket machines in stations.

Note that in some Italian cities (including Milan, Turin, Genoa, Naples, and Rome) there are two or more main-line stations, although one is usually the principal terminal or through-station. Be sure of the name of the station at which your train will arrive, or from which it will depart.

There is refreshment service on all long-distance trains, with mobile carts and a cafeteria or dining car. Tap water on trains is not drinkable.

To save money, **look into rail passes.** But be aware that if you don't plan to cover many miles, you may come out ahead by buying individual tickets.

➤ FROM THE U.K.: **British Rail** (☎ 0171/834–2345). **French Railways** (☎ 0891/515–477); calls charged at 49p a minute peak rate, 39p all other times.

CUTTING COSTS

To save money **look into rail passes.** But be aware that if you don't plan to cover many miles, you may come out ahead by buying individual tickets.

If Italy is your only destination in Europe, **consider purchasing an Italian Railpass,** which allows unlimited travel on the entire Italian Rail network. The Italy Flexi Rail Card allows a limited number of travel days within one month: $216 for four days of travel in first class ($144 second class); 8 days of travel ($312 first class, $202 in second class); and 12 days of travel ($389 first class, $259 second class). Passes for travel on consecutive days are also available: 8 days ($273 first class, $182 second class); 15 days ($341 first class, $228 second class); 21 days ($396 first class, $264 second class); and 30 days ($478 first class, $318 second class).

The Italian Kilometric Ticket is valid for two months and can be used by as many as five people to travel a total of 3,000 km (1,800 mi). The price is $289 for first class and $181 second class.

Once in Italy, **inquire about the Carta Verde (Green Card) if you're under 26** (40,000 lire for one year), which entitles the holder to a 20% discount on all first- and second-class tickets. Those under 26 should also inquire about discount travel fares under the Billet International Jeune (BIJ) and Euro Domino Junior schemes. Also in Italy, you can **purchase the Carta d'Argento (Silver Card) if you're over 60** (40,000 lire for one year), which allows a 40% discount for first-class rail travel and a 20% discount on second-class travel. For further information, check out the Ferrovie dello Stato (FS) Web site (www.fs-on-line.com).

Italy is one of 17 countries in which you can **use Eurailpasses,** which provide unlimited first-class travel in all of the participating countries. If you plan to rack up the miles, get a standard pass. Train travel is available for 15 days ($554), 21 days ($718), one month ($890), two months ($1,260), and three months ($1,558). You can also receive free or discounted fares on some ferry lines.

If your plans call for only limited train travel, **look into the Europass,** which costs less money than a Eurailpass and allows train travel in France, Germany, Italy, Spain, and Switzerland within a two-month period ($348 for five days of travel; $368 six days; $448 eight days; $528 10 days; and $728 15 days). Rail travel to Austria/Hungary, Portugal, Greece, and Benelux can be added for additional fees ($60 one country, $100 two countries). You can receive discounts for two or more people.

Please note that these fares are subject to change in 2000.

In addition to standard Eurailpasses, **ask about special rail-pass plans.** Among these are the Eurail Youthpass (for those under age 26), Eurail Saverpass and Eurail Saver Flexipass (which give a discount for two or more people traveling together), Eurail Flexipass (which allows a certain number of travel days within a set period), and the EurailDrive Pass, which combines travel by train and rental car.

Whichever pass you choose, remember that you must **purchase your Eurailpass or Europass before you leave** for Europe. You can get further information and order tickets at the Rail Europe Web site (www.raileurope.com).

Many travelers assume that rail passes guarantee them seats on the trains they wish to ride. Not so. You need to **book seats ahead even if you are using a rail pass.** Seat reserva-

tions are required on some European trains, particularly high-speed trains, and are a good idea on trains that may be crowded—particularly in summer on popular routes. You will also need a reservation if you purchase sleeping accommodations.

➤ INFORMATION AND PASSES: Eurail- and EuroPasses are available through travel agents and **Rail Europe** (✉ 226-230 Westchester Ave., White Plains, NY 10604, ☎ 914/682–5172 or 800/438–7245; ✉ 2087 Dundas E., Suite 105, Mississauga, Ontario L4X 1M2, ☎ 416/602–4195). **DER Tours** (✉ Box 1606, Des Plaines, IL 60017, ☎ 800/782–2424, FAX 800/282–7474). **CIT Tours Corp.** (✉ 342 Madison Ave., Suite 207, New York, NY 10173, ☎ 212/697–2100, 800/248–8687, 800/248–7245 in western U.S.). Italian rail passes can be purchased through DER Tours or CIT Tours as well.

➤ UNIQUE GUIDEBOOK: *Italy by Train* by Tim Jepson (Fodor's Travel Publications, ☎ 800/533–6478 or from bookstores); $16.

➤ TRAIN INFORMATION: The main train station in Campania is the **Stazione Centrale** in Naples (✉ Piazza Garibaldi, ☎ 1478/88088 toll-free). The Ferrovia Circumvesuviana leaves for points east from the **Stazione Circumvesuviana** (✉ Corso Garibaldi, ☎ 081/779–2144); all trains also stop on the lower level of Stazione Centrale. Destinations include Herculaneum, Pompeii, and Sorrento. SEPSA manages two railway lines that leave from the **Stazione Cumana** (✉ near Montesanto Metro station, ☎ 081/735–4111). Both end at Torregavata, at the west end of the Bay of Naples; the Cumana line goes along the coast and stops at Pozzuoli and Baia, among other places. Salerno's train station (✉ Piazza V. Veneto, ☎ 1478/88088 toll-free) is a stop on the Milan–Reggio di Calabria line.

TRANSPORTATION
AROUND ITALY

Public transportation is the fastest mode of travel among Italy's cities. It is also relatively inexpensive in comparison to the costs of renting a car and paying for gas and tolls. Italy's cities are served by an extensive state

THE GOLD GUIDE / SMART TRAVEL TIPS

railway system (FS, ☞ Train Travel, *above*), with fast service on main lines (Milan–Venice–Florence–Rome–Naples) that in some cases beats plane travel in time and cost. A complete schedule of all trains in the country and fares can be bought from most newsstands for about $8.

Buses (☞ Bus Travel, *above*), somewhat less comfortable than trains and slightly less expensive, offer more frequent service to certain smaller cities and towns that are served only by secondary train lines. Buses are also better relied upon in more rugged areas. Ferries and hydrofoils ply among the islands; some islands, such as Capri and Ischia, have helicopter service, a more expensive alternative.

Italy has an intricate network of autostrade routes, good highways, and secondary roads, making renting a car (☞ Car Rental, *above*) for travel among most cities a feasible but expensive alternative to public transportation (not to mention complaints of white-knuckle driving by those inexperienced with autostrade speeds). A car can be a good investment if you are interested in carefree countryside rambles, offering time to explore more remote towns. Having a car in Naples, however, often leads to parking and traffic headaches, plus additional expense in the form of garage and parking fees.

TRAVEL AGENCIES

A good travel agent puts your needs first. Look for an agency that has been in business at least five years, emphasizes customer service, and has someone on staff who specializes in your destination. In addition **make sure the agency belongs to a professional trade organization.** The American Society of Travel Agents (ASTA), with 27,000 agents in some 170 countries, is the largest and most influential in the field. Operating under the motto "Integrity in Travel," it maintains and enforces a strict code of ethics and will step in to help mediate any agent-client disputes if necessary. ASTA also maintains a website that includes a directory of agents. (Note that if a travel agency is also acting as your tour operator, *see* Buyer Beware *in* Tours & Packages, *above*.)

➤ LOCAL AGENT REFERRALS: **American Society of Travel Agents** (ASTA, ☎ 800/965–2782 24-hr hot line, FAX 703/684–8319, www.astanet.com). **Association of British Travel Agents** (✉ 55–57 Newman St., London W1P 4AH, ☎ 0171/637–2444, FAX 0171/637–0713). **Association of Canadian Travel Agents** (✉ 1729 Bank St., Suite 201, Ottawa, Ontario K1V 7Z5, ☎ 613/521–0474, FAX 613/521–0805). **Australian Federation of Travel Agents** (✉ Level 3, 309 Pitt St., Sydney 2000, ☎ 02/9264–3299, FAX 02/9264–1085). **Travel Agents' Association of New Zealand** (✉ Box 1888, Wellington 10033, ☎ 04/499–0104, FAX 04/499–0786).

VISITOR INFORMATION

TOURIST INFORMATION

➤ AT HOME: **Italian Government Tourist Board** (ENIT; ✉ 630 5th Ave., New York, NY 10111, ☎ 212/245–4822, FAX 212/586–9249; ✉ 401 N. Michigan Ave., Chicago, IL 60611, ☎ 312/644–0990, FAX 312/644–3019; ✉ 12400 Wilshire Blvd., Suite 550, Los Angeles, CA 90025, ☎ 310/820–0098, FAX 310/820–6357; ✉ 1 Pl. Ville Marie, Suite 1914, Montréal, Québec H3B 3M9, ☎ 514/866–7667, FAX 514/392–1429; ✉ 1 Princes St., London W1R 8AY, ☎ 0171/408–1254, FAX 0171/493–6695).

➤ TOURIST OFFICES IN ITALY: **Rome** (✉ Via Parigi 5, 00185, ☎ 06/48899255). **Naples** (✉ Piazza dei Martiri 58, 80121, ☎ 081/405311); for further listings of tourist offices in Naples and the Amalfi Coast, *see* the A to Z section at the end of each regional chapter in this book.

➤ U.S. GOVERNMENT ADVISORIES: **U.S. Department of State** (✉ Overseas Citizens Services Office, Room 4811 N.S., 2201 C St. NW, Washington, DC 20520; ☎ 202/647–5225 for interactive hot line; 301/946–4400 for computer bulletin board; FAX 202/647–3000 for interactive hot line); enclose a self-addressed, stamped, business-size envelope.

WEB SITES

Do check out the World Wide Web when you're planning. You'll find everything from up-to-date weather forecasts to virtual tours of famous cities. Fodor's Web site, www.fodors.com, is a great place to start your on-line travels.

➤ SUGGESTED WEB SITES: For more information specifically on Italy, visit www.initaly.com, www.wel.it, and www.enit.it. The site for Ferrovie dello Stato, www.fs-on-line.com, is a good source for train information. The official site for the Italian Government Tourist Board is located at www.italiantourism.com. The official web site for Campania is www.regione.campania.it. A good web site for information about towns along the Amalfi Coast is www.ecostieramalfitana.it (then add the following: /costfoto/cost, then first four letters of town name directly following, and finally,.htm). Two handy sites for Capri are: www.caprinet.it and www.caprionline.com/.

WHEN TO GO

Campania is not always at its best in high summer: Naples can become a sweltering inferno, the archaeological sites swarm, and the islands and Amalfi Coast resorts are similarly overrun with tour buses and bad tempers. Any other time of year would be preferable, including even winter, when the temperature rarely falls below the comfort threshold and rain is relatively rare. Optimum times are May–June and September–October. Due to the temperate climate, bougainvillea and other floral displays can bloom through Christmas, while swimming is possible year-round, though you will only see the hardiest bathers out between October and May.

Summer is also the worst time for ascents to Vesuvius; the best visibility occurs around spring and fall. Watch the clock, however, as the days get shorter; excursions to Vesuvius, Pompeii, Herculaneum, and the islands all require some traveling, and it's easy to get caught with little daylight left. At most archaeological sites, you are rounded up two hours before sunset, but by that time most crowds have departed so late afternoon is an optimum time to enjoy Pompeii and Herculaneum in peace and quiet. Remember that a good number of hotels, restaurants, and other tourist facilities in Sorrento, the Amalfi Coast, and the islands close down from November until around Easter.

If you can avoid it, don't travel at all in Italy in August, when much of the population is on the move, especially around Ferragosto, the national holiday period which begins August 15 and generally extends to the beginning of September; at this time, Naples is fairly deserted and many of its restaurants and shops are closed. Of course, with residents away on vacation, this makes crowds less of a bother for tourists.

CLIMATE

Weatherwise, the best months for sightseeing are April, May, June, September, and October—generally pleasant and not too hot. The hottest months are July and August, when humidity can make things pretty unpleasant. However, most of the places covered in this book lie along the seashore, if not actually in the sea (Capri, Ischia, Procida) which takes some of the curse off the heat. Winters are relatively mild but cold fronts can arrive and stay for days.

NAPLES

Jan.	53F	12	May	72F	22C	Sept.	79F	26C
	40	4		54	12		61	16
Feb.	55F	13C	June	79F	26C	Oct.	71F	22C
	41	5		61	16		54	12
Mar.	59F	15C	July	84F	29C	Nov.	63F	17C
	44	6		65	18		48	9
Apr.	65F	18C	Aug.	84F	29C	Dec.	56F	14C
	48	9		65	18		44	6

➤ FORECASTS: **Weather Channel Connection** (☎ 900/932–8437), 95¢ per minute from a Touch-Tone phone.

1 DESTINATION: NAPLES AND THE AMALFI COAST

NAPOLI EVER AFTER

HE ACUTE STAGES ARE EASY to diagnose: the symptoms cry out. Utter the words *Bay of Naples, Positano,* or *Capri,* and patients will close their eyes and sigh—or roll their eyeballs and moan. If it's an advanced case, they will embark on a monologue in which you will be able to discern such phrases and fragments as ". . . the lure of the Mediterranean," ". . . the magic of the Southern sun," ". . . water that out-sapphires the jewels at Tiffany's," ". . . the song of the sirens." Every ailment—physical, mental, or social—reflects a need. Acute and widespread Campania mania—the hopeless infatuation with Campania and its myriad sun-wreathed resorts and starlighted isles—simply proves (with or without spots) that there is something in the organism, blood, and mental makeup of every modern-day escapist that requires a good dose of this relentlessly romantic corner of the world.

It has been this way ever since the Roman emperors escaped overheated Rome by building pleasure palaces around the Bay of Naples—and, in the process, inventing the very idea of the vacation. Back then, some Roman travel agent urged his countrymen to "See Naples and Die." Ever since, up to today, this pithy phrase has been interpreted in contrasting, equally viable ways. Lovers of Naples, asking what there is on earth that you can't find here, get the slogan's true meaning. The hard-liners, noting the murderous traffic, Mafia doings, ever-present threat of Vesuvius erupting, and the region's earthquakey history, say, "See Naples and die." As it turns out, the saying originally advised travelers to visit the city on the bay, then check out the nearby town of Mori (Latin for "to die"). And it is in this sense that this guidebook proceeds. It is simply a given that you must first explore this relentlessly fascinating city, then move on to the rest of Campania, a province that stacks snazzy resorts, grandly Baroque palaces, Edenic gardens, the most satisfying hundred miles of coastline to be found in tourist Europe, and some of the oldest ruins this side of Constantinople into one mammoth must-see sandwich.

However, if you limit your tour to Sorrento, Ravello, Capri, Ischia, Positano, Pompeii, and Amalfi, you will "see" Campania, but you won't understand it. To do that, you must get to know Naples itself. Most guidebooks approach this capital of Campania with a degree of circumspection, treating her as the cousin who would be presentable if only she toned down her makeup, watched her mouth, and didn't try to palm her date's wallet. But it could also have something to do with the array of things to see in Naples: the supreme, sun-drunk, natural setting with Dame Vesuvius tapping her feet across the Bay of Naples; the richest museum of Greco-Roman antiquities in the world; one of the finest collections of Renaissance paintings; outstanding examples of architecture from medieval to modern; and a kaleidoscope of colorful vignettes. But you don't come to Naples to see things, as such; you come to Naples to *be*. Naples is a kinetic gust of 3-D garlic-and-basil aromatherapy for the soul, a vital and revitalizing splash of reality; Naples is rediscovering the "simple things" and finding them exalted into ecstasies of complication; Naples is fluidity among stasis, fertility spawning misery, infinite intelligence circumventing colossal stupidity. Naples is intense, and intensely poetic. Naples doesn't need defending—it does that quite well by itself, thank you. And it is not rational, despite the many grids that various rulers vainly laid down to tame it. Naples is about falling in love, not blindly—that wouldn't last long, in any case—but instead by having your senses and sensibilities shamelessly charmed into full bloom.

It's not only the scenery that will incessantly engage your senses; it's also the Neapolitans themselves. More so than in any Italian city, the engine driving Naples is its people. Sophia Ponti, *née* Loren, the most famous living Neapolitan (okay, so she's from the suburb of Pozzuoli) recently confided that her *concittadini* "had many virtues: fantasy, sincerity, generosity, boastfulness, a sense of humor . . . Neapolitans do not have defects . . . or at least I've never noticed any." Not everyone has been so complimentary: Throughout history foreigners of all stripes have sustained a positively unseemly orgy of righteous indignation and disdain for the Neapolitans and their anarchic and passionate approach to morality. Already in ancient times, the entire Neapolitan area (of Baia in particular) was notorious as a fleshpot. The goings-on in the court of Joan I in the 14th century make that old 1980s soap opera *Dynasty* look like an unimaginative Romper Room model of treachery and lust. Naples's reputation for sexual permissiveness was sealed when the French troops of Charles VIII, chased out of Naples, took back with them an epidemic they later termed "the Neapolitan disease": syphilis. Epidemiological historians still argue over the origins of the disease in Europe, but the damage was done. The very Victorian philosopher Walter Benjamin simply dismissed Naples as "a lost city."

Yes, contrary to native daughter Sophia, others have looked upon the Neapolitans with a less generous eye, put off by their robust earthiness, their physicality, their volatility. The truth is, on deeper acquaintance, the mannerisms of the Neapolitans are found to be merely the prickly nettles that must be navigated before reaching the ripe center. Their mode of life is simply an inextinguishable belief that the art of living lies in enjoying what surrounds you, not passively, but with enthusiasm—be it the sunshine, a glass of wine, romance, a scam, a prayer, a song, an argument, a traffic jam. Sublime artists of existence, Neapolitans are skilled players in the larger, more serious world. And yet, far from being bitterly cynical, they take the same delight in the ingeniousness, the virtuosity as it were, of a crook as they do of an artist. They are free of cynicism and loaded with courage (Naples was the only city in World War II to rout the Nazi occupiers in a spontaneous revolt).

Naples is almost as old as Rome, and the main components of the historically constructed mentality are Greek and Spanish—testimony to the city's ancient Greek founders and its 16th-century Spanish rulers—rather than Italian as such. Greek was commonly spoken in Naples, even under the Roman Empire, and Naples was considered an outpost and living remnant of Greek culture in Italy, much as New Orleans retained its Frenchness in 19th-century America; the Neapolitans' brilliant,

argumentative, and impossibly charming nature is ancient Greek, and a number of words in the widely spoken present-day dialect retain concepts of the founders. To this have been added Spanish pride and an intransigent sense of honor.

Once experienced deeply and openly, Naples remains a reference point while exploring the rest of Campania—at once a grounding in reality and a glimpse into the stratosphere of fantasy. There are a fair number of sights to see in this region, but many visitors find such pursuits beside the point, for they look upon Campania as a playground, a school, a way of life that insists on having its way with you. Who but the Neapolitans could have invented dolce far niente—the sweetness of doing nothing? But fulfillment under the Campanian sun comes in various guises. The legions of honeymooners, Main Streeters, and deadline slaves could be lounging in the very sand once trod by Nero, Tiberius, and Hadrian. Virgil's *Georgics* and Wagner's *Parsifal* came to life in view of these waters. Passion—pairs on the scene have included Admiral Nelson and Lady Hamilton and Elizabeth Taylor and Richard Burton—has a way of percolating under these skies. Numerous great and once-great names spent time here, writing, painting, philosophizing, or just drinking in the grand scenery.

Like them, you will want to depart Campania with that final sense of beauty unparalleled, with the echoes of Capri's grottoes still resounding in your ears and the perfume of the flowers of Ravello still in your nostrils, with the austere classicism of Paestum oddly blending in your mind with the Cave of the Cumaean Sibyl, and with the panorama from your window in Naples, with its splendid bay and ever-threatening volcano, all comprising one vast picture in your mind. If you're lucky, that celebrated Neapolitan vista will be yours to enjoy from your hotel room on a spring morning when the sun is just warm enough to be comfortable. Step out onto your balcony for the first time and drink in the panorama. Down below your balcony will be the Bay of Naples, with its gently curving shoreline, docks, and palm-lined avenues. Farther along will be the Castel Nuovo of Charles I of Anjou, its eternal and primitive shape contrasting sharply with far more modern buildings near it. Follow the bay with your eyes to the horizon and Vesuvius itself. Look to your right to see a little islet that seems to spring directly out of the the bay. This is Capri. Ischia is probably a little out of your vision's range, as are Pozzuoli and Cumae, but no matter. Far below you the bay is shimmering blue. In the distance gentle little waves fleck it with white. The air is fragrant with flowering vines and trees. A violently purple bougainvillea cluster clings to the hotel trellis within a few feet of your head. It would be pleasant just to sit there in the warmly comfortable sun and relax for the rest of the day—maybe for a week or so. That's what a Neapolitan would do. But we haven't time.

—Gregory W. Bailey

WHAT'S WHERE

Campania is a region of names—Capri, Sorrento, Pompeii, Paestum, Positano, Amalfi, Ravello—that evoke visions of cliff-shaded coves, sun-dappled waters, and mighty ruins. And Naples, a tumultuous, animated city, the very heart of Campania, stands guard over these treasures. Campania stretches south in flat coastal plains and low mountains from Baia Domizia, Capua, and Caserta to Naples and Pompeii on the magnificent bay; past the isles of Capri and Ischia; along the rocky coast to Sorrento, Amalfi, and Salerno; and farther still past the Cilento promontory to Sapri and the Calabria border. Inland lie the bleak fringes of the Apennines and the rolling countryside around Benevento.

Many of Campania's attractions are on the Golfo di Napoli (Bay of Naples)—including the city itself and its satellite islands, Capri and Ischia, and the archaeological sites of Pompeii, Herculaneum, and the Campi Flegrei (Phlegrean Fields), at the northern end of the bay. At the southern end, Sorrento also lies within this charmed circle, within easy distance of Positano, Amalfi, and the pleasures of the Amalfi Coast. Farther afield, Paestum offers more classical sights, and inland, Caserta and Benevento have a Bourbon palace and more majestic Roman remains.

Naples

The most operatic of Italy's cities, Naples is extraordinary, and it is the Neapolitans who make it so. Their capacity for warmth, friendliness, and *amore* is amazing. They love you, they love their city, and they want you to love it back. But to win her loving heart, you must woo her, just as Clark Gable did Sophia Loren in the 1956 film *It Happened in Naples*. That heart is the Spaccanapoli, the kaleidoscopic 5-km-long (3-mi-long) pedestrian ribbon that cuts the inner city in two. This is the historic center of Naples, and any city tour should include this open-air museum of a neighborhood, studded with some of the city's most famous churches and palaces, including the Gesù Nuovo, the Cappella Sansevero, and the city duomo. In the streets, the atmosphere is almost carnival-like, as crowds at one of the many sidewalk cafés overflow into the narrow, canyonlike roadways.

Spaccanapoli is an oasis sheltered from the grandeur of classical Naples, which is centered around the Piazza del Plebiscito, a vast square laid out in the Napoleonic era and today the eye of the urban storm swirling around it. Around this square and the nearby Piazza Municipio are the great urban monuments—whose style is best described as overblown imperial—erected by many of Naples's invaders and conquerors: the brooding medieval keep of the Castel Nuovo; the Palazzo Reale, where the Bourbon kings lived in awe-inspiring splendor; the glittering 19th-century Teatro San Carlo opera house; and the elegant Church of San Francesco di Paola. Just to the north is Via Toledo (often called Via Roma)—the "Broadway" of Naples, which bisects the city north to south and stretches from the harbor to the hill of Capodimonte. This grand thoroughfare runs by the world-famous Museo Archeologico Nazionale, packed with archaeological relics of the Classical era, and a must-see before venturing out of town to see Pompeii and Herculaneum. Their most important finds are on display here—everything from sculpture to carbonized fruit—and seeing them will add to the pleasure of your trip to the two excavated towns. Near the museum is the neighborhood of I Vergini, where some famous Baroque palaces designed by Ferdinando Sanfelice can be seen. From here, footsore and weary, you deserve a taxi or bus to reach the Capodimonte hill, high over Naples, where the Museo di Capodimonte, the greatest of the Bourbon palaces, has artistic masterpieces and royal apartments to ogle as well incomparable views over the entire city from its Bosco di Capodimonte (park).

Just to the south of the Piazza del Plebiscito is Naples's famous harbor and the elegant stretch of waterfront that runs from the Lungomare over to the Riviera di Chiaia. Here is Castel dell'Ovo, a 12th-century fortress built over the ruins of an ancient Roman villa, whose site commands a view of the whole harbor—proof, if you need it, that the Romans knew a premium location when they saw it. Nestled under the walls of the castle is the Borgo Marinaro, a toylike fishing village built at the end of the 19th century for the fishermen of the Santa Lucia district. Nearby is the diamond-shape Piazza dei Martiri, center of chic Naples and surrounded by streets lined with elegant boutiques and antiques shops. Other must-dos include the world-famous Aquarium; the sumptuous Villa Pignatelli; the historic Pizzofalcone quarter; and the grand 19th-century bayside promenades of Via Partenope and Via Caracciolo, lined with luxury hotels and Belle Epoque mansions and backdropped by a vista of Vesuvius.

Funiculars link this part of town with Naples's steep Vomero Hill, today a gentrified residential quarter and home to three important museums: Villa La Floridiana, the Castel Sant'Elmo, and the Certosa di San Martino. They have treasures galore, but you might be content just to take in the heart-stopping views from the slopes of the Vomero neighborhood. If you can adapt to its ways, Naples may become your favorite city in Italy. After all, who really needs stoplights?

On the outskirts of the city are three areas that make interesting day excursions. To the west of the city, strumming mandolins can still be heard at the *ristoranti* (restaurants) found in Posillipo, a district once favored as a seaside getaway by the Spanish and French aristocracy. To the northeast is Caserta, a spectacular 18th-century palace built by the Bourbons to be the Italian answer to Versailles. Farther east is Benevento, site of the Arch of Trajan, one of the most beautiful ancient Roman triumphal arches extant.

Around the Bay: From Pompeii to the Phlegrean Fields

The area surrounding Naples has a Greco-Roman history that makes the city look like the new kid on the block. The Greeks set out to Hellenize Italy's boot in the 6th and 7th centuries BC by settling here at Cumae. Later, the Romans used the area as one giant playground, paving the roads from their colonies to numerous pleasure villas along the sea. Both groups left ruins for modern-day explorers to peruse. West of Naples is the Campi Flegrei—the fields of fire—alternatively condemned by the ancient Greeks as the entrance to Hades and immortalized as the Elysian Fields, a paradise for the righteous dead. This whole area floats freely on a mass of molten lava very close to the surface (Italy's two major seismic faults intersect here). Such sights as the Solfitara, or "little Vesuvius," inspired Dante when he wrote his *Inferno*. Here is where Nero and Hadrian had summer villas, Virgil composed his poetry, and the Apostle Paul landed to spread the Gospel. Also here are ancient sites, such as the Greeks' first mainland city, Cumae—home of the fabled Antro della Sibilla (Cave of the Cumaean Sibyl); Nero's Baths of Baia; the ancient Roman amphitheater of Pozzuoli, the third-largest arena in Italy; and the Lago d'Averno (Lake Avernus), which the ancients thought to be the very gates of hell. Today water-skiers glide over its surface without getting sucked in.

To the east of Naples around the bay lie Pompeii and Herculaneum (Ercolano), the most completely preserved cities of classical antiquity, along with their nemesis, the dream volcano, Vesuvius. Volcanic ash and mud from Il Vesuvio preserved these towns almost exactly as they were on the day it erupted in AD 79, leaving them not just archaeological ruins but testimonies of daily life in the ancient world. All three sites can be visited from either Naples or Sorrento using the Circumvesuviana railway, the suburban line which provides fast, frequent, and economical service. Pompeii, noted for its romantic legend (thanks to Sir Edward Bulwer-Lytton's Victorian potboiler *The Last Days of Pompeii*) as well as its actual artifacts, is the most famous system of Roman excavations anywhere, but perhaps Herculaneum—Pompeii's smaller but wealthier and more cultured neighbor—is the more interesting. Above all looms the profile of Vesuvius, the cause of all this ruin and, as a concomitant, of all this preservation. Its ominous, towering profile is so inseparable from the Bay of Naples area and the ferocious power it can unleash so vivid as you tour the sights of the cities that it destroyed, you may be overwhelmed by the urge to explore the crater itself.

The Islands: Capri, Ischia, and Procida

History's hedonists have long luxuriated on Campania's famous islands. The Roman emperor Tiberius built a dozen villas on Capri to indulge his sexual whims. Later residents have included dancer Rudolf Nureyev and droves of artists and writers. These days day-trippers make up the bulk of the visitors, and they can easily turn Capri from a pint-size paradise into pure purgatory on summer weekends, when the fabled isle is packed with far too many people. Yet even the crowds are not enough to destroy Capri's very special charm. The town is a Moorish opera set of shiny white houses, tiny squares, and narrow medieval alleyways hung with bougainvillea. Although there are famous man-made sights— the Villa of Tiberius, the Certosa di San Giacomo, and the Villa San Michele, among them—it is the island's natural wonders that are the main lure. The famed Blue Grotto is but one of many such caverns, and some connoisseurs think it's not even the most beautiful of the grottoes, instead giving the laurel variously to its Green, Yellow, Pink, or White counterpart. Elsewhere are the geologic marvels of the Arco Naturale, the Pizzolungo stone pinnacle, and the famed I Faraglioni rocks, which anchor the island's southern coast. At night everyone congregates on the Piazzetta to search for heavenly bodies—of the Hollywood, not the astral, variety.

Twice the size of Capri, the neighboring island of Ischia promises more peace and quiet, although the hordes of Germans who take over in the summer can make this island as congested as Capri. Ischia's volcano, Monte Epomeo, shoots up to a height of 2,585 ft, but don't be alarmed— it hasn't erupted for nearly seven centuries. Around the rim of the island are Campania's most beautiful white-sand beaches and a number of towns, including Casamicciola and Lacco Ameno, which trade on the island's greatest drawing cards: spas, thermal baths, and mineral springs. For a break from a mud bath, explore the Castello at Ischia Porto or La Mortella, the gardens designed by Sir William Walton, which are at Forio. The nearby island of Procida is a wild and rugged island of great charm. Its small population of fishermen, vineyard workers, domed houses, and sweeping views were all immortalized in the Academy Award–winning film *Il Postino*.

Sorrento and the Amalfi Coast

Emperors and kings, popes, the greatest musicians, writers, and artists have made Sorrento their preferred abode for more than 2,500 years——and it just takes one look at the view over the Bay of Naples to tell you why. Directly across the water from Naples, Sorrento was until the mid-20th century a small, genteel resort favored by central European princes, English aristocrats, and American literati. Now the town has grown and spread out along the crest of its famous cliffs, and apartments stand where citrus groves once bloomed. Still, the old historic town is a Belle Epoque treasure, with picturesque alleyways, palm tree–shaded cafés, and some of Italy's most gorgeous hotels. Like most resorts, Sorrento is best off-season, either in spring and early autumn or in winter, when Campania's mild climate can make a stay pleasant anywhere along the coast.

Sorrento is the leading jewel of the Sorrentine peninsula, but there are other destinations to explore along the promontory: the gracious villa-hotels of Sant'Agnello; the idyllic fishing port of Massa Lubrense; the mountaintop aerie of Sant'Agata sui Due Golfi (which offers a Cinerama vista over both the bays of Naples and Salerno); the beach at Marina del Cantone; and the ancient Roman villas of Castellamare di Stabia.

Heading south from Sorrento the south side of the peninsula leads to the dramatically scenic, spectacularly beautiful Amalfi Coast, linked together by a road that must have a thousand turns, each with a different view, on a dizzying 69-km (43-mi) journey from Sorrento to Salerno. Crystal lagoons where the water is emerald-green, small boats lying in sandy coves like brightly colored fish, vertiginous cliffs hollowed out with fairy grottoes where the air is turquoise and the water an icy blue, and white, sunbaked villages dripping with flowers all join together in a single scenic masterpiece. Whatever town you pick as your favorite, you'll have a battle on your hands if you insist that it deserves the title of Most Beautiful. Some prefer Positano, the world's most photographed fishing village and once called "the poor man's Capri" until the jet set discovered it. Others choose Amalfi, a city adorned with medieval monasteries, Arab-Sicilian cloisters, souk-like passageways, and the coast's grandest cathedral. Creative souls, from Boccaccio to Greta Garbo, have always preferred Ravello, perched 1,500 ft over the famously blue Bay of Salerno, a town blessed with some of Italy's most beautiful gardens and villas. To the south, beyond modern Salerno, lies ancient Paestum, where three of the best-preserved ancient Greek temples anywhere, including Greece itself, stand sharp against the cobalt sky.

PLEASURES AND PASTIMES

The Art of Enjoying Art

You could select almost any three paintings in Naples's museums or churches and spend not only weeks or months but a lifetime in their company. But when you get all that beauty wholesale—a slew of Titians, great Baroque altarpieces, acres of painted Annunciations—your eyes can glaze over from the heavy downpour of images, dates, and names, and you begin to lean, Pisa-like, on your companion for support. The secret, of course, is to act like a turtle—not a hare—and take your sweet time. Instead of trotting after briskly efficient tour guides, allow the splendors of the age to unfold—slowly. Get out and explore the actual settings—medieval chapels, Rococo palaces, and Romanesque cloisters—for which these marvelous examples of Italy's art and sculpture were conceived centuries ago and where many of them may still be seen in situ.

Museums are only the most obvious places to view art; there are always the trompe l'oeil renderings of Assumptions that float across Baroque church ceilings and piazza scenes that might be Renaissance paintings brought to life. Instead of studying an 18th-century altarpiece in the Museo di Capodimonte, spend an hour in the Rococo cloisters of the Church of Santa Chiara. An hour walking through the open-air museum of Naples's Spaccanapoli district will reveal more about the artistic energy of Naples than a day spent in its art collections. Of course, chances are you'll also see a Caravaggio altarpiece so perfect, so beautiful, that your knees will buckle.

Buon Appetito!: The Pleasures of Dining

It's no wonder Neapolitan food has won the hearts (and stomachs) of millions: The rich volcanic soil and fertile waters surrounding the city provide abundant and varied seafood, Vesuvian wines, vine-ripe tomatoes, and luscious fruits. Simple, earthy, at once wholesome and sensual, as sophisticated in its purity as the most complex cuisine, as inspired in its aesthetics as the art and architecture of its culture, the cooking of Campania strikes a chord that resonates today as it did when it was served up centuries ago. Its enduring appeal can be traced to an ancient principle: respect for the essence of the thing itself. Naples—the homeland of pizza—is most famous for pizza *alla Margherita* (with tomato, mozzarella, and basil) and marinara (with tomato, garlic, and oregano). Nothing could be simpler, yet nothing is more delicious. That is the wonder of the cuisine of Campania. Like Michelangelo freeing the prisoners that dwelt within the stone—innate, organic—a chef in Campania seems intuitively to seek out the crux of the thing he is about to cook and flatter it, subtly and with the purest of ingredients.

Today the newest trend in southern Italian cooking is to serve up the old—the simple, rustic, time-honored forms of *cucina simpatica, rustica,* and *trattoria*—with a nouvelle flair. Just venture to Campania's greatest restaurant, Don Alfonso 1890, in Sant'Agata sui Due Golfi, and discover how famed chef Alfonso Iaccarino's gastronomic brilliance has made *la nouvelle cucina* newer still. Yet Signore Iaccarino also stays true to Campania's roots, using spices brought to the region by Arab traders and luxuries *à la française* that would have delighted the Bourbons who ruled Naples in the 18th century (try his cannelloni stuffed with asparagus, truffles, *and* foie gras). Above all, this chef insists that Campanian cooking remains *puro* and *sincero*—true to the region's culinary traditions.

Whether a slice of pizza from a street vendor in Naples or a culinary extravaganza at Don Alfonso 1890, dining is a marvelous part of the total southern Italian experience, a chance to enjoy authentic specialties and ingredients. Visitors have a choice of eating places, ranging from a *ristorante* (restaurant) to a trattoria, *tavola calda,* or *rosticceria.* The line separating ristoranti from trattorie have blurred of late, but a trattoria is usually a family-run place, simpler in decor, menu, and service than a ristorante and slightly less expensive. Some rustic-looking spots call themselves *osterie* but are really restaurants (a true osteria is a basic, down-to-earth tavern.) At a tavola calda or rosticceria, prepared food is sold to be consumed on the spot or taken out; you choose what you want at the counter and pay at the cashier. An *enoteca* is a wine bar where you can order wine by the glass or bottle; most have tables, and many serve savory light meals and snacks.

None of the above eateries serves breakfast; in the morning you go to a *caffè* (coffee bar), where you can also find sandwiches, pastries, and other snacks that are perfect for later in the day. Tell the cashier what you want, pay for it, and then take the stub to the counter, where you restate your order and then drink and eat standing at the counter. Remember that table service costs extra, almost double; don't sit at a table unless you want to be served. On the other hand, if you do sit down, you'll be allowed to linger as long as you like.

In eating places of all kinds the menu is posted in the window or just inside the door so you can see what you're getting into (in a snack bar or tavola calda the price list is usually displayed near the cashier). In all but the simplest places there's a *coperto* (cover charge) and usually also a *servizio* (service charge) of 10%–15%, only part of which goes to the waiter. A *menù turistico* (tourist menu)—which usually means you've stepped into tourist territory, beware—includes taxes and service, but beverages are usually extra.

Generally, a typical meal in a restaurant or trattoria consists of at least two courses: a first course of pasta, risotto, or soup and a second course of meat or fish. Side dishes such as vegetables and salads cost extra, as do desserts. There is no such thing as a side dish of pasta; pasta is a course in itself, and Italians would never think of serving a salad with it; the salad comes later. Years ago pasta dishes were inexpensive because restaurateurs made their profit on the total of the first and second courses. Now tourists and even some diet-conscious Italians tend to order only one course—usually a pasta, perhaps followed by a salad or vegetables—so hosts have jacked up the price of first courses. Now, about antipasti: many a misunderstanding arises over a lavish offering of antipasti, which literally means "before the pasta." No matter how generous and varied the antipasti, the host expects you to order at least one other course. Pizza is in a category by itself and is a one-dish meal, even for the Italians. But some replace the starter course of pasta with a small pizza.

Tap water is safe almost everywhere unless labeled *"non potabile."* Most people order bottled *acqua minerale* (mineral water), either *gassata* (carbonated), or *naturale,* or *nongassata* (without bubbles). In a restaurant you order it by the *litro* (liter) or *mezzo litro* (half-liter); often the waiter will bring it without being asked, so if you don't like it or want to keep your check down, make a point of ordering *acqua semplice* (tap water). You can also order *un bicchiere di acqua minerale* (a glass of mineral water) at any bar. Italians mostly go heavy on the salt: If you are on a low-sodium diet, ask for everything (within reason) *senza sale* (without salt).

Lunch is served in Campania from 1:30 to 3:30, dinner from 8:30 to 10:30, or later in some restaurants. Almost all eating places close one day a week and for vacations in summer, especially during the last two weeks in August.

Il Dolce Far Niente

The idea of vacation was probably invented when some hardworking Roman emperor escaped Rome for a villa on the Bay of Naples, and ever since the denizens of Campania have been fine-tuning what they call il dolce far niente—the sweet art of idleness. In today's hectic age, even relaxing can feel like a chore, but thanks to Campania's opulent villas, picture-perfect coastal resorts, and dreamy hill towns, you can idle here more successfully than anywhere else. But it takes more than trading in a silk tie for a T-shirt; you have to adjust to the deeper, subtler rhythms of leisure Italian style. Hours spent over a Campari in a sun-splashed café; days spent soaking up the sun on the beach at Positano; an afternoon spent painting a watercolor at the gardens of Ravello's Villa Cimbrone: You may be pleasantly surprised to find that such pursuits prove more beneficial than forced marches through the obligatory sights of Naples, Pompeii, or Amalfi. The luxury is often in the lingering.

GREAT ITINERARIES

If art and antiquity are high on your list, consider spending a few days in Naples before retreating to the beauty of Capri, Ischia, or the Amalfi Coast. Now that the city has made great strides in combating urban decay, practically everyone who takes the time and trouble to discover its artistic riches and appreciate its vivacious nature considers it well worth the effort. Naples is close to Italy's most fabled classical ruins, and you should dedicate at least a morning or afternoon to Pompeii or Herculaneum.

If You Have 3 Days

In 🏛 **Naples,** a visit to the **Museo Archeologico Nazionale** is an essential preparation (or follow-up) for an expedition to **Herculaneum** (Ercolano) and **Pompeii,** indispensable sights for anyone visiting Campania. The islands of 🏛 **Ischia** and 🏛 **Capri** can also be reached from Naples and make an ideal antidote to the city's noise. It is worth spending at least one night outside Naples, and a good alternative to the islands would be 🏛 **Sorrento,** an easy hydrofoil ride away and a good base from which to tour the nearby Amalfi Coast, where you could visit small towns—🏛 **Positano,** 🏛 **Amalfi,** 🏛 **Ravello,** and/or **Vietri sul Mare,** for instance—on a third day's excursion.

If You Have 5 Days

In 🏛 **Naples,** more time will enable you to take in one of the region's greatest palace-museums, the **Museo Capodimonte,** housed in one of the Bourbon royal palaces. Outside town you could also see more than

just one of the classical sights, including a visit to the Greek temples of **Paestum,** highly recommended for a glimpse at some of Magna Graecia's most stunning relics. You might also venture north to **Caserta** to wander around the royal palace. Back in the Bay of Naples, spend your fourth and fifth days exploring 🏛 **Ischia** and 🏛 **Sorrento,** both undemanding holiday resorts with plenty of natural beauty.

If You Have 7 Days

A week in Campania will allow you to discover some of the more esoteric pleasures that Naples has to offer. Apart from the sheer vibrancy of its shopping streets and alleys and the glorious views over the waterfront, 🏛 **Naples** has plenty of diversions within its tight mesh of streets, and you should make time for visiting some of the many famous churches of the historic Spaccanapoli district, including the **Duomo,** of course, but also **Santa Chiara** and the **Cappella Sansevero,** with its 18th-century sculptures. Outside town head west to the volcanic region of the **Phlegrean Fields,** where Roman remains lie within a smoking, smoldering area rich with classical history. Spend three nights on the Amalfi Coast, making sure to visit inland 🏛 **Ravello,** and pass some time in pretty 🏛 **Positano,** which requires at least a day and a half. 🏛 **Capri,** too, deserves a couple of nights to appreciate fully its beauty— of secluded coves and beaches, not to mention the famous Blue Grotto—easily eclipsing the island's more lurid tourist trappings. You might pass a last day, perhaps en route out of Campania, in **Benevento,** which holds a well-preserved Roman theater and the renowned Arco di Traiano.

FODOR'S CHOICE

No two people will agree on what makes a perfect vacation, but it's fun and helpful to know what others think. Here's a compendium drawn from the must-see lists of hundreds of tourists. We hope you'll have a chance to experience some of these great memories-in-the-making yourself while visiting Campania. For detailed information about entries, refer to the appropriate chapters within this guidebook.

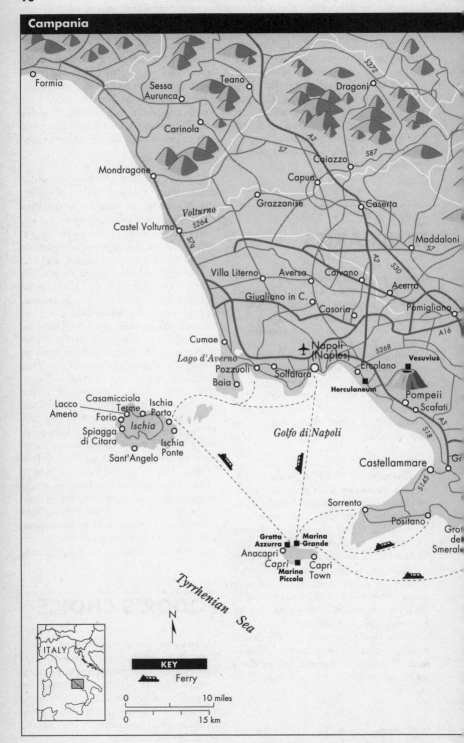

Formia

Sessa
Aurunca

Teano

Dragoni

S372

Carinola

A2

S7

Caiazzo

S87

Mondragone

Capua

Volturno

S264

Grazzanise

Caserta

Castel Volturno

S7a

Maddaloni

S7

Villa Literno

Aversa

Calvano

Acerra

Giugliano in C.

S30

A2

Pomigliano

Casoria

A16

Cumae

Napoli
(Naples)

S268

Lago d'Averno

Vesuvius

Pozzuoli

Solfatara

Ercolano

Herculaneum

Baia

Casamicciola
Terme

Lacco
Ameno

Ischia
Porto

Forio

Ischia

Golfo di Napoli

Pompeii

Scafati

A3

Spiaggia
di Citara

Ischia
Ponte

Sant'Angelo

Castellammare

Gr

S145

Sorrento

**Grotta
Azzurra**

**Marina
Grande**

Anacapri

Positano

Gro
de
Smerale

Capri

Capri
Town

**Marina
Piccola**

Tyrrhenian Sea

N

ITALY

KEY

🚢 Ferry

0   10 miles

0   15 km

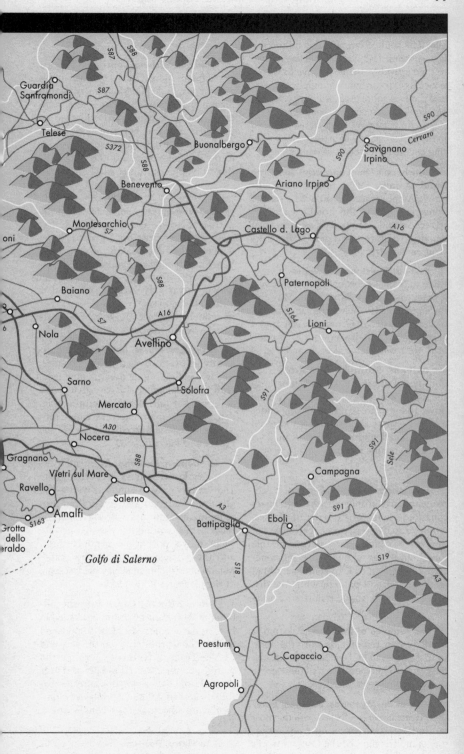

Moments

⭐ **Dawn Concert at the Villa Rufolo, Ravello.** The soul of serenity, this hilltop village, suspended between sea and sky, is home to the Fèstival Musicale di Ravello. Experience its extraordinary midnight concerts and the even more extraordinary *concerto all'alba*—a dawn concert that serenades the rising sun beginning at 4 AM, usually held in the first week of August—to enjoy a fitting encore to Ravello's stirring scenery.

⭐ **Luncheon at the Cappuccini Convento Hotel, Amalfi.** Set so high atop a cliff above Amalfi it seems you need a pair of wings to reach it, this hotel's legendary terrace-veranda frames a view of medieval Amalfi so picturesque it practically clicks your camera for you.

⭐ **Festa di San Gennaro, Naples.** Everything in Naples is brought to a boil twice a year—on the first Saturday in May and on September 19—when the Liquefaction of the Blood of San Gennaro is celebrated at the city duomo. If you want to "assist" at *Il Miracolo*, arrive as early as 7 AM.

⭐ **Twilight, Positano.** The utter tranquillity of Positano at sunset is a balm to the soul. Whitewashed houses tumble down to the azure sea, shimmering under a blood-orange sky. Reserve an alfresco table at a café and let it all soak in. *This* is why you came to Italy.

Places

⭐ **Spaccanapoli, Naples.** For perfect people-watching, promenade through Spaccanapoli, the historic district of Naples, whose packed streets, pungent aromas, and operatic hawking offer an unforgettable Punch-and-Judy show. Towering tenements (the tallest of 19th-century Europe) jostle with grand palazzi, while the district's swirling Baroque architecture melts even the stoniest hearts.

⭐ **The Temples of Paestum.** Paestum is blessed by its remoteness from the main tourist routes. The best times to absorb the grandeur and desolation of these noble ruins are daybreak and dusk.

⭐ **Villa of the Mysteries, Pompeii.** Enter this private house—adorned with the most famous frescoes surviving from antiquity—and the days of the Caesars won't seem that remote.

⭐ **Villa Cimbone, Ravello.** No one should miss the breathtaking gardens of this villa—whose roses once warmed Greta Garbo's chilly heart—and its sky-touching Belvedere of Infinity.

⭐ **Villa San Michele, Capri.** Join the cast posed for an Alma-Tadema painting at this antique-inspired villa. Make a wish standing on the Sphinx Parapet—here, high atop Anacapri, your spirit will shed its earthly bonds, and, hey, you never know. When you return by bus, be sure to be nice to the driver—you're 2,000 ft above the Bay of Naples on this road.

Comforts

⭐ **Bellevue-Syrene, Sorrento.** Long the darling of crowned heads (and heads that were once crowned), this legendary hotel is a fantasia of ducal salons, violet posies, Venetian chandeliers, and muted champagne corks. Today old-world guests still arrive—invariably greeting each other with "Haven't I seen you . . ."—to savor its unique ambience and to marvel at its grand vista of the Bay of Naples. *$$$$*

⭐ **Excelsior-Vittoria, Sorrento.** Magnificently set overlooking the Bay of Naples, this is a Belle Epoque dream come true, with gilded salons elegant enough to make a Proust heroine swoon, stunning gardens, and a romantic terrace where musicians lull guests with equal doses of Cole Porter and Puccini. *$$$$*

⭐ **Le Sirenuse, Positano.** As legendary as its namesake sirens, this hot-cool, exquisite 18th-century palazzo shimmers with stylish glamour: Venetian and Neapolitan museum-quality antiques, vine-entwined terraces with breathtaking views, a private yacht, Italy's most beautiful pool terrace, and the priciest—probably the best—restaurant on the Amalfi Coast are just some of the pleasures here. *$$$$*

⭐ **Punta Tragara, Capri.** Pity the billionaire who thinks his ship has sailed in but has never enjoyed a blissful stay here. Built by Le Corbusier, set at the very end of Via Tragara (Capri's, perhaps the world's, prettiest street), and perched over the rocks of I Faraglioni, this hotel has baronial guest rooms and a poolside restaurant whose beauty stops conversation. *$$$$*

⭐ **San Pietro, Positano.** Set like a gull's nest high over the Bay of Positano, this is the favorite Amalfi Coast "forgetaway" of Julia Roberts, Princess Caroline of

Monaco, and a gaggle of Agnellis. Part De Mille, part de Milo—the giddily pretty rooms here are accented with antique statues—the San Pietro remains the hotel wonder of the Amalfi Coast. *$$$$*

⭐ **Caruso Belvedere, Ravello.** With regal Empire-era salons and terraced gardens offering spellbinding views of the blue Bay of Salerno, this aristocratic hotel fairly purrs with gentility and style. No wonder authors like Virginia Woolf, Graham Greene, and Tennessee Williams often booked this place. *$$$–$$$$*

⭐ **Cappucini Convento, Amalfi.** Like Richard Wagner, you may be tempted to abandon your room and camp out under the stars on this hotel's legendary veranda, set high on a cliff over the sea. Originally a medieval convent, then a fabled inn in the Grand Tour era, this is still southern Italy's most sublime hotel. Touched by peace and quietude, guests enjoy more than a hint of the blessed isolation in which the monks once lived. *$$$*

⭐ **La Fenice, Positano.** All the scenic magic of the Amalfi Coast is distilled into one tiny package at this hotel, whose castaway cottages cascade down a hill in an ambuscade of bougainvillea. *$$–$$$*

⭐ **Lorelei et Londres, Sorrento.** *O Sole Mio!* The 19th-century music-box tinkle of Sorrento can still be clearly heard at this pensione, once favored by *Room with a View* ladies from England. With a terra-cotta facade sunburned by a century of sun and a café that seems to levitate over the Bay of Naples, this albergo (small hotel) should be declared a national monument by the Italian government. *$*

⭐ **Soggiorno Sansevero, Naples.** Set in the former palazzo of the Princes Sansevero, just a block away from the floridly magnificent Capella Sansevero and right on the most charming square of Spaccanapoli, this tiny pensione can't be beat for the location—or price. *$*

Flavors

⭐ **Don Alfonso 1890, Sant'Agata.** Haute-hungry pilgrims know the road up to mountaintop Sant'Agata is the *strada* to culinary glory: a table at Don Alfonso, southern Italy's finest restaurant. We recommend *gamberi crude al caviale blue con sucito di limone*, or red shrimp with blue caviar—it's also Prince Rainier's favorite. *$$$$*

⭐ **Eolo, Amalfi.** The room is small, elegant, with an Gothic window framing a view of the harbor; the kitchen is superlative, with an eye for the spectacular (just order the scampi risotto, adorned with a jewel-like crustacean). Opened in 1998, this is run by the Gargano family, whose famous Hotel Santa Caterina is just across the bay. *$$$$*

⭐ **Villa Pompeiana, Sorrento.** Here, on the site of the seaside villa where Emperor Augustus once dined on moray eels fattened on human flesh, William Waldorf Astor built a re-creation of the glory that was Rome—a tiny villa set with Pompeiian murals, mosaic floors, and a stone terrace worthy of a Caesar. Now it's the restaurant of the Hotel Bellevue Syrene, and you can dine here on fine regional delicacies like Li Galli lobster with melon pearls. No moray eels, however. *$$$$*

⭐ **O' Capurale, Positano.** Positano is all about easy elegance, and this dining spot sums it all up. Graced with a coved ceiling awash with colorful Fauvist-style frescoes, the dining room vibes with happy, stylish diners unwinding before your eyes. All it takes is one blissful lunch here to forget all about those newspaper headlines. *$$*

⭐ **Lo Scoglio, Marina di Cantone.** Dramatically set on a pier by the beach, you can hear, smell—even *taste*—the waves from here on a rough day. The cuisine, not unexpectedly, is freshly caught seafood, but even if you only stop by for a gelato at this informal ristorante, you'll enjoy yourself immensely (especially if you're a water baby, or are accompanied by one). *$–$$*

⭐ **O' Guarracino, Positano.** Just maybe the prettiest pizzeria anywhere, this tree house overlooking the cliffs, the sea, and Torre Trasìta has a setting to make you fall in, or rekindle, love (choose carefully with whom you sit). *$–$$*

⭐ **Pizzeria Brandi, Naples.** Since Pavarotti considers this an obligatory stop when in Naples, why shouldn't you? The birthplace of *pizza Margherita*—created in 1889 to honor a former queen of Italy—this is an adorably cozy spot with full-blast Neapolitan charm. One glorious bite here and you'll forget about those Little Caesar pies back home. *$*

FESTIVALS AND SEASONAL EVENTS

Campania's top seasonal events are listed below, and any one of them could provide the stuff of lasting memories. It is revealing that the Italian *festa* can be translated either as "festival or holiday" or "feast"—food is usually the most fundamental aspect of Italian celebrations. For further information contact the **Italian Government Tourist Board** (☞ Visitor Information *in* Smart Travel Tips A to Z) and the **regional visitor centers,** listed in the A to Z section at the end of each chapter in this book.

ning from Piazza del Plebiscito over to Piazza Municipio, concluding with fireworks over the Stazione Marittima along the bay. Fashionable merrymakers zero in on Capri, where islanders stir from their wintry pace to welcome hordes for days-long celebrations.

JAN. 5–6:➤ **Epiphany Celebrations** (Epifania). Roman Catholic Epiphany decorations are evident throughout Campania. Notable is the celebration in Naples when the Befana witch arrives on the Piazza del Plebiscito. "Good" children line up for sweets on Via Foria.

San Gennaro—a procession of the saint's relics—through the streets of Spaccanapoli to the Church of Santa Chiara.

EARLY MAY:➤ **Maggio dei Monumenti** (Monuments of May) opens Neapolitan palazzi, churches, and landmarks usually closed to the public. The month also sees the **Notti d'Arte,** a series of concerts and performances in historic settings, such as the Capella Palatina of the Castel Nuovo, the Salone da Ballo of the Museo di Capodimente, and the Salone d'Ercole of the Palazzo Reale.

DEC.:➤ **Christmas in Naples** (Natale a Napoli) is celebrated through December until January 6 (Epiphany). The season officially opens December 8 on the day of the Immacolata (Immaculate Conception), when the mayor lays wreaths on the Guglia dell'Immacolata and when the *Presepe* (crèche) shops of Via Gregorio Armeno are thronged by Neapolitans. Historic crèches are on view in many churches, including Santa Chiara, San Domenico Maggiore, and the Gesù Nuovo.

DEC.–JUNE:➤ The **Opera Season** is in full swing at Teatro San Carlo in Naples. ✉ *Via San Carlo 101–3,* ☎ *081/797-2111.*

DEC. 31:➤ Naples stages a rousing **New Year's Eve** celebration, along a processional route run-

SPRING

EARLY APRIL:➤ **Easter in Naples** (Pasqua a Napoli) is celebrated around Easter Monday (Pasquetta). Throughout the Settimana Santa (Holy Week), choral concerts are offered in churches. Sorrento hosts a torch-lighted Good Friday **Incappucciati** (Brotherhoods) procession.

EARLY MAY:➤ In Naples the first of the two annual celebrations of the **Feast of San Gennaro** is marked on the first Sunday in May at the Duomo of Naples (the ceremony of the Liquefaction of the Blood begins at 9 AM, but arrive by 7 or you'll wind up far from the altar and the action). Unlike the similar festa held in September, this one includes a *Processione di*

SUMMER

EARLY JUNE:➤ The **Regatta of the Great Maritime Republics** (Regatta Storica dell Antiche Repubbliche Marinare) sees keen competition among the four former maritime republics—Amalfi, Genoa, Pisa, and Venice. The regatta is held every four years in Amalfi, with the next scheduled for the first Sunday in June 2000.

LATE JUNE:➤ On the fourth Sunday of every June, the **Festa di Gigli** (Feast of the Lilies) is held in Nola, just to the north of Naples. Spectacular wooden floats, often bearing orchestras, celebrate the homecoming of Bishop Paolino from Africa in 394.

LATE JUNE–LATE SEPT.:➤ **Estate a Napoli** (Summer in Naples) is a summer-long schedule of concerts and performances. Past special events have included *concerti a mezzanotte* (midnight concerts, which actually start at 11 PM) in parks; Baroque, Neapolitan, and jazz concerts at the Borgo Marinaro; and a Comedy Festival at the Castel Nuovo. During the last week of June the **Napoli Cinefest Film Festival** is held in the city, featuring outdoor movies.

JULY 16:➤ The Feast of the **Madonna del Carmine** is held on Naples's Piazza Mercato and is celebrated by the "burning" of the campanile of Santa Maria del Carmine with fireworks.

JULY–AUG.:➤ **Estate Musicale Sorrentina** is the summer music festival in Sorrento. Concerts are held in historic cloisters and churches.

JULY–AUG.:➤ The **Fèstival Musicale di Ravello** actually schedules concerts throughout most of the year (except January–March) at Ravello's

spectacular Villa Rufolo, but the annual highlights are the operatic concerts scheduled during July to commemorate the 1880 visit of Richard Wagner to the villa's famous gardens. ✉ *Piazza Vescovado, Ravello,* ☎ *089/858149.*

AUG. 15:➤ The traditional beginning of the **Ferragosto,** the traditional vacation period in Italy, is marked by an exodus from Naples and many regional celebrations, including the Assunta, or Feast of the Assumption of the Virgin Mary, in Positano, which commemorates the defeat of the Saracens with a procession and mass held on the main beach.

AUTUMN

EARLY SEPT.:➤ The first week in September usually sees both the **Vittorio da Sica Film Festival** and the **Premi Leonide Massine**

dance awards, held in Positano.

MID-SEPT.:➤ You can't see *Il Vesuvio* erupt on command, but many regional organizations sponsor dinner sunset cruises on the Bay of Naples, with a **fireworks display to recreate the eruption of Vesuvius.** One celebrates the Festa di S. M. del Lauro a Meta di Sorrento in mid-September, leaving from the Molo Beverello of Naples. For information contact: *Ascultur Campania,* ☎ *081/ 665532; Associazione Aliseo,* ☎ *081/5265780.*

SEPT. 19:➤ The main celebration of the **Feast of San Gennaro** is held at Naples's duomo on this day. *Il Miracolo* begins (hopefully) at 9 AM, but the best seats are grabbed hours earlier. Once the blood of St. Gennaro liquefies, a ceremonial cortege is paraded from Piazza del Duomo to Piazza del Carmine. For details contact: *Comitato Diocesano S. Gennaro,* ☎ *081/446103.*

2 NAPLES

A kinetic gust of 3-D garlic-and-basil aromatherapy for the soul, Naples is a destination no one ever forgets. The most operatic of cities, it blasts you with a confounding mix of beauty, chaos, and a glorious past. If your eye is greedy for splendor, many treasures beckon—the world's finest museum of classical antiquities, opulent Baroque palaces, and bravura Caravaggio altarpieces—but the greatest treasure of all is the Neapolitan people themselves. Today, nearby Vesuvius may slumber, but Naples itself is erupting in a renaissance of cultural identity and pride.

By Gregory
W. Bailey

BUILT LIKE A GREAT AMPHITHEATER around her beautiful bay, Naples is an eternally unfolding play acted by a million of the best actors in the world," Herbert Kubly observed in his *American in Italy.* "The comedy is broad, the tragedy violent. The curtain never rings down." Is it a sense of doom from living in the shadow of Vesuvius that makes many Neapolitans so volatile, perhaps so seemingly blind to everything but the pain or pleasure of the moment? Poverty and overcrowding are the more likely causes. But whatever the reason, Naples remains the most vibrant city in Italy—a steaming, bubbling, reverberating minestrone in which each block is a village, every street the setting for a Punch-and-Judy show, and everything seems to be a backdrop for an opera not yet composed. It is said that northern Italians vacation here to remind themselves of the time when Italy was *molto Italiano—really* Italian. In this respect, Naples—Napoli in Italian—-doesn't disappoint: Neapolitan rainbows of laundry wave in the wind over alleyways open-windowed with friendliness, mothers caress children, men break out into impromptu arias at sidewalk cafés, street scenes offer Fellini-esque slices of life, and everywhere contrasting elements of faded gilt and romance, rust and calamity, grandeur and squalor form an intoxicating pageant of pure *Italianità*—Italy at its most Italian.

From the moment you arrive at swirling Piazza Garibaldi, the city blasts you with a confounding mix of beauty, chaos, and a glorious past. The piazza, which is home to the Stazione Centrale, the main railroad terminal, seems at first glance a battered place—crowded, polluted, and inhospitable. Journalists used to joke darkly that at any given moment, one in three of those on the scene were major criminals, and the other two hadn't been caught yet. Vespas, Fiats, and city buses careen insanely through its streets, heeding neither traffic light nor hapless pedestrians. It is this first impression that has been the wrong impression for so many travelers, for once away from this piazza, the pace changes, and your point of view changes with it. Naples unfolds as a cornucopia of elegant boulevards, treasure-stocked palaces, the world's greatest museum of classical antiquities, the stage-set neighborhood of Spaccanapoli, and hundreds of historic churches. For the serious-minded, walking, cathedral-visiting tourist, Naples becomes *Napoli la bella,* a city centuries of romantics have deemed one of the most beautiful in the world, a designation that owes much to its location on the breathtaking Bay of Naples, an immense past attested to by its historic and grand monuments of architecture, and a mode of life that never fails to fascinate.

Despite these attributes, by the 1970s a different, rather seedy image had emerged: *Napoli la terribile.* Horror stories abounded about the *scippatori,* Vespa-riding muggers who yanked purses from sightseeing strollers; hospitals so terrible that patients were said to dial 113, the emergency number, from their bedside phone because they despaired of ever seeing the ward nurse; and the juvenile *scugnizzi,* the street children who would pry off your license plate at one traffic light only to sell it back to you at the next. Unemployment reached 30%, the infrastructure was rotting (government subsidies were simply being *mett'in tasca*—or "put into pocket,"—as the local phrase had it, by the Camorra, the Neapolitan equivalent of the Mafia), while the threat of earthquakes and ever-present gridlock made sectors into an Italian Los Angeles.

By the early 1980s Neapolitans had had enough. Baroness Mirella Barocco mobilized the city's rich and powerful into Committee Naples Ninety-Nine, an organization whose mission was to uplift both the city's historic structures and its public image. When Antonio Bassolino became mayor in 1992, he jump-started the city's economic development, cleaned up the streets, and crowded more policemen than travelers into the main railway terminal. By the time global leaders like Clinton and Yeltsin convened in the city in 1992 for the G7 summit meeting, many palaces had been restored, churches reopened, conferences held; the Camorra was out and Art—many city museums received a renovation—was in. Today a decade later, it is Naples that has erupted in an unending flow of cultural excitement while Il Vesuvio (Vesuvius) still sleeps its long sleep. The Future of Italy, capital letters intended, is now the ascendant motif, as some of artists have taken up residence near the city's new modern art museum at the Capodimonte Palace; a renaissance of southern Italian cooking is making headlines around the world; and more and more travelers with a been-there-done-that take on Rome, Florence, and other capitals of northern Italy, are setting their course southward. Only a few years ago, Naples was a "don't," and almost all the thousands who traveled to the city's Stazione Centrale only did so because it was the gateway to Pompeii, Sorrento, Capri, and the Amalfi Coast. Now you can travel to the city to discover that Naples is more than a railway station—it is a civilization.

The origin of Naples, once called Parthenope and later Neapolis, can be traced to what are now the nearby ruins of Cumae, the earliest Greek colony in Italy, founded around 750 BC. Greek civilization flourished for hundreds of years along this coastline, but there was nothing in the way of centralized government until the Roman Empire, uniting all Italy for the first time, surged southward and, with little opposition, absorbed the Greek colonies in the 4th century BC. The Romans were quick to appreciate the sybaritic potential of the region, and wealthy members of the empire flocked here to build palatial country residences. Generally, the peace of Campania was undisturbed during the centuries of Roman rule.

Naples and Campania, with the rest of Italy, decayed with the Roman Empire and collapsed into the abyss of the Middle Ages. In 1130 the Norman king Roger II, King of the Two Sicilies, made Naples the capital of his Norman empire, until Henry VI of Hohenstaufen captured it in 1194; his enlightened son, Frederick II, endowed the city with the Castel Nuovo and the Castel dell'Ovo and founded a university that attracted many scholars and poets. By now the popes had an eye on Naples, and together with the French king Louis IX and Charles of Anjou, their French Angevin government conquered the Hohenstaufen forces in 1268. Charles of Anjou and Robert the Wise sponsored the construction of several important buildings, including the Church of Santa Chiara, which introduced the style of Provençal Gothic to the city. Aragonese rule arrived in 1442 with the siege of Alfonso I of Aragon, but his line was driven from the city in turn by the alliance between King Louis XII of France and Ferdinand of Spain. The nobles who served under the Spanish viceroys in the 16th and 17th centuries, when their harsh rule made all Italy quake, enjoyed their libertine pleasures, resulting in the flourishing of taverns and gaming houses, even as Spain milked the citizenry with burdensome taxes. During this time Naples became Europe's second-largest city, after Paris (and also its most densely populated—to accommodate the crowds, tenements rose as high as seven stories, possible because of the solidity of Neapolitan tufa rock).

After a short-lived Austrian occupation, Naples became the capital of the Kingdom of the Two Sicilies, established by the Bourbon kings in 1738. This somewhat garbled kingdom was made up of Naples (which included most of the southern Italian mainland) and Sicily, which were united in the Middle Ages, then separated and unofficially reunited under Spanish domination during the 16th and 17th centuries. With the rule of the Bourbon kings, the Neapolitan golden age began in earnest, as their rule was generally benevolent, as far as Campania was concerned, and their support of the papal authority in Rome was an important factor in the development of the rest of Italy. The rule of Charles III of Bourbon, along with that of his son Ferdinand IV, was important artistically: Both kings not only built many of the architectural showpieces of the city—the Palazzo Reale, Palazzo Capodimonte, Teatro San Carlo, and the Palace of Caserta, to name just a few—they also sponsored noted musicians, artists, and writers, who were only too willing to submit to court life in such magnificent natural surroundings. But the modern world was knocking in the person of Napoléon, whose forces dethroned the Bourbons in 1799. The glamour of the Empire style came to the city when Napoléon appointed his brother-in-law, Joachim Murat, as the king of Naples. In 1815 the Bourbons returned to power, Murat was shot, and Ferdinand IV exclaimed that the poor general had been a better upholsterer than an administrator. In 1816, with Napoléon out of the way on St. Helena, Ferdinand officially remerged the two kingdoms, proclaiming himself Ferdinand I of the Kingdom of Two Sicilies. His reactionary and repressive rule earned him a few more colorful titles among his rebellious subjects. Finally, Giuseppe Garibaldi launched his expedition, and in 1860 Naples was united with the rest of Italy.

Clearly, as the historic capital of Campania, Naples has been perpetually and tumultuously in flux. Neapolitans are instinctively the most hospitable of people, and they've often paid a price for being so, having unwittingly extended a warm welcome to wave after wave of invaders. Lombards, Goths, Normans, Spanish viceroys, Napoleonic generals, and French Bourbons arrived in turn, and most of whom were greedy and self-serving. Still, if these foreign rulers bled the populace dry with taxes, they left the impoverished city with a rich architectural inheritance.

Much of that inheritance is on display on the Piazza Gesù Nuovo—a showplace for the city's most beloved churches and a showcase for the city's greatest attraction, the Neapolitan people themselves. On the piazza, watch and rub elbows with them. Listen to them—or rather watch them—talk. Let their charm, their gaiety, their effervescence, their completely undiluted spontaneity sweep you into their unique but glorious concept of life and living. You begin to realize there's something about Naples that makes the Neapolitans the happiest people in the world. In an hour or two you'll feel like part of the Neapolitan *familia* yourself. Compared to most other great metropolises of the world, Naples has little tourist infrastructure, so it allows you to become a native very quickly, as you'll find out if you spend some time on the Piazza Gesù Nuovo. Lost? You'll be escorted (probably by way of mamma's house). Hungry? Hey, *paisan,* bring a slice! Can't think of a phrase? A translation is shouted out over the din, and a single word is never sufficient when 10 will do—as you could have seen one September afternoon when an English couple asked for directions to the Church of Pio Monte delle Misericordia. One passerby started explaining, but another man suddenly thought of a still shorter way and butted in. In no time 8 or 10 people were kindly proffering their own versions. The arguing that ensued was not severe. There was nearly one casualty. The inquiring couple never learned the shortest—or, for that matter, any other—way to Pio Monte. But the sun was hot, the sky was blue, and there are plenty of other beautiful churches in Naples.

Pleasures and Pastimes

La Cucina Napolitano—*And* It's Good for You!

Anyone who loves food will love Naples. After all, this is the birth-place of several of the world's most popular dishes and culinary delights: pizza, spaghetti *al pomodoro* (with tomatoes), mozzarella cheese, as well as most of the pasta shapes everyone knows, such as ziti, vermicelli—what most Italians call spaghetti—fusilli, *bucatini,* and linguine, as well as some of the most *delicioso* coffee and desserts served up anywhere. For the most part, these dishes reflect the schizophrenic split of rich and poor that has always characterized the city. Since most Neapolitans as well have long been both very poor and very creative, *cucina povera*—subsistence nourishment alchemically raised to culinary gold—is at its best here. This species of "poor peoples' food" is best represented by pizza. By the 18th century fishermen were eating like kings and kings like fishermen: Neapolitan royalty was known for its love of the sturdy and virtuous "common" food: forks were supposedly invented so that Ferdinand II could indulge in spaghetti at state banquets in a dignified manner, and Ferdinand IV used the porcelain kilns at Capodimonte for cooking pizza, so he didn't have to go out late at night to satisfy his cravings.

Beyond pizza and pasta, a number of other specialties take cheap, abundant ingredients and produce solid and dazzlingly delicious nourishment: the local version of Italian bean stew, *pasta e fagioli,* can suffice for a meal. The profusion of fried foods, and small take-out eateries—the *frig-gitorie*—serving only those items, grew out of the resilience of the many poor Neapolitans, who couldn't afford cooking facilities, if they had a home at all, and so took whatever items they had down to the local fryer and then either brought them home to eat or ate them standing up. There are more variations on fried dough than you will ever want to try, but no one should miss the famous pea-studded rice croquettes bound with béchamel, best enjoyed at the pizzeria Da Matteo. *Arancione,* large rice croquettes with tomato meat sauce and cheese, make a great snack, and zucchini flowers are a popular appetizer at pizzerias. Neapolitan *ragù,* cooked endlessly, makes ambrosia out of humble cuts of meat (cut but not ground), and simple pasta with tomato sauce is always a good bet, given the quality of the tomatoes. A number of dishes bear witness to the importance of communal eating (not to mention efficiently recycled leftovers), including *sartù,* an aristocratic and suitably elaborate rice casserole and, if you're around at Easter, *castiello,* a golden ring of tender dough filled with everything on hand. Spaghetti *all puttanesca,* tarted up with olives and capers, is a superquick pasta dish said to have been cooked up, as its name indicates, by ladies of the night who didn't have time to slave over the stove.

In part, Neapolitan cooking tastes so wonderful because of its superb local ingredients: the rich volcanic soil surrounding the city, nurtured by abundant sun and benevolent breezes, has from ancient times been famous for the quality of its produce. *Friarelli* are a local type of broccoli, almost all stems and no flower, which are blanched like collard greens and tossed on pizza or sautéed with garlic and red pepper and served, delicious and remineralizing, with grilled sausage (*salsiccia e friarelli*). True mozzarella is the property of Campania; the best is made from 100% water-buffalo milk and has a unique tang and velvety consistency. Most *bufala* is mixed (legally) with cow's milk, which tends to dilute its character, and the most common mozzarella is *fior di latte,* made entirely from cow's milk. But be sure to try a good bufala while in Naples—it's a revelation: the cheese must be eaten very fresh (the same day is best) and doesn't like to travel. An absolutely simple dish, though, such as the *insalata caprese* (tomato, mozzarella, and basil salad), becomes a voluptuous Titianesque masterpiece when all the ingredients are right—typical of the best dishes of *cucina napoletano*. To top it all off, critics consider southern Italian cooking among the healthiest in the world—unlike the cholesterol-ladden butters used in northern Italian cuisine, most Campanian dishes use olive oils. And don't forget that Campania is really one great wine flask. Among the region's wines, Gragnano, Falerno, and Greco di Tufo are fine whites. Ischia and Ravello also produce good white wine. Campania's best-known reds are Aglianico, Taurasi, and the red version of Falerno. The most famous wines, of course, are the Lacryma Cristi whites—supposedly named because Christ, looking down on the beautiful Bay of Naples, wept at the sins of the people.

Lodging: A View with a Room

Naples has the range of accommodations you would expect of any bustling metropolis, from the squalid *alberghetti* (little hotels) around the Piazza Garibaldi railway station to the grand landmarks of luxury on the Lungomare and the Vomero. Since Naples is very much a businessperson's city, the better hotels can be quickly booked up by conventioneers (who are willing to pay top prices and even supplements for amenities like air-conditioning), so reserve well in advance for the finer hotels. Unfortunately, the equivalent of the genteel *pensiones* of yesteryear are few and far between: usually small and intimate, several in Naples do still exist, and they often have a quaint appeal that fortunately does not preclude modern plumbing. Whether you are in a five-star hotel or a more modest establishment, you may enjoy one of the greatest pleasures of all: a room with a view. In this case it's not *any* view, but the lay-down-and-die panorama of the Bay of Naples and Vesuvius, so be sure to ask for a bayside room if your hotel can provide one (and when making reservations, be sure to inquire if breakfast is included in the room rate, if there is a supplement for air-conditioning, and if parking facilities come with an extra fee). When you get to your bayside room, step out onto the balcony. You will gasp, of course. Everyone does.

Beyond Baroque: Neapolitan Art and Architecture

Naples is commonly categorized as a Baroque city, and it is true that this 17th- and 18th-century style produced defining monuments for the city, but it is a mistake to define Naples simply as Baroque. The city is so much older than that—almost as old as Rome (which was the city that actually gave rise to the Baroque style). In any case, the "baroque" exuberance of Naples goes back to ancient times; it was just that the style found fertile ground here underneath the volcano. But this chapter aims to introduce the reader to other facets of the city as well, by including unjustly neglected monuments, for Naples has ancient Greek and Roman ruins, vertical heaven-seeking medieval churches, first-rate chapels of the Renaissance, elegant 19th-century Empire and Neoclassical palaces, and important Modernist buildings from the 20th century as well, much of which tends to be obscured by all the polychrome-marble flourishes of the Baroque style. In the end, the Naples of today is the sum of all these periods—and something timeless as well.

Passion on the High C's: Opera at Teatro San Carlo

Opera is an art form peculiarly suited to the Neapolitan temperament. You can attend a performance of *Lucia di Lammermoor* at the Teatro San Carlo (where it received its premiere in 1835). Some may find its stylized acting and great singing a bad mixture esthetically, some will be embarrassed by the naked emotion on display and the clichéd sentimentality or incomprehensibility of the plot, and some may ridicule

the convention that permits a dying Edgardo to rise and sing a powerful aria and perhaps an encore before lying down again to die. But
whatever naysayers may think, opera is the lifeblood of Neapolitans,
a reflection of the drama of their existence, a sublimation of their personal mythology; their melodrama, burlesque, pantomime, circus, and
celebrity concert all rolled into one. Back when the Teatro San Carlo
was built (1737), Naples was the musical capital of Italy, and here many
of the greatest operas of the melodious trio of Rossini (1792–1868),
Bellini (1801–35), and Donizetti (1797–1848) received their loudest
ovations, since they often showcased bel canto singing to bravura effect. The bel canto style—in which libretto and dramatic tension are
sacrificed to virtuoso singing—produced a typically Neapolitan human
being: the prima donna, haughty, tempestuous, temperamental, a
despot in all her glory. The greatest singers flocked to the San Carlo
since they knew Neapolitans were more prepared to stomach over-the-
top emotional excess (on and off the stage) more than anyone else in
Italy. Today opera in Naples is a medium that grows neither old nor
old-fashioned. The season lasts from early December to June, and the
audience's dress and jewelry on premiere nights sometimes matches the
extravagant red-and-gold decor of the auditorium. Under huge clus-
ters of candelabra, the full house resembles an overflowing basket of
flowers—a sight to remember, even before the curtain has gone up.

EXPLORING NAPLES

Naples, a bustling city of some 1.2 million people, presents a particular challenge for visitors because of its hilly geographic terrain and its
twisty, earthquakey, and often congested streets. Though large, however, Naples invites walking; the bus system and funiculars are also options for surmounting the problem of weary legs. Sightseeing days should
begin no later than 9, as most churches are usually open only from 7:30
AM until noon or 12:30, reopening only after the afternoon siesta from
4 or 4:30 PM until about 7. In addition, many museums open at 9 but
close at 2; exceptions are the Aquario, the Museo di Capodimonte, and
the Museo Archeologico Nazionale (which sometimes host extended
hours in the summer). If you come to Naples by car, park it in a garage
as fast as you can, agree on the cost in advance, and then forget it for
the duration of your stay (otherwise, theft is a constant risk). Use the
funiculars to get up and down the hills (for information, ☞ Getting
Around *in* Naples A to Z, *below*), and take the Metropolitana—the
city's subway system—to such destinations as Piazza Garibaldi, Chiaia, Mergellina, and Pozzuoli; for Pozzuoli and the Phlegrean Fields,
Pompeii, Herculaneum, and the towns of the Amalfi Coast, take the
Circumflegrea, Cumana, and Circumvesuviana lines.

The heart of Naples stretches along the Bay of Naples from Piazza
Garibaldi in the east to Mergellina in the west, with its back to the
Vomero Hill. From Stazione Centrale, on Piazza Garibaldi, Corso Umberto I (known as the "Rettifilo") heads southwest to the monumental city center around the piazzas Bovio, Municipio, and Trieste e
Trento; here is the major urban set piece of the Palazzo Reale, Teatro
San Carlo, and Galleria Umberto Primo. To the north are the historic
districts of old Naples; to the south is the port. Farther west along the
bay are the more fashionable neighborhoods of Santa Lucia and Chiaia, and finally the waterfront district of Mergellina. The residential
area of Vomero sits on the steep hills rising above Chiaia and downtown. Just to the east is Naples's picturesque quarter, Spaccanapoli—
the heart of the *centro istorico* (historic center)—once called the
Decumano Inferiore in Roman times and today a street that changes

names several times on its way through the heart of old Naples (it comprises Via Benedetto Croce and Via San Biagio dei Librai, among others).

Tying much of this geographic layout together is the "spine" of the city, Via Toledo—Naples's major north-south axis, which begins at Piazza Trieste e Trento and heads up all the way up to Capodimonte. It's basically one straight road with four different names (five if you count the official name of Via Roma, which all the locals know it as anyway). Via Toledo links Piazza Trieste e Trento with Piazza Dante. Going further north you get into Via Pessina for about 100 yards which takes you up to the mega junction with the Museo Archeologico Nazionale. North of that, you head up to the peak of Capodimonte by traveling along Via Santa Teresa degli Scalzi and then Corso Amedeo di Savoia. To make things a bit more confusing, parts of Via Toledo are pedestrianized—and that means no buses or scooters, thankfully—which is from just south of Piazza Carità (where Via Toledo/Roma intersects with Via Diaz) all the way to Piazza Trieste e Trento. Currently Via Diaz is closed to through traffic, which means that southbound buses from Piazza Dante have to turn left in Piazza Carita, pass in front of the main post office and then join the maelstrom downtown towards Piazza Bovio and Corso Umberto. Bear in mind that mobility is further disrupted at the moment thanks to the various works on the new Metropolitana extension line running through the heart of the city: Piazza Dante is boarded off, as is Piazza Bovio, and much of Piazza Municipio. As you can see, walking is often the least complicated mode of transportation.

That noted, promenading through Naples takes a little practice. In a city where a red light is often looked at as merely a suggestion, walking across a busy avenue can be like a game of chess—if you hesitate, you capitulate. Most residents just head out into the unceasing flow of traffic, knowing cars invariably slow down to let them cross (trick for the fainthearted: look for an elderly couple—when they cross, you *know* it will be safe). Essentially, you should cross big streets one or two lanes at a time, and don't ever hesitate in the middle of a lane—keep moving so motorcycles can avoid you. In any event, once you've dealt with the hurtling traffic at Piazza Trieste e Trento, nothing in life should faze you.

Numbers in the text correspond to numbers in the margin and on the Naples maps.

Great Itineraries

IF YOU HAVE 1 DAY

Begin with the Naples you have always imagined: Spaccanapoli—the historic quarter where palaces and slums, neon-lighted pizzerias and gilded cathedrals, organ-grinders and Mercedes create an open-air museum. Ground zero here is Piazza Gesù Nuovo, site of the churches of the Gesù Nuovo and Santa Chiara and entryway to the spectacular 5-km-long (3-mi-long) pedestrian ribbon called the Spaccanapoli. Explore the memorable sights of this quarter—the Capella Sansevero, the crèche shops of Via Gregorio Armeno, the Caravaggio altarpiece at the Pio Monte, and the Chapel of San Gennaro at the Duomo—by first walking east along the Spacca, then returning west one block north along Via Tribunali. After lunch at a Spacca pizzeria or café, head over to Via Toledo, Naples's main thoroughfare, and walk back to the ceremonial center of the city: Piazza del Plebiscito, bookended on one side by the Church of San Francesco di Paola, and on the other by the Bourbons' palace, the Palazzo Reale. Combine sightseeing with shopping by touring the Galleria Umberto I and the shops of nearby Via Chi-

24

Naples

aia, which leads to the *"salone"* of Naples, chic Piazza dei Martiri. Continue south to the bayside Lungomare and walk over to the Castel dell'Ovo for a sunset dinner—with Vesuvius front and center—at one of the restaurants at the harbor port, the Borgo Marinaro.

IF YOU HAVE 3 DAYS

Having survived your first whirlwind day in Naples, begin your second day at the world-famous Museo Archeologico Nazionale (be there when the doors open in the morning to get a jump on the crowds). Packed with archaeological relics of the classical era, it's a must before venturing out of town to see Pompeii and Herculaneum. After viewing the *Hercules Farnese* and other ancient masterworks, you deserve a taxi or bus to reach Museo di Capodimonte, high above the city center and the greatest of the Bourbon palaces. Amble through its grand ballrooms and take in the great art collection, then promenade in its park to admire the views over the bay and city. Return to the city center and bustling Piazza Municipio to view the collections on view at the brooding Castel Nuovo. For your third day take the Funiculare Centrale opposite Galleria Umberto I up the Vomero Hill to explore the Certosa di San Giacomo, a Baroque extravaganza of a monastery, and the mighty Castel Sant'Elmo. Then walk through the pretty residential quarter to the Villa La Floridiana's decorative-arts museum and sylvan park, which has wonderful views high over the city. Take the Funiculare di Chiaia back down to the Lungomare to visit the aristocratic Villa Pignatelli (get there before it closes at 1 PM) and the celebrated Aquario. Head over to the west end of the Riviera di Chiaia by foot or bus to Mergellina for dinner and an evening boat tour of the waterfront, or opt for an opera performance at the Teatro San Carlo.

IF YOU HAVE 5 DAYS

On your fourth day, take a vacation from your Neapolitan vacation by heading out of town to the nearby 18th-century Palace of Caserta, built by the Bourbon king Charles III. Tour the gilded salons, majestic park, and English Garden designed by Sir William Hamilton and his wife, the celebrated Emma. Or, instead, venture out past Posillipo to the Phlegrean Fields and pay a call on the Cave of the Cumaean Sibyl. On your fifth day devote more time to the museums and galleries mentioned above—along with the many others covered in the pages below—that interest you most. Return to further explore a kindred neighborhood—the elegant Chiaia and Vomero or the picturesque Spaccanapoli—allowing plenty of time for poking into odd corners and courtyards and churches, and for café-sitting to watch the passing Neapolitan parade.

Napoli Nobilissima: The Monumental City Center

Naples's setting on the most beautiful bay in the world has long been a boon for its inhabitants—the expansive harbor has always brought great mercantile riches to the city—and, intermittently, a curse. Throughout history, a who's who of Greek, Roman, Norman, Spanish, and French despots has quarreled over this gateway to Campania. Each set of conquerors recognized that the area around the city harbor—today occupied by the Molo Beverello hydrofoil terminal and the 1928 Stazione Maritima—was the veritable welcome mat to the metropolis and consequently needed to be turned into a fitting showcase of regal and royal authority. This had become imperative because of the explosive growth of Naples's population, which, by the mid-16th century, had made it into the second-largest city in Europe after Paris. With the mass migration of the rural population to the city, Naples had grown into a capricious, unplanned, disorderly, and untrammeled capital. Thus, the central aim of the ruling dynasties became the creation of a *Napoli nobilissima*—a noble Naples.

The monuments they created remain a prominent feature of the city center today: One of the most magnificent opera houses in Europe, a palace that nearly rivals Versailles, an impregnable *castello*, a majestic church modeled on Rome's Pantheon, and a 19th-century shopping galleria are landmarks that marked the shifts among the ruling powers, from the French Angevins and Spanish Habsburgs to the French Bourbons and, later, the postunification rise of the bourgeoisie and the regime of Mussolini. This historic sector is the much-put-upon Cinderella—as Naples is seen by many of her fans—but all dressed up in her princess-to-be jewels and finery and ready to wow the onlookers at the royal ball. In contrast to the intense intimacy of the Spacca (☞ Spaccanapoli: The Heart and Soul of Naples, *below*), the official center of Naples unrolls its majesty with great pomp along wide avenues and monumental piazzas.

A Good Walk

In a day filled with monarchist grandeur, it's only fitting to start out with breakfast at **Caffè Gambrinus,** on Piazza Trieste e Trento, the very center of Naples and set between Piazza del Plebiscito and Piazza Municipio. Gilded and mirrored, this 19th-century café was once the rendezvous for Italian dukes, prime ministers, and writers like Oscar Wilde, Guy de Maupassant, and Gabriele d'Annunzio. Treat yourself to a *cappuccino* and a pastry as rich and velvety as the surroundings, then head directly outside the door to the grand Piazza del Plebiscito. Neapolitans are too often caught up in the present to appreciate their past, and one sad example of this was the decades-long use of this urban showpiece as a parking lot. Now it makes an imposing setting for **San Francisco di Paola** ①, the domed 19th-century church built by Ferdinand I and its grand Doric hemicycle. Inside, the Roman-style basilica is Naples at its most Neoclassic—imperial, aloof, funereal, and Olympian. From here head directly across the piazza to the main entrance of Naples's Royal Palace. Note the niches on its facade, filled in 1888, on order of King Umberto I of Italy, with a series of rather ungainly statues of the kings of Naples, including, on the far right, his own static and unexpressive father, Victor Emanuel II, who had seized the palace (and the kingdom) from the Bourbons. Of all these figures, Joachim Murat comes out looking the most dignified, even if, as Vittori Gleisejes writes, he appears "a bit too . . . virile in his revealing uniform."

At the **Palazzo Reale** ②, walk up the grand staircase of its Scalone d'Onore and tour the spectacular 18th- and 19th-century salons of the Museo dell'Appartmento Reale. You can't use the hallway constructed by the Bourbon kings to take them directly to the Royal Box of the adjacent **Teatro San Carlo** ③, so head back down to the piazza and make a right turn to the Piazza Trieste e Trento, where opera lovers will want to take a guided tour of the famous red-and-gold theater (weekends only; if a rehearsal is going on, porters at the theater will allow you to see the auditorium for a tip). Directly across the way is the fastidiously elegant vastness of the **Galleria Umberto I** ④. Walk to the far end of this ancestor of the shopping mall to Via Santa Brigida and tour the Church of **Santa Brigida** ⑤, burial place of renowned artist Luca Giordano. Head back through the Galleria and then gently downhill the Via San Carlo and the Via Vittorio Emanuele III to the usually light-drenched **Piazza Municipio,** with the delightfully discreet Church of San Giacomo ai Spagnoli camouflaged within the bay side of the Banco di Napoli building and a pile of Greek ruins, forming an island in the middle of the square across its daunting expanse of vehicular chaos. Above this piazza rises the civilized fortress of the **Castel Nuovo** ⑥, with the bay as a backdrop. Outside, study its great sculpted triumphal arch of Alfonso of Aragon; inside, explore the museum and Hall of the Barons. Head across Piazza Municipio to Via Medina until you reach the important 20th-century complex at **Piazza Matteotti** ⑦. Then trip across the centuries by continuing up Via Monteoliveto and its piazza, where you'll find both the quiet Church of **Sant' Anna dei Lombardi** ⑧, which is in fact a fascinating and very digestible museum of Renaissance sculpture (with a great frescoed sacristy), and the **Palazzo Gravina** ⑨.

Make a left leaving Sant'Anna dei Lombardi and head over to Piazza Carita and the Broadway of Naples, Via Toledo (often also referred to as Via Roma). On the opposite side of the wide throughfare are some of Naples's most fascinating (sometimes dangerous) *quartieri*, including the famous Spanish Quarter, or Quartieri Spagnoli. If you don't opt to make this detour, walk the 15 or so blocks back down Via Toledo to the Piazza Trieste e Trento; along the way, take in the **Banco di Napoli** ⑩, do some window-shopping, and pick up a hot, flaky *sfogliatella* pastry at Pinturchio or some cool chocolates at Gay-Odin. Back around Piazza Trieste e Trento make a stop for a leisurely lunch: Ciro a Santa Brigida and Amici Miei are in the neighborhood, as well as a number of places on nearby Via Santa Lucia, while Pizzeria Brandi is just up Via Chiaia. From here on you can take things easy.

Timing

Not including time spent in the enormous Palazzo Reale and Castel Nuovo museums, walking this route will take approximately three leisurely hours. There's no chance of escaping the crowds—this is the very heart of metropolitan Naples, but it's always best to get up early and get a head start—especially as this allows you to see the spectacular Piazza del Plebiscito *senza popolo* (without people). With no backpacks or Ray-Bans to be seen, the square looks little changed from the early 19th century.

Sights to See

⑩ **Banco di Napoli** (Bank of Naples). The oldest credit institution in Italy (founded as the *Monte di Pietà* in 1539, the present building is an imposing marble swath designed by Marcello Piancentini, leader of the Historical Monumentalism school of early 20th-century architecture and "official" architect of the fascist regime. ⊠ *Via Toledo 178.*

★ ⑥ **Castel Nuovo.** Brooding over the modern traffic that swirls around it, this castle is one of the most famous landmarks of the city and is often referred to by Neapolitans as the Maschio Angioino (Angevin Keep, in reference to its Angevin builders). Today it is the current seat of the city government, with its courtyard filling up in June with couples registering their wedding vows, and the moat outside is the site of a morning flower market. The castle's shadows, however, hide some legend-haunted events that played out within the dark, *piperno*-stone walls, along with—rumor once had it—King Ferrante's crocodile, which was said to dispatch live prisoners. The founder of the Angevin dynasty, Charles I d'Anjou, first built this fortress, known from its beginning, in 1279, as the "new castle" (to differentiate it from the Castel dell'Ovo and the Castel Capuano). Under his successor Robert the Wise, it became a great center of culture, with the castle library attracting such luminaries as Petrarch and Boccaccio. Alfonso d'Aragona took up residence here when he conquered Naples in 1443 and marked his arrival with a fairly complete rebuilding, including the five defensive towers now visible and, especially, the impressive marble **Arco di Trionfo** at the entrance. This highly important work of the first Renaissance (1443–68) consciously takes its inspiration from ancient Roman triumphal arches, recombining the elements, however, in a completely innovative composition of two superimposed arches so as to fit the tall, narrow space; many noted sculptors worked on the arch. The most celebrated was Francesco Laurana, who carved the bas-relief above the lower arch, which shows, appropriately, the triumphal official entrance of Alfonso into Naples on February 26, 1443. This grand depiction effectively overrides any memory of Alfonso's earlier foray through the city's underground sewer system (in the middle of the night of June 12, 1442, he emerged from underground into the home of a Neapolitan matron by the name of La Ceccarella, who, betraying her rightful king, guided the regal-looking intruder and his dashing band of armed men to the gates of the city, which they threw open to allow their troops to advance).

Once inside the Arco di Trionfo, you'll find the ticket office on the left. Across the imposing courtyard is the Palatine Chapel, one of the few remaining structures of the Angevin Palace, its austere facade graced by a portal with delicate reliefs and a Madonna by Francesco Laurana (1474). Decorated inside by Giotto and friends in the 14th century, the frescoes are now reduced to a few fragments, none of which can be attributed to the master. The chapel now houses paintings from the 14th through the early 16th centuries and graceful sculptures by Laurana and Domenico Gagini. Next to it in the left corner is the **Sala dei Baroni,** or Barons' Room, built for Alfonso by the Majorcan architect Guglielmo Sagrera in 1446–54. Its simple volume is topped with a late-Gothic Moorish-inspired octagonal star vault whose ribs, in gray *piperno,* provide a harmonious accent to the the yellow-tufa walls. The hall gets its name from a famous party held here in 1486, when Ferdinand I of Aragon invited a number of troublesome, powerful lords to dinner and then had them arrested and executed. For souvenirs of the event, he had several of the victims embalmed; their bodies were brought out from time to time to entertain more fortunate guests, who still must have been a bit nervous. The dungeons where the unlucky lords were to await death are below the Palatine Chapel (you would think that their moans would have disturbed mass) and can be viewed today.

The rest of the public space of the castle houses the **Museo Civico,** which is an interesting, low-key collection of painting and sculpture, especially strong in 19th-century landscapes with views of a lost or transformed Naples, but also with some nice 17th-century paintings and the bronze doors that Ferrante commissioned from William the Monk in 1475 to record his victory over John d'Anjou. ⊠ *Piazza Municipio,* ☎ *081/795-2023.* 🎫 *10,000 lire.* 🕐 *Mon.–Sat. 9–7.*

❹ **Galleria Umberto I.** In 1885, in reaction to the devastating cholera epidemic of the previous year, authorities hastily implemented a massive urban renewal plan whose "clean-up" of Naples especially entailed the destruction of slum areas between Spaccanapoli and the Palazzo Reale. With facades on Via Toledo—the most animated street in Naples at the time—and across from the Teatro San Carlo, this galleria, built in 1887–90 according to a design by Emanuele Rocca, had a prestigious and important location from the start. As with its larger predecessor, the Galleria Vittorio Emanuele II in Milan, the Galleria Umberto Primo exalts the taste of the postunification commercial elite (the "jackals" of Lampedusa's famous historical novel *Il Gattopardo*) in a virtuoso display of new technology clothed in traditional style. Here are the iron-ribbed glass barrel vault and 188-ft-high dome by Paolo Boubée), which represented the latest advance in modern form yet is layered over with the reassuring architectural ornament of the 14th century (another era when the bourgeoisie triumphed in Italy). The ground floor was designed to offer weatherproof shopping for the new class of spenders; professional studios, fashion ateliers, and newspaper offices occupied the three upper stories. A small underground theater, the *Salone Margherita*, was constructed near the Via Toledo entrance for chamber-music concerts, but within a few months of its opening evolved into a legendary nightclub and a center of Naples's turn-of-the-century nightlife.

Neapolitans used to come here for a leisurely Campari; today they occasionally visit for a quick espresso, since the grand gallery has a somewhat forlorn air. Still, it makes a soothing soothing passageway by virtue of its sumptuous marble inlay, while the block of light streaming through one of the upper-level loggias into the magnificent vastness of the arcade makes for a great scene. At Christmastime a huge public Nativity crèche is set up, and the space becomes quite festive. ⊠ *Entrances on Via San Carlo, Via Toledo, Via Santa Brigida, Via Verdi.*

❾ Palazzo Gravina. A dignified Renaissance palace in the Tuscan style with a vigorous *bugnato* (diamond-point) facade, the palazzo was begun in 1513 for Ferdinando Orsini, duke of Gravina, by Gabriele d'Angelo, a student of Alberti and Brunelleschi. The monumental doorway was added by Mario Giuffredo in a restoration of 1762–72, and an extra story was added in 1839, which is clearly visible from the beautiful courtyard. Largely burned down in 1848 by Swiss Guards trying to flush out a group of armed patriots, it now houses the modern School of Architecture, so feel free to wander around to observe how old and new coexist. ⊠ *Via Monteoliveto 3.*

★ ❷ Palazzo Reale. One of the showplaces of Naples, the Palazzo Reale, or Royal Palace, was meant to be the apotheosis of Bourbon power in the city. Renovated and redecorated by successive rulers in a style that can only be called overblown imperial, once lorded over by a dim-witted king who liked to shoot his hunting guns at the birds in his tapestries, and filled with salons designed in the most deliciously lavish 18th-century Neapolitan taste, it remains a palatial pile. Commissioned by the Spanish viceroys in 1600, who ordered the Swiss architect Domenico Fontana to build a suitable new residence for Philip III, should he chance to visit Naples (which he didn't), the immense complex was not in fact completed until 1843 (by Gaetano Genovese). The palace saw its greatest moment of splendor in the 18th century, when Charles III of Bourbon became the first permanent resident; during that century Luigi Vanvitelli filled in half the arcades in the lower register of the facade to strengthen it, and Ferdinando Fuga created the State Wing after the accession of Ferdinand IV in 1759. Today this wing comprises the Museo dell'Appartamento Storico, or **Royal Apartments**, which can be visited to get a glimpse of Bourbon glory.

To view these 30 rooms on the first floor, enter the courtyard and ascend the monumental Scalone d'Onore on the left (the ticket booth is at the bottom of the staircase), going up the left side of the stairs. Montesquieu, the French 18th-century writer, considered this to be the finest staircase in Europe, and it sets a tone for the glitter and grandeur to come. The first doors on the right open up into the **Court Theater**, built by Ferdinando Fuga for Charles III, who in 1763 had created an opera company for private performances of comic opera. It was inaugurated in 1768 with *Peleo e Teti*, by Giovanni Paisiello, but soon afterward fell into disuse. Damaged by World War II bombs, it was restored in 1950; note the resplendent royal box, which abandons the lure of monumentality for intimate luxury. Following are the suite of rooms around the courtyard that constitute the royal apartments. Room IV is the **Throne Room**, with wine-red striped-silk walls and gilded stuccos representing the 12 provinces of the Kingdom of the Two

Sicilies; the ponderous Empire-style throne in fact dates from after 1850. Giuseppe Bonito painted the two portraits of the ambassadors from Turkey and Tripoli in 1741; the entourage from Tripoli (to the right of the throne) looks like they'd be much more fun, but of course they were still pirates.

The decoration picks up in the **Room of the Ambassadors** (Room V), where a pair of choice 18th-century Gobelin tapestries grace the light green walls together with a lovely Annunciation by Artemisia Gentileschi. The ceiling painting honoring Spanish military victories is by local artist Belisario Corenzio and his school (1610–20). Room VI, with pale gold walls and a simple white vault, was the bedroom of Charles's queen, Maria Amalia of Saxony, and hides a small, brilliantly gold private oratory in the corner, with beautiful paintings by Francesco Liani of Parma (1760). Above the exit door is a Madonna and Child attributed to the charming Spanish mannerist Ruviales. This door takes you a bit toward the courtyard to rejoin the inner rooms along the third side.

Room VII, small and square, has wonderful ceiling frescoes by Battistello Carraciolo (1610–16)—all velvet, fire, and smoke, they reveal the influence of the recent visit by Caravaggio to Naples—a jolly series by Federico Zuccari depicting 12 Proverbs on small wood panels, along with, last but not least, a Titian portrait (circa 1543) of Pier Luigi Farnese. Room VIII has an ugly red 19th-century ceiling (how royal taste had fallen) but is redeemed by a great 18th-century "Nocturnal" clock by Charles Clay and a spectacularly overdone enamel and gilt-bronze birdcage on a flower stand, given by Czar Nicholas I to Ferdinand when he visited in 1846; the table flaunts views of the czar's various palaces. As for paintings, there is a simpatico portrait of a flutist by Alexis Grimou and a wonderfully hard-edged and cynical depiction of two tax collectors by van Roymerswaele (1538).

Room XIII was **Joachim Murat's writing room** when he was king of Naples; he brought with him from France some regal furniture by the great French *ébeniste* (cabinet-maker) Weisweiller, originally commissioned by Marie Antoinette and completed by commissions of his own (including the desk and two dignified clocks) in 1812. The next few rooms combine ponderous 19th-century furnishings and rather better Baroque paintings: Room XVII, in particular, has a good selection of paintings by followers of Caravaggio; Room XVIII has an intensely colored Guercino depiction of Joseph dreaming; and Room XIX is full of still lifes from the important Neapolitan school. The huge Room XXII, painted in green and gold with kitschy *faux* tapestries, is known as the **Hercules Hall,** for in a moment of glory it once housed the *Hercules Farnese.* The authentic tapestries are from the Royal Factory of Naples (1783–89), but the things to look at here are the porcelain creations from Sévres, including the Atlas with his starry globe and the huge green-chrome vase (1812), painted by Louis Béranger.

The **Palatine Chapel,** redone by Gaetano Genovese in the 1830s, is a disappointing affair as chapels go, having been gussied up with too much gold, but it has a stunning Technicolor intarsia altar from the previous chapel (Dionisio Lazzari, 1678). Note the false-perspective panels, which almost propel the altar into the stratosphere of bad taste. Also here on a long-term loan is the famous *Presepio* (Nativity) scene of the Banco di Napoli—it may lack the spectacular setting of the *Presepio Cuciniello* in the Museo di San Martino but has even better sculpture, with pieces by important sculptors such as Giuseppe Sammartino (the shepherdess at the table in the tavern scene on the right), Francesco and Antonio Viva, Francesco Celebrano, and others. There are some pleasant 19th-century landscapes in the next few rooms, as well as Queen

Maria Carolina's Ferris wheel–like reading lectern (which enabled her to do a 19th-century reader's version of channel surfing).

The last room on your way out is the **Bodyguards' Room,** which backs up to the Throne Room and displays some finely worked and fascinating architects' models for the palace and an astonishingly frank wax portrait bust of Queen Maria Carolina of Austria. With no court maquillage, her face is eerily similar to Jacques-Louis David's brutal sketch of Maria's cousin Marie Antoinette in a cart on the way to the guillotine—perhaps a fitting and final note to your visit to this Bourbon extravaganza of a palace. Another wing of the complex holds the **Biblioteca Nazionale Vittorio Emanuele III,** the largest in southern Italy and one of the most important in the country. Begun, as with so many other Bourbon collections, with Farnese bits and pieces, it was enriched with the priceless papyri from Herculaneaum found in 1752 and opened to the public in 1804. You can view these and a splendid choice of manuscripts and rare editions in the elegant rooms open to visitors. To actually use the library for research, you need to apply for a card. The library also has a lovely garden, which looks out on the Castel Nuovo. ⊠ *Piazza del Plebiscito,* ☎ *081/580–8111.* ▨ *8,000 lire.* ⊙ *Mon.–Tues. and Thurs.–Fri. 9–9, Sat. 9–midnight, Sun. 9–8.*

❼ Piazza Matteotti. In 1925 Mussolini issued a famous (now notorious) call for "good Italian architecture," hoping to revive the glories of Italian architecture and underline the power of the modern Italian state; he was fortunate in having a flood of talented architects answer the call, in a wildly creative and polemical exploration of modernism, but the troublesome political context of the resulting constructions has tended to push a number of magnificent structures into oblivion. The area between Piazza della Carità and Piazza Municipio in Naples represents one of the most significant and successful urban transformations of this period, and the pride of this vast program is the Piazza Matteotti, object of an important 1927 competition.

The piazza, which combines a number of important civic buildings in a modern forum, is dominated by the strong parabolic curve of the post office, or **Palazzo dell Poste e Telegrafi,** a surprisingly contemporary building by Bolognese architect Giuseppe Vaccaro, who combines elements of the Rationalist Functional style—in which the plan and decoration of the building clearly articulate its functions—with subtle historical references. The lower band of dark gray diorite not only alludes to the gray *piperno* of local Renaissance construction, it also delineates the large public spaces on the ground floor. Inside, the building refreshingly retains its original interior furnishings, and the streamlined decoration of the public rooms buffers the boredom of waiting in endless lines with their Deco-ized *Metropolis*-style elegance.

The other jewel of the piazza is the **Palazzo della Provincia,** to the left of the post office, by the young Neapolitan engineer Marcello Canino, which is a good example (along with the Banco di Roma) of the other predominant architectural current in the fascist era: Historical Monumentalism, which sought to translate ancient forms (arches, colonnades, basilical structures, and so forth) into a modern idiom. The Rational Functionalist school was generally judged too international and rootless a style for an Italy intent on reviving its own specific past glory, although in fact projects to combine elements of the two schools. Although the **Questura** looks every bit the totalitarian police station that it once was, with a stubbornly horizontal and forbiddingly spartan mass of travertine crying out "Abandon hope, all ye who enter here," in its defense, at least its form expresses function. ⊠ *At intersection of Via Monteolivedo, Via A. Diaz, and Via Battisti.*

Quartieri Spagnoli (Spanish Quarter). The Spanish garrison was quartered in the now-decaying tenements aligned in a tight-knit grid along incredibly narrow alleys in this neighborhood roughly between Via Toledo (downhill border) and Via Pasquale Scura (western leg of Spaccanapoli). It's a hectic, impoverished (occasionally dangerous) area—chock-full of local color—brooding in the shadow of Vomero, but it's showing signs of improvement.

★ ❶ **San Francesco di Paola.** Modeled after Rome's Pantheon, this circular basilica is the centerpiece of the Piazza del Plebiscito and remains one of the most frigidly voluptuous examples of the Stil Empire, or Neoclassic style, in Italy. Commissioned by Ferdinand I in 1817 to fulfill a vow he had made in order to enlist divine aid in being reinstated to the throne of the Kingdom of the Two Sicilies, it rose at one end of the vast parade ground built several years earlier by Joachim Murat, and it managed to transform Murat's inconveniently grandiose colonnade—whose architect was clearly inspired by the colonnades of St. Peter's in Rome—into a setting for restored Bourbon glory. The church also usefully fulfilled a prophecy by the 15th-century saint Ferrante d'Aragona, for whom it is named, that one day a large church and square would occupy the crowded site. Pietro Bianchi from Lugano in Switzerland won a competition and built a slightly smaller version of the Pantheon, with a beautiful coffered dome and a splendid set of 34 Corinthian columns in gray Mondragon marble, but the overall lack of color (so different from the warm interior of the Pantheon) combined with the severe geometrical forms produces an almost defiantly cold space. To some, this only proves the ancients did sometimes know their own architecture better. Art historians find the spectacle of the church to be the ultimate in Neoclassic *grandezza*; others think this Roman temple is only fitting to honor Jove, not Christ. In any event, the main altar, done in gold, lapis lazuli, and other precious stones by Anselmo Caggiano (1641), was taken from the destroyed Church of the Santi Apostoli and provides some relief from the oppressive perfection of the setting. ⊠ *Piazza del Plebiscito,* ☎ *081/764–5133.* ☉ *Mon.–Sat. 7:30–11 and 3:30–6, Sun. 8–1.*

❺ **Santa Brigida.** The Lucchesi fathers built this church around 1640 in honor of the Swedish queen and saint who visited her fellow queen, Naples's unsaintly Giovanna I, in 1372 and became one of the first persons to go on record as denouncing the loose morals and irrepressible sensuality of the Neapolitans. The height of the church's dome was limited to prevent its interfering with cannon fire from nearby Castel Nuovo, but Luca Giordano, the pioneer painter of the *trompe l'oeil* Baroque dome, effectively opened it up with a spacious sky serving as the setting for an *Apotheosis of Saint Bridget* (1678), painted (and now in need of restoration) in exchange for his tomb space, marked by a pavement inscription in the left transept. ⊠ *Via Santa Brigida 72,* ☎ *081/552–3793.* ☉ *Daily 7:30 AM–12:30 PM and 5:30–7 PM.*

❽ **Sant' Anna dei Lombardi.** Long favored by the Aragonese kings, this church, simple and rather anonymous from the outside, houses some of the most important ensembles of Renaissance sculpture in southern Italy. Begun with the adjacent convent of the Olivetani and its four cloisters in 1411, it was redone in the Baroque style in the mid-17th century by Gennaro Sacco, although this is no longer so visible, as the bombs of 1943 rather radically altered the decoration and led to a modern restoration that has tended to restore the original *quattrocento* (15th-century) lines. The wonderful coffered wooden ceiling, currently under restoration, will add a bit of pomp. Inside the porch is the tomb of

Domenico Fontana, one of the major architects of the late 16th century, who died in Naples after beginning the Palazzo Reale. Once inside the entrance door, you enter a simple single-nave church with side chapels. Turn around and you will see, on either side of the entrance wall, two fine Renaissance tombs. The one on the left of the entrance, as you face the wall, belongs to the Ligorio family (whose descendant Pirro designed the Villa d'Este in Tivoli) and is a work by Giovanni da Nola (1524); the tomb on the right is a masterpiece by Giuseppe Santacroce (1532) for the del Pozzo family. To the left of the Ligorio Altar (the corner chapel on the immediate right as you face the altar) is the Correale Chapel, whose altar contains precious reliefs of the *Annunciation* and *Scenes from the Life of Jesus* (1489), by Benedetto da Maiano, a great name in Tuscan sculpture. On the other side of the entrance is the Piccolomini Chapel, with a Crucifixion by Giulio Mazzoni (circa 1550), a refined marble altar (circa 1475), a funerary monument to Maria d'Aragona by another prominent Florentine sculptor, Antonello Rossellino (circa 1475), and on the right, a rather sweet fresco of the Annunciation by an anonymous follower of Piero della Francesca.

The true surprises of the church, however, are off to the right of the altar, in the presbytery and adjoining rooms. The chapel just to the right of the main altar, belonging to the Orefice family, is richly decorated in pre-Baroque (1596–98) polychrome marbles and frescoes by Luis Rodriguez; from here you continue on through the Oratory of the Holy Sepulcher, with the tomb of Antonio d'Alessandro and his wife, to reach the church's showpiece: a potently realistic life-size group of eight terra-cotta figures by Guido Mazzoni (1492), which make up a Pietà; the faces are said to be modeled from actual people at the Aragonese court. Toward the rear of the church is Cappella dell'Assunta, with a fun painting of a monk in its corner by Michelangelo's student Giorgio Vasari, and the lovely Old Sacristy, adorned with one of the most successful decorative ensembles Vasari ever painted (1544), and breathtaking wood-inlay stalls by Fra' Giovanni da Verona and assistants (1506–10) with views of famous buildings (ask the attendant for the key). ⊠ *Piazza Monteoliveto 3.* ☉ *Tues.–Thurs. and Sat. 8:30–12:30.*

★ ❸ **Teatro San Carlo.** La Scala in Milan is more famous, but San Carlo is more beautiful, and Naples is, after all, the most operatic of cities. First built in eight months and 10 days in 1737 by Angelo Carasale for Charles III of Bourbon—and opened on the king's saint's name day—it burned down in 1816 and was rebuilt, with its facade of five rustic arches in gray *piperno* surmounted by an elegant loggia, in only nine months. This time the architect was Antonio Niccolini, working under the impetus of Domenico Barbaja, the Milanese director appointed by Joachim Murat in 1810. Barbaja, San Carlo's most legendary director, started out as a waiter in a tavern and enriched himself through a talent for gambling. He obviously wanted to keep his job under the new regime and therefore made a bet with the king to have the theater open within nine months. More importantly, he also managed in the same year to convince Gioacchino Rossini to come to Naples as conductor and house composer; Stendhal hailed Ferdinand's wise retaining of Barbaja and his prompt sponsorship of the theater as a "coup d'état" for the deep and immediate bond it created between the ruler and his opera-loving populace. This was further cemented by the many operas composed for the house, including Donizetti's *Lucia di Lammermoor* and Rossini's *La Donna del Lago.*

Nearly 200 boxes are arranged on six levels, and the huge stage (12,000 square ft) permits productions with horses, camels, and elephants and even boasts a removable backdrop that can lift to reveal the Palazzo

Reale Gardens. Above the rich red-and-gold auditorium is a breathy ceiling fresco, by Giuseppe Camarano, suitably representing Apollo presenting poets to Athena. At many performances, however, all eyes were on the sumptuous royal box, which seats 15 and is topped by a gigantic gilded crown. Check the local newspaper *Il Mattino* or the *Qui Napoli* for information on performances (☞ also Nightlife and the Arts, *below*,), or pick up a schedule at the ticket office and get ready for a great evening of opera. Standards are among the highest in Europe at the San Carlo—even the great Enrico Caruso was hissed here. Even if you can't catch a performance, try to take the guided tour to see the splendid theater—as Stendhal once wrote: "The first impression one gets is of being suddenly transported to the palace of an oriental emperor. There is nothing in Europe to compare with it, or even give the faintest idea of what it is like." ⊠ *Via San Carlo 101–103*, ☎ *081/797–2330 (gate), 081/797–2331 or 081/797–2412 (ticket office),* FAX *081/797–2309.* ☑ *Guided Tours: Sat., Sun. 2–3:30 PM; 5,000.*

Spaccanapoli: The Heart and Soul of Naples

If you arrive in Naples just to do the sights, you'll see the city, but you won't get to its essence. To do that, you need to discover Spaccanapoli, the unforgettable neighborhood that is the heart of old Naples. A buzzing hive of daily chaos in a constantly re-created grid of ancient patterns, this densely populated neighborhood presents perhaps the city's most familiar and joyfully pungent face. This is the Naples of peeling facades spackled with enough drying laundry to suggest a parade; of arguments in the streets (or are they arguing? it's sometimes hard to tell) swelling to operatic proportions, often with onlookers adding contributions to supplement the lyrical principals; of small alleyways with freshly laid flowers at the many shrines to the Blessed Virgin. Here, where the cheapest pizzerias in town feed the locals like kings, the full raucous street carnival of Neapolitan popular culture is punctuated with improbable oases of spiritual calm. All the contradictions of Naples—splendor and squalor, palace and slum, triumph and tragedy—meet here and sing a full-throated chorale. The amazing thing is that it seems, somehow, more real in its conscious theatricality. And, paradoxically, it also seems impossible to remain stressed out in the midst of all this ricocheting vitality.

Spaccanapoli (literally, "Split-Naples") is actually the name of the ruler-straight street that divides the neighborhood in half—a fantastic 5-km-long (3-mi-long) pedestrian ribbon that was originally the ancient Roman Decumanus Maximus, or main thoroughfare. Today the street changes names six times along its route, with Via Benedetto Croce and Via S. Biagio dei Librai among the most prominently used. This breathtaking roadway-cum-piazza is a palisade of towering 19th-century tenements (once the highest in Europe, they soared up to eight floors because of the population density), faded palazzi, and Baroque churches. Contrasting elements of faded gilt and romance, joy and calamity, neon-lighted pizzerias and gilded cathedrals produce a dizzying ragout. Cinderella would feel right at home. Thanks to the warmth of the locals, you will, too.

The Spacca is not simply picturesque. It also contains some of Naples's most important sights, including a striking conglomeration of churches—Lombard, Gothic, Renaissance, Baroque, Rococo, and Neoclassical. Here are the majolica-adorned cloister of Santa Chiara; the sumptuous Church of the Gesù Nuovo; two opera-set piazzas; the city duomo (where the Festa di San Gennaro is celebrated every September); the Capella Sansevero; the greatest painting in Naples—Caravaggio's

Seven Acts of Mercy altarpiece—on view at the Church of Pio Monte; and Via Gregorio Armeno, where shops devoted to *Presipio* (crèche) wares nearly transform every morning into Christmas. This region is best explored by heading up the Spacca to the Duomo, then back along Via Tribunali. The Via Tribunali is often referred to as part of the city's Decumano Maggiore, but as it is only one block over from the Spacca, the entire region is also commonly grouped under the name Spaccanapoli. Wherever you head, you'll find half of Naples's populace crowded at your elbow, with everyone pursuing life *con gusto*. The beautiful thing is that despite the Punch and Judy appearance of things, almost everyone turns out to be a sweetheart. If the Spacca is the heart of Naples, it pumps for all.

Numbers in the text correspond to numbers in the margin and on the Naples map.

A Good Walk

Begin at Piazza Gesù Nuovo with a visit to the Church of **Gesù Nuovo** ⑪ (1584) to give a shot of Jesuit pomp to your morning cappuccino. As you exit, admire the piazza's extravagant carved-stone spire that honors the Virgin Mary, the Guglia dell'Immacolata, whose saints and cherubs, sculpted by Francesco Pagano and Matteo Bottigliero after a design by Giuseppe Genuino (1743), are considered a high point of 18th-century Neapolitan sculpture. Across the square, relax your eyes at **Santa Chiara** ⑫, a broodingly severe Gothic monument of the 14th century, built by Robert of Anjou. In noisy Spaccanapoli, peace breaks out in the cloisters of the district, none more beautiful here than the Chiostro delle Clarisse, transformed in 1742 into a Rococo-era showpiece by a colorful majolica-tile overlay on its columns and benches. At this point the piazza debouches into the pedestrian roadway nicknamed the Spaccanapoli. Past a block full of moldering palazzi—note Palazzo Filmarino at the corner of Via S. Sebastiano, the home of Benedetto Croce, the noted aesthete and philosopher, and now site of his library—is the Piazza San Domenico Maggiore, where the Guglia di San Domenico (1737) and the apse of San Domenico Maggiore create one of Naples's most charming urban set pieces. Residents of the district move into this piazza during spring and summer months, making it a "living room"—the furniture is the umbrellaed tables of Scaturchio, Naples's celebrated *gelateria* (ice-cream parlor). After enjoying a time-out here, head up the right-hand side of the piazza to Via Francesco de Santis and the **Cappella Sansevero** ⑬ (1590), the tomb-chapel of the Sangro di San Severo family, which features three showstopping 18th-century sculptures, including Giuseppe Sanmartino's *Veiled Christ*.

Backtrack to the Spaccanapoli roadway and take in the pretty 18th-century Church of **Sant' Angelo a Nilo** ⑭ and picturesque Largo Corpo di Napoli, where the statue of the Egyptian river god Nile reclines on a pedestal. Farther down the Spaccanapoli—whose name changes here from Via Benedetto Croce to Via S. Biagio dei Librai—is the tiny Church of San Nicola a Nilo, whose horseshoe-shape steps serve as an open-air antiques store. Just across the street is the **Monte di Pietà** ⑮, whose Cappella della Pietà and spectacularly opulent 17th-century salons can be found just beyond the courtyard (open Saturday only). Continue down the Spacca to view the storefront Ospedale delle Bambole—a doll hospital—at No. 81, then make a right turn on Via Duomo to the atmospheric **Museo Civico Filangieri** ⑯. Head back up Via Duomo two blocks to Via Tribunali and make a right to the **Pio Monte della Misericordia** ⑰, whose church contains one of the greatest 17th-century altarpieces in Europe, Caravaggio's *The Seven Acts of Mercy*. Head back to the Via Duomo and turn right to the **Duomo di San Gennaro** ⑱, the majestic cathedral built for Charles I of Anjou in the 14th century and home to the Cappella del Tesoro di San Gennaro. If you have more adrenaline to burn for Baroque, turn right from the Duomo up the avenue to Via Apostoli to see **San Giuseppe dei Ruffi** ⑲ and **Santi Apostoli** ⑳. Nearby is a monument of Neapolitan Gothic, **Santa Maria di Donnaregina Vecchia** ㉑.

Head back down Via Duomo one block to the Via dei Tribunali—the other great historic thoroughfare of the district. Turn right along the street and discover the first of the street's many imposing churches— the elegant **I Girolamini** ㉒ and the gigantic **San Lorenzo Maggiore** ㉓, whose 18th-century facade hides a Gothic-era nave. The church is at the corner of Via San Gregorio Armeno, probably the most charming street in Naples. Famed for its lavishly Rococo Church of **San Gregorio Armeno** ㉖, whose towering campanile arches over the street, this thoroughfare is lined with nearly a dozen *presipi* (crèche) stores. After exploring the shops along the street, head back up to Via dei Tribunali, turn left and head east for about 10 blocks—passing the mammoth **San Domenico Maggiore** ㉗ on your way—to find pretty Piazza Bellini, whose cafés are perfect for a time-out and restorative espresso. You'll learn that, for the price of an aperitif or an ice cream, the cafés of the Spaccanapoli bestow instantaneous club membership on a patron. From the moment you settle into a chair, you belong.

TIMING

Because many churches open at 7:30 AM and close for the afternoon around 1 PM, it's imperative to get an early start to fit in as many sights before the midday break. The famous Cappella Sansevero is open through the day, while the Monte di Pietà is only open Saturday morning. During the midday break, wander around savoring couleur locale and enjoy lunch at any of a number of good inexpensive restaurants in this neighborhood (it's best to plan on paying cash for this lunch), with Scaturchio in Piazza San Domenico the perfect place for after-lunch espresso. Then fit in a bit of shopping by browsing around Piazza Dante and the Via Santa Maria di Constantinopoli for used books and antiques, or head over to the Via San Gregorio Armeno to pick out a manger figure to take back home. By 4 many of the churches reopen. Plan on a good two hours to walk this route, plus a quarter to a half hour for each of the principal churches you decide to visit.

Sights to See

★ ⑬ **Capella Sansevero.** Rightly one of the emblematic monuments of Naples in the popular imagination, this dazzling masterpiece, the funerary chapel of the Sangro di Sansevero princes, combines noble swagger, overwhelming color, and a touch of the macabre—which is to say, it expresses Naples perfectly. The di Sangros were renowned military leaders as far back as the Dark Ages, and they boast no fewer than six saints in their family (who are portrayed in the chapel's painted roundels between the windows). The chapel was begun in 1590 by Giovan Francesco di Sangro, the result of a vow to be fulfilled if he were cured of a dire illness. He lived for another 14 years, which was good for the building campaign, but the present aspect of the chapel is due to his descendant Raimondo di Sangro, prince of Sansevero, who had it completely redone between 1749 and 1770.

Youthful portraits show this fascinating character with a pronounced pointy chin. Confident and sophisticated in his tastes, obviously brilliant, and an important mover in Naples's Enlightenment, this princely, intellectual mad scientist, and inventor was accused of just about everything then considered base: atheism, alchemy, and Freemasonry. The last two are likely: he seems to have been in fact a Grand Master of the Freemasons, and his claim to be able to reproduce the miracle of St. Gennaro's blood got him kicked out of the Fraternity of the Treasure of St. Gennaro. He left a personal touch in the basement, down the stairs to the right, where two glass cases house a pair of "anatomical machines," which are astonishing even if fake. Purporting to be an encyclopedic reconstruction of the blood vessels of an adult male and a pregnant female, they are supposedly based on two of the prince's servants, who fell victim to his curiosity when he injected them while still alive with what is conjectured to be a mercury solution that hardened their arteries.

Prince Raimondo is generally credited with the design of the splendid marble-inlay floor; he hired Francesco Maria Russo to paint the ceiling with a *Glory of Paradise* (1749) and also hired a young team of up-and-coming sculptors, whose contributions remain the focal point for most visits here: the showpiece is smack in the middle of the chapel, Giuseppe Sammartino's *Veiled Christ* (1753). The artist was only 33 years old when he sculpted this famous work, which was originally meant to be placed in the crypt. It was too good to leave down below with *those things* and the audacious virtuosity of the clinging drapery showing the wounds underneath is one of the marvels of Neapolitan sculpture. A taste for the *outré* and extravagant had already been demonstrated by other statues in the chapel, especially Francesco Quierolo's *Disillusion,* to the right of the altar, with its chisel-defying net making a spectacular transition to empty space. This Genovese sculptor also did the female statue representing *Sincerity* on the right and the commemorative *Altar to St. Odorisio* between the two Allegories. Antonio Corradini, who came to Naples from the Veneto region via Rome, is responsible for the allegorical statue to the left of the altar, *Veiled Modesty* (1751), also widely considered his masterpiece; he also sculpted the funerary monument and Allegory of *Decorum,* on the inside of the front wall to the right of the exit. The main altar and its reliefs are the work of Francesco Celebrano, and the angels on either side are by a sculptor from nearby Sorrento, Paolo Persico. Celebrano also contributed the wonderful funerary monument above the front door, with Cecco di Sangro leaping out of his coffin in commemoration of one of his most famous exploits—when, having been left for dead, he suddenly reappeared, fully armed, in the thick of the battle. Celebrano also did the tomb on the left of this monument. This team of sculptors is essentially responsible for the remainder of the sculptural decor as well, with the notable exception of the three 17th-century tombs in the front bays of the side walls. ⊠ *Via Francesco di Sanctis 19,* ☎ *081/ 551–8470.* ☉ *Mon. and Wed.–Sat. 10–5, Tues. and Sun. 10–1.*

★ ⑱ **Duomo di San Gennaro.** The shrine to the paterfamilias of Naples, San Gennaro (St. Gennaro), the city's cathedral is home to the saint's devotional chapel, among the most spectacular—in the show-biz sense of the word—in the city. With a colonnade leading to an apse bursting with light and Baroque splendor, the duomo's nave makes a fitting setting for the famous **Miracle of the Blood,** when the blood of the martyred San Gennaro liquifies (hopefully) in its silver ampule every September 19 before an audience of thousands massed in front of the duomo's altar. *San Genna, fa'o miracolo! Fa ampresso! Nun ce fa suffri!* yell the congregants during the ritual—"Saint Genna, do the miracle! Hurry up! You'll pay for it if you don't do it!" If St. Januarius (to use his ancient Latin name) doesn't cooperate, however, it's usually the city that winds up paying, or so the locals believe: Eruptions of Vesuvius, cholera outbreaks, and defeats of the Naples's soccer team have all been blamed on the saint if the *miracolo* doesn't occur.

THE GLITTER AND THE GOLD: NEAPOLITAN BAROQUE ART AND ARCHITECTURE

TIME, LIKE A RIVER, has dropped its silt over Naples, leaving in each age its characteristic deposit. Today, however, this deposit is not neatly layered, waiting for a distant spade to uncover, as at Pompeii, but one that is capricious, unplanned, and disorderly. Naples is a city of dramatic pairings: Baroque with medieval, plenty with want, grandeur with muddle. Of the numerous artistic styles that comprise this feast, however, none suited the Neapolitan temperament better than the Baroque—the style that came to the fore in the 17th century and continued in the 18th century under the Bourbon kings.

In a city of volcanic passions, the flagrantly emotional, floridly luxurious Baroque—an art that seems perpetually on the point of bursting its bonds—found immediate favor. The departure of the austere Spanish viceroys in the 17th century gave free rein to the city's natural inclination for this extroverted style, allowing artists like Caravaggio and the Spaniard Il Ribera, and architects like Ferdinando Sanfelice and Cosimo Fanzago, to strut their aesthetic stuff.

With untrammeled individualism given full play, the results—most still visible today—were theatrical, dramatic, dynamic, vivid, alive, and sometimes wonderfully showy. Venture into the Gesù Nuovo (mother church of the *Padri Gesuiti*, or Jesuit Fathers) and note the buoyant swirl of stucco, inlaid marble, and gilt work, a florid tangle that mirrors the chaos of the piazza outside its door. Like the city outside the doors, the decorative scheme is diffuse and disjunctive, with little effort to organize everything into a easily understood scheme. Throughout the city, artists loved using illusionistic trompe l'oeil tricks of ingenious device on church cupolas, as in the Capella di San Gennaro at the Duomo. Here, as in other churches, you'll see reliquaries studded with semiprecious stones and covered with gold, gold, and more gold. Elsewhere, statues were made

hyper-real, either thanks to amazing technique—such as the marble figures in the Capella Sansevero, where fishing nets and veils were carved from pure stone—or by being dressed in silk and velvet garments. Thanks to the Counter-Reformation, the Catholic church was then busy making an overt appeal to the congregant, using emotion and motion to get the message across—no more so than in 17th- and 18th-century Naples, a city which, incidentally, had some 20,000 clerics, more than in Rome itself.

The most representative practitioner of Neapolitan Baroque was Cosimo Fanzago (1591–1678). A Lombard by birth, he arrived in Naples to study sculpture, so even when he decorated a church, he usually covered it head to toe with colored and inlaid marbles, as in his work at the Church of San Martino in the Certosa (charterhouse) that sits atop the Vomero Hill. Two decades earlier, Caravaggio (1571–1610) had arrived in Naples from Rome and this great painter of chiaroscuro took the city by storm. He was on the point of bringing the Baroque style back to earth in Naples—thanks to the unflinching truthfulness and extroverted sensuality in his paintings—but other forces prevailed.

Neapolitan Baroque painters were generally a mediocre bunch. Many, in fact, banded together to form a *"Facione de' Pittori"* headed by the favored painter of the Spanish vice royals, Il Ribera. These *Dependentii*, or disciples, formed more than just a "union": they were a full-fledged gang and led to the persecution that plagued most painters who came to Naples for work, such as the noted Domenichino and Guido Reni, both of whom fled the city and the cabal to save their lives (or nearly so: it was widely believed that Domenichino was mysteriously poisoned shortly after leaving the city). Thanks to the disciples of Spagnoletto (Il Ribera's nickname), pride, pomposity, glitter, and gold conquered all.

The duomo was first established by Charles II of Anjou, using imported French architects, on the site of a previous structure, the Cattedrale Stefania (AD 570), and next to an even earlier structure, the still-extant Basilica di Santa Restituta (4th century AD). Already restored in 1456 and 1484, it was largely redesigned in 1787 and 1837. The original facade collapsed in the earthquake of 1349, and the present pseudo-Gothic concoction is a modern (1877–1905) fake by Enrico Alvino and Giuseppe Pisanti, which, however, reemploys the doors—still majestic in spite of extensive damage—from the 1407 facade. The central door, by Antonio Baboccio, features a *Madonna and Child* by Tino da Camiano under its arch. Inside, the splendid nave welcomes all, with a gilt wooden ceiling (1621) and golden roundels painted above the pillars by Luca Giordano and his school depicting various saints. The nave's magnificent pillars are decorated and reinforced by 110 ancient granite columns. Above the entrance door is the reconstructed monument of the church's founder, Charles II d'Anjou (circa 1285), reconstructed in 1599 by Domenico Fontana for the viceroy Enrico Guzman, the famous count of Olivares. From the nave head to the right side of the church to see the chapel devoted to the city's patron saint.

The **Cappella del Tesoro di San Gennaro**, or Chapel of the Treasure of San Gennaro, was built in 1608–37 by the Theatin architect Francesco Grimaldi to fulfill a vow pronounced by city father made in desperation during an outbreak of the plague (January 13, 1527), some 80 years earlier. The chapel honors San Gennaro (250–305), one of the earliest Christian martyrs; as bishop of Benevento, he was executed at Pozuoli during the rule of the emperor Diocletian. The entrance to the chapel is marked by a heavy gilt-bronze grille (1668–86) by noted architect Cosimo Fanzago, who also designed the chapel's superb floor, and is flanked by statues of Sts. Peter and Paul by Giuliano Finelli. Inside, the elegant Greek-cross plan is decorated everywhere possible with gold, colored marble, bronze, and paint, but nothing could be too overdone for the home of St. Gennaro's most famous DNA sample and the fabulous treasure of jeweled offerings bestowed by numerous sovereigns. The 40-odd *brocatello* columns, with their musty tones of dried roses, were sent from the quarries of Tortosa in Valencia, Spain. Numerous bronze statues of saints keep permanent watch over the chapel. The high altar on the back wall, designed by the painter Francesco Solimena (1689–90), seems to swell as it tries to contain the opulence of the central relief, created in silver (circa 1692) by Giovan Domenico Vinaccia (who inserted into it a portrait of himself holding eyeglasses). Above the altar, against the wall, is a large bronze of St. Gennaro on his bishop's throne, by onetime Bernini assistant Giuliano Finelli. Also behind the altar are two silvered niches donated by Charles II of Spain to house the reliquaries containing the blood of the Saint (the right-hand one) and his skull. This latter reliquary consists of the famous gilded medieval bust done by three French artists (1305) set on a silver base from 1609, the actual repository of the precious vials of the saint's blood.

Most of the frescoes are by the Bolognese artist Domenichino, but his compatriot Guido Reni was originally engaged to paint the cycle, and thereby hangs a tale. The celebrated painter came to Naples only to find his life made miserable by jealous local artists indignant at seeing such an honor given to an outsider. Ultimately, the commission went to the great Domenichino, who came to Naples only after the viceroy himself guaranteed his protection. He started painting under armed guard in 1630 and had almost completed the ensemble in 1641 when he died suddenly. Poisoning was suspected, and the committee at this point refused to even consider any Neapolitan painter, so the Roman Giovanni

Lanfranco was called in to bravely (and quickly) finish the dome, and it was he who painted the dome's frescoed vision of Paradise. Also note Il Ribera's *St. Gennaro in the Furnace* (1647), on the right-hand wall— perhaps the most beautiful church painting in Naples. Dating from his early Neapolitan period, it shows the clear but well-digested influence of Velasquez visible in the figures on the left, and it is imbued with a Mediterranean luminosity that is rare in his work. The chapel, a veritable church-within-a-church, also has its own sacristy, which contains a luxurious washbasin by Cosimo Fanzago. This room leads into a suite of rooms with frescoes by Giacomo Farelli and a splendid altarpiece by Massimo Stanzione; at the back are kept the 51 statues of the "co-patron" saints, displayed in the chapel proper in May and September and which accompany the reliquary of the blood on its annual procession to Santa Chiara.

The main altar sits in the resplendent apse redesigned in 1744 by Paolo Tosi and framed by two magnificent jasper columns found in a dig in 1705. The paintings in the apse are the work of Stefano Pozzi (ceiling and left wall) and Corrado Giaquinto (right wall). A staircase on either side of the entrance to the presbytery (high altar area) descends to the Caraffa Chapel, better known as the **Succorpo di San Gennaro,** or, more simply, the crypt (currently closed for restoration), a Renaissance masterpiece by Tommaso Malvito (1497–1506) in the form of a rectangular room divided into three naves by rows of columns. Malvito also carved the imposing statue of Cardinal Oliviero Caraffa, who commissioned the chapel. A simple antique terra-cotta vase underneath the main altar contains the bones of San Gennaro.

Coming back up into the nave and continuing in a counterclockwise direction, you find the Chapel of San Lorenzo, with highly restored frescoes by Lello da Orvieto (circa 1314–20). This chapel hides an elevator that ascends one of the corner towers to the roof, which offers an intimate yet panoramic view of the historic quarter. Nearby is the tomb of Pope Innocent, sculpted in 1315, redone in the 16th century by Tommaso Malvito. The middle tomb belongs to Andrea of Hungary, the unfortunate consort of Queen Joan I, who allegedly had him strangled in Aversa (at least the dogs at the foot of the deceased show a little sadness). Beyond the tombs of Pope Innocent XII and the late-Renaissance chapel of the Brancaccio family, a door leads to the Chapel of Santa Restituta.

The **Capella di Santa Restituta** is in fact the oldest church in Naples, dating from the 4th century AD and, according to tradition, built by order of the first Christian emperor, Constantine, on the site of a temple to Apollo. It was dedicated to St. Restituta in the 8th century when the martyr's relics were transferred to the church. Originally having five naves, the church was reduced to a side chapel when Charles II d'Anjou built the present cathedral, then given a Baroque redo in the 1730s, but the Gothic structure is readable under the stucco decoration. Recent interventions have revealed the original Paleochristian pavement and the bases of the columns. To the left is a ticket booth for the visit to the baptistery and underground archaeological area (entrance: 5,000 lire), a fairly dry exhibit of ancient fragments; however, the Baptistery of San Giovanni in Fonte, is in itself worth the ticket price— a square room with an octagonal dome, built by Bishop Soterus in the middle of the 5th century, it still dazzles with its rare and important early Christian mosaics. The figurative language here still belongs firmly to the late-antique imperial tradition, even while adopting new Christian motifs. Divided into eight trapezoidal sections by lush garlands of fruit on a gold ground (here to express luxury rather than eternity), with a ring of birds in the center (notice the phoenix, symbol of resurrection, with its fiery halo), the eight figurative panels, with a blue background colored by lapis lazuli, follow an iconographical scheme from Roman art. Note the pendentives with the symbols of the evangelists: Only a bit of St. Luke's oxen remains, which is unfortunate because the two remaining compositions are thoroughly regal: the angel of St. Matthew—a young man with a pronounced Roman nose, large expressive eyes, and close-cropped hair, wearing a toga— rendered in large Impressionist-like tessera, and a hallucinatory lion, symbol of St. Mark, with orange hellfire rising in its eyes. ⊠ *Via Duomo 147,* ☎ *081/449097.* ⊙ *Daily 8–noon and 5–7:30.* ▧ *Santa Restituta Chapel: 5,000 lire.*

★ ⓫ **Gesù Nuovo.** *Opulenza* and *magnificenza* are the words that come to mind when describing this floridly Baroque church, the centerpiece of the Piazza del Gesù Nuovo. Its formidable diamond-point facade is actually a remnant of the Renaissance palace of the Sanseverino princes (1470, architect Novello di San Lucano), destroyed to make way, in 1584–1601, for a generically stupendous exercise in the full-throated Jesuit style, albeit one with an unusual Greek-cross plan. The dome has been rebuilt twice (this is an earthquake zone); the present version dates from the early 19th century. The bulk of the interior decoration took more than 40 years and was completed only in the 18th century. You will find the familiar Baroque sculptors (Naccherino, Finelli) and painters. The gracious *Visitation* above the altar in the second chapel on the right is by Massimo Stanzione, who also contributed the fine frescoes in the main nave: they are in the presbytery (behind and around the main altar). In the chapel to the left of this are some interesting frescoes by the young Francesco Solimena, who became a leading Baroque painter, and to the left of that is a wonderful gallery of reliquary portraits, each placed in its own opera box, and around the corner is a small devotional room where statues are draped head to toe with silver body-part votive offerings. ⊠ *Piazza del Gesù Nuovo,* ☎ *081/551–8613.* ⊙ *Mon.–Sat. 6:30–12:45 and 4:15 –7:30, Sun. 6:30–1:30.*

㉒ **I Girolamini.** The Girolamini is another name for the Oratorians, followers of St. Philip Neri, to whom this splendid church is dedicated. Built in 1592–1619 by the Florentine architect Giovanni Antonio Dosio, the dome and gray-and-white facade were rebuilt after a design by Ferdinando Fuga (circa 1780) in the most elegant Neoclassic style. Hit by Allied bombs in 1943, the intricate carved-wood ceiling is still being restored, and the place is essentially closed off for the current restoration of the complex, which also includes the Pinacoteca and its high-quality, intimate collection of 16th- and 17th-century paintings. Here, too, is one of the most gloriously decorated 18th-century libraries in Europe, the 60,000-volume Biblioteca dei Girolamini, now used by scholars. But you can still get a good look at the grandiose fresco on the inside of the entrance wall, by Luca Giordano (1684). The Oratorians also built the Casa dei Padri dell'Oratorio, down the block at Via Duomo 142. Step through its gate for a moment to see the two improbably calm and disciplined cloisters, designed by the Florentine architects Giovanni Antonio Dosio, Dionisio di Bartolomeo and Dionisio Lazzari sometime around 1600.

The area around Piazza Giromamini was an important nucleus of intellectual life in the Renaissance and Baroque period, thanks to the presence of the Girolamini Library. Directly across the street as you exit the Girolamini is the run-down (and closed) Church of Santa Maria della Colonna (Antonio Guidetti, 1715), which was the church for the adjacent orphanage. This orphanage not only housed and clothed its charges but also taught them the rudiments of grammar and, especially, music, eventually becoming a renowned conservatory (whose most famous pupil is the great Neapolitan composer Giambattista Pergolesi). To the right, note an inscription by Naples's profusely subtle philosopher, historian, and politician Benedetto Croce (1866–1952) to mark the house in which his illustrious predecessor, Giambattista Vico, lived for nearly 20 years. On the left is the Palazzo Manso, where the Marchese di Villa hosted the noted 16th-century poet Torquato Tasso. ⊠ *Piazza Girolamini 107,* ☎ *081/294444.* ☉ *Daily 9:30–1.*

★ ⑮ **Monte di Pietà.** As Spaccanapoli was home to both Naples's poorest and richest residents, the latter formed several charitable institutions, of which the Monte di Pietà was one of the most prominent. At the beginning of the 16th century, it constructed this palazzo (F. Cavagna, 1605), with a grand courtyard leading to the Capella della Pietà, with gilt stuccoes and beautiful frescoes by B. Corenzio. Leading off the chapel are a number of salons, including the Sala dell Cantoniere, with inlaid marbles and precious intarsia wood work. Since most Neapolitan residential palace interiors are private or have disappeared, this 17th-century enfilade of salons offers a rare glimpse of Naples at its most sumptuous. Concerts and theatrical performances are often held in the courtyard during the summer. Today the palazzo is an office for the Banco di Napoli. ⊠ *Via Biagio dei Librai 114,* ☎ *081/551-7074.* ☉ *Sat. 9–2.*

⑯ **Museo Civico Filangieri.** Housed in the Florentine-style Palazzo Cuomo, this is now a unique museum—the residue of a once-important collection created by the Princes Filangieri, who donated it to the city in 1888. The palazzo was originally built in the Tuscan Renaissance style, only to be demolished when Via Duomo was laid out. It was reconstructed (1879), then World War II scattered the important canvases. Still, it preserves the private air of a connoisseur's house, with weapons, paintings, furniture, medallions, and costumes displayed in 19th-century-style salons. ⊠ *Via Duomo 288,* ☎ *081/203175.* ▨ *5,000 lire.* ☉ *Mon.–Sat. 9:30–2, 3:30–7, Sun. 9:30–1:30.*

㉕ **Napoli Sotterranea.** Outside San Paolo Maggiore (on your right as you're coming out) on Piazza San Gaetano along Via Tribunali is one of the entrances to *Napoli Sotterranea*—Underground Naples. This is a fascinating tour (be prepared to go up and down a lot of steps and squeeze through some tight spaces) through a portion of Naples's fabled underground city and a good initiation into the complex layering of history in the city center. Most of the tufa mound on which Naples rises is honeycombed with successive layers of tunnels, well shafts, and underground halls whose interconnections permit a passage from Porta Capuana to the Palazzo Reale without ever seeing the light of day. Used by the soldiers of Belisarius in the 6th century AD, and again by the troops of Holy Roman Emperor Otto IV of Brunswick in the Middle Ages, the complicated network remained largely forgotten until the Neapolitan architect and engineer Guglielmo Melisurgo undertook a well-documented exploration beginning in 1880. Melisurgo identified three main strata: the sewer system underneath the modern city, a network of water conduits and wells that underlay ancient Naples, and an even lower layer of caves carved out of the rock. One day he emerged in the middle of the Military Hospital of the Trinità, causing quite a commotion among nurses and military guards. But the tunnels, as with the catacombs in Rome, originated principally as quarries, greatly expanded after the Spanish viceroys forbade the importation of raw building materials. The surprisingly large caves served a vital military purpose during the popular uprising against the Nazis in 1943, allowing the safe passage of soldiers and arms and providing bomb shelters. The Germans, cognizant of the location of some of the principal caverns but unable to mount a credible assault given the general chaos in the streets, bombed a number of entrances in a departing act of gratuitous vengeance, trapping the crowds underground. The arriving American soldiers, informed by locals, dug out thousands of desperate, hungry people just in time to avert a rampant typhus outbreak. Tours are provided, usually Saturday and Sunday at 10 AM and noon. ✉ *Piazza San Gaetano,* ☎ *081/449821.*

★ ⑰ **Pio Monte della Misericordia.** One of the defining landmarks of Spaccanapoli, this octagonal church was built around the corner from the duomo (practically in front of its constantly used side door) for a charitable institution founded in 1601 by seven noblemen to carry out acts of Christian charity: feeding the hungry, clothing the poor, nursing the sick, sheltering pilgrims, visiting prisoners, ransoming Christian slaves, and burying the indigent dead—acts immortalized in the history of art by the famous altarpiece painted by Caravaggio (1571–1610) depicting the *Seven Acts of Mercy* and now the celebrated focus of the church. In this haunting work the artist has brought the Virgin in palpable glory, unforgettably borne atop the shoulders of two angels, right down into the street—and not a rhetorical place, but a real street of Spaccanapoli (scholars have in fact suggested a couple of plausible identifications) populated by figures in whose spontaneous and passionate movements the people could see themselves given great dignity. Along with other paintings in the church, the sculptures by Andrea Falcone on its porch refer to this commitment. The original church was considered too small and destroyed in 1655 to make way for the new church, designed by Antonio Picchiatti in 1658–78. Pride of place is given to the great Caravaggio above the altar (for a discussion of this work, see the Close-Up box, "Chiaroscuro Plus: Caravaggio's *Seven Acts of Mercy*," *below*) but there are other important Baroque-era paintings on view here; some hang in the church while others are in the adjoining Pinacoteca, or picture gallery.

The extraordinary expressiveness and efficiency of the Caravaggio altarpiece can be judged by comparison with the church's other paintings, commissioned from Neapolitan painters after Caravaggio hit the road again (to Malta) to stay one step ahead of the law. In particular, in the painting to the left of the altar, *St. Peter Rescuing Tabitha* (1612), Fabrizio Santafede is clearly struggling to modify his Technicolor formalist style to suggest the dramatic impact of the altarpiece—but the figures here merely occupy the space of the painting, rather than animate it. Upon seeing Caravaggio's altarpiece, a number of artists changed their style radically, although often giving a personal interpretation to one aspect of Caravaggio's style. The painting to the right of the exit door is a beautiful work by one of the best of the Neapolitan Caravaggesques, Giovan Battista Carraciolo, who was 29 years of age when the slightly older artist came to town. Depicting the *Liberation of St. Peter* (1615), the composition is almost shockingly spartan, nearly all dark brown with contained blocks of white, red, and flesh tones. For more paintings of the Neapolitan Seicento, head up the staircase in the courtyard around the left of the church to the church's small museum of 17th- and 18th-century paintings. ✉ *Via Tribunali 253,* ☎ *081/446973.* ☉ *Weekdays 9:30–1:30; Pinacoteca museum Thurs.–Sat. 9–1.*

CHIAROSCURO PLUS: CARAVAGGIO'S *SEVEN ACTS OF MERCY*

THE MOST UNFORGETTABLE painting in Naples, Michelangelo Merisi da Caravaggio's *Seven Acts of Mercy* takes pride of place in the Church of Pio Monte della Misericordia, as well as in nearly all of southern Italy, for emotional spectacle and unflinching truthfulness. Painted in 1607, it combines all the traditional seven acts of Christian charity in sometimes abbreviated form in a tight, dynamic composition under the close, compassionate gaze of the Virgin (the original title was *Our Lady of Mercy*). She flutters down with the Christ child into a torchlit street scene borne by two of the most memorable angels ever painted.

Illuminated in the artist's landmark chiaroscuro style (featuring pronounced contrasts of light, *chiaro*, and deep shadow, *scuro*), a man is being buried, a nude beggar is being clothed, and—this artist never pulled any punches—a starving prisoner is being suckled by a woman. Caravaggio, as with most geniuses, was a difficult artist and personality, and his romantic bad-boy reputation as the original bohemian, complete with angry, nihilistic, rebel-with-a-cause sneer and roistering and hippy-like lifestyle, has dominated interpretations of his revolutionary oeuvre and tend to present him as an antireligious painter. This is perhaps understandable—most of the documents pertaining to his life relate to his problems with the law and make for a good story indeed (he came to Naples after killing a man in a bar brawl in Rome, where his cardinal patrons could no longer protect him).

But in spite of (or perhaps because of) his personal life, Caravaggio painted some of the most moving religious art ever produced in the West, whittling away all the rhetoric to reveal the emotional core of the subject. His genuine love of the popular classes and for the "real" life of the street found expression in his use of ordinary street folk as models, though if his art seems to surge directly from the gut, his famous "objectivity" of observation and reduced palette have clear antecedents in paintings from his home region in northern Italy. The simplicity and warts-and-all depictions of his characters show a deeply original response to the Counter-Reformation writings on religious art by Carlo Borromeo, a future saint, also from Lombardy.

The *Seven Acts of Mercy,* the first one commissioned for the new church of the charitable institution, has been called "the most important religious painting of the seventeenth century" by the great 20th-century Italian art critics Roberto Longhi and Giuliano Argan, and if that may not be immediately obvious, it's nevertheless easy to imagine the impact this astonishing painting had on artists and connoisseurs in Naples. It is easy to imagine that Caravaggio was a natural Neapolitan of the heart, like the recent soccer player–turned–hero Maradona, and had his maverick virtuosity similarly appreciated. And like Maradona, he came, dazzled them, and left, though in the year he spent in Naples he managed to paint at least three other major works, now in Vienna, London, and the Museo di Capodimonte (the *Flagellation*) as well as a few lost works. Naples affected his style, too: it began to express visual relations purely in terms of dramatic light and shadow, which only further exalted the contrasts of human experience.

NEED A
BREAK?
When leaving the Pio Monte during the summer months, note that a
street vendor named **Ciro** often sets up in the small square directly across
from the church and sells a silky homemade lemon slush (*limonata*) given
a shy blush by a dose of strawberry juice. Smoothly tart, ice cold, and—
well—*real*, it makes for a uniquely satisfying complement to Caravaggio's vision of daily grace.

㉗ San Domenico Maggiore. One of the largest churches of Spaccanapoli,
this Dominican house of worship was originally constructed by Charles
I of Anjou in 1238. Legend has it that a painting of the Cruxifixon
spoke to St. Thomas Aquinas when he was at prayer here. This early
edifice, however, was nearly gutted by a fire three centuries later and,
in 1850, a neo-Gothic edifice rose in its place, complete with a nave
of awe-inspiring dimensions. In the second chapel on the right are remnants of the earlier church—14th-century frescoes by Pietro Cavallini,
a Roman forerunner of Giotto. Along the side chapels are also some
noted funerary monuments, including those of the Carafa family,
whose chapel, to the left of the altar, is one of the most beautiful Re-
naissance-era setpieces in Naples. ⊠ *Piazza San Domenco Maggiore
8/a,* ☎ *081/557–3204.* ☉ *Daily 7:30–noon, 4:30–7 PM.*

㉙ San Giuseppe dei Ruffi. Half a block from the Duomo, this late-17th-
century church, built by Dionisio Lazzari, features one of the most impressively solid and dramatically Baroque facades in Naples. The order
must have spent most of its money on it, since they wound up painting the nave walls in faux marble to keep up appearances. This place
can be a relaxing stop in the morning if the nuns are singing.

㉖ San Gregorio Armeno. Landmarked by a picturesque campanile that
spans Via San Gregorio Armeno, this convent was one of the oldest
and most important in Naples. The nuns (often the daughters of
Naples's richest families) who lived here must have been disappointed
with Paradise when they arrived—banquets here outrivaled the royal
court's, hallways were lined with paintings, and the church groaned
with an an orgy of gilt stucco and semiprecious stones. Described as
"a room of Paradise on Earth" by Carlo Celano and designed by Nic-
colò Taglicozzi Canle, the church has a highly detailed wooden ceiling, unique papier-mâché choir lofts, a nuns' gallery disguised by
18th-century jalousies, a shimmering organ, candlelighted shrines, and
important Luca Giordano frescoes of scenes of the life of St. Gregory,
whose relics were brought to Naples in the 8th century from Byzantium. Inside, the convent's cloister has a grand view of the Bay of Naples,
while rooms such as the Salottino della Badessa—generally not on view,
as this is still a working convent—are preserved as magnificent 18th-
century interiors. ⊠ *Piazzetta San Gregorio Armeno 1,* ☎ *081/552–
0186.* ☉ *Daily 9:30–noon.*

㉓ San Lorenzo Maggiore. One of the grandest medieval churches of the
Decumano Maggiore, San Lorenzo features a very unmedieval facade
of 18th-century splendor—-due to the effects and threats of earthquakes, the church was reinforced and reshaped along Baroque lines
in the 17th and 18th centuries, and remaining from this phase is the facade by Ferdinando Sanfelice (1742), which is based on the sweeping
curves of Borromini's Filomarino altar in the Church of Santi Apostoli.
Begun by Robert d'Anjou in 1265 on the site of a previous 6th-century
church, the church's single, barnlike nave reflects the desire of the Fran-
ciscans for simple spaces with enough room to preach to large crowds.
Numerous statues and paintings from the 14th century are indicative
of San Lorenzo's importance during this period. In 1334, in fact, Boccaccio met and fell in love with his fabled Lady Fiammetta here, and in

1343 another great Italian poet, Petrarch, resided in the monastery next
door. During the 20th century late-Baroque accretions were stripped off
to reclaim the original Gothic design. Entering the huge nave and then
beginning at the right, view a number of notable tombs and chapels,
including the tomb of the Admiral Ludovico Aldomorisco in the second chapel, a fine Renaissance composition by Antonio Baboccio
(1421), and the Cacace Chapel, a Baroque masterpiece with a typically
sumptuous marble-inlay display from the workshop of Cosimo Fanzago.
The transept is announced by a grandiose triumphal arch, while the main
altar (1530) is the sculptor Giovanni da Nola's masterpiece; notice the
fascinating historical views of Naples in the reliefs.

The apse was built by an unknown imported French architect of great
caliber, who gives here a brilliant essay in the pure French Angevin style,
complete with an ambulatory of nine side chapels that is covered by a
magnificent web of cross arches. The most important monument in the
church is found here: the tomb of Catherine of Austria (circa 1323),
by Tino da Camaino, one of the first sculptors to introduce the Gothic
style into Italy. The left transept contains the 14th-century funerary monument of Carlo di Durazzo and yet another Fanzago masterpiece, the
Cappellone di Sant'Antonio—Cappella being too diminutive a word,
especially in this behemoth of a church. Outside the 17th-century
cloister is the entrance to the excavations under San Lorenzo, which
are a good initiation to the Roman and Greek cities beneath the modern one. Near the area of the forum, these digs have revealed streets,
markets, and workshops of another age. ⊠ *Via dei Tribunali 316,* ☏
081/454948. ▣ *Excavations: 5,000 lire.* ☉ *Daily 8–12 and 4–7; excavations Mon. and Wed.–Sat. 9–1 and 4–6:30.*

㉔ **San Paolo Maggiore.** Like Santi Apostoli, this church was erected for
the Theatin fathers in the late 16th century (1583–1603), the period
of their order's rapid expansion. This was another instance where
Francesco Grimaldi, the (ordained) house architect, erected a church
on the ruins of an ancient Roman temple, then transformed into a Christian basilica. Spoils from the temple survive in the present incarnation,
especially the two monumental Corinthian columns on the facade
holding up a piece of their architrave to form a portal over the entrance
door. The cloaked torsos of the ancient gods, which used to lie under
the statues of Peter and Paul, have been moved. An earthquake knocked
down the original facade in 1688, and World War II did further damage, but note the paintings of Massimo Stanzione in the fourth chapel
down the right aisle. The most beautiful space in the church is the sacristy, to the right of the altar, with bright, clear painted decor by
Francesco Solimena. ⊠ *Piazza San Gaetano,* ☏ *081/454048.* ☉ *Mon.–
Sat. 9–2.*

⑭ **Sant' Angelo a Nilo.** Originally built by Cardinal Brancaccio in the late
1300s, this church was redesigned in the 16th century by Arcangelo
Guglielminelli. Inside the graciously beautiful interior is the earliest evidence of the Renaissance in Naples: the cardinal's funerary monument,
sculpted by the famous Donatello, assisted by the almost-as-famous Mich-
elozzo, in 1426–27. The front of the sarcophagus bears a bas-relief *Assumption of the Virgin,* testament to Donatello's legendary *"stiacciato"*
trompe-l'oeil technique. Beyond the small courtyard is the Palazzo
Brancaccio, where the learned prelate opened the first public library in
Naples in 1690. ⊠ *Piazzetta Nilo, along Via San Biagio dei Librai.*

★ ⑫ **Santa Chiara.** Across from the Gesù Nuovo and offering a stark and
telling contrast to the opulence of that church, Santa Chiara is the leading monument of Angevin Gothic in Naples. The fashionable church
for the nobility in the 14th century, and a favorite Angevin church from

the start, the church was intended to be a great dynastic monument by Robert d'Anjou. His second wife, Sancia di Majorca, added the adjoining convent for the Poor Clares to a monastery of the Franciscan Minors so she could vicariously satisfy a lifelong desire for the cloistered seclusion of a convent; this was the first time the two sexes were combined in a single complex. Built in a Provençal Gothic style between 1310 and 1328 (probably by Guglielmo Primario) and dedicated in 1340, the church had its aspect radically altered, as did so many others, in the Baroque period, when the original wooden roof was replaced with a vault dripping in stuccos. A 48-hour fire started by Allied bombs on August 4, 1943, put an end to all that, as well as to what might have been left of the important cycle of frescoes by Giotto and his Neapolitan workshop: Giorgio Vasari, writing in the mid-16th century, tells us that the paintings covered the entire church.

Basically only the walls remain of the original building, with their powerful buttresses, and some grandiose royal tombs cobbled together from the bits left over. The interior, a large, luminous rectangular hall, nevertheless offers ample serenity, the 18th-century marble floor by Domenico Antonio Vaccaro has been decently restored, and the tombs, in the back, are worth a look. The most important tomb, in the church towers behind the altar and sculpted by Giovanni and Pacio Bertini of Florence (1343–45), is, fittingly, the tomb of the founding king: the great Robert d'Anjou, known as the Wise. Unfortunately it was devastated in World War II, but you can still make out the members of the royal family in the arches underneath the sarcophagus. The altar merits a special mention: by an unknown hand working in the 1320s or '30s, its slender torsaded columnettes house the liveliest sculpture in the church. To the right of the altar is the tomb of Carlo, duke of Calabria, a majestic composition by Tino da Camaino and assistants (1326–33) and answering it on the side wall is Tino's last work, the tomb of Carlo's wife, Marie de Valois. A separate room behind the altar, the Poor Clares' Choir, permitted the nuns to attend mass and receive communion through a grate while observing their rules of seclusion. This lofty Gothic space also retains the only traces of the Giotto-school decoration (and they are traces). Near the front door is the Chapel of St. Francis, with sturdy and expressive statues by Giovanni Domenico d'Auria.

Around the left side of the church at Via Santa Chiara 49/c is a gate leading to the **Chiostro delle Clarisse**, the most famous cloister in Naples. It's clear here that we are not dealing with any normal convent; the benches and octagonal columns upholding the trellis of vine shading this privileged garden comprise a light-handed masterpiece of painted majolica designed by Domenico Antonio Vaccaro, with a delightful profusion of landscapes and light blue and orange floral motifs realized by Donato and Giuseppe Massa and their studio (1742). Where the real vines leave off and the painted ones took over was once hard to say, but much of the cloister is now being replanted, so the complete effect is missing. The elegant 14th-century porch around the garden is enlivened by fading frescoes. In the back corner you can enter the Museo dell'Opera, built on the visible remains of an old Roman bath establishment and containing some interesting sculptural fragments (look for Giovanni da Nola's moving wooden *Ecce Homo* of 1519) and objects illustrating life in the cloister. ⊠ *Via Benedetto Croce,* ☎ *081/552–6209.* ☉ *Church daily 7–12:30 and 3:30–6:30; cloister Mon.–Sat. 8:30–12:30 and 3:30–6:30, Sun. 9:30–1.*

㉑ **Santa Maria di Donnaregina Vecchia.** The towering Gothic funeral monument of Mary of Hungary, wife of Charles II of Anjou (circa 1254–1309), who is said to have commissioned the frescoes in the church at a cost of 33 ounces of gold, is contained within this church. Don't confuse this church with another, nearby in the piazza, of the same name, but Baroque. ⊠ *Vico Donnaregina.* ⊙ *Daily 9–1.*

㉔ **Santi Apostoli.** This Baroque church in a basic Latin-cross style with a single nave shares the piazza with a contemporary art school in a typically anarchic Neapolitan mix. Built (1610–49) by the ordained architect Francesco Grimaldi for the Theatin fathers above a previous church, itself built on the remains of a temple to Neptune, it is worth a quick peek inside for its coherent, intact Baroque decorative scheme, featuring excellent paintings on the inside of the entrance wall and on the ceiling by Giovanni Lanfranco (circa 1644), with a good number painted by his successors Francesco Solimena and Luca Giordano. The gorgeous terra-cotta and marble floor is a work of the late 17th century by Francesco Viola. For lovers of Baroque architecture, there is an altar in the left transept by the great architect Francesco Borromini. Commissioned by Cardinal Ascanio Filmarino, this is the only work in Naples by this architect, whose freedom from formality so inspired the exuberance of the Baroque in southern Italy, although its massive virile flourish of monochrome gray stone comes as a bit of a shock in the midst of this polychromed city. As you exit the church, in the next-to-last chapel on the aisle to your left, is the tomb of Vincenzo Ippolito (1776), by Giuseppe Sammartino, famous for the virtuosity of his *Dead Christ* in the Cappella Sansevero. The two self-satisfied putti flouncing around the cinerary urn here, however, seem to prefigure the Pompier-style kitsch of the late 19th century. ⊠ *Largo Santi Apostoli 9,* ☎ *081/299375.* ⊙ *Mon.–Thurs. 8–11:30 and 5:30– 8, Sun. 8:30–1.*

Art and Antiquity: From the Museo Archeologico Nazionale to the Museo di Capodimonte

It is only fitting that the Museo Archeologico Nazionale—the single most important and remarkable museum of Greco-Roman antiquities in the world (in spite of itself, some observers say)—sits in the upper *decumanus,* or neighborhood, of ancient Neapolis, the district first colonized by the ancient Greeks and Romans. Repository of many of the greatest surviving art treasures of antiquity—including most of the celebrated finds from Pompeii and Herculaneum—the museum has so many rooms it almost constitutes its own walking tour. As Naples's preeminent treasure trove, it deserves your undivided attention early in the day, but if two hours is your limit for gazing at ancient art, discover other nearby sights of the Decumanus Maggiore, off the beaten track but prized by connoisseurs of Naples: the finest palace designed by Ferdinando Sanfelice, who helped define Neapolitan Baroque; the Orto Botanico, the city's botanical gardens; and the historic Church of San Giovanni a Carbonara. The final leg of the tour leads to the northern suburbs of the city, whose highest point is crowned by the Museo di Capodimonte, the greatest of the Bourbon palaces, now a regal museum.

A Good Walk

Provided your feet don't call a sit-down strike after touring the enormous complex of the **Museo Archeologico Nazionale** ㉘, walk eastward along Piazza Cavour until it becomes Via Foria. Here, opposite the picturesque Porta San Gennaro, a relic of the old 15th-century city walls, you should make a left turn onto Via Crocette and enter I Vergini—a densely packed working quarter—where you'll find two of Ferdinando Sanfelice's greatest works, the Palazzo dello Spagnolo, on the Largo Vergini, and, farther along on Sanità, the architect's own house, **Palazzo**

Sanfelice ㉙, which boasts one of Europe's most astounding Baroque staircases. Backtrack to Piazza Cavour and continue one block to Via Domenico Cirillo, where you'll make a right turn two blocks to Via Carbonara and the important Church of **San Giovanni a Carbonara** ㉚. If you prefer lush gardens to great architecture, simply head up Via Forio for some 10 blocks (many buses run along this street) until you reach the **Orto Botanico** ㉛. Backtrack to the Museo Archeologico Nazionale and take Bus No. R4 up Via Santa Teresa Degli Scalzi (an extension of Via Toledo/Via Roma) up the Corso Amedeo di Savoia Duca D'Aosta until you reach the Tondo di Capodimonte and the **Museo di Capodimonte** ㉜.

TIMING

The Museo Archeologico Nazionale and the Museo di Capodimonte are Naples' two most famous museums and, as such, both enjoy extended evening hours (dependent on annual municipal subsidies)—on Saturdays, the archaeological museum might even be visited up to midnight. However, a good portion of the rooms in these museums usually close up at 2 PM, leaving only the center core of the collections to be seen later. If you want the full feast, get an early morning start. This tour could easily take six hours, not including transportation time between the center city and Capodimonte.

★ ㉘ **Museo Archeologico Nazionale** (National Museum of Archaeology). Those who know and love this legendary museum have a tendency, upon hearing it mentioned, to heave a sigh: it is famous not only for its unrivaled collections but also for its off-limit rooms, missing identification labels, poor lighting, billows of dust that attack the unwary visitor, suffocating heat in summer, and indifferent personnel—a state of affairs often seen by some critics as an encapsulation of everything that's wrong with southern Italy in general. Precisely because of this emblematic value, the National Ministry of Culture has decided to lavish attention and funds on the museum in a complete reorganization. This process has been ongoing for for some time and looks as if it will continue for a while longer. The much-vaunted new hours (until 7 PM, with later evening openings projected as well) also deserve half a cheer because many rooms still close at 2 PM, including the Egyptian collection, the prehistoric collection, the bronzes, the rooms with the frescoes from the Temple of Isis, and what's viewable of the glass and jewelry collection. This leaves only the core of the museum, but it says a lot that this reduced nucleus still puts most other museums to shame—and is still worth a detour. For it includes the legendary Farnese collection of ancient sculpture, together with local sculptural finds, and almost all the good stuff—the best mosaics and paintings—from Pompeii and Herculaneum. The quality of these collections is unexcelled and, as far as the mosaic, painting, and bronze sections are concerned, unique in the world.

History of the Museum. The museum was born in the mind of Charles III, who had inherited the various Farnese collections from his mother. The Farnese family had collected antiquities quite aggressively in Rome during the 16th century, when there were still quite a few important pieces to be found—their excavations of the Baths of Caracalla, in particular, produced a number of marvels, including the Farnese Bull and Farnese Hercules—and these pieces, together with the paintings, made an ideal endowment for a new museum. In addition, Charles's wife, Amalia of Saxony, inherited a rich collection from her father, Augustus, which had been recently augmented with statues dug up in the Herculaneum area by Prince d'Elboeuf (1711). Charles originally intended to house the collection, together with the Farnese collection of paintings and precious objects, in a new palace at Capodimonte, which would be at once a dynastic monument and an avant-garde intellectual endeavor of the Enlightenment, but the antiquities collection soon outstripped the available space. In 1738, the same year the definitive project for Capodimonte got underway, excavations began at the site explored by Prince d'Elboeuf—Resina, in the Herculaneum area—which yielded a stunning sample of marble and bronze statues. And then, in 1748, a new site opened up that surpassed every archaeologist's dreams: Pompeii. By 1750 a makeshift museum had been set up in the royal villa at Portici to house the rapidly growing finds, and Naples, with its exciting excavations, had become an obligatory stop on travelers' Grand Tour. The digs continued, often under frightful standards: bronze statue fragments were regularly melted down as being of no value, and paintings considered unworthy of the royal collections were systematically destroyed. However, it should be said in the archaeologists' favor that the paintings they removed and varnished with their makeshift wax solution are in better condition today than those left in place, and to a large extent, modern archaeology is already present in the thorough visual documentation of the excavations—plans, drawings, and engravings—by artists and architects of the 18th century.

After a time the question of a fitting museum became an international issue, and given the precarious position of Portici (it lies under Vesuvius), a solution was deemed urgent—even if it did not seem so to the king. (When Vesuvius erupted in 1767, and ministers pleaded with him to find a safe, permanent home for the collection, Charles of Bourbon replied that if the worst happened and they were buried anew, they would be the joy of excavators 2,000 years later). A decision was made in 1777 to utilize a former university, the Palazzo degli Studi, on the hill of Santa Teresa. Ferdinando Fuga was given orders to draw up a plan, but his innovations as usual stirred up controversy, and when he died in 1782, nothing had been built, and the project was passed on to the Roman architect Pompeo Schiantarelli. During this decade the Farnese collection of ancient sculpture finally arrived. This was totally illegal, of course—Cardinal Alexander Farnese's will of 1587 specifically stipulated that the collection was to stay in Rome. But Ferdinand IV, son of and successor to Charles III, politely ignored the strident complaints of the pope and various other personages, including Goethe, and calmly packed up the loot for transfer. The theft must have been all the more galling for the Romans because the pieces had been scattered around Naples for a long time while they awaited their new home (the celebrated Bull, for example, was set up as a fountain in Chiaia and only brought to the museum in 1826).

The museum, named the Royal Library of Naples, finally opened in 1801—perhaps a bit late, given that Ferdinand had just massacred nearly all of his city's intellectual élite in "appreciation" of their Republican ideas. On the whole, however, the museum, if not the Neapolitans themselves, did well from the Napoleonic wars. The French had already packed up the Farnese Hercules for transport to the new Louvre, but the new king of Naples, Joachim Murat, was able to use his considerable military clout within Napoléon's empire to keep the museum's contents in Naples (the rest of Italy was thoroughly and expertly plundered). Murat's wife, Caroline (who rather usefully happened to be Napoléon's sister), herself collected antiquities; so Ferdinand proudly added her collection to the museum in 1816, once he had reestablished himself on the throne with the help of his friends. Just in case anyone had any doubts about who the owner was, or what sort of government had set it up, he renamed it the Royal Bourbon Museum. The building was finally finished in 1822, just in time to house the spectacular mosaics uncovered in the 1830s in the House of the Faun in Pompeii. With the fall of the Bourbons and unification with the emergent Italy, the collection was reorganized as a so-called National Museum. The result of course was immediate mismanagement and a number of scandals, concerning not only the ideological content underlying the display program but also the large number of pieces that simply went missing, including important items from the Boscoreale treasure now in the Louvre. Damage inflicted on the building by the 1980–81 earthquakes was the impetus for the last two decades' campaign of modernization.

Room-by-Room Tour of the Collections. As you enter the building, the ticket booth is immediately on the left, with a sign indicating which rooms are open and which closed (read this before buying your ticket). Ahead of you is the large **Atrium of the Magistrates,** which contains a dignified but discreet introduction to the sculpture collections, including a pair of Dacians from Trajan's Forum in the middle aisle and a number of toga-wearing figures and members of the Balbi family from Herculaneum. If you want to continue with marble sculpture, wend your way back to the door near the ticket takers, the one framed by two columns of antique Numidian yellow marble, and enter the Room of the Tyrannicides. It makes more sense, however, to start your visit on the top floor of the museum, which contains some of the more demanding works on the eye, and work your way down. Placed unavoidably at the bottom of the stairs is a ridiculous statue of Ferdinand IV in the guise of Athena, by Canova (which shows that some people should just never wear drag, especially if they have a regal dignity to maintain). While the text found below has an extensive description of the entire collection, you might wish to invest in an up-to-date printed museum guide, as exhibits are poorly labeled.

Go up two flights of stairs to the first floor (that's by Italian accounting; the mezzanine only counts for half a floor—except when it comes to subsidies). To the right is the important collection of bronzes. The first room (CXV) presents a delightful collection of small decorative bronzes (Silenus heads, children's portraits, leopard antefixes), while an adjoining room (closed but visible) houses a mosaic floor and a few lost fresco fragments. The big room (CXVI) ahead contains statues that most museums would sell their souls to get, as virtually all metal objects from antiquity, especially bronze statues, were melted down. Here you have a treasury of life-size masterpieces, with a splendid set of heads along the left wall illustrating the ancient themes of illustrious men—Hellenistic princes, philosophers, poets—and generic, ideal figures referring to aspects of civilized life: theatrical figures and athletes (note the head of Thespis with the bronze curls soldered on separately). In front of these sit a pensive *Hermes* from a local workshop and the famous *Drunken Satyr,* a pair of deer, the two running athletes (copies after Lysippus) with their original encrusted eyes, and, in the corner next to the left window, a bust of Dionysius with extravagant, meticulously rendered hair. The far wall has a celebrated set of five female *Dancers* (recently reinterpreted as water carriers and identified with the Danaids, who were condemned to draw water endlessly) in the stiff but expressive Severe style. The last room (CXVII), just beyond, contains another fine series of bronze Herm heads, an impressive 1st-century BC copy of a lance-throwing *Athena Promachos,* which replicates the moumental statue that once decorated the Acropolis in Athens, and the justifiably renowned portrait head known as the *Seneca,* whose world-weary expression will still move you deeply, even if he is placed too low for the viewer to receive its full impact (bend down low). An equally impressive collection of small bronzes will eventually be displayed in the rooms along the courtyard.

Back through the bronze galleries and to the right at the staircase, you come into the large **Sala della Meridiana,** designed as the reading room of the library and presently wasted space, gussied up with a series of huge 19th-century mediocrities detailing the family history of the fabulous Farnese. At the far end of the room is a famous statue of the titan *Atlantis* from the Farnese collection, which bears the oldest known complete depiction of the constellations of the zodiac. Off the door to the right, a suite of rooms along the front facade of the *palazzo* houses newly renovated displays of findings from the pre-Roman Campagna, with lots of the usual pottery. On the other side of the Sala della Meridiana, a pair of Trajan-era kneeling Persians in white and purple *pavonazzetto* marble drapery provides a suitable announcement of the celebrated ancient fresco collection beyond.

Room 1 (or CXVI; most rooms are numbered in both Arabic and Roman styles) starts off with some excellent *Fourth-Style painted-stucco friezes from the House of Meleager* in Pompeii that refer to the cults of Dionysius and Hercules, but this is just an antechamber to the cream of the crop, spread around the rooms branching off from Room 2 (CXVIII). Handy English-language displays of information, on the left as you enter, give a good presentation of the so-called Four Styles of Roman painting as seen in Pompeii and Herculaneum, evidence of the "golden age" of Roman wall painting. The room to the right displays what's left of the Third Style *paintings from the villa at Boscoreale,* discovered in 1900; the next room (LXX) contains two versions of the *Three Graces* on the right. The third bay (LXXI) has a display case in the center with some exquisite monochrome paintings on marble, including an exquisite *Fight with a Centaur* rendered in a confident precise line reminiscent of Ingres. The bay with the window shows off the famous paintings from the Basilica of Herculaneum, discovered in 1739, including a panel of an oddly nonchalant Hercules discovering his son Telephus being nursed by a doe in Arcadia. Room LXXII has a wonderful *Perseus Freeing Andromeda* from the House of the Dioscuri in Pompeii, plus the celebrated image of *Theseus and the Minotaur* next to the exit door. The last room (LXXIII) along the front facade houses a number of panels in the refined but cold antiquarian current of the Third Style, a reflection of Augustan classicism. Nearby are the six rooms (LXXIX–LXXXIV) that feature material recovered from the Temple of Isis.

Room LXXXV starts the **Glass Collection,** with one of the museum's showstoppers in the center: the *Blue Vase from Pompeii,* an astonishing example of antique cameo glasswork, with white swirls of vegetation and wildlife surrounding Dionysius and Ariadne against an intense cobalt blue. In the room in the back corner, you come to the spectacular scale model of Pompeii made in 1879. The main part of the glass and jewelry collection is not visible at present. Room LXXXVII has a fun selection of gladiators' armor. Stairs take you back down to the mezzanine, site of the **Mosaic Collection.** And what mosaics they are! The first room, which gives just a taste of things to come, sports a striking spotted leopard and a small panel showing Theseus doing unspeakable Greek things to the Minotaur. The next room on your right (LVIII) concentrates on *nymphaeum* and fountain mosaics in glass paste but also features the much-reproduced black-and-white depiction of Death and a stunningly sensitive portrait of a woman in micro-mosaic. The finest works are saved for the last two rooms: the world-renowned *opus vermiculatum* mosaics from the House of the Faun in Pompeii. The star piece here is the gigantic *Alexander and Darius at the Battle of Issus* on the far wall. Considered to be a copy of a famous painting by Philoxenos of Eretria done for King Cassander of Macedonia (end of the 4th century BC), this mosaic copy, which dates to 125–120 BC, would be, even if clumsily rendered, of priceless documentary value for our knowledge of the lost art of Greek painting; as it turns out, the mosaic itself is a masterpiece. Nearby, cat fans will appreciate the small panel with the cat attacking a bird, while the scene of the *Satyr and Nymph* next to the window of the first room presents lust in an astringently frank manner.

Once back on the ground floor, cross the **Atrium of the Magistrates** and go through the yellow columns on the side wall near the ticket takers to the **Room of the Tyrannicides** (Room 1), named for the group in the center, a 2nd-century AD Roman copy of a famous bronze by Kritios and Nesiotes cast in 477 BC. To the right, notice the beautiful fragmentary *head of Apollo from Baiae,* with traces of red paint still in his hair. Through the door to the left of this head, you enter the **Gallery of the Great Masters** (Rooms II–VI), which contains mostly copies of works by Greek masters, but some of these copies are among the finest, or they are the only such examples known, including the *Apollo Citharedos,* between Bays II and III, with his rich, flowing hair, and the *Dorophoros of Polycletes,* in Bay II. The window-side of the leftmost bay (Room VI) shows off a pair of gorgeous, if damaged, Greek originals of the 4th or 3rd century BC: Nereids with flowing "wet" drapery carved in succulent honeycomb-color stone. Back into the Room of the Tyrannicides and to your right is the **Gallery of Flora** (or, Gallery of the Carracci, Room VIII), with a beautifully intact *Artemis of Ephesus* in basalt and antique yellow marble, her fecundity underlined by her multiple breasts and the numerous animals adorning her raiment. In the middle of the gallery stands a voluptuous *Aphrodite Callipygos* ("of the beautiful buttocks"), originally found in the area of Nero's Domus Aurea in Rome.

The collections of ancient sculpture culminate in the **Gallery of the Farnese Bull** (Rooms XI–XV), whose monumentality is no less than the grandiose sculptures from the Baths of Caracalla deserve. The right end of the gallery is dominated by the awesomely powerful *Farnese Hercules,* a signed ("Glykon of Athens made this") copy of a 4th-century BC bronze by Lysippus. His left arm is a restoration, and the nearby set of legs was made by Guglielmo della Porta in the 16th century to complete the statue when it was first discovered; the originals, found afterward, were long judged inferior to these and were not reintegrated until much later. At the left end, the splendid *Farnese Bull*—the largest sculptural group to come down to us from antiquity—answers the Hercules in magnificence. Yes, it has been highly restored (this is well documented on the wall), but all in all, the restorers did a decent job, and the strong composition, with its calm depiction of murder, still inspires awe, as it has with numerous artists who have been influenced by this sculpture in the past, from Michelangelo to Picasso.

Behind the Hercules is a discreet door leading into two small rooms (which both close at 2) housing the **Farnese Collection of Gems,** mostly ancient cameos. The centerpiece of the collection is the fabled *Farnese Cup,* a true stunner, carved out of a solid layered block of agate and sardonyx to translucent thinness, with various color layers brilliantly used to portray a group of mythological figures on the interior and a Medusa's head on the exterior. Probably a royal commission of the court of the Ptolemies in Egypt from the 2nd or 1st or first century BC, this masterpiece most likely became Roman imperial property before passing through the court of Frederick II Hohenstaufen in Palermo and ending up in Rome, where Lorenzo the Magnificent bought it in 1471. It takes good eyes to appreciate the rest of the collection because the pieces are small, but the ensemble as a whole is fascinating.

Once back out of the Gallery of the Farnese Bull and into the Gallery of Flora, turn right toward the rear of the building; this second half of the inner gallery contains more masterpieces, including one of the best versions of *Antinous* as well as a pliant *Ganymede* with a threatening eagle farther down on the left. Below the stairs is the **Egyptian Collection.** The courtyard makes for a delightful resting place, in which you can lie in the midday Mediterranean sun atop an inscribed block of marble humid with history. The courtyard on the other side is closed off for eventual restoration, but the gallery along the back side has been fitted out with striking glass panels that illuminate a stretch of sarcophagi. Is this a foretaste of the museum to come? ⊠ *Piazza Museo,* ☎ *081/ 440166.* ▣ *12,000 lire.* ☉ *Mon.–Sat., 9–2, Sun. 9–8. Closed Tues. Extended summer schedule (Wed.–Fri. and Sun.–Mon. 9–7:30, Sat. 9–8, 9–midnight) may go into effect dependent on whether special monies are budgeted season-by-season by municipal government; call 081/440166 to determine if extended schedule is in effect.*

★ ㉜ **Museo di Capodimonte.** The grandiose 18th-century Neoclassic Bourbon royal palace, in the vast Bosco di Capodimonte (Capodimonte Park), which served as the royal hunting preserve and later as the site of the Capodimonte porcelain works, is a spectacular setting for Naples's finest collection of old master paintings and decorative arts. Perched on top of a hill overlooking all of Naples and the bay, the palace was built in 1738 by Charles III of Bourbon as a hunting retreat, then expanded by Antonio Medrano—architect of the Teatro San Carlo—to become the repository of the fabled Farnese art collection he inherited from his mother, Elizabeth Farnese. For this art-loving king, however, collecting was not enough; to compete with his father-in-law, Frederick Augustus, the Elector of Saxony, who had founded the celebrated Meissen porcelain factory, Charles decided to set up his own royal factory, opposite the Capodimonte Palace (today still an art college), and before long, the "soft-paste" porcelain figurines of Pulcinello, biscuit vendors, and pretty nymphs were the chicest collectibles for Europe's rich. Fittingly, the most unique room in the palace is entirely crafted from porcelain (3,000 pieces of it)—**Queen Maria Amalia's Porcelain Parlor** (1757–59), built for the royal palace at Portici but relocated here.

But Capodimonte's greatest treasure is the excellent collection of paintings, well displayed in the **Galleria Nazionale** on the palace's first and second stories. Before you arrive at this remarkable collection, a magnificent staircase leads to the royal apartments, where you'll find beautiful antique furniture, most of it on the splashy scale so dear to the Bourbons, and a staggering collection of porcelain and majolica from the various royal residences. The walls of the apartments are hung with numerous portraits, providing a close-up of the unmistakable Bourbon features, a challenge to any court painter. The main galleries on the first floor are devoted to work from the 13th to the 18th centuries, including many familiar masterpieces by Dutch and Spanish masters, as well as by the great Italians: Simone Martini's *St. Louis Crowning King Robert* (1317), Masaccio's *Crucifixion* (1426), Giovanni Bellini's *Transfiguration* (1480), Annibale Carracci's *Pietà* (1600), Parmigianino's *Antea* (1531), Gentileschi's *Judith and Holofernes* (1630), Caravaggio's *Flagellation* (1607–10), and a bevy of famous Titians, including the *Danaë* (1545).

On the top floor, a new set of galleries features international contemporary art—including Andy Warhol's *Mount Vesuvius,* painted when the artist visited Naples in 1985—while the second floor holds extensive collections of 14th- to 19th-century Neapolitan painting and decorative arts, including plenty of dramatic renditions of Vesuvius in all its raging glory. When you've had your fill of these, take time to admire the genuine article from the shady parkland outside, designed by Ferdinando Sanfelice and then adapted into the "natural" English style, which affords a sweeping view of the bay. You can get to the museum via Bus No. 24 from Piazza Municipio or Piazza Carità. ✉ *Via Miano 2 (Porta Piccola), Via Capodimonte,* ☎ *081/744–1307.* 💰 *14,000 lire.* ◷ *Tues.–Sat. 10–7, Sun. 9–8. Closed Mon.*

OFF THE
BEATEN PATH

CATACOMBE DI SAN GENNARO – Many of these catacombs in Naples predate the Christian era by two centuries. The church was inspired by St. Peter's in Rome. The niches and corridors of the catacombs are hung with early Christian paintings. ✉ *Via Capodimonte, next to Madre di Buon Consiglio church on Via Capodimonte,* ☎ *081/7411071.* 💰 *5,000 lire.* ◷ *Guided tours daily every 45 mins 9:30–11:45* AM.

㉛ Orto Botanico. Founded in 1807 by Joseph Bonaparte and Prince Joachim Murat as an oasis from hectic Naples, this is one of the largest of all Italian botanical gardens, comprising some 30 acres. Nineteenth-century greenhouses and picturesque paths hold an important collection of tree, shrub, cacti, and floral specimens from southern Italy. ✉ *Via Foria 223,* ☎ *081/449759.* 💰 *Free.* ◷ *Apr.–May, Mon.–Fri. 9–1; other times and seasons, by appointment only.*

★ ㉙ **Palazzo Sanfelice.** Ferdinando Sanfelice (1675–1748) is perhaps the most brilliant of all Neapolitan Baroque architects, so much so that he really was father of the evolution of the style into Neapolitan Rococo. For his own family palazzo, he designed his greatest architectural flourish—the staircase *ad ali di falco,* so named because it resembles a falcon's wing. Because the city was so overcrowded, many palazzi towered as high as seven stories, and consequently staircases became a prominent status symbol, often built as openwork double-flight stairs on exterior courtyards. Sanfelice designed his with a series of rhythmic, perforated arcades that mirror the look of a bird in flight. Climbing this four-story extravaganza—the actual structure is so spectacular, no excess ornamentation was needed—will make you feel like you are also soaring. There is another smaller, interior staircase here, which frames a garden like a stage set. The palazzo is generally closed except for public holidays 8 AM–7 PM, but if you ring the bell and ask the custodian, you may be permitted to view the courtyard staircase. Other important Sanfelice staircases can be seen nearby at the Palazzo di Maio (✉ Discesa della Sanità 69) and the Palazzo della Spagnola (✉ Via Vergini 19). ✉ *Via Sanità 2–4.*

㉚ **San Giovanni a Carbonara.** This sadly neglected church—given the short shrift many guides give it, if they don't omit it altogether—is a coherent complex of Renaissance architecture and sculpture that can hold its own against any church in Florence or Rome in terms of quality, if not size. Its curious name is the result of its location during medieval times near the city trash dump, where refuse was burned (carbonized); this location is just outside the Capuana Gate of the old city walls. Its history starts in 1339, when the Neapolitan nobleman Gualtiero Galeota gave a few houses and a vegetable garden to a small convent of Augustinian monks who ministered to the poor neighborhood nearby. Four years later, in admiration of the monks' simplicity and piety, he added another two contiguous gardens and built a church to his family's patron saint, John the Baptist. At this point, some monks moved out, judging the new complex too luxurious; however, King Ladislas judged it too small and 50 years later started a new church, enriching the complex enough to serve as a suitable site for his tomb (together with his sister and successor to the throne, Joan II). Redone in the 18th century and badly damaged in 1943, the church has been returned to its original appearance thanks to a conservation scheme.

To enter the church, go up the dramatic staircase in *piperno* stone with a double run of elliptical stairs—modeled after a 1707 design by Ferdinando Sanfelice (similar to other organ-curved stairways in Rome, such as the Spanish Steps); together with the courtyard on top, this staircase formed the scene of one of the first major battles of the Neapolitan revolt against the Nazis in September–October 1943 (known as the Four Days of Naples). Upon entering the rectangular nave, the first thing you see is the Monument of the Miroballo family, which is actually a chapel on the opposite wall, finished by Tommaso Malvito and his workshop in 1419 for the Marchese Bracigliano; the magnificent statues in the semicircular arch immediately set the tone for this surprising repository of first-class Renaissance sculpture. The small altar to the right of this chapel is known as the *Presepe,* or Nativity scene, and features wooden figures by Pietro and Giovanni Alamanno (1478).

The main altar was reframed in the exuberant Baroque manner with a marble-inlay balustrade from 1746; however fancy the altar is, it is completely dwarfed by its spectacular backdrop, the suitably royal (59 ft tall), if not megalomaniacal, funerary monument of King Ladislas (who died in 1418) and Joan II, finished by Marco and Andrea da Firenze in 1428. Four monumental female statues of Virtues hold up the sarcophagi of Ladislas and his sister, as well as statues of the two monarchs seated on thrones, and, finally, an energetic armed Ladislas on horseback being blessed by a bishop (the king died excommunicate, but you can buy anything in Naples).

A door underneath this monument leads to the **Ser Carraciolo del Sole Chapel,** with its rare and beautiful original majolica pavement—the oldest (1427) produced in Italy, from a workshop in Campania, and showing the influence of Arab motifs and glazing technique. Constructed on a circular plan, the chapel's walls are painted with a provincial but charming mid-15th-century fresco series representing various scenes from monastic life together with the life of the Virgin. The chapel is dominated by the imposing tomb of Sergianni Caracciolo, duke of Canosa and lover of Queen Joan II. He was murdered, perhaps with her consent (there are different versions, of course) during the night of August 8, 1432, in the nearby Castel Capuano by a group of noblemen; his ambition, resented by his numerous enemies, had apparently outstripped his utility to her.

Coming back out into the nave and immediately turning right at the altar, you enter another circular chapel, the **Carraciolo di Vico Chapel.** This cohesive, sophisticated ensemble shows how Italian art history, first written by Tuscans with a regional agenda, tends to simplify the evolution of Renaissance art and architecture at the expense of other centers. The dating for the chapel is the object of debate; usually given as 1517, with the sculptural decor complete by 1557, the design (usually attributed to Tommaso Malvito) may go back to 1499 and thus precede the much more famous Tempietto in Rome, by Bramante, which it so resembles. In fact, the chapel's superlative quality has led some scholars to reject the traditional attribution and give it to Bramante himself or one of the Sangallos under the assumption that such a fine work should naturally be by someone quite famous. The architect suavely subverts the purity of the white-marble decor with colored-marble backgrounds for the niches and the lunettes of the wall monuments, which deepen and expand the space, together with a sober red, gray, and white marble pavement in a concentric circular layout. The main altar, in a shallow apse in front of you as you enter, is embellished with statues by the Spanish sculptors Diego de Siloe and Bartolomeo Ordonez. A few 17th-century statues of later family members take their place discreetly without destroying the harmony of this Renaissance masterpiece.

Coming once again into the nave, see if the next door on the right is open (or ask the custodian): this leads to the small rectangular room of the **Old Sacristy,** commissioned by the Carraciolo di Sant'Erasmo, whose walls are decorated with 18 richly colored fresco panels depicting scenes from the Old and New testaments as well as saints and doctors of the Church, painted by Giorgio Vasari, that disciple of Michelangelo and godfather of Renaissance art history; the marble washbasin is worth a closer look (the sacristy was closed for restoration at press time). Outside the church in the courtyard there is a chapel on the right (the Chapel of the Crucifix), with a *Crucifixion* by Giorgio Vasari, and the tomb of Antonio Seripando (1539). You can be thankful this great church is off the path of tour groups so you can absorb the ordered beauty of the decoration in peace. ⊠ *Via San Giovanni a Carbonara 5,* ☎ *081/295873.* ⊙ *Mon.–Sat. 9–1.*

OFF THE
BEATEN PATH
MUSEO NAZIONALE FERROVIARIO – Children love to see the old-fashioned engines, cars, and railroad equipment on display in the restored railway works, east of the center, founded by the Bourbon rulers of Naples in the last century. ⊠ *Corso San Giovanni a Teduccio,* ☎ *081/ 472003.* ⊞ *Free.* ⊙ *Mon.–Sat. 8:30–1:30.*

Funiculì, Funiculà: The Vomero to the Lungomare

When the French writer and philosopher Montesquieu visited Naples in 1728, he exclaimed: "Nothing is more beautiful than the siting of Naples in the gulf: Naples is like an amphitheater on the sea." Start at the top of that theater—the Vomero Hill—then go back down to explore Naples's elegant waterfront area, the Lungomare, which runs from the Riviera di Chiaia to the Castel dell'Ovo, the harbor castle. Neapolitans often say their town's glories are vertical—the white *guglia* obelisks that festoon the historic quarter, the eight-story tenements of Spaccanapoli, and Vomero, the towering hill that overlooks the city center. Even longtime residents love to head up here to gaze in wonder at the entire city from the balcony belvedere of the Museo di San Martino. Before them, a big rich spread of southern Italian amplitude fills the eye: hillsides dripping with wedding-cake hotels, miles of villainously ugly apartment houses, streets short and narrow—leading to an unspeakable as well as unsolvable traffic problem—countless church spires and domes, and far below, the reason it all works, the intensely blue Bay of Naples. To tie together the lower parts and upper reaches of the city, everyone uses the *funavia*—the cable car system that run on three separate routes up and down the Vomero. Before you know it, you can be hopping and skipping over the city with these funiculars, whistling, of course, "Funiculì-funiculà," the famous 1880 song composed by Neapolitans Peppino Turco and Luigi Danza to celebrate the opening of the first line.

Thanks to the funiculars, you can readily take in many of Naples's aristocratic pleasures and treasures: the chic Piazza dei Martiri sector; the gilded 19th-century Villa Pignatelli; three museums that crown the Vomero Hill—the Villa La Floridiana, the Certosa di San Martino, and the Castel Sant'Elmo; the Lungomare, the most champagne stretch of waterfront in Naples; and finally, the historic Pizzofalcone quarter. In the 19th century Naples's waterfront harbored the picturesque quarter that was called Santa Lucia, a district dear to artists and musicians and known for its fishermen's cottages. The fishermen were swept away when an enormous landfill project extended the land out to what is now Via Nazario Sauro and Via Partenope, the address for some of Naples's finest hotels. Today, the waterfront promenade has lost much of its former color, but it still retains a uniquely Neapolitan charm.

A Good Walk

Begin at the main station of the Funiculare Centrale, on the tiny Piazza Duca d'Aosta, just opposite the Via Toledo entrance to the Galleria Umberto I. After two hillside stops, get off at the end of the line, Stazione Fuga, near the top of the Vomero Hill. To get to the Castel Sant'Elmo/Certosa di San Martino complex, head out from the station, turning right on Via Cimarosa, then left on Via Morghen. At the next street, Via Scarlatti—the main thoroughfare of the neighborhood—turn right and walk up the steps of the hill, then follow the path around the left side of the Montesanto funicular until you run into the Via Tito Angelini. This street, lined with some of Naples's best Belle Epoque mansions, leads to the **Castel Sant'Elmo** ㉝ and the adjoining **Certosa di San Martino** ㉞, which commands magnificent vistas over city and sea to Vesuvius. After viewing this enormous complex (its star exhibition is the collection of *Presepe,* or Nativity, scenes), backtrack to Via Scarlatti until you make a left on Via Bernini at Piazza Vanvitelli. This piazza, with no shortage of smart bars and trattorias, remains the center for the Vomero district. Walk right onto Via Cimarosa for two blocks until you reach the entrance to the **Villa La Floridiana** ㉟, today a museum filled with aristocratic knickknacks and surrounded by a once-regal park. After viewing the villa, make a left from the park entrance on Via Cimarosa for two blocks until you reach the Stazione Cimarosa of the Chiaia funicular, which will take you back down to the Lungomare area. From the Amedeo funicular station walk down Via del Parco Margherita, past Piazza Amedeo, making a left onto Via Colonna, a right onto Via Bausan, a right onto Via Santa Teresa a Chiaia, and then make a left down Via Ascensione to the Riviera di Chiaia (*chiaia* means "beach" in the Neapolitan dialect), where a final right turn brings you to the **Villa Pignatelli** ㊱, whose red-velvet salons still seem warm with the spirits of the Rothschilds, Actons, and other aristos who once called this home. From here cross the Riviera to the waterfront park of the Villa Comunale and its **Aquario** ㊲, which is open afternoons from March to October.

For a late lunch, follow the Riviera past the Piazza della Vittoria onto Via Partenope and the spectacular **Castel dell'Ovo** ㊳. In its shadow is the enchanting **Borgo Marinaro** ㊴—a dollhouse of a fishermen's village, where seafood restaurants offer good food. From here return to the Piazza dei Martiri, venture up Via Caterina until you reach Via Chiaia, lined with shops, food stores, and the immense Palazzo Cellamare. Halfway up the street there is the elegant Empire-era Ponte di Chiaia, a 17th-century gateway restored in the 1880s. Near it you'll find an elevator that can carry you up to the historic hill of **Pizzofalcone,** the very first settlement of the ancient Greeks, which was transformed into an elegant residential quarter in the Baroque and Rococo periods. View Naples's finest 18th-century palace courtyard at the **Palazzo Serra di Cassano** ㊶; then explore the churches of **Santa Maria degli Angeli** ㊵ and **Santa Maria Egiziaca** ㊷ (by 4:30, churches should open for evening hours). Check out if there is any theatrical performance you wish to attend at the Pizzofalcone's theater, the Politeama, then you can take the elevator back down—*never* take the neighboring stairway, as its deserted route makes it a haunt for juvenile delinquents—to the elegant shopping and dining of the Chiaia district. If you're looking for a place for a pizza dinner, not far away is Naples's most historic pizzeria, Brandi, at Via Miano 27. Head back along Via Chiaia to the Piazza dei Martiri to join chic Neapolitans on their evening *passeggiata,* shopping the boutiques, bookstores, and antiques shops lining the streets that radiate off the piazza (particularly the designer-dense stretch of Via dei Mille). The Metropolitana Piazza Amadeo station is nearby, while the R3 bus route, Tram 1, and Bus 140 follow the Riviera di Chiaia, which is the main avenue of the Lungomare.

TIMING

As always in Naples, it's best to start out early in the morning to fit most of your sightseeing in before the luncheon break—and the midday heat. Try to finish the sights on the Vomero Hill before noon so you can catch the funicular back down to the waterfront's Villa Pignatelli, which closes at 2 PM.

Numbers in the text correspond to numbers in the margin and on the Naples map.

Sights to See

37 Aquario (Aquarium). For a city named by the Greeks after the mermaid Parthenope (who slew herself after being rejected by Odysseus, at least in the version according to the poet Virgil), it is only fitting that Naples should have established one of Europe's first public aquariums in 1872. At this time—when, not so incidentally, the public imagination was being stirred by the fictional creations of Jules Verne's Captain Nemo and Hans Christian Andersen's Little Mermaid—technological innovations came into place to funnel seawater directly from the bay into the aquarium tanks, which showcase some 200 species of fish and marine plants (undoubtedly better off here than in the highly polluted Bay of Naples, their natural habitat). Officially named the Stazione Zoologica, founded by the German scientist Anton Dorhn, and housed in a Stil Liberty building designed by Adolf von Hildebrandt, the aquarium quickly became the wonder of Naples for children and art-exhausted adults. Today the ground floors contain the aquarium tanks—fishy "living rooms" decorated with rocks and plants of the region and all illuminated by skylights. Upstairs are research facilities and the library, which is decorated with Hans von Marées's magnificent mosaics showing the Lungamare area as it looked when the Aquario opened, which was then set directly on the water. To see the library, you need to make a special request when buying your tickets. ⊠ *Stazione Zoologica, Viale A. Dohrn,* ☎ *081/ 583–3111.* 🎫 *3,000 lire.* ◷ *May–Sept., Tues.–Sat. 9–6, Sun. 9:30–7:30; Oct.–Apr., Tues.–Sat. 9–5, Sun. 9–2.*

★ **39 Borgo Marinaro.** If your thoughts of Naples involve the strumming of a mandolin, fishermen singing "Santa Lucia," and idyllic seaside sunsets, the city can be a sad disappointment—that is, until you venture to the Borgo Marinaro, a toy fishermen's village nestling under the shadows of the mighty Castel dell'Ovo. After the cholera epidemic of 1884, entire quarters of the city were demolished and the rubble was transported to the Santa Lucia quarter as *colmata,* or landfill. For the most part, picturesque fishermen's houses were replaced by the Lungomare's luxurious hotels, but something of old Naples remains here at this little harbor port, officially called the Porto di Santa Lucia. Adorned with kitschy seafood restaurants, lovely outdoor cafés, and thriving boat shops, it inhabits the small islet called Megaris by the ancients and now connected to the mainland by the mole of the Castel dell'Ovo. From the Santa Lucia shrine (just under the mole), stroll along the Lungomare past the Hotel Excelsior to the **Fontana dell'Immacolatella** (1622), sculpted by Pietro Bernini, father of the famous Gianlorenzo, which frames a great vista of Vesuvius. ⊠ *Via Partenope, at Castel dell'Ovo.*

㊳ Castel dell'Ovo. The oldest castle in Naples, the Castel dell'Ovo sits on the most picturesque point of the bay, standing guard over the city it protects. Occupying the isle of Megaris, it was originally the site of the Roman villa of Lucullus—proof, if you need it, that the ancient Romans knew a premium location when they saw one (for the same reason, some of the city's top hotels share the same site today). By the 12th century, it had become a fortress under the Normans; it was once the prison of Conradin and of Beatrice, daughter of Manfred, last of the Hohenstaufen rulers. Its name refers to the legend that the poet Virgil saw a magical egg rise from the waves here. This must have been one tough egg to crack, as the fortress still looks awe inspiring and impregnable, although it lost many of its towers and battlements centuries ago. Today, it is used as a conference and convention center, and if you can attend one of the events here, such as the September Antiqua show, do so: The castle's gigantic rooms, rock tunnels, and belvederes over the bay are among Naples's most striking sights. ⊠ *Via Partenope, at the Borgo Marinaro,* ☎ *081/415002.* ⊙ *Open for special events and exhibitions only.*

㉝ Castel Sant'Elmo. Long a powerful symbol of foreign and governmental domination, the imposing fortress of the Castel Sant'Elmo broods over the city center from its hilltop perch atop the Vomero and seems to be policing you wherever you walk in Naples. Originally built by Charles I of Anjou in 1275 and enlarged by the Angevin kings in the 1330s, it was transformed in the 16th century by Pedro Scrivà under viceroy Don Pedro de Toledo into its present stoutly fortified six-point-star configuration. The castle cells housed many prisoners over the centuries, including the philosopher monk Tomasso Campanella (1568–1639), leaders of the Masaniello rebellion, and even patriots of the Italian Risorgimento. From the ramparts panoramic views of the city extend in all directions. Today the great rooms of the castle often host temporary exhibitions and conferences. ⊠ *Largo San Martino,* ☎ *081/578–4030.* 🎟 *4,000 lire.* ⊙ *Tues.–Sun. 9–2.*

★ **㉞ Certosa di San Martino.** Atop a rocky promontory with a fabulous view of the entire city, and with majestic salons that would please any monarch, the Certosa di San Martino is a monastery that seems more like a palace. In fact, by the 18th century Ferdinand IV was threatening to halt the order's government subsidy, so sumptuous was this *certosa,* or charterhouse, which had been started in 1325 under the royal patronage of Charles of Anjou. With the Carthusians's vast wealth and love of art, it was only a matter of time before dour Angevin Gothic was traded in for varicolor Neapolitan Baroque, thanks to the contributions of many 17th- and 18th-century sculptors and painters—note particularly the paintings in the Certosa Church by Luca Giordano and Il Ribera (his *Descent from the Cross,* over the main altar, is one of his masterpieces). The signature style note was set by Cosimo Fanzago (1591–1678), an architect, sculptor, and decorator who was as devout as he was mad, as you can see from his work in the **Chiosto Grande.** Fanzago's ceremonial portals at each corner of the cloister are among the most spectacular of all Baroque creations—aswirl with Mannerist volutes and Michelangelo-esque ornament, they serve as mere frames for six life-size statues of Carthusian saints, who sit atop the doorways, judging all with deathless composure. Fanzago worked at the Certosa from 1623 to 1656; he laid on the luxe in the church's Cappella di San Bruno (1631) and the grand staircase that leads to the **Quatro del Priore,** the prior's apartment, which was the residence of the only monk who had any contact with the outside world—an extravaganza filled with frescoes, 18th-century majolica ornaments, and paintings, with extensive gardens where scenic pergolati overlook the bay.

Nearby is the **Sezione Presepiale**, the greatest collection of Nativity crèches in the world. Ranging in size from a nutshell to an entire room, they offer supreme evocations of 18th-century life. Many figures are garbed in exquisite costumes and with portraitlike faces. The most noted is the *Presepe Cuciniello*, with more than 160 shepherds, eight dogs, countless angels, Moors, chickens, cheese wheels, beggars, and dwarfs, all worshiping the holy family against a brilliant blue sky. The crèche collection is just one section of the **Museo Nazionale di San Martino**, a collection dealing explicitly with Neapolitan subject matter, which moved into the Certosa when the religious orders were suppressed in the 19th century (some rooms are closed for an ongoing renovation). Before leaving the Certosa, be sure to visit Room 25, whose parapet frames *the* panoramic view of Naples. ✉ *Museo Nazionale di San Martino, Largo San Martino,* ☎ *081/578–1769.* ▣ *9,500 lire.* ☉ *Tues.– Sun. 9–2.*

❸ La Nunziatella. In 1736 the Jesuits asked Ferdinando Sanfelice, then at work several blocks away on the magnificent Palazzo Serra di Cassano (☞ *below*), to transform a novitiate into a church; the result is one of the jewels of 18th-century Neapolitan architecture, with rich but not overwhelming marble-inlay work and an excellent series of contemporary frescoes by Francesco de Mura. The interior of the church can occasionally be viewed in the morning if you ask the guard or chaplain at the adjoining military college, but usually you need official permission from the Ministry of Defence. ✉ *Via Generale Parisi,* ☎ *081/ 764–1520.*

★ ❹ Palazzo Serra di Cassano. By the late 18th century, Via Monte di Dio had become one of Naples's poshest addresses. Lined with palazzi and villas, it was chosen by Prince Aloisio Sera di Cassano for his family palace, designed by Ferdinando Sanfelice, the most important architect of domestic architecture in Naples. In this city where spectacle and love of show have always been important, the appropriately gigantic double-flight staircase that Sanfelice built in the palace courtyard wouldn't have been out of place in a lavish 1950s MGM musical. The regal staircase was reduced to back-door status when the palazzo's main door was closed by the prince in honor of his son Gennaro, executed as one of the participants in the 1799 revolution. Today the Istituto Italiano per gli Studi Filosofici, an institute devoted to philosophy studies, occupies much of the palazzo; they offer a full calendar of courses and lectures throughout the year. ✉ *Via Monte di Dio 14–15,* ☎ *081/ 764–2652.* ☉ *Weekdays 7:30–7:30; Sat. 7–noon.*

Pizzofalcone. In the 7th century BC, Pizzofalcone (Falcon's Beak) *was* Naples. The ancient Greeks had settled here because, legend says, the body of the siren Parthenope had been found washed ashore on the beach at the foot of the Pizzofalcone Hill, then known as Monte Echia. Nearly two millennia later, in the 18th century, the hill, mere feet from the bay and the Castel dell'Ovo, became a fashionable address as Naples's rich and titled sought to escape the congestion and heat of the city center. The rocky promontory soon became studded with Baroque palaces and and Rococo churches. You can walk up to Pizzofalcone by taking Via G. Serra just to the right-hand colonnade of the Church of San Francesco di Paolo, on Piazza del Plebiscito, to Pizzofalcone's main Piazza del Santa Maria degli Angeli, or take the elevator (never the dark staircase) from Via Chiaia. The leading sights are the palazzi along Via Monte di Dio—including Palazzo Serra di Cassano (☞ *above*)—and the churches of La Nunziatella, Santa Maria degli Angeli, and Santa Maria Egiziaca (☞ *above* and *below*). Like other parts of Naples, Pizzofalcone harbors both palaces and slums; unlike other parts, it's off the beaten path, so don't stop to answer questions from seemingly innocuous strollers. ✉ *Piazza Santa Maria degli Angeli, accessed via the elevator at the Ponte di Chiaia on Via Chiaia.*

NEED A
BREAK?

Walking up the fashionable Via Chiaia, in the shadow of the Pizzofalcone hill and behind Piazza del Plebiscito, you'll come upon **Caflisch** (✉ Via Chiaia 144, ☎ 081/416477), closed Monday, a historic café serving snacks and high-quality chocolates and pastries to nibble over a cappuccino or espresso.

㊵ Santa Maria degli Angeli a Pizzofalcone. In 1590 the princess of Sulmona, Costanza del Carretto Doria, commissioned this church not far from her palace on Pizzofalcone. In the 17th century the church was given to the Theatine order and enlarged by an architect belonging to the order. The lively vault and dome frescoes are by Giovanni Beinaschi, better known as a painter of genre scenes, and there are some good paintings by Luca Giordano and Massimo Stanzione. ✉ *Piazza Santa Maria degli Angeli,* ☎ *081/764–4974.* ☉ *Daily 7:30–noon and 5–7.*

㊷ Santa Maria Egiziaca a Pizzofalcone. This church is probably the masterpiece of Cosimo Fanzago, a Lombard architect and sculptor who became one of the leading innovators of Neapolitan Baroque. The octagonal form of the church was to influence the work of many of his contemporaries, and its luminous white dome comes as somewhat of a surprise compared with his several furiously polychrome marble-inlay chapels he left around town; a taste of that exuberance appears in the florid high altar, which features a fine painting of the titular Virgin by another renowned creator of the Neapolitan Baroque, Domenico Antonio Vaccaro. ✉ *Via Egiziaca 30,* ☎ *081/764–5199.* ☉ *Daily 9:30–1 and 5–7.*

㉟ Villa La Floridiana. Now a pretty residential neighborhood, the Vomero Hill was once the patrician address of many of Naples's most extravagant estates. La Floridiana is the sole surviving 18th-century villa, built in 1817 on order of Ferdinand I for Lucia Migliaccio, duchess of Floridia—their portraits greet you as you enter. Only nine shocking months after his first wife, the Habsburg Maria Carolina died, when the court was still in mourning, Ferdinand secretly married Lucia, his longtime mistress. Scandal ensued, but the king and his new wife were too happy to worry, escaping high above the city and court gossip to this elegant little estate. Designed by architect Antonio Niccolini in Neoclassic style, the house is now occupied by the **Museo Nazionale della Ceramica Duca di Martina**, a museum devoted to the decorative arts of the 18th and 19th centuries. Countless display cases are filled with what Edith Wharton described as "all those fragile and elaborate trifles the irony of fate preserves when brick and marble crumble": Sevres, Limoges, and Meissen porcelains, gold watches, ivory fans, glassware, enamels, majolica vases. Sadly, there are no period rooms left to see. Outside is a park designed in the English style by Degenhardt, who also designed the park at Capodimonte. Nannies and their charges walk along the winding paths to the stepped terraces, which offer spectacular views. Unfortunately, the park is not well tended—graffiti defaces the Grecian Tempietto, the pools are dry, the grass is parched—as yet another treasure is wasted by the city government. ✉ *Via Cimarosa 77,* ☎ *081/578–8418.* 🎟 *5,000 lire.* ☉ *Mon.–Sat. 9–2.*

㊱ Villa Pignatelli. More officially known as the Museo Diego Aragona Pignatelli Cortes, this is one of the few patrician homes of old Naples that is open to the public. When built in 1826 by architect P. Valente for the aristocratic Acton family (Sir Harold Acton, who died in the mid-1990s, was the author of many books on Neapolitan history; Princess Acton, whose family to this day hosts the best New Year's Eve parties in Naples, still occupies the family palazzo, which towers over nearby Via Chiaia), it was one was of the city's premier houses, with a Grecian-temple front and a beautiful park. In 1841 the barons Rothschild took over and redid rooms in Second Empire splendor, including the leather-lined smoking salon and the Sala Rosso, a red velvet-and-gold jewel box. Prince Pignatelli Cortes's daughter donated the house to the city in 1952, and he must be spinning in his grave at the shoddy state of the house today, with dim lighting, enough dust to cover Pompeii, and rooms used as warehouses. The house may be spruced up for some of the temporary exhibitions held here from time to time, but it usually looks like a set for Violetta's death scene in *La Traviata*. On the grounds is a carriage house that contains the **Museo delle Carozze** (Carriage Museum), with coaches from the late 1800s to the early 1900s. A stroll in the park here is a pleasant respite from the noisy city streets. ⊠ *Riviera di Chiaia 200,* ☎ *081/669675.* ▩ *5,000 lire.* ☾ *Tues.–Sun. 9–2.*

<table><tr><td>OFF THE
BEATEN PATH</td><td>**PARCO VIRGILIANO AND POSILLIPO** – At the far western end of the city lie two of Naples's most tranquil spots—the Parco Virgiliano, named after the great ancient Roman poet Virgil, and the suburb of Posillipo. The park is still beautiful and is, according to legend, the site of the poet's tomb, which is now judged to be an anonymous Roman *columbarium* (funerary monument). It is set not far from both the Crypta Neapolitana, an ancient Roman tunnel now caved in, and the tomb-memorial of Giacomo Leopardi, the noted 19th-century poet. The vista from the bluff overlooking the bay and city is world famous. Gain access to the park from Piazza Sannazzaro, which lies at the far west end of the Riviera di Chiaia, opposite the pretty Porto Sannazaro in the Mergellina district (take a train to the Stazione di Mergellina station). Farther to the west along the coast is the seaside suburb of Posillipo (☞ West of Naples map *in* Chapter 3), whose name comes from the ancient Greek *Pausilypon* ("respite from pain"). This was once the place for Naples's most idyllic shoreline and villas, but is now sadly overrun with apartment buildings. Still, the beaches and coves here harbor picturesque spots like the hamlet of Marechiaro ("clear sea")—home to two of Naples' best restaurants—and not far from the Palazzo Donn'Anna, built by Cosimo Fanzago for the wife of the Spanish viceroy in 1637 and one of the city's most romantic, legend-haunted structures; another fabled abode, the former casino-villa of Sir William Hamilton, is nearby (both villas are still private). Bus route No. 20 runs along Via Posillipo and the sea. ⊠ *Parco Virgiliano, Via Salita Grotta 20,,* ☎ *081/081/669390.*</td></tr></table>

DINING

Let's be honest: you really want a traditional Neapolitan dinner with lots of tomato sauce and a great show of Neapolitan love songs to get you crying into your limoncello. There's no reason to feel guilty, because even the natives love to get into the spirit. But listening to somone warble "Santa Lucia" while feasting on a pizza *Margherita* (with basil, mozzarella, and tomatoes) from a table overlooking the Bay of Naples is just one example of the pleasures awaiting diners in Naples. From *vitello alla Principe di Napoli* (veal garnished with truffles) to sea bass in *aqua pazza*—that is to say, poached in water "maddened" with anchovy, bay leaves, *peperoncino*, and olive oil—to Neapolitan pastries like ricotta-rich *babà al Rhum*, the city expresses its gastronomic self in many ways. The *haute*-hungry should look elsewhere (particularly

HEY, IT NEVER TASTED LIKE THIS BACK HOME

THERE'S NO PIZZA like real Neapolitan pizza. If you don't believe it, try one at *Ciro a Santa Brigida* (✉ Via Santa Brigida 71, ☎ 081/552–4072). This restaurant is a little more upscale than a typical Neapolitan pizzeria, but its pizza is the real thing, and it's proper to eat it with your napkin stuffed into your shirt to avoid tomato stains. The restaurant's owner, Antonio Pace, president of the True Neapolitan Pizza Association, is behind an unusual initiative to upgrade the quality of pizza worldwide. Mr. Pace and Professor Carlo Mangoni di Santo Stefano, a nutritionist at the University of Naples, have written what they call a Pizza Discipline, a treatise that discusses everything from the history of pizza to the perfect ingredients for the perfect Neapolitan pie. Based on the Pizza Discipline, the city of Naples recently registered a logo that pizzerias can hang in their window if, and only if, they serve true Neapolitan pizza. That means using sinfully luscious buffalo-milk mozzarella made in certain areas near Naples, kneading the dough for exactly 30 minutes, and letting it rise for four hours. (The "discipline" includes photos of dough taken through a microscope before and after it has risen.)

It may take a while before pizzerias around the globe actually hang the logo in their windows. But the city of Naples wants it to eventually be a sign of quality as distinctive as the DOC (*Denominazione di Origine Controllata*, or denomination of controlled origin) on wine labels. The logo will be blue, with Mt. Vesuvius in the background, a red pizza with mozzarella in the center, and PIZZA NAPOLETANA written across the foreground. Make sure you're the first to spot it!

Some pizza history, as recounted by Professor Mangoni (who scoffs at claims that pizza was invented in the United States):

Pizza marinara, which doesn't have mozzarella at all but is simply a pie with tomatoes, garlic, oregano, and olive oil, first appeared in Naples around 1760. King Ferdinand of Naples liked the pizza, but his wife, a Habsburg princess, wouldn't allow pizza in the palace. The king would often sneak out to one of the world's first pizzerias, making the places famous.

Even earlier, there's a mention of plates of flour with other food on top in Homer's *Iliad,* but Professor Mangoni says this was just a precursor to pizza, not the real thing. Tomato sauce, says Mangoni, dates back to 1733.

Mozzarella came later. The pizza margherita was invented in 1889, when Naples chef Raffaele Esposito was called on to prepare a meal for the Italian Queen, Margherita. He made a pizza with tomato sauce and mozzarella, and his wife had the idea of adding basil to honor Italy's red, white, and green flag.

According to the Pizza Discipline, the only true pizzas are marinara and margherita. Anchovies, pepperoni, and so on are heresy. So don't expect to see the logo with Mt. Vesuvius at your local pizza joint anytime soon.

In Antonio Pace's family, pizza goes back a long way. He claims his grandfather's grandfather made pizza in 1856. Pizza fact or fiction aside, at Ciro a Santa Brigida, everything is delicious. Ask for a taste of plain buffalo mozzarella and just savor it in your mouth. If you have a lactose intolerance, there's still hope—Professor Mangoni and his team of scientists are developing lactose-free mozzarella. If they manage to match the taste of real mozzarella, he says, pizzerias will be allowed to use it and still display the Pizza Napoletana logo. Go figure.

Ristorante Don Alfonso 1890, just across the bay in Sorrento) and so should those in search of newer-than-now nouvelle flights of fantasy, designer plates, and *dernier-cri* fusion dishes. In Naples it is still the old reliables that apply, the recipes time-tested by centuries of mammas that still manage to put meat on your bones and smiles on your faces.

This means pizzerias aplenty. As the birthplace of pizza (☞ Close-Up box, "Hey, It Never Tasted Like This Back Home," *above*), Naples prides itself on its vast selection of pizzerias, the most famous of which—Da Michele, Brandi, or Trianon—deserve the encomium "incomparable." Many Neapolitans make lunch their big meal of the day, then have a pizza for supper or—just watch the jeweled operagoers at the Teatro San Carlo head over to Ciro a Santa Brigida—a late-night treat.

When it comes to *i secondi*—or main dishes—you can find a first-rate chicken offering, but the reason visitors to Naples want to eat seafood is a good one: geography. Naples's position, hugging a rich bay, has guaranteed that marine creatures feature prominently on local menus. Marinated seafood salad (*insalata di frutti di mare*) is a classic antipasto, as well as marinated white anchovies (*alice*). Spaghetti *con le vongole veraci* (with clams, garlic, and a baby's fistful of chopped flat-leaf Italian parsley) is of course a popular and dependable standard, as are myriad variations on linguine or fresh pasta with mixed seafood (mussels, shrimp, clams, and so forth), usually "stained" with fresh cherry tomatoes. If you come across it, try spaghetti *alle neonate*—with minuscule whole newborn fish (Herod's Massacre of the Innocents applied to seafood pasta)—this is usually an off-the-menu item, but you can ask the waiter or check out the seafood display. As for seafood Neapolitan style, the best—*spigola* (sea bass), *pesce spada* (swordfish), and, if you can find it, the *San Pietro* (sort of a sole for grown-ups) is grilled simply and ennobled with a splash of olive oil and a squeeze of lemon. Fresh calamari, kissed lightly by a grill, can be exquisitely delicate, but the fried version, which can be uniquely satisfying, is, alas, too often done these days with frozen squid. Shrimp, too, are often frozen even in upmarket establishments, so caveat emptor. Fish in restaurants is usually out on display, so you can easily check if your bass has clear, firm eyes—not cloudy. Another good way to have fish is *all'acqua pazza* (literally, in crazy water), poached with anchovy bay leaves, red pepper, and olive oil, a brew said to have been invented by returning fishermen using seawater to cook up a meal on the beach; this makes marvelous use of less expensive fish, such as the dorata.

In the end, veterans know that the best restaurants in Naples are the simplest. But no matter where you head, you'll be delighted (or exasperated—depending on how critical you are): after all, you're in Naples and the mise-en-scène—Vesuvius as a backdrop to your flambéed chicken Vesuvio or a table on a charming alleyway—can't be beat. Note that many restaurants in Naples close up for at least a week around August 15 to celebrate the Ferragosto holidays.

CATEGORY	COST*
$$$$	over 85,000 lire
$$$	60,000–85,000 lire
$$	25,000–60,000 lire
$	under 25,000 lire

per person, excluding drinks and service

City Center
Appropriately, the monumental city center features some of Naples's most famous restaurants.

$$$ ✕ **Ciro a Santa Brigida.** Off Via Toledo near the Castel Nuovo, Ciro
★ has been an obligatory entry on any list of Neapolitan cooking (as op-
posed to cuisine) since 1932 and the days when Toscanini and Piran-
dello used to eat here. Popular with business travelers, artists, and
journalists who prefer food over frills, Ciro is famous for a wide va-
riety of canonical favorites with an emphasis on rustic food, from the
very fine pizzas and their justly famed versions of *pasta e fagioli* to the
classic *sartù*—rice loaf first conjured up by Baroque-era nuns—and the
splendid *pignatiello e vavella,* or shellfish soup. The *scaloppe all Ciro*
(veal scallops with prosciutto and mozzarella) and penne with smoked
mozzarella and eggplant are also wonderful. The menu looks too large
for all its items to be good, but the owners must be doing something
right, since the place is often packed with Neapolitan regulars. The old
waiters are darling wherever you sit, but try to get a table upstairs, which
has a pleasanter atmosphere. ✉ *Via Santa Brigida 71,* ☎ *081/552–*
4072. AE, DC, V. Closed Sun. and last 2 wks in Aug.

$$ ✕ **Amici Miei.** A place favored by meat eaters who can't take eat another bite of sea bass, this small, dark, and cozy den of comfort is well
loved for its specials such as tender carpaccio with fresh artichoke hearts
and a rice and arugula dish featuring duck breast. Happily, there are
also excellent pasta dishes, such as *orecchiette* with chickpeas, or that
extravaganza, the *carnevale lasagne,* an especially rich concoction used
to sustain the taste buds over the Lenten period. Everyone ends with
the homemade fruit tart. ✉ *Via Monte di Dio 78,* ☎ *081/764–6063.*
AE, DC, V. Closed Mon. and Aug. No dinner Sun.

$$ ✕ **La Fila.** To the north of the Stazione Centrale at Piazza Garibaldi,
this family-run establishment was considerably brightened up in a
1997 remodeling. If the hostess insists on you having something, trust
her: the simplest dishes, so often done indifferently elsewhere, are here
exquisite voyages of discovery: baked pasta with meatballs and pizza
with pungent sausage kissed awake by the wood-fired oven, or the ubiq-
uitous potato croquette, here made with respect, real mashed potatoes,
and smoked provolone. Fish is usually excellent and at reasonable prices.
Also on tap is true sourdough pizza—the house specialty is topped with
prosciutto, mushrooms, and mozzarella. ✉ *Via Nazionale 6/c,* ☎ *081/*
206717. No credit cards. Closed Mon.

$ ✕ **Brandi.** If you haven't been to Brandi, you haven't been to Naples.
★ Forget that this historic place gave the world pizza Margherita—the clas-
sic combo of tomato sauce, mozzarella, and basil, named after King Um-
berto's queen. This is, hands down, one of the most picturesque
restaurants in Italy. Set on a cobblestone alleyway just off chic Via Chi-
aia, it welcomes you with an enchanting wood-beamed salon festooned
with 19th-century memorabilia, saint shrines, gilded mirrors, and bou-
quets of flowers, beyond which you can see the kitchen and some of
Naples's most famous *pizzaioli* (pizza makers) at work. Upstairs are two
tiny, low-ceiling rooms (evidence of the venerable date of the restau-
rant) adorned with mirrors and celeb photos. Most Neapolitans stay
away, but it's their loss: join Luciano Pavarotti, Chelsea Clinton, and
groups of Japanese tourists to enjoy the most *delicioso* ambience in the
city. In addition to the Margherita, the menu features an array of other
pizza choices plus a few meat and fish main courses. ✉ *Via Miano 27–*
29, ☎ *081/741–0455. No credit cards. Closed Mon.*

$ ✕ **Triunfo.** A strikingly clean place in a neighborhood near the Stazione
Centrale that has seen better times, this restaurant sticks out for the
quality of its pizza as well, with a devoted clientele of regulars. The
selection of cold antipasti, with lots of simply prepared vegetables, is
a welcome change from the usual fried offerings, and the house pizza,
with prosciutto and artichokes, makes a wonderful summer dinner. ✉
Vicolo II Duchesca 10, ☎ *081/268948. No credit cards. Closed Sun.*

68

Restaurants

'A Canzuncella, **31**

'A Fenestella, **5**

'A Taverna é Zi Carmela, **15**

Amici Miei, **16**

Brandi, **25**

Caruso, **18**

Casanova Grill, **20**

Cibo, **35**

Ciro a Santa Brigida, **26**

Da Cicciotto, **6**

Da Corrado, **50**

Da Gennaro e Titina, **34**

Da Michele, **39**

I Re di Napoli, **17**

La Bersagliera, **21**

La Cantina di Triunfo, **7**

La Cantina di Via Sapienza, **52**

La Cantinella, **23**

La Fila, **48**

La Taverna dell'Arte, **33**

La Sacrestia, **1**

Lombardi a Santa Chiara, **36**

Lombardi a Via Forio, **51**

Marino, **24**

Mimì alla Ferrovia, **47**

Porta Venosa, **32**

Sorbillo, **54**

Trianon, **40**

Triunfo, **45**

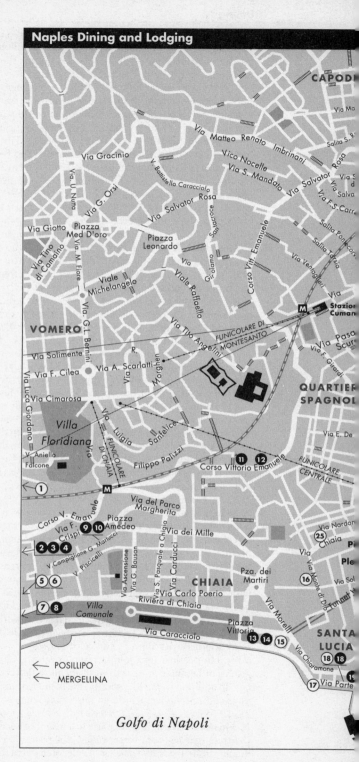

Naples Dining and Lodging

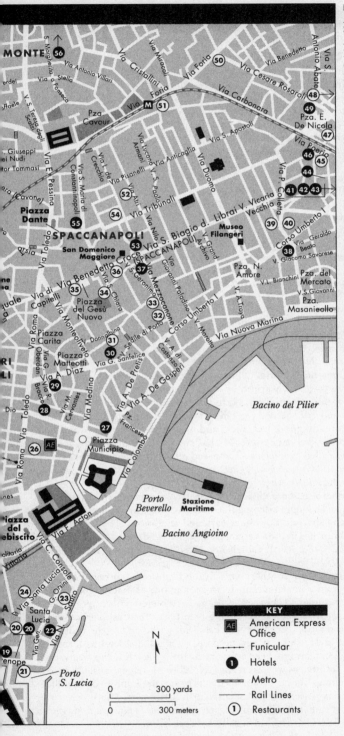

Lodging

Albergo
Sansevero, **55**
Ausonia, **8**
Britannique, **11**
Collegio Europeo, **37**
Delle Terme, **3**
Excelsior, **20**
Executive, **30**
Grand Hotel Oriente,
29
Hotel Eden, **42**
Hotel Ginevra, **43**
Hotel Santa Lucia, **19**
Le Fontane al
Mare, **14**
Mediterraneo, **28**
Mercure Napoli
Angioino, **27**
Mexico, **49**
Miramare, **22**
Paradiso, **2**
Parker's, **12**
Parteno, **13**
Pensione Mancini, **46**
Pinto Storey, **9**
Ruggiero, **10**
San Pietro, **44**
Soggiorno
Sansevero, **53**
Splendide, **4**
Suite Esedra, **38**
Terminus, **41**
Vesuvio, **18**
Villa Capodimonte, **56**

Spaccanapoli and Environs

For *cucina povera e vero*—the truest Neapolitan cuisine— head to the restaurants and pizzerias of Naples's most picturesque quarter.

$$$ ✕ **'A Canzuncella.** Here is one of those places where you can come for a traditional Neapolitan dinner with a show of Neapolitan crooners— a performance only an entrenched curmudgeon would fail to enjoy. In fact, you can eat very well here, and they don't go overboard on the tomato sauce. ✉ *Piazza Santa Maria La Nova 17/18,* ☎ *081/551–9018. MC, V.*

$$$ ✕ **Mimì alla Ferrovia.** This Neapolitan version of a grand Parisian
★ brasserie is an institution—whose clients have included Fellini and that magnificent true-Neapolitan comic genius and fake noble, Totò—but even so, Mimì manages to live up cheerfully to its history, proudly serving fine versions of everything from pasta e fagioli to fresh fettuccine with lobster, or the sea bass *al presidente,* baked in a pastry crust and enjoyed by any number of Italian presidents on their visits to Naples. Not so much a place to see and be seen as a common ground where the famous and unknown can feast and be of good cheer, Mimi is dressed in sober beige and green hues and accented with updated Art Deco features, white tablecloths, and retro bentwood chairs—all of which pleasantly tone down the bustle. ✉ *Via. A. D'Aragona 19/21,* ☎ *081/ 289004. AE, DC, MC, V. Closed Sun. and last 2 wks in Aug.*

$$ ✕ **Da Gennaro e Titina.** If you just want mamma to take care of you, head to this trattoria to choose from a reassuring menu of basic Italian home-style classics. Decor is minimal and spotlessly clean, and all dishes are served up with steady love. ✉ *Via Santa Chiara 6,* ☎ *081/ 552–9080. No credit cards. Closed Mon.*

$$ ✕ **La Taverna dell'Arte.** On a small side street near the university, this gracious trattoria, warmed up with touches of wood, prides itself on its fresh interpretations of Neapolitan classics: excellent salami, mozzarella and *frittate* (fried vegetables) among the appetizers, cabbage soup redolent with good beef stock, and meat and fish grilled over wood. Typical Neapolitan desserts—babas and the familiar crunchy almond cookies called *cantuccini*—are served up with homemade liqueurs. ✉ *Rampe San Giovanni Maggiore 1/a,* ☎ *081/552–7558. V. Closed Sun. and last 2 wks in Aug.*

$$ ✕ **Lombardi a Santa Chiara.** One of the city's most famous pizzerias, this is packed night after night. Compared to many other pizzerias, it's large and spacious but rather dark and lugubrious. The second Lombardi branch is in the I Vergini district. ✉ *Via Benedetto Croce 59,* ☎ *081/552–0780. AE, V. Closed Sun. and last 2 wks in Aug.;* ✉ *Via Foria 12,* ☎ *081/456220. AE, DC, MC, V. Closed Mon.*

$$ ✕ **Porta Venosa.** Affable owner Bruno Esposito has brought his years of experience in restaurants to fruition in one of Naples' most pleasant new establishments. The decor is resolutely contemporary and discreetly hip; The ever-changing menu features fresh variations on Mediterranean specialties (chicken with garlic and citrus fruit, Portuguese-style fish soup, vegetarian pasta alla bolognese) with enough rotating standards to keep everyone happy (grilled fish and meats, fried anchovies, etc.) as well as creative selections for vegetarians. On Thursday evenings, the chef concocts theme menus presenting a different foreign cuisine (Mexican, Brazilian, North African, etc.) for those of you who just can't take any more pasta. ✉ *Largo San Giovanni Maggiore 15,* ☎ *081/552–6127. AE, MC, V. Closed Sun.*

$–$$ ✕ **Cibo.** Young, noisy, and hip, this new restaurant/bar is a friendly mixing spot at night and a great place for a take-out pizza or sandwich at lunch while you're discovering Spaccanapoli. They have a wide and innovative selection of pizzas and a stimulating selection of sandwiches for vegetarians who are tired of tomato and mozzarella. ⊠ *Piazza del Gesù Nuovo 26,* ☎ *081/551–8427. No credit cards. Closed Sat.*

$ ✕ **Da Corrado.** In this smoky, boisterous hall near the Orto Botanico Gardens, you can delight yourself by discovering just how good inexpensive Neapolitan food can be. All the usual suspects on the menu are here, plus a revolving selection of traditional but forgotten specialties, such as rabbit cacciatore style or pasta with sardines. ⊠ *Via Foria 122,* ☎ *081/553–4655. No credit cards.*

$ ✕ **Da Michele.** You have to love a place that has, for more than 130
★ years, offered only two types of pizza—with or without cheese—and a small selection of drinks, and still manages to line them up. The prices have something to do with it, but the pizza itself suffers no rivals, and even those waiting in line are good humored, as the boisterous, joyous atmosphere wafts out with the smell of yeast and wood smoke into the street. ⊠ *Via C. Sersale 1/3,* ☎ *081/553–9204. No credit cards. Closed Sun. and last 2 wks in Aug.*

$ ✕ **La Cantina di Via Sapienza.** There's a strong whiff of 1920s Paris intelligentsia in this hangout of students and young professionals, although the garb is now in Technicolor shades and every dish is spiced up with garlic. Busy and not big enough (expect to share a table—and if they're not shy, why should you be?), but the prices can't be beat, and the daily selection of a good dozen vegetable side plates merits a detour on its own, even if you're not a vegetarian. ⊠ *Via Sapienza 40,* ☎ *081/459078. No credit cards. Closed Sun.*

$ ✕ **Sorbillo.** The locals still wait in line for their turn to sit down and devour a basic Neapolitan pizza cooked to perfection—after all, the third generation of pizza-makers runs this place. Try the unique Pizza al pesto. Don't expect tablecloths. ⊠ *Via dei Tribunali 32,* ☎ *081/446643. No credit cards. Closed Sun.*

$ ✕ **Trianon.** Across the street from its arch rival Da Michele, this is a classic pizzeria with a simple yet upscale Art Nouveau ambience expressed in soothing tile and marble. The classics (Margherita, marinara), of course, are done in an exemplary manner, but you can also feast on pizza with sausage and broccoli greens, while the signature pizza Trianon comes with eight different toppings. ⊠ *Via P. Coletta 46,* ☎ *081/553–9526. No credit cards. Closed Sun. lunch.*

Santa Lucia and Chiaia

The obvious spot for both chic and touristy fish restaurants, the area also has a number of reasonable alternatives, some with great views as well.

$$$–$$$$ ✕ **Caruso.** When you get the urge to dress up, head to the panoramic rooftop restaurant of the Hotel Vesuvio—a very chic locale that is not as expensive as you might think. The food wisely declines to compete with the view of the bay but instead accompanies it suavely. Seafood predominates, from the marinated *frutti di mare* and fish-stuffed ravioli to the classic grilled sea bass, but if you're tired of shrimp and such, try the delicate lemon risotto or the *bucatini all Caruso*—tubular spaghetti with fresh tomatoes, sweet peppers, and sautéed zucchini. ⊠ *Hotel Vesuvio, Via Partenope 45,* ☎ *081/764–0044. AE, DC, MC, V.*

$$$–$$$$ ✕ **La Cantinella.** A cool, curvy decor with bamboo armchairs and wrought-iron lamps, La Cantinella is a well-known address for sophisticated seafood dishes and a relaxed but luxurious atmosphere. A wide selection of appetizers, with all the Neapolitan specialties, including a very well-done insalata di frutti di mare and a house appetizer with salmon in a zucchini crust on an eggplant ragout, leads into rigatoni with swordfish, onions, capers, and cherry tomatoes or pasta with tiny shrimp, clams, and green pepper. The abundant scampi *al gratin* are justly famous, but this is also a good place to try the less expensive

John Dory in *aqua pazza*. There is an extensive, reasonable, and well-organized wine list. ✉ *Via Cuma 42*, ☎ *081/764–8684. AE, DC, MC, V. Closed Sun.*

$$$ ✕ **Casanova Grill.** Soft lights and a trendy art-deco look set the tone at Hotel Excelsior's restaurant. The seasonal specialties and antipasti arranged on the buffet will whet your appetite for such traditional Neapolitan dishes as the simple spaghetti al pomodoro and the classic *carne* (meat) alla pizzaiola. ✉ *Hotel Excelsior, Via Partenope 48*, ☎ *081/7640111. AE, DC, MC, V.*

$$–$$$ ✕ **La Bersagliera.** On the port at Santa Lucia, in the shadow of the looming medieval Castel dell'Ovo, this spot is touristy but fun, with an irresistible combination of spaghetti and mandolins. Dalí and De Chirico, Sophia and Marcello all came here in the grand old days to enjoy uncomplicated timeworn classics, such as spaghetti with mixed seafood and eggplant *alla* parmigiana. But as any Neapolitan will tell you, simple grilled fish always tastes better when you season it with sea air. ✉ *Borgo Marinaro 10*, ☎ *081/764–6016. AE, DC, MC, V. Closed Sun. and 2 wks in Aug.*

$$ ✕ **'A Taverna é Zi Carmela.** Not far from the Villa Comunale gardens, this is a reasonable, family-run alternative in the pricey Santa Lucia area. Don't pay attention to the haphazard decor; the pizza is excellent, from the ubiquitous basics to such original specialties as the *incazzata*, a calzone stuffed with spicy pasta *all'arrabbiata* (for those who can't decide if they want pizza or pasta). If you do want pasta, try the hearty gnocchi with beans, or the superb house spaghetti with fresh tomato and a perfectly-cooked medley of fresh seafood. ✉ *Via Nicolò Tommaseo 11/12*, ☎ *081/764–3581. AE, DC.*

$$ ✕ **I Re di Napoli.** With its inviting blue-and-green custom-tile interior and tables set along the seafront drive, this chic pizzeria is an essential hangout for Naples's gilded youth and really gets going toward midnight on weekends. The various stuffed pizzas named after kings are classics with a modern twist: try the *Boccone di Re Ferdinando*, filled with *speck* (lean cured pork), *provola* cheese, and artichokes. ✉ *Via Partenope 29/30*, ☎ *081/764–7775. AE, DC, V.*

$ ✕ **Marino.** This famous pizzeria offers up its delights in a cool white-and-blue room. Try the house specialty, the Anastasia, with cherry tomatoes and lots of premium mozzarella. ✉ *Via Santa Lucia 11/81/20*, ☎ *081/764–0280. AE, V. Closed Mon. and Aug.*

Mergellina and Posillipo

These bayside suburbs feature some of the most popular restaurants in Naples.

$$$$ ✕ **La Sacrestia.** Naples' most famous restaurant was founded in 1972
★   by Arnaldo Ponsiglione, a passionate scholar of historical Neapolitan recipes; his son Marco continues this tradition while amplifying it with contemporary improvisations. This "temple of Neapolitan gastronomy" is appropriately perched on the heights above Mergellina in a superb location with a terrace. For starters try the risotto with baby squid or the pasta with shrimp, artichokes and olives, or, if you're feeling regal, the *bucatini alla Principe di Napoli*, pasta noodles ennobled by an abundance of un-Neapolitan truffles. Wonderful grilled fish and fritto misto follow, as well as a changing selection of innovative seafood dishes. ✉ *Via Orazio 116*, ☎ *081/664186. AE, DC, MC, V. Closed Aug. No dinner Sun., no lunch Mon.*

$$$ ✕ **La Cantina di Triunfo.** Founded by Carmine Triunfo in 1890 as a wine shop with food, this warm and inviting establishment, run by his grandson (also named Carmine) still features the original marble counter behind the wooden tables. The specialty here is well-prepared *cucina povera* ("poor peoples' food"), from the antipasta of hot pep-

pers, salami, and cheese to the famous *vermicelli alle vongole fujute* (pasta with "escaped" clams, flavored with a dose of seawater) and the "meatballs" made of bread, but more aristocratic specialties take their place on the menu as well: sartù—the famous rice-based dish— or the fabulous shrimp au gratin in lemon leaves. The wine selection is appropriately vast, so you'll be sure to find happiness. ⊠ *Riviera di Chiaia 64,* ☎ *081/668101. DC, V. Closed for lunch, Sun., and Aug.*

$$$ ★ ✕ **'A Fenestella.** One of the most beloved of Neapolitan restaurants, this is picturesquely perched over a beach in Posillipo near the end of a long winding side road (taxi is the preferred mode of transportation). In the 19th century, a legend had grown up surrounding this house's seaside window, or fenestella—any Juliet would promise herself simply by showing herself in the window to the Romeo sailing in the boat below, or so the story, and famous Neapolitan folk song that was inspired by it, goes. Today, the restaurant is blatantly traditional with a comfortable decor and the usual suspects on the menu (for stylish food and people, head just across the road to Da Cicchiotto). Still, sitting at a window table overlooking the sea here remains a quintessential Neapolitan memory for many old-timers. ⊠ *Calata del Ponticella a Marechiaro 23,* ☎ *081/769–0020. AE, DC, V. Closed Wed.; Sun. in summer.*

$$-$$$ ★ ✕ **Da Cicciotto.** Want to dine among Naples' rich and fashionable? Most of them prefer to dine at the city's *circoli,* or private clubs, and don't patronize restaurants—but there's a fair chance you'll find a Neapolitan count or a world-famous decorator enjoying this jewel, one of Naples' best-kept secrets. With a tiny stone terrace overlooking a pleasant anchorage (and the famous Fenestrella restaurant), centered around an antique column, and with seats and canopy exquisitely upholstered in blue-and-white matching-but-mixing fabrics, this is the dreamy setting for *cucina vera*—real Neapolitan food. To appreciate that outdoor setting, come here for lunch, not dinner. If you're a regular, you don't even bother with a menu but just start digging into the sublime antipasti and go with the owner's suggestions. ⊠ *Calata del Ponticella a Marechiaro 32,* ☎ *081/575-1165. AE, DC, MC, V. Closed Wed.*

Caffès and Coffee

Naples is ground zero for coffee lovers, and a snappy, definitive antidote to the hysterical pretensions of Seattle. Espresso was invented here and is still considered by the Neapolitans to be an essential and priceless part of their cultural patrimony (the word *espresso,* by the way, should probably be understood here in its meaning "pressed out," rather than the more common interpretation of "quick"). For many cognoscenti, Naples has the best coffee in the world. Almost any bar you walk into, no matter how dingy or how close to the train station, is likely to serve up an espresso that would make any Malibu hot spot wilt in envy. Even Italian bars do not specialize in alcoholic beverages per se and are generally tied to, as English pubs once were with brewers, a coffee roaster/distributor. The sponsoring brand is indicated with a sign on the outside, so you can choose your bar by looking for the sign of your favorite brand. Brands tend to be highly regional; the classic Naples brand is Kimbo. Monaldo and Toraldo are also safe bets; the Caffè Gambrinus serves the former. Some small, family-run caffès roast their own.

But just what makes Neapolitan coffee so good? Superior blends—it's hard to get an espresso in Naples that isn't 100% arabica—the excellent quality of spring or well water used, and the great care taken in the roasting (most "Italian-roast" coffee in the United States simply tastes burned). And let's not forget that the local masters at the espresso machines tend to use more coffee per serving and pack it in tighter to build up pressure under the powerful jolt of steam, resulting in a concentrated squirt of liquid with the consistency of motor oil lurking under an seductive mousse topping—nirvana for coffee lovers.

You won't find any double low-fat mochas with extra vanilla here; in Naples you take your coffee like a grown-up. Individuals do have a choice of certain permitted variations—*corretto*, with a shot of grappa or the local moonshine thrown in; *al vetro*, in a glass; *macchiato*, "stained" with a burst of steamed milk; and, of course, cappuccino. On the whole, coffee is a Neapolitan sacred ritual with precise rules. Cappuccino, for instance, is essentially a breakfast beverage, accepted in the afternoon with a pastry but looked strangely at after a meal (they claim it's bad for the liver). Many Italians like to order a glass of water (*bicchiere d'acqua*) with their coffee as a chaser. As for flavored coffees, Neapolitans, like all Italians, will stubbornly and instinctively believe that you only add flavorings to coffee to hide imperfections in the original grind. Coffee is perhaps the one feature of life in which Neapolitans don't gild the lily. Why fix what works?

For a true Neapolitan coffee, go to **Scaturchio** (✉ Piazza San Domenico Maggiore 19, ☎ 081/551–6944), which constitutes a complete and essential Neapolitan experience in itself (☞ Pastry Shops and Pasticcerie, *below*). This is a stand-up affair, as is the small **Caffè del Professore** (✉ Piazza Trieste e Trento 46, ☎ 081/403041), which offers a superb espresso, as well as a house specialty, the *espresso Napolitano,* which has a third more coffee in the dose and is sweetened with a coffee syrup (it's quite sweet; you can ask for it *amaro*—bitter—and add your own sugar). If you want to sit down and milk the experience, the most famous coffeehouse in town is the **Caffè Gambrinus** (✉ Via Chiaia 1/2, ☎ 081/417582), catty-corner to the Palazzo Reale across the Piazza Trieste e Trento. Founded in 1850, this 19th-century jewel, which functioned as a brilliant intellectual salon in its heyday, has unfortunately fallen into a Sunset Boulevard–type place, relying on remembrance of past glamour, at the mercy of the Japanese tourists and their pitiless cameras, and with often indifferent service. **La Caffeteria** (✉ Piazza dei Martiri 30, ☎ 081/764–4243) is a classic address in the chic Chiaia district, and and it has a second space in Vomero (✉ Piazza Vanvitelli 10/B, ☎ 081/558–2592). Both addresses sell their famous coffee-flavored chocolates in the form of tiny coffeepots. The **Gran Bar Riviera** (✉ Riviera di Chiaia 181–183, ☎ 081/665026) also has good profiteroles and fresh tiramisu. If you're in Santa Lucia, **Megaride** (✉ Via Borgo Marinaro 1, ☎ 081/764–5300), on the port under the shadow of the Castel dell'Ovo, provides a romantic outdoor setting for a coffee or aperitif. Piazza Bellini, in the Spaccanapoli area, contains a gaggle of good and hip cafés, and almost any of the pastry shops mentioned below will have an excellent brew.

Pastry and Gelati Shops

On the whole, Neapolitan pastry tends to suffer from the excesses that mar most southern Italian desserts: Falstaffian enthusiasm rather than precision in technique, ricotta clogging up everything, embarrassingly sentimental glops of glaze, and overeffusive dousings of perfumed syrups: one local specialty, the Babà al rhum, often succumbs to this latter vice. But the Neapolitan tradition of pastry is an old and venerable one, and the most classic Neapolitan invention in matters of *pasticceria* (pastry making), the *sfogliatella*, is a true Baroque masterpiece, with puff pastry cut on a bias and wrapped around a nugget of cinnamon-sugar ricotta to form a simple but intricate shell. These are best eaten hot, and they are easy to find in Naples this way: the classic address is **Pintauro** (⊠ Via Toledo 275, ☎ 081/317339), at the entrance to the Galleria Umberto I. If you need a hot-out-of-the-oven morsel as soon as you get off the train, **Attanasio** (⊠ Vico Ferrovia 2, ☎ 081/285675), directly off Piazza Garibaldi, is also justifiably famous. Better hotels often serve them warm with breakfast. *Torta caprese,* a simple, rich chocolate cake with ground almonds, is another Neapolitan favorite, as are eclairs of all flavors and forms.

Scaturchio (⊠ Piazza San Domenico Maggiore 19, ☎ 081/551–6944), closed Tuesday, is the essential Neapolitan pastry shop. Although the coffee is top of the line and the ice cream and pastries quite good—including the specialty, the *ministeriale,* a pert chocolate cake whipped with rum-cream filling—it's the atmosphere that counts here. In the heart of Spaccanapoli, it's where nuns, punks, businessmen, and housewives commune on the good things they all have in common. Up in Vomero, **Daniele** (⊠ Via Scarlatti 104, ☎ 081/578–0555) features refined renditions of traditional specialties and a stellar orange mousse. The largest number of good pastry shops are in the upscale Chiaia neighborhood. **Caflisch** (⊠ Via Chiaia 143, ☎ 081/404588) has an elegant wood-paneled salon atmosphere and famous *cassette* and *semifreddi* (iced cakes and mousses. **Moccia** (⊠ Via San Pasquale a Chiaia 21, ☎ 081/411348) is often said to be the finest pasticceria in the city, and they have great babas and an out-of-this-world pound cake injected with just the right dose of intense lemon curd. But connoisseurs will say the most refined and tasty pastry in town can be found at **Gran Caffè Cimmino** (⊠ Via G. Filangieri 12/13, ☎ 081/418303). Stop here on your afternoon shopping marathon (or late at night) for the wonderful coffee accompanied by crisp, light cannoli, airy lemon eclairs, *choux* paste in the form of a mushroom laced with chocolate whipped cream, and delightful wild strawberry tartlets, precise and Lolita-innocent, with only a dew spray of ruby glaze as a discreet and knowing enticement to perdition.

All these addresses will have exemplary ice cream as well, but you may prefer a more informal setting. **Scimmia** (⊠ Piazza Carita 4), in the center of town, scoops out a luscious variety of flavors, while young Neapolitans often go down to Mergellina to have a cone at one of the outdoor chalets in the garden along the port: **Chalet Ciro** (⊠ Via F. Carracciolo, 1 block west of Mergellina hydrofoil pier, ☎ 081/669928) is the best; they also whip up astonishing milk shakes and smoothies using a wide selection of fruit that looks as if it grew in fruit paradise. A number of ambulant vendors around town sell absolutely first-rate lemon ice, or granita, for derisory prices; this can be a godsend in summer.

Chocolate lovers will be relieved to know that **Gay Odin** (⊠ Via Toledo 291, ☎ 081/421867), Naples's most famous *cioccolateria,* has seven stores distributed around town, including, handily, along the shopping street Via Chiaia—all recognizable by their inviting dark-wood Art Nouveau decor; try the signature chocolate forest cake (*foresta*) or their unusual "naked" chocolates (*nudi*), a suave mixture of chestnuts and walnuts. A small alleyway leading off the side of the Gesù Nuovo toward Via Toledo hides a little-known jewel that is worth the detour: **Gallucci** (⊠ Via Cisterna dell'Olio 6, ☎ 081/551–3148), founded in 1890, specializes in fruit-filled chocolates (the cherry and grape are memorable) and also produces a delightfully original local cult item, chestnuts filled with marsala.

Food Shopping

The makings of delicious sandwiches can be had at any neighborhood *salumerie,* which specialize in cured meats and cheese. You'll find the cheapest and freshest fruits and vegetables in the open-air markets; look up one of the large outdoor markets in the Shopping section, *below.* Cubbyhole mom-and-pop groceries offer basic food stuff and sometimes produce. For exotic (including American) ingredients, **Codrington** (✉ Via Chiaia 94, ☎ 081/418257), founded in 1886, is the only international specialty-foods store in town. For a peanut butter fix, you might try the area around any NATO base, or the American market down Via Forcella, between the duomo and Corso Umberto I.

LODGING

Since Naples is not known for peace and quiet, it's good news that it features a bevy of hotels that deliver exactly that—most accommodations are cool and tranquil sanctums, with the emphasis on cool (as one of Europe's hottest and busiest cities, its hotels feature some of the strongest air-conditioning around). Unfortunately, rare is the hotel that fills every measure on our yardstick—character, national aura, centrality to interesting locations. Yet there are grand hotels that still conjure up the days of steamship travel and whose window views allow you to indulge in reveries of Vesuvius, several options that set out to be ideal business hotels (with faxes, copiers, and modems at the ready), and even a pensione that occupies the former palace of the Princes di Sangro. When booking, inquire if there is an additional fee for air-conditioning, parking facilities, and breakfast.

CATEGORY	COST*
$$$$	over 350,000 lire
$$$	200,000–350,000 lire
$$	100,000–200,000 lire
$	under 100,000 lire

All prices are for a double room, excluding tax and service.

Lungomare and Santa Lucia

This prominent stretch of seacoast, with an unsurpassed view of the Bay of Naples, naturally attracts the greatest concentration of luxury hotels in the city, although more reasonable lodging is available on the side streets.

$$$$ ▦ **Excelsior.** A swarm of maharajahs, emperors, and Hollywood legends has stayed at this hotel, which has maintained the grand tradition since 1909. The exterior—with the hotel's name magnificently picked out in Pompeiian red—is awash in elegant detail, while the interior is a symphony of soaring columns, gilded French doors, and Venetian chandeliers. Guest suites features the best views of Vesuvius in Naples. Today the hotel caters to corporate chiefs, its ballrooms host company meetings, the breakfast is delicious, but there's not a maharajah or Hollywood legend in sight. ✉ *Via Partenope 48, 80121,* ☎ *081/764–0111,* FAX *081/764–9743. 136 rooms with bath. Restaurant, bar, air-conditioning, meeting rooms, parking. AE, DC, V.*

$$$$ ✕▦ **Vesuvio.** Caruso died here, Queen Sophia of Sweden stayed here (just after a cholera epidemic, as a gesture of good will), Oscar Wilde and his lover Lord Alfred Douglas escaped here—but you'd never know that this is the oldest of Naples's great seafront hotels from its exterior, now defaced with one of the ugliest modern facades in existence. Once you get past the sickly gray and Miami Beach–pink, the interior soothes your eye with a vaguely art deco decor and a spectacular view of Vesuvius and the bay, which diners can drink in from the famous Caruso rooftop restaurant. Guest rooms are traditional modern with cove moldings, parquet floors, and gleaming bathrooms. ✉ *Via Partenope 45, 80121,* ☎ *081/764–0044,* FAX *081/764–4483. 165 rooms*

with bath. Restaurant, bar, air-conditioning, exercise room, meeting rooms, parking. AE, DC, V.

$$$–$$$$ ✕⊡ **Hotel Santa Lucia.** There may be luxury hotels in Naples as fetch-
★ ing as this one (the Grand Hotel Parker springs to mind), but none en-
joys this dreamy location: Directly opposite the Borgo Marinaro, the
tiny fishermen's marina on the bay. Open your window here to find
the port immortalized in the song "Santa Lucia," bobbing with hun-
dreds of boats, lined with charming seafood restaurants, and with a
backdrop of the medieval Castel dell'Ovo directly below your balcony.
Even if your room doesn't have this view, the hotel's luxurious, qui-
etly understated polish will win you over. In 1997 a renovation spruced
up the decor, now aglow with antiques, chandeliers, and full-length por-
traits of Neapolitan aristocrats. The brocaded and very comfortable
guest rooms are traditional in style, with bathrooms paved in terra-
cotta and often equipped with whirlpool bath. Just off the lobby, the
restaurant Megaris is one of the best hotel restaurants in town. ⊠ *Via
Partenope 46, 80121,* ☏ *081/764–0666,* 𝔽𝔸𝕏 *081/764–8580. 107 rooms
with bath. Restaurant, bar, air-conditioning, meeting rooms. AE, DC,
MC, V.*

$$$ ⊡ **Miramare.** Like a relic of a more gracious age, this turn-of-the-cen-
tury town house in the Liberty (or Art Nouveau) style sits above the
frantic traffic of Via Nazario Sauro like a dowager at a disco party.
Once the American consulate, it still offers the air of a private home,
an air much fostered by manager Enzo Rosalino. He often presides over
guests in the main parlor, seeing to their comfort with a courteous attention to detail, as shown by the electric teapots and the selection of
videocassettes available in the rooms. Guest rooms, with an airy Deco
feel to them, are handsome, quiet, and exquisitely air-conditioned. The
hotel looks directly onto the bay (and that traffic) and you can enjoy
a breakfast atop the roof garden. A 10-minute walk takes you to the
Piazza del Plebiscito and the center of Naples. ⊠ *Via N. Sauro 24, 80132,*
☏ *081/764–7589,* 𝔽𝔸𝕏 *081/764–0775. 31 rooms with bath. Air-conditioning. AE, DC, MC, V.*

$$ ⊡ **Parteno.** Owner Adele Gentile has installed an exclusive and elegant
bed-and-breakfast right on the seafront near the Villa Comunale. The
spacious and serene rooms are tastefully decorated with period etch-
ings and gouache views of Naples, and all possess a small balcony; the
front room looks over the bay. ⊠ *Via Partenope 1, 80121,* ☏ 𝔽𝔸𝕏 *081/
245–2095. 6 rooms with bath. Air-conditioning. AE, DC, MC, V.*

Piazza Garibaldi and Environs

This is by no means the nicest or most interesting part of town to stay
in, but it's convenient to the train station, and there's almost always
a room somewhere.

$$$ ⊡ **Mexico.** A warm and inviting Art Deco lobby with multicolor in-
laid marble floors provides an apt welcome to this hotel. Upstairs, guest
rooms are cozy and air-conditioned, with wooden floors and ice-green
fabric-covered walls. Clean and comfortable, the Mexico also features
friendly personnel. ⊠ *Via C. Rosaroli 13/15, 80139,* ☏ *081/266330,*
𝔽𝔸𝕏 *081/266554. 40 rooms with bath. Bar, air-conditioning, parking.
AE, MC, V.*

$$$ ⊡ **Suite Esedra.** Hidden on a tiny piazza off frantic Corso Umberto,
this is a hotel that's convenient to transportation as well as to the ro-
mantic neighborhood of Spaccanapoli. The hotel's decor, based on an
astrological theme, takes itself lightly enough to work. Each guest
room expresses a different planet or sign of the zodiac, all in the
coolest faux-Memphis style, with plenty of sleek woods and Philippe
Starck–esque touches. However, the hotel is in a densely packed dis-
trict (reach out your window and you can practically touch the build-

ing across the way), so the building has sliver dimensions with guest rooms on the petit side, except for two suites which have their own private terrace with whirlpool. Still, the lobby, library, and dining room are all suavely decorated. ⊠ *Via A. Cantani 12, 80133,* ☎ FAX *081/553–7087. 15 rooms with bath. Bar, air-conditioning, exercise room. AE, MC, V.*

$$$ ⊞ **Terminus.** Immediately to your left as you come out of the train station onto hectic Piazza Garibaldi, this hotel is a cool pastel oasis of calm—sleek, clean, and stylish, with up-to-date, comfortable rooms and a good breakfast buffet. A real plus is the excellent staff. ⊠ *Piazza Garibaldi 91, 80142,* ☎ *081/779–3111,* FAX *081/206689. 145 rooms with bath. Restaurant, bar, air-conditioning, exercise room. AE, DC, MC, V.*

$$ ⊞ **San Pietro.** Situated in the middle of the action, off the Piazza Mancini market on the west side of Piazza Garibaldi, the San Pietro is a surprisingly calm family-run hotel. Guest rooms are spare and luminous, usually dominated by a large comfortable bed. All in all, this is a reasonably priced and pleasantly clean option. ⊠ *Via San Pietro ad Aram 18, 80142,* ☎ *081/553–5914. 50 rooms, 18 with bath. Bar. AE, MC, V.*

$ ⊞ **Hotel Eden.** Just off Piazza Garibaldi to the right as you exit the station, this is the best inexpensive lodging near the station. Brothers Nicòla and Enzo furnish friendly advice and functional rooms. No breakfast is provided. ⊠ *Corso Novara 9, 80142,* ☎ *081/285344,* FAX *081/ 285690. 44 rooms with bath.*

$ ⊞ **Hotel Ginevra.** This inexpensive, family-run pensione is around the corner from the Eden, but up two flights of stairs (no elevator). Guest rooms are basic but clean and reliable. ⊠ *Via Genova 116, 80142,* ☎ *081/554–1757,* FAX *081/283210. 13 rooms, 6 with bath. AE, MC, V.*

$ ⊞ **Pensione Mancini.** Around the corner from the San Pietro, this new pensione is a safe and comfortable outpost in the middle of the daily carnival of Neapolitan street life. ⊠ *Via Mancini 33, 80142,* ☎ *081/ 553–6731. 6 rooms, 3 with bath. Bar. No credit cards.*

Spaccanapoli and Piazza Municipio
Spaccanapoli is a good choice if you're traveling on a budget and want to enjoy the flavor of Naples's most historic quarter; the area around Piazza Municipio, although close by, sports a collection of upscale large-capacity business hotels.

$$$$ ⊞ **Grand Hotel Oriente.** This is an excellent businessperson's hotel with all the conveniences and in a great location. After a long, hard day it's a boon to return here and find comfortable, soundproof guest rooms. ⊠ *Via Diaz 44, 80134,* ☎ *081/551–2133,* FAX *081/551–4915. 132 rooms with bath. Restaurant, bar, air-conditioning. AE, DC, V.*

$$$ ⊞ **Executive.** Near Santa Maria la Nuova, this restored convent still ★   grants a privileged solace from the busy world. The airy, well-insulated rooms come complete with a phone in the bathroom. The bar area is an exquisitely decorated nook. ⊠ *Via del Carriglio 10, 80134,* ☎ FAX *081/552–0611. 19 rooms with bath. Bar, air-conditioning, sauna, exercise room. AE, DC, MC, V.*

$$$ ⊞ **Mediterraneo.** A large, modern, efficient business hotel, this place is within walking distance of both the Teatro San Carlo and Spaccanapoli. Reasonable and personable for its category, it also features a beautiful roof garden. ⊠ *Via Nuova Ponte di Tappia 25, 80133,* ☎ *081/ 551240,* FAX *081/552–5868. 252 rooms with bath. Restaurant, bar, air-conditioning. DC, MC, V.*

$$$ ⊞ **Mercure Napoli Angioino.** Right off Piazza Municipio and close to the Teatro San Carlo, this popular place has a sober yet luminous lobby and quiet, tastefully appointed guest rooms, some of which are reserved

for nonsmokers. This is a good choice if you are taking a boat from the nearby Mole Beverello. The restaurant is set in the historic Villa Virgilliana. ⊠ *Via De Pretis 123, 80133,* ☎ *081/552–9500,* 𝖥𝖠𝖷 *081/552–9509. 85 rooms with bath. Restaurant, air-conditioning, meeting rooms. AE, DC, V.*

$$ **Albergo Sansevero.** This is a superbly located option—as handy to the
★ main thoroughfare of Via Toledo as it is to the historic enchantments of Spaccanapoli. Ten blocks away from its sister establishment, the Soggiorno Sansevero (☞ *below*), this albergo, or small hotel, is just off cafè-set Piazza Bellini, the prettiest of the Spacca's squares, and its address is one of the city's great 19th-century boulevards. Rooms are pricier than at the Soggiorno, but all have private baths, and breakfast is served to guests. ⊠ *Via S. Maria di Constantinopoli 101, 80131,* ☎ *081/210907,* 𝖥𝖠𝖷 *081/211698. 11 rooms with bath. AE, MC, V.*

$–$$ 🏠 **Collegio Europeo.** Right around the corner from Piazza San Domenico Maggiore, this is an excellent choice if you are looking for a clean firm bed at budget prices in the middle of the university quarter. You need to take 200-lire coins for the elevator, however (or walk four flights of stairs). The international student atmosphere extends to dorm rooms available downstairs. No breakfast is offered, but you're right around the corner from Scaturchio. ⊠ *Via Mezzocannone 109/c, 80131 (look for the Cinema Astra),* ☎ 𝖥𝖠𝖷 *081/551–7254. 17 rooms, 7 with bath. AE, MC, V.*

$ 🏠 **Soggiorno Sansevero.** If you want to soak in the atmosphere of old
★ Naples, this is ground zero. Within the very heart of Spaccanapoli, this pensione occupies a floor in the former palace of the princes di Sangro di San Severo, who built the famous family chapel directly behind this building. Although the palazzo overlooks the opera-set Piazza San Domenico, the tiny Soggiorno is on the palazzo's quiet inner courtyard. Rooms are simply furnished—linoleum floors, modern beds, great-grandmama's boudoir bureau—and may even come with ghosts: Carlo Gesualdo, inventor of the madrigal song, murdered his wife and her lover on the palace's staircase October 16, 1590. Breakfast is not included, but Scaturchio is right outside across the piazza. The staff is very friendly and helpful. ⊠ *Piazza San Domenico 9 (Palazzo Sansevero), 80131,* ☎ *081/555–5949,* 𝖥𝖠𝖷 *081/211698. 16 rooms, 12 with bath. No credit cards.*

Chiaia–Vomero–Posillipo
Chiaia is the ritziest residential neighborhood of Naples, studded with 19th-century mansions and an elegant shopping district bordering the Villa Comunale gardens by the water. Above Chiaia rises the Vomero Hill, offering great vistas of the bay. The bayside atmosphere continues at Mergellina, a transportation hub set at the far western end of the Riviera di Chiaia, and beyond at the suburban coastal district of Posillipo.

$$$$ ✕🏠 **Parker's.** Opened in 1870, this grand hotel continues to serve up
★ a supremely elegant dose of old-style atmosphere and now welcomes a good number of visiting V.I.P.s, ranging from rock stars to Boris Yeltsin. The Russian leader probably enjoyed the hotel decor, which is a homage to the Neoclassical style, brought to Naples by Napoléon and his general Joachim Murat: gilt-trimmed Empire bureaux, 19th-century paintings, shimmering chandeliers, fluted pilasters, and ornate ceilings all create a splendid environment, now newly aglitter thanks to a renovation in 1997. Set midway up the Vomero Hill (and convenient to funicular lines), the hotel's perch offers great views of the bay and distant Capri, but if your room doesn't have one of these breathtaking vistas, drink it all in from the excellent rooftop-garden restaurant. Off the lobby is the soigné bar, a favored spot for refined relaxation. ⊠ *Corso Vit-*

torio Emanuele 135, 80121, ☎ 081/761–2474, 🖹 081/663527. *83 rooms with bath. Restaurant, bar, air-conditioning, meeting rooms, parking. AE, DC, MC, V.*

$$$ ⊞ **Britannique.** Adjacent to Grand Hotel Parker's, this reserved and traditional hotel above Piazza Amedeo has light, well-appointed rooms with even better views across the bay and city, thanks to the small private garden across the street reserved for guests for prevents any obstruction. Guest rooms are very comfortably furnished. ⊠ *Corso Vittorio Emanuele 133, 80121, ☎ 081/761–4145, 🖹 081/660457. 86 rooms with bath. Restaurant, bar, air-conditioning, meeting rooms, parking. AE, DC, V.*

$$$ ⊞ **Paradiso.** This impressive hotel on the hillside of Posillipo is famous for the views of the Bay of Naples from its rooms, roof-garden restaurant, and garden terrace over the Bay of Naples. From your own flower-bedecked balcony you can also take in the immediate neighborhood, less enchantingly filled with apartment buildings. While located at the western edge of the city, the nearby funicular takes you efficiently to the harbor port and transportation hub of Mergellina, at the end of the Riviera di Chiaia. ⊠ *Via Catullo 11, 80122, ☎ 081/761–4161, 🖹 081/761–3449. 74 rooms with bath. Restaurant, bar, air-conditioning, parking. AE, DC, MC, V.*

$$$ ⊞ **Splendide.** Next to the top of the Mergellina funicular, facing the Gulf of Aeneas, this hotel is a pleasant alternative for panoramic views. ⊠ *Via A. Manzoni 96, 80123, ☎ 081/714–1955, 🖹 081/714–6431. 50 rooms with bath. Bar, air-conditioning. AE, DC, MC, V.*

$$$ ⊞ **Villa Capodimonte.** Far from the hurly-burly of the city, set in a park near the majestic Museo di Capodimonte, this recently opened "villa" enhances gracious Neapolitan hospitality with thoroughly modern comfort. The spacious rooms have panoramic views over the city, and there is a tennis court for those who can't do without. ⊠ *Via Moiarello 66, 80131, ☎ 081/459000, 🖹 081/299344. 64 rooms with bath. Restaurant, air-conditioning. AE, DC, V.*

$$ ⊞ **Ausonia.** The spic-and-span rooms of this hotel are decorated in a nautical motif and it retains a homey feel. In the courtyard of a building on the waterfront at Mergellina, this is quite handy if you are taking a boat from the Mergellina pier. ⊠ *Via Carracciolo 11, 80122, ☎ 081/682278, 🖹 081/664536. 20 rooms with bath. AE, MC, V.*

$$ ⊞ **Delle Terme.** In the same complex as the Agnano Spa in the Campo Flegrei, this recently remodeled hotel in a park is an ideal spot if you are travelling by car (it's easy to get to, and you don't have to drive into Naples) and want a relaxing and convenient base for a few days. Access is provided to Naples via a frequent hotel shuttle which takes you to the Metro stop at Campo Flegrei. The spa gives discounts on their various services to hotel guests. ⊠ *Via Agnano Astroni 24, 80125, ☎ 081/570–1733, 🖹 081/762–6441. 62 rooms with bath. Restaurant, bar, air-conditioning, parking. AE, DC, MC, V.*

$$ ⊞ **Le Fontane al Mare.** Come here for semi-luxury accommodations at a relatively low price. Most of the elegant rooms have balconies overlooking the sea (although only five rooms have private bath), and you're a short walk from the Villa Comunale, the pleasant park on the bay. ⊠ *Via Niccolà Tommaseo 14, 80125, ☎ 081/764–3811, 🖹 081/764–3470. 22 rooms, 5 with bath. AE, DC, MC, V.*

$$ ⊞ **Pinto Storey.** A fascinating old pensione, overflowing with warmth and charm, this is located on the third floor of an elegant late-19th century building off the chic Piazza Amedeo. Guest rooms are simple and airy. ⊠ *Via G. Martucci 72, 80125, ☎ 081/681260, 🖹 081/667536. 25 rooms with bath. Air-conditioning. AE, DC, MC, V.*

$$ ☎ **Ruggiero.** In the same building as the Pinto Storey, this bright, cheerful pensione has clean rooms at reasonable prices with convenient access to the Metropolitana, the funicular to Vomero, and the Villa Comunale gardens. ✉ *Via G. Martucci 72, 80125,* ☎ *081/681260,* FAX *081/667536. 28 rooms, 14 with bath. DC, MC, V.*

NIGHTLIFE AND THE ARTS

The Arts

By Frank
Gerard
Godlewski

A vast array of opera, music, dance, and film is offered in Naples. Schedules of events are published in daily newspapers, particularly *Il Mattino* and the excellent monthly periodical *Qui Napoli* (available in an English-language version and usually gratis at hotels and visitor centers). Information and ticket sales are provided by the following ticket agencies: **Box Office** (✉ Galleria Umberto I 15–16, ☎ 081/551–9188); **Concerteria** (✉ Via Schipa 21, ☎ 081/761–1221); **Botteghino** (✉ Via Pitloo 3, ☎ 081/556–4684); **MC Teatro e Musica** (✉ Via Giulio Palermo 124, ☎ 081/546–2264); **Napoli Frakcomoda** (✉ Via Duomo 33, ☎ 081/265161).

Concert Halls and Theaters

In addition to the world-famous Teatro San Carlo (☞ Opera and Classical Music, *below*), Naples has several other leading concert halls and theaters. Each theater generally plans its entire season—which usually runs October through May—in advance with a printed schedule. **Auditorium RAI-TV** (✉ Via Marconi, ☎ 081/725–1111) is a modern facility within the television studio complex at Fuorigrotta. The **Augusteo** (✉ Piazza Augusteo, ☎ 081/414243) is a large, centrally located theater off Via Toledo that usually presents commercial Italian theater and concerts. **Galleria Toledo** (✉ Via Montecalvario 36, ☎ 081/425824) attracts the hip set with avant-garde theater presentations. **Teatro Bellini** (✉ Via Conte di Ruvo, ☎ 081/549–9688) is a gilded Belle Epoque theater that presents plays and concerts of a more academic flavor. **Teatro Cilea** (✉ Vomero, ☎ 081/643705) is a modern facility on the grounds of the Domenico Martuscelli Institute for the Blind. **Teatro della Palme** (✉ Via Vetriera 12, ☎ 081/418134), a rather ugly postwar plywood auditorium, usually hosts concerts presented by the Associazione Alessandro Scarlatti. **Teatro Mercandante** (✉ Piazza Municipio, ☎ 081/551–3396) is a Belle Epoque theater that hosts the Corto-Circquito (Short Circuit) Video Festival from time to time. Taking the thousands of miles into consideration, the **Teatro Politeama** (✉ Via Monte di Dio a Pizzofalcone, ☎ 081/764–5016) could almost be considered another off-Broadway playhouse, considering its challenging bill of fare. For a satisfying Neapolitan "soul" experience, catch a local singer like Lina Sastri or Lara Sansone warbling at the **Teatro Sannazaro** (✉ Via Montecalvario 16, ☎ 081/551–3396); traditional Neapolitan plays by Edoardo di Filippo are also often presented here. Finally, the **Palapartenope** (✉ Via Barbagallo, ☎ 081/570–6806) is an enormous hangar at Fuorigrotta where most pop concerts are performed.

Film

Naples has many cinema and video stores and rental outlets. The city's love fest with the movies reaches its high point every year with the Napoli Cinefest Film Festival, usually presented every June at the **Cinema Modernissimo** multiplex (✉ Via Cisterna del Olio, ☎ 081/551–1247). Other cinemas in the city center include **Ambasciato** (✉ Via Crispi, ☎ 081/680266), **Arlecchino** (✉ Via Alardieri, ☎ 081/416731), **Delle Palme** (✉ Via Vetriera, ☎ 081/418124), and **Santa Lucia** (✉ Via Santa Lucia, ☎ 081/764–8837). Consult *Il Mattino* for further listings.

Opera and Classical Music

The historic **Teatro San Carlo** (✉ Via San Carlo, ☎ 081/797–2111; ☞ *Exploring Naples, above*) is the luxury liner of all the opera houses in southern Italy. Today the concert hall still gleams with its mid-19th-century gilded furnishings and thick red-velvet drapes. For the opera season (December through June), many seats are presold by subscription but there are usually some seats available if you go along to the box office some days before the performance (unless, say, Pavarotti is performing, when tickets might get sold out as soon as they are available). How far in advance can you book? This depends on the opera and time of year. For some opera performances tickets could only be bought five days before the performance, but at other times it might be weeks in advance. Unlike many leading opera companies in the United States, the San Carlo does not operate on a revolving repertory schedule: Each opera or ballet presentation is usually scheduled for a mini-run, generally in a 10-day period.

Prices vary due to both location and date. The front rows of the stalls, known as *poltronissime,* might be as much as 350,000 lire for a performance on the first night of an opera, while up in the sixth tier, the Balconata VI, you would pay a fifth of that price, or much less if you went on a later night. Prices are always highest at first nights with the best opera *dive,* then fall off as top performers are sometimes substituted after a few nights. If you get a box seat, keep in mind that there are as many as six people sharing a box, so it is worth getting there early to get a front seat. Some people tip the *maschere* (ushers) and this is especially appreciated if they have fixed you up with a better seat than the one you were allocated originally (maybe a season ticket holder didn't show up). Ballet and concert performances are up to 50% less expensive than opera presentations. One way of getting into the San Carlo for much less would be to go on a guided tour (Saturdays and Sundays only, 2 to 3:30 PM). At 5,000 lire a shot, you soak up some of its magnificence and it might be preferable to paying 50 times as much and sitting through five hours of the Ring cycle. For complete information, contact the box office (☎ 081/797–2331 or 081/797–2412) which is open Tuesday to Sunday, 10–1 PM and 4:30–6:30 PM.

The **Conservatorio San Pietro a Maiella** (✉ Via San Pietro a Maiella, ☎ 081/459255) is home to the **Associazione Alessandro Scarlatti** (✉ Piazza dei Martiri 58, ☎ 081/406011) and is one of Italy's most noted music conservatories. Naples features a full calendar of classical and chamber music concerts; check the newspaper listings and street posters for information about concerts frequently held in the historic churches of the city.

A classical music festival known as **International Music Weeks** takes place throughout May in Naples. Concerts are held at the Teatro San Carlo, the Teatro Mercadante, and in the Neoclassic Villa Pignatelli. For information contact the Teatro San Carlo box office (☞ *above*).

Nightlife

As soon as the sun goes down, nightlife ignites everywhere in Naples with more pubs and piano bars than you can shake a pizza at. There is something for everyone—from 19th-century-style *caffè-concerts* at the **Caffè Gambrinus** (✉ Via Chiaia 1/2, ☎ 081/417582) in Piazza Trieste e Trento until 1 AM to the cutting-edge hangouts favored by the crowd now called Tendenza by the Neapolitan press. In many of the cafés and discos of Mergellina, Piazza Vittoria, Piazza dei Martiri, Via Partenope, and the Borgo Marinaro, baby Sophia Lorens and Frank Sinatras swarm the streets and alleys, while a bohemian crowd lingers on in Piazza Bellini until 3 AM. Even at this late hour many streets and piazzas in the historic Spaccanapoli quarter are alive with youth. The chic and stylish postyuppie crowd sticks to Piazza dei Martiri, Via dei Mille, and Piazza Amedeo, frequenting old-guard watering holes. But unlike those places, many nightspots open and close with alarming frequency, so be sure to call ahead when planning a club tour of Naples.

Bars, Cafés, and Discos

Most disco clubs issue a 17,000-lire drink card at the door that must be returned when you leave, stamped to show you've consumed at least one drink. After the first or second drink, other drinks usually run less (about 8,000 lire). Discos host nights devoted to various themes and trends—techno/house, gay, retro-1970s—organized by talented Neapolitan art directors and DJs. The youth set goes crowd-hopping in the Centro Storico, particularly Spaccanapoli, from Wednesday to Sunday nights from 10:30 PM to 4 AM, with some places becoming so crowded that the street scene outside becomes a key part of the experience. Hordes of postpunk and grunge night owls begin by regrouping in the main squares of Spaccanapoli, such as Piazza San Domenico Maggiore and Piazza Gesù Nuovo, to plan their strategies for the evening, usually around the **Lazzerella Bar** (⊠ Calata Trinità Maggiore), the adjacent SKA Social Center, and a nearby hot spot: the **Velvet Garage** (⊠ Via Cistern dell'Olio 11). The next stop on the loop is **Notting Hill** (⊠ Piazza Dante 88/A, ☎ 081/564–2830), a steamy disco that features theme nights. **Tongue** (⊠ Via Manzoni 207, ☎ 081/7690800) appeals especially to gays and techno-heads.

In Spaccanapoli, the bar crowd heads instead to Piazza Bellini, where the arty and literary take up residence at the **Caffè Intramoenia** (⊠ Piazza Bellini 70, ☎ 081/290720) and the **Caffè 1799** (the date of the Neapolitan Revolution) (⊠ Piazza Bellini). Others prefer to or to make the scene at the **Art Cafe** (⊠ Piazza San Domenico Maggiore) or the **Hayli Club** (⊠ Via San Giovanni Maggiore Pignatelli 45, ☎ 081/552–0340). Near the Piazzetta Nilo, crowds descend on **Frame Caffè** (⊠ Via Giovanni Paladino 10), the **Blu Colbalto** (⊠ Via Giovanni Paladino 3), and the **Vineria del Centro** (⊠ Via Giovanni Paladino 8) for a bit of artistic anything. A bit off the beaten track, **Ferdinandstrasse** (⊠ Piazza Porta Nova 8, ☎ 081/207390) began life as a gay disco bar but now attracts a wide array of figures from the art world.

A dressier crowd hangs out in the Chiaia zone. The center for Naples's *jeunesse dorée* is Piazza dei Martiri, where the elegant **La Caffèterria** (⊠ Piazza dei Martiri 25/26, ☎ 081/764–4243) draws night owls. Nearby is **Vinariam** (⊠ Via Capella Vecchia 7, ☎ 081/764–4247), a refined wine bar. This hip area also has a number of discos, including **My Way** (⊠ Via Cappella Vecchia 30/c, ☎ 081/764–4735) and the fashionable **Beloved** (⊠ Via dei Mille), a hotbed of 1970s looks and sounds. Along elegant Via dei Mille are a number of old-guard nightclubs, such as **La Mela** (⊠ Via dei Mille 40, ☎ 081/413881) and **Chez Moi** (⊠ Parco Margherita 13, ☎ 081/407526), which is particularly simpatico for Neapolitan aristocrats. Along the Via Partenope, traffic jams occur outside the new nightspot **Pinterré** (⊠ Via Partenope)—but who knows what the scene is like? It's just too packed to enter! A savvy group heads to **Gabbiano** (⊠ Via Partenope 26, ☎ 081/7645717), where live music is usually on tap. Farther-flung options include the **Otto Jazz Club** (⊠ Salità Carlati 23, ☎ 081/552–4373), the disco **Upstroke** (⊠ Via Coroglio, ☎ 081/670–8992), and in a district just beyond Vomero, **Madison Street** (⊠ Via Scambati 47, ☎ 081/546–6566), a vast, fun, and tacky disco that allows all persuasions to trip the night fantastic.

OUTDOOR ACTIVITIES AND SPORTS

By Frank
Gerard
Godlewski

For complete news and information about sporting events, check the local newspaper *Il Mattino* and the free English-language monthly guide *Qui Napoli*. Many sporting facilities in Naples, such as those for golf and horseback riding, are run as private clubs, so they are not listed here. The major sports area of Naples is the Mostra d'Oltremare area, to the west of the city center, site of the Stadio San Paolo (soccer stadium). Here, too, is **Edenlandia,** the largest amusement park in Campania. ⊠ *Viale Kennedy,* ☎ *081/239–1182.* 🎫 *3,000 lire, 15,000 lire all rides.* ⊙ *Oct.–Mar., weekdays noon–8, weekends 10:30 AM–midnight; Apr.–Sept., weekdays 3–10, weekends 10:30 AM–midnight.*

Participant Sports

Beaches, Spas, and Water Sports

Beaches are few and far between in Naples proper, although out of desperation Neapolitans like to take to the Lungomare rocks that line the waterfront from the Castel dell'Ovo to the little port of Mergellina (swimming here is officially banned, although the young and reckless disregard the law). For true swimming pleasure, head to the Posillipo coast that lies just west of the Mergellina harbor. Here are three ancient fishing ports: **Giuseppone a Mare,** at the end of Via Ferdinando Russo; **Marechiaro,** at the end of Discesa Marechiaro; and **La Gajola** (local dialect for "The Cage"), at the end of Discesa Gajola. These are quite picturesque spots immortalized in Neapolitan songs, landscape paintings, and poetry. The more policed and costly facilities in the Posillipo zone are: the **Elena** (⊠ Via Posillipo 14, ☎ 081/757–5058); **Gabbiano** (⊠ Via Marechiaro 115, ☎ 081/575–5650); **Le Rocce Verdi** (⊠ Via Posillipo 68, ☎ 081/575–6716); **Marechiaro** (⊠ Discesa Marechiaro, ☎ 081/769–1215); and **Villa Imperiale** (⊠ Via Marechiaro 90, ☎ 081/575–4344). Paradisiacal beaches can be found throughout the entire Bay of Naples region. *Il Mattino,* the local Neapolitan newspaper, has a page entitled "Per Che Parte" (For Those Who Leave) listing all the ferry and hydrofoil schedules for transportation to and from the nearby bathing spots that are perfect for a day trip (such as Amalfi, Positano, Capri, Sorrento, and, particularly, Ischia, famous for its white-sand beaches).

With millennia of volcanic activity in the region, the Bay of Naples area is home to many spas. Two ancient Roman period structures, or *sudatorium,* are still active today as spa facilities near Naples: the **Stuffe di Nerone** (⊠ Via Stuffe di Neroni 37, Bacoli, ☎ 081/868–8006) and the **Stuffe di San Germano** (⊠ Via Agnano Astroni 24, ☎ 081/570–2122). Both offer thermally heated spring pools and natural steam caves where you can enjoy lava mud baths and massages using eucalyptus leaves.

Sci Nautico Partenopeo (⊠ Lago d'Averno, Pozzuoli, ☎ 081/866–2214) offers waterskiing sessions and courses at what was once believed the mouth of hell, at Lago d'Averno, west of Naples.

Bicycling

The traffic of Naples creates hazards for bikers, but there are three areas that enable them to experience flora (sometimes even fauna), cityscapes, and views of the Bay of Naples all in one healthy shot: the Parco di Capodimonte; the stretch of road from Piazza del Plebiscito down across the Lungomare waterfront to Mergellina; and the steep, uphill, and literally breathtaking ride on Via Posillipo to Parco Virgiliano. For biking information contact **Cicolverde** (⊠ Piazza degli Artisti 27, ☎ 081/291184).

Fitness Facilities

Parco Virgiliano has a beautiful outdoor running and gymnastics area. The locals are friendly and courteous to out-of-town *salutisti* (health-conscious travelers) and usually just let you join in. Two major facilities are in Neapolitan suburbs: **Magic World** (☎ 081/804–8389), at Licola, is a new large-scale outdoor fitness and swimming facility; the **Piscina Scandone** (✉ Via Giochi dei Mediterraneo, ☎ 081/570–9154) is a public swimming and fitness center in Fuorigrotta. Closer to the center of town is the **Skorpion Club** (✉ Via dei Mille 16, ☎ 081/407334) and the **Hotel Vesuvio Fitness Center** (✉ Via Partenope 45, ☎ 081/764–0044).

Running

The same courses mentioned in Biking (☞ *above*) may be enjoyed by runners, but the temperature of the summer months should be taken into consideration; Neapolitans habitually run only at sunset or in the evening and comment bemusedly at foreign runners baking themselves under the sun like pepperoni pizza. Periodic excursions are organized by the **Club Alpino Italiano** (☎ 081/764–5343).

Tennis

At the Villa Communale near the American Consulate (✉ Piazza della Repubblica) is the **Tennis Club Napoli** (✉ Viale Dohrn, ☎ 081/761–4656). Other facilities include the **Sporting Club Virgilio** (✉ Via Tito Lucrezio Caro, ☎ 081/575–5261) and the **Tennis Club Vomero** (✉ Via Rossini, ☎ 081/688912). All of these clubs are private, but inquire about special privileges and passes.

Spectator Sports

Soccer

Considering the position of importance and the popularity of *calcio*, or soccer, for the Neapolitan people, the San Paolo Stadium is probably a shrine only a fraction less important than the duomo. This shrine's last "saint" was Diego Maradona, who, in 1987, led the town team (their name, incidentally, is just Napoli) to first place in the Italy's national championships. Matches are played at the **Stadio San Paolo** (☎ 081/239–5582), in a suburb to the west of Mergellina (beware: raucous crowds on their way to a game can clog up public transportation throughout the city). Tickets range from about 34,000 lire (at the top of the giant stadium) to 510,000 lire (for the new Top Club facility). The stadium is across the piazza from the Ferrovia Cumana train station at Mostra and can also be reached via the Metropolitana stop at Piazzale Vicenzo Tecchio. Other than the box office, tickets are available through Concerteria (✉ Via Schippa 23, ☎ 081/764–1221).

SHOPPING

Naples is a fascinating and largely underrated city for shopping. From the delightful *Presepe* (Nativity scenes) shops that transform Via San Gregorio Armeno into a perpetual Christmas morning to its noted leather-goods emporia, the city's rich history of skilled workmanship means it abounds in unique souvenirs and gifts, including some of the world's best ties (**Marinella**), crèche figures (**Ferrigno**), masks (**Nel Regno della Pulcinella**), shoes (**Lerre**), and intarsia tabletops (**Domenico Russo**). At the other end of the price scale are world-famous, dirt-cheap bootleg cassettes and CDs of Italian and Neapolitan music for you to check out. A sense of adventure is once again the key, especially in the open markets, which are worth a visit just as a social experience—watch your wallets and leave the expensive extra camera lenses at the hotel; bargaining here is an art.

Shops are generally open from around 9 in the morning to 1, when they close for lunch, reopening around 3:30 or 4 and staying open until 7 or 7:30. Most stores are closed Sunday, but certain higher-volume addresses have procured a license allowing them to open on Sunday morning. Sales run twice a year, from mid-January (after the Befana) to mid-March for the fall/winter collections and from mid-July to early September for the spring/summer collections, with half-price discounts common.

Department Stores and Shopping Malls

La Rinascente (⌧ Via Toledo 343, ☎ 081/411511) is a good, basic department store with a wide variety of clothes, cosmetics, household items, and so forth; the same goes for **Coin** (⌧ Via Santa Caterina in Chiaia 23, ☎ 081/245–1938). Both of these are conveniently located in the central shopping district and stay open through the lunch hour. **Coin** also has a store in Vomero (⌧ Via Scarlatti 100, ☎ 081/578–0111). **Standa** (⌧ Via Solimene 143, ☎ 081/578–0480), in Vomero, is a less expensive chain, with a supermarket attached; **Upim** has a wide variety of inexpensive goods available, with stores in Vomero (⌧ Via Scarlatti, ☎ 081/556–2817), Chiaia/Piazza Amedeo (⌧ Via dei Mille 59, ☎ 081/417520), and Piazza Matteotti (⌧ Piazza Matteotti 7, ☎ 081/ 552–1279).

There are two elegant 19th-century shopping centers in Vomero— **Galleria Scarlatti,** on Via Scarlatti, and **Galleria Vanvitelli,** in Piazza Vanvitelli—as well as the more famous (though somewhat lackluster) **Galleria Umberto I,** across from the Teatro San Carlo, if you want to browse indoors and under cover.

Markets

Shopping in an outdoor market is an essential Neapolitan experience; do prepare yourself against pickpockets (now you've been warned, so relax and don't wear your tiara). Food markets are all over town, offering a Technicolor feast for the eyes as well as free street theater. Some of the principal ones are: the **Mercato di Porta Nolana** (⌧ Via Carmignano) open Monday–Saturday 8–6, Sunday 8–2, just south of Piazza Garibaldi, with a great display of seafood; the **Mercato di Sant'Antonio** (⌧ Via Sant'Antonio Abate) open daily 9–8 and north of the Porta Capuana; the **Mercatino della Pignasecca** (several blocks to the west of Piazza Carità, off Via Toledo), open Monday–Saturday 8–2; the **Mercatino di Antignano,** in Vomero (⌧ Piazza degli Artisti), which is open daily 8–1; and the **Mercatino della Torretta** (⌧ Viale Gramsci), which is open Monday–Saturday 8–1 and has everything from fresh fish and vegetables at thrillingly low prices to clothes and appliances. Specialty markets also abound. Photographers will want to explore the flower market, which opens at dawn every day in the moat of the Castel Nuovo. On the last two weekends of each month there is an **antiques market** in the Villa Comunale, where junk from grandmother's attic nuzzles up to some surprisingly fine furniture and objects; it's open daily 8–4.

Clothes merit a special mention. Neapolitans are the world masters of the used-clothing trade and also specialize in—well, let's call them unofficial brand-name knockoffs, sometimes of excellent quality. If you trust your eye, you can have a field day: excellent shoes often made by the same factories that turn out top brands, quality leather purses, secondhand cashmere at the price of discount-store cotton. Of course, quite often you have to wade through a lot of dismal stock of no interest in order to get to the good stuff, but that's part of the fun. The best stomping ground is the **Mercato di Ponte Casanova** (⌧ Porta Capuana), which is open Monday–Saturday 8–sunset and which must have the world's greatest collection of jeans and a surprising number of untagged name-brand items at half price. The above-mentioned markets of **Antignano** in Vomero and **Torretta** on Viale Gramsci in Mergellina also have a good selection of clothing.

Shopping Districts

Most of the luxury shops in Naples are along a crescent that descends the Via Toledo to Piazza Trieste e Trento and then continues along Via Chiaia to Via Filangieri and on to Piazza Amedeo, as well as continuing south toward Piazza dei Martiri and the Riviera di Chiaia. Within this area, the Via Chiaia itself probably has the greatest concentration and variety of shops (and café-pastry shop Cimmino, on the corner of Via Filangieri and Via Chiaia, makes for an excellent rest stop along this route). The area around Piazza Vanvitelli, and Via Scarlatti, in particular, in Vomero also has a nice selection of shops outside the tourist zone, with the **Galleria Scarlatti,** on Via Scarlatti, and **Galleria Vanvitelli** in Piazza Vanvitelli, and can be conveniently reached by funicular from Piazza Amedeo or the Cumana station. Used-book dealers tend to collect in the area between Piazza Dante, Via Port'Alba, and Via Santa Maria Constantinopoli toward Piazza Bellini. The shops specializing in *Presepe* (Nativity scenes) are in Spaccanapoli, on the Via San Gregorio Armeno.

Specialty Stores

BOOKS AND PRINTS

Naples is a paradise for bibliophiles. It helps if you read Italian, of course, but you can find a reasonable selection of delightful surprises in French- or English-language publications as well. The best area to hunt is between Piazza Bellini and Piazza Dante, along the streets of Via Santa Maria di Constantinopoli, Via San Sebastiano, and Via Port'Alba. **Libreria Guida** (⊠ Via Port'Alba 20/23, ☎ 081/446377) has a wide selection of current publications in English and is a good place to mingle with the locals. Rare-book enthusiasts will want to check out **Casella** (⊠ Via Carlo Poerio 92, ☎ 081/764–2627), just above the Riviera di Chiaia, a famous source that also specializes in authors' autographs; and **Colonnese** (⊠ Via San Pietro a Maiella 33, ☎ 081/445–9858), near Via Port'Alba, which also has a wide assortment of antique postcards and magical objets d'art. If you're an art history student and pictures are what matter, browse the booksellers near Piazza Bellini and take Via Port'Alba to Piazza Dante, where **ALPHA** (⊠ Via Sant' Anna dei Lombardi 10, ☎ 081/552–5013) has a great selection of cut-rate art books. For antique prints and engravings, the best shop in town is **Bowinkel** (⊠ Piazza dei Martiri 24, ☎ 081/764–4344), in the Chiaia area; it also has antique postcards, watercolors, photographs, and fans. **Arethusa** (⊠ Riviera di Chiaia 202/b, ☎ 081/411551) specializes in collectible posters and has an excellent selection of both rare and inexpensive editions.

CLOTHING AND ACCESSORIES

Neapolitans are famous for their attention to style, and Naples abounds in clothing stores for every pocketbook. National chains are present, of course, and a good selection of stylish, affordable clothes can be found at **G. B. Pedrini** (⊠ Via Toledo 330, ☎ 081/404949), **Benetton** (⊠ Via Chiaia 203/204, ☎ 081/405385), and **Camomilla** (⊠ Via Scarlatti 185, ☎ 081/578–2004). Up the price scale, **Emporio Armani** (⊠ Piazza dei Mille 64, ☎ 081/425816) is in the Via dei Mille/Via Filangieri area of the Chiaia district. Here, too, is **Versace** (⊠ Via Calabritto 7, ☎ 081/764–4210) and **Prada** (⊠ Via Calabritto 9, ☎ 081/764–1323).

A number of smaller, local, or more exclusive shops are also worthy of notice. **Amina Rubinacci** (⊠ Via dei Mille 16, ☎ 081/415486) is the queen of knitwear, featuring her famous "ostrich" pullover and a wide range of colors in sweaters. **Maxi Ho** (⊠ Via N. Nisco 23/27, ☎ 081/427530) has the latest in men's and women's fashion trends. **Eddy Monetti** (⊠ Via dei Mille 45 a/b/c, ☎ 081/407064 for men's shop; ⊠ Piazza Santa Caterina a Chiaia for women) offers classic, elegant sportswear. Young people flock to the **Magazzini Generali** (⊠ Via dei Mille 26/28, ☎ 081/413872) for its huge assortment of up-to-date items for all budgets, as well as to **Bamba** (⊠ Via Chiaia 209, ☎ 081/414767), which sells original designs.

Women can find provocative clothes by the local designer and erstwhile pal-of-Andy-Warhol Ernesto Esposito at **Stafelli** (⊠ Via Carlo Poerio 12, ☎ 081/764–6922), off the Piazza dei Martiri above Riviera di Chiaia. If your taste runs along more subdued lines, **Alta Moda Pirone** (⊠ Via San Pasquale a Chiaia 29, ☎ 081/411927) is an old-fashioned house on the second floor of a historic palazzo with classic original designs for an exclusive clientele (great cashmere coats and silk raincoats); or try **Barbaro** (⊠ Galleria Umberto I 3/7, ☎ 081/411284), for a stylish choice of name designers, **Mediterraneo** (⊠ Vico Satriano 10, ☎ 081/407064), for chic, up-to-date fashions at accessible prices; and **Livio de Simone** (⊠ Via D. Morelli 15, ☎ 081/764–3827), whose choice of hand-painted fabrics in vibrant colors reflects the city so well.

Naples is a surprisingly good city for male fashion and tends to completely spoil its male clotheshorses (many would use the word *peacocks*). **Pour les Amis** (⊠ Piazza dei Martiri 28, ☎ 081/764–3103) is a good example of what is meant by spoiling; the careful and refined selection of clothing and accessories is complemented by impeccable service. Another excellent address is the hip but easygoing **Giorgio** (⊠ Via Calabritto 29, ☎ 081/764–4122). Finely tailored shirts with hand-sewn buttonholes can be found at **Luigi Borelli** (⊠ Largo Sant'Orsola a Chiaia, ☎ 081/410070). If you feel like indulging in a custom-made suit, try **Blasi** (⊠ Via dei Mille 27/35, ☎ 081/415823), which also has some superb ready-to-wear items, or the **Sartoria dal Cuore** (⊠ Piazza Vittoria 6, ☎ 081/245–1056). You'll find high-class souvenirs that are more immediate and more accessible at **Marinella** (⊠ Riviera di Chiaia 287, ☎ 081/764–4214), where Maurizio Marinella, grandson of the founder, Eugenio, cuts made-to-measure ties for the world's royalty and other sensitive necks—these are widely considered by globe-trotting VIPs to be the finest ties in the world, and most important, they are never considered vulgar. The selection of fabrics is so vast it's impossible *not* to find the perfect tie. **Argenio** (⊠ Via Filangieri 15, ☎ 081/418035) is another famous and exclusive address for men's accessories, and former supplier of scarves, cuff links, buttons, tiepins, and so forth, to the royal Bourbons of the House of the Two Sicilies.

Lerre (⊠ Via Calabritto 21, ☎ 081/764–3884) sells original shoes for "an emancipated and evolved woman" (the New York gallery owner Ileana Sonnabend bought 18 pairs in one visit). **Mario Valentino** (⊠ Via Calabritto 10, ☎ 081/764–4262) offers fine handmade shoes in his fashionable shoe store. **Spatarella** (⊠ Via Calabritto 1, ☎ 081/764–3794) is a top source for shoes by local craftsmen, as well as for high-quality belts, purses, and luggage. The best address in town for hats is **Piscopo** (⊠ Via San Pasquale 17). For gloves to match, head to **Pistola** (⊠ Via Santa Caterina a Chiaia 12, ☎ 081/422058), famous for more than 100 years for the quality of its craftsmen, who in addition to the classic models, offer a surprising selection of chic, high-tech sports gloves.

CRAFTS AND GIFTS

The classic handicraft of Naples is the *Presepe*—or Nativity crèche scene—with elaborate sets and terra-cotta figurines and elements of still life. The tradition goes back to the medieval period, but its acknowledged golden age arrived in the 18th century, when famous sculptors churned out stunningly lifelike figurines, which were then custom-dressed by the chicest tailors to the aristocracy, providing a delightfully picturesque, if idealized, view of Neapolitan street life. The most stunning masterpieces from this period are the Presepe Cucinello, in the Museo di San Martino; one that belongs to the Banco di Roma displayed in the Palazzo Reale; and the Royal Nativity Scene in Capodimonte. The tradition is alive and flourishing; although the sets and figurines retain their 18th-century aspect, the craftsmen keep their creativity up to date with famous renditions of current political figures and other celebrities: porn star and member of parliament Ilona Staller, better known as La Cicciolina, was a big hit a few years back (not as the Virgin Mary—there's a limit to everything, even in Naples), as was exiled political leader Benedetto Craxi, represented, with typical Neapolitan humor, in Arab dress (he's hiding out in Tunisia) as one of the wise men. In 1998 Clinton and Lewinsky made an appearance. The scenes are appropriately completed with a profusion of domestic animals and food of all sorts, meticulously rendered. A number of the smaller articles make great Christmas tree ornaments, if you don't feel up to adopting an entire Bethlehem-on-the-bay Nativity scene. Shops cluster along the Via di San Gregorio Armeno in Spaccanapoli, and they're all worth a glance, but the undisputed master is **Giuseppe Ferrigno** (⊠ Via di San Gregorio Armeno 10, ☎ 081/552–3148), who still faithfully uses 18th-century techniques. If you're seriously bitten by the collecting bug, you can find rare antique Nativity figures at **Marisa Catello** (⊠ Via Santa Maria Constantinopoli 124, ☎ 081/444169) or **Salvatore Iermano** (⊠ Via Domenico Morelli 30, ☎ 081/764–3913). Another popular shop is **Gramendola** ⊠ Via di San Gregorio Armeno 51, ☎ 081/712–3164) where the creations of Matteo Prencipe are on view.

The **Ospedale delle Bambole** (⊠ Via San Biagio in Librai 81, ☎ 081/203067)—a tiny storefront operation—is a world-famous "hospital" for dolls, a wonderful photo-op, and a great place to take kids. But once you've whetted their appetite, take them to **Baracca e Burattina** (⊠ Piazza Museo 2, ☎ 081/347946), where they can choose a new handcrafted doll, or to the unnamed but colorful shop at Via Martucci 73. **Nel Regno di Pulcinella** (⊠ Salita Arenella 56, ☎ 081/578–6450), another great address for kids and adults alike, specializes in handmade Neapolitan masks.

Music lovers can get a prestigious violin, mandolin, or lute at **Liuteria Calace** (⊠ Via San Domenico Maggiore 9, ☎ 081/551–5983) or **Liut-officina** (⊠ Vico San Pietro a Maiella 6, ☎ 081/290852). You'll get a spontaneous and more accessible musical experience at any of the *bancarelle,* or ambulant sellers, specializing in bootleg cassettes and CDs; you'll find them in most outdoor markets, or along Corso Umberto I, or walking around the city center with ghetto blasters marketing the latest songs.

For unique personal items, try **Del Porto** (⊠ Via Santa Lucia 165, ☎ 081/764–0093), whose tortoise-shell creations are true works of art. Elegant office supplies—notebooks, pens, and stationery—can be had at **P & C** (⊠ Largo Vasto a Chiaia 86, ☎ 081/418724), a treasure trove for writing enthusiasts; the **Bottega Artigiana del Libro e della Carta** (⊠ Calata Trinità Maggiore, ☎ 081/551–1280); and the **Bottega della Carta** in Chiaia (⊠ Via Cavalerizza a Chiaia 20/23, ☎ 081/421903). **Acampora Profumi** (⊠ Via G. Filangieri 71, ☎ 081/414162) is a famous local perfume maker selling prized fragrances in signature minimalist aluminum flasks.

HOUSEHOLD DECORATION, ART, AND ANTIQUES

For household linens, **La Cage** (✉ Largo Duca della Ferrantina 10, ☎ 081/403811) has the most exclusive selection in Naples, although the national chain **Frette** (✉ Via dei Mille 2, ☎ 081/418728) is justifiably famous throughout Italy for the quality of its sheets, towels, and bedspreads.

Galeria Elena (✉ Viale Gramsci 15/c, ☎ 081/667822) crafts luxury floors in wood, marble inlay, mosaic and terra-cotta and has a splendid collection of high-quality reproductions of Renaissance majolica tiles. Another good address for hand-painted ceramic tiles include **Antica Manifattura Ceramica F.lli Stingo,** in the industrial zone south of the central train station (✉ Via Breccia a Sant'Erasmo 111, ☎ 081/261617). **Domenico Russo e Figli** (✉ Via Bisignano 5, ☎ 081/764–8387) continues the centuries-old Neapolitan tradition of marble-inlay work, creating precious tables and console tops. The Muscariello brothers produce museum-quality replica furniture (they copied the ancient furniture from Herculaneum for the Getty Museum) at **I Cirmolo** (✉ Via Sapienza 8, ☎ 081/451140), and **Salvatore Molino** (✉ Via Alabardieri 21/22, ☎ 081/426505) also painstakingly handcrafts furniture, using time-tested techniques. Fine bronze reproductions can be found in the area of Capodimonte at the founders **Patrizio di Pietro** (✉ Corso Amedeo di Savoia 248, ☎ 081/741–0217) and **Chiurazzi** (✉ Via dei Ponti Rossi 271, ☎ 081/751–2685).

If you're interested in original antiques, reputable addresses include **Arte Antica** (✉ Via Ferrigni 9, ☎ 081/764–6897), with a fine display of porcelain objects. The largest selection of prestigious shops is on the Via Domenico Morelli south of Piazza dei Martiri: **Gennaro Brandi** (✉ Via Domenico Morelli 11, ☎ 081/764–3906); **D'Amodio** (✉ Via Domenico Morelli 6/bis, ☎ 081/764–3872); and **Florida** (✉ Via Domenico Morelli 13, ☎ 081/764–3440). Fine collectible 20th-century furniture and objects (basically Art Nouveau and Art Deco) can be seen in Chiaia at **Nabis** (✉ Via Cavalerizza a Chiaia 52, ☎ 081/422493) and **Fabbrini** (✉ Vico Satriano 2, ☎ 081/764–3753); and for current designs, go by **Agorà** in Posillipo (✉ Via Orazio 138/a, ☎ 081/651056), **Novelli** in Piazza Amedeo (✉ Piazza Amedeo 21/22, ☎ 081/413233), or **San Patrignano Casa d'Arte** (✉ Via Santa Lucia 133, ☎ 081/764–0878), which shows high-quality, limited-edition, handcrafted furnishings and objects and is worth a visit even if you have no intention of buying.

Back in the late 1970s, the late Lucio Meglio operated the finest contemporary art gallery in Naples and succeeded in luring international superstars like Andy Warhol and Joseph Beuys to the city (Warhol wound up lingering on past his summer holidays and contributed paintings of Mt. Vesuvius to the Terra Motus show, held to benefit the city after the earthquake of 1980). Lia Rumma, together with her late husband Marcello Rumma and art critic Achile Bonito Olivo, helped create the Arte Povera and Transavantguardia movements, while the standard bearers of the Neapolitan aesthetic—Francesco Clemente in painting; Philip-Lorca diCorcia in photography—maintain worldwide reputations. They and other leading contemporary artists frequently exhibit in the city's leading art galleries: **Galleria Lucio Amelio** (✉ Piazza dei Martiri 58, ☎ 081/422023); **Galleria Vera Vita Gioia** (✉ Vico Fonesca, ☎ 081/544–0553); **Galleria Beppe Morra** (✉ Via Calabrito 20, ☎ 081/764–3337); **Galleria Lia Rumma** (✉ Via Vannella Gaetani 14, ☎ 081/764–3619); and **Galleria Trisorio** (✉ Riviera di Chiaia 215, ☎ 081/414306).

JEWELRY

The best selection of goldsmiths' and jewelers' shops is, appropriately enough, in the traditional zone on and around Via degli Orefici (Street of the Goldsmiths) in Spaccanapoli. A leading address here is **Gioiel-leria Caso** (✉ Piazza San Domenico Maggiore 16, ☎ 081/551–6733), which has antique jewelry and silver. **Brinkmann** (✉ Piazza Munici-pio 21, ☎ 081/552–0555) creates pieces using rare coins, including an exquisite collection of watches. **Ventrella** (✉ Via Carlo Poerio 11, ☎ 081/764–3712) is a posh salon showing original designs by the most exclusive contemporary workshop. Naples has also long been famous for its coral and cameos, and although the raw material now comes most often from the Far East, it is Neapolitan technique and inspira-tion that transform the shells and coral into works of art. A number of touristy cameo shops along the Sorrento coast sell cameos of vary-ing quality and price, but if you want to see how beautiful they can get, go to Torre del Greco and visit **Bianca Lombardi** (✉ Via Tironi 10, ☎ 081/881–6344) or **Giovanni Apa** (✉ Via de Nicola 1, ☎ 081/881–1155). **Caso** (☞ *above*) has the best selection in Naples.

SIDE TRIPS

Caserta is the Italian answer to Versailles, while if you proceed to Ben-evento, you'll view an almost perfectly preserved Roman arch. Ben-evento was badly damaged by World War II bombings, but among the modern structures there are some medieval and even older relics still standing in the old town. If you go by car, make a brief detour to the medieval hamlet of Caserta Vecchia on the hillside, where there is a very old cathedral and one or two good restaurants.

For location of destinations, see the Campania map near the front of this book.

Caserta

★ *11 km (7 mi) northeast of Herculaneum; 25 km (16 mi) northeast of Naples.*

The royal palace known as the **Reggia di Caserta** is exemplary of mid-18th-century Bourbon royalty living. Architect Luigi Vanvitelli de-voted 20 years to its construction under Bourbon ruler Charles II, whose son, Charles III, moved in when it was completed in 1774. Both king and architect were inspired by Versailles, and the rectangular palace was conceived on a massive scale, with four interconnecting courtyards, 1,200 rooms, and a vast park. Though not as well maintained as its French counterpart, the main staircase puts the one at Versailles to shame, and the **royal apartments** are sumptuous. It was here, in what Eisen-hower called "a castle near Naples," that the Allied High Command had its headquarters in World War II, and here German forces in Italy surrendered in April 1945. Most enjoyable are the gardens and parks, particularly the Cascades, where a life-size Diana and her maidens stand. ✉ *Piazza Carlo III,* ☎ *0823/321400.* 🎫 *Royal apartments: 8,000 lire; park: 4,000 lire; minibus: 1,500 lire.* 🕐 *Royal apartments: Apr.–Sept., Tues.–Sun. 9–6; Oct.–Mar., Tues.–Sun. 9–1:30; park: Apr.–Sept., Tues.–Sun. 9–1 hr before sunset; Oct.–Mar., Tues.–Sun. 9–3.*

Benevento

35 km (22 mi) east of Caserta; 60 km (37 mi) northeast of Naples.

Benevento owes its importance to its establishment as the capital of the Lombards, a northern tribe that invaded and settled what is now Lombardy when they were ousted by Charlemagne in the 8th century. Tough and resourceful, the Lombards moved south and set up a new duchy in Benevento, later moving its seat south to Salerno, where they saw the potential of the natural harbor. Under papal rule in the 13th century, Benevento built a fine cathedral and endowed it with bronze doors that were a pinnacle of Romanesque art. The cathedral, doors, and a large part of the town were blasted by World War II bombs. The **duomo** has been rebuilt, with the remaining panels of the original bronze doors in the chapter library. Fortunately, the majestic 2nd-century AD **Arco di Traiano** survived unscathed. Roman emperor Trajàn, who sorted out Rome's finances, brought parts of the Middle East into the empire and extended the Appian Way through Benevento to the Adriatic. The ruins of the **Teatro Romano,** which had a seating capacity of 20,000, are still in good enough shape to host a summer opera and theater season. ⊠ *Take Via Carlo from the duomo.* 🖼 *4,000 lire.* ☉ *Daily 9–1 hr before sunset.*

NAPLES A TO Z

Arriving and Departing

By Boat

If you're heading to the Aeolian Islands, other parts of Sicily, or Sardinia, Naples may be a convenient departure point. The major long-distance carriers are **Tirennia** (departs from Stazione Marittima, near Piazza Municipio, ☎ 0147/899000 or 081/580–0340) and **Linee Lauro** (departs from Molo Belvedere below Castel Nuovo, ☎ 081/551–3352). Boats leave occasionally (not every day) for Tunis (18 hours southwest, 170,000 lire), Sardinia (14 hours west, 50,000–100,000 lire), Palermo (11 hours southwest, 61,600–90,500 lire), and the Aeolian Islands (8–14 hours, 66,500–75,500 lire), among other places. Departure times and additional info on some routes, including the local ferry and hydrofoil lines listed below, can be found in *Qui Napoli* or in the newspaper *Il Mattino.*

For trips around the Bay of Naples, the main port is **Molo Beverello,** below Castel Nuovo. Many carriers send boats to the islands all day until 7 or 8, though in the off-season service is less frequent. Carriers include **Linee Lauro** (☎ 081/551–3352), **Caremar** (☎ 081/551–3882), and **Navigazione Libera del Golfo** (☎ 081/552–7209). Hydrofoils (but not ferries) also leave from the port at Mergellina, a short walk below the Mergellina train station; these are run by **SNAV** (☎ 081/761–2348) and **Alilauro** (☎ 081/761–4909). Major destinations from both ports include Capri (hydrofoils: 40 minutes southeast, 16,000 lire; ferries: 1 hour 20 minutes, 9,800 lire), Procida (hydrofoils: 30 minutes southeast, 14,500 lire; ferries: one hour, 8,800 lire), and Ischia (hydrofoils: 40 minutes south, 18,000 lire; ferries: 1 hour, 20 minutes, 10,000 lire). Several hydrofoils also ply to Sorrento (25 minutes southeast, 12,000 lire), Positano (one hour southeast, 25,000 lire), and Amalfi (1½ hours southeast, 26,000 lire).

By Bus

Medium- and long-distance buses out of Naples are handled by two companies. **ACTP** (☎ 081/700–1111) buses usually leave from Piazza Garibaldi; **SITA** (☎ 081/552–2176) buses leave from either Piazza Garibaldi or Via G. Pisanelli, just south of Piazza Municipio, for destinations that include Bari and the Amalfi Coast. Some major routes are listed in *Qui Napoli,* available free at EPT offices, but in general, avoid buses if you can take a train to the same place.

By Car

Naples is located on the major north-south Autostrada del Sole, more commonly known as the A1 to Rome and Milan and the A3 to Salerno. The A30 acts as an express highway through Campania; the A16 winds southeast in the direction of Bari. As they near Naples, the autostradas meet the Tangenziale di Napoli (2,000-lire toll), which travels a circuit around the city center. The ring road, Tangenziale Ovest di Napoli, borders the city's northern sector, and meets the A1 for Rome and the A2 to Capodichino Airport in the east, continuing on to Pozzuoli and the Phlegrean Fields region to the west of the city center. The A3 for Salerno can be reached from Corso Arnaldo Lucci, southeast of Piazza Garibaldi.

By Plane

Capodichino Airport, 8 km (5 mi) north of Naples (☎ 081/789–6259), has many domestic and international connections. **Alitalia** (☎ 081/542–5111), **Lufthansa** (☎ 081/551–5440), and **British Airways** (☎ 081/780–3087) all fly from here. **Bus 14** runs from Piazza Garibaldi to the airport (hourly, 25 minutes) between 5:15 AM and 10:05 PM. A **shuttle bus** (☎ 081/531–1706) also runs from 6 AM to midnight between the airport and Piazza Municipio (hourly, 30 minutes, 3,000 lire), stopping in Piazza Garibaldi along the way. If you take a taxi from Piazza Garibaldi, expect to pay 40,000 lire (agree on a price beforehand) for the 15-minute trip.

By Train

Stazione Centrale (☎ 1478/88088 toll-free) overflows onto Piazza Garibaldi, northeast of old Naples and the port. Services in this hectic station include a pharmacy, money exchange office, 24-hour luggage check (5,000 lire every 12 hours), post office, and visitor information office. A **Wasteels branch office** (☎ 081/201071) sells BIJ train tickets Monday–Saturday 9–7:30. Trains leave at least hourly for Rome (2½ hours northwest, 18,000 lire) and several times daily for Milan (7 hours northwest, 64,000 lire) and Reggio di Calabria (4½ hours southeast, 38,500 lire). If you're staying in Mergellina, many trains stop first at **Stazione Mergellina** (✉ C. Vittorio Emanuele 4, ☎ 01478/88088), also near a hydrofoil port. If you arrive at night, consider taking a taxi to your hotel, but be sure you and the driver agree on a price ahead of time—many Neapolitan taxi drivers like to pretend the meter doesn't work.

Naples has two sets of commuter rail lines, each with its own tickets. The **Ferrovia Circumvesuviana** leaves for points east from the Stazione Circumvesuviana (☎ 081/779–2144), on Corso Garibaldi; all trains also stop on the lower level of **Stazione Centrale** (✉ Piazza Garibaldi). Destinations include Herculaneum, Pompeii, and Sorrento. **SEPSA** (☎ 081/735–4111) manages two railway lines that leave from the **Stazione Cumana** (✉ Nar Montesanto Métro station). Both end at Torregavata, at the west end of the Gulf of Naples; the Cumana line goes along the coast and stops at Pozzuoli and Baia, among other places.

Getting Around

A major saving grace in the city's transit system is the **Giranapoli** (1,500 lire), a 90-minute ticket that works for the Metropolitana (subway), tram, *funicolari* (funiculars), and **ATAN** city buses, as long as you are within the city limits. You can purchase tickets at most tobacco shops (look for the TABACCHI sign) or newsstands. If you buy a day pass (4,500 lire), remember to stamp it the first time you use it.

By Bus

Bus routes in Naples change frequently, the signs posted at bus stops aren't too helpful, and there's no bus map available. That said, they have recently reorganized the system around a small network of frequent routes that shuttle you efficiently among a few major junctions. These are the **R1,** which runs between Piazza Medaglie d'Oro in Vomero and Piazza

Bovio (at the end of Corso Umberto near Piazza Municipio) by way of Via Toledo and Via Diaz; the **R2,** which runs between Piazza Garibaldi and Piazza Municipio; the **R3,** which runs between Piazza Municipio and Piazza Trieste e Trento and Mergellina; and the **R4,** which runs from Piazza Bovio and the Ospedale Cardarelli above Vomero by way of the Museo Archeologico Nazionale. Other useful buses include the **24,** which takes you from downtown (Piazza Castello by way of Via Monteoliveto) to Capodimonte; the **C25,** which connects Piazza Bovio, Piazza Municipio, Via Santa Lucia, and Piazza Amedeo; the **C59,** which takes you from Piazza Garibaldi to the Duomo and on to Piazza Cavour, near the Museo Archeologico Nazionale; the **105,** which will get you to the duomo from Piazza Municipio by way of the port; the **140,** which takes you from Via Santa Lucia to Posillipo by way of Piazza Sannazaro; and the **152,** which runs between Posillipo and Piazza Garibaldi. The **E1** is handy in the city center; it makes a loop from Piazza del Gesù Nuovo around the Museo Archeologico Nazionale and the duomo and back by way of Via Monteoliveto. Since transfers are free, a few mistakes won't deplete your bank account. For further information call **Giranapoli** (⌧ Via G. B. Marino 1, ☎ 081/763–2177).

By Car

Traveling by car through Naples calls to mind the many circles described in Dante's *Inferno.* Congestion and stunt driving are par for the course, as is the rush-hour gridlock that sets in on weekdays. Weekends aren't much better: Suburbanites like to pile into their cars, enter Naples from Via Marina and do a traffic loop to Mergellina and the Via Carracciolo waterfront. This nightlife traffic-jam phenomenon takes hours and seems to now be a favorite pastime. At peak hours, even buses (which usually have their own separate traffic lanes) get blocked. Clearly, walking is the best alternative.

For those who decide to tempt fate, it is advisable to leave your car only in designated parking areas. The *parcometro,* the Italian version of metered parking in which you put coins into a machine for a stamped ticket that you leave on the dashboard, has been introduced in Naples, but the safest option is to park your car in a garage. Most of the hotels in the Santa Lucia district have (expensive) garages, but the following are some of the more centrally located and reasonably priced options. In Santa Lucia: **Garage Chiatamone** (⌧ Via Chiatamone 26, ☎ 081/764–2863); **Garage dei Fiori** (⌧ Via Colonna 21, ☎ 081/ 414190). In the historic center: **Garage Santa Chiara** (⌧ Pallonetto Santa Chiara 30, ☎ 081/551–6303). In the Molo Beverello zone by the harbor: **Garage Turistico** (⌧ Via dei Gaspari 14, ☎ 081/552– 5442). Near the Mergellina train and Metropolitana stations: **Garage Mergellina** (⌧ Via Mergellina 112, ☎ 081/761–3470); **Garage Sannazzaro** (⌧ Piazza Sannazzaro 142, ☎ 081/681437).

Gas and service stations (most open at night) can be found in some rather civilized locations: Piazza Municipio (Mobil); Piazza Mergellina (AGIP); Via Manzoni (Esso); Via Ugo Foscolo (APE); Via Falcone (IP); and Corso Europe (AGIP).

By Funiculare and Tram

If you're heading up to the Vomero Hill, **funicolari** (cable cars) make the trek (**ANM:** ☎ 081/763–1111). The Funicolare Centrale from its Via Toledo station links the city center with the Piazza Fuga station atop the Vomero Hill. The Funicolare di Chiaia links Via del Parco Margherita to the Via Domenico Cimarosa station on the Vomero Hill. The Funicolare di Montesanto travels from Piazza Montesanto to the station at Via Morghen. In addition, the Funicolare di Mergellina links the waterfront at Via Megellina with Via Manzoni. The basic funicu-

Finally, a travel companion that doesn't snore on the plane or eat all your peanuts.

MCI WORLDCOM   WorldPhone®

123 456 7891 2345
J.D. SMITH

When traveling, your MCI WorldCom Card is the best way to keep in touch. Our operators speak your language, so they'll be able to connect you back home—no matter where your travels take you. Plus, your MCI WorldCom Card is easy to use, and even earns you frequent flyer miles every time you use it. When you add in our great rates, you get something even more valuable: peace-of-mind. So go ahead. Travel the world. MCI WorldCom just brought it a whole lot closer.

You can even sign up today at www.mci.com/worldphone or ask your operator to make a collect call to 1-410-314-2938.

EASY TO CALL WORLDWIDE

1 Just dial the WorldPhone access number of the country you're calling from.
2 Dial or give the operator your MCI WorldCom Card number.
3 Dial or give the number you're calling.

France ◆	0-800-99-0019
Germany	0800-888-8000
Ireland	1-800-55-1001
Italy ◆	172-1022
Spain	900-99-0014
Sweden ◆	020-795-922
Switzerland ◆	0800-89-0222
United Kingdom	
To call using BT	0800-89-0222
To call using CWC	0500-89-0222

For your complete WorldPhone calling guide, dial the WorldPhone access number for the country you're in and ask the operator for Customer Service. In the U.S. call 1-800-431-5402.

◆ Public phones may require deposit of coin or phone card for dial tone.

EARN FREQUENT FLYER MILES

American Airlines®
A'Advantage®

Continental Airlines
OnePass®

▲ Delta Air Lines
SkyMiles·

■ MILEAGE PLUS.
United Airlines

U·S AIRWAYS
DIVIDEND MILES

MCI WorldCom, its logo and the names of the products referred to herein are proprietary marks of MCI WorldCom, Inc. All airline names and logos are proprietary marks of the respective airlines. All airline program rules and conditions apply.

MCI WORLDCOM

The first thing you need overseas is the one thing you forget to pack.

FOREIGN CURRENCY DELIVERED OVERNIGHT

Chase Currency To Go® delivers foreign currency to your home by the next business day*

It's easy—before you travel, call 1-888-CHASE84 for delivery of any of 75 currencies

Delivery is free with orders of $500 or more

Competitive rates— without exchange fees

You don't have to be a Chase customer—you can pay by Visa® or MasterCard®

CHASE

THE RIGHT RELATIONSHIP IS EVERYTHING.®

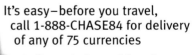

1•888•CHASE84
www.chase.com

lar fare is 1,500 lire, valid for 90 minutes. The funiculars usually run from 7 AM to 10 PM with departure every 10 minutes. The city's **tram** system runs northeast–southwest; Tram 1 will take you from Piazza Garibaldi to Mergellina along the waterfront and on to Campi Flegrei and Bagnoli.

By Metropolitana

Naples's main urban Metro line, **Metropolitana Napoli** (☎ 081/748–4111), runs through the city from Gianturco, east of Stazione Centrale, through the lower level of Stazione Centrale, and takes you as far west as Pozzuoli. Useful stops include **Piazza Cavour** (just up the street from the Museo Archeologico Nazionale), **Montesanto** (near the Cumana railway station and Montesanto funicular line), **Piazza Amedeo** (in the tony Chiaia district and near the Chiaia funicular line), and the **Stazione Mergellina** (near the Mergellina funicular line). Subway tickets cost 1,500 lire each; the main line usually runs from 6:40 AM to 10:54 PM, with departures every 15 minutes.

A line extending to the suburbs and hospital district north of Naples is also operational: the Metropolitana Collinare. The Naples nexus for this line is Piazza Vanvitelli, atop the Vomero Hill. This line will be connected with the main center-city line, when the brand new Metropolitana route (no name as of yet) is completed, hopefully by the end of 2000. After coming down from the Vomero Hill, this new line will stop off in Piazza Dante/Museo, then dart south to Via Diaz, Piazza Municipio, and then bend east toward Piazza Garibaldi via Piazza Bovio.

By Taxi

Neapolitan taxi drivers are famous for making up fares *"a la testa del cliente"*—that is to say, whatever they think they can get away with, which can be a sometimes shocking amount. However, the current city administration has made major inroads in bringing discipline to the situation, and taxis are now an efficient and reasonable way to get around. Take some precautions, though. Never take an "unofficial taxi" (the people who accost you at the airport and train station, offering you a taxi: real taxi drivers wait at a taxi stand)—they always cost twice as much and are almost never a good idea. Do make sure that the meter has been turned on. It will start at 4,000 lire, although the minimum fare is 6,000 lire. Regular supplements are charged for the following services: 3,000 lire for weekends and holidays, 4,000 lire for nighttime service (10 PM to 7 AM), 1,000 lire for each bag (this is why they're so eager to put your shoulder bag in the trunk), 5,000 lire for service to or from the airport, and 1,500 lire for a radio call. Expect to pay from 10,000 to 25,000 lire for most trips in town during the day, and 50,000 lire to or from the airport.

If you arrive with a suspiciously high fare (especially combined with an excuse that the meter wasn't working), complain. Get all your things out of the taxi (if you're staying at a hotel, call the porter for help, and expect to tip him). You might try a Neapolitan ruse and get your camera out and take a few pictures of the license plate of the car and the driver's door with the taxi identification painted on it (a city name followed by a number). By this point it's likely the driver will be quickly trying to bargain you down. If the driver is being particularly stubborn, ask for a receipt (*una ricevuta,*) which they are required by law to give, and if all else fails, blithely say, "Okay, *chiaiamo la polizia*"—let's call the cops—and smile. Don't try this in isolated suburbs, and do try to keep your sense of humor.

Taxis in Naples do not cruise, but if empty they will stop if you flag them down. Taxis wait at stands or can be paged by telephone. **Radio**

taxi numbers include: ☎ 081/570–7070, 081/556–0202, 081/556–4444, and 081/551–5151. It's usually cheaper and quicker to call a nearby taxi stand. The principal ones are: **in the center,** Piazza Garibaldi (☎ 081/553–8700) and Piazza Carità (☎ 081/552–0700); **near the seafront,** Via Partenope (☎ 081/764–0700), Piazza Vittoria (☎ 081/415200), and Piazza Mergellina (☎ 081/680900); and **on the hills,** Piazza Amedeo (☎ 081/680700), Piazza Medaglie d'Oro in Vomero (☎ 081/556–3841), and Piazza Mazzini in Vomero near the Museo Archeologico Nazionale (☎ 081/549–3357).

Being Streetwise in Naples

After a decade-long offensive against crime, Naples is now as safe as any other modern metropolis. Employment is up, poverty is down, and armies of *polizia* now patrol the city's main thoroughfares. Provided you stay clear of the remaining pockets of crime (most of these neighborhoods, like the Forcella district and the Spanish Quarter, are well off the beaten tourist path) you can enjoy a safe stay. That noted, some advice is in order. In the city's picturesque quarters, streets aren't just streets—they are literally "living rooms," so act as you would as a guest in someone else's house: Don't gawk at residents as you stroll through Spaccanapoli or the Pignasecca market. Have fun taking photographs— most Neapolitans are extremely proud of their neighborhoods—but don't make a production number out of it. In the poorer sectors, don't wave a 20-carat diamond around, nor an expensive Nikon, or, for that matter, your guide book. It's best to blend in with the natives, so you might even camouflage yourself by storing your camera and pocketbook in a shopping bag from one of the city stores.

Note that there is a "safe" and "unsafe" side to the street when dealing with the main arteries that circle the foot of the Vomero hill: Via Chiaia, Via Toledo, and Via Roma. Don't walk on the side which borders the hill itself: *scugnizzi* (street kids) like to scoot out on rollerblades from the densely packed residential quarters at the base of the hill, grab a pocketbook, then dash back into the crowds. Also be aware of two men riding the same Vespa—one generally drives, the other yanks. Wear a concealed money belt or remain aware of the stray pickpocket on the jammed buses and subways. As they are fond of saying in Naples, if you think something bad is going to happen to you, it will: So, smile and enjoy yourself.

Contacts and Resources

Car Rentals

Be careful if you rent a car outside Campania; there is always extra insurance for this region, and most companies refuse to let you take a Mercedes or BMW into Campania and make you sign a retainer accepting all responsibility for the car if you do take it there. Car thieves here are some of the fastest and most organized in the world; the car is usually dismantled and in Eastern Europe the next day (there's a big market with the new Eastern European mafiosi for relatively inexpensive trophy cars). Agencies in Naples include: **Avis** (✉ Stazione Centrale, ☎ 081/553–7171; ✉ Via Partenope 23, ☎ 081/764–5600); **Europcar** (✉ Via Partenope 38, ☎ 081/764–5070, as well as the airport and central train station); **Hertz** (✉ Aeroporto di Capodichino, ☎ 081/780–2971; ✉ Piazza Garibaldi 93, ☎ 081/206228); **Maggiore** (✉ Via Cervantes 92, ☎ 081/552–1900, as well as the airport and central train station).

Changing Money

If you want convenience and aren't changing a big wad, use the **Ufficio di Cambio** inside Stazione Centrale (☞ Coming and Going by Train, *above*); it's open daily 7:15 AM–8:30 PM. If you have a moment, **Cambio San Pietro** (✉ Corso Umberto 292), on the right just as you leave

Piazza Garibaldi, has much better rates. There are also other exchange offices just below on Via Cristoforo Colombo, one of which is open until 7 PM. If you want to compare rates, you can also go to the financial district around Piazza Municipio where there are many banks that also offer currency exchange services. However, you'll find the best way to change money in Italy, for which you get the best rate without paying any fees, is to use your ATM card at whatever bank is close at hand. The only charge will be whatever your bank charges for using a bank not your own and the rate you'll get is whatever the rate you would get charging something on a credit card. The only disadvantage is you won't know the exact rate until you get home and look at your bank statement to see precisely how many dollars were deducted from your account.

Consulates
United Kingdom (✉ Via Francesco Crispi 122, off Piazza Amedeo, ☎ 081/663511; ☉ weekdays 9–12:30 and 2–4:30). **United States** (✉ Piazza della Repubblica 2, at west end of Villa Comunale, ☎ 081/583–8111; ☉ weekdays 8–1).

Doctors and Dentists
Call 081/751–3177.

Emergencies
General emergencies: (☎ 113). **Police:** (☎ 112).

Ambulance: (☎ 081/752–0696). **Fire:** (☎ 115). **Medical emergency:** after 8 PM (☎ 081/761–3466) and ask for an English-speaking nurse. The main **police station** (✉ Via Medina 75, ☎ 081/794–1111) has an *ufficio stranieri* (foreigners' office) that usually has an English speaker on staff.

Naples has some excellent general hospitals: **Ospedale Cardarelli**: (✉ Via Cardarelli 9, ☎ 081/757–2956); **Universitaria Policlinco Federico II** (✉ Via S. Pansini, ☎ 081/746–2937); **Ospedale dei Pellegrini** (✉ Via Portamedina 41, ☎ 081/563–3234); and **Ospedale San Paolo** (✉ Via Terracina 219, ☎ 081/768–6284).

English-Language Books
For romance, philosophy, or a handy thesaurus, head to **Universal Books** (✉ Via Rione Sirignano I, just off Riviera di Chiaia, ☎ 081/663217; ☉ weekdays 9–1 and 4–7, Sat. 9–1).

Guided Tours
Giranapoli, the city's public transportation authority, offers bus tours of the city's principal monuments, lasting around 2½ hours, for the price of a regular bus ticket. You can arrange this service, called **Arte Bus,** through your hotel, or call Giranapoli (☎ 081/763–2177). You can book tours to Pompeii, Vesuvio, and the islands with **CIT** (✉ Piazza Municipio 70, ☎ 081/552–5426). If you're a spelunker at heart, call the **Libera Associazione degli Escursionisti Sottosuolo** (✉ Via Santa Teresa degli Spagnoli 24, ☎ 081/400256) for adventurous tours of Naples's underground (weekends, 10 AM at the Piazza Trieste e Trento). Other exciting tours of Naples's underground are offered weekends at 10 AM by **Napoli Sottoteranea** (meet in Piazza San Gaetano to the left of San Paolo Maggiore, ☎ 081/449821). Agencies in town offering guided tours with official guides include: **Carrani Tours** (in Rome, ☎ 06/488–0510 or 06/474–2501; **Milleviaggi** (✉ Riviera di Chiaia 252, ☎ 081/754–2064); **Tourcar** (✉ Piazza Matteotti 1, ☎ 081/552–3310); and **STS** (✉ Piazza Medaglie d'Oro 41, ☎ 081/578–9292). And you can hire an individual guide by contacting **Sirlat** (✉ Via Gramsci 22, ☎ 081/761–1192).

Late-Night Pharmacies

Try the **pharmacy** in Via Carducci above the Villa Comunale (✉ Via Carducci 21–23, ☎ 081/417283), as well as in the hallway of Stazione Centrale. If these are closed, they will post the addresses of those that are open (the others take turns staying open late); you can also call 192 or buy a copy of the newspaper *Il Mattino* for a daily list of pharmacies that are open nights and weekends in your neighborhood.

Mail and Phones

The best place to make long-distance calls is at **Telecom** (✉ Via A. Depretis 40, between Piazza Bovio and Piazza Municipio; ⊘ Mon.–Sat. 9:30–1 and 2–5:30). The main **post office** (✉ Piazza Matteotti off Via Diaz, ☎ 081/551–1456; ⊘ weekdays 8:15–7:20 and Sat. 8:15–1:30) has *fermo posta* (held mail). The postal code is 80100. Branch offices are usually open weekdays 8:15–1:30 and Saturday 8:15–12:10.

Travel Agencies

Every Tour travel agency (✉ Piazza Municipio 5–6, ☎ 081/551–8564; ⊘ weekdays 9–1:30 and 3:30–7, Sat. 9–1) provides the entire range of American Express services. Dedicated to helping students, **Euro Study Travel** (✉ Mezzocannone 119, ☎ 081/552–0947; ⊘ weekdays 9:30–1:30 and 3–6) is across from the central university building. The ticket office (✉ Via Mezzocannone 87) is also open Saturday 9:30–12:30.

Visitor Information

The numerous tourist offices in Naples aren't always open when they claim to be, but most are generally open from Monday to Saturday 9–7 and Sunday 9–2 except where noted. There's an **EPT** office (☎ 081/268779) in **Stazione Centrale**, where the people are quite friendly and helpful; the main administrative center (with an atmosphere of Baroque mothballs) is in **Piazza dei Martiri** (✉ Piazza dei Martiri 58, ☎ 081/405311; ⊘ weekdays 8:30–2). Branches are also at **Stazione Mergellina** (☎ 081/761–2102) and at the airport (☎ 081/780–5761). An **AACST** office (✉ Piazza Gesù Nuovo, ☎ 01/552–3328) specializes in information on old Naples but generally just gives out brochures. A second office is in front of the **Castel dell'Ovo** (☎ 081/764–5688; closed Sun.).

3 AROUND THE BAY: FROM POMPEII TO THE PHLEGREAN FIELDS

From steaming volcanic craters to peaceful archaeological sites, the area around the Bay of Naples has lost none of the fascination it held for the ancient Greeks and Romans. Here, within sight of Mt. Vesuvius are Pompeii, Herculaneum, Cumae, and Baiae—towns that now look like abandoned Cecil B. DeMille movie sets. Blessed with centuries-old traditions of fine gastronomy and hospitality, Campania Felix—Campania, the Happy Land, as the Romans called it—remains a lush landscape where the dividing line between myth and reality is so very tenuously drawn.

By Mark
Walters

▌F YOU'RE HEADING TO NAPLES, YOU CAN EITHER GET
THERE by train, bus, and car or you can "arrive" aboard
a boat. If you're lucky enough to travel by water, a peacock's tail of splendor unfolds as you enter the vast Golfo di Napoli,
or Bay of Naples. Enshrined in 1,001 travel posters, this nerve-tingling
vista offers a turquoise-rimmed crescent of isles, hills, azure sky and
sea, ancient cities, and modern villas, all arrayed around the bay east
and west of Naples. But to each side of the city, the earth fumes and
grumbles, reminding us that all this beauty was born of cataclysm. Along
the coast to the west are the Campi Flegrei, or the Phlegrean Fields of
the ancients, where the crater of the Solfatara spews satisfyingly Dante-
esque gases and where hills like Monte Nuovo have a habit of emerging overnight. Nearby are the dark, deep waters of Lago d'Averno, the
lake that was allegedly the ancient doorway to hell, or Hades, as it was
then called. To the southeast is slumbering Vesuvius, the mother of all
mounts, looking down from its 4,000-ft height at the coastal strip stretching from modern and ancient Pompeii all the way to Naples. With potential death and destruction so close at hand, it is small wonder that
southern Italians—and in particular the inhabitants of Campania
around Naples—plunge so enthusiastically into living life to its fullest,
obeying to the letter Horace's precept—carpe diem.

If the most famous volcano in the world looms over the scene like a
perpetual and living tombstone, every visitor should feel perfectly safe.
The observatory on Vesuvio's slopes keeps its scientific finger on the
subterranean pulse and will warn when signs of misbehavior become
evident, so no one need worry about becoming an unwilling exhibit
in some future Pompeii. You can simply concentrate on the memorable
sights that can fringe the spectacularly blue bay. The whole region is
fraught with legend and immortal names. Sixteen kilometers (10 miles)
to the west of Naples lies an area where the emperors Nero and
Hadrian worked on their suntans, Virgil composed his poetry, and the
Apostle Paul landed to spread the Gospel. Here are ancient sites, such
as the Greeks' first colony, the city of Cumae, home of the famed
Cumaean Sybil; Baia, the luxury-loving Baiae, whose hot springs made
it the largest and most dissolute spa of ancient Italy; and the Amphitheater
of Pozzuoli, whose subterranean galleries are far better preserved than
even Rome's Colosseum. Here are the Campi Flegri—inspiration for
Dante's *Inferno,* and the sulfur-ridden Solfitara, the "Little Vesuvius."
Heading east of Naples are the glittering Bourbon palaces of Portici,
the ancient palace at Oplontis, and, under the shadow of Vesuvius, Herculaneum and Pompeii—two of the largest archaeological sites in Europe. Nowhere else in Italy is there such a spectacular mingling of natural
beauty with the remains of antiquity.

Rich archaeological and literary evidence shows that there has been a
continuous human presence in the area for millennia. Used as outposts
probably by the Minoans and Myceneans in the second millennium
BC, the area was first colonized by Greeks from Euboea in the 8th century BC, who settled on the island of Pithekoussai (modern day Ischia)
and later on the mainland at Cumae. So much we learn from a very
valuable literary source, the Greek geographer Strabo (64 BC–after AD
21), who must have traveled extensively in the area. The early Greeks
traded widely with the Etruscans and local Italic peoples, eventually
extending their sphere of influence to Neapolis and southward and northward along the shores of the Tyrrhenian Sea.

Greek civilization flourished for hundreds of years along this seaboard,
but there was nothing in the way of centralized government until cen-

turies later when the Romans surged southward and began to set up colonies of their own for added protection, especially after incursions by foreign forces such as Pyrrhus and Hannibal, in the 3rd century BC.

From the 1st century BC onward, Campania became synonymous with sybaritic wealth. It was here that the wealthy Romans built their palatial residences, tapping the naturally hot springs for their fabled baths and harnessing the rich volcanic soils in the area to produce wines lauded by Latin poets. Emperors indulged in vices that would have been unseemly in the capital, and there was the usual complement of public baths and theaters to keep the plebeians happy.

The merrymaking on the other side of Naples was truncated in AD 79 by Vesuvius, which was believed by few at the time to harbor any danger for those living at its base. We are fortunate to have a memorable description by Pliny the Younger of his uncle being overwhelmed by the surge cloud and dying of asphyxiation in Stabiae, now Castellammare di Stabia. Although written some years after the event, Pliny's letter to Tacitus is a unique and moving account of the disaster. But as so often happens in history, other people's cataclysms are an archaeologist's dream: Pompeii, Herculaneum, and outlying lesser-known villages such as Oplontis were spared the ravages of the centuries and have been remarkably preserved for posterity.

Following the fall of the Roman Empire and the period of general decay that prevailed during Byzantine times, more than 1,000 years were to pass before the area's classical greatness was once again appreciated, this time by young, well-heeled 18th- and 19th-century travelers from northern Europe, for whom a visit to Vesuvius and the various ancient sites was the culmination of their Grand Tour.

Many would say that the region is now experiencing a second Renaissance. Increasingly, conventional modes of tourist development are being scaled back in favor of a more global appreciation of the landscape. The designation of Vesuvius as a national park in 1996 and, together with the villas on its lower slopes, as a UNESCO World Heritage Site in 1998, points the way toward sustainable development, guaranteeing travelers an enthralling mix of archaeology, history, folklore, gastronomy, and nature for years to come.

Pleasures and Pastimes

Dining

If *Betae garo cum olivis capparibusque* and *Cassata oplontis* seem a somewhat unusual listing on a menu, fitting perhaps for an antiquarian Vatican dinner party, further surprises will be in store when dining out in Pompeii. At the Principe restaurant, Roman banquets are re-created with ingredients that would have been used 2,000 years ago. You might even be able to taste one of the dishes mentioned above (the first is beet with fish sauce, olives, and capers). Fortunately, the ancients committed much of their culinary expertise to writing, thanks mainly to authors like Cato, Cicero, and the renowned gourmet in Augustan times, Apicius.

To the west of Naples, Cumae is thought to have been the setting for part of Petronius's *Satyricon,* a picaresque novel probably written in the 1st century AD, containing the memorable scene of a dinner hosted by the nouveau-riche Trimalchio. In the same area of the Campi Flegrei, the tradition of abundance, if not excess, continues in a host of local restaurants and trattorias. This is where many local Neapolitans migrate on weekends to buy their *frutti de mare* (seafood) or dine in Lucullan style at the many waterside restaurants in the area, at half the price they would spend at restaurants nearer home.

The wines, too, are unlikely to disappoint: the white-grape variety Falanghina, from the Campi Flegrei, has justifiably built up a reputation as a fine accompaniment to fish-centered meals, while the slopes of Vesuvius produce Lacryma Christi (red, white, and rosé). If available, try the range of wines produced at competitive prices by the local bottler Cantina Grotta del Sole.

CATEGORY	COST*
$$$$	over 85,000 lire
$$$	60,000–85,000 lire
$$	25,000–60,000 lire
$	under 25,000 lire

*per person, excluding drinks and service

Hiking

For challenging hikes off the beaten track, parts of Vesuvius have been mapped out with trails for public access. What looks like a barren wasteland from down below turns out to be a profusion of well-adapted plant and animal life, which is at its best in spring and early summer. Deserted paths cut across ancient lava fields and pyroclastic material, through lunarlike terrain and then suddenly into Mediterranean scrub and woodland. As an alternative, on torrid summer days, take an eight-minute cable-car ride from Castellammare di Stabia up to Monte Faito, which rises impressively to almost 4,000 ft on the southeastern sweep of the Bay of Naples. A short walk takes you into shady beech woods reminiscent of Italy's Apennine backbone, while more ambitious trails marked by the Club Alpino Italiano lead across imposing landscapes to the Amalfi Coast.

Lodging

To avoid what might seem like glorified Pompeian *lupanares*—those favored abodes of ancient ladies of the night—the choice of hotel merits special attention throughout the area. Most hotels will give excellent value for money compared with locations in the city of Naples and will be a good deal quieter as well. However, where hotels are close to main roads—and that means motor scooters at night—ask for quiet rooms at the back, especially in the busy towns of Pompeii and Pozzuoli. As throughout Italy, high season is usually at Christmas, Easter, and during the summer, when temperatures, prices, and visitor numbers reach a crescendo. At Pompeii avoid visiting during religious festivities if at all possible, as local hotels are likely to be booked up with pilgrims months in advance. As a general rule, to ensure you get the right room at the right time, book well ahead of your visit.

CATEGORY	COST*
$$$$	over 300,000 lire
$$$	160,000–300,000 lire
$$	100,000–160,000 lire
$	under 100,000 lire

*All prices are for a double room, excluding tax and service.

Wildlife

If you're suffering from a surfeit of archaeology or feel the need to compensate for overindulging in the local *cucina,* a visit to one of the extinct volcanic craters near Naples could produce dividends. The Astroni crater, now an preserve run by the World Wide Fund for Nature, offers breathtakingly beautiful walks amid Mediterranean woodland only 16 km (10 mi) from the very heart of Naples. Picnic sites have been thoughtfully laid out in various shady spots within the crater perimeter. At the base, there is the added interest of small brackish lakes overlooked by an observation hide, so there's a good chance of seeing a variety of bird species. Like so many places here, the crater is steeped in history: used by the Romans for its natural thermal baths, this whole area became the hunting domain of the Aragonese in the 15th century and then of the Bourbon kings in the 18th and 19th centuries.

A smaller crater near the coast to the west of Pozzuoli offering shorter and less shady walks is Monte Nuovo, whose cone formed in just eight days of explosive activity in 1538. Innovatively run by the town council of Pozzuoli together with a local school, the cone still exhibits some residual volcanic activity in the form of fumaroles. This is the place to hone your botanical skills, with many of the main species of the Mediterranean maquis having been planted and clearly labeled close to the site offices.

Exploring Pompeii, Herculaneum, and Mt. Vesuvius

The lower slopes of Vesuvius, which is the most densely inhabited volcanic region in the world, are crisscrossed by major roads and several railway lines, providing easy access to most of the archaeological sites. Start with Pompeii, work your way clockwise around the volcano to Oplontis and Herculaneum, and then shoot off at a tangent to the Museo Archeologico Nazionale in Naples to study the many artistic treasures once buried in these towns. To make a chronological departure from classical times, while in Ercolano do a short detour to visit the sumptuous Royal Palace of Portici and a Vesuvian villa such as the attractively restored Villa Campolieto, both built during Bourbon rule in the 18th century. The best form of transportation is the Circumvesuviana light railway, with its stations never more than a 10-minute walk from the major sites.

Numbers in the text correspond to numbers in the margin and on the East of Naples, Pompeii, and West of Naples maps.

Great Itineraries

With limited time at your disposal, priority should be given to the sites of **Herculaneum** ② and **Pompeii** ⑥–㉖, although one day will be only enough to whet the appetite. A practical minimum for really absorbing the splendors of this area and getting a healthy balance of archaeology, history, museums, and cuisine is about three days. To take in the entire span from the Campi Flegrei to Pompeii, including some of the undeservedly less-visited sites such as **Oplontis** ⑤ in Torre Annunziata and **Baia** ㉜, you would be advised to make a weeklong trip with at least two base camps, one on either side of Naples.

IF YOU HAVE 3 DAYS

Begin at **Pompeii** ⑥–㉖, allowing at least half a day for the archaeological site, which will be just enough to take in the main civic buildings and a representative sampling of villas, and the hot spots of ancient Roman entertainment, such as the Amphitheater. Given the part it played in AD 79, **Vesuvius** ③ also merits a visit, though temperatures at the peak in winter months can be pretty frigid. To complete the threesome, head for **Herculaneum** ②, for its less-visited but more evocative ruins.

IF YOU HAVE 5 DAYS

More time in the area will enable you to head west of Naples into the Campi Flegrei, where a little exploring will pay immediate dividends. To experience the volcanic nature of this otherworldly terrain, walk across the crater of the **Solfatara** ㉗ and then soak up the archaeological sites of **Pozzuoli** ㉘ and **Baia** ㉜. Reserve half a day for the site of **Cumae** ㉝ and appreciate the sweeping views of Italy's Tyrrhenian coastline from its impressive acropolis.

With a little more time to unwind and appreciate the diversity of this remarkable landscape, try to fit in a visit to one of the extinct craters—now nature reserves—of **Monte Nuovo** ㉛ or the **Astroni** ㉙, west of Naples. With time left over, sample the opulence of a Vesuvian villa on the so-called Miglio d'Oro, or Golden Mile, built by the aristocracy in Bourbon times close to the Royal Palace of **Portici** ①.

This part of the Mediterranean is at its best in spring and fall. Winter months occasionally reserve chill surprises for visitors, with roads on the upper slopes of Vesuvius becoming dangerously icy at times. In April and May watch out for the hordes of (nonpaying) schoolchildren at archaeological sites and, as a general rule—to avoid the crowds—visit sites first thing in the morning or late afternoon before closing time (usually an hour before sunset). Pompeii rewards its overheated summer visitors with open-air theatrical performances on the site during the evenings, while other sites such as Cumae and Oplontis have rival attractions. For nature lovers, this part of the Mediterranean, especially the verdant Campi Flegrei, becomes a floral feast at springtime, while the north-facing slopes of Vesuvius are still awash with color as late as June and July.

UNDER THE SHADOW OF VESUVIUS: PORTICI TO HERCULANEUM

Though barely more than a third as high as Mt. Etna, its Sicilian counterpart, Vesuvius with its relatively modest 4,189 ft has achieved unparalleled status in the collective consciousness of the Italians and the world. "Vesuvius is nature committing suicide," Madame de Staël reported back to Parisians during the Age of Enlightenment. For centuries this still-active volcano had offered a spectacle to visitors who flocked to the Bay of Naples to marvel at its small-scale eruptions, ever-present flumes of smoke, and thundering fumaroles. In the mid-18th century, in fact, the entire court of Naples set up shop Portici, at the foot of the mountain, building summer villas that served as ringside seats to the volcano's pyrotechnics. Artists painted the mountain in eruption, streams of lava rendered in lurid hues of blood. Romantic poets climbed the peak under the full moon to create odes extolling its sublime and terrible power. Duchesses (fashionably attired with earrings of lava stone) would hire chairmen to bear them up to the rim, where, down below, rainbow mounds of sulfurous ash, vents of hissing steam, lunarlike boulders—everything it seems but little imps dashing about with long Luciferian pitchforks—presented a hellish sight. All the while, inhabitants living around the cone would study Vesuvius for signs of impending destruction. "*Napoli fa i peccati e la Torre li paga*," the residents of nearby Torre del Greco used to mutter—"Naples sins and the Torre suffers." When reports of depraved behavior circulated about Neapolitans across the bay, chastisement was only to be expected.

In the 18th century, the Roman towns of Pompeii and Herculaneum—buried by the devastation wrought by the famous AD 79 eruption—were first excavated and became the most celebrated archaeological sites in Europe. Today, thousands of visitors arrive every day, most with one eye monitoring Il Vesuvio, just a few miles away. There have been many major and minor eruptions of the volcano in the past 2,000 years, the most recent in 1944. The fact remains that there have been around 30 eruptions since AD 79 with only two in the 20th century. This might be construed as good news, but many vulcanologists think it is ominous when a living volcano is so silent, and they now maintain a constant watch. Today Vesuvius may have lost its plume of smoke, but it has lost none of its fascination.

Portici

❶ *7 km (5½ mi) southeast from Naples; 1 km (½ mi) northwest from Ercolano.*

All set rather incongruously within the urban sprawl of the Comuni Vesuviani is Portici, whose Reggia di Portici, or Royal Palace, its little known botanical garden, and numerous villas, of which the Villa Campolieto is the most celebrated, still offer a peek into the gilded lives of the 18th-century rich and famous. A little more than 250 years ago, the area was chosen by the first Bourbon king of the Two Sicilies, Charles III, as the site for a royal palace that would be sufficiently close to Naples for him to be able to return to the capital at a moment's notice, yet far enough away for the king and his entourage to indulge in hunting, one of the main Bourbon pursuits. No matter that courtiers were worried by the proximity of Vesuvius; Charles refused to show concern at any imminent danger, proclaiming, "God, the immaculate Virgin, and San Gennaro will protect us." The royal presence in the area triggered a boom in real estate, with more than 120 ducal villas being built in the subsequent half century on a stretch of land that came to be known as the "Miglio d'Oro" (Golden Mile). Here life became one long *fête champêtre,* with costume balls, picnics, concerts, and entertainment, some of which enchanted the likes of Goethe and Lord Byron. Today, progress is being made by the *Ente per le Ville Vesuviane* (Vesuvian Villa Agency) to purchase and restore the villas to their former glory.

The showpiece is Portici's *Reggia* (palace), or **Palazzo Reale.** Straddling the Via Nazionale delle Calabrie (Statate 18), the main road that led south of Naples in past centuries, now renamed Via Università, this royal palace was designed by the architect Canevari, complete with a layout of 75 acres of woodland, and executed by another architect, Ferdinando Fuga, 1738–42. It stands impressively at the foothills of Vesuvius and enjoys sweeping views across the Bay of Naples from both the south-facing inner courtyard and its upper floors. Although the agriculture department of Naples University still occupies most of the palace, the cultural heritage ministry has taken over a few of the rooms on the *piano nobile* and currently uses them for temporary exhibitions, thereby restoring to the public one of the main landmarks of Bourbon history and architecture.

The palace is conveniently located on a trolley-bus route (No. 255) between Ercolano and Portici about 1,000 ft northwestward up the road from the Herculaneum archaeological site. The bus stop is unmistakable, right in the middle of the courtyard right between the northern and southern wings. Head for the university porters' lodge on the seaward side (a parking lot just beyond) and mount the monumental staircase leading up to the piano nobile. At the risk of developing a crick in your neck, admire the well-preserved 18th-century trompe l'oeil frescoes decorating the walls and the ceiling and generally enjoy these now-hallowed halls of academia. Horatio Nelson would have walked up the same staircase on his way to a royal banquet held in his honor by King Ferdinand IV and Queen Carolina in 1798, where he sat opposite and first met Sir William Hamilton and his wife, Emma. At the time the palace was used as a repository for many of the early finds from Herculaneum, now in the Museo Archeologico in Naples, and it was noted particularly for the decorative 18th-century panels from the finest salon—called the porcelain, or china, room—which were sub-

East of Naples: Portici to Pompeii

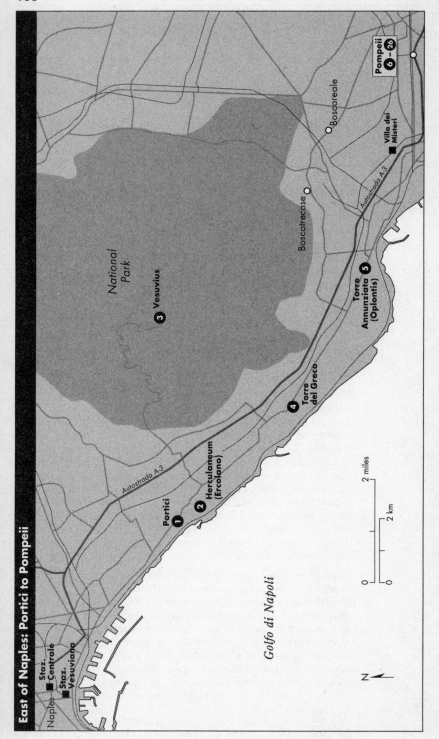

Naples

Staz.
Centrale

Staz.
Vesuviana

Autostrada A-3

National
Park

Vesuvius ③

Portici ①

② Herculaneum
(Ercolano)

④ Torre
del Greco

Boscatrecase ○

Boscoreale ○

Autostrada A-3

Villa dei
Misteri ■

Pompeii
⑥ – ㉖

Torre
Annunziata ⑤
(Oplontis)

Golfo di Napoli

N

0   2 miles

0   2 km

sequently moved to the Royal Palace of Capodimonte, where they can still be admired today. ✉ *Via Università 100,* ☎ *081/775–1251.* ✉ *Free.* ⊙ *Sept.–July, weekdays 8:30 AM–7 PM.*

Opposite the entrance to the Royal Palace of Portici lies the **Orto Botanico** (Botanical Garden), founded in 1872, which is housed within the palace grounds and abuts the magnificent Holmoak Wood, the hunting preserve of the Bourbon kings. The original collection was severely damaged in World War II, when the botanical institute was requisitioned and the garden used as a vehicle parking area by Allied forces. Since then the botanical collection has recovered and expanded, with new acquisitions especially from Madagascar and the Caribbean, a delightfully shady palmery, an impressive variety of cycads, and some unusually large specimens of the exotic Asian tree *Ginkgo biloba.* If assistance or guidance is at hand, ask to see the rare southern African desert plant *Welwitschia mirabilis,* and the native but endangered primrose *Primula palinuri.* In addition to normal opening hours, guided visits can also be arranged by appointment with the curator. ✉ *Via Università,* ☎ *081/775–5109.* ✉ *Free.* ⊙ *Daily 7–1.*

Leaving the archaeological site of Herculaneum and heading southeast along Corso Resina with Vesuvius on your left and the Bay of Naples on your right, after about 980 ft you'll pass the entrance to **Villa Campolieto,** one of the most attractive villas, which—like most historic buildings still standing in the area—has survived centuries of volcanic eruptions, earthquakes, and post-Bourbon neglect. Go in through the well-tended gardens past the information kiosk (leaflets available in English) and turn left into the main building. If you're motorized, ask at the kiosk to use the parking facilities at the far end of the gardens.

The construction of Villa Campolieto was commissioned by Prince Luzio of Sangro and entrusted to no less than four architects during its troubled conception from 1755 to 1775, with the final touches added by the architect Luigi Vanvitelli, better known for his work on the Royal Palace of Caserta, and his son Carlo. After entering through the gardens—this was in fact the original main entrance, as the large doorway on the Via Nazionale delle Calabrie (now Corso Resina) would have been reserved for carriages—proceed up the Vanvitellian staircase (similar to the one at the palace at Caserta) to the piano nobile, currently used for art exhibitions and as lecture halls. Note the classical scenes in most of the frescoes on this floor, with fine illusionist work by Jacopo Cestaro, including depictions of Minerva and Mercury set in a Vanvitelli-style colonnade. Cestaro was also responsible for the beautifully restored frescoed ceilings in both front rooms facing Vesuvius.

At ground-floor level, the main peculiarity is the elliptical rotunda, which provides a picturesque setting for outdoor concerts and theatrical performances during the Vesuvian Villas Festival in July. Note the natural gray shading of the steps and lower facade, characteristic of many buildings erected in the Bourbon era, from the local volcanic *piperno* stone. This villa is the headquarters for the Ente per le Ville Vesuviane association. ✉ *Corso Resina 283, Ercolano,* ☎ *081/732–2134.* ✉ *Free.* ⊙ *Tues.–Sun. 10–1.*

Dining

$–$$ ✕ **Trattoria da Calcagno.** This is the one of the best present-day eateries in Ercolano, catering to locals and foreigners alike: freshly cooked food washed down by lively Vesuvian wines only 325 ft up from the excavations of Herculaneum just off Via 4 Novembre. Dishes and wines vary according to the season, with pasta with beans a winter favorite and richly garnished spaghetti with clams for summer months.

✉ *Corso Italia 17, Ercolano,* ☎ *081/739–0405. No credit cards. Closed Sun.*

$ ✕ **A' Cantinella do Cunvento.** A short walk down Via Università from the Royal Palace of Portici brings you to this unpretentious ristorante-pizzeria, known to the locals as Da Peppino, after its owner-manager Giuseppe. Although crowded with staff from the nearby college at lunchtime, there is nothing donnish about the down-to-earth service or prices. The all-in-one price of about 15,000 lire includes first course (pasta or rice), main course (octopus salad is a specialty), and fruit. ✉ *Via Università 64, Portici,* ☎ *081/775–5301. No credit cards. Sometimes closed weekends.*

Shopping

Donadio Manifattura Coralli (✉ Via del Corallo, Ercolano, ☎ 081/490686) is first and foremost a cameo factory; it also sells directly to the public. Local artisans can be observed making the cameos, an age-old tradition in which shells are meticulously carved to produce mythological scenes in relief, exploiting the natural layering and contrasting colors of the raw material.

Herculaneum (Ercolano)

★ ❷ *12 km (8 mi) southeast of Naples; 40 km (25 mi) northwest of Salerno.*

A visit to the archaeological site of Herculaneum neatly counterbalances the hustle of its larger neighbor, Pompeii. And although close to the heart of the busy town of Ercolano—indeed, in places right under it—the ancient site seems worlds apart, and you have the sensation of being catapulted back into the past. Like Pompeii, Herculaneum was buried by Vesuvius's eruption in AD 79. Unlike Pompeii, it was submerged in a mass of volcanic mud that sealed and preserved wood and other materials (at Pompeii these were consumed by red-hot cinders). Much smaller than its famous neighbor, Herculaneum was wealthier, more select, and more of what has been found has been left in place. Several villas have inlaid marble floors that evoke the same admiration as the mosaics in Naples's Museo Archeologico. Elsewhere it is possible to walk through a typical Roman tenement, climbing the original stairs to the cramped, poorly lighted rooms that overlook the central courtyard. Here there is more of a sense of a living community than Pompeii is able to convey. When you've gorged yourself on Roman antiquities, sample the sumptuousness of one of the newly restored Vesuvian villas or the Royal Palace of Portici. Like all the other sites in the Vesuvian area, Herculaneum is served efficiently by the Circumvesuviana railway, which provides fast, frequent, and economical connections; from Naples's Stazione Centrale or Stazione Vesuviana, take the Circumvesuviana train to the Ercolano stop (5 per hour, 20 minutes east, 2,000 lire). The ruins are a five-minute walk down Via Novembre toward the Bay of Naples. Archaeology buffs will want to bring a flashlight to better see into the dark corners of the excavated houses.

Lying more than 60 ft below the town of Ercolano, the **Scavi di Ercolano** (Excavations of Herculaneum) are set among the acres of greenhouses that make this area one of Europe's chief flower-growing areas. It was named, like several other Greek colonies around the Mediterranean, after its legendary founder Heracles (Hercules), but details surrounding its foundation date or the exact provenance of its Greek settlers life have yet to be revealed. Certainly the grid layout of the town plan suggests affinities with nearby Neapolis (now Naples), so it could have been an offshoot of its neighbor on the Bay of Naples. Like many Greek sites in southern Italy, in about the 4th century BC it fell under Samnite influence and finally became a *municipium* under Roman dominion in

89 BC. At the time of its destruction in AD 79, it had about 5,000 inhabitants (as compared to Pompeii's 20,000), many of whom were fishermen, craftsmen, and artists, while a lucky few patricians owned villas overlooking the sea. In contrast with Pompeii, most of the damage here was done by volcanic mud. This semiliquid mass seeped into the crevices and niches of every building, covering household objects and enveloping textiles and wood—sealing all in a compact, airtight tomb.

Casual excavation—and haphazard looting—began at the beginning of the 18th century under the prince of Elbeuf, who purchased the land after a farmer had made several chance finds in marble. The excavation technique at the time consisted of digging vertical shafts and horizontal galleries, and whenever possible, gunpowder was used to speed up the work—techniques that make those of the much-maligned Hermann Schliemann, discover of Troy, sound positively scrupulous. It was precisely through this network of underground tunnels that 18th-century visitors from northern Europe on their Grand Tour—such as Horace Walpole and Thomas Gray—were to experience the buried city. As Gray wrote to his mother, "The passage they have made with all their turnings and windings is now more than a mile long." As you walk you see parts of an amphitheater, many houses adorned with marble columns encrusted with the same, the point of a temple, several arched vaults of rooms painted in fresco. Systematic digs were not initiated until the 1920s, by which time many of the cherries buried within the cake had already been damaged or removed. Today less than half of Herculaneum has been excavated; with present-day Ercolano and the unlovely Resina quarter (famous among bargain hunters as the area's largest secondhand clothing market) perched on top of the site, progress is understandably limited. On entry, in addition to getting a good overview of the site, you get an idea of the amount of volcanic matter that had to be removed during excavations as you walk down the ramp to the lower entrance on the seaward side, with the neatly laid-out streets and well-preserved edifices to your right.

If you feel closer to the past at Herculaneum than at Pompeii, it's in part because there are fewer jarring reminders here of the present era: not so many hawkers or tacky souvenirs for sale, no babel of languages at the ticket office, no tour group leader booming, "Now you can take some photos of these lovely old ruins . . . although you may already have enough snaps of your dear hubby." Also, though Herculaneum had only one-fourth the population of Pompeii and has only been partially excavated, what has been found is generally better preserved. In some cases you can even see the original wooden beams, staircases, and furniture. Lending a touch of verdant life, some of the peristyle gardens have been replanted. Today much excitement is focused on one excavation in a corner of the site, the **Villa dei Papiri**, built by Julius Caesar's father-in-law. The building takes its name from the 1,800 carbonized papyrus scrolls dug up here in the 18th century, leading scholars to believe it may have been a study center or library. Now Italian archaeologists and geologists have uncovered part of the villa itself and hope to unearth more of the library—given the right funds and political support. Little of the villa can be seen above ground, though visitors to the J. Paul Getty Museum in California can see a modern version of the villa, modeled according to drawings made by the Swiss antiquarian Carl Weber in the 18th century and now the repository for the Getty's important collection of classical antiquities.

Walk through the ticket office down the slope to the southern end of the site toward another ticket check, near the large modern structure of the Antiquarium (yet to be opened). This is a good point at which to view the grid system of roads, with the three *cardines* (from north-east to southwest) being intersected by two *decumani* from left to right. The blocks, as in Pompeii, are referred to as *insulae,* each containing four or five main villas and sometimes a row of shops. In general, and unsurprisingly, the best mosaics, wall paintings, and any organic remains such as wooden furniture are found in those parts that were excavated in the 20th century. The 19th-century open-air excavators—though systematic—took few precautions to preserve the upper stories (just note the ruinous state of Insula II, in the southwest corner as you go in) and, in addition, the artwork has been exposed to the air for an extra century. At the southern (lower) end of the site was the small port, which means that thanks to various eruptions (especially AD 79 and AD 1631), the topography of the land has changed beyond all recognition. It is now hard to believe that Herculaneum lay *"inter duos fluvios infra Vesu-vium"* (between two rivers below Vesuvius).

Take advantage of the first few—less spectacular—villas to get a feel for the layout of a typical Italic house, although here no two plans are the same. After the entranceway, most houses had a long narrow corridor called the fauces, or *vestibulum* opening onto an *atrium* (court-yard) with an *impluvium* in the middle in which to collect rainwater, often channeled to an underground cistern. At the back of the atrium was a *tablinum,* the main reception room where the *patronus* (host) would receive his *clientes* (guests). In some houses there would have been a screen to provide more privacy for the master of the house. Where there was space, a colonnaded garden (peristyle) was considered desirable, complete with fountains and a *triclinium* (open-air dining room). *Cubicula* (bedrooms) were sometimes on either side of the entrance, al-though this is by no means the rule in Herculaneum. Also try to spot the service area (kitchen), with the servants' quarters immediately above.

If you're looking for decorations, these are especially delicate in the **Casa del Atrio a Mosaico** (House of the Mosaic Atrium), with a geo-metrically patterned flooring in the vestibulum leading into a black-and-white checkerboard pattern in the atrium, with the tablinum in the background. The tablinum is unusually elaborate, with its three aisles separated by two rows of pillars topped by Corinthian capitals, conforming to the design described by the great Roman architect Vit-ruvius as *"oecus aegyptius,"* or Egyptian-style room. Like many other houses in both Herculaneum and Pompeii, this may be kept locked, and you could be restricted to a peek through the entrance. This villa enjoyed a sweeping view of the sea, a vantage point utilized by the many rooms that had windows. ⊠ *Insula IV, 1–2.*

The **Casa del Nettuno ed Anfitrite** (The House of Neptune and Am-phitrite) takes its name from the mosaic that still sports its bright blue coloring and adorns the wall of the small secluded nymphaeum, or shrine, at the back of the house. According to legend, in the time-honored fash-ion of the Olympians, Neptune (or Poseidon) saw her dancing with the Nereids on the island of Naxos, carried her off, and married her. The adjacent wall, in similar mosaic style though less well preserved, has a hunting scene with a stag being pursued by a dog. Annexed to the same house is a remarkably preserved wineshop, where amphorae still rest on carbonized wooden shelves. ⊠ *Insula V, 6–7.*

An even better-preserved example of carbonized remains is in the **Casa del Tramezzo di Legno** (House of the Wooden Partition), as it has been prosaically labeled by archaeologists. Following renovation work in the mid-1st century AD, the house was designed to have a frontage on three sides of Insula III and included a number of storerooms, shops, and sec-ond-floor habitations. This suggests that the owner was a wealthy *mer-*

cator, a member of the up-and-coming merchant class that was starting to edge the patricians out of their privileged positions. The fauces in this house lead into an airy atrium, with a lovely garden. Look closely at the impluvium, and you'll see the original impluvium flooring below, which was later replaced with marble, perhaps under a change of owners. Next to the impluvium is an elegant marble table, or *cartibulum,* while behind is the tablinum partially screened off by a bronze-studded wooden partition (the central part of which is missing) that would also have had hooks for hanging *lucernae* (lamps). ⊠ *Insula III, 11–12.*

Stories of Roman licentiousness are belied by the **Terme del Foro** (Forum Baths), where there were separate sections for men and women. Here you see most of the architectural ingredients of *thermae* (baths). But besides the mandatory trio in the men's section (a round *frigidarium,* a cool swimming pool; a *tepidarium,* a semi-heated pool; and a *calidarium,* or heated pool), there is also an *apodyterium,* or changing room, with partitioned shelves for depositing togas and a low podium to use as seating space while in line to use the facilities. For more attractive mosaics—particularly a spectacular rendition of Neptune—go around into the women's baths (with seemingly no frigidarium). The heating system in the tepidarium was also different (no hot air piped through or under, only braziers). Note the steam vents ingeniously built into the bath's benches and the small overhead cubbies in which bathers stored their togas. ⊠ *Insula VI.*

The **Casa del Bicentenario** (House of the Bicentenary) was a patrician residence with smaller rooms on the upper floor, which may have been rented out to artisan tenants who were probably Christians because they left an emblem of the cross embedded in the wall. Visual treats here include a tablinum painted with mythical scenes and paved in mosaic. The house derives its name from its discovery by the grand old man of archaeology, Amedeo Maiuri, in 1938, which coincided with the 200th anniversary of the beginning of excavations in Herculaneum. Incidentally, Maiuri's surname is never mentioned by local archaeologists as it is supposed to bring bad luck, so he is usually referred to just by his first name. ⊠ *Insula V, 15–16.*

There are many other houses that have important remains, including the **Casa dei Cervi** (House of the Stags), which once featured marble sculptures of dogs attacking deer and still has a lavish mosaic floor, a triclinium decorated with frescoes in the Third Style, and a *pergula* (arbor) overlooking the sea; the **Casa del Rilievo di Telefo** (House of the Relief of Telephus), which has one of the largest and most beautiful atriums in the town, a room with colored marble ornamentation, and a famous 1st-century BC relief of the myth of Achilles and Telephus; and the **Casa del Bel Cortile** (House of the Beautiful Courtyard) which also has a reception room with frescoes in the Second Style. Two ramps lead from the lower end of the excavation to the shoreline where 12 arcades hold the remains of a group of skeletons, all that survives of a large group of people caught by Vesuvius's blast as they tried to escape by boat to the sea.

One of the more spectacular sights at Herculaneum is also a well-guarded secret: the **underground theater** dating to about the 1st century BC, in the northwest corner of the site but only accessible by prior arrangement with site guides or local travel operators. Access is gained from a small square building painted in Pompeian red at Corso Resina 23, about 325 ft farther along the road to Portici, opposite the Church of Santa Caterina. If you're visiting in summer months, you can get some extra atmosphere by seeing the evening show, performed in Italian, that's set in the various houses down in the archaeological site. Ask at the ticket office or local Azienda di Soggiorno (Information Bureau) for information. ✉ *Corso Resina, Ercolano,* ☎ *081/739–0963.* 🎫 *12,000 lire.* ⊙ *Daily 9–1 hr before sunset (ticket office closes 2 hrs before sunset).*

Vesuvius

★ ❸ *16 km (10 mi) east of Naples; 8 km (5 mi) northeast of Herculaneum; 40 km (25 mi) northwest of Salerno.*

Although the destructive powers of Vesuvius are undoubtedly diminished, the threat of an eruption is ever present for the local population crowded at its base. While the local administrators in the 13 *comuni* surrounding the volcano are well versed in risk-management procedures, because its slopes are more densely populated than any other volcano in the world, the practicalities of evacuating over half a million people are daunting. In bygone ages the task of protecting the local inhabitants fell to the martyred patron saint of Naples, San Gennaro, or St. Januarius, whose statue was often borne aloft through the streets of Naples in attempts to placate the volcano's wrath. Nowadays, volcanic activity is attentively monitored by the Osservatorio Vesuviano, founded under Bourbon king Ferdinand II in the mid-19th century and the facility where the seismic scale was invented. The original observatory, conspicuous with its Pompeian red facade, has survived unscathed on the volcano's upper slopes and now serves as a small conference center, while being flanked by an operations center that houses antiquated equipment used by seismologists in previous centuries. Access is currently restricted to scientific groups and associations, but plans are afoot to create a proper visitor center housing a mineralogical museum, characteristic landscape gouaches, early seismographs, and information panels. For further details phone the Osservatorio (☎ 081/777–7149 or 081/777–7150).

Seen from the other side of the Bay of Naples, Vesuvius appears to have two peaks: on the northern side is the steep face of Monte Somma, possibly part of the original crater wall in AD 79; to the south is the present-day cone of Vesuvius, which has actually formed within the ancient crater. The AD 79 cone would have been considerably higher, perhaps peaking at more than 2,150 ft. The upper slopes bear the visible scars left by relatively recent eruptions, the most striking being the lava flow from 1944 lying to the left (north side) of the main approach road from Ercolano on the way up. On earlier lava flows such as that of 1872, the grayish lichen named after the volcano, *Stereocaulon vesuvianum,* has had more time to break up the volcanic rocks and prepare the way for pioneer plants like red valerian and the characteristic leggy Mt. Etna broom, which transform the upper slopes into a blaze of dark pink and yellow in late spring.

Under its new status as a national park and world biosphere reserve, Vesuvius currently enjoys substantially greater protection from urban encroachment and other land uses that have ravaged the towns lying at its base. The park office (☎ 081/771–7549) has mapped out a series of trails open to the public; a popular one includes the Valle del Gigante (Giant's Valley) and the Valle dell'Inferno (Hell's Valley). To reach this, head downhill from the summit parking lot on the north side and look for the footpath descending on the other side of the guardrail at the first bend. Those seeking a barren lunar landscape will be disappointed: the flora here is remarkably diverse, boasting 23 species of orchids set amid an interesting combination of montane vegetation and Mediterranean maquis. Birders should watch out for peregrine falcons soaring over Monte Somma and for ravens at lower altitude, in addition to various warbler species that have found their eco-niches on the upper slopes of Vesuvius.

For public transport users, the Vesuvius bus run by Trasporti Vesuviani (☎ 081/739–2833 or 081/739–1674) leaves the Circumvesuviana railway station in Pompeii–Villa dei Misteri about five times a day (tickets are 4,500 lire), does another pickup at the Ercolano station, snakes its way up the mountain to the foot of the long-defunct *seggiovia* (chairlift) and the aborted *funicolare* (cable car) of the 1980s (2,943 ft), and then after a brief stop heads farther uphill to Quota 1000, the car park near the top. This is the end of the road for all but service vehicles up to the crater and the best place to reward yourself with a drink after the ascent (take a seat outside the café, weather permitting (unlike much of Italy, it's the same price whether sitting or standing). For those driving up, the road is sometimes confusingly signposted, but as a general rule look for the brown or yellow VESUVIO signs from the Herculaneum (Ercolano) or Torre del Greco autostrada exits and keep heading upward for about 20 minutes (incidentally, for taxi rides up Vesuvius from Torre del Greco or Pompei, expect to pay about 120,000 lire roundtrip). The road is not much better than in the days of Lord and Lady Hamilton, but it is certainly much dirtier. When you get to the parking lot at the top, for extra security opt for paying the 3,000-lire parking charge. The parking lot and bus terminal at Quota 1000 lie roughly 30 minutes' walk (about a 400-ft climb) from the nearest viewing point down into the crater. You will be handed a sturdy walking stick on leaving the parking lot (a small tip is appreciated on your return). The path is kept in a good state of repair but bring nonskid shoes (not sandals) and come prepared for strong winds. You have to pay a fee near the crater of 9,000 lire (open from 9 AM to two hours before sunset), which covers the cost of a compulsory but somewhat elusive guiding service. Once you've seen the fumaroles and gazed down as much as 600 ft into the wondrous depths of the crater, take in the broad sweep around the Bay of Naples—though you'll probably find the city of Naples more photogenic from lower down its slopes near the observatory. As you walk up the volcano path, you cannot look too long or unwarily at the splendid views without worrying about your feet— there are some spots where a little chain fence is all that prevents you from taking a steep fall. Near the top is the ticket seller's booth and a postcard stand—in typically enterprising Neapolitan fashion, postcards here cost several thousand lire, while the same cards cost a thousand lire less at the bottom of the mountain.

Torre del Greco

❹ *16 km (10 mi) southeast of Naples; 11 km (7 mi) northwest of Pompeii.*

Being in an area of high volcanic risk, Torre del Greco has borne the brunt of Vesuvian eruptions over the centuries. The demolition work of the historic center begun by Vesuvius was almost completed by the postwar building boom, and with more than 100,000 inhabitants Torre del Greco is now close behind its neighbor Portici as one of the most densely populated towns in the world. However, some architectural jewels have survived—including the 18th-century Vesuvian villa Palazzo Vallelonga, on Via Vittorio Emanuele and the Museo dei Coralli on Piazza Palomba—will show you why the Torresi (the townspeople) are still considered the world's best fashioners of coral. This is also a good base camp for exploring the Vesuvian area, with well-paved, clearly signposted roads north of the Torre del Greco autostrada exit.

Dining and Lodging

$$–$$$ ✕ **La Mammola.** A secluded restaurant on the grounds of the Hotel Marad, Torre del Greco, La Mammola has departed in an interesting way from the standard platters found around the Bay of Naples. It has succeeded in achieving a touch of stylishness without succumbing to pretension. Ask for a sample of its seafood *primi piatti* (first courses), including the dark gnocchi dish *gnocchetti neri con vongole e asparagi* (with clams and aspargus), and wash it down with some fine Pietro-torcia wine from Ischia, a blend of two ancient grape varieties, Bian-colella and Forastera, that Tiberius and Nero might have enjoyed. ✉ *Via San Sebastiano 24,* ☎ *081/882–5664. Reservations essential Sat. eve. AE, DC, MC, V. Closed Mon. No dinner Sun.*

$$$ 🏨 **Hotel Marad.** Dominated by huge spreading umbrella pines and con-veniently close to the Torre del Greco exit of the Naples–Salerno A3 au-tostrada, the Marad bristles with efficiency and is an obvious base for exploring the area around Vesuvius and Herculaneum. Booking in ad-vance makes good sense, as the hotel doubles as a conference center. Lying at the lower end of the price range, it offers four-star facilities at three-star prices, and a choice of two excellent restaurants. Travelers without cars will appreciate the pickup car service from the nearest Circum-vesuviana station. ✉ *Via San Sebastiano 24, 80059,* ☎ *081/849–2168,* 🖷 *081/882–8794. 74 rooms with bath. 2 restaurants, air-conditioning in some rooms, outdoor pool, meeting rooms, parking. AE, MC, V.*

Torre Annunziata (Oplontis)

★ ❺ *20 km (12 mi) southeast of Naples; 5 km (3 mi) west of Pompeii.*

Surrounded by the fairly drab urban landscape of Torre Annunziata, thrown up in the 1960s, Oplontis justifies its reputation as one of the most spectacular archaeological sites to be unearthed in the 20th cen-tury. The villa complex has been imaginatively ascribed—from a mere inscription on an amphora—to Nero's second wife, Poppaea Sabina, whose family was well known among the landed gentry of neighbor-ing Pompeii. As Roman villas go, Poppaea's Villa, or Villa A, as it is called more prosaically by archaeologists, is way off the top end of the scale. What has so far been excavated is more than 325 ft by 225 ft, and because the site is bound by a road to the west and a canal to the south, we are unlikely ever to gauge its full extent. Complete with por-ticoes, a large peristyle, *piscina* (pool), baths, and extensive gardens, besides the standard atria, triclinia, and a warren of cubicula, the villa has been thought by some to have been a training school for young philosophers and orators. Certainly, for those overwhelmed by the throngs at Pompeii, a modern-day visit to the site of Oplontis offers a chance for contemplation and intellectual refreshment.

Access is easiest from the Circumvesuviana station of Torre Annunzi-ata (about 200 yards away). Outside the station turn left and then right downhill, and the site is just after the crossroads down on the left. If coming by car, take the Torre Annunziata turnoff from the Naples–Salerno autostrada, turn right, and then look for signs on the left for Oplontis at the first major crossroads. The main entrance to the site is from the north—you basically go into the villa through the gardens, with the atrium on the southern side lying under about 16 ft of pumice and pyroclastic material from Vesuvius. This is a good time to have a close look at the stratigraphy of the volcanic deposits: note the thin layers of the lighter surge flow deposit near the base of the profile. Al-though pumice fallout presented few problems for local inhabitants dur-ing the eruption, it was the surge cloud which proved lethal, leading rapidly to asphyxiation.

Oplontis offers the full gamut of Roman wall paintings, with its occupants showing a particular penchant for the illusionist motifs of the so-called Second Pompeian Style. There are some good examples in the west wing of the villa, especially in the triclinium (Room 14—look for the room numbers above the doors) giving onto the small portico (Room 13), which abuts the west end of the site and the road above. Although the stucco work in the thermae, or baths, is less impressive than in Pompeii and Herculaneum, the calidarium (Room 8) has a delightful miniature landscape scene surmounted by a peacock in a niche at its eastern end. Nearby, in the tepidarium (Room 8) there is an interesting glimpse into the structural design of Roman baths; here the floor is raised by *suspensurae,* small brick supporting pilasters, enabling warm air to pass beneath.

Such initial opulence sets the scene for the rest of the site. Although there are exceptions to the rule—for example, from their relatively small size and less elaborate frescoes, the cubicula, or bedrooms, are perhaps conspicuous by their simplicity—a visit to the eastern wing confirms the earlier impression. The warren of rooms gives way to much larger spaces, featuring long corridors, peristyles fit for large gaggles of stoics, and a large piscina, or swimming pool, with its complement of porticoes and terraces, at the eastern end. ✉ *Via Sepolcri 1, Torre Annunziata,* ☎ *081/862–1755.* ✇ *4,000 lire.* ☉ *Daily 9–1 hr before sunset.*

POMPEII: CITY OF VESUVIUS

Mention Pompeii and most travelers will think of ancient Roman villas, prancing bronze fauns, writhing plaster casts of Vesuvius's victims, and the fabled days of the Caesars. Mention Pompeii to many southern Italians, however, and they will immediately think of the Santuario della Madonna, the 19th-century basilica in the center of town, with the archaeological ruins taking second place. Although millions of culture seekers worldwide head for ancient Pompeii every year, the same number of Italian pilgrims converge on the basilica as a token of faith—joining processions, making *ex-voto* offerings, or just honoring a vow. Wealthy Neapolitans come to make their donations to assist the Church carry out its good deeds. New-car owners come to get their vehicles blessed—and given driving standards in these parts of the world, insurance coverage from on high is probably a sensible move.

Caught between the hammer and anvil of cultural and religious tourism, the modern town of Pompeii has shaken off its rather complacent approach and is now endeavoring to polish up its act. In attempts to ease congestion and improve quality at street level, parts of the town have been pedestrianized and parking restrictions tightened. Departing from the rather sleazy reputation of previous years, several hotels have filled the sizable niche in the market for quality deals at affordable prices. As for recommendable restaurants, if you deviate from the archaeological site and make for the center of town, you will be spoiled for choice.

Unlike many archaeological sites in the Mediterranean region, those around Naples are almost all well served by public transport. Pompeii has all of three railway stations, and it's a short hop from here to the impressive villa of Oplontis, in Torre Annunziata. For transportation details, *see* Around the Bay A to Z, below.

Pompeii

★ *24 km (15 mi) southeast of Naples; 11 km (7 mi) southeast of Herculaneum.*

Tomb of a civilization, petrified memorial to Vesuvius's eruption on the morn of August 23, AD 79, the **Scavi di Pompei** is probably the most famous system of excavations anywhere. It is certainly the most accessible and one of the largest. Two hours are the absolute minimum for a visit, while buying the guidebook is a necessity unless you don't mind getting lost three or four times during your independent tour. That may not be such a bad thing. Today Pompeii is choked with both the dust of 25 centuries *and* hundreds of thousands of tourists every year; only by escaping the hordes and lingering along its silent streets can you truly fall under the site's spell. On a quiet backstreet, all you need is a little imagination to sense the shadows palpably filling the dark corners, to hear the ancient pipe's falsetto and the tinny clash of symbols, to envision a rain of rose petals gently covering a Roman senator's dinner guests. Come in the late afternoon when the site is nearly deserted, and you will understand that the true pleasure of Pompeii is not in the seeing but in the feeling.

Ancient Pompeii was much larger than Herculaneum; a busy commercial center with a population of 10,000–20,000, it covered about 160 acres on the seaward end of the fertile Sarno Plain. In 80 BC the general Sulla turned Pompeii into a Roman colony, a place where wealthy patricians could escape the turmoil of city life. The town was laid out in a grid pattern, with two main intersecting streets. The wealthiest took whole blocks for themselves; those less well endowed built a house and rented out the front rooms, those facing the street, to shopkeepers. The facades of these houses were relatively plain and seldom hinted at the care and attention lavished on the private rooms within. An arriving visitor entered into an open atrium, in the rear of which was a reception room. Behind this was another open area, called the peristyle, with rows of columns and perhaps a garden with a fountain. Only close friends ever saw this private part of the house, which was surrounded by the family's bedrooms and a dining area.

Pompeian houses were designed around an inner garden so that families could turn their backs on the outside world. Today we install picture windows that break down visual barriers between ourselves and our neighbors; the people in these Roman towns had few windows, preferring to get their light from the central courtyard—the light within. How pleasant it must have been to come home from the Forum or from the baths to your own secluded holding, with no visual reminders of a life outside your own preserve. Not that public life was so intolerable. There were wineshops on almost every corner, and frequent shows were given at the Amphitheater. The public fountains and toilets were connected to huge cisterns by lead pipes beneath the sidewalks. Since garbage and rainwater collected in the streets of Pompeii, the sidewalks were raised, and huge stepping stones were placed at crossings so pedestrians could keep their feet dry. Herculaneum had even better drainage, with an underground sewer system that led to the sea.

The ratio of freemen to slaves was about three to two. A small, prosperous family had two or three slaves, although many had far more. Since manual labor was considered degrading, the slaves did all the housework and the cooking, including the cutting of meat, which family members ate with spoons or with their fingers. Everyone doted on grapes, and figs were also popular. Venison, chicken, and pork were the main dishes. People ate the fruit of the quince tree (a good source of vita-

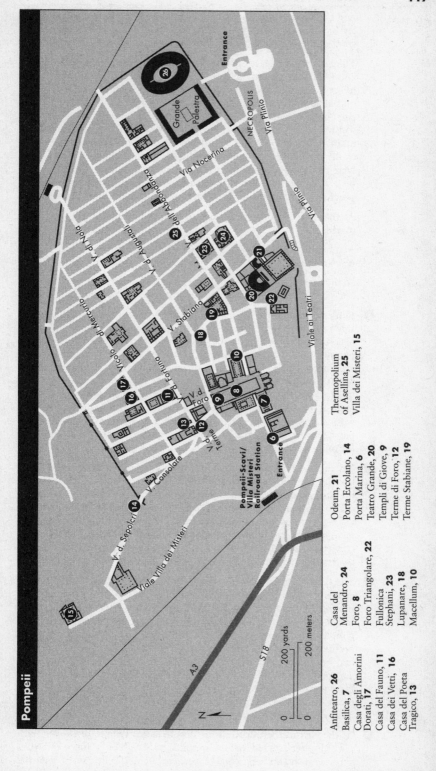

Pompeii

Anfiteatro, **26**
Basilica, **7**
Casa degli Amorini Dorati, **17**
Casa del Fauno, **11**
Casa dei Vetti, **16**
Casa del Poeta Tragico, **13**

Casa del Menandro, **24**
Foro, **8**
Foro Triangolare, **22**
Fullonica Stephani, **23**
Lupanare, **18**
Macellum, **10**

Odeum, **21**
Porta Ercolano, **14**
Porta Marina, **6**
Teatro Grande, **20**
Templi di Giove, **9**
Terme di Foro, **12**
Terme Stabiane, **19**

Thermopolium of Asellina, **25**
Villa dei Misteri, **15**

min C) to guard against scurvy. Bread was made from wheat and barley (rye and oats were unknown) and washed down with wine made from grapes growing on the slopes of Vesuvius.

The government was considered a democracy, but women, gladiators, and Jews were denied the vote. They did, however, express their opinions on election day, as you'll see from campaign graffiti still visible on public walls. Some 15,000 instances of graffiti were found in Pompeii and Herculaneum. Many were political announcements—one person recommending another for office, for example, and spelling out his qualifications. Some were bills announcing upcoming events—a play at the theater, a fight among gladiators at the Amphitheater. Others were public notices—that wine was on sale, that an apartment would be available on the Ides of March. A good many messages were personal and lend a human dimension to the disaster. Here are a few:

At the baths: "What is the use of having a Venus if she's made of marble?"

At a hotel: "I've wet my bed. My sin I bare. But why? you ask. No pot was anywhere."

At the entrance to the front lavatory at a private house: "May I always and everywhere be as potent with women as I was here."

6 Enter through **Porta Marina**, so called because it was on the seaward side prior to the eruption in AD 79 (the sea would have accessible from here via a narrow canal). The layout here is less gridlike than in other parts of town because you're in the oldest section of Pompeii, originally a smallish Oscan or pre-Roman settlement. In Roman times the road up to Porta Marina itself would have been steep and difficult for larger conveyances to negotiate—fortunately there were seven other gates to choose from—although this was by far the quickest way of getting to the hub of civic life, the Forum. In this case there were two passages, the one on the left for pedestrians and the one on the right for animals and light vehicles.

7 Beyond the Porta Marina and past the Temple of Venus is the **Basilica**, the law court and the stock exchange of the town. These oblong buildings ending in a semicircular projection (apse) were the model for early Christian churches, which had a nave (central aisle) and two side aisles separated by rows of columns. Standing in the Basilica, you can recognize the continuity between Roman and Christian styles of architecture, though here, instead of a sacral area being placed at the end, there was the tribunal.

8 The Basilica opens onto the **Foro** (Forum), with which it shares some elements of its design: a large rectangular area with a colonnade surmounted by a loggia, running along three sides. This served as the political, commercial, and religious center of city life, with the main temples, law courts, commercial and government buildings grouped around it. It was here that elections were held and speeches and official announcements made. In AD 79 the Forum would have been adorned with statues of the great and the good, many of them probably equestrian, as testified by some bases left on the south side. One of the bases is wider and more massive than the others, indicating that it may have been the *suggestum,* or orator's rostrum.

9 At the far (northern) end of the Forum is the **Tempio di Giove** (Temple of Jupiter), sacred to the Capitoline triad of Jupiter, Juno, and Minerva, with the brewing cone of Vesuvius behind. Little more than the base of this 2nd-century BC temple has been preserved. Like many buildings in Pompeii, it was severely damaged in an earthquake in AD 62 and was still in a ruined state at the time of the eruption in AD 79.

⑩ On the eastern side of the Forum fronted by an elegant three-column portico is the **Macellum**, the covered meat and fish market dating back to Augustan times. Like the ancient Greek *agora* in Athens, the Forum was a busy shopping area, complete with public officials to apply proper standards of weights and measures.

⑪ The renowned **Casa del Fauno** (House of the Faun) gets its name from the small bronze statue in the middle of its spacious impluvium. The original—like so many of the best works of art unearthed in Pompeii—is housed in the Museo Archeologico Nazionale in Naples. This is both one of the earliest and most sumptuous private dwellings in Pompeii. The front part of the house is arranged around two atria, behind which is the peristyle with a portico of 28 Ionic columns. On its discovery in 1830, particular attention was focused on the fine mosaic all done in tiny tesserae depicting the Battle of Issus fought between Alexander the Great and the Persian emperor Darius III in 330 BC, found in the *exedra* (discussion room) fronted by stuccoed columns immediately behind the first peristyle. The exedra was flanked by two *triclinia* (dining rooms) giving onto a megaperistyle at the back.

⑫ The **Terme di Foro** (Forum Baths), on Via delle Terme, are smaller than the Terme Stabiane (☞ *below*), but have more delicate decoration. The tepidarium and calidarium in the men's section are extremely well preserved and provide a useful insight into heating systems. The tepidarium was warmed by a brazier while beneath the calidarium were brick pillars, or *suspensurae,* which together with hollow walls, ensured the passage of hot air. Note the inscription in bronze letters around the great *labrum* (fountain) recording the names of the officials who installed the labrum, as well as its cost (5,420 sesterces) in the years AD 3–4.

⑬ The **Casa del Poeta Tragico** (House of the Tragic Poet), opposite the Forum Baths, is a typical middle-class house from the last days of Pompeii. On the floor is a mosaic of a chained dog and the inscription CAVE CANEM ("Beware of the dog"). The house owes its name and fame to a mosaic found in the tablinum representing a *choregos,* or theatrical sponsor, along with, on the walls of the atrium and peristyle, a superb series of pictures, now in the Naples museum, of mythological subjects like the Sacrifice of Iphigenia.

⑭ The beautiful **Porta Ercolano** (Herculaneum Gate) was a main gate that led to Herculaneum and Neapolis. The gate has three archways—the central one for wheeled conveyances and the two side openings for pedestrians. It is thought to have been constructed without a defensive strategy in mind. This would imply a fairly late construction date, when the colonization of southern Italy was well consolidated and the native Italic peoples were no longer restless.

★ **⑮** One of the most evocative roads in Pompeii, the Via dei Sepolcri, leads out from the Porta Ercolano and is lined with tombs—a favorite spot for painters and photographers of the early 20th century. This road leads to the celebrated **Villa dei Misteri** (Villa of the Mysteries), lying 490 ft outside Pompeii's walls and therefore in theory not part of the ancient town. It contains what some consider the greatest surviving group of paintings from the ancient world, telling the story of a young bride (Ariadne) being initiated into the mysteries of the cult of Dionysus. Bacchus (Dionysus), the god of wine, was popular in a town so devoted to the pleasures of the flesh. But he also represented the triumph of the irrational—of all those mysterious forces that no official state re-

BURIED PLEASURE: UNLOCKING THE VILLA OF THE MYSTERIES

A FUNNY THING HAPPENS on the way to the forum as you walk through Pompeii. Covered with dust and decay as it is, the city seems to come alive. Perhaps it is the familiar signs of life observed along the ancient streets: the beer shops with tumblers' rings still fresh in the counter, the stanchion where horses were tethered outside the taverna, the tracks of chariot wheels cut in the pavement. Coming upon the *thermapoli* (the drinking bar), you imagine natives calling out, "One for the road." The *macellum* (marketplace) would be crowded with *palinquine* (litters); the dentist booth, iron implements at the ready for reluctant customers. But a glance up at Vesuvius, still brooding over the scene like an enormous headstone, reminds you that these folks— whether imagined in your head or actually wearing a mantle of lava dust—have not taken a breath for centuries.

In its day, Pompeii was celebrated as the Côte d'Azur, the seaside Brighton, the Fire Island of the ancient Roman empire. Evidence of a Sybaritic bent are everywhere. In the town's grandest villas as well as rowdiest *lupanari* (brothels), murals still reveal a worship of hedonism. Images of satyrs, bacchantes, hermaphrodites, and acrobatic couples indulge in hanky-panky. Even entryways are adorned with the Roman guardian against the Evil Eye— a painted Phallus. People came here to do the things Greeks had a word for, and there is no more astounding, magnificently memorable evidence than the world famous frescoes on view at the Villa dei Misteri, or Villa of the Mysteries, a palatial abode build at the far northwestern fringe of Pompeii. Unearthed in 1909, this villa had over 60 rooms painted with frescoes, but the finest are the series that represent the Dionysian rites of initiation, found in the *triclinium,* or banquet room.

Painted in the most glowing Pompeiian reds and oranges, the panels relate the saga of Ariadne, a young bride, and her initiation into the sacred mysteries of the cult of Dionysus, a god imported to Italy from Greece and then given the Latin name of Bacchus. The Villa of the Mysteries frescoes were painted circa 50 BC, most art historians believe, and represent the peak of the Second Style of Pompeiian wall painting. The triclinium frescoes are thought to have been painted by a local artist although the theme may well have been copied from an earlier cycle of paintings from the Hellenistic period.

Tour groups permitting (though detached from the rest of Pompeii, this room gets its fair share of through-traffic), try to stand by the protective chain and study the paintings from left to right. In all there are ten scenes, beginning with the reading of the ritual by a child (Dionysus, perhaps) assisted by a seated matron, followed by a servant pouring libations to carry out some type of sacrificial ceremony. The third picture (on the left-hand wall) depicts a Silenus with his musical accompaniment, somehow connected with the fourth, a frightened woman. The slightly damaged frescoes on the front wall depict Dionysus (recognized by his staff, or *thyrsus*) slumped over an enthroned Ariadne, flanked by a Silenus and satyrs on the left and, on the right, a kneeling woman (perhaps a bacchante) unveiling a phallus with a winged figure wielding a *flagellum* standing over her. The south wall (on the right) depicts a woman being flogged while a naked bacchante does a twirl—but is the woman being flogged or does she simply want to veil her eyes from the phallus? The last two scenes show a seated woman, possibly preparing for a bridal ceremony, while the last portrays a mantled woman, perhaps the spouse and priestess of the god. Unlike with Greek vase painting, for example, we are not assisted in the interpretation by inscriptions with the names of the main characters, so some of the above construct—now the verdict of most archaeologists—is debatable. Today, all visitors here must ponder love among the ruins as they wander through the silent villa and contemplate the mysteries of its celebrated frescoes.

ligion could fully suppress. The cult of Dionysus, like the cult of the Cumaean Sibyl, gave people a sense of control over fate, and in its focus on the Other World, helped pave the way for Christianity. For more information on these fabled frescoes, ☞ Close-Up box, "Buried Pleasure: Unlocking the Villa of the Mysteries," *below*.

★ ⑯ The **Casa dei Vettii** (House of the Vetti) is the best example of a house owned by wealthy *mercantores* (merchants), which has been faithfully restored with vivid murals—a magnificent *pinacoteca* (picture gallery) within the very heart of Pompeii. The scenes here—except for the two wings off the atrium—were all painted after the earthquake of AD 62. Within this visual feast, cast an admiring glance at the delicate frieze around the wall of the triclinium, depicting cupids engaged in various activities, such as selling oils and perfumes, working as goldsmiths and metalworkers, acting as wine merchants, or performing in chariot races. This is definitely the place to refresh your memory of Greek mythology. In another *oecus* (room) facing onto the peristyle are other masterpieces of the Fourth Style of Pompeiian painting, including one scene of Daedalus showing Pasiphaë, Minos's wife, a wooden cow, a disguise which would enable her to consummate her divine-inflicted passion for a bull. Opposite this scene is the omnipresent Dionysus surprising Ariadne while asleep, and on the end wall is Ixion bound to a wheel by Hephaestus with Hera standing by disdainfully—a torture devised by Zeus to punish Ixion for having dared to seek the love of Hera, Zeus's wife. Given Zeus's amply testified philandering, Ixion could have been forgiven for thinking the coast was clear.

⑰ The **Casa degli Amorini Dorati** (House of the Gilded Cupids) is an elegant, well-preserved home with original marble decorations in the garden. The house may well have belonged to the Poppaei family, better known for their family connections with Nero, who married the notorious Poppaea the second time around. Its pictorial decorations express elegant and refined theatrical tastes dating to Nero's time (AD 54–AD 69). The house is named after the cupids engraved in gold leaf that adorn one of the *cubicula* (bedrooms). Stroll around the peristyle in the garden, which would have been adorned with sculptures, marble tables, and a pool.

⑱ On the walls of the well-preserved **lupanare** (brothel) are the scenes of erotic pastimes in which clients could engage. Several of the rooms were on the upper floor, served by an independent staircase, suggesting separate facilities for customers who wanted to keep a lower profile. At ground level, small painted panels above the entrances illustrated the specialty offered by each *meretrix* (courtesan).

⑲ The **Terme Stabiane** (Stabian Baths) were heated by underground furnaces whose warmth circulated among the stone pillars supporting the floor, rose through flues in the walls, and escaped through chimneys. The water temperature could be set for cold, lukewarm, or hot. Bathers took a lukewarm bath to prepare themselves for the hot room. A tepid bath came next and then a plunge into cold water to tone up the skin. A vigorous massage with oil was followed by rest, reading, horseplay, and conversation. The Stabian Baths are the most complete in Pompeii and among the oldest baths from Roman times. This was the basic pattern used for the grand imperial baths of antiquity, such as the Baths of Caracalla in Rome, although the latter were built to a massive scale. Like the Forum Baths, these had a palaestra, or porticoed area, where athletes could train, play a *sphaeristerium* (ball game), and then remove dirt and oils from their bodies with a strigil before cooling off in the the frigidarium.

⓴ Not far from the Stabian Baths was the theater area on the southern side of town. The **Teatro Grande** (large theater), originally dating from the 2nd century BC but subsequently restored, had a seating capacity of about 5,000. It was designed to fit in to the natural slope of the hill, so that spectacles would be performed against a backdrop of the Lattari Mountains. Little remains of the original *cavea* (seating area) except for some of the lower tiers, some of the *media cavea* halfway up, and the framework of the *summa cavea* (top gallery). Behind the theater lie the gladiators' barracks, though this porticoed area is thought to have served as a space for the audience to unwind in between plays. Of course, with the advent of racier entertainment down in the Amphitheater, this large theater lost much of its pull.

⓲ Adjacent to the Teatro Grande is the **Odeum**, also called **Teatrum Tectum** (Covered Theater). Built between 80 BC–75 BC and with a seating capacity of 1,000, the Odeum is a gem of theatrical architecture, which was far less heavily restored in antiquity than its predecessor next door. The semicircular cavea was truncated and transformed into an almost square-shape design so as to facilitate the building of a roof. With theatrical performances often held on hot summer days, ancient Pompeians would have welcomed the shade provided.

⓶ Some of the oldest structures in Pompeii are to be found in the **Foro Triangolare** (Triangular Forum), west of the theater complex. In the middle of the Forum are the remains—just a few column capitals in Doric style—of a temple dating as far back as the 6th century BC, originally dedicated to Hercules, the founder of the city. This is one of the quietest areas of the archaeological site, and the ample shade afforded by trees here makes it a good spot to pause and muse on what you've seen.

The main street running most of the way from the Forum to the Amphitheater was the bustling **Via dell'Abbondanza** (incidentally, the name is not authentic and was made up by archaeologists). Shops were by no means restricted to the Forum area, and many were located along the Via dell'Abbondanza. Shops can easily be distinguished from private houses by their much broader fronts about 6–10 ft wide with wooden shutters for nighttime security. Private houses had narrower—almost poky—entrances, thereby reducing exposure at street level to an absolute minimum.

⓳ Togas, the required Roman attire, were washed at **Fullonica Stephani**. The cloth was dunked into a tub full of water and chalk, and stomped upon like so many grapes. Once clean, the material was stretched across a wicker cage and exposed to sulfur fumes. The fuller (cleaner) carded it with a long brush, then placed it under a press. The harder the pressing, the whiter and brighter it became. When excavated in 1911, the entrance to the fuller's premises was still shuttered and locked. Behind was a body clutching a bagful of sesterces. Could these have been the last takings of the *fullonica*? Or had a passerby, carrying his worldly wealth, stopped inside and sought refuge behind the door from the hail of lapilli outside?

⓴ Many paintings and mosaics were executed at the **Casa del Menandro** (House of Menander), a patrician's villa. The Greek comic poet Menander is depicted in a rectangular niche on the far wall in the peristyle, although you need go no farther than the *atrium* to see three scenes from the Trojan war in a small exedra to the left: the death of Laocoön and his sons (right); Cassandra trying to dissuade the Trojans from making the fatal mistake of bringing the Wooden Horse into Troy; and (left) one of the Greek heroes with Helen. This impressive residence also had a small complex of private baths, just next to the kitchen to the right of the peristyle. The siting of the baths next to the kitchen quarters was common practice in many of the larger villas, enabling heat from cooking to be exploited for warming the caldarium.

㉕ The **Thermopolium of Asellina** (Asellina's Inn), on the Via dell'Abbondanza, is the most complete example of an inn to be discovered in Pompeii. On the ground floor was the characteristic *thermopolium,* a counter with built-in earthenware containers holding snacks and hot drinks—perhaps that famed delicacy *garum,* made from marinated fish innards (or anchovies, if you were lucky)—while the upstairs part had guest rooms. At street level, customers ate standing up or on the move, as there were few taverns that offered a choice of either sitting or standing.

★ **㉖** The **Anfiteatro** (Amphitheater) was the ultimate in entertainment for local Pompeians and offered a gamut of experiences, but essentially this was for gladiators rather than wild animals. Unlike the amphitheater at Pozzuoli, there are no underground *cellae* for the penning of animals and, besides, *venationes* (combats with wild animals) only really became popular from well into the 1st century AD onward. With the large palaestra close by and the gladiatorial barracks near the theater area, there were extensive facilities to train gladiators in many types of combat. Teams worked for impresarios, who hired them out to wealthy citizens, many of whom were running for office and hoping that the gory entertainment would buy them some votes. Most gladiators were slaves or prisoners, but a few were those from the far-flung reaches of the empire who enjoyed fighting. When a gladiator found himself at another's mercy, he extended a pleading hand to the president of the games. If the president turned his thumb up, the gladiator lived; if he turned his thumb down, the gladiator's throat was cut. The arena got pretty bloody after a night's entertainment and was sprinkled with red powder to camouflage the carnage. The victorious gladiator got money, or a ribbon symbolizing his exemption from further fights. If he was a slave, he was often set free. If the people of Pompeii had trading cards, they would have collected portraits of gladiators; everyone had his favorite. Says one piece of graffiti: "Petronius Octavus fought thirty-four fights and then died, but Severus, a freedman, was victor in fifty-five fights and still lived; Nasica celebrates sixty victories."

By Roman standards, Pompeii's Amphitheater was quite small (seating capacity: 20,000). Built in about 80 BC, it was oval and divided into three seating areas, like a theater. There were two main entrances—at the north and south ends—and a narrow passage on the west, called the *Porta Libitinensis,* through which the dead were most probably dragged out. A wall painting found in a house near the theater (now in the Naples Museum) depicts the riot in the Amphitheater in AD 59 when several citizens from the nearby town of Nucera were killed. After Nucerian appeals to Nero, shows in the Amphitheater were suspended for 10 years.

Just behind the Amphitheater is the second entrance to Pompeii (at Villa dei Misteri there is only an exit), with the main square and its basilica a short walk to the east. To get the most out of Pompeii, allow at least three or four hours. You should have a pocketful of small change (500-lire coins) for tipping the guards who are on duty at the most important villas. They will unlock the gates for you, insist on explaining the attractions, show you some soft Pompeian pornography if you ask for it, and expect a tip for their services. If hiring a guide, make sure the guide is registered for an English tour and standing inside the gate; agree beforehand on the length of the tour and the price. Pompeii has its own stop (Pompei–Villa dei Misteri) on the Circumvesuviana, close to the main entrance at the Porta Marina, which is the best place from which to start a tour. ⊠ *Pompei Scavi,* ☎ *081/861–0744.* 🎫 *12,000 lire.* ☉ *Daily 9–1 hr before sunset (ticket office closes 2 hrs before).*

Dining and Lodging

$$$–$$$$ ✕ **Il Principe.** This is the closest you'll get to experiencing the tastes of
★ ancient Pompeii, though the wines (fortunately) will be quantum leaps better. Also the food is so artistically presented that it seems boorish to pick up a knife and fork. Try the *pasta vermiculata garo,* otherwise known as spaghetti with *garum pompeianum,* a fish-based sauce consumed widely in Roman times. Don't forget to round off the meal with the *cassata Oplontis,* reconstructed from Apicius's recipe and inspired by a famous still-life fresco found on the site. On several evenings between September and March the restaurant offers theme menus devoted to ancient Roman cooking. The decor is luxe, with echoes of Stil Liberty (Art Nouveau) in its style. ⊠ *Piazza B. Longo 8,* ☎ *081/850–5566,* FAX *081/863–3342. AE, DC, V. Closed Mon. in winter.*

$$–$$$ ✕ **Ristorante President.** The Gramaglia father-and-son team are well
★ versed in top-level catering and make sure that customers sigh with satisfaction after every course. For something different, try the *astice ubriacata* (drunken lobster) accompanied by some imaginative side dishes, like *sfoglie di zucca in agrodolce* (sweet and sour pumpkin strips). Beautiful presentation, impeccable service, and excellent value for money all add up to a stellar meal. ⊠ *Piazza Schettini 12,* ☎ *081/850–7245,* FAX *081/863–8147. AE, DC, MC, V. Closed Mon.*

$–$$ ✕ **Ristorante Pizzeria Carlo Alberto.** This is a small, efficiently run restaurant with an impressive repertory comfortably out of the reach of large tour groups. If you're a vegetarian, try *pizza con mozzarella, rucola, e mais* (pizza with mozzarella, rocula, and corn) or just have a plain *focaccetta* instead of bread to accompany your meal. Those who make it through to the *dolce* (desserts) should sample the delicate *Grappa del Vesuvio,* made from Lacryma Christi grape varieties. ⊠ *Via Carlo Alberto 15,* ☎ *081/863–3231. Reservations essential weekends. DC, MC, V. Closed Mon. in winter.*

$$$ 🏨 **Hotel Amleto.** *Appassionati* and connoisseurs of historical styles of furnishings will find this hotel a real treat. Enjoy the Pompeian-type mosaic in the reception room and the mesmerizing House-of-the-Vettii–type scene in the breakfast room before retiring to your quarters, either 19th-century Neapolitan in style or Venetian in taste. Convenient to say the least, this spot is near the archaeological site and close to Pompeii's cathedral. There is a solarium and roof garden. ⊠ *Via B. Longo 10, 80045,* ☎ *081/863–1004,* FAX *081/863–5585. 26 rooms with bath. Air-conditioning, parking. AE, MC, V.*

$$ 🏨 **Hotel Forum.** Handily close to the ancient site, though set back enough from the road to be fairly quiet, the Forum is an excellent base for a short stay. Linger over breakfast downstairs with its well-kept garden as a backdrop. ⊠ *Via Roma 99, 80045,* ☎ *081/850–1170,* FAX *081/ 850–6132. 24 rooms with bath. Air-conditioning, meeting rooms, parking. AE, DC, MC, V.*

$$ 🏨 **Villa Laura.** This is an unusual hotel (with a mini-museum of antiques in the reception area), attentively run under the guidance of its owner, *Signora* Antonella. Ask for one of the more spacious, quieter rooms at the back overlooking the garden. ⊠ *Via de la Salle 13, 80045,* ☎ *081/863–1024, 081/863–1036,* FAX *081/850–4893. 25 rooms with bath. Air-conditioning, parking. AE, DC, MC, V.*

Nightlife and the Arts

Pompeii's late-summer festival of the performing arts, known as the **Panatenee Pompeiane,** hosts a series of classical plays in July and August. For information contact the tourist office in Pompeii just off the main square or one of the tourist offices in Naples (☞ Visitor Information *in* Around the Bay A to Z, *below*).

WEST OF NAPLES: THE PHLEGREAN FIELDS

Extinct volcanoes, steaming fumaroles, natural spasms, and immortal names, all steeped in millennia of history, are the basic ingredients of the Campi Flegrei, or Phlegrean Fields (from the ancient Greek word *phlegraios,* or burning). Pompeii and Herculaneum, to the east of Naples, may be the most celebrated archaeological sites in Campania, but back in the days of the Caesars they were simple middle-class towns compared to the patrician settlements to the west of Naples. Here, at Baiae, famed figures like Cicero, Julius Caesar, Nero, and Hadrian built sumptuous leisure villas (*villae otiorum*) and ports for their gigantic pleasure barges; here St. Paul arrived at Pozzuoli on board an Alexandrian ship; here the powerful came to consult the oracles of the Cumaean Sibyl; and here Virgil visited Lago d'Averno—the legendary entrance to the underworld—to immortalize it in his *Aeneid.* Although many villas have now sunk beneath the sea, there are many archaeological sights still extant: the Flavian Amphitheater, which, if not as imposing above ground as the Colosseum at Rome, is far better preserved in the galleries and cages below the arena in which wild beasts, gladiators, and stage props were kept in readiness; the ruins of the Sibyl's Cave in Cumae; and the ancient baths of Baia. To such archaeological riches, add a pinch of local hospitality and an essence of gastronomy, and you'll soon see why the area holds so much fascination for the present-day traveler.

The Solfatara

㉗ *8 km (5 mi) west of Naples; 2 km (1 mi) east of Pozzuoli.*

Here at the sunken volcanic crater Solfatara you can experience firsthand the otherworldly terrain of the Campi Flegri. In fact, the only eruption of this semiextinct volcano was in 1198, though according to one legend, every crater in the area is one of the mouths of a 100-headed dragon named Typhon that Zeus hurled into the crater of Epomeo on the island of Ischia. According to another, the sulfurous springs of the Solfatara are poisonous discharges from wounds the Titans received in their war with Zeus. Both legends, of course, are attempts to dramatize man's struggle to overcome the mysterious and dangerous forces of nature. Appropriately, it was given the name of *Forum Vulcani* by the ancient Romans, who thought it the residence of the god Vulcan. The Solfatara has been a powerful magnet for travelers over the past 300 years. No self-respecting 18th-century aristocrat taking the Grand Tour would have returned to northern Europe without visiting the site, which has always been much more accessible from the center of Naples than the better-known Vesuvius on the other side of Naples.

The Solfatara lies on two bus routes out of Naples (152, M1), with stops just outside the main entrance, and is a 15-minute walk uphill (1 km/½ mi) from the Metropolitana station of Pozzuoli. By car take the *tangenziale* (bypass) from Naples toward Pozzuoli, getting off at the Agnano, Exit 11, about 4 km (2½ mi) away from the crater. Then follow signs to Pozzuoli and look for the VULCANO SOLFATARA sign when beginning the descent into Pozzuoli. Enter the Solfatara through the arch of the turn-of-the-20th-century, long defunct baths complex (parking facilities and ticket office inside). You approach the volcanically

West of Naples: Campi Flegri (The Phlegrean Fields)

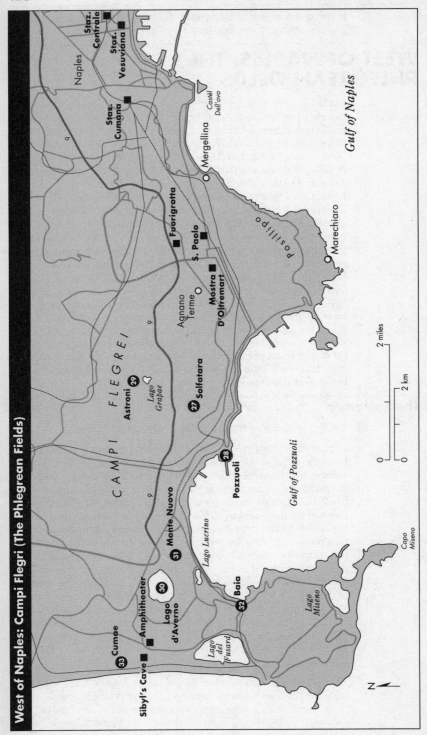

Naples

Staz. Centrale

Staz. Vesuviana

Staz. Cumana

Castel Dell'ovo

Mergellina

Gulf of Naples

Fuorigrotta

S. Paolo

Agnano Terme

Mostra D'Oltremart

Marechiaro

Posillipo

CAMPI FLEGREI

Astroni 29

Lago Grabae

27 Solfatara

28 Pozzuoli

Gulf of Pozzuoli

Monte Nuovo

31

Lago Lucrino

30 Amphitheater

Lago d'Averno

Baia 32

Lago del Fusard'

Lago Miseno

Cumae 33

Sibyl's Cave

Capo Miseno

N

0   2 km
0   2 miles

active area down an avenue of holm oak trees, with the attractive Solfatara campsite making full use of all available shade on either side. Complete with year-round bar, and seasonal restaurant (☎ 081/526–8144, 081/526–2341), open April–October, providing honest fare to campers and other visitors, this must be one of the best-appointed volcanic craters in the world. After you have cleared the refreshment area, emerge from the vegetation into a light clay expanse that in bright sunlight makes you reach instinctively for your sunglasses. Helpful information panels both on the surrounding vegetation and the volcanic action at the core of the crater will steer you past the century-old brick *stufe* (ovens) resembling a Roman *sudatorium* (sauna), where you could until recently (it's now been bricked up) be parboiled in a matter of seconds. The sulfur fumes were supposed to cure those afflicted with diseases of the respiratory tract, the skin, and the joints. While musing on advances in modern medicine, move on to the fenced-off area of the fumaroles, known as the *Bocca Grande,* where steam whooshes out at about 160°C. Continuing the circuit, note the *fangaia,* or mud baths, which produce highly prized mineral-rich mud for medicinal purposes. The dark veining on the mud surface consists of bacteria that are superresistant to high acidity and temperature. The walk continues past a 19th-century well that was sunk to tap mineral water from an underlying aquifer 30 ft below and which was in active use until the 1920s. ⊠ *Via Solfatara 161, Pozzuoli,* ☎ *081/526–2341.* 🎫 *8,000 lire.* ☉ *Daily 8:30–1 hr before sunset.*

Dining and Lodging

\$–\$\$ ✕ **Taverna Viola.** Lying just 165 ft down the road from the Solfatara, this rustic-style restaurant/pizzeria has a pleasing view over the Bay of Pozzuoli and the added attraction of serving pizzas at lunchtime. This is the place to deviate from a pizza margherita and have one *con prosciutto e rughetta* (with ham and rucola) or even branch out into a fish-based dish, depending on the season and weather conditions at sea. ⊠ *Via Solfatara 76, Pozzuoli,* ☎ *081/526–9953. MC, V.*

\$\$ 🏨 **Hotel Solfatara.** A clean functional hotel built in 1983, and since recently refurbished, this is handily located just outside the Solfatara exit. For extra peace and quiet, ask for a room at the back (no view). ⊠ *Via Solfatara 163, 80078,* ☎ *081/526–7017,* 𝔽𝔸𝕏 *081/526–3365. 34 rooms with bath. Air-conditioning, parking. AE, DC, MC, V.*

\$ 🏨 **Camping Vulcano Solfatara.** With its gamut of bungalows, caravans, and tents for hire, this campsite set in Mediterranean woodland within the Solfatara crater offers tranquillity, unique ambience, and good facilities at very reasonable prices. Reservations are essential for bungalows. ⊠ *Via Solfatara 161, 80078,* ☎ *081/526–7413,* 𝔽𝔸𝕏 *081/526–3482. Restaurant, pool, shop, parking. AE, DC, MC, V. Closed end Oct.–end Mar.*

Pozzuoli

㉘ *8 km (5 mi) west of Naples.*

Legendary spirits populate Pozzuoli. St. Paul stepped ashore at the harbor here in AD 61 en route to Rome: His own ship had been wrecked off Malta, and he was brought here on the *Castor and Pollux,* a grain ship from Alexandria that was carrying corn from Egypt to Italy. Not far away from the harbor esplanade, San Gennaro, patron saint of Naples, earned his holy martyrdom by being thrown to the lions at an imperial gala staged in the town's enormous amphitheater, constructed by the Flavian emperors (the wild beasts were said to have torn the rags from Gennaro's body but to have left him unharmed—at which point he was taken to the public square and finished off). More recently, that latter-day goddess Sophia Loren was born in a house still standing on a backstreet, later to set off to Naples and celluloid fame. Today Pozzuoli is a well-connected busy town with about 70,000 inhabitants, who live chiefly on its fisheries, shipping, and tourism. Built on geologically unstable land, the area near the port was partially evacuated in the early 1980s due to a phenomenon known locally as bradyseism, or the rise and fall of the land surface. Since then it has been gradually recolonized and partially gentrified: many of the buildings in the Centro Storico have been given a face-lift, the main park (Villa Avellino) has become a mecca for open-air summer festivals, and the town's reputation as a center for gastronomy has been firmly established. Pozzuoli has also capitalized on its strategic position close to two of the islands in the Bay of Naples, Procida and Ischia. One of its main selling points is its main arena—apart from Rome, Puteoli (to use the ancient Latin name of the town) was the only place in the empire to boast two amphitheaters—offering glimpses into the life of *panem et circenses* (bread and circuses) in classical times, when Puteoli was one of the busiest ports in the Mediterranean and easily eclipsed Neapolis (today's Naples).

★ The **Anfiteatro Flavio** (seating capacity, 40,000) is a short walk from the Pozzuoli Metropolitana railway station and about 15 minutes' walk down from the Solfatara. Despite the wear and tear of the millennia and the loss of some of the masonry to lime making in the Middle Ages, the site is one of the marvels of Roman architecture in the Campi Flegrei area. The foundation date is open to question. Like many sites in antiquity, the period from conception to final execution could stretch over decades. It was probably built under Vespasian (AD 70–AD 79), as testified to by various inscriptions reading COLONIA FLAVIA AUGUSTA PUTEOLANA PECUNIA SUA, although some maintain that work may have started under Nero (AD 54–AD 69), and had merely completed later. As you approach the site, note the external part in *opus reticulatum* (masonry arranged in a pattern) and brick, which is typical of the Flavian emperors, while the pillars of the external portico are all in brick, which would suggest a 2nd-century addition. Although we now get a fairly good idea of the horizontal ground plan in ancient times, comparison with the Colosseum in Rome shows that much of the superstructure has been lost: the outside part consisted of three stories surmounted by an *atticus* (decorative attic) while the *cavea* or sitting area would have had a portico above the top row of seats decorated with a number of statues and supported by columns (now found in the underground part). At ground level there was an *ambulacrum* (walkway) along which spectators would have passed to reach the *vomitoria* (exits) or outlets inside.

As testified to by the complex underground network of *carceres*, or cells, which definitely merit a visit, entertainment consisted mainly of venationes, or fights, often involving exotic animals like lions and tigers brought from far-flung corners of the Roman Empire, through the port of Puteoli. The *fossa*, or large ditch in the middle of the arena, may well have contained the stage setting, which could be raised when necessary to provide a scenic backdrop. According to tradition, several early Christians—including the Naples protector St. Januarius, or San Gennaro—were condemned to be savaged by wild beasts in Puteoli under the Fourth Edict, passed in AD 305, but the sentence was later commuted to a less spectacular *decapitatio* carried out farther up the hill on Via Solfatara at a site now commemorated by the Church of St Januarius.

Down near the port, 325 ft from the Cumana railway stop of Pozzuoli in Piazza Serapide, are the evocative remains of the ancient **macellum,** or food market, a porticoed courtyard with a *sacellum* (shrine) at its northern end. Known commonly—but erroneously—as the Temple of Serapis and proven to have been below sea level (see the perforations in the columns made by mollusks) for much of its history, this is almost all that remains of the ancient harbor district of Puteoli. The macellum is closed to the public but easily visible and photographed from Via Roma on the waterfront. ✉ *Anfiteatro Grande, Via Terraciano 75,* ☎ *081/526–6007.* 🎟 *4,000 lire.* ☉ *Daily 9–1 hr before sunset.*

Dining

$$ ✗ **Antica Trattoria da Ciuffello.** With fish browning invitingly on the barbecue outside and a welcoming roomy feel to the interior, this *caratteristica* trattoria is conveniently—and appropriately—located very close to the ancient macellum, the food market. Sample its much vaunted *zuppa di pesce* (fish soup), which is a *primo* and *secondo* courses rolled into one. ✉ *Via Dicearchia 11bis,* ☎ *081/526–9397. DC, V. Closed Wed. in winter.*

$–$$ ✗ **Ristorante Don Antonio.** Despite its unflattering location up a *vicolo* one block away from the Pozzuoli waterfront, this restaurant has achieved cult status in Neapolitan circles for its fresh seafood and unbeatable prices. Unlike other hostelries, which will happily serve well into the afternoon siesta or late at night, Don Antonio's rolls down the shutters as soon as the day's catch has been consumed. ✉ *Via Magazzini 20,* ☎ *081/526–7941. Reservations not accepted. No credit cards. Closed Mon.*

Astroni

㉙ *7 km (4 mi) west of Naples; 3 km (2 mi) northeast of Pozzuoli.*

The extinct volcanic crater of the Astroni is one of the natural marvels of the Campi Flegrei. Its peaceful shady avenues running through attractive Mediterranean woodland have made it a popular retreat for families and nature lovers alike. It also has something of a historical pedigree: The Romans came for the sulfur-rich waters, although their thermae have yet to be physically located. The Aragonese dynasty in the 15th century made the crater a royal hunting reserve, which was further consolidated by the Bourbons under Charles III in the mid-18th century. Most structures in the crater, as well as the high wall around the perimeter, date to the latter period. Saved from further decline and neglect only in the 1980s, it was converted into a wildlife refuge managed by the World Wide Fund for Nature (WWF) and now serves as a center for environmental education in the Naples area.

Access to the reserve is gained through the ancient Bourbon gatehouse at the top of the crater on the southern side. Maps and suggested itineraries are displayed at the ticket office. The best walks, combining splashes of history amid scenic trails, lead downhill to the base of the crater. On the road down (only service vehicles are allowed along its 2-km/1-mi stretch) take in the sweeping views of thick woodland and the lakes at the base of the crater, a landscape reminiscent of those painted by the 18th-century court artist Hackert—and certainly not what you'd expect to find within a 10-minute drive of the city of Naples. Continue on down past the wildlife information panels. Although many of the birds illustrated thereon may be heard, even seen, it is very unlikely that you will see any of the mammals illustrated, such as the *volpe* (fox) and the *ghiro* (dormouse), as they are either shy and retiring or else nocturnal. At the end of the road there is a shady picnic site with walks that branch out in various directions around the *laghi* (lakes) and toward the *Vaccheria*, a Bourbon hunting lodge. Have a discreet look through the spy holes at the various raptor species housed in aviaries behind the picnic site. These injured birds—mainly buzzards (*Buteo buteo*)—are sober reminders of the harm caused to wildlife in many parts of Italy by the illegal use of firearms.

Allow at least two or three hours for exploring the crater. On your way the vegetation changes quite noticeably, from a Mediterranean-type woodland with holm oaks at the crater sides into a more temperate woodland at the base, where chestnut and elm are found. This is due to what experts call vegetational inversion. The cooler, damper microclimate around the lakes at the crater base has encouraged the growth of tree species normally found at 1,500 ft or more above sea level. If you have binoculars, cast an eye over the lakes for various aquatic bird species; spring and autumn migration activity occasionally produces some pleasant surprises. The Astroni Reserve can be best reached by car; from Naples take the tangenziale Exit 11 at Agnano and turn right toward Pianura; you'll see the entrance on your left after about 2 km (1 mi) (free parking outside). As an alternative, you can take Bus C2, which starts from outside the Campi Flegrei Metropolitana station and ask the driver or fellow passengers for the nearest stop to Astroni (about a 15-minute walk). Special guided tours are available on Sunday. ⊠ *Riserva degli Astroni Oasi WWF, Agnano,* ☎ *081/588–3720.* 🎫 *8,000 lire (free for WWF members).* ⊘ *Daily 9–4:30 (last admission 2).*

Lago d'Averno

> ③⓪ *11 km (7 mi) west of Naples; 3 km (2 mi) north of Baia.*

When the great poet Virgil wrote *"Facilis descensus Averno"*—"The way to hell is easy"—it was because he knew the way. Regarded by the ancients as the doorway to Hades, the fabled Lago d'Averno (Lake Avernus) was well known by the time the great poet settled here to write *The Aeneid.* Today the scene is little changed from his day and is best appreciated at sunset or when the moon is rising. Forested hills rise on three sides, the menacing cone of Monte Nuovo rises on the fourth. The smell of sulfur hangs over this lonely landscape, seemingly at the very gates of hell. No place evokes Homer, Virgil, and the cult of the Other World better than this silent, mysterious setting. On the approach road from Lago Lucrino (Lake Lucrino) less than 1 km (½ mi) to the south, look for remnants of the Roman channel dug in the 1st century BC, which transformed Avernus into a protected inner harbor and linked it to the Lucrine lake and the sea beyond. An even greater feat of engineering was the tunnel (now blocked off) from the northwestern side of Avernus leading to the center of Cumae. Also not far away is the Mare Morto of ancient Romans, who identified it as the Stygian Lake of the Dead, where Charon plied his trade and ferried souls across into the underworld. Nearby is the spring that was thought to flow directly from the River Styx, and it was there that Aeneas descended into Hades with the guidance of the Cumaean Sibyl, as famously recounted in *The Aeneid* of Virgil. To reach the Lake Avernus, take the Cumana railway to Lucrino (a 10-minute walk away); by car, drive westward from Pozzuoli, hugging the coast where possible, and turn right (inland) at Lucrino, about 4 km (2½ mi) away.

Dining

$$$–$$$$ ✕ **La Ninfea.** In antiquity, the site of some of the most celebrated oyster beds and fish farms, Lake Lucrino is now the setting for this stylish restaurant, which treats cooking as one of the fine arts. On your way in, admire the aquarium brimming with crustaceans of all shapes and sizes, and if overwhelmed by the choice of seafood, consult the waiter or even Antonio, the experienced sommelier. For a *primo piatto* with a difference, pamper yourself with the *tagliolini alla Sofia,* with its gar-

nish of lobster, cream, and cheese. ✉ *Piazza Italia, Lucrino,* ☎ *081/ 866–1326. AE, DC, MC, V. Closed Tues. in winter.*

$$ ✕ **La Cucina di Ruggiero.** Starting from a bizarre but *simpatico* welcome announced through a booming megaphone, this occasion is likely to be very different from anything you've previously experienced. Besides running this homely restaurant on the western shore of Lake Lucrino, Ruggiero is also a writer and poet—though his clients would insist that the real artist is his wife, Maria, whose culinary repertory and imagination are boundless. No written menus here and no choice—you eat what has been prepared that day: a family meal with a difference. ✉ *Via Intorno al Lago Lucrino, Lucrino,* ☎ *081/ 868–7473. Reservations essential. No credit cards. Closed Mon.–Tues. No lunch Wed.–Thurs.; no dinner Sun.*

Monte Nuovo

③① *10 km (6 mi) west of Naples; 3 km (2 mi) west of Pozzuoli.*

Monte Nuovo is the youngest volcano in the Campi Flegrei and the only one to have formed in historical times. Overlooking the Bay of Pozzuoli and lying between the town of Arco Felice and Lake Lucrino, at its highest point on the eastern side the volcanic cone rises more than 400 ft above sea level. The center consists of a funnel-shape crater with a maximum diameter of 1,300 ft. When Monte Nuovo erupted in 1538, it destroyed the ancient site of Tripergole on its lower western slopes, filled in much of Lake Lucrino and some of Lake Avernus, thus burying a considerable amount of archaeological evidence. Thanks largely to the volcano's protected status, the crater sides and the slopes of the cone now have a thick cover of Mediterranean *maquis* vegetation, intersected with trails of varying lengths and dotted with a few fumaroles, especially on the southeastern side.

The access road to Monte Nuovo (Via Virgilio) branches off Via Milliscola, linking Pozzuoli and Lucrino at roughly the midpoint between the Cumana stations of Arco Felice and Lucrino (about a 15-minute walk). The area is jointly run by the municipality of Pozzuoli and a local scientific school whose pupils first adopted the site in 1996. Much of the lower part has been landscaped and restored for educational purposes. A series of trails start from the visitor center (ask here about evening concerts) whose duration varies between one and two hours, with the possibility of descending into the heart of the crater. ✉ *Oasi Naturalistica di Monte Nuovo, Via Virgilio, Arco Felice, Pozzuoli,* ☎ *081/804–1462.* ▨ *Free.* ☉ *Daily 9–1 hr before sunset.*

Baia

③② *12 km (7 mi) west of Naples; 4 km (2½ mi) west of Pozzuoli.*

Now largely under the sea, ancient Baiae was once the most opulent and fashionable resort area of the Roman Empire, the place where Sulla, Pompey, Cicero, Julius Caesar, Tiberius, and Nero built their holiday villas. Petronius's *Satyricon* is a satire on the corruption, intrigue, and wonderful licentiousness of Roman life at Baiae. (Petronius was hired to arrange parties and entertainment for Nero, so he was in a position to know.) It was here that Cleopatra was staying when Julius Caesar was murdered on the Ides of March (March 15) in 44 BC; here that Emperor Claudius built a great villa for his third wife, Messalina (who is reputed to have spent her nights indulging herself at local brothels); and near here that Agrippina (Claudius's fourth wife and ultimate murderer) is believed to have been killed by henchmen sent by her son Nero in AD 59. Unfortunately, the Romans did not pursue the custom of writing—"Here lived Crassus" would help—so it is difficult to assign these historical events to specific locations. Consequently, conjecture is the order of the day: Julius Caesar's villa is now thought to be at the top of the hill behind the archaeological site and not near the foot of the Aragonese castle, though we cannot be absolutely certain. We do know, however, that the Romans found this area staggeringly beautiful. A visit to the site can only confirm what Horace wrote in one of his Epistles: *"Nullus in orbe sinus Baiis praelucet amoenis"* (No bay on Earth outshines pleasing Baiae).

★   Access to the **Parco Archeologico e Monumentale di Baia** (Archaeological Park) is delightfully straightforward on the Cumana railway (trains leave every 15–20 minutes from Montesanto in Naples, travel time 30 minutes). Outside the Baia station cross the railway line on a footbridge, noting the impressive dome of the so-called Temple of Diana, part of the ancient baths complex sundered from the rest of the archaeological site by the railway, obviously built well before the days of impact assessment. Continue upward for about five minutes until you reach the entrance to the site (limited parking facilities also available). Unlike Pompeii, Oplontis, and Herculaneum, where visitors are left stranded with very little site information—it's good for sales of guidebooks and guiding services—at the Baia ticket office you should receive a small map to the site while information panels in readable English are at strategic intervals. In antiquity this whole area was the Palatium Baianum (the Palace of Baiae), dedicated to otium—the ancient form of dolce far niente—and the residence of emperors from Augustus to as late as Septimius Severus in the 3rd century AD. The first terrace, the aptly named Villa dell'Ambulatio, is one of the best levels from which to appreciate the topography of the site: the whole hillside down to the level of the modern road near the waterfront has been modeled into flat terraces, each sporting different architectural features. While up on this terrace, look for the exquisite stuccoed artistry with its depictions of dolphins, swans, and cupids in the *balneum* (bathroom) (Room 13) and admire the elaborate theatrical motifs in the floor mosaic in Room 14. Below the balneum and inviting further exploration is a nymphaeum, or miniature theater, which can be reached from the western side. The suggested itinerary around the site is somewhat confusing, especially as part of the site is roped off. This regrettably includes the Temple of Mercury, on the lowest level, which has held so much fascination for travelers from the 18th century onward. It has been variously interpreted as a frigidarium and as a *natatio* (swimming pool) and is the oldest example of a large dome (50 BC–27 BC), predating the cupola of the Pantheon in Rome. If possible, have a peek inside the temple and test the impressive echo within.

If visiting during weekends and you have some surplus energy after touring the main archaeological site, continue up Via Fusaro away from Baia and branch left at the next roundabout. After about 150 yards along Via Bellavista look for a large gate on the left with a panda symbol. This marks the entrance to the newly created archaeological heritage park run by dedicated WWF volunteers. A short walk through small vegetable plots and vineyards will take you up to the summit and what is now believed to be Julius Caesar's villa, complete with the remains of a World War II gun emplacement and a commanding view both east and west. The park now hosts traditional concerts and poetry readings throughout much of the year (entrance is free but donations are welcome) and provides a focal point for local *contadini* (farmers) to sell their produce. For the schedule of events, ask at the archaeological site ticket office or at the Museo Archeologico dei Campi Flegrei (☎ 081/523-3797; ☞ *below*). ✉ *Parco Archeologico e Monumentale di Baia, Via Fusaro 75, Baia,* ☎ *081/868–7592.* ✆ *4,000 lire.* ☉ *Daily 9–1 hr before sunset.*

Housed in the Castle of Baia commanding a fine 360-degree view—eastward across the Bay of Pozzuoli and westward across the open Tyrrhenian—is the recently established **Museo Archeologico dei Campi Flegrei.** Regular bus service leaves the Baia station (in the direction of Bacoli; buy a ticket for the return journey, too, at the kiosk outside the Baia railway station) and stops about 2 km (1 mi) away, just opposite the ramp ascending to this impressively located castle. Though its foundation dates to the late 15th century, when Naples was ruled by the House of Aragon and an invasion by Charles VIII of France looked imminent, the castle was radically transformed under the Spanish viceroy Don Pedro de Toledo after the nearby eruption of Monte Nuovo in 1538. Indeed, its bastions bear a striking resemblance to the imposing Castel Sant'Elmo in Naples, built in the same period. This is an ideal spot for museumphobes: spacious, uncluttered display rooms with tastefully contextualized finds, a virtual absence of large tour groups, access to bastion terraces if required, and a viewing time of approximately one hour at the most. The south side of the castle is also the venue for outdoor classical music recitals and other performances (on summer evenings; ask at the ticket office about forthcoming events).

Of the three main exhibitions, the first on the suggested itinerary consists of plaster casts from the Roman period found at the Baia archaeological site. This gives valuable insights into the techniques used by the Romans to make copies from Greek originals in bronze from the Classical and Hellenistic periods. Displayed in the cases are plaster molds and casts from a local sculptor's workshop active around the 1st century BC, which were then used to produce marble copies of well-known works, such as that of the Athenian Tyrannicides, which would have stood in the Agora of Athens. Thanks to the Romans' love of Greek art and their fondness for marble copies of the bronze originals, we have been able to reconstruct much of the history of ancient Greek sculpture.

Pride of place in the museum goes to the sacellum, or small sanctuary, transported from nearby Misenum and tastefully displayed inside the Aragonese tower, *Torre Tenaglia.* Standing about 20 ft high, the sacellum has been reconstructed, with two of its original six columns (the rest in steel) and a marble architrave with its dedicatory inscription to the husband-and-wife team of *Augustales* (imperial cult devotees), who commissioned restoration of the sanctuary in the 2nd century AD, this surmounted by a pediment depicting the beneficent couple. Behind the facade are the naked statues of Vespasian (left) and Titus (right) in a flattering heroic pose, at least from the neck downward. To the right outside the sanctuary is a bronze equestrian statue (1st century AD) originally depicting Domitian. After his death and the subsequent *damnatio memoriae* (the imperial decree issued by emperors who wanted to disgrace predecessors by destroying all sculpted likenesses of them) was extensively—but all too visibly—remodeled to represent his successor, Nerva. Such changes in favor and falls from grace were common in the 1st century AD, and there are cases where faces were resculpted so many times that the statues ultimately became unrecognizable.

Moving on to the upper floor of the tower, you come to the other *capolavoro*, or showpiece, of the museum, the reconstruction of Emperor Claudius's nymphaeum, discovered in 1959 but only systematically excavated in the early 1980s, which now lies together with much of the ancient site of Baiae under 20 ft of water in the Bay of Pozzuoli. The sculptural elements salvaged from the seabed include a recognizable scene of a headless Odysseus plying Polyphemus (statue never found) with wine, aided by a companion with a wineskin. The other statues filling the niches along the two longer walls of the nymphaeum include Claudius's mother, Antonia, and a rather poignant sculpture of perhaps one of his daughters who died young. She is depicted holding a butterfly about to take wing, thought to be symbolic of the spirit of life departing. In contrast, there are two statues of the youthful Dionysus (one crowned, the other with panther), making any thematic connections between the statues rather hard to draw. The function of the nymphaeum is suggested by the marble supports for *klinai* (couches) set on the floor near the entrance: this must have been a showy triclinium, with its full complement of statues and fountains designed to ease the weight of imperial cares and provide due source for reflection and inspiration. ⊠ *Via Castello 39, Bacoli,* ☎ *081/523–3797.* ⊠ *4,000 lire.* ⊘ *Mon.–Sat. 9–1 hr before sunset, Sun. 9–2.*

Dining and Lodging

$$ ✕⊞ **Azienda Agrituristica Il Casolare.** Il Casolare offers the rare chance of dining and lodging within a 10,000-year-old crater (thankfully extinct). This place is particularly known for its restaurant, perched on the inner slopes of the volcano, offering a view of the patchwork of farmed plots on the crater floor. Specializing in *cucina contadina napoletana,* the owner Tobia serves whatever is in season. No agonizing over menus here: expect about a cornucopia of different antipasti (including possibly goat's ricotta, and *poppacelle,* or peppers done in vinegar) and some novel vegetarian dishes like pasta *e chicerchia* (vetching). The four rooms, or *mini-appartmenti,* are small but tastefully renovated, a perfect base for exploring the surrounding area. Transfers can be arranged from the Baia railway station. There is also convenient parking, situated up an unbelievably narrow lane (Via Selvatico) almost opposite the entrance to Baia Castle. If you're coming to dine, a flashlight is provided evenings for descending to the restaurant in the crater. ⊠ *Via Selvatico, Contrada Coste dei Fondi di Baia, 80070,* ☎ *081/523–5193. Reservations essential. 4 rooms with bath. Restaurant, parking. No credit cards. Closed Mon. No dinner Sun.*

Cumae

㉝ *16 km (10 mi) west of Naples; 5 km (3 mi) north of Baia*

Being perhaps the oldest Greek colony on mainland Italy, Cumae overshadowed the Phlegrean Fields and Neapolis in the 7th and 6th centuries BC, since it was home to the **Antro della Sibilla,** the fabled Cave of the Cumaean Sibyl—one of the three greatest oracles of antiquity who is said to have presided over the destinies of men. In about the 6th century BC the Greeks hollowed the cave from the rock beneath the ridge leading up to the present ruins of Cumae's acropolis. Today you can walk—just as Virgil's Aeneas did—through a dark, massive 350-ft-long stone tunnel that opens into the vaulted Chamber of the Prophetic Voice, where the Sibyl delivered her oracles. Standing here in one of the most venerated sites of ancient times, the sense of the *numen*—of communication with invisible powers—is overwhelming. "This is the most romantic classical site in Italy," wrote H. V. Morton. "I would rather come here than to Pompeii."

Cumae was founded in the third quarter of the 8th century BC by Greek colonists. The name has legendary origins: Myth has it that Euboean mariners found a woman who had miscarried a baby on the beach here, and the fetus was washed out to sea by great breakers on the shore. Thinking this an omen from the gods of fertility, the mariners built an altar here and called their new settlement *kuema* (or "fetus" in Greek). Centuries later Virgil wrote his epic of *The Aeneid,* the story of the Trojan prince Aeneas's wanderings, partly to give Rome the historical legitimacy that Homer had given the Greeks. On his journey, Aeneas had to descend to the underworld to speak to his father, and to find his way in, he needed the guidance of the Cumaean Sibyl. Virgil did not dream up the Sibyl's Cave or the entrance to Hades—he must have actually stood both in her chamber and along the rim of Lake Avernus, as you yourself will stand. When he described the Sibyl's Cave in Book VI of *The Aeneid* as having "*centum ostia*"—a hundred mouths—and depicted the entrance to the underworld on Lake Avernus so vividly, "*spelunca alta . . . tuta lacu nigro nemorum tenebris*"—"a deep cave . . . protected by a lake of black water and the glooming forest"—it was because he was familiar with this awesome landscape. In Book VI of *The Aeneid,* Virgil describes how Aeneas, arriving at Cumae, sought Apollo's throne (remains of the Temple of Apollo can still be seen) and "the deep hidden abode of the dread Sibyl/An enormous cave . . ." On either side of the entrance to the cave today are inscribed one of Virgil's most powerful verses: "On one side of the Eubean rock/Is cut a huge cavern. To it lead/A hundred broad ways, a hundred mouths/From which there tumble out as many voices,/The Sibyl's answers. As they all arrived/Upon the threshold of the cave the virgin/Cried out: 'The time to question fate is now!/The god is here, the god!' As she spoke/Before the temple doors her countenance/Changed suddenly, her color changed, her hair/Fell loose about her shoulders and she panted/Violently, her wild heart grew great within her,/She seemed taller, her voice was not a mortal's/Because the god's power had breathed upon her."

In general, Sibyl was the title given to inspired prophetesses, usually of Apollo. As the god of light who pierced through all darkness, Apollo was also the god of divination, and there were oracles throughout the ancient world interpreting his will. Although Cumae never achieved the status of Delphi, it was the most important oracular center in Magna Graecia, and the Sibyl would have been consulted on a whole range of matters. Foreign governments consulted the Sibyl before mounting campaigns. Wealthy aristocrats came to consult with their deceased relatives. Businessmen came to get their dreams interpreted or to seek favorable omens before entering into financial agreements or setting off on journeys. Farmers came to remove curses on their cows. Love potions were a profitable source of revenue; women from Baiae lined up for potions to slip into the wine of handsome charioteers who drove up and down the street in their gold-plated four-horsepower chariots. Still, it was the Sibyl's prophecies that ensured the crowds here, prophecies written on palm leaves and later collected into the corpus of the Sibyline books. However, with the coming of the Olympian gods, the earlier gods of the soil were discredited or given new roles and names. Ancient rites, such as those surrounding the Cumaean Sibyl, were now carried out in secret and known as the Mysteries. The Romans—like the later Soviets—tried in vain to replace these Mysteries by deifying the state in the person of its rulers. Yet even the Caesars appealed to forces of the Other World. And until the 4th century AD, the Sibyl was consulted by the Christian bishop of Rome—one reason why Michelangelo portrayed the Cumaean Sibyl—one of his most magisterial creations—on the Sistine Chapel ceiling.

However little of ancient Cumae now stands above ground—and the Temple of Apollo has suffered woefully over the millennia—the underground passages are virtually intact, though not entirely visitable. There are detailed information panels to guide you through the site, with extra information on flora and fauna supplied by the local Worldwide Fund for Nature. As you walk through, you'll soon appreciate what a good choice it was to colonize this site: it was surrounded by fertile land, offered opportunities for development on various levels, had relatively easy access to the sea (though no natural harbor), and an acropolis at the top providing an excellent vantage in all directions. Allow at least two hours for this visit to soak up the ambience, study the ruins, and reach the top level overlooking the Acherusia Palu—now Lago Fusaro—to the south and part of the Silva Gallinaria, the thick holm oak ground cover to the north, once an immense forest stretching almost all the way to Rome. Unlike in Greek and Roman times, when access to Cumae was through a network of underground passages, an overground bus service leaves the Baia station at regular intervals. If driving, leave the Naples tangenziale (bypass) at the Cuma exit and then continue to follow signs for about 3 km (2 mi). There is a free parking lot. ⊠ *Via Acropoli 39, Cuma,* ☎ *081/853–3060.* ✉ *4,000 lire.* ☉ *Daily 9–1 hr before sunset.*

AROUND THE BAY A TO Z

Arriving and Departing

By Car

Most archaeological sites are fairly accessible by car and usually have reasonably safe parking facilities. Pompeii is a very short distance off the A3 autostrada (toll from Naples or Salerno: 1,600 lire), though this major highway with only two lanes in each direction can get very congested with ill-disciplined drivers.

A car could be useful for exploring the Campi Flegrei region on the west side of Naples, especially for sites like Cumae and Lake Avernus where public transport is either infrequent or nonexistent, as well as the Astroni and Monte Nuovo craters. From Naples travel toward Pozzuoli on the Tangenziale—the Naples bypass (toll: 1,100 lire)—exiting at the appropriate junction.

By Train

The main station in Naples (Stazione Centrale, at Piazza Garibaldi) is also the main interchange node for public transport both east and west of Naples. A branch of the aptly named Circumvesuviana railway (☎ 081/772–2444) serves the main archaeological sites at the foot of Vesuvius. Trains leave from the Corso Garibaldi station in Naples, then make a stop at the main terminal at Piazza Garibaldi just 10 blocks away, and then head southeast for Sorrento (about two trains per hour, 2,200 lire to Ercolano, 3,100 lire to Torre Annunziata and Pompei Scavi-Villa Dei Misteri). Confusingly, the station called "Pompei" lies on a different line which will leave you not at the main entrance to the archaeological site but just behind the cathedral, close to the amphitheater.

For the Phlegrean Fields to the west of Naples, take the Cumana line run by SEPSA (☎ 081/551–3328), with trains every 15–20 minutes) from the terminus at Piazza Montesanto near Montesanto Metropolitana station. Alternatively, take the Metropolitana all the way to Pozzuoli from one of the railway stations in Naples (Piazza Garibaldi or the more welcoming station of Mergellina (☎ 081/554–3188), with one departure every 10–15 minutes. This will drop you near the amphitheater and the Solfatara crater.

Getting Around

By Bus

In general, in this area it's best to travel on rails than on wheels, as local roads can be frustratingly slow. However, for the trip up Vesuvius the bus run by **Transporti Vesuviani** (☎ 081/739–2833; 5,000 lire from the Pompei–Villa dei Misteri Circumvesuviana station, 3,000 lire from Ercolano station) will take you up to the car park and the starting point of the path up to the top of the cone.

By Car

Off the main highways, signposting is sometimes poor, with road signs suffering intense competition from advertising placards, so navigating becomes an invaluable skill. The westbound Tangenziale (Napoli–Pozzuoli) should be avoided Saturday evenings and Sundays in summer (crowds heading out of Naples for nightlife or beaches). Road surfaces are usually fair, though conditions near the top of Vesuvius can become icy in winter. Take customary precautions when parking and leaving your vehicle: use a *parcheggio custodito* (attended parking lot) and avoid on-street unattended parking when possible.

By Taxi

Pompeii: Piazza Santuario (☎ 081/863–2686); Piazza Esedra (☎ 081/536–7852). **Ercolano:** Stazione Circumvesuviana (☎ 081/739–3666). **Pozzuoli:** Piazza della Repubblica (☎ 081/526–5800).

By Train

When not affected by wildcat strikes or landslides, the railway network either side of Naples is cheap and reliable, though with the many stops along the way you're unlikely to experience nerve-tingling velocity. As in any mass transit system through a fairly depressed area, not all your fellow-passengers will be well versed in train etiquette so brace yourself for smoking in nonsmoking compartments, etc., especially on the Circumvesuviana.

Contacts and Resources

CURRENCY EXCHANGE

Pompeii: Banco di Napoli (✉ Piazza B. Longo 37, ☎ 081/863–1001). There are also several exchange bureaux around and off the main square, Piazza Longo, near Porta Marina, and an ATM conveniently located by the main ticket office at Porta Marina. **Ercolano: Exchange Bureau, Alesi Travel International** (✉ 1 Traversa IV Novembre 12, ☎ 081/739–7587). **Pozzuoli: Banco di Napoli** (✉ Via N. Terracciano 18, ☎ 081/525–6111).

EMERGENCIES

Pompeii: Police (☎ 081/850–6172). **Ambulance** (☎ 081/863–7816). **First Aid** (✉ Via Colle San Bartolomeo 50, ☎ 081/535–9111).

Ercolano (Herculaneum): Police (☎ 081/732–1858). **Ambulance** (☎ 081/777–5600). **Hospital** (✉ Ospedale Maresca, Via Montedoro, Torre del Greco, ☎ 081/882–4033).

Pozzuoli: Police (☎ 081/804–1100). **Ambulance** (☎ 081/526–6954). **Hospital** (✉ Ospedale S. Maria delle Grazie, Via Domiziana, ☎ 081/855–2111).

TRAVEL AGENCIES AND GUIDED TOURS

Pompeii: Amorini Viaggi (✉ Via Lepanto 235, ☎ 081/850–2614, FAX 081/856–1689).

Ercolano (Herculaneum): Alesi Travel International: (✉ 1 Traversa IV Novembre 12, ☎ 081/739–7587, FAX 081/777–2872).

Pozzuoli: Campi Elisi Viaggi e Turismo (⊠ Via Solfatara 13, ☏ 081/526–6466, FAX 081/526–6845).

Pompeii: Azienda Autonoma di Cura Soggiorno e Turismo (⊠ Via Sacra 1, ☏ 081/850–7255), open 9–2, closed Sunday. **Ufficio Informazione** (⊠ Piazza Porta Marina 12, ☏ 081/850–8277), open 9–2, closed Sunday.

Ercolano (Herculaneum): Ufficio Turistico (⊠ Via IV Novembre 82, ☏ 081/788–1243), open 9–2, closed Sunday.

Pozzuoli: Azienda Autonoma di Cura Soggiorno e Turismo (⊠ Piazza Matteotti 1/a, ☏ 081/526–5068), open 9–2, closed Sunday.

4 CAPRI, ISCHIA, AND PROCIDA

Emperors, kings, and artists have all made the Bay of Naples's sea-wreathed isles their abodes for more than 2,000 years. And well they might, for Capri, Ischia, and Procida are compact realms of undiluted beauty. Bathed in 24-karat sunshine, Capri has been a chic resort ever since the Caesars made it their private playpen; Ischia is famous for its volcanic spas where there's nothing between you and the world except for a layer of fango mud; while lizards far outnumber the tourists in Procida's quiet hills, immortalized in the Oscar-winning film *Il Postino*. The locals dare you to find lovelier islands, even in your own imagination.

By Mark
Walters

THE ISLANDS OFF NAPLES ARE SO DIFFERENT that you
wonder how they can possibly be in the same bay—
indeed, some would insist they are not, that they all
lie just beyond its outer fringes. The contrast goes beyond the mere
geology and vegetation of the three islands. They all occupy different
niches in the traveler's mind, with Capri pandering to the whims of
the international great-and-good, Ischia servicing the needs of its predominantly German and Italian clientele, and Procida—the closest to
the mainland—being more dependent on the weekend and summer influx of Neapolitans. Chosen by the Greeks, the great connoisseurs and
aesthetes of antiquity, as their first base in Italy, the islands of Capri,
Ischia, and Procida combine a broad gamut of experiences.

When the three islands—two of which were rebellious daughters of a
distant volcanic eruption, and the third, Capri, part of the limestone
chain of the Apennines—demanded to be compensated for their rocky
complexions, the master of the universe seemed to have agreed to
their every peculiar request: Capri got magnificent grottoes, rampa-
geous wildflowers, and beautiful views that are vacations in themselves;
Ischia, catch basins, natural hot springs, and paradisiacal white-sand
beaches; Procida, plunging cliffs and verdant hills. Little wonder history's hedonists have long luxuriated on them.

But islandophiles have always had a special love for Capri (pronounced
with the accent on the first syllable). Erstwhile pleasure dome to Roman
emperors, and still Italy's most glamorous seaside getaway, this craggy,
whale-shape island tips one of the two points of the crescent of the Bay
of Naples (Ischia tips the other). The island's beauty is an epic one:
cliffs that are the very embodiment of time, bougainvillea-shaded pathways overlooking the sea, trees seemingly hewn out of rock by the Greeks.
It's little wonder tales tell of German tourists who would rent villas
while their wives were buying postcards and American industrialists
who wired home to sell their factories. Capri has always been a stage
that lesser mortals could share with the beautiful people, often an eclectic potpourri of duchesses who have left their dukes home, fading
French film actresses, pretenders to obscure thrones, waspish cou-
turiers, and sireny supermodels.

Today Capri's siren song continues to seduce thousands of visitors. The
summer scene calls to mind the stampeding of bulls through the narrow streets of Pamplona: if you can visit in the spring or fall, do so.
Yet even the crowds are not enough to destroy Capri's very special charm.
The town itself is a Moorish opera set of shiny white houses, tiny squares,
and narrow medieval alleyways hung with flowers, while its hillsides
are spectacular settings for luxurious seaside villas. The mood is mod-
ish but somehow unspoiled. The upper crust bakes in the sun in private villas; the secret is that you also should disappear while the
day-trippers take over—offering yourself to the sun at your hotel pool
or exploring the hidden corners of the island. Even in the height of summer, you can enjoy a degree of privacy on one of the many paved paths
that wind around the island hundreds of feet above the sea.

In terms of settlements, conquests, and dominion, the history of the
islands is a microcosm of that on the mainland. For eastern Mediterranean traders in the second and first millennia BC, Capri and Ischia
were both close enough to the mainland to provide easy access to trade
routes and impervious enough to afford natural protection against invaders. Ischia, or Pithekoussai, as it used to be called—a word probably derived from the Greek for a large earthenware jar (*pithos*) rather

than the less plausible word, *pithekos*, meaning monkey—is renowned in classical circles as being the first colony founded by the Greeks on Italian soil, as early as the 8th century BC. Capri, probably colonized a century or so later, is amply described in the early years of the Roman Empire by authors such as Suetonius and Tacitus, as this was the island where Tiberius chose to spend the last 10 years of his life.

After the breakup of the Roman Empire, the islands, like many parts of the Mediterranean, suffered a succession of incursions. Saracens, Normans, and Turks all laid siege to the islands at some stage, interspersed with periods of relative stability under the Schwabians, the Angevins, the Aragonese, and the Spanish. After a short interregnum under the French at the beginning of the 19th century, a period of relative peace and prosperity ensued.

Over the next century, from the opening of its first hotel in 1826, Capri saw an influx of visitors that reads like a Who's Who of literature and politics, especially in the early decades of the 20th century. Ischia and Procida established themselves as holiday resorts much later, with development taking place from the 1950s onward. Recent years have seen a diversification in the type of experiences offered on the three islands. From being entirely dependent on its thermal springs, Ischia is now the archaeological front-runner in the bay, with the opening of a new museum in Lacco Ameno. Procida is starting to capitalize on its chief natural asset, the unspoiled island of Vivara, as well as the pastel colors of its main harbor, the set for the widely acclaimed film *Il Postino*. On Capri, for those seeking peace and quiet away from its main thoroughfares, a number of walks have been mapped out past some of the major geological landmarks and through delightfully species-rich Mediterranean maquis.

Pleasures and Pastimes

Dining
Though relatively close together, the three islands enjoy different culinary traditions. Capri has lent its name to two dishes that can also be widely consumed on the mainland: *insalata caprese,* a dish with a color scheme like the Italian flag—made with alternating slices of mozzarella and tomato and served with a sprig of basil; and *torta caprese,* a plain cake combining chocolate and finely chopped almonds and topped with a sprinkling of powdered sugar. Unlike Capri and Procida, where seafood tends to predominate, the Ischitani exploit their naturally fertile volcanic soils to good effect: wine flows—notably from Biancolella and Forestera grape varieties—and is a pleasing accompaniment to the renowned dish from Ischia, *coniglio all'ischitana,* rabbit in a rich tomato-based sauce together with aromatic herbs like basil, rosemary, thyme, and marjoram. The sauce is also used as an accompaniment to *bucatini,* spaghetti-shape pasta with a hole running from one end to the other. Note that restaurant listings for both Capri Town and Anacapri are united in one section.

CATEGORY	COST*
$$$$	over 85,000 lire
$$$	60,000–85,000 lire
$$	25,000–60,000 lire
$	under 25,000 lire

per person, excluding drinks and service

Lodging
Although island prices are generally higher than those on the mainland, it is definitely worth paying the difference for an overnight stay.

On Capri, once the day-trippers have left center stage and headed down to the Marina Grande for the ferry home, the streets regain some of their charm and tranquillity. Again, although Ischia can be sampled piecemeal on day excursions from Naples, given the size of the island, you'd be well advised to arrange a stopover. Bear in mind that there is considerable competition for hotel rooms, especially at moderate prices. Weekends on the islands are popular with the Italians from the mainland, as are the months of July and especially August. On Capri hotels seem to fill almost as quickly as your wallet empties, so book well in advance to be assured of getting first-pick accommodations. Note that hotel listings for Capri Town and for Anacapri are united in one section.

CATEGORY	COST*
$$$$	over 350,000 lire
$$$	200,000–350,000 lire
$$	100,000–200,000 lire
$	under 100,000 lire

All prices are for a double room, excluding tax and service.

Exploring Capri, Ischia, and Procida

Lying equidistant from Naples (about 10 km [6 mi]), Ischia and Capri stand like guards at the main entrance to the Bay of Naples, with Ischia to the west and Capri to the south, while Procida is like a small stepping-stone halfway between Ischia and the Capo Miseno (Cape Misenum), on the mainland. The islands can be reached easily from various points in and near Naples, with the port of Pozzuoli offering the closest access to Procida and Ischia, and the port of Sorrento lying almost opposite Capri.

All the islands are well served by road networks, with buses plying the main roads and a funicular on Capri to reach the main town from the Marina Grande, as well as a chairlift to the top of Monte Solaro (1,932 ft) from Anacapri. Note that on a few of Capri's major roads only cars, taxis, and buses are permitted—elsewhere on the island foot power is the preferred mode of transportation. Life on Capri gravitates around the two centers of Capri Town (on the saddle between Monte Tiberio and Monte Solaro) and Anacapri, higher up (984 ft). Ischia's larger population is distributed into about six larger urban areas and countless smaller villages and farmsteads dotted around the slopes of Monte Epomeo, the highest point on the island (2,582 ft). Both Ischia and Capri contrast strikingly with Procida, much of which is built-up apart from the less developed southwestern end and the island of Vivara, linked by a pedestrian causeway to the harbor of Chiaiolella.

Great Itineraries

If archaeology and history are at the top of your list of priorities, choosing between Ischia and Capri can be difficult. Moving around Capri to the main sites is generally easier—and can be done in a day if pushed—while Ischia calls for more chilling out at your destination, especially in summer months. With limited time, Procida can be tacked on to your stay as a day trip from Ischia or from the mainland.

IF YOU HAVE 1 DAY
With no chance of overnighting, take an early ferry from the mainland to Capri so that you get to the main sites before the human tsunami hits the island. Take a quick tour of glamorous Capri—**La Piazzetta** ②, the idyllic Via Tragara, and the famed **I Faraglioni** ⑧ and **Punta Tragara** ⑨. Return by route of the romantic **Certosa di San Giacomo** ⑩, then, if you're up for a hour hike, head up to the **Villa Jovis** ④ to gaze

in wonder at Tiberius's Leap and the sea views. After lunch, take a breath-less bus ride up to Anacapri to visit the mountaintop gardens of Axel Munthe's **Villa San Michele** ⑬. From Anacapri catch the bus to the **Grotta Azzurra** ⑱—the matrix-blue light at this grotto scintillates even in late afternoon and by then the crowds are gone.

IF YOU HAVE 4 DAYS

After the day outlined above, overnight on Capri—even more magi-cal when the day-trippers have departed—and enjoy more of its sights on your second day. Begin with a morning jaunt around the Giro del-l'Arco Naturale to view the **Grotta di Matermania** ⑥ and the **Villa Mala-parte** ⑦. For more scenic splendor, head back up to Anacapri and the chairlift up **Monte Solaro** ⑭, then explore the churches of **Santa Maria a Cetrella** ⑮ and **San Michele** ⑰. If you just want to be busy doing nothing, opt instead to laze the afternoon away at the bathing lido at **Marina Piccola** ⑫. On day three head to Ischia. Visit Ischia Ponte and the "doorman" to the island—the magnificent Castello Aragonese—then visit the museum of Roman antiquities at **Lacco Ameno** ㉓ and **Forio** ㉔, where you'll find the island's most picturesque church, the Sanc-tuario del Soccorso, and the famous gardens of La Mortella. On your final day you'll want to save time for a welcome dip into Ischia's soothing waters, either at Citara Beach, or at one of the noted spas: if you want crowds and children, head to Poseidon in Forio; for more stylish surrounds, check out Negombo in Lacco Ameno. Or take the ferry and explore nearby Procida.

IF YOU HAVE 7 DAYS

A week should be enough to sample a gamut of pleasures ranging from natural saunas to trails winding through thick Mediterranean maquis, with plenty of time left over for experiencing the local brands of dolce vita in the evenings. On Capri go for a round-the-island boat trip and spend a lazy day on Procida combining a walk on Vivara with a lin-gering lunch at a quayside restaurant at the quiet marina of Chi-aiolella.

WHEN TO TOUR CAPRI, ISCHIA, AND PROCIDA

Lying at a latitude of just more than 40 north, the islands in the Bay of Naples enjoy a typical Mediterranean climate, with hot dry sum-mers, which means the area can be pretty torrid in July and August. Spring is excellent for wildflowers and birds, although it also attracts large numbers of vacationers, especially from northern Europe. If you're looking for a quiet break, the holiday season calms down con-siderably from the end of September, while sea temperatures are still pleasantly warm by Mediterranean standards even to the end of Oc-tober. At any time of year outside the summer, conditions can be stom-ach churning in the Bay of Naples and on exceptionally rough days ferry services to the mainland may be canceled.

In winter *la caccia* (hunting) is a common pursuit, especially on Ischia, so it's best to schedule country walks for nonhunting days (usually Tues-day and Friday, check locally). Watch out for Pasquetta (Easter Mon-day), when the ferries to the islands are crammed with Neapolitans hell-bent on their annual country picnic. This is definitely a no-go day for travel or country walks.

CAPRI: A SIREN LANDSCAPE

D. H. Lawrence once called Capri "a gossipy, villa-stricken, two-humped chunk of limestone, a microcosm that does heaven much credit, but mankind none at all." He was referring to its once rather farouche reputation as well as its unique natural beauty. Fantastic grottoes, soaring conical peaks, caverns great and small, plus villas of the emperors and thousands of legends combine with the ancient Roman tales of Suetonius's "exquisite tortures" to give the isle an air of whispered and mysterious evil and an intoxicating quality as heady as its rare and delicious wines. Emperor Augustus was the first to tout the island's pleasures by nicknaming it Apragopolis, the city of sweet idleness, and ever since Capri has drawn escapists of every ilk. Ancient Greek and Roman goddesses are no longer worshiped here, having been supplanted by the likes of Jacqueline Kennedy, Elizabeth Taylor, and Brigitte Bardot, who made the island into a papparazzo's paradise in the 1950s and 1960s.

Of all the peoples who have left their mark on the island during its millennia of history, the Romans and the sybaritic wealth they displayed here have had the greatest effect in modeling the island's psyche. Capri became the very center of power in the ancient Roman Empire when Tiberius built 12 villas scattered over the island and decided to spend the last 10 years of his life here, refusing to return to Rome even when he was near death. Far from being a dirty old man who was only interested in orgies, this poor, misunderstood gentleman used Capri as a base to set up many of the governmental edicts that literally created the ancient Roman Empire. All his hard work and happy play—he indulged his secret passion for astronomy here—were overlooked by ancient scandalmongers, prime among them Suetonius, who wrote: "In Capri they still show the place at the cliff top where Tiberius used to watch his victims being thrown into the sea after prolonged and exquisite tortures. A party of mariners were stationed below, and when the bodies came hurtling down, they whacked at them with oars and boat-hooks, to make sure they were completely dead." Thankfully, present-day Capri is less fraught with danger for visiting dignitaries or travelers from afar. The main risks now are overexposure to the Mediterranean sun and overindulgence in pleasures of the palate.

Capri Town and Environs

From the main harbor, Marina Grande, you can take a bus or funicular to reach the hub of the island, Capri Town. This white-on-white fantasy of Capriote architecture, window boxes filled with blooms, and stylish boutiques rests on a saddle between rugged limestone cliffs to the east and west, where huge herds of *capre* (goats) once roamed, hence the name of the island. Beyond Capri Town lies some of the island's most spectacular sights, including I Faraglioni and the Villa Jovis. As you disembark at the marina quay, note that unlike the other islands in the Bay of Naples, Capri is not of volcanic origin but was formed by marine deposits laid more than 100 million years ago and then uplifted during plate tectonic activity in the Pleistocene era (as recently as 1–2 million years ago), as Monte Tiberio, to the left of the Marina Grande, and Monte Solaro, to the west, powerfully attest.

A Good Walk

Once you get off the ferry and have picked up a decent map of Capri (1,500 lire at the information office on the main jetty), take a funicular ride up from the harbor area of **Marina Grande** ① to Capri Town (only one stop, 1,700 lire one-way; if for any reason it's not working, there's a bus and taxi service). For the energetic, there's a former mule track starting from a small square on the quayside called Largo Fontana that will get you up in about 15 minutes, emerging just below the clock tower in Capri Town. The top funicular station brings you out onto Piazza Umberto I, better known locally as **La Piazzetta** ②. On peak days in the summer this area gets so crowded it's rumored the local police

Capri

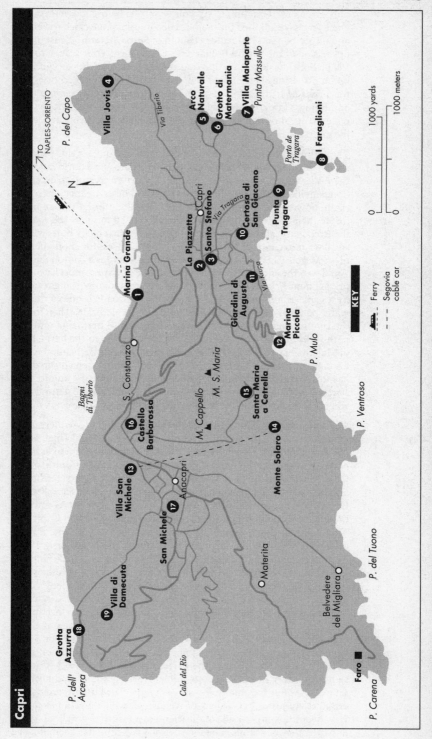

TO NAPLES-SORRENTO

P. del Capo

Villa Jovis 4

Via Tiberio

Arco Naturale 5
Grotto di Matermania 6
Villa Malaparte 7
Punta Massullo

Porto de Tragara

I Faraglioni 8

Capri
La Piazzetta
Santo Stefano 3
2
Via Tragara
Certosa di San Giacomo
10
Punta Tragara 9

Marina Grande 1

Giardini di Augusto
Via Krupp
11

Marina Piccola 12

P. Mulo

S. Constanzo

Bagni di Tiberio

M. S. Maria
M. Cappello
Santa Maria a Cetrella 15

P. Ventroso

Castello Barbarossa 16

Monte Solaro 14

Villa San Michele 13
San Michele
Anacapri
17

Materita

Belvedere del Migliara

P. del Tuono

Villa di Damecuta 19

Grotta Azzurra 18
P. dell' Arcera

Cala del Rio

Faro

P. Carena

KEY
Ferry
Segovia cable car

1000 yards
1000 meters

only give you 20 minutes to sip your Campari before moving you on. Once you have admired the majolica decoration of the clock tower dial and inspected the 17th-century church of **Santo Stefano** ③, just off the upper side of the square in Piazzetta Cerio, forge your way across to Via Le Botteghe. If you are thinking about a picnic lunch, you can stock up on provisions here. Try Sfizi di Pane, a baker at Via Le Botteghe 4 for a slice of frittata *di maccaroni* or a more orthodox *panino* (roll) and fixings. Look on the right for the discreet supermarket, to complete the meal or just to stock up with liquid refreshments at accessible prices.

The farther you get away from La Piazzetta, the quieter this pedestrianized road becomes. Via Le Botteghe becomes Via Fuorlovado and then Via Croce, developing gradually into an avenue fringed by bougainvillea and spreading oleander trees. This is an area where real estate now changes hands for at least 10 million lire a square meter (more than $500 per square ft). After about 10 minutes the road to the Arco Naturale branches off to the right. Archaeology buffs will instead want to continue straight on up Monte Tiberio for about 45 minutes to reach Tiberius's famous mountaintop **Villa Jovis** ④—on the way you'll pass the entrance to the Villa Lysis, one of Capri's most legendary private homes, built by the poet Baron Fersen and now being restored by a Chilean millionaire. The café at the crossroads is one of the last watering holes before heading out to the Arco Naturale. Then follow the ceramic signs for Arco Naturale along Via Matermania until the path forks after about 15 minutes (Arco Naturale, to the left; Grotta di Matermania, to the right). Peer at the **Arco Naturale** ⑤ (Natural Arch), keeping in mind that the path is a cul-de-sac, so every step you go down has to be retraced. Then, knee joints permitting, take the hundreds of steps down to the **Grotta di Matermania** ⑥, an impressive natural cave where the ancient Romans worshiped the goddess Cybele every dawn.

The path continues down and southward through fine Mediterranean maquis vegetation (most of the evergreen trees are holm oak) high above the shoreline, affording fine views of Punta Massullo where **Villa Malaparte** ⑦—possibly the most important creation of 20th-century Italian architecture—perches over the sea. Two hundred yards farther on is a panoramic point from which you can gaze at the three **Faraglioni** ⑧, Capri's striking offshore rocks, which now loom into sight. As you continue westward, look first for the most romantic house on Capri, the Villa Solitaria—once home to novelist Compton MacKenzie, it is set on a bluff high over the sapphire sea and was built in the early 1900s by architect Edwin Cerio—then look for the towering rock pinnacle Pizzo Luongo (High Point), which the ancients thought was the petrified form of Polifemo, the giant who was blinded by Odysseus's men. The end of the Giro dell'Arco Naturale (Natural Arch Circuit) is reached at another panoramic point, the Punta Tragara, which marks your arrival back in Capri Town. From here take Via Tragara—lined with elegant hotels and villas, it is the most beautiful street on Capri (some say the world)—until it joins with Via Camerelle. Look for a left turn down Via Cerio to the **Certosa di San Giacomo** ⑩ (Carthusian Monastery of St. James) to enjoy Capri's grandest architectural set piece. About five minutes' walk away up Via Matteotti are the **Giardini di Augusto** ⑪ (Gardens of Augustus), which give an excellent view over the southern side of the island towards the Faraglioni. Here, however, the road stops. The impressive Via Krupp has been blocked off, making access to Marina Piccola impossible from this point. So retrace your steps until you get to Via Serena—you'll recognize it from the vast oleander bushes on either side of the walkway which form a picturesque arch, which is a mere five-minute walk from the Piazzetta.

Once back at base, reward yourself with a granita or a fruit-based cocktail (perhaps fresh peaches or strawberries with spumante) at the Gran Caffè, the very first bar to grace the square 40 years ago. As standard drinks like caffè espresso and cappuccino are outrageously expensive, you might as well splurge on something really memorable.

TIMING

Allowing time for a refreshment stop, a little shopping, and a fair amount of camera lens focusing, the walk will take between three and five hours. Those who aren't up for a lot of hiking should choose either the trek to the Villa Jovis or the Giro dell'Arco Naturale; the latter is a cliff-side path that includes hundreds of steps (going downhill mostly), so be prepared. Most of the sites and shops are open throughout the day, but as there's more than a fair amount of up-and-down, you'd be well advised to avoid the stickiest hours—weather-wise—from 12 AM to 3 PM during the peak summer season.

Sights to See

⑤ Arco Naturale. One of Capri's most famous natural wonders, this geologic arch is all that remains of a large limestone cave which has suffered the erosive effects of wind and rain over the millennia. Once a cave likely to have been hollowed out by wave action, it then broke apart when uplifted to its present position in relatively recent geological times (about 1–2 million years before present) to its present position hundreds of feet above sea level. Engraved by 19th-century artists, it became a favorite pictorial landmark for travelers in the era of Romanticism. ⊠ *Via Arco Naturale, at the end of Via Matermania.*

★ ⑩ Certosa di San Giacomo (Charterhouse of St. James). Nestled between the Castiglione and Tuoro hills, this grand, palatial complex was a Carthusian monastery for centuries dedicated to St. James. It was founded between 1371 and 1374 by Count Giacomo Arcucci, who was given the lands and the means to create the monastery by Queen Giovanna I of Naples; both the count and queen died during the upheaval of the Angevin monarchy. Shortly after the monastery was sacked by the pirate Dragut in the 16th century, it was restored and rebuilt—heavily so, since the friars within were often detested by the Caprese, since they exacted heavy taxes on the populace yet refused to open their gates to minister to them when the plague broke out through the centuries.

You enter the complex via a spectacular entryway, which leads to a public library, the **Biblioteca Comunale Popolare Luigi Bladier,** and the spacious **Church of San Giacomo** (built in 1690). After admiring the church's Baroque frescoes, follow the signpost down toward the Parco, which leads down an avenue flanked by pittosporum and magnolia toward the monastery gardens and some welcome benches. Beyond a covered road lies the **Chiostro Grande** (Large Cloister)—originally the site of the monks' cells and now the temporary home of a local high school. Nearby is the much prettier 15th-century **Chiostro Piccolo** (Small Cloister), now the venue for summertime open-air concerts. Before leaving be sure to visit the **Museo Diefenbach,** a collection of large canvases by the German painter K. W. Diefenbach, who visited Capri in 1900 and stayed until his death in 1913. Not even a protracted stay on such an uplifting island was able to cure Diefenbach of his chronic depression, and his tormented soul emerges clearly in his powerful paintings, most filled with apocalyptic storms and saintly apparitions. Also on view here are four Roman statues of marine goddesses found in the Grotta Azzura several decades ago. From La Piazzetta take Via Vittorio Emanuele and then Via F. Serena to reach this beautiful monastic complex. ⊠ *Via Certosa, Capri Town,* ☎ *081/837–6218.* ⊑ *Free.* ☉ *Daily 9–2, park 9–1 hr before sunset.*

⑪ **Giardini di Augusto** (Gardens of Augustus). You'll see some spectacular views of the southern side of Capri from the southernmost terrace of this well-kept park lying on both sides of Via Matteotti. The pretty gardens are only that (a tacky fountain doesn't help). In one corner of the gardens is a monument to Lenin, who visited Gorky and his Capri-based school for revolutionaries between 1907 and 1913. Above the gardens is the Villa Krupp, now a hotel of the same name. This was the home of the German industrialist Friedrich Alfred Krupp, who commissioned the zigzagging Via Krupp, now closed to the public, designed by Emilio Mayer and built in 1902. An amateur marine biologist, Krupp fell in love with Capri after coming to Naples to visit to its aquarium. Although heir to a munitions fortune, Krupp was the most peaceful of men and bestowed monies on many island charities. For his troubles, he was hounded to death by malicious gossip that he carried on orgies at his villa and the island grottoes, and he committed suicide in 1902. More than one critic has observed that Via Krupp shows that roads can be works of art as well as functional structures. Currently undergoing a massive renovation, it usually connects Giardini di Augusto and the Punta del Cannone with the Marina Piccola. ⊠ *Via Matteotti, Capri Town.*

⑥ **Grotta di Matermania.** Set in the bowels of Monte Tuoro, this legend-haunted cave was dedicated to Cybele, the Magna Mater, or Great Mother of the gods, hence the somewhat corrupted name of the cave. A goddess with definite eastern origins, Cybele did not form part of the Greek or Roman pantheon: her worship was introduced to Italy in 204 BC at the command of the Sibylline oracle, supposedly for the purpose of driving Hannibal out of Italy. At dawn the cave is touched by the rays of the sun, leading scholars to believe it was originally a shrine where the Mithraian mysteries were celebrated. Hypnotic rituals, self-castration, ritual sacrifice of bulls, and other orgiastic practices made this cave a place of myth, so it was not surprising when later authors believed (erroneously) that Emperor Tiberius used it for his orgies. Nevertheless, the cave was adapted by the Romans into a luxurious nymphaeum (small shrine), but little remains of the original structure aside from the walls, which would have been covered by tesserae, polychrome stucco, and marine shells. If you want to see the few ancient remains, you have to step within the now-unprepossessing cavern. ⊠ *Giro del'Arco Naturale.*

★ ⑧ **I Faraglioni.** Few landscapes set more artists dreaming than that of the famous Faraglioni—three enigmatic, pale-ochre limestone colossi that loom out of the sea, just off the Punta Tragara on the southern coast of Capri. Soaring almost 350 ft out of the water, the Faraglioni have become for most Italians an immediately recognizable symbol of Capri and have been poetically compared to Gothic cathedrals or modern skyscrapers. The first rock is called Stella or di Terra, since it is attached to the land; at its base is the famous restaurant and bathing lido Da Luigi, where the luncheon menus come with beach mattresses. The second is called di Mezzo, and little boats can often be seen going through its picturesque tunnel, which was caused by sea erosion. The rock farthest out to sea is Scopolo and is inhabited by a wall lizard species with a striking blue belly, thought by some to be endemic to this particular area, while mainstream biologists just consider it a local variant; legend has it that they were originally brought as pets from Greece to delight ancient Roman courtiers.

The "three sons of Capri" can be best seen from the belvedere at Punta Tragara at the end of Via Tragara. At this point, a path—marked by a plaque honoring the poet Pablo Neruda, who loved this particu-

lar walk—leads down hundreds of steps to the water and the feet of I
Faraglioni, and perhaps lunch at one of the two lidos at the rock base:
Da Luigi, a household name in the Bay of Naples, or La Fontelina, an
exclusive sun-drenched retreat nearby. After lunch, habitués then hire
a little boat to ferry them back to nearby Marina Piccola and the bus
back to town. Another place to drink in the view of I Faraglioni,
which is most romantic at sunset, is the Punta Del Cannone, a hilltop
belvedere reached beyond the Certosa di San Giacomo and the Giardini di Augusto. ⊠ *End of Via Tragara, Capri Town.*

② La Piazzetta. The English writer and Capriophile Norman Douglas called
this square, officially known as Piazza Umberto I, "the small theater
of the world." The rendezvous point for international crowds, this *"salone"* became famous as the late-night place to spot heavenly bodies—
of the Hollywood variety, that is: Frank Sinatra, Rita Hayworth, Julie
Christie, and Julia Roberts are just a few of the celebs that made La
Piazzetta the place where the rich and famous come to watch other rich
and famous folk. Today, at the height of summer, it's rumored that the
polizia give you 20 minutes on the square before moving you on. If,
in fact, *le tout Capri* bothers to make an appearance any longer, they
show up at 8 in the evening to enjoy an aperitif and some peppery *taral-
lucchi* breadsticks, only to return for a late-night limoncello.

In any event, the square is never less than picturesque and has been a
natural crossroads and meeting point on the island since Roman times.
The religious complex of Santo Stefano was built around the square
in the 17th century, but the clock tower and Municipio, or town hall
(once the archbishop's palace) are the only remnants of its cathedral.
Capri's Big Ben—the characteristic bell tower, or Torre de'Orologio—
is perched over the ancient gateway. Just above the gateway on the lower
side is a Latin inscription erected by an American man of letters,
Thomas Spencer Jerome, at the beginning of the 20th century, who
wished to restore "honor and dignity" to the much-maligned Emperor
Tiberius. ⊠ *At intersection of vias Botteghe, Longano, and Vittorio
Emanuele, Capri Town.*

① Marina Grande. Besides being the main gateway to Capri and the
main disembarkation point for the mainland, Marina Grande is usually the starting point for round-island tours and trips to the Blue Grotto.
Originally a conglomeration of fishermen's houses, it is now an extended
hodgepodge of various architectural styles, with buildings that almost
exclusively service the tourist industry. Warehouses and storerooms in
which fishermen once kept their boats and tackle have now become
shops, restaurants, and bars, most either tacky or overpriced. The marina has faded in the glare of neon since the days when it was Sophia
Loren's home in the 1958 film *It Started in Naples.* To the west lies
the historic Church of San Costanzo, Palazzo a Mare (the former
palace of emperor Augustus), and the chic Baths of Tiberius beach.

⑫ Marina Piccola. Just a 10-minute ride from the main bus terminus in
Capri (Piazzetta d'Ungheria), Marina Piccola is a delightfully picturesque inlet that provides the Capresi and other sun worshipers with
their best access to reasonable beaches and safe swimming. The entire
cove is romantically lined with *stabilimenti*—elegant bathing lidos
where the cabanas are often air-conditioned and the bodies can be
Modigliani-sleek. The most famous of these (a fee must be paid if you
wish to use their facilities), found closest to I Faraglioni, is La Canzone del Mare, once presided over by the noted British music-hall singer
Gracie Fields and for decades favored by the smart set, including Noël
Coward and Emilio Pucci (who set up his first boutique here). La
Canzone del Mare's seaside restaurant offers a dreamy view of I

Faraglioni and a (pricey) luncheon here can be an iconic Capri moment. Jutting out into the bay is the **Scoglio delle Sirene**, or Sirens' Rock—a small natural rock arch—which the ancients believed to be the haunt of the Sirens, whose song seduced Odysseus in Homer's *Odyssey*. This rock separates the two small beaches: Pennaulo, to the east, and Marina di Mulo, site of the original Roman harbor, to the west. ⊠ *Via Marina Piccola*.

❸ Santo Stefano. Towering over La Piazzetta, with a dome that is more sculpted than constructed and with *cupolettas* that seem molded from frozen zabaglione, Capri's mother church is a prime example of *l'architectura baroccheggiante*—the term historians use to describe Capri's fanciful form of Baroque architecture. Often using vaults and molded buttresses (since there was little wood to support ceilings on such a scrubby island), Capri's architects became sculptors when they adapted Moorish and Grecian styles into their own "homemade" architecture. Sometimes known unglamorously as the ex-cathedral, the church was built in 1685 by Marziale Desiderio from Amalfi on the site of a Benedictine convent (founded in the 6th century), whose sole relic is the clock tower campanile across the Piazzetta. As in so many churches in southern Italy, there has been a good deal of recycling of ancient building materials: the flooring of the high altar was laid with polychrome marble from Villa Jovis, while the marble in the Cappella del Sacramento was removed from the Roman villa of Tragara. Inside the sacristy are exhibited some of the church treasures, including a silver statue of San Costanzo, the patron saint of Capri, whose holy day is celebrated every May 14. Opposite the church on the tiny Piazzetta I. Cerio are the Palazzo Cerio, which houses the Centro Caprense, the Palazzo Farace, which houses the Biblioteca Caprense I. Cerio (I. Cerio Library), and the Palazzo Vanalesti, the executive offices of the Capri tourist board. Ignazio Cerio's son, Edwin, is the author of many eloquent books about Capri. ⊠ *Piazza Umberto I, Capri Town.*

★ ❹ Villa Jovis. Named in honor of the ancient Roman god Jove, the villa of the emperor Tiberius is riveted to the towering Rocca di Capri like an eagle's nest, perched overlooking the strait separating Capri from Punta Campanella, the tip of the Sorrentine peninsula. Lying near the easternmost point of the island, the villa is reached by a well-signposted 50-minute walk that climbs gradually from the Piazzetta in Capri town and offers several opportunities along the way to slake your thirst and draw breath if necessary (if possible, resist temptation until you get to the welcoming Bar Jovis, about 650 ft from the site on Via Tiberio). Although criticized by locals for the state of neglect in which it is kept, Villa Jovis is nonetheless a powerful reminder of the importance of the island in Roman times. What makes the site even more compelling are the accounts of the latter years of Tiberius's reign from Capri, between AD 27 and AD 37, written by authors and near-contemporaries Suetonius and Tacitus. They had it that this villa was famous for its sybaritic living, thus sounding a leitmotif that extends down to the luxurious hotels of today.

There are remarkably few discrepancies between the two historiographers. Both point to Tiberius's mounting paranoia in Rome, while Tacitus outlines his reason for choosing Capreae (*Annals,* Book IV). "Presumably what attracted him was the isolation of Capreae. Harborless, it has few roadsteads even for small vessels; sentries can control all landings. In winter the climate is mild, since hills on the mainland keep off gales. In summer the island is delightful, since it faces west and has open sea all round. The bay it overlooks was exceptionally lovely, until Vesuvius's eruption transformed the landscape." Capri

in Roman times was the site of 12 spacious villas, but Villa Iovis is both
the best preserved and must have been the largest, occupying nearly
23,000 square ft. It was believed by ancient tattletales that Tiberius,
fearful of assassination, slept in different villas every night, even putting
wax effigies of himself in all of them to confuse evildoers. Although
Tacitus spits with characteristic venom in his account, Suetonius leaves
little to the imagination: Tiberius's character is systematically vilified
and pilloried, while the atrocities committed at Villa Jovis are described in gory detail in *The Twelve Caesars*.

The entrance to the site lies just beyond the *pharos* (lighthouse) built
under Tiberius and used until the 17th century to warn ships of the
narrows between Capri and the mainland. Pick up a site map at the
ticket office, which gives a useful breakdown of the various areas of
the villa to be visited. This is also the area with the **Salto di Tiberio**
(Tiberius's Leap), the place where ancient gossips believed Tiberius had
enemies, discarded lovers, and even unfortunate cooks hurled over the
precipice into the sea, some 1,000 ft below. After taking stock of this
now-harmless viewing platform with the information panels, take the
upper path past the baths complex around the palace residential quarters to the heavily restored Chapel of Santa Maria del Soccorso with
its large bronze statue of the Madonna. This walk round the perimeter of the site gives an idea of the overall layout of the palatial residence, which in places rose to five stories in height. From here descend
some steps and then a ramp to the *ambulatio* (walkway) or belvedere,
which offer additional spectacular views and plenty of shade, as well
as a *triclinium* (dining room) halfway along. The center of the site is
a complex devoted to cisterns. Unlike in Pompeii, there was no aqueduct up here to provide fresh running water, so the cisterns next to the
bath complex were of prime importance.

The villa was occupied and adapted during medieval times, with the
servants' quarters on the western side suffering the most damage. Unfortunately, by the time the site was finally excavated in the 1930s, most
of the finer mosaic pavements had already been removed—mainly to
adorn the Church of Santo Stefano in Capri town and some of the private villas on the island, with any frescoes having by then faded through
millennia of wear and tear. ⊠ *Via A. Maiuri,* ☎ *081/837–0381.* 📠
4,000 lire. ☉ *Daily 9–1 hr before sunset.*

❼ Villa Malaparte. Nicknamed the *Casa Come Me* (House Like Myself)
and perched out on the rocky Punta Massulo, this villa is considered
one of the monuments of modern 20th-century architecture yet looks
like it saw the first dawn of history. Built low to be part of the ageless
landscape, the red-hued villa was designed in Rationalist style by the
Roman architect Adalberto Libera in the late 1930s for its owner
Curzio Malaparte (author of the novel *La Pelle,* which recounts various World War II experiences in Naples). However, Malaparte was unhappy with the design and made a number of alterations during the
construction phase, including the famous trapezoidal staircase that seems
to grow out of the roof. The villa is private, but if you want to see it
up close, it was featured as a suitably striking backdrop for Brigitte
Bardot in Jean-Luc Godard's underrated film *Contempt* (1963). ⊠ *Giro
dell'Arco Naturale.*

From Anacapri to the Blue Grotto

A tortuous road up from Capri town (465 ft) leads 3 km (2 mi) up a
dramatic escarpment to sky-swimming Anacapri (930 ft), the island's
only other town and leading settlement on the island's peaks, poetically referred to as the Monte Sireni (Siren Heights). Crowds are thick-

est around the square that is the starting point of the chairlift to the top of Monte Solaro and close to Villa San Michele, the main magnet up here for tour groups. To get here, take the bus from the terminus in Via Roma (Capri Town) or go directly from the port of Marina Grande (1,700 lire one-way). Allow plenty of time for getting back down again, as space on the local buses can come at a premium. The athletically inclined could try the 900 steps of the Scala Fenicia, or Phoenician Stairway (more likely to have been built by the Greeks than the Phoenicians), leading all the way down to Marina Grande. Long in a state of disrepair, this ancient pathway has only recently been restored and reopened. As a fitting finale, take the convenient bus down the hill from Anacapri to the water's edge and the fabled Blue Grotto.

A Good Walk

From Anacapri's main square of Piazza Vittoria, take Via Capodimonte to **Villa San Michele** ⑬, about 980 ft down on the right, past a formidable array of boutiques, bars, and liqueur factories, all vying to ensnare unwitting passersby. As with many sites on the island, it's best to get to the villa shortly after it opens, or in the early evening when the day-trippers have moved through. After browsing through its rooms and strolling through the gardens and the ecomuseum, retrace your steps to Piazza Vittoria and make for the lower station of the *Seggiovia* (or chairlift) to **Monte Solaro** ⑭ (5,000 lire one-way, 7,000 lire round-trip). You will soon be whisked out of town over whitewashed houses and carpets of spring-flowering broom and rockrose to the viewing platform at the top of Solaro. From here a path leads northward downhill toward the highly picturesque Church of **Santa Maria a Cetrella** ⑮ through some of the most beautiful wooded countryside on Capri. During both spring and autumn look out for migrating birds. A splash of yellow combined with an undulating flight could be the golden oriole while the multicolor bee-eater also migrates via Capri in May and September. On the way back down from Cetrella follow the signs to Anacapri along Via Monte Solaro (downhill), which will pass by close to the ruins of the **Castello Barbarossa** ⑯ and then emerge right by Villa San Michele. If you have time and energy left over, make for Via Orlandi, a useful street for stocking up on provisions. Pass the impressive Casa Rossa (Red House), on your right, and then take the next right turn (Via San Nicola) to Piazza San Nicola and the Church of **San Michele** ⑰. Savor its magnificent majolica tile floor depicting the Garden of Eden from the choir loft and head back to the Piazza Vittoria. By mid- to late afternoon, the crowds will have vanished from the **Grotta Azzurra** ⑱ (Blue Grotto), at the sea below Anacapri. Catch the convenient bus that links the town with the grotto and enjoy this fabled sight around 4 PM or 5 PM, when connoisseurs swear that the light is best (not from 10 AM to 1 PM, as is often believed—those hours were said to be prime by native Caprese, who, in truth, actually preferred to siesta their early afternoons away).

TIMING

The walk takes approximately three hours in all, allowing at least one hour for the visit to Villa San Michele and its gardens, and a further two hours' leisurely ambling on the round-trip. If armed with a packed lunch, you're most likely to find a picnic site near Cetrella—in attempts to discourage low-spending day-trippers from the mainland, consumption of picnics is made fairly difficult on Capri.

Sights to See

Casa Rossa. Capri is famous for its turn-of-the-century villas built by artists, millionaires, and poets, who became willing prisoners of Capri during the Gilded Age. Elihu Vedder, Charles Coleman, Lord Algernon, and the Misses Wolcott-Perry were some of the people who constructed lavish Aesthetic Movement houses. This particular villa, near the center of Anacapri, was built between 1876 and 1898 with walls hued in distinctive Pompeian red around a 14th-century Aragonese tower by the American colonel J. C. MacKowen from Louisiana. A historian and archaeologist, MacKowen wrote a guide to Capri and brought to light marble fragments and statues inside the Blue Grotto, thus showing its importance as a nymphaeum in Roman times. The house is closed to the public. ⊠ *Via G. Orlandi, Anacapri.*

⑯ Castello Barbarossa. The foundation of this castle, almost clinging to the side of the cliff above Villa San Michele, dates to the late 10th century, when Capri was ruled by the ancient maritime republic of Amalfi. Named after the admiral of the Turkish fleet, Khair-Eddin, or Barbarossa (Redbeard), who stormed and took the castle in 1535, much of the original layout was changed over the centuries. The castle is part of the Swedish-run Axel Munthe Foundation, which organizes weekly guided visits on Thursday afternoons from May to October (telephone the Foundation to reserve a place and for precise time of visit) besides carrying out ornithological research in the surrounding area. ⊠ *Axel Munthe Foundation, Anacapri,* ☎ *081/837–1401.*

★ **⑱ Grotta Azzurra** (Blue Grotto). Only when the spectacular Grotta Azzurra was "discovered" in 1826 by the Polish poet August Kopisch and his Swiss friend, the artist Ernest Fries—it had long been known to the island residents—did Capri become a tourist heaven. The watery cave's breathlessly blue beauty quickly became a symbol of the era of Romanticism—a monument in man's return to nature and revolt from reason. The pair's discovery triggered widespread interest and began the flow of Grand Tour visitors to the island. In fact, however, the grotto had been an island landmark since time immemorial. In the Roman era, as testified by the extensive remains primarily below sea level together with several large statues, now at the Certosa di San Giacomo, it had been the elegant, mosaic-decorated nymphaeum of the adjoining roman villa of Gradola. Historians can't quite agree if it was simply a lovely little pavilion where rich patricians would cool themselves for midday picnics or if it was truly a religious site where sacred mysteries were practiced. The extraordinary sapphire color makes the Mediterranean itself look gray and is caused by a hidden opening beneath the surface of the walls that refracts light through the blue water from the outside. At highest illumination, the very air inside looks tinted blue.

The Grotta Azzurra can be reached from Marina Grande or from the small embarkation point below Anacapri on the northwest side of the island, reached by bus from Anacapri. If you're pressed for time, skip this sometimes frustrating and disappointing excursion. You board one boat to get to the grotto, and you have to transfer to another smaller one in order to get inside (the opening is only just over 3 ft high). If there's a backup of boats waiting to get in, you'll be given precious little time to enjoy the gorgeous color of the water and its silvery reflections. Instead, tour Anacapri first, then head to the Piazza Vittoria for the bus that connects the town with the seaside grotto. Be prepared to dicker with the boatmen at the grotto entrance. Swimmers are "free." Yes, adventuresome types (who know that this type of activity is officially banned here) can enjoy the intoxicating experience of a grotto swim, but only after hours (☞ Close-Up box, "My Blue Heaven: Swimming in the Grotta Azzurra," *below*). Note that the Blue Grotto is just one of Capri's many seaside caves: there are also a Grotta Bianca (White Cave), Grotta Verde (Green Cave), Grotta Rossa (Red Cave),

MY BLUE HEAVEN: THE LURE OF THE GROTTA AZZURRA

CERTAINLY ONLY a completely soulless being could fail in his mind's eye to people Capri with nymphs, dryads, and centaurs, its grottoes and caverns with mermaids and dancing fauns, while in the imagined palatial villas strewn about the island Greeks and Romans mingle with pirates, Saracens, Norman princes, and Renaissance courtiers in a vast and gay time-forgetting revel. But nowhere is Capri's hold on the imagination greater than at its Blue Grotto, or Grotta Azzurra.

Once thought to be the haunt of Emperor Tiberius—it was thought that the old gent stayed incognito at the nearby Villa di Dame Occulte (the modern Capri landmark Damecuta is said to derive from the name) and gained access to the wondrous grotto by a secret passage, which many thought to be the *cloaca maxima* (sewer) of Anacapri—the Grotta Azzurra was only "rediscovered" on August 18, 1826 by the two painters August Kopisch and Ernst Fries, with their Capri host Don Giuseppe Pagano. Then, believe it or not, it was forgotten again. Only when, two years later, the young German poet Wilhelm Waiblinger came to Capri and wrote an ode about the blue cave, which became an overnight sensation back in Germany and which inspired Hans Christian Andersen to use the Grotta Azzurra as a setting in his 1835 novel, *The Improvisor*, was the Blue Grotto's modern fame assured.

As one of the most famous tourist attractions in the world, it can be overrun with tour boats during peak midday hours. Perhaps this is why, after hours, Capri's prowling young and daring often steal into the watery cavern, its midnight-blue waters and opaline walls—once so dear to Emperor Tiberius's heart—the irresistible lure. Legend claims a ship with a cargo of Tyrian purple dye (a color the exclusive province of Roman emperors) sank below the grotto and has forever colored its waters a wine-dark blue, so swimmers might half expect to emerge tinted themselves. Its walls the color of opals, the Grotta Azzurra is a very enchantment of blue—its color is neither like the sky nor like a jewel, not yet like the sea, but partakes of the colors of all three. But making Emperor Tiberius's reputed retreat your own is frowned upon and officially banned by the authorities. Since local convention (and Fodor's) never considers such unofficial dunking, hail instead a magic carpet over to your hotel pool to indulge your own craving for lavish soaking.

If thrill-seekers cannot avoid the grotto's lure, they attempt to swim into the cave early in the morning or after 5:30 in the evening when the boats have left. Needless to say, they do this only if the sea is perfectly calm—fatalities have occurred in rougher weather—and always with companions at hand. Swimming in the Blue Grotto can be an ethereal experience, and is now enjoyed by many who arrive and leave their clothes at the bar just above the entrance (no doubt it would be politic to have an *aperitivo* there after the swim).

Swimmers enter the cave by holding onto the chain that threads the entrance—but all swimmers should keep in mind that the only resting place inside is on a ledge on the back wall and the distance to it a good 100 ft. This area was once the site of an ancient Roman nympheum, and marble statues that were found here are now on view at Capri's Certosa di San Giacomo museum. With a face mask, snorkel, and flippers, experienced snorkelers like to swim into the cave in the usual way, then about-face and dive under for 10 or so ft, then swimming toward and under the huge undersea arch to finally pop up in the sea outside. The distance is about 65 ft, so this should only be attempted by professional snorkelers with companions. Old-timers tell you to watch out for the small purple jellyfish that deliver a rather annoying sting. If you decide to be venturesome here, always take extra precautions and be ever alert for your own safety.

and numerous other caves, many of which can be explored if you hire a boat for a classic *giro*, or tour, of the island. ⊠ *Grotta Azzurra*. 📱 *23,500 lire from Marina Grande, 15,500 lire by rowboat from Grotta Azzurra near Anacapri.* ☉ *9–1 hr before sunset, closed if sea is even minimally rough.*

⑭ Monte Solaro. An impressive limestone formation and the highest point on Capri (1,932 ft), Monte Solaro affords gasp-inducing views toward both bays of Naples and Salerno. A 12-minute chairlift ride will take you right to the top (refreshments available at bar), which is a starting point for a number of scenic trails on the western side of the island. Picnickers should note that even in the summer it can get windy at this height, and there are few trees to provide shade or refuge. ⊠ *Piazza Vittoria, Anacapri,* ☎ *081/837–1428.* 📱 *5,000 lire one-way, 7,000 lire round-trip.* ☉ *Daily 9–5:30.*

⑰ San Michele. The octagonal Baroque church of San Michele on Piazza San Nicola, finished in 1719, is best known for its exquisite majolica pavement, designed by Solimena and executed by the *mastro-riggiolaro* (master tiler) Chiaiese from Abruzzo. A walkway skirts the rich ceramic carpet depicting Adam and a duly contrite Eve being expelled from the Garden of Eden but you can get a breathtaking overview from the organ loft, reached by a winding staircase near the ticket booth (a privileged perch you have to pay for). Outside the church is the Via Finestrale, which leads to Anacapri's noted **Le Boffe quarter.** This section of town, slightly lower on the hillside, is centered around the Piazza Ficacciate and the Church of Santa Sophia and owes its name to the distinctive domestic architecture prevalent here, which uses vaults and sculpted groins instead of cross beams. The word *boffe*, as it turns out, comes from the Neapolitan dialect for "swollen." ⊠ *Piazza Nicola, Anacapri,* ☎ *081/837–2396.* 📱 *2,000 lire.* ☉ *Nov.–Mar., daily 10–3; Apr.–Oct., daily 9–7.*

★ ⑮ Santa Maria a Cetrella. Scenically perched on the slopes of Monte Solaro, this small sanctuary in late Gothic style—with its older parts dating to the late 14th century—offers a truly picturesque frame for a panorama that takes in much of the island. It also marks the top of the second access route (Il Passetiello) used in ancient times, which linked Capri town with Anacapri. This is the pathway that the Carthusian monks of San Giacomo would have used to reach their properties in the upper part of the island. The church was substantially rebuilt by Franciscan monks in the early 17th century, when a sacristy was added. To reach Santa Maria, you can climb a path leading off Viale Axel Munthe (an hour-long walk); an alternative is to descend a path leading from the Monte Solaro chairlift. ⊠ *Monte Solaro.*

⑲ Villa di Damecuta. Sited strategically on a ridge with views sweeping across the Bay of Naples toward Procida and Ischia, the main access to this Roman villa would have been from the landing stage right by the Blue Grotto at Gradola. This was probably one of the villas mentioned by Tacitus in his *Annals* as having been built by Tiberius: "Here on Capreae, in twelve spacious, separately named villas, Tiberius settled." Like Villa Jovis to the east, Villa di Damecuta was extensively plundered over the centuries prior to its proper excavation in 1937. Below the medieval tower (Torre Damecuta) there are two rooms (*domus* and *cubiculum*) that are thought to have been Tiberius's secret summer refuge. Affinities with Villa Jovis may be seen in the *ambulatio* (walkway) complete with seats with its stunning backdrop. To reach Villa Damecuta, get the bus from Anacapri to Grotto Azzurra and ask the driver to let you off at the right stop. Alternatively, you can walk from the center of Anacapri down the bus route (about 30

minutes, but no sidewalks) or try your luck in the network of virtually traffic-free little alleyways running parallel to the main road. ✉
Via A. Maiuri. 🖂 *Free.* ☉ *Daily 9–1 hr before sunset.*

★ ⑬ **Villa San Michele.** Henry James called this villa and garden "the most
fantastic beauty, poetry, and inutility that one had ever seen clustered
together," and this encomium can't be topped. At the ancient entranceway to Anacapri just at the top of the Scala Fenicia and occupying the
site of an ancient Roman villa, Villa San Michele was built (beginning
in 1896) in accordance with its owner's instructions, Axel Munthe (1857–
1949). Physician to the Swedish royal family, Munthe practiced both
in Paris and in Rome, thereby building up a substantial fortune, much
of which he plowed into real estate in Anacapri. He was also known
as a philanthropist because of his lifelong dedication to the sick and
destitute. Munthe's *The Story of San Michele* is an evocative—if not
entirely reliable—autobiography.

Those 19th-century artists Alma-Tadema and Lord Leighton—specialists in painting scenes *all'antica*—would have set up their easels in a minute
at the villa, since it is set around Roman-style courtyards, marble walk-
ways, and atriums. Rooms display the doctor's varied collections, which
range from bric-a-brac to classical antiquities (once thought so important J. Pierpont Morgan arrived to spend millions on them, but the good
doctor knew that most were fakes so refused all offers). Medieval choir
stalls, Renaissance lecterns, and gilded statutes of saints comprise the
esthetic setting, with some rooms preserving the doctor's personal memorabilia, enabling the visiting public to find out more about this enigmatic patron of the arts and humanist. The villa is connected by a
spectacular pergola path overlooking the entire Bay of Naples. This leads
to the famous Sphinx Parapet, where an ancient Egyptian sphinx sits
and looks out over to Sorrento (you cannot see its face—on purpose).
It is said that if you touch the sphinx's hindquarters with your left hand
while making a wish, it will come true. The parapet is connected to the
little Chapel of San Michele, which once stood on the grounds of one
of Tiberius's villas. When Munthe bought the property, its missing bells
were said to ring as a sign that Tiberius was seeking forgiveness for having sentenced a certain carpenter from Galilee to death. Oddly enough,
the only person who ever lived at the Villa San Michele (the doctor's
home was the Torre di Materita, up the mountainside) was the March-
esa Casati, the notorious fin de siècle fashion plate who was fond of
walking diamond-collared leopards down the Champs Élysees.

Besides hosting summer concerts, the Axel Munthe Foundation has a
recently established ecomuseum that fittingly reflects Munthe's fond-
ness for animals, where you can learn about various bird species—accompanied by their songs—found on Capri. Not only did Munthe aid
people, he bought up the hillside as a sanctuary for birds, which pre-
vented the Caprese from capturing quail by terrible means (lured by
songbirds that had been blinded to make them sing better). Today, thanks
to the good Dr. Munthe, this little realm is still an Eden. ✉ *Via Capodimonte, Anacapri,* ☎ *081/837–1401.* 🖂 *8,000 lire.* ☉ *Jan.–Feb., daily,
10:30–3:30; Mar., daily 9:30–4:30; Apr., daily 9:30–5; May–Sept.,
daily, 9–6; Oct., daily 9:30–5; Nov.–Dec., daily 10:30–3:30.*

Dining and Lodging
Even basic accommodations come at a premium on Capri and all the
zeroes on the hotel bills are likely to make you feel dizzy. Some hotels
charge extra for breakfast, so you might just wish to enjoy a coffee
and *cornetto* at a town café. Note that while many hotels close for the
winter months, some of these reopen to celebrate the Christmas and
New Year holidays.

Since cars are generally not permitted on Capri, most hotels will arrange porterage from the Marina Grande port if you tell them when you're arriving (on what boat/hydrofoil, etc.) Sometimes this is a complimentary service. Porterage services can be obtained for a fee down at the port (☎ 081/837–0896).

$$$ ✕ **I Faraglioni.** With natural shade provided by a 100-year-old wisteria plant, this is a popular, fairly stylish restaurant which is both centrally located and yet almost immersed in Mediterranean greenery. Meals here usually kick off with *uovo alla Monachina,* an egg-shape dish stuffed with mystery ingredients. For first course, try the *straccetti con gamberi e pomodorini* (fresh green pasta with shrimps and small tomatoes). ✉ *Via Camerelle 75, Capri Town,* ☎ *081/837–0320. Reservations essential eves. AE, DC, MC, V. Closed Nov.–Mar.*

$$$ ✕ **La Canzone del Mare.** This is the legendary bathing lido of the Marina Piccola, erstwhile haunt of Grace Fields, Emilio Pucci, Noël Coward, and any number of 1950s and '60s glitterati. The VIPs may have departed for the Bagni di Tiberio beach but the setting is as magical as ever: Enjoy luncheon (no dinner served) in the thatched-roof pavilion looking out over the sea and I Faraglioni in the distance—this is Capri as picture-perfect as it comes. You need to pay a fee to actually use this bathing *stabilimenti* but why not make a day of it—after all, the menu comes with a beach mattress. ✉ *Via Marina Piccola 93, Capri Town,* ☎ *081/837–0104. No credit cards. Closed Nov.–Mar.*

$$$ ✕ **La Capannina.** Isn't that Whitney Houston at the table by the door?
★ Known as one of Capri's most celebrity-haunted restaurants, La Capannina is only a few steps from the busy social hub of the Piazzetta. It has a vine-draped veranda for dining outdoors by candlelight in a garden setting and most of the regulars can't stand the stuffy indoor rooms. The specialties, aside from an authentic Capri wine with the house label, are homemade ravioli and *insalada caprese.* ✉ *Via Le Botteghe 14, Capri Town,* ☎ *081/837–0732. Reservations essential. AE, DC, MC, V. Closed Wed. (Oct.–May) and mid-Jan.–mid-Mar.*

$$$ ✕ **La Fontelina.** Lying just below Punta Tragara at the base of Capri's
★ impressive offshore rocks known as the Faraglioni, this is the place to enjoy a delightfully comatose day on the island. Given its position right on the water's edge, seafood is almost de rigueur. For a slightly different starter, try the *polpette di melanzane,* and then dip into the vegetable buffet. Highly recommendable is the house sangria, a blissful mix of white wine and fresh fruit. If overwhelmed by large-size portions of pasta, order half portions (and pay half). This also functions as a lido, with steps and ladders affording access into fathoms-deep blue water. Access by boat from Marina Piccola or on foot from Punta Tragara (10 minutes). Only lunch is served. Just across the way is its archrival lido-restaurant, Da Luigi, with a more evocative setting but now a bit too famous for its own good. ✉ *I Faraglioni, at end of Via Tragara, Capri Town,* ☎ *081/837–0845. AE. Closed for dinner and mid-Oct.–Easter.*

$$–$$$ ✕ **Le Grottelle.** This is an extremely informal trattoria built up against the limestone rocks above the Arco Naturale, with the cave at the back doubling up as the kitchen and wine cellar. The menu is chiefly seafood, with *linguine con gamberetti e rucola* (pasta with shrimp and arugula) one of the more highly prized specialties. ✉ *Via Arco Naturale 13,* ☎ *081/837–5719. Reservations essential eves. AE. Closed mid-Nov.–Mar.*

$$–$$$ ✕ **Ristorante Pizzeria Aurora.** Though often frequented by celebri-
★ ties—photographs of famous guests adorn the walls inside—this restaurant offers courtesy and *simpatia* irrespective of your persona. If you want to eat out and be seen, reserve one of the tables outside on one of Capri's most chic thoroughfares; otherwise go for extra privacy and

ambience within. Try the *sformatino alla Franco* (a rice pie in a prawn sauce) but hold something back for the homemade sweets at the end. ⊠ *Via Fuorlovado 18–20, Capri Town,* ☎ *081/837–0181. Reservations essential eves. AE, DC, MC, V. Closed Jan.–Feb.*

$$ ✕ **Al Grottino.** This small and friendly family-run restaurant, which is handy to the Piazzetta, has arched ceilings and lots of atmosphere; autographed photos of celebrity customers cover the walls. House specialties are gnocchi with tomato sauce and mozzarella, and linguine *ai gamberetti* (with shrimp and tomato sauce). ⊠ *Via Longano 27, Capri Town,* ☎ *081/837–0584. Reservations essential. AE, MC, V. Closed Tues. and Nov. 3–Mar. 20.*

$$ ✕ **Da Gelsomina.** Set amidst its own terraced vineyards with inspiring views across to the island of Ischia and beyond, this is much more than just a well-reputed restaurant. It has an immaculately kept swimming pool and is located close to the island's finer walks—an excellent base for a whole day or longer. There is also a six-room pensione, with free transfer service by request from Anacapri center. ⊠ *Via Migliera 72, Anacapri,* ☎ *081/837–1499. AE, MC, V. Closed Jan. and Tues. in winter.*

$$ ✕ **Da Tonino.** It is well worth making the short detour off the beaten track to the Arco Naturale to be pampered by creative chef Tonino. With the emphasis more on land-based dishes, try the *terrina di coniglio* (rabbit terrine) or ask for the pigeon dish with pesto, rosemary, and pine nuts, accompanied by wine from an unbelievably well-stocked cellar. ⊠ *Via Dentecala, Capri Town,* ☎ *081/837–6718. AE, DC, MC, V. Closed Jan. 10–Mar. 15.*

$$ ✕ **Il Cucciolo.** Nestling in thick maquis high above the Blue Grotto and a five-minute walk from the Roman site of Villa Damecuta, this must be one of the most romantic locations in the Mediterranean. The cucina is refreshingly inventive: ask for their specialty *fagottini all'ortica*, pasta stuffed with cheese and stinging-nettles. There is evening chauffeur service to and from Anacapri. ⊠ *Via Le Fabbrica 52, Anacapri,* ☎ *081/837–1917. Reservations essential eves. AE, DC, MC, V. Closed Tues. and Nov.–mid.-Mar.*

$$ ✕ **La Rondinella** This is an airy ristorante-pizzeria looking onto the main pedestrianized street of Anacapri. In summer, make sure you reserve a table out on the popular terrace. If you have difficulty choosing from the extensive menu, ask for advice or opt for one of their favorite pasta dishes, *linguine macchiavelle*, with capers, olives, and cherry tomatoes. ⊠ *Via Orlandi 295, Anacapri,* ☎ *081/837–1223. AE, DC, MC, V. Closed Jan. 10–Feb. and Thurs. Oct.–May.*

$–$$ ✕ **La Giara.** Only about two minutes' walk from the bustling Piazza Vittoria in Anacapri, this pizzeria-ristorante has a wide range of palatable piatti served briskly and courteously. For a change from seafood, try their *pennette aum aum*, pasta pleasingly garnished with eggplant, mozzarella, cherry tomatoes, and basil. ⊠ *Via Orlandi 67, Anacapri,* ☎ *081/837–3860. AE, DC, MC, V. Closed Dec.–Jan. and Wed.*

$–$$ ✕ **Mamma Giovanna.** This ristorante-pizzeria sits just below Piazza Diaz in the heart of the old town of Anacapri, facing the 16th-century church of Santa Sofia. The no-frills ambience belies the quality of the cucina: besides *pizze* (served midday and evenings), Mamma Giovanna specializes in *primi piatti*, such as *maccheroncelle al cartoccio* (pasta cooked in the oven with seafood). ⊠ *Via Boffe 3/5, Anacapri,* ☎ *081/837–2057. Reservations essential eves. No credit cards. Closed Jan.–Feb.; Wed. Oct.–Apr.*

$–$$ ✕ **Serena Snack Pub.** Despite the somewhat off-putting name, the cucina is 100% authentic. The *antipasto misto di contorni* has a good selection of grilled vegetables while you can expect a variety of homemade pasta, with the flagship being *ravioli maison*, (with a pesto and

In case you want to see the world.

At American Express, we're here to make your journey
a smooth one. So we have over 1,700 travel service locations in over 130 countries ready to help. What else
would you expect from the world's largest travel agency?

do more

Travel

Call 1 800 AXP-3429 or visit
www.americanexpress.com/travel

In case you want to be welcomed there.

We're here to see that you're always welcomed at establishments everywhere. That's why millions of people carry the American Express® Card – for peace of mind, confidence, and security, around the world or just around the corner.

do more

Cards

To apply, call 1 800 THE-CARD
or visit www.americanexpress.com

In case you're running low.

We're here to help with more than 190,000 Express Cash locations around the world. In order to enroll, just call American Express at 1 800 CASH-NOW before you start your vacation.

do more AMERICAN EXPRESS

Express Cash

And in case you'd rather be safe than sorry.

We're here with American Express® Travelers Cheques. They're the safe way to carry money on your vacation, because if they're ever lost or stolen you can get a refund, practically anywhere or anytime. To find the nearest place to buy Travelers Cheques, call 1 800 495-1153. Another way we help you do more.

do more

Travelers Cheques

prawn sauce). You eat as much or as little as you want—just a *panino* (sandwich), perhaps—all within a minute of the Piazzetta. ✉ *Via Vittorio Emanuele 19, Capri Town,* ☎ *081/837–3860. DC, MC, V. Closed Tues. and Nov. 3–Mar. 20.*

$$$$ **Europa Palace Hotel.** A modern resort atmosphere pervades this large Mediterranean-style hotel set in lovely gardens. Each of four junior suites has a private swimming pool and terrace. The bedrooms are tastefully decorated in bright contemporary style, with white predominating, and have marble bathrooms. The position in Anacapri offers relative seclusion from the summer crowds. ✉ *Via Capodimonte, Anacapri 80071,* ☎ *081/837–3800,* FAX *081/837–3191. 93 rooms with bath. Restaurant, bar, air-conditioning, pool, spa. AE, DC, MC, V. Closed Nov.–Mar.*

$$$$ **La Scalinatella.** If you're bronzed and beautiful, or just bronzed, or
★ even just beautiful, this is your kind of hotel. A white Moorish mansion out of the Arabian Nights, it conjures up Capri in finest Hollywood fashion. The name means "little stairway," and that's how this charmingly small hotel is built, on terraces following the slope of the hills, with winding paths and bougainvillea arbors. Inside, the decor is *Architectural Digest*–opulent, with Venetian blackamoor statues, Empire-era consoles, and Valentino fabrics. Guest rooms have overstuffed sofas, bright colors, large terraces, and his-and-her bathrooms (with whirlpool baths). Outside, one of Capri's bluest pools is the fetching setting for delicious luncheons. ✉ *Via Tragara 8, Capri Town 80073,* ☎ *081/837–0633,* FAX *081/837–8291. 30 rooms with bath. Restaurant, bar, air-conditioning, pool, tennis court. No credit cards. Closed Nov.–mid-Mar.*

$$$$ **Punta Tragara.** When you factor in everything, this place must be
★ the finest hotel on Capri. Clinging to the Punta Tragara, it has a hold-your-breath perch directly over the rocks of I Faraglioni. Originally a villa enjoyed by Churchill and Eisenhower, it was renovated by Le Corbusier, then opened as a hotel in the 1970s by Countess Manfredi. Baronial fireplaces, gilded antiques, and travertine marble set the style in the main salons, while guest rooms—no two are alike—are sumptuously cozy-casual. The garden area is out of a dream, set with two saltwater pools, one adorned with exotic trees and cacti, the other, with jet-powered water and next to an arbor-covered restaurant. To top it all off, the staff seems to have been sent to the finest finishing schools. If you really want to taste the good life, stay here. ✉ *Via Tragara 57, Capri Town 80073,* ☎ *081/837–0844,* FAX *081/837–7790. 47 rooms with bath. Restaurant, bar, air-conditioning, 2 pools. AE, DC, MC, V.*

$$$$ **Quisisana.** This was one of Capri's first and most celebrated hotels and, today, still packs them in. This seems to be the operative phrase, for this place seems nearly as elephantine as a Las Vegas hotel. The mile-long lobby leads to the pool area—gorgeous, yes, but the size of a set for an Esther Williams MGM movie. The Quisisana remains a favorite with some because of its shiny and luxe restaurants, see-and-be-seen bars, professional service, array of facilities, and location (just down the street from the crowded Piazzetta, this is *too* convenient). Spacious guest rooms have arcaded balconies—the only problem is that there are floors and floors of them. ✉ *Via Camerelle 2, Capri Town 80073,* ☎ *081/837–0788,* FAX *081/837–6080. 143 rooms with bath. Restaurant, bar, pool, sauna, tennis court. AE, DC, MC, V. Closed Nov.–mid-Mar.*

$$$$ **Villa Brunella.** This quiet family-run gem nestles in a garden setting just below the lane leading to the Faraglioni. Comfortable and tastefully furnished, the hotel also has spectacular views, a swimming pool, and a terrace restaurant known for good food. ✉ *Via Tragara 24, Capri Town 80073,* ☎ *081/837–0122,* FAX *081/837–0430. 18 rooms with bath. Restaurant, bar, air-conditioning, pool. AE, DC, MC, V. Closed Nov.–Mar.*

$$$–$$$$ ☷ **La Palma.** Though the oldest hotel on Capri (1822) this attentively run hotel has certainly not rested on its laurels. When you arrive at its front door you're immediately given a blast of island glamour, with gleaming lobby, palm trees, and majolica-tiled rooms providing a delightful contrast to the hustle at street level outside (this is just down the street from La Piazzetta). Room prices dip substantially outside peak season, making it more affordable to enjoy this aura of style and tranquillity in the town center. ⊠ *Via V. Emanuele 39, Capri Town 80073,* ☎ *081/837–0133,* FAX *081/837–6966. 72 rooms with bath. Restaurant, bar, air-conditioning, meeting rooms. AE, DC, MC, V. Closed Jan.– Easter.*

$$$ ☷ **Biancamaria.** This tastefully refurbished hotel with its pleasing facade and whitewashed spreading arches lies in a traffic-free zone close to the heart of Anacapri. The front rooms have large terraces looking towards Monte Solaro, while those at the back are quieter and more private. ⊠ *Via G. Orlandi 54, Anacapri 80073,* ☎ *081/ 837–1000,* FAX *081/837–2060. 25 rooms with bath. Air-conditioning. AE, MC, V. Closed Nov.–Mar.*

$$$ ☷ **Gatto Bianco.** A literary atmosphere pervades this spacious but discreet hotel located only two minutes' walk from the Piazzetta. This was where Jacqueline Kennedy sought refuge when hounded by paparazzi. It now provides old-world charm and character with a distinct local flavor. ⊠ *Via Vittorio Emanuele 32, Capri Town 80073,* ☎ *081/ 837– 0203,* FAX *081/837–8060. 44 rooms with bath. Air-conditioning. AE, DC, MC, V. Closed Nov.–mid-Mar.*

$$$ ☷ **San Michele.** You'll find this large white villa-hotel next to Axel Munthe's home. Surrounded by luxuriant gardens, the San Michele offers solid comfort and good value, along with spectacular views. It's modern, with some Neapolitan period pieces adding atmosphere. Most rooms have a terrace or balcony overlooking either the sea or island landscapes. ⊠ *Via G. Orlandi 5, Anacapri 80071,* ☎ *081/837–1427,* FAX *081/837–1420. 59 rooms with bath. Restaurant, pool. AE, DC, MC, V. Closed Nov.–Mar.*

$$$ ☷ **Villa Krupp.** Occupying a beautiful house overlooking the Gardens of Augustus, this historic hostelry was built by the tortured German munitions millionaire and was once the home of Maxim Gorky, whose guests included Lenin. Rooms are plain but spacious. ⊠ *Viale Matteotti 12, Capri Town 80073,* ☎ *081/837–0362,* FAX *081/837–6489. 12 rooms with bath. MC, V. Closed Nov.–Feb.*

$$$ ☷ **Villa Sarah.** This whitewashed Mediterranean building has a homey look and bright, simply furnished rooms. It's close enough to the Piazzetta (a 10-minute walk) to give easy access to the goings-on there, yet far enough away to ensure restful nights. There are a garden and a small bar. ⊠ *Via Tiberio 3/a, Capri Town 80073,* ☎ *081/837–7817,* FAX *081/837–7215. 20 rooms with bath. Bar, air-conditioning in some rooms. AE, DC, MC, V. Closed Nov.–Mar.*

$$–$$$ ☷ **Aida.** A 10-minute walk from the town center in a tiny lane that borders the Gardens of Augustus, the Aida offers a tranquil haven from Capri's bustle and hard sell. The staff is sociable, and the rooms, which look onto a small garden, are spacious, comfortably furnished, and immaculately clean. ⊠ *Via Birago, Capri Town 80073,* ☎ *081/ 837–0366. 10 rooms with bath. No credit cards. Closed mid-Oct.–Apr.*

$$ ☷ **Villa Eva.** Named after its dynamic owner-manageress, this is a popular international stopover for young *Wandervögel* (travelers) who have a more laid-back approach to traveling. Accommodation is in small, low-impact villas set in luxuriant gardens. When not tending the grounds, Vincenzo, Eva's husband, will take you down to the nearby Blue Grotto for a late-afternoon swimming expedition. ⊠ *Via La Fab-*

brica 8, Anacapri 80073, ☎ 081/837–1549, FAX 081/837–2040. 24 rooms with bath. AE, DC, MC, V. Closed mid-Nov.–mid-Feb.

$$ ☒ **Villa Helios.** The charming Villa Helios is set in a 19th-century, lilac-hued, Moorish-inspired villa, surrounded by extensive orchards and located on a quiet Capri lane. Don't come here for luxe—floors are linoleum-covered and some rooms share baths. Do come here for peace—a lovely chapel occupies part of the first floor. For a small fee (4,000 lire) all guests become members of the Centro Italiano Turismo Sociale, a Christian organization operating Italy-wide. Profits from the operation are thoughtfully channeled by the villa's owners (Franciscan nuns) into a local hospice. ☒ *Via Birago 18, Capri Town 80073, ☎ 081/837–0240, FAX 081/837–0240. 25 rooms, 20 with bath. MC, V. Closed mid-Oct.–Apr.*

Nightlife and the Arts

As would be expected, Capri offers a fair spread of evening entertainment, especially on weekends and during the busier months of July and August, when many upper-crust Italians from the mainland occupy their holiday homes on the island. For music that is fairly gentle on the ears, try one of the traditional *taverne,* which are peculiar to Capri Town. There are also a number of discos and piano bars from which to choose. Christmas on Capri is a special time, when most of the island visitors are Italians. On New Years' Eve, the Piazzetta is definitely the place to be seen, with dancing and music culminating in a magnificent fireworks display. On New Year's Day there are marching bands, pageants, and all the revelry you would expect on this exuberant island.

DISCOS

For 360° music almost any night of the year, **Underground** is the clubbing spot for cognoscenti of various ages. Unlike most other discos in Italy, no admission fee is charged, though you are expected to knock back the odd drink (about 10,000 lire each). On Tuesdays in July and August, make a point of going down to Antonio Beach near the Faro, where Underground arranges open-air discos by the water's edge (☒ Via Orlandi 259, Anacapri, ☎ 081/837–2523) beginning at 10:30 PM.

TAVERNE

Anema e Core (☒ Via Sella Orta 39/e, Capri Town, ☎ 081/837–6461) means "soul and heart" in Caprese dialect. This popular place is tucked down a quiet side street two minutes' walk from the Piazzetta. Admission (40,000 lire) includes an eclectic range of lightish live music (after 11 PM and a drink from the bar. No food is served so come well primed. There's no dancing here officially, though some guests—including celebrities—occasionally take to the tables. The spot is closed Mondays and is usually open 9 PM to 3 PM. Reservations are essential on weekends. Other favorites are **Guarracino** (☒ Via Castello 7, Capri Town, ☎ 081/837–0514) and **Settebello** (☒ Via Longano 51, Capri Town, ☎ 081/837–5960).

The Arts

Culturally speaking, Capri has a fairly long hibernation. June through September, however, comes alive with various events, including an outdoor concert season. It is a magical experience to see works performed at the Villa San Michele or in the Certosa di San Giacomo. In general, for information about cultural events and art exhibitions, ask at the local tourist information office or scan the posters in shop windows.

MUSIC AND CONCERTS

Concerts are held regularly at the Certosa di San Giacomo (☞ Sights to See, *above*) in the attractive setting Chiostro Piccolo from June through September (usually Wednesday and weekends), while the Axel Munthe Foundation lays on cosponsored free concerts on the grounds of Villa San Michele (☞ Sights to See, *above*) on weekends. This means that if you're interested, you'll also have to arrange an overnight stay on the island.

Outdoor Activities and Sports

Although there are several tennis courts on the island, most are restricted access, so the vast majority of people looking to burn up excess energy do so at sea level or below. For naturalists, bird-watching is particularly good in spring and autumn as Capri lies on a migration pathway, while botany lovers will be thrilled by the various walks, especially from April to June.

SCUBA DIVING

For those who want something more adventurous than a little snorkeling off Marina Piccola, scuba diving can be arranged from Marina Grande, and you can hire your own Zodiac (no license required) to take you round the coast to one of the many lesser-known grottoes on the island. As a general rule, avoid weekends, as island sea traffic makes navigation trying. When scuba diving, always use safety buoys to signal your presence underwater. The main outfitter is **Whales** (⊠ Via Colombo 17, Marina Grande, Capri, ☏ 081/837–5833), which charges 65,000 lire per hour to hire a six-seater *gommone* (Zodiac). For the inexperienced, the **Capri Diving Club** (⊠ Località Punta Carena, ☏ 081/837–3487) organizes diving courses leading to internationally recognized diplomas.

SWIMMING

Capri is not noted for its fine beaches. The habitués cram onto **Marina Piccola,** generally considered to have the best beach on the island. It's certainly the most historic: Homer believed this to be the legendary spot where the Sirens nearly snared Odysseus. Social go-getters seem to prefer the less picturesque Bagni di Tiberio beach near Marina Grande. At Marina Piccola, expect to pay about 20,000 lire per person for the use of showers, lockers, and a sun chair/sun bed. It is definitely worth investing in snorkeling gear, as the sea is rich in marine life, and visibility is often excellent. For information on swimming in the Blue Grotto, ☞ Close-Up box, "My Blue Heaven: Swimming in the Grotta Azzurra," *above*.

TENNIS

Almost right in the town center but pleasingly secluded are three clay courts at **Tennis Capri** (⊠ Via Camerelle 41, Capri Town, ☏ 081/837–0261, ☝ 30,000 lire per hour per court, 50,000 per lesson, racquets for hire). Access is off Via Sella Orta.

Shopping

Although Capri is hardly likely to be a bargain hunter's paradise, shopping here is almost an experience in its own right. In the main town near the Piazzetta, the shop windows are usually immaculately dressed, while the shops themselves are generally designed to be low impact and pleasing on the eye. Large neon signs are definitely out. Frustratingly though, goods are often displayed without price tags, which means you have to shop Italian-style: Decide whether you like an article first and then inquire as to its price, rather than vice versa.

BOOKSTORES

An antiquarian's delight and one of the most elegant bookstores in Italy, **La Conchiglia** not only offers the largest selection of books on Capri and the Bay of Naples islands but publishes many sumptuous tomes through their own imprint. In addition to books, an attractive array of prints, gouaches, and old editions of English books on Capri and the south of Italy is offered at their art gallery–cum–store (⊠ Via

Camerelle 18, Capri Town, ☎ 081/837–8199), although a greater variety of titles is offered at their other location (✉ Via Le Botteghe 12, Capri Town, ☎ 081/837–6577). There is also a branch in Anacapri (✉ Via Orlandi 205, Anacapri, ☎ 081/837–2646).

GELATERIE

For those with a soft spot for homemade Italian ice creams, head straight for the **Bar Embassy** (✉ Via Camerelle 16, Capri Town, ☎ 081/837–7066) with its imaginative assortment of different flavors (changed each day). Competition is stiff, though, from the **Gelateria Buonocore** (✉ Via Vittorio Emanuele 35, Capri Town, ☎ 081/837–7826), where you can see (and smell) wafer cones being made by hand.

JEWELRY

The extra security of being on a virtually crime-free island means that you can actually wear the expensive items you might want to buy. Some tax-free "bargains" might be possible from **Cartier** (✉ Via Vitttorio Emanuele 47, Capri Town, ☎ 081/837–0618), though their range of goods is unlikely to vary worldwide. Alternatively, try **Alberto and Lina** (✉ Via Vittorio Emanuele 18, Capri Town, ☎ 081/837–0643) for perhaps a distinctive locally crafted brooch or some cuff links displaying ancient Roman coins.

PERFUME

If you're looking for something that is easily portable to take back from Capri, then eau de toilette, some potpourri, or perfumed soap might be just the thing. **Carthusia** has been making perfumes since 1948, but—as they will proudly tell you—the tradition of perfumery on the island stretches back hundreds of years to the days of Queen Giovanna of Anjou. *Factory:* ✉ *Via Matteotti, Capri Town,* ☎ *081/837–0368; showrooms:* ✉ *Via Camerelle 10, Capri Town,* ☎ *081/837–0529;* ✉ *Via Capodimonte 26, Anacapri,* ☎ *081/837–3668.*

RESORTWEAR

Capri's main shopping streets—the Via Vittorio Emanuele and Via Camerelle—are crammed with world-famous names (Fendi, Gucci, Benetton, Ferragamo, Hermès) but if you are are overwhelmed by the choice and are looking for something stylish but Capri-distinctive—in an astonishing range of colors—then try the resortwear sold at one of the many stores run by Roberto Russo. His larger boutiques are: **Capri Uomo** (✉ Piazzetta Quisisana, Capri Town, ☎ 081/838–8200) and **Capri Donna** (✉ Via Vittorio Emanuele, Capri Town, ☎ 081/837–8204). Alternatively, browse round **Rubinacci** (✉ Via Camerelle 9, Capri Town, ☎ 081/837–7295) for something smart yet casual in cotton, linen or cashmere. Sandals are a Capri speciality. With a family business stretching back 82 years, **Giuseppe Faiella** (✉ Via Vittorio Emanuele 49, Capri Town) is justifiably proud of his made-to-measure footwear. Expect to pay 65,000–95,000 lire for a carefully handcrafted pair.

ISCHIA: THE SEASIDE CURE

Although Capri leaves you breathless with its charm and beauty, Ischia takes its time to cast its spell. In fact, an overnight stay is definitely not long enough for the island to get into your blood. Here you have to look harder for the signs of antiquity, the traffic is reminiscent of Naples—albeit on a good day—and the island displays all the hallmarks of rapid, uncontrolled urbanization. Ischia does have its jewels, though. There are the wine-growing villages beneath the lush volcanic slopes of Monte Epomeo, and unlike Capri, it enjoys a life of its own that survives when the tourists head home. Ischia has some lovely hotel-resorts high in the mountains, offering therapeutic programs and rooms with dramatic views. Should you want to plunk down in the sun for a few days and tune out the world, then go down to sea level: against the stunning backdrop of Monte Epomeo and with the one of the island's inviting beaches—or natural hot baths—close to hand, you might wonder whether the Emperor Augustus knew what he was doing when he surrendered Ischia to the Neapolitans in return for Capri.

Unlike Capri, Ischia is volcanic in origin. From its hidden reservoir of seething molten matter comes the thermal springs said to cure whatever ails you. As early as 1580, a doctor named Lasolino published a book about the mineral wells at Ischia. "If your eyebrows fall off," he wrote, "go and try the baths at Piaggia Romano. Are you unhappy about your complexion? You will find the cure in the waters of Santa Maria del Popolo. Are you deaf? Then go to Bagno d'Ulmitello. If you know anyone who is getting bald, anyone who suffers from elephantiasis, or another whose wife yearns for a child, take the three of them immediately to the Bagno di Vitara; they will bless you." Today the island's main industry, tourism, revolves around the 100 or so thermal baths, some of which are attached to hotels while others just operate as day centers. In the height of summer, the island's population of 60,000 swells more than sixfold, with considerable strain placed on local water resources and public transport facilities and with decibel counts rising notably. However, most of the *confusione* is concentrated within the island's six towns and along its main roads, and it is relatively easy to find quiet spots even close to the beaten path.

Ischia Ponte to Lacco Ameno

With easy access to the coastline, the area from Ischia Ponte to Lacco Ameno is almost a continuum of *stabilimenti balneari* (private bathing establishments) during the summer months, set against the scenic backdrop of Monte Epomeo and its verdant slopes. Most port traffic to the island—mainly ferries and hydrofoils from the mainland—is channeled into Ischia Porto and Casamicciola, both towns also being burgeoning resorts and busy spa centers. The Castello Aragonese in Ischia Ponte, which is in fact a vast medieval complex rather than just a castle, is probably the island's main historic sight, while Lacco Ameno with its immense archaeological heritage and more upmarket ambience is a good base for exploring the north of the island. Buses between the main towns are both frequent and cheap, though somewhat overcrowded.

Ischia Ponte

20   *2 km (1 mi) southeast of Ischia Porto.*

★ Marked by the spectacular **Castello Aragonese,** the harbor at Ischia Ponte is Ischia's main gateway. From afar you can make out the brooding, towering castle, which sits atop an islet just off the main shore at Ischia Ponte (or Ischia Bridge), so-called because of the artificial causeway built in the mid-15th century to connect it with the rest of Ischia. The little island was settled as early as the 5th century BC, when the tyrant Hiero of Syracuse came to the aid of Cumae in its power struggle against the Etruscans. This was his reward: an almost unassailable natural offshore island more than 300 ft high, on which he erected high watchtowers to monitor movements across the Bay of Naples. The island changed hands in the succession of centuries, with Greeks from Neapolis, Romans, Visigoths, Vandals, Ostrogoths, Saracens, Normans, Schwabians, and Angevins, all staking successful claims to the island and modifying the fortifications and settlements. This was where the population of Ischia sought refuge in 1301, when Epomeo's last eruption buried the town

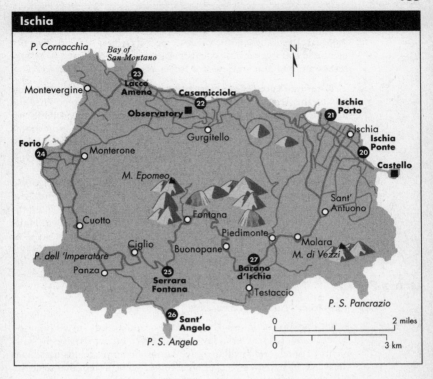

Ischia

of Geronda on the other side of the causeway. The new influx of inhabitants led to a flurry of building activity, most notably the construction
of **Cattedrale dell'Assunta,** built above a preexisting chapel that then
became its crypt. In the following century the Angevin castle was rebuilt by Alfonso of Aragon (1438), who gave it much of its present form.
However, its turbulent history continued well into the 19th century, when
it was seriously damaged by the English in their attempts to dislodge
the French during the Napoleonic Wars (1809). Parts of the citadel were
then used to house political (anti-Bourbon) prisoners until the Risorgimento and Italy's unification in 1861.

Two hours should be enough to give you a feel of the citadel, stroll along
its ramparts, and visit its key religious sites. Don't miss the frescoed 14th-
century crypt beneath the cathedral (Giotto school), while the ruined
cathedral itself with its noticeable 18th-century additions—such as the
Baroque stucco work—is quite atmospheric. Access to the citadel is via
an elevator from the base, and the various walks at the top are clearly
signposted. While taking in the whole site, enjoy the stunning views from
the various vantage points. ⊠ *Castello Aragonese, Ischia Ponte,* ☎ *081/
992834.* ⊠ *10,000 lire.* ☾ *Summer, daily 9:30–7; spring and autumn,
daily 9:30–5. Closed mid-Nov.–Dec. 26 and Jan. 7–Mar. 1.*

Dining and Lodging

With signs like BIER VOM FASS and SPAGHETTI-EIS HIER, you could be forgiven if you thought you were actually in northern Europe rather than
on the Mediterranean. Fortunately, the Germans who flock to Ischia
tend to be fairly discerning customers when it comes to dining and lodging, and standards in both departments tend to be high when measured
against respective prices. In general, when choosing a hotel on Ischia,
make sure it does not look onto the busy Strada Nazionale, the main
road linking the six towns on the island. In restaurants, seek personal

advice where possible: it is worth asking the serving staff what they recommend rather than choosing willy-nilly off the menu. When choosing wines, the draught house wines—especially whites—are usually quite palatable and significantly cheaper than the bottled variety. Note that restaurant and hotel reviews for Ischia are listed under each town.

$$–$$$ ✕ **Ristorante Cocò Gelo.** This inviting restaurant sits on the causeway linking the Aragonese castle to the rest of Ischia and is renowned for its fresh fish, which is highly prized by the Ischitani. For specialties try the linguine *ai calamaretti* (with squid), while a good starter in winter months is the vegetable-based *zuppa di fagioli e scarola* (bean and escarole soup). ✉ *Via Aragonese 1,* ☎ *081/981823. AE, DC, MC, V. Closed Jan. and Wed. Oct.–Mar.*

$–$$ 🏨 **Pensione Il Monastero.** Uniquely located within the Castello Aragonese
★   at Ischia Ponte and with fairly rustic rooms that peer down into the Mediterranean, hundreds of feet below, this is the ultimate in ambience combined with the peace and quiet of a traffic-free area. Half-board is compulsory at all times. This is a highly popular hotel, so book way in advance. ✉ *Castello Aragonese 3, 80077,* ☎ *081/992435. 22 rooms. No credit cards. Closed Oct. 20–end Mar.*

Ischia Porto

㉑ *4 km (3 mi) east of Casamicciola.*

Ischia Porto is the largest town on the island and the usual point of debarkation. It's no workaday port, however, but a pretty resort with plenty of hotels and low flat-roofed houses on terraced hillsides above the water. Its narrow streets often become flights of steps that scale the hill, and its villas and gardens are framed by umbrella pines. The port area was originally a landlocked volcanic crater through which the Bourbon king Ferdinand II had a channel cut to create an opening seaward and then converted it into a sheltered port (1854). As you walk into the town along the waterfront, note the grandiose facade of the ancient municipal baths, where Ferdinand II used to take the waters, now used for town council offices and occasional art exhibitions.

Dining and Lodging

$$ ✕ **Da Gennaro.** This small family restaurant on the seafront at Ischia Porto serves excellent fish in a convivial atmosphere. Specialties include spaghetti with clams and linguine *all'aragosta* (with lobster). ✉ *Via Porto 66,* ☎ *081/992917. AE, DC, MC, V. Closed Nov.–mid-Mar.*

$$$ 🏨 **Villa Rosa.** A highlight at this gracious family-run hotel, in a villa with bright and airy rooms, is the thermally heated pool in the villa garden. In high season half-board is required, and you must reserve well in advance. Prices fall into the lower end of this category. It's in the heart of Ischia Porto and only a short walk from the beach. ✉ *Via Giacinto Gigante 3, 80077,* ☎ *081/991316,* 📠 *081/992425. 37 rooms with bath. Restaurant, air-conditioning in some rooms, pool. AE, MC, V. Closed Nov.–Easter.*

$–$$ 🏨 **Del Postiglione.** This attractive pink Mediterranean-style edifice is smaller than it appears, with only 15 guest rooms. Its aura of understated luxury is created by marble floors, tropical plants adorning the outside, and generous balconies overlooking one of Ischia Porto's quiet back streets, a couple of minutes from the seafront. Half-board only is accepted in August. ✉ *Via Giacinto Gigante 19, 80077,* ☎ *081/ 991579,* 📠 *081/985956. 15 rooms with bath. Restaurant, bar, babysitting. No credit cards.*

Casamicciola

㉒ *2 km (1 mi) east of Lacco Ameno.*

Known properly as the spa town of Casamicciola Terme, the town revolves around the busy Piazza Marina with its statue of the Italian king Vittorio Emanuele II and its marble plaque to Henry Ibsen, who was inspired by the beauty of the area to write *Peer Gynt* here. The town has retained some charming examples of 19th-century architecture. About 2 km (1 mi) from the center is a small **geophysical observatory** from the 19th century, set up to monitor the seismic activity on the island. The *osservatorio* has various antique monitoring devices and a cranky seismic tank designed by the scientist Giulio Grablovitz. ⊠ *Osservatorio Geofisico, Località Sentinella,* ☎ *081/996163.* ⊙ *By appointment only.*

Lacco Ameno

㉓ *6 km (4 mi) west of Ischia Porto; 3 km (2 mi) north of Forio.*

The smallest of the six *comuni* on the island, Lacco Ameno is a mecca for some of Italy's rich and famous. Italian magnate Gianni Agnelli anchors every summer close to the Fungo, a most distinctive mushroom-shape rock in volcanic tufa sculpted by wave action in the small marina, now one of the most notable natural landmarks in the Bay of Naples. Luchino Visconti, the noted realist film director and opera designer, had his Villa La Colombaria nearby in Baia San Montano, now used by the local council to promote the film industry on the island. The Bay of San Montano, a brilliant blue-sapphire buckle along the coast, is now the setting for Negombo, the most stylish of the thermal complexes on the island. Colonized by the Greeks as early as the 8th century BC, the landscape here has remained epic: it was used as the backdrop for the barge scene in Elizabeth Taylor's *Cleopatra*. The main road along the seafront in Lacco Ameno (Corso Rizzoli) thankfully has been pedestrianized and is now virtually a large promenade flanked by low-key shops, cafés, and restaurants. Lacco Ameno is also home to a fine spa, the Giardini Nogombo (☞ Outdoor Activities and Sports, *below*).

★ Lacco Ameno's archaeological importance—it lies just below the very first Greek settlement on the island at Monte Vico (380 ft) to the west—is amply reflected by the finds displayed in the new **Museo Archeologico of Villa Arbusto** and the ancient site beneath the Church of Santa Restituta. Villa Arbusto, built by Carlo d'Aquaviva in 1785 on top of a Bronze Age settlement, houses a large range of Greek pottery unearthed at the ancient necropolis site near the Baia di San Montano, much of it dating to the earliest years of the Greek colony (late 8th century BC), including Nestor's Cup, a kotyle vase in geometric style. ⊠ *Villa Arbusto, Lacco Ameno,* ☎ *081/900356.* 🎟 *10,000 lire.* ⊙ *Summer: Daily 9:30–1, 5–9; Winter: Daily 9:30–1, 3–7.*

From the nearby Church of Santa Restituta, almost completely rebuilt following a catastrophic earthquake in 1883, you can gain access to the underground excavations at the **Museo e Scavi Santa Restituta,** which are a memorable lesson in stratigraphy. Discovered in 1950 when the old majolica pavement above was removed, the underground site shows the building activities of several different periods (archaic Greek, Hellenistic, Roman, and early Christian), faithful reconstructions of an ancient loom and a miller's workshop, and the various finds discovered in situ. Although the structures are poorly labeled and it takes an expert eye to discern which buildings belong to which periods, this gives you a good idea of historical continuity on the island in ancient times. ⊠ *Piazza Santa Restituta, Lacco Ameno,* ☎ *081/980538.* 🎟 *5,000 lire.*

⊘ *Mar.–May and Sept.–Oct., weekdays 9–noon and 3–6, Sun. 9–noon; June–Aug., weekdays 9:30–12:30 and 5–7, Sun. 9:30–noon.*

Lodging

$$$$ 🏨 **Grande Albergo Mezzatore.** Far from the madding, sunburnt crowds
★ that swamp Ischia, this luxurious forgetaway perches in splendid isolation on the extreme promontory of Punta Cornacchia. Standing on the terraces of this renovated castello, set over the blue Bay of San Montano, with yachts parading below you, it's not hard to understand why film director Luchino Visconti chose to live just up the hill. This hotel has nearly everything to tempt its privileged guests to just stay put and *relax*: storybook cove, glamorous pool area, full health and beauty treatments—although the vast Nogombo spa is just down the road—serious chef, and hundreds of pine trees for true peace and quiet. The ancient fortress has been sleekly renovated—perhaps too much so from the look of its umber-red exterior. Inside, all is white-on-white with antiques and ancestral portraits as accents. The official address is Forio but this is much closer to Lacco Ameno, where you should get off if you're using the bus. ⊠ *Località San Montano, Forio d'Ischia, 80075,* ☎ *081/ 986111,* ℻ *081/986015. 58 rooms with bath. Restaurant, air-conditioning, pool, beauty farm, sauna, spa, tennis court, parking. AE, DC, V. Closed Nov.–Apr.*

$$$$ 🏨 **Regina Isabella.** Built in the early 1960s (not the most elegant of eras) and tucked away in an exclusive corner of the beach in Lacco Ameno, Ischia's largest luxury hotel has full resort facilities and pampers guests with spa treatments as well. The rooms are ample and decorated in warm Mediterranean colors, and most have terraces or balconies. Don't miss the fun of socializing with chic vacationers in the elegant bar or restaurant or at poolside. When filming *Cleopatra* on Ischia, Elizabeth Taylor and Richard Burton camped out here. ⊠ *Piazza Santa Restituta, 80076,* ☎ *081/994322,* ℻ *081/990190. 134 rooms with bath. Restaurant, bar, air-conditioning, indoor and outdoor pool, spa, tennis court, beach. AE, DC, MC, V. Closed mid-Oct.–mid-Apr.*

$$$$ 🏨 **San Montano.** Modern San Montano, replete with nautical motifs and ceramic-tile floors, overlooks the sea in a quiet spot. The rooms have compact maritime-style furnishings, color TVs, and minibars. The hotel also has all resort facilities and provides spa treatments, too. ⊠ *Via Montevico 1, 80076,* ☎ *081/994033,* ℻ *081/980242. 67 rooms with bath. Restaurant, air-conditioning, pool, spa, tennis court. AE, DC, MC, V. Closed Nov.–Mar.*

$$$ 🏨 **Hotel Della Baia.** A small tastefully furnished hotel on a pedestrianized road, this is near the magical bay of San Montano and just opposite the elegant Negombo Gardens, with their luxuriant thermal pools. Half-board terms include free entry to Negombo, except in August. ⊠ *Baia di San Montano, 80076,* ☎ *081/995453,* ℻ *081/ 986342. 20 rooms with bath. Bar, air-conditioning. AE, DC, MC, V. Closed Nov.–Mar.*

From Forio to Barano

Although the northern side of the island has the lion's share of history and archaeology, the south and west sides offer the best beaches. Vacationers flock to the water's edge at Citara and Maronti, where you can seek out the underwater geothermal vents and enjoy your own thermal bath free of charge. On the south side is the unspoiled village of Sant'Angelo, a restful antidote to the hectic towns elsewhere on the island. Higher up on the slopes of Epomeo is Serrara Fontana, the starting point for an excursion up to the highest point on Ischia.

Forio

㉔ *9 km (6 mi) west of Ischia Porto.*

Lying close to the main wine-producing area of the island, Forio is a busy seaside resort with beaches barely a minute's walk from its town center. At first glance, it seems to provide sad evidence of suburban sprawl, and its natural setting of flat coastline is not the most alluring. However, the island's most picturesque church is here: the 14th-century whitewashed Church of Santa Maria della Neve, down at the ★ harbor, better known as the **Sanctuario del Soccorso.** This is a good spot for a sunset evening stroll and for getting a clearer overview of the rest of the town, with the Torrione, one of 12 towers built under Aragonese rule in the 15th century to protect Forio's inhabitants from the ever-present threat of pirate raids.

Two kilometers (1 mile) north of Forio is one of the most stunningly ★ beautiful gardens in Mediterranean Italy, **La Mortella.** The garden was a labor of love designed in 1956 by the famous landscape architect Russell Page for Sir William Walton and his Argentine-born wife, Susana. It was created within a wide, bowl-shape rocky valley, originally not much more than a quarry, overlooking the Bay of San Francesco and with spreading views toward Monte Epomeo and Forio. This is where Lady Walton, now a talented gardener in her own right, first planted the flowering trees of her childhood, such as jacaranda and the rare bromeliad. Native wild plants were encouraged in the upper reaches of the gardens, with dainty vetches and orchids as well as myrtle, from which the garden got its name, La Mortella. Besides some soothing strolls among the well-labeled flower beds and landscaped rock gardens, try to spend some time in the museum dedicated to the life and works of the late English composer, William Walton. The gardens have excellent facilities, including a shop selling Sir William's music and Lady Walton's lively biography of her husband, *Behind the Facade,* as well as light, homemade refreshments. Needless to say, there is a concert series scheduled in the gardens during summertime. ⊠ *Via Calise 35, Forio,* ☎ *081/986237.* ⊡ *12,000 lire.* ☼ *Tues., Thurs., and weekends 9–7.*

Dining and Lodging

$$ ✕ **Bar-Ristorante Bagno Teresa.** This is an unpretentious restaurant on Citara Beach (no dress code) that offers a range of fresh seafood at reasonable prices served with lively local wine. This is the place to come if you want to stay light for the afternoon swim—there's no need to order a full Mediterranean splurge. ⊠ *Baia di Citara,* ☎ *081/907647. No credit cards. Closed Nov.–Mar.*

$$$ ▣ **La Bagattella.** *The* place to stay in Forio, this high-style oasis has a
★ white wedding-cake, arabesque ambience, with flower-covered balconies, sleek illuminated pool, exotic plants, and palm trees. The lobby is handsomely accented with wood antique furniture, while most guest rooms are modern and as spacious as apartments. A new wing has the less desirable accommodations, but everyone here can enjoy the truly orchidaceous atmosphere. ⊠ *Via Tommasso Ciglino 8, 80075,* ☎ *081/ 986072,* ℻ *081/989637. 26 rooms with bath. AC, MC, V. Closed Nov.– Mar.*

$$ ▣ **Hotel Semiramis.** A quiet family-run hotel, this is within a minute's walk of Citara Beach and the vast Giardini Poseidon. The rooms are decorated tastefully in thematic styles, with the best and most expensive in the panoramic new wing on the upper terrace. To cap it all, there is a child-friendly, secluded swimming pool tapping water from geothermal aquifers 30 ft down. ⊠ *Spiaggia di Citara, 80075,* ☎ *081/907511,*

FAX *081/907511. 33 rooms with bath. Bar, pool. No credit cards. Closed Nov.–Mar.*

$–$$ 🏠 **La Pergola.** One of the very few opportunities to stay on a working farm on Ischia, La Pergola is a whitewashed villa perched attractively on the slopes of Monte Epomeo and surrounded by vineyards and olive and fruit trees, with sweeping views westward over Citara Beach. Its dynamic young owners also operate a thriving restaurant serving local specialties including the fabled rabbit dish *coniglio all'ischitana*. The owners also offer cooking courses on occasion and have a small farm shop with homemade jams, liqueurs, and olive oil. ✉ *Via San Giuseppe 8, 80075,* ☎ *081/909483,* FAX *081/909483. 7 rooms with bath. No credit cards.*

Serrara Fontana

㉕ *8 km (5 mi) southeast of Forio.*

The name of this town reflects the merging of two small hill communities, Serrara and Fontana, into one larger *comune*. Apart from being a primarily agricultural community, Fontana is also known as the departure point (take Bus CS or CD from Ischia Porto, get off in the Piazzetta) for the hike up **Monte Epomeo** (mules can be rented near the parish Church of Santa Maria della Sacca). You should allow about two hours for this hike. Though it is rather underwhelming in terms of wildlife—sadly, hunting has decimated the numbers of larger birds and small mammals—the view at the very summit of Monte Epomeo, more than 2,500 ft above sea level, makes you feel that the two-hour round-trip was well worthwhile.

Sant'Angelo

㉖ *2 km (1 mi) south of Serrara Fontana.*

A sleepy fishing village out of season, Sant'Angelo, with its promontory of La Roia, has preserved its character remarkably well over the years. The area has been spared much of the *speculazione edilizia* (speculative building, often without planning permission) that has hit the rest of the island, and the steep winding paths by the sea are closed to traffic. Well connected by public transport (Bus CS from Forio or Ischia Porto, Bus CD from Ischia Porto only), this is a perfect site for an early evening passeggiata: you can peek into local pottery shops or tasteful boutiques, and then nestle into a café near the quayside for an aperitivo.

Dining

$$ ✕ **Pizzeria dal Pescatore.** A pizzeria with pleasing decor, this spot enjoys a fine view from the terrace overlooking the promontory of La Roia at Sant'Angelo. Some imaginative pizzas are served here—try the pizza *a fiori di zucchini* (zucchini pizza) or just trust in the chef's special. ✉ *Piazza Ottorino Troia 7,* ☎ *081/999206. AE, DC, MC, V. Closed Nov.–Apr.*

Barano D'Ischia

㉗ *6 km (4 mi) east of Serrara Fontana; 6 km (4 mi) south of Ischia Porto.*

Perched on a ridge 650 ft up, Barano combines the two industries of agriculture and tourism. Life here revolves around the main Piazza San Rocco with its two churches, San Sebastiano (the town's patron saint) and San Rocco (17th century). Like many churches on the island, San Sebastiano has undergone profound changes since its original foundation as an Augustine monastery in the 17th century. The pale yellow-and-white campanile was an 18th-century addition contemporary with the paintings by Di Spigna within. Barano is also the staging post for the south-facing Beach of Maronti, which is well worth a visit outside the busy months of July and August.

Nightlife, Sports, and Shopping

Nightlife

In the town of Ischia Porto, nightlife tends to concentrate around what the locals know as the Rive Droite, the eastern side of the port, while Ischia Ponte (☞ *below*) has a well-known discotheque actually within the Aragonese Castle, which in its heyday (1960s and 1970s) used to attract world celebrities (now it's a magnet for the teenage scooter brigade). In some private gardens, occasional concerts and cultural events are offered during the summer months. In general, nightlife on Ischia—especially of the cultural variety—is extremely seasonal, with events peaking in the summer when organizers are most assured of a large paying public. There is a rich tradition in local festivals, with the feast of Sant'Anna (July 26) holding pride of place with its skillful chore-ography and floating procession in the marina at Ischia Ponte below the Aragonese Castle.

On the eastern side of the harbor in Ischia Porto is a cluster of restau-rants and *enoteche* (wine bars) sometimes offering evening entertain-ment along the street known as the Rive Droite. Nightlife on Ischia is geared to start late in the evening, and you should be prepared to stay the course until the early hours. **Valentino Club** (☒ Corso Vittorio Colonna 97, Ischia Porto ☎ 081/982569), in the center of Ischia Porto, is the focal point for anyone but the gel-and-scooter set, with clientele in its early twenties and above. Admission varies between 25,000 lire and 35,000 lire, depending on what's on offer. Music-wise, it's pretty eclectic, though there's usually a fair dose of disco revival. Doors open at about 11:30 PM, with most habitués rolling in at about 1:30 AM and then heading up the road for an early morning cornetto at Calise in Piazzetta degli Eroi. No wonder so many of the young crowd hit the beach toward lunchtime or early afternoon.

The Arts

There is no theater as such on Ischia, although a few of the cinemas occasionally operate as theaters to put on local plays (in Italian). In season (from April to the end of October) town hall premises—such as Lacco Ameno and Ischia Porto—may be used to display paintings and sculptures, primarily by local artists. The main theatrical arena (out-door) on the island is in the Giardini Negombo, which has hosted some pretty big music and rock stars, although both Villa Arbusto (Lacco Ameno) and La Mortella (Forio) are used to hold classical music con-certs and recitals.

For information on forthcoming cultural events, check at the Azienda Autonoma di Cura, Soggiorno e Turismo (information office) in Ischia Porto or inquire at a local *agenzia di viaggi* (travel agency). In June the William Walton Foundation often arranges a busy schedule of concerts during the late afternoon within the magical gardens of La Mortella, admission to which is included in the price of the ticket. Villa Arbusto combines musical *serate*, or evening soirées, in summer months with visits to the new antiquities museum. From June to September the **Giardini Negombo** (☒ Baia di San Montano, Lacco Ameno, ☎ 081/986152) offers a variety of entertainment in its spacious outdoor arena.

Outdoor Activities and Sports

Tennis has the most facilities of any sport on the island, with an average of three to four clubs in each town, in addition to those attached to private hotels. In terms of water sports, virtually every beach offers windsurfing, waterskiing, and sailing facilities in season.

CANOEING

Unlike on Capri, aficionados of water sports are unlikely to leave Ischia dissatisfied. On a calm day a canoe will take you round into that secluded bay you've spotted from afar, perhaps with its sea cave that's worth exploring. A good place to start—considered by locals to be one of the best beaches on the island—is Citara, near the Giardini Poseidon. Canoe and boat rental from many beaches on Ischia is run by **Dario Mazzara Marine Service** (⊠ Via F. Di Lustro 10, Forio, ☎ 081/507–1328). For a rowboat, go to the outfitters along the oceanfront at Lacco Ameno such as **Isola Verde Viaggi** (⊠ Piazzetta Pontile 1/3, Lacco Ameno, ☎ 081/980455). Expect to pay 10,000–15,000 lire per hour for nonmotorized boat rental.

TENNIS

Playing at a well-established club with good clay courts is likely to set you back about 20,000 lire per hour. The **Tennis Club Pineta** (⊠ Corso Vittorio Colonna, Ischia Porto, ☎ 081/993300) is a centrally located club that accepts temporary members.

THEMAL BATHS

If you visit one of the island's many *terme,* or spa baths, you will not only be following a well-established tradition stretching back more than 2,000 years but also sampling one of the major contemporary delights of Ischia. You should allow at least half a day for this experience, as it is a pity to rush through. If you do decide to restrict yourself to half a day, then go in the afternoon, when the hefty entrance fee is lowered. The larger establishments have a plethora of pools offering natural hydromassage at different temperatures and in different settings, with a complement of bars and restaurants to enable customers to stay on the premises right through the day. Most terme are equipped with beauty centers, offering an unbelievably broad range of services, from mud-pack treatments and manicures to tattoo removal and bioenergetic massage.

For the ultimate Ischian escape, try the tastefully landscaped park of **Giardini di Negombo.** Designed around a beach of the finest sand, by the scenic bay of San Montano, it was created decades ago by Duke Luigi Camerini, a passionate botanist (who named his resort in honor of its resemblance to a bay in Sri Lanka). There are 12 saltwater or thermal pools here, plus facilities for hydromassage, a beauty center with sauna and Turkish bath, sports facilities for diving, windsurfing, volleyball, yoga, a bar, restaurant, and, according to the brochure, "a boutique for irresponsible purchases." All this is set in gardens with 500 species of Mediterranean plants and several panoramic views. Everything here—modern stone waterfalls, elegant poolside tables with thatched-leaf umbrellas, sensitive landscaping—is in the finest taste. Also on the grounds is a large outdoor arena, where stars like Tina Turner and Mireille Mathieu have performed. ⊠ *Baia di San Montano, Lacco Ameno,* ☎ *081/986152.* ☞ *35,000 lire all day, 27,000 lire after 2 PM, 19,000 lire after 4:30 PM.* ☉ *Apr.–Oct., daily 8:30–7.*

The largest spa on the island, with the added boon of a natural sauna hollowed out of the rocks, is the **Giardini Poseidon Terme.** Here you can sit like a Roman senator on a stone chair recessed in the rock and let the hot water cascade over you. A fairly tacky spectacle with countless thermally regulated pools and lots of toga-clad statues of the Caesars, Poseidon is usually overrun with Germans, most of them grandparents shepherding grandchildren. ⊠ *Citara Beach, Forio,* ☎ *081/907122.* 🖾 *40,000 lire all day, 35,000 lire after 1 PM, 8,000 lire for visitors (no bathing) 1 hr before closing time.* ⊙ *Apr.–Oct., daily 8:30–7.*

Shopping
The best shops in Ischia are to be found along the pedestrianized streets of Ischia Porto, Forio, Ischia Ponte, and to a lesser extent, Sant'Angelo, though the island as a whole is not renowned as a shoppers' paradise.

For books try **Libreria Pickwick** (⊠ Via de Luca 157, opposite Hotel Jolly, Ischia Porto, ☎ 081/981138). For leather goods and clothing boutiques, most islanders head straight for Via Roma in Ischia Porto, just a two-minute walk from the harbor. A number of shops sell competitively priced leather articles such as bags and belts, while there is also a fair array of clothing boutiques. But don't expect any of the big names you find on Capri. With all the beauty farms on Ischia, ladies may enjoy visiting the main cosmetics factory on the island, **Ischia Thermae** (⊠ Via Schioppa 17, Forio, ☎ 081/997745), which occupies an 18th-century palazzo in the town center of Forio. Besides poring over some of the formidably named articles in their retail outlet (such as Thermal Mud Purifying Mask Exfoliator), you can join a guided tour of the factory twice a week (Wednesday and Friday at 5) and get a free sample of their products. Finally, while you're out and about, stop by **Ciccio,** near the ferry piers (⊠ Via Jasolino, Ischia Porto), for the best gelati on Ischia. In Casamicciola, make for **Gelateria Calise** (⊠ Piazza Marina, Casamicciola), again just opposite the landing stage.

PROCIDA: ISLAND OF CONTRASTS

Lying barely 3 km (2 mi) from the mainland and 10 km (6 mi) from the nearest port of Pozzuoli, Procida is an island of enormous contrasts. It is the most densely populated island in Europe—almost 11,000 people crammed into less than 3½ square km (2 square mi)—and yet there are oases like Marina Corricella and Vivara, which seem to have been bypassed by modern civilization. The inhabitants on the island—the Procidani—have an almost symbiotic relationship with the Mediterranean: many join the merchant navy while others either fish or ferry vacationers around local waters. And yet land traffic here is more intense than on any other island in the Bay of Naples.

In scenic terms this is the place to admire what the Italians call "Spontaneous," or folkloric Mediterranean, architecture: Look for the tall archways on the ground floor, which signals places where boats could be stowed in winter, the outside staircases providing access to upper floors without cramping interior living space, and the delicate pastel colors of the facades contrasting with deeper, bolder blues at sea. Picturesquely scenic, it is no surprise that Procida has strong artistic traditions and is widely considered the painters' island par excellence.

Terra Murata and Abbazia di San Michele

Close to Marina Grande Sancio Cattolico, the main port of Procida, the town of Terra Murata is a fascinating cluster of ancient buildings, including churches, palazzi, fortifications, ancient walls, and gateways, mostly in yellow-gray tufa stone. A Benedictine abbey was founded here in the 7th century, safely tucked away from mainland marauders, and the area became the focal point for the inhabitants of the island. Perched precariously at the top of a cliff facing the small bay of Corricella is the 16th-century **ex-convent of Santa Margherita Nuova,** which is currently undergoing restoration. The easily distinguishable **Palazzo Reale** built at the same time—confusingly, sometimes called Il Castello—was used as a prison until 1986. Rumor has it that its inmates were a little miffed at having to abandon the perks of being on the sun-drenched island of Procida.

Within Terra Murata is the **Abbazia di San Michele.** San Michele (St. Michael) is the island's patron saint and a key figure in its history and traditions. Legend has it that in 1535, when the sultan of Algeria's admiral laid siege to the island, San Michele appeared above the pirate force and put them to flight (the 17th-century painting depicting the scene is in the choir of the abbey's 17th-century church, while one of the invaders' anchors can also be viewed). On the wall close to the richly coffered ceiling of the church is another depiction of San Michele, this time by the grandmaster Luca Giordano (1699). As you walk around the church, note the holes in marble flagstones on the floor, which were in effect trapdoors through which bodies could be lowered to the underground cemetery below. There are also a remarkable number of statues, several of which are still borne through the streets of Procida during its Easter processions. ⊠ *Terra Murata,* ☎ *081/896–7612.* 🔢 *Free but donations welcome. Guided tours available on request at the bookstore at entrance to abbey.* ☉ *Spring–fall, Mon.–Sat. 9:45–12:45 and 3–6; winter, Mon.–Sat. 3–5.*

Corricella

Singled out for the waterfront scenes in *Il Postino*—the 1995 Oscar-winner for Best Foreign Film that was the last movie in which Massimo Troisi starred—the inhabitants of Corricella have been relatively immune to life in the limelight, and apart from the opening of an extra restaurant and bar, there have been few changes in this sleepy fishermen's village. This is the type of place where even those of us with failing grades in art classes feel like reaching for a paintbrush to record the delicate pinks and yellows of the waterfront buildings.

Dining and Lodging

With such a strong seafaring tradition on Procida, you'd be wise to stick primarily to seafood, especially in summer. And if you have space left over at the end of the meal, try the local variety of *torta di limone,* made from the island's wondrously large lemons.

$$–$$$ ✕ **La Gorgonia.** This atmospheric restaurant sits right on the waterfront down at Corricella. The specialty here is a combination of seafood and locally grown vegetables, such as pasta *con fagioli e cozze* (with beans and mussels). ⊠ *Marina Corricella,* ☎ *081/810–1060. AE, DC, MC, V. Closed Nov.–Feb. and weekdays Mar.–May and Oct.*

$$ 🏨 **Casa Gentile.** This is a very quiet hotel with spacious rooms overlooking Corricella, designed to blend in tastefully with the local Mediterranean architecture. If interested in fishing, ask the owner, Vincenzo, if you can join him on his nighttime travels around the Bay of Naples. The hotel offers a water-taxi service to and from port. ⊠ *Marina Corricella 88, Procida,* ☎ *081/896–7799,* 🆔 *081/896–9011. 10 rooms with bath. MC, V. Closed Nov.–mid-Mar.*

Vivara

Vivara, a crescent-shape island and terminal segment of a volcanic cone, is a living museum of natural history with unsullied Mediterranean maquis vegetation. It has miraculously survived the designs of property speculators over the past 30 years and is now awaiting a proper management plan from the Regione Campania. Apart from a few historic buildings on the island, including a Napoleonic fort near the entrance gateway, the main cultural interest lies in its rich archaeological finds dating to prehistoric times, especially the Bronze Age, as testified to by a wealth of Mycenean pottery fragments.

The island is at its best in springtime, with most of its plants in flower and lots of birds on the move. The path winds up from the causeway to a cluster of abandoned settlements at the highest point of the island (357 ft). On the way admire the dense maquis on either side with characteristic plant species like tree heather, the strawberry tree, and rockrose, the latter of which sports delicate pink flowers in spring. Although you'll hear birds—especially the blackcap—don't expect to see any of these skulking warblers except perhaps around the clearing at the center of the island. At migration time look out for two of the Mediterranean's more exotic-looking summer visitors, the hoopoe, a bird that looks more in keeping with the African savanna, and the bee-eater, a splash of unusually vivid colors. For information about access and guided tours on Vivara, contact the **Azienda Autonoma di Cura, Soggiorno e Turismo** (✉ Via Roma, Procida, ☎ 081/810–1968) before trekking out to the island.

Lodging

$$ 🏨 **Crescenzo Hotel-Ristorante.** A short walk from Vivara, this is a three-story whitewashed hotel overlooking the small yachting marina of Chiaiolella. Half-board only in August, though with specialties like spaghetti *ai ricci di mare* (with sea urchins) you should consider half-board at other times of the year as well. ✉ *Marina di Chiaiolella,* ☎ *081/896–7255,* 𝙵𝙰𝚇 *081/810–1260. 10 rooms with bath. Restaurant, bar, free parking. AE, DC, MC, V.*

Nightlife and Sports

Nightlife

Procida's nightlife revolves around Via Roma in the port town of Marina Grande Sancio Cattolico, though there are a number of late-closing bars and restaurants around the Marina di Chiaiolella, too. Interest in the arts is less flourishing here, especially as there is no natural focal point for exhibitions and shows. If on the island at Easter, make sure you see the striking Good Friday procession through the island's major streets.

The **Birreria Pub Sotto Sopra** (✉ Via Roma 11, Procida, ☎ 081/810–1013) serves good draft lager almost around the clock in a fairly congenial quasi-nautical setting.

The Arts

Procida was the setting for Elsa Morante's novel, *L'Isola di Arturo,* which has lent its name to the literary competition held every September on Procida. Art exhibitions are occasionally held down at the port in several of the palazzi along Via Roma, while the Abbazia di San Michele in Terra Murata lays on special exhibitions connected with religious and literary themes. Ask about forthcoming events at the Azienda Autonoma di Cura, Soggiorno e Turismo (information office) in Marina Grande Sancio Cattolico.

Outdoor Actvities and Sports

With its famous nautical school and centuries-old seafaring traditions, Procida is an ideal base for chartering yachts of various sizes or just exploring the seabed with one of the diving schools on the island.

SAILING

One of the market leaders in Italy is **Sail Italia** (✉ Via Roma 10, Procida, ☎ 081/896–9264 or 081/896–9962). Except for the even-pricier month of August, chartering a 10-berth 40-ft yacht for a week—enough time to visit the other islands in the bay as well as the gorgeous island of Ponza, farther afield—will set you back about 7 million lire inclusive of skipper and final clean. If reckoned on a daily per-person basis, this is an interesting alternative to hotel stays on the various islands.

SCUBA DIVING

The **Procida Diving Center** (✉ Lido di Procida, Marina Chiaiolella, Procida, ☎ 081/896–8385) organizes courses and provides equipment for divers of all levels. You may be taken into shallower waters, like Secca delle Formiche, near Vivara, or shown the coral formation off one of the headlands on the island. The cost for a session averages about 50,000 lire per person, and the season runs roughly from May to October.

CAPRI, ISCHIA, AND PROCIDA A TO Z

Capri

Arriving and Departing

By Hydrofoil or Ferry

Capri is well connected with the mainland in all seasons, though there tend to be more sailings between April and October. However, you can't return to Naples after about 8 PM, so if you want to see an evening concert, you'll have to look for hotel accommodations. Ferries, hydrofoils, Seacats, and similar vessels leave from Molo Beverello (below Piazza Municipio) in Naples and from Sorrento's Marina Piccola, while *aliscafi* (hydrofoils) also sail from the small marina of Mergellina, a short distance west of the Villa Comunale in Naples. Departure schedules are listed every day in several daily papers (*Corriere della Sera, Il Mattino, La Repubblica*). If you are planning to move on from Capri to Ischia or the Amalfi Coast, there is regular service from May to October, when demand is higher. As for ferry costs, there is little to be gained—sometimes nothing—from buying a round-trip ticket, which will just tie you down to a return schedule of only one shipping line. For locals in Naples there are restrictions on taking cars onto the island, while non-Italians can move relatively freely. Bear in mind that much of Capri town is pedestrianized, and a car on the island may well be more of a hindrance than a help.

Caremar (☎ 081/551–3882). Five hydrofoil departures from Molo Beverello; 16,500 lire high season, 15,900 lire low; travel time 40 minutes. Six ferry departures per day; 9,800 lire high season, 8,800 low season; travel time one hour 15 minutes; supplement of about 4,000 lire for fast craft.

Linee Marittime Partenopee (☎ 081/878–1430, 081/807–1812). One–three hydrofoil departures every hour from Sorrento, 12,000 lire, travel time 30 minutes. Seven ferries per day from Sorrento, 7,500 lire, 50 minutes. One hydrofoil per day from Ischia (in AM), 20,000 lire, one hour.

Navigazione Libera Del Golfo (☎ 081/552–0763). Roughly one hydrofoil departure per hour, 16,000 lire, travel time 40 minutes, one late-afternoon hydrofoil from Positano and Amalfi, approximately 20,000 lire, travel time 50 minutes.

SNAV (☎ 081/761–2348). Hydrofoil every hour from Mergellina, 18,000 lire, travel time 40 minutes.

Getting Around

Most of Capri's sights are reasonably accessible by either boat or bus, except for Villa Jovis and Cetrella, which involve some walking (about 40 minutes). Bus service is relatively cheap and frequent, while taxis are likely to cost 10–20 times the cost of public transport. Access to the Blue Grotto is usually from Marina Grande in a 20-seater boat, decanting into smaller rowboats near the grotto. Some prefer to take the bus to Anacapri and then change onto another line that passes close to the grotto on the northwest side of the island. This operation involves taking just one boat and will reduce overall your cost by about 3,000 lire. However, don't always set your heart on an excursion to the Blue Grotto, as visits cannot be made when the sea is even minimally choppy. An alternative is the Giro dell'Isola (round island tour; for operators, ☞ Guided Tours, *below*), which is a better value for money compared with the Blue Grotto excursion.

Off the major bus routes, many roads are pedestrianized. The trails close to Villa Jovis and the Arco Naturale are all well paved and well maintained, while those on the steeper parts of Monte Solaro are the only ones where walking shoes are advisable. If you go down the Scala Fenicia footpath from Anacapri, take your time. Although not dangerous, some stretches are quite steep and should be walked with caution.

By Taxi
Capri Town: Taxis (☎ 081/837–0543). **Anacapri: Taxis** (☎ 081/837–1175).

Contacts and Resources

Currency Exchange
Capri Town: Cambio (⊠ Via Roma 33, ☎ 81/837–0785). **La Piazzetta** (⊠ Piazza Umberto I 10, ☎ 081/837–0557).

Anacapri: La Piazzetta 2 (⊠ Piazza Vittoria 2b, ☎ 081/837–3146).

Emergencies
Capri: Police (☎ 081/837–4211); **First Aid** (☎ 081/838–1205); **Hospital** (⊠ Ospedale Capilupi, ☎ 081/838–1111).

Anacapri: Police (☎ 081/837–1011); **First Aid** (☎ 081/838–1205); **Hospital** (⊠ Ospedale Capilupi, ☎ 081/838–1111).

Guided Tours
Gruppo Motoscafisti (⊠ Molo del Porto, Marina Grande, Capri, ☎ 081/837–5646). Excursions to Blue Grotto from Marina Grande (23,500 lire, with Sunday supplement) and round island tour, or *giro,* taking in other grottoes and getting good close-ups of the Faraglioni (19,000 lire, with Sunday supplement).

Laser Capri (⊠ Via Ruocco 45, Marina Grande, Capri, ☎ 081/837–5208). Excursions to Blue Grotto from Marina Grande (22,500 lire, with Sunday supplement) and round island tour (15,000 lire).

Cooperativa Battelieri Capresi (⊠ Via C. Colombo 23, Marina Grande, Capri, ☎ 081/837–0973). This company manages the rowboats covering the short distance into the Blue Grotto.

Travel Agencies
Grotta Azzurra (⊠ Via C. Colombo 64, Capri, ☎ 081/837–0410, FAX 081/837–7528). This travel agency can arrange ticketing for flights,

trains, etc., on the mainland as well as providing incoming services such as hotel reservations, customized tours of the island, mainland tours to Herculaneum, Pompeii, the Amalfi Coast, as well as scooter rentals.

Visitor Information

Capri: Azienda Autonoma di Cura, Soggiorno e Turismo (⊠ Banchina del Porto, Marina Grande, Capri, ☎ 081/837–0634). Open 8:30–8:30 in season and 9–1 and 3–7 approximately in winter.

Azienda Autonoma di Cura, Soggiorno e Turismo (⊠ Piazza Umberto I, Capri Town, ☎ 081/837–0686). Open 8:30–8:30 high season and 9–1 and 3–7 approximately in winter.

Anacapri: Azienda Autonoma di Cura, Soggiorno e Turismo (⊠ Via G. Orlandi, 19/A, Anacapri, ☎ 081/837–1524). Open 8:30–8:30 in high season, 9–1 and 3–7 approximately in winter.

Ischia

Arriving and Departing

By Hydrofoil or Ferry

Like the other islands in the Bay of Naples, Ischia is well connected with the mainland in all seasons. However, the last sailings leave for Naples and Pozzuoli at about 8 in the evening, and you should allow plenty of time for getting to the port and locating the relevant ticket office. Unlike Capri and Procida, Ischia has three separate ports—Ischia Porto, Casamicciola, and Forio (hydrofoils only)—so you should choose your ferry or hydrofoil according to your destination. The closest port to Ischia is that of Pozzuoli, where you have the added bonus—besides paying lower fares—of walking through the colorful fish market on your way to the jetty. Many of the sailings go via Procida, giving you an attractive glimpse of its waterfront but also extending travel time by 10–15 minutes. Departure schedules are listed every day in several daily papers (*Corriere della Sera, Il Mattino, La Repubblica*). Buy a single ticket rather than a round-trip, which would tie you to the same shipping line on your return journey. Like Capri, local Italians are subject to restrictions on taking cars over to the island, while non-Italians can move relatively freely.

Alilauro (☎ 081/761–1004). Roughly one hydrofoil per hour from Mergellina, Naples to Ischia Porto, 18,000 lire, travel time 40 minutes. Five hydrofoils per day May–September to Forio, 20,000 lire, travel time, 50 minutes.

Caremar (☎ 081/551–3882). Six hydrofoil departures from Molo Beverello, Naples to Ischia Porto, 16,500 lire high season, 15,000 lire low, travel time 50 minutes. Eight ferry departures per day, 9,800 lire high season, 9,000 low, travel time, 1½ hours.

Linee Lauro (☎ 081/552–2838). Roughly one hydrofoil every two hours from Molo Beverello, Naples to Ischia Porto, 18,000 lire, travel time 40 minutes. Eight ferry departures per day to Ischia Porto, 10,000 lire, travel time 1¼ hours.

SNAV (☎ 081/761–2348). Hydrofoil every two hours from Mergellina, Naples, to the marina of Casamicciola, 18,000 lire high season, 16,000 low, travel time 50 minutes.

Traghetti Pozzuoli (☎ 081/526–7736). Ferry every hour from Pozzuoli, sometimes docking at Casamicciola, 9,000 lire, travel time 1 hour.

Getting Around

Ischia has an excellent, competitively priced bus network, with all the major sites and beaches within easy reach of one of its 10 lines. Runs continue on some routes until well after 10 PM, making evening sorties feasible even if you haven't got your own transport. Ischia also has taxis and microtaxis, which are basically three-wheelers with a cabin at the back. A number of car and scooter rental facilities are available, although Ischia already has more than its fair share of motorized two-wheelers on the roads and many have undergone engine tampering to improve performance (and boost noise levels). If you use a bicycle on the island, be prepared for lots of ups and downs, and where possible take to the minor roads. Boat and Zodiac rentals are possible at most of the major beaches, and ferrying service is sometimes arranged to reach out-of-the-way beaches.

By Bicycle

About 100 yards from Ischia Porto's ferry terminal, **Del Franco** (⊠ Via Alfredo De Luca 121, opposite Hotel Jolly, Ischia Porto, ☎ 081/991334) has a fair range of sturdy bicycles—surprisingly, some without gears—costing 20,000 lire per day.

By Bus

The main bus terminus is in Ischia Porto at the start of Via Cosca from where buses run by the company **SEPSA** (☎ 081/991808) radiate out around the island. There are also convenient *fermate* (stops) at the two main beaches of Citara and Maronti, with timetables displayed at the terminus. At 1,700 lire per ticket, the service may be considered a good value though conditions can get very hot and crowded at peak beach-visiting times.

By Car

Given the much larger size of Ischia compared to the other islands Capri and Procida (where cars are virtually redundant), having your own transport on Ischia could be handy, especially if you have to schlep large quantities of diving equipment, say, around the island. However, in most towns now there are strict parking restrictions, and *vigili urbani* (traffic police) are constantly on the lookout for aberrant motorists. The police are also clamping down on the use of seat belts, so if you do drive, be sure to wear yours even on the shortest journey.

By Taxi

Taxis—and microtaxis—are to be found near the major ferry and hydrofoil terminals, and there are taxi ranks close to all the town centers on the island. Though perhaps a novelty, microtaxis can be both expensive and noisy, so you should be prepared to suspend intelligent conversation during the journey. By law all taxis and microtaxis have to use their meters, so make sure the meter is activated as soon as your journey begins. If the taxi doesn't have a meter, beware: many drivers seem to be pirates in disguise, so work out a flat fee before you set out. If you just go along for the ride, you could wind up being very unpleasantly surprised when you're charged $15 for a three-minute trip.

Contacts and Resources

Car Rentals

Del Franco (⊠ Via Alfredo De Luca 121, opposite Hotel Jolly, Ischia Porto, ☎ 081/991334).

Currency Exchange

In general look for exchange bureaus or signs saying WECHSEL (German for "exchange"). Commission rates may be marginally higher than in the local banks, but red tape is virtually nonexistent, and service is likely to be considerably faster.

Alilauro Biglietteria (⊠ Hydrofoil ticket office, Ischia Porto, ☎ 081/761–1004). **Viaggi e Turismo Di Leva** (⊠ Piazza Medaglia d'Oro 11, Forio, ☎ 081/997711).

Emergencies
Island of Ischia Porto: **Police** (☎ 081/991336); **First Aid** (☎ 081/994044); **Hospital** (⊠ Ospedale Rizzoli, Lacco Ameno, ☎ 081/994044).

Guided Tours and Travel Agencies
Most travel agencies supply the following services: hotel booking, car rentals, guided tours, flight and ferry bookings, and day excursions to the mainland and other islands.

Isolaverde Viaggi (⊠ Piazzatta Pontile 1/3, Lacco Ameno, ☎ 081/980455, FAX 081/995329). **Sud Italia Incoming & Citara Travel** (⊠ Via Schioppa, Forio, ☎ 081/507–1308, FAX 081/507–1237). **Viaggi Romano** (⊠ Via Porto 5/9, Ischia Porto, ☎ 081/991215, FAX 081/991167).

Visitor Information
Azienda Autonoma di Cura, Soggiorno e Turismo (⊠ Ufficio Informazioni, Banchina Porto Salvo, Ischia Porto, ☎ 081/507–4231, FAX 081/507–4230, ⊙ 9–1:30 PM; Apr.–Oct. also open 3–7:30 PM).

Procida

Arriving and Departing
By Hydrofoil or Ferry
Procida's ferry timetable caters to the many daily commuters who live on the island and work in Naples or Pozzuoli. The most frequent—and cheapest—connections are from the Port of Pozzuoli. As with the other islands, buy a single ticket rather than a round-trip (there is virtually no saving on a round-trip ticket, which is usually twice the single fare, and it ties you down to one operator on your return). After stopping at Procida's main port, Marina Grande Sancio Cattolico, many ferries and hydrofoils continue on to Ischia, for which Procida is considered a halfway house.

Caremar (☎ 081/551–3882). Six hydrofoil departures from Molo Beverello, Naples, 13,900 lire high season, 12,500 lire low, travel time 40 minutes. Seven ferry departures per day from Molo Beverello, Naples, 8,300 lire high season, 7,500 low, travel time one hour, 10 minutes. There are three ferry departures per day from Pozzuoli, 4,700 lire high season, 4,300 low, travel time 40 minutes.

SNAV (☎ 081/761–2348). Hydrofoil every two hours from Mergellina, Naples, 14,000 lire high season, 13,000 low, travel time 35 minutes.

Procida Lines 2000 (☎ 081/896–0328). Ferry is roughly every hour from Pozzuoli, 4,500 lire, travel time 40 minutes.

Getting Around
There are four main bus lines that will take you to practically every corner of the island as well as a fleet of microtaxis operating round island tours and plying the route between the port and the Marina di Chiaiolella, on the southwest of the island. To get to Vivara, a road climbs westward out of Chiaiolella, and motorized access is barred shortly before reaching the causeway linking the two islands. Though Procida has fewer hills than either Ischia or Capri, cycling is really only feasible when the roads are closed to motorized traffic (evenings in sum-

mer). Most islanders get around on mopeds and scooters, which means the streets between the port and the center of the island are both noisy and loaded with pollutants, making casual strolling and window-shopping stressful. Beaches can be reached by sea or land, with local fishermen improvising as water-taxi drivers.

By Bicycle
Signor Basilea Luoni of **Associazione Azione Verde** has a cycle shop opposite the Scuola Media (✉ Piazza Sant'Antonio da Padova, Marina Grande Sancio Cattolico, ☎ 081/896–7395), which is about a 30-minute walk from the ferry terminal. The shop can arrange for bike delivery to the port.

By Bus
The bus terminus in Procida is at the disembarkation point in Via Roma. Provided there is no traffic gridlock along the island's narrow streets, the buses run by the company **SEPSA** (☎ 081/810–1241) will get you to most destinations within about 10 minutes for 1,700 lire. Chiaiolella is the most frequently served destination (about every 15 minutes) and timetables are displayed—and tickets bought—at a newsstand close to the landing stage. In summer the bus service runs until about 4 in the morning.

By Taxi
For about 20,000 lire, microtaxis with a capacity of about five passengers will take you from the port to Chiaiolella. This can be a welcome service in summer, when buses get overcrowded and steamy. For the round island tour, expect to pay upwards of 50,000 lire. However, this includes frequent stops along the way plus a shotgun-quick visit to the Abbazia. Although by law all microtaxis have to use their meters, it may be worth your while to agree on a fixed price beforehand. Taxis can be hired at **Marina Grande** (☎ 081/896–8785) or at **Marina Chiaiolella** (☎ 081/896–8816).

Contacts and Resources

Currency Exchange
Credem (✉ Via Roma 102, Procida).

Emergencies
Police (☎ 081/896–8539); **First Aid** (☎ 081/896–9058); **Hospital** (☎ 081/810–1213).

Guided Tours and Travel Agencies
Graziella Travel (✉ Via Roma 117, Procida, ☎ 081/896–9594, FAX 081/896–9190).

Visitor Information
Azienda Autonoma di Cura, Soggiorno e Turismo (✉ Stazione Marittima Ferry ticket office, Via Roma, Procida, ☎ 081/810–1968), open April–October, daily 9:30–1 and 4–7:30, November–Easter, daily 9:30–1.

5 SORRENTO AND THE AMALFI COAST

Not all of Paradise was lost. A dollop of it—the Sorrentine peninsula and the Amalfi Coast—remains, to be found again and again in one of the most gigglingly gorgeous corners on earth: Sorrento—Italy at its Belle Epoque best; perfect Positano—a claim that is more than alliteration; Amalfi—a shimmering medieval city; and romantic mountaintop Ravello. Connecting these towns is the Amalfi Drive, a cliff-hugging stretch of road that tests one's faith in civil engineering. This roller-coastal route offers views that are drop-dead breathtaking (literally, it sometimes seems).

By Lea Lane

THANK ODYSSEUS FOR LETTING THE SIRENS LURE HIM to their lair near Sorrento. Here, as the *Odyssey* tells us, the first tourist of record resisted the seductive song of the Sirenusiae—three half-women, half-mermaids. Homer doesn't fill in the details, but the wily navigator outwitted them by tying his men to the ship's mast and sealing their ears with wax. While John Donne said no man is an island, it was left to ancient mariners to speak for the ladies: According to them, the three Sirens spitefully chose to live out eternity as rocky outcrops, right here on the Li Galli islands, in the waters off Positano. Even today, it is difficult for modern steersmen—whether of plane, train, or boat—to resist the allure of this part of southern Italy, a palmy and balmy land stretching south from the Bay of Naples and the Sorrentine peninsula to the Amalfi Coast and the Bay of Salerno, rimmed by the true-bluest waters of the Mediterranean. Like Homer, you'll be able to spin your own tale of lemony breezes, emerald grottoes, sun-kissed vistas, sea-fresh food, and an embracing, generous people. Like a 21st-century Odysseus, to leave these blessed shores willingly you may have to hang on to the ferry rail, close your eyes, and turn your Discman up to full blast.

The Sorrentine Peninsula was put on the map by the ancient Romans. The emperors—who knew a great thing when they saw it—claimed the region for their own, crowning the golden, waterside cliffs of what was then called "Surrentum" (or Land of Sirens), with their palatial villas. Where they staked out their vacation spots, resorts now stand, the broken columns and capitals and marble busts of the Caesars now scattered among orange trees and terraces, attesting to their power—and its decline. Sorrento goes as far back as the Etruscans, but for much of its existence has focused on pleasure, and was a major stop on the elite's Grand Tour itinerary beginning in the late 18th century. Thanks to reports from Goethe, Lord Byron, Shelley, and Richard Wagner, the word was out. By the mid-19th century, grand hotels and wedding-cake villas had sprung up to welcome princes, khans, and tycoons.

Gently faded like a stereopticon image, and set with sherbet-hued villas, Sorrento still exudes a special pull—from its bustling piazza named for the famous 16th-century poet Tasso, a local boy, to the belvederes framing the slowly setting sun. For anyone suffering *"nostaglie di Napoli"*—a longing for tarantellas, strumming mandolins, and dolce far niente—this is the ideal place, since Naples itself has become so urbanized. As a hub for must-see sites—Pompeii, Naples, Capri, and the Amalfi coast to the south—Sorrento is unequaled. Because of its convenient location the city can become overrun with visitors during the summer months, so it's fortunate that the rest of the Sorrentine peninsula, with plains and limestone outcroppings, watchtowers and Roman ruins, groves and beaches, monasteries and villages, winding paths leading to isolated coves and panoramic views of both the bays of Naples and Salerno, remains relatively undiscovered. The peninsula's tip was, eons ago, connected to Capri and it seems you can practically jump there. Separating grande dame Sorrento from the relatively arriviste Amalfi coast, this hilly, forested peninsula provides the famed rivals breathing space, along with incredible restaurants and an uncrowded charm all its own.

Heading south, the Amalfi coast—or the Costiera Amalfitana—from Positano to Vietri sul Mare, is arguably the most divinely sensual 48-km (30-mi) stretch of water, land, and habitation on earth. Legends abound, but Greeks were early colonizers at Paestum to the south, and Romans fled their own sacked empire in the 4th century to settle the steep coastal ridge now called the Lattari mountains (because of the milk, or *latte,* produced there). Coveted by Lombards, Saracens, and other hopefuls held literally at bay (some of the time), the medieval Maritime Republic of Amalfi dominated the seas and coast until the Normans conquered southern Italy from the 11th century. By the end of the 13th, Naples, the capital of the Angevin kingdom, became the dominant ruler of the region until Italy unified in the mid-19th century.

By the late 19th century, with the creation of the two-lane Amalfi Drive, tourism blossomed, and what a road show. One of the most exciting drives in the world, it seems to be pasted onto the faces of dizzying precipices and far-flung headlands. All along the drive, wind and water erosion has carved limestone mountains into spires and crags that seem to defy gravity, cliffs plummet straight to the sea, and crushed rock washes up along turquoise inlets. Ravines and valleys, formed by torrential flows from the highlands, are folded into the limestone coast, softening the scene with meadows and chestnut woods. Thanks to this feat of engineering that is the Amalfi Drive, the world soon discovered what has come to be called the "Divina Costiera." The justly famed jewels along this coastal necklace are Positano, Amalfi, and Ravello, but today's traveler will find the satellite baguettes—including Conca dei Marini, Atrani, Scala, and Cetara—just as sparkling. The top towns along the Amalfi Drive may fill up in high season with Nikons, tour buses, and elbows, but in the countryside, not much seems to have changed since the Middle Ages: mountain are still terraced and farmed for citrus, olive, wine, and dairy, and the sea is dotted with fishermen's dories. Vertiginous villages are dominated by duomos; crammed with houses on, into, above, and below hillsides to the bay; crossed by mule paths; and navigated by flights of steps called *scalinatelli,* often leading to outlooks and belvederes that take your breath away—in more ways than one. Songs have been composed about these serpentine stone steps, and they may come to haunt your dreams. After all, some *costieri* (natives of the coast) like to count them one by one to get to sleep.

Semi-tough realities lurk behind the scenic splendor of the Divina Costiera, most notably the extremes of driving, the endless steps, and nonexistent parking. Furthermore, it rains in the spring, the hills can burn dry in the summer, and museums are few. Until you adjust, people seem to talk in maximum decibels. So what. For a precious little time, you are in a land of unmarred beauty.

Pleasures and Pastimes

Beaches
Beaches are typically considered disappointing, as they usually consist of small patches of coarse gray sand, or just a few rocks below the precipices. It's the water that compels: infinite shades of aquamarine, lapis, and amethyst, shimmering in sunshine, glowing silver in moonlight, and becoming transparent in coves. The best regional beaches are on the Sorrentine peninsula, to the west and south, many of them reachable only by footpath or boat. The longest and widest beaches on the Amalfi Coast are in Maiori and Minori, but there are many small beaches and coves from which to choose. As space is at a premium, few organized beachside activities are available—the best bet is at Positano. For exercise, folks descend (and later ascend) the scalinatelli to rocky coves, where adults dip and sunbathe and children play hide and seek.

Boating
People take to boats here with the ease others use buses and subways. Ferries and hydrofoils are regularly scheduled during high season. The

waters are calm and beckoning, and boating for pleasure frees you from the tension of coastal driving, so try to arrange to spend at least one day on the water. Bright red-and-blue fishing boats are for hire by the day or for a few hours at the major harbors of Sorrento, Positano, and Amalfi, and by almost any beach wherever you see fishermen. Boats can take you around the Sorrento area and peninsula to the Emerald Grotto, to Capri and offshore islets, to major towns, and otherwise inaccessible cove beaches. They will drop you off and pick you up, or stay with you, depending on your budget. Look for established sites on major beaches and come a day or so ahead to reserve and bargain, especially if you're with a group. Pricing could be around $20 an hour, more or less, depending on the market, the season, and your talent at haggling. If in doubt, ask for suggestions about local boatmen at your hotel or at the town tourist board. And don't expect fishermen to speak much English; you'll have to speak with with your hands, as many Italians do.

Dining: La Cucina Costiera

Locals say they have "one foot in the fishing boat, one in the vineyard"— and a fortunate stance it is, as you can count on eating simple, fresh, seasonal food, and lots of it, with *tutti i sapori della Campagnia verace* (all the true flavors of Campagna). From the gulfs come *pesce alla griglia* (grilled fish), *calamari* (squid), *aragosta* (lobster) and *gamberone* (shrimp). Wood-oven-baked thin-crust pizzas start with *salsa alla margherita*—tomato sauce, basil, and cheese—and marinara—with tomato, garlic, and oregano—and go from there to infinity.

Food seems more sensuous amid all this beauty. Sun-dried tomatoes hang in bright red cascades on balconies and shopfronts ("VIAGRA NATURALE" boasts a hand-lettered sign in Amalfi). After spring and autumn rains, peasants still search the ravines for snails, to serve up with hot sauce. Oranges are as big as grapefruits, and lemons (*sfusati*) as big as oranges are cultivated on seemingly endless net-covered pergolas. From linguine with lemon at trattorias to lemon soufflés at fancy restaurants, the yellow citrus is everywhere, and all parts are used, as in *passolini* (raisins or figs baked in lemon leaves, bound by thin red thread). Not only are lemons a main component of meals and drinks, but they are used to remedy everything from flu to bunions.

Ingredients grown in terraced plots include plump olives pressed into oil or eaten fresh, tiny spring *carciofi* (artichokes), and sweet figs. *Sponzino,* or *pomodoro del pendelo,* the tomatoes carried from Egypt long ago by fishermen, grow in the mountains and muddy fields of Furore and Conca dei Marini. Eggplant, asparagus, mushrooms, and eggplant thrive in the Tramonte uplands, while tomatoes come from Campora. Soft *caprese* and *fiore di latte* sheep cheeses are from the high hill pastures of Agerola, while the world's best buffalo mozzarella comes from Paestum. Unusual fruits worth seeking out are carobs, and *ponceri*—citrus the size of a melon, often used in pastries.

Pasta is often served with seafood, but regional dishes include *crespelle al formaggio*—layers of crepes with bechamel cheese sauce, and *scialatielli,* similar to fettucini, sometimes a house specialty, served with varied sauces. Clams and pasta baked in a paper bag—*"al cartoccio"*— is popular in Amalfi. In Positano, try traditional squid with potatoes, stuffed peppers, and slow-simmering ragu (tomato sauce with meat, garlic, and parsley). Around Cetara, salted anchovies, eggplants, and peppers in oil are the base of the famed sauce callled *"garum,"* handed down from the Romans. A lighter version is *colatura di alici,* an anchovy sauce developed by Cistercian monks near Amalfi, served on spaghetti as a traditional Christmas Eve treat. Holidays and celebrations especially inspire the sweet tooth, with *zeppole, mustacciuoli,*and *struffoli* pastries at Christmas and New Year's, and eggy fruit tarts and almond cakes at Easter time. On their saint day, different villages serve different specialties. Residents in Conca dei Marini devour *"Santarosa sfogliatella"*—cakes in the shape of a nun's hood, made from milk, sugar, dried cherries, and dough mixed with San Nicol wine.

Wine here is light, drinkable, and inexpensive, and often consumed only months after crushing; don't be surprised if it's the color of beer, and served from a jug (*"sfuso"*–loose wine). Practically all of it comes from Campania, often from the town or village in which it's poured, perhaps even from the restaurant's own centuries-old vines. Little of it transports well. Furore, Gragnano, and Ravello produce good bottled wines, both rosso and bianco, with Furore's Cuomo perhaps the finest white. In Sorrento look for rosolio, a liqueur traditionally served to Neapolitan nobles, created by the court of the French king Louis XIV. But the most renowned local local digestif is limoncello, capturing in a bottle the color, fragrance, and taste of those tart-sweet lemons. Drink it cold in a tiny, frosty glass or after a shot of hot espresso—a golden memory quenched with each sip.

Although a few restaurants are world renowned, most are family affairs, with pappa out front, the kids serving, and mamma, aunts, and even old *nonna* in the kitchen. Smile a bit, compliment the cuisine, and you're apt to meet them all.

CATEGORY	COST*
$$$$	over 85,000 lire
$$$	60,000–85,000 lire
$$	25,000–60,000 lire
$	under 25,000 lire

per person, excluding drinks and service

Festivals

Holy week tableaux and processions in Sorrento, Christmas trees fashioned from bougainvillea in Positano, crèches under water at the Emerald Grotto, ancient regattas and pageants in Amalfi, music festivals overlooking the gardens and coastline in Ravello—here, festivals and holidays celebrate the sea, the mild nights, and the beauteous, historic surroundings as well. And each town has its own Saint's Day, with huge quantities of special foods and revelry long into the night. Check out individual listings for further information on these celebrations, and other seasonal cultural festivities. And if possible, consider them when booking.

Lodging

The ghosts of a trysting Garbo in Ravello or ailing Caruso in Sorrento haunt the hotel corridors. Because of logistics, major chains are absent for the most part, and, consequently, the lodging scene offers a true sense of place. Sorrento's 18th- and 19th-century cliffside villas and palazzos, with their big gardens and grand staircases, huge baths and tile floors, have been transformed into spacious hotels, as have Amalfi's former convents with their peaceful cloisters. *Agriturismo* (country living) sets up farmhouse stays in rural and upland areas; check with local tourist boards.

Great vistas, and balconies from which to ponder them, are available at most lodgings along these coasts. Air-conditioning, phones, and cable TVs are usual at all but the most basic establishments, and a light breakfast is usually included in the price. Few business or fitness centers are available—who needs them here?—even at luxury establishments. Reserve ahead, as hotel rooms are scarce in high season and may be closed altogether in low. Some hotels offer or require half or even full board and minimum stays in July and August, and around holidays. Inquire when booking.

Most lodgings in this part of Campania have been owned by the same families for generations, and whether the owner is plain mamma-and-pappa or an heir to a ducal line, personality is evident. Along with local management may come quirks, even in the fanciest establishments—floors that dip a bit, faucets off-center, wake-up calls when you're already brushing your teeth. But you just may get your hand kissed or an invitation to chat, or get to know a glossy family dog named Lorenzo, or a cat named Luca, and isn't that sort of thing more memorable in the long run?

CATEGORY	COST*
$$$$	over 350,000 lire
$$$	200,000–350,000 lire
$$	100,000–200,000 lire
$	under 100,000 lire

All prices are for a double room, excluding tax and service.

Shopping
In the 19th century, travelers to Sorrento loved shopping for regional trifles—local crafts, embroideries, ceramics, inlaid wooden furniture (intarsia), music boxes, dolls in tarantella costumes—and, today, these rather kitschy gifts still enchant the hordes of shoppers along Sorrento's Via Cesario. The most esteemed products in the Amalfi Coast area are ceramics from Vietri sul Mare, but some towns also produce local pottery. Amalfi still produces some fine handmade paper, an industry since the Middle Ages. Ravello offers coral jewelry and wines; and Positano is world famous for its handmade, blazingly colorful resort wear. Lemon-based goods of all sorts are available, and foodstuffs include honey, citrus and olive products, and pasta. Bargaining is acceptable sometimes, and as everywhere, prices are best where the locals trade. Shops stay open late, till 9 or so, but close from about 3 to 5.

Vistas
Dolce far niente—literally "the sweetness of doing nothing"—seems the major leisure activity around here, and balustrade bend, belvedere gaze, and bench butt are byproducts of gazing. The Sorrento area and the Amalfi coast are studded with belvederes ("beautiful sights") and rest stops built on the roadside for you to pull off safely, especially important if you're the driver and miss what your passengers are oohing and ahhing about. Sorrento's cliffside bay vistas are wider and more serene than the Amalfi Coast's mountain-meets-sea drama. Positano and Ravello have the most dramatic in-town vistas, although great ones peek out and pop up just about everywhere. The Lattari mountains behind the coast are exceptional for wider panoramas. When booking hotels, ask to be on the water side, throw open the shutters, and, at least once, worship the sun: rising on the Amalfi coast, setting in Sorrento, or doing both on the peninsula.

Walking and Hiking
Throughout this entire region, walking *is* hiking, so be prepared. Positano, where streets usually take the form of staircases, is a resort where you may leave in better condition than when you arrived. These towns are picturesque for a reason, and you've probably never seen so many flights of steps—those bothersome scalinatelli: thousands of them, down to the beaches, up to churches, across the hills. Getting around will take a healthy set of lungs, strong calves, time-outs for rest, comfortable shoes, and a big bottle of Pellegrino water—slow and steady

is the way to go. As for intentional hiking, mule paths and footpaths were the only land-means to get around before the car, and most remain in place for hikers' delight. The Sorrentine peninsula has many downhill paths from hubs such as Sant' Agata sui due Golfi, and you can even hike the highlands from Positano to Ravello. Check out Julian Tippet's excellent walking book, *Landscapes of Sorrento and the Amalfi Coast* (Sunflower Press), often to be found at bookstores and newsstands in the area. Even if you're not in shape, you can still participate: take transportation uphill, and let gravity help get you down.

Exploring Sorrento, the Sorrentine Peninsula, and the Amalfi Coast

From Castellammare di Stabia on the north edge of the Sorrentine peninsula to Vietri at the eastern edge of the Amalfi coast, from the Bay of Naples on the north to the Bay of Salerno on the south, this small ledge of land is a poem of compressed beauty, with two main "verses" and a bridge. Sorrento, on the Bay of Naples, is set solidly on a steep cliff, and neighboring towns slope over the gulf, with deep valleys breaking the terraced watershed behind. The rural, sometimes mountainous peninsula is rimmed by both bays, and two narrow, winding roads, Statale (or State Highways) 145 and 163, feed into the Amalfi Drive at the peninsula's southern edge, which faces the Bay of Salerno, near Positano. If you think a road is just for getting from here to there, the twisty Amalfi Drive is not for you. The natives joke that to journey it from end to end by car in the English manner takes three hours; in the Italian style, a half hour. The going is wild until Amalfi, then tapers off; expect the ride of your life.

Numbers in the text correspond with numbers in the margin and on the Sorrento, Sorrentine Peninsula, Amalfi Coast, and Amalfi maps.

Great Itineraries

The coastal sections—steep, winding, and ultrascenic—can only be traversed by boat or by two-lane roads. When driving round-trip, many choose to go only in one direction on the coastal roads, going the other way via the highway at Salerno or by train from Salerno or by boat from Amalfi or Positano. If a once-over of the region's most fascinating sights is enough, three days will allow you to see Sorrento, Amalfi, and Ravello—the musts. A practical minimum for an overview of the splendors to be found on the Sorrentine peninsula, and in Positano, Paestrum, and smaller villages along the coast, is five days. To take in the entire span from Sorrento to Paestum, you can put together a glorious 10-day trip.

IF YOU HAVE 3 DAYS

If staying in one place is a priority, and you aren't going exploring, start by picking a favorite base. If you want to comb the coasts, it's best to plan at least two overnight destinations. **Sorrento** ①–⑧ should be one hub, especially if you're interested in heading north or to the peninsula. You can get to the Amalfi Coast by private or public transport, and by boat, ferry, and hydrofoil, and also to Naples and environs, and the islands of Capri or Ischia. And the train from Sorrento will deposit you right in front of Pompeii. You'll need a day to enjoy the Sorrento area, plus another leisurely day exploring the Sorrentine peninsula, enjoying the best beaches in the area or a rural hike. For the third day, whizzing past the Sorrentine peninsula, it's a rise-early, full-day excursion along the Amalfi Drive with a drive through **Positano** ⑮, a stop at the Emerald Grotto in **Conca dei Marini** ⑳, and brief stops in **Amalfi** ㉑–㉛, at least for the Duomo, and in **Ravello** ㉝ for the villas and a panoramic view; if you want to linger, you can return from Salerno to

Sorrento at night via the highway and Sorrentine coast. If you prefer more time along the coast rather than the peninsula, or if you want to visit **Paestum** ④⓪, spend one of your nights in Amalfi; in so doing, you'll also be able to enjoy nearby adorable **Atrani** ㉜. If you don't mind staying overnight in three different places, a day each in Sorrento and Amalfi and a third day in Ravello or Positano would maximize this brief regional experience. If you're travelling by water, remember that Sorrento, Positano, and Amalfi have the most frequent connections. And although these itineraries start in Sorrento, you could travel east to west on the coastal roads just as easily—but remember if you want to stay late and return to Sorrento, you don't want to take rural, scenic roads at night.

IF YOU HAVE 5 DAYS

With the three-day itinerary as a base, add the extra two days wherever you feel you want to spend more time relaxing or sightseeing. You might stay two days each in **Sorrento** ①–⑧ or **Amalfi** ㉑–㉛, and spend the fifth either in **Positano** ⑮, with its shops and resort atmosphere, or **Ravello** ㉝, with its gardens, villas, and panoramic views. After reading this chapter, you'll have a better idea.

IF YOU HAVE 10 DAYS

With a 10-day tour, you'll have the luxury of staying on at your favorite places, and still being able to see just about everything of note in the region. After enjoying **Sorrento** ①–⑧ and environs, work your way slowly south across the Sorrentine peninsula, then along the Amalfi coast, with a day trip to **Paestum** ④⓪. You can take the highway or train back from **Salerno** ㊴ to Naples, Rome, or wherever, on the tenth day. A possible itinerary would be three days in Sorrento and environs; one day at a rural town by a beach, such as **Massa Lubrense** ⑬ or **Marina del Cantone** ⑭; one day in **Positano** ⑮; two in **Amalfi** ㉑–㉛; and two in **Ravello** ㉝. Perhaps spend the additional day visiting Paestum, in the agricultural highlands of Agerola, or on a long day at sea exploring coves, islets, and grottoes.

When to Tour Sorrento and the Amalfi Coast

Sheltered by the Lattari mountains arcing east to west across the peninsula and inland from the Amalfi coast, and exposed to cool breezes from two bays, the region of the Sorrentine peninsula and the Amalfi Coast enjoys a climate that is among the mildest in Italy; the temperature rarely falls below 50 degrees Fahrenheit (10 degrees Celsius) in winter, or climbs above 80 degrees Fahrenheit (26 degrees Celsius) in summer. Winter is least crowded but is sometimes overcast, and many hotels close from November to March. Easter time can also be rainy—locals call it *passione de Pascua* ("tears of passion"), and assume it will rain on Good Friday. Although May is sublime, Italian students are on a break and can overrun major sites. Summer is filled with festivities and offers the best weather for sunning and swimming, bringing dense crowds, especially during the last two weeks of August, when Italians vacation, en masse.

SORRENTO AND THE SORRENTINE PENINSULA

Like the familiar song "Come Back to Sorrento," with its long-held closing notes like a mournful cry—listen to the Pavarotti version and you may shed a tear yourself—Sorrento's beauty is tinged with melancholy. Its streets seem like 19th-century sepia photographs, vestiges of the Roman Empire's ruins are strewn about, and banks of votive offerings of hopeful Sorrentines flicker in the crypt of the basilica of St.

Antonino. Vesuvius looms in the distance. And with the sun's heart-stopping descent into the Bay of Naples, the isle of Capri fades into the purple twilight, as if disappearing forever.

But touched with sadness or not, Sorrento is a temptress above all. Around the 6th century BC, the Greeks named it Surrentum—"city of the Sirens." Etruscans and their mysteriously vanished civilization left its traces. Then Oscans and Romans came, and rulers from Goth and Byzantium, followed by sacking Lombards, Saracens, and Amalfitans. Next were the Normans, in the early part of the 12th century, and the beneficent Aragonese. Decimated in 1558 by the Turks, the city later rebuilt its walls, and in the early 1700s began a comeback which peaked in the following century when Sorrento became a prescribed stop for "Grand Tour" travelers, who sopped up its culture and history, along with sun and sea and tomato sauce. Among the literati who played and wrote here were Byron, Keats, Scott, Dickens, Goethe, Wagner, and Ibsen. According to a letter from his traveling companion in 1876, the philosopher Nietzsche, not known for effervescence, "laughed with joy" at the thought of going to Sorrento, and French novelist Stendahl, called it "the most beautiful place on earth."

The tourist industry that began centuries ago is still dominant, although the lords and ladies of bygone days have been replaced with (mainly English) tour groups. Sorrento has become a jumping-off point for visitors to Pompeii, Capri, and Amalfi, but you will probably come to love it for itself. The Sorrentine people are fair-minded and hard-working, bubbling with life and warmth. The tufa cliff on which the town rests is like a great golden pedestal spread over the bay, absorbing the sunlight in deepening shades through the mild days, and orange and lemon trees waft a luscious perfume in spring. In the evening, people fill cafés to nibble, sip, and talk nonstop; then, arms linked, they stroll and browse through the maze of shop-lined lanes. The central piazza is named after the poet Torquato Tasso, born here in 1544. What greater delight than a cozy, burnished town that commemorates a poetic native son—and serves great pasta too? Chances are, you will *torna a Surriento* ("Come back to Sorrento"), as the famous song's lyrics predict. Or, at least, hope to.

The Sorrentine peninsula is bounded on the east by Monte Faito, to the west by Punta della Campanella, to the south by Monti Lattari, and to the north by the Bay of Naples. Filled with forests, vineyards, and groves, its largely rural landscape belies its role as a center of hedonism, starting when Roman emperor Augustus designated Sorrento as a "place of delights," and it has been one ever since. Use the town as a hub and take a day to go north on busy, two-lane Statale 145 to visit some of the prosperous coastal towns, their watchtowers rising from the Piano (plain) di Sorrento, which evolved as trading centers and shipyards under the Angevin viceroys. To reach the more relaxing, rural western and southern sections of the peninsula, follow Statale 145 or 163 for a one- or two-day excursion. Or hire a boat to take you around the coast to some of the isolated beaches, set among ruins and watchtowers reachable only by footpath or boat.

Sorrento

48 km (30 mi) south of Naples; 50 km (31 mi) north of Salerno.

A city of under 20,000, Sorrento's population swells with tourists in season. Winding along a cliff above a small beach and two harbors, the town is split in two by a narrow ravine formed by a former mountain stream. To the east, dozens of hotels line busy Via Correale along the cliff—many

Sorrento

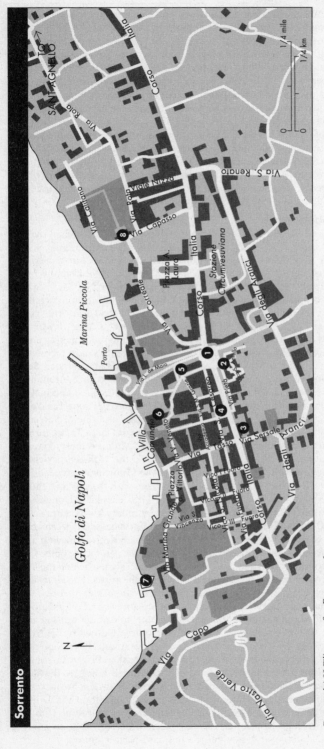

Golfo di Napoli

SAN'AGNELLO

Marina Piccola

Porto

Marina Grande

Capo

Duomo dei SS Filippo
e Giacomo, **3**
Marina Grande, **7**
Museo Correale di
Terranova, **8**
Palazzo Correale, **2**
Piazza Tasso, **1**

San Francesco, **6**
Sant' Antonio, **5**
Sedile Dominova, **4**

N

1/4 mile

1/4 km

"grand" according to their names, and some, indeed still are. Farther east (and usually out of sight of most tourist itineraries) is modern Sorrento, engulfed in a wave of "concretitis." To the west, the old town around the piazzas is relatively flat, with winding, stone-paved lanes bordered by balconied buildings, some joined by medieval stone arches. This part of Sorrento is a delightful place to walk, especially in the mild evenings, when people are out and about, and everything is open. Craftspeople are often at work in their stalls and shops, and are happy to let you watch; in fact, that's the point. Most people arrive at the Stazione Centrale, the end of the line for the Circumvesuviana Railway; a 10-minute walk to the left along Corso Italia will bring you to the Piazza Tasso and the center of the historic quarter. At the station (which also functions as the main bus terminal), note the bust of Ernesto De Curtis, composer of *Torna a Surriento,* that music-box anthem you'll find yourself humming or whistling long after you return home.

A Good Walk

Begin at Sorrento's historic center, **Piazza Tasso** ①, watched over by the statues of the eponymous poet, and the city's patron saint, St. Anthony Abbot. Avoid congested Corso Italia and head instead to the southeast corner of the piazza to Via Pietà to take a look at the noted Palazzo Veniero (No. 14) and the **Palazzo Correale** (No. 24) ②, whose 18th-century majolica courtyard (1768), now a flower shop, overflows with charm. Follow this street until you reach the Largo Arcivescovado, site of the **Duomo dei SS Filippo e Giacomo** ③. After viewing this grand cathedral, head for its wedding-cake campanile, making a right off Corso Italia down Via Giuliani to enter Sorrento's most picturesque quarter. Here, on Via S. Cesareo is the beautifully frescoed **Sedile Dominova** ④, the ancient, open-air site of civic discourse. At night, its little square, called the Largo Dominova, is illuminated and makes a fetching backdrop for diners at Caffé 2000. Return to Piazza Tasso along Via S. Cesareo, lit with 19th-century lanterns and one of Sorrento's prettiest streets. When you arrive at the edge of Piazza Tasso, turn left toward the bay, a block or so along Via De Maio, to pretty Piazza S. Antonino, the site of stately palm trees and the 11th-century church of **Sant' Antonio** ⑤. Across the piazza is the Municipio (town hall), the former monastery of S. Maria delle Grazie, with cloister and church. From there, take Via Santa Maria delle Grazie and Via Donnorso to the Church of **San Francesco** ⑥, and its legendary 14th-century "Paradise" cloister. Relax in the adjoining Villa Comunale gardens and enjoy their Cinerama-wide view of the Bay of Naples. Keep going west along Via Veneto to the Piazza della Vittoria. Here the rear facade of the Hotel Tramontano bears a faded "Casa della Tassa" sign, marking the birthplace of the revered poet. Cross the piazza to the aristocratic Hotel Bellevue Syrene, perhaps to enjoy a drink on the hotel's garden belvedere or a lunch at its Villa Pompeiana, a re-creation of a Pompeiian villa built for Lord Astor. Continue past the hotel to exit the walls near the Porta Greca (Greek gate), and take the stairway down to the fishing port of **Marina Grande** ⑦, where seafood restaurants have good deals. Catch a bus back up to the old town. Once back at Piazza Tasso, walk east along the Via Correale, lined by villas-turned-hotels, to the **Museo Correale di Terranova** ⑧, where its collection of ancient artifacts is set within a pretty garden. End the walk by heading left on Via Califano to the Albergo Lorelei et Londres, a relentlessly picturesque 19th-century pensione, whose terrace café offers a perfect place to enjoy a drink, a nibble, and, hopefully, a postcard-perfect sunset.

TIMING
This complete walk is most enjoyable if you leave sufficient time for discovery and rests; if you wish to include everything, allow at least

half a day. If you're not planning to tour the Museo Correale (which is usually open in the morning and from 5 to 7 PM), you may want to throw a sweater over your shoulders the way the Italians do and start your walk—but call it a promenade—in late afternoon.

Sights to See

Antiche Murae. Not much remains of the ancient stone walls (antiche murae) which once ringed the old city—they were constructed in the Greek era, added to in Roman times, and rebuilt in the 16th century after the Turkish invasion. Originally they contained two access gates leading from the sea, and three from the land, as well as strategically placed towers. The Romans also built over the Greek urban layout of the city, which in some sections is much the same as in ancient times. ⊠ *Under the road at the Porta Parsano Nuova by Piazza Tasso, near the Marina Grande, and in the western end in Via Sopra Le Mura.*

❸ **Duomo dei SS Filippo e Giacomo.** Ancient, but rebuilt from the 15th-century right up to 1924, the town's cathedral follows a Latin cross design, its nave and two side aisles divided by thick piers with round arches. A Renaissance-style door and artworks, including the archbishop's 16th-century marble throne and ceiling paintings attributed to the 18th-century Neapolitan school, are easily viewable. Outstanding 19th- and 20th-century marquetry ornaments a magnificent choir loft, entrance panels, and representations of the stations of the cross. Look for the unusual 10th-century marble slab used as a gravestone, with a lioness on the front and a depiction of the deceased on the back. The delightfully florid three-story campanile, topped by a clock and a belfry, has an open, arcaded base and recycled Roman columns. ⊠ *Largo Arcivescovado, at the corner of Corso Italia and Via. R.R. Giuliani.*

NEED A BREAK?	Espresso and sweet, raisin-stuffed lemon leaves make a fine afternoon delight at **Piemme** (⊠ Corso Italia 161, ☎ 081/807–2927).

❼ **Marina Grande.** Close to the historic quarter, the port, or "borgo," of the Marina Grande is Sorrento's fishing harbor. There is a small beach area, colorful changing cabins, bright umbrellas on *stabilimenti* (breakwaters), and a few good seafood restaurants. It's especially picturesque in early morning, when water-weary fishermen head in, their primary-color boats brimming with the day's catch. Don't confuse this harbor with Marina Piccola, at the base of the cliff, below Piazza Tasso; that is the area where ferries and hydrofoils drop anchor. ⊠ *On the bay, off Via Marina Grande.*

❽ **Museo Correale di Terranova.** Set in a 18th-century villa and lovely garden on land given to the patrician Correale family by Queen Joan of Aragon in 1428, this museum has an excellent private collection amassed by the count of Terranova and his brother. The building itself is fairly charmless, with few period rooms, but the garden offers an allée of palm trees, citrus groves, floral nurseries, and an esplanade with a panoramic view of the Sorrento coast. The collection itself is one of the finest devoted to Neapolitan paintings, decorative arts, and porcelains, so for connoisseurs of the Seicento (Italian 17th century), this museum is a must. Magnificent 18th-century inlaid tables by Giuseppe Gargiulo, Capodimente porcelains, and Rococo portrait miniatures remind us of the age when pleasure and delight was all. Also on view are regional Greek and Roman archaeological finds, medieval marble work, glasswork, old master paintings, 17th-century majolicas—even Tasso's death mask. ⊠ *Via Correale,* ☎ *081/878–1846.* 🎫 *8,000 lire.* ☉ *Wed.–Fri. 3–5, Sat.–Mon. 9:30–12:30.*

★ ❷ **Palazzo Correale.** Just off the southeast corner of Piazza Tasso, this palazzo was originally built in the 14th century in Catalan style but transformed into a Rococo-era showstopper, thanks to its exquisite **Esedra Maiolicata** (Majolica Courtyard, 1772), one of the many examples of majolica and faienceware, an artisanal highlight of Campanian craftsmen (other notable examples are the Chiosto del Clarisse in Naples' Santa Chiara and the grand terrace of Positano's Hotel San Pietro). In 1610 the palazzo became the Ritiro di S. Maria della Pietà and, today, remains private, but all can view the courtyard just beyond the vestryway. Its back wall—a trompe l'oeil architectural fantasia, entirely rendered in majolica tile—is now a suitably romantic setting for the Ruoppo florist shop. Buy a rose here and bear it through the streets of old Sorrento, an emblem of your pleasure in the moment. Leaving the palazzo, note the unusual arched windows on the palace facade, a grace note also seen a few doors away at **Palazzo Veniero** (No. 14), a 13th-century structure with a Byzantine-Arab influence. ✉ *Via Pietà 24.*

❶ **Piazza Tasso.** This was once the site of Porta Catello, the summit of the old walls that once surrounded the city. Today, it remains a symbolic portal to the old town, overflowing with apricot-awninged cafés, *stil Liberty* (Italian Art Nouveau) buildings, the people who are drawn here day and night, and horse-drawn carriages clip-clopping by. In the center of it all is Torquato Tasso himself, standing atop a high base and rendered in marble by sculptor Giovanni Carli in 1870. The great poet was born in Sorrento in 1544, and died in Rome in 1595, just before he was to be crowned Poet Laureate. He is best known for his heroic poem, *Jerusalem Delivered.* At the northern edge of the piazza, where it debouches into Corso Italia, is the Church of Maria del Carmine, with a Rococo wedding-cake facade of gleaming white and yellow stucco. Step inside to note its wall of 18th-century tabernacles, all set, like a jeweler's display, in gilded cases, and the fine ceiling painting of the Virgin Mary. ✉ *Center of the town, along Corso Italia and above the Marina Piccola, at the western edge of the historic district.*

Piazza della Vittoria. Tree-shaded Piazza Vittoria is book-ended by two fabled hotels, the Bellevue Syrene and the Imperial Tramontano, which was home to famed 16th-century writer Torquato Tasso. Set by the bayside balcony, the facade of the **Casa della Tasso** is all the more exquisite for its simplicity and seems little changed from his day. The poet's house originally belonged to the Rossi family, into which Tasso's mother married, and was set with beautiful gardens (not surprisingly, Tasso's most famous set piece—the meeting of Rinaldo and the nymph Arminda—takes place within a sylvan setting). The piazza itself is supposedly the site where a temple to Venus once stood, and the scattered Roman ruins make it a real possibility. ✉ *Via Veneto and Via Marina Grande.*

★ ❻ **San Francesco.** Near the Villa Communale gardens and sharing its vista over the Bay of Naples, this church is celebrated for its "Paradise Cloister," or **Chiostro della Paradiso.** Filled with greenery and flowers, the Arab-inspired 14th-century cloister has interlaced pointed arches of tufa rock, alternating with octagonal columns topped by elegant capitals, supporting smaller arches. The church portal is particularly impressive, with the original 16th-century door featuring intarsiated (inlaid) work. Note the exterior bronzework by sculptor A. Nena. The interior has 17th-century decoration including a wooden cross of St. Francis of Assisi and a 17th-century crucifix. The convent is now an art school, where students' works are often exhibited, while the cloister is the romantic setting for concerts and theatrical presentations during the summer. ✉ *Via S. Maria delle Grazie and Via Donnarso.*

❺ Sant' Antonio. Gracing Piazza di S. Antonino and one of the largest churches in Sorrento, Sant' Antonio honors the city's patron saint, St. Anthony Abbot. The church and the portal on the right side date from the 10th century. Its nave and side aisles are divided by recycled ancient columns, and the interior is done in the Baroque style, with fine paintings, including one on the nave ceiling, painted by Giovan Battista Lama in 1734. Directly opposite across the piazza is the turn-of-the-century *Municipio* (town hall). ✉ *Piazza di Sant' Antonino.*

★ **❹ Sedile Dominova.** Showpiece of the Largo Dominova—the little square that is the heart of the historic quarter—this is a picturesque open loggia with expansive arches, balustrades, and a green-and-yellow-tile cupola, originally constructed in the 15th century. The open-air structure is frescoed with Baroque-era trompe l'oeil columns and the family coats of arms which once belonged to the *sedile* (seat), the town council where nobles met to discuss civic problems as early as the Angevin period, in the 15th century. The sediles resolved regional differences and members were granted privileges by powerful Naples during the days of the Spanish occupation. Today, Sorrentines still like to congregate around the umbrella-topped tables near the tiny square; in the evening, under the still vibrant and now softly illuminated frescoes, men sitting in the forecourt may still be discussing civic problems while playing cards. ✉ *Largo Dominova, at the corner of Via S. Cesareo and Via R. R. Giuliani.*

★ **Villa Comunale.** The finest public gardens in Sorrento, this offers benches, flowers, palms, and people-watching, plus a seamless vista of the Bay of Naples and Vesuvius. ✉ *Adjoining the Church of San Francesco.*

OFF THE
BEATEN PATH

CAPO DI SORRENTO AND THE BAGNO DELLA REGINA GIOVANNA – Just 2 km (1 mi) west of Sorrento, turn right off Statale 145 toward the sea, then park and walk a few minutes through citrus and olive groves to get to Punta del Capo, the craggy tip of the cape, with the most interesting ancient ruins in the area. They were identified by the Latin poet Publio Papinio Stazio as the ancient Roman villa of historian Pollio Felice, patron of the great authors Virgil and Horace. Next to the ruins is Bagno della Regina Giovanna (Queen Joan's Bath). A cleft in the rocks allows the sea to channel through an archway into a clear, natural pool, with the water turning iridescent blue, green, and violet as the sunlight changes angles. The easiest way to see all this is to rent a boat at Sorrento, and later you can go on to the fishermen's haven of Marina di Puolo by sailing westward for lunch at a modest restaurant with fresh catch.

Dining and Lodging

$$$$ ✗ **Ristorante Caruso.** A classic international and operatic theme is carried out from "preludio" appetizers, such as Malossal caviar, to the "rapsodia delicatesse" desserts, including crepes Suzette. Sorrentine favorites are tweaked creatively as well, including ravioli with broccoli sauce, and squid with almonds. The staff is warm and helpful, the singer on the sound system is the long-departed "fourth tenor" himself, and the operatic memorabilia with posters and old photos of Caruso is viewed in a flattering pink-blush light. This elegant restaurant deserves its longtime reputation and popularity. ✉ *Via S. Antonino 12,* ☎ *081/807–3156. AE, DC, MC, V. Closed Mon. Nov.–Easter.*

$$$ ✗ **"La Favorita"—O' Parrucchino.** This restaurant is set in a sprawling, multi-level, high-ceilinged greenhouse and orchard, with tables and chairs amid enough tropical greenery to fill a Victorian conservatory—the effect is enchantingly 19th century in tone. Opened in 1890 by an ex-priest (O' Parrucchiano means "the priest's place" in the local di-

alect), La Favorita continues to serve classic Sorrentine cuisine. Though the white bean soup, cheese baked in lemon leaves, ravioli caprese, lemon tart, and profiteroles are all excellent, they can't compete with the unique decor. ✉ *Corso Italia 71,* ☎ *081/878–1321. AE, DC, MC, V. Closed Wed. Nov.–Easter.*

$$$ ✕ **L'Antica Trattoria.** Is there a more charming restaurant in Sorrento? Built in the 1800s and set behind an iron gate, room after room in this old house is filled with tiled floors, candles, copper, ceramics, antiques, soft music—and lusty Sorrentine standbys. Choose from a tasting menu or gourmet selection featuring a huge choice of antipasti, and seek out the sea bass in salt crust, and fresh-fruit gelati. Some prefer the more informal, flower-spilled terrace; either way, you're in for a sense-of-place experience, set conveniently between the public gardens and the Duomo. ✉ *Via P.R. Giuliani 33,* ☎ *081/807–1082. AE, DC, MC, V. Closed Feb.*

$$$ ✕ **Zi 'ntonio.** The sixth generation of Uncle Tony's family now runs this rustic restaurant serving huge portions of sensational food. Choose antipasti from a spread of more than 25 dishes, and then try specialties including St. Peter's fish with artichokes; lobster and lemon risotto; and savory Parma ham served with mozzarella (*delicioso!*—from the same distributor since the 1950s). Local wines are well priced. Up a chestnut-wood staircase, it's fun to eat aloft in the balcony, but any of the three floors and several rooms is evocative, filled with tiles, flags, murals, plates, and hearty diners. ✉ *Via Luigi de Maio 11,* ☎ *081/878–1623. AE, DC, MC, V. Closed Wed.*

$$–$$$ ✕ **La Lanterna.** On the site of ancient Roman thermal baths (you can still see ruins under a glass section in the floor), this is an historic venue as well as a beloved eatery. Outdoor dining under the lanterns, or indoor under the beamed ceiling and stucco arcades, you'll enjoy *cucina tipica, locale e nazionale,* including old favorites such as scaloppini marsala. ✉ *Via S. Cesareo 23/25,* ☎ *081/878–1355. AE, DC, MC, V. Closed Wed.*

$–$$$ ✕ **Aurora-'O Canonico.** This 100-year-old, award-winning institution in the heart of Sorrento is the place for wood-oven pizza with a choice of 50 toppings, homemade gnocchi, and fresh seafood. The outdoor café, informal trattoria, and more formal ristorante sit side by side, and all are excellent. Try the *"scarzette del Cardinale"* (the Cardinal's hat)—a special pastry here—and choose from a list of over 400 wines. ✉ *Piazza Tasso 7,* ☎ *081/878–3277. AE, DC, MC, V. Closed Mon.*

$$ ✕ **Lanterna Mare.** Either on a terrace overlooking the bay of Naples or indoors in a woodsy atmosphere, enjoy the fish and seafood hauled just a few feet from the Marina Grande docks—usually, the finny specialties are among the freshest around; try some topping a pizza. This is a sibling of in-town La Lanterna, more informal, and in its own way, just as great. ✉ *Via Marina Grande 44,* ☎ *081/807–3033. AE, DC, MC, V. Closed in winter.*

$ ✕ **Delfino.** Right on the sea, you can eat in the sunshine or in a glassed-in nautical-motif dining area. Cod, anchovies and octopus are fresh and flavorful, and this informal, economical venue also has a snack bar for light meals. You can even swim off the pier—but please: a half an hour after eating! ✉ *Marina Grande,* ☎ *081/878–2038. No credit cards.*

$ ✕ **Giardiniello.** The garden is the seating of choice at this big, inexpensive, simply decorated enterprise with a congenial owner out front and mamma in the kitchen, typical of Sorrento trattorias catering to tourists as well as locals. Pizza is best for lunch; if you stick to pastas, however, you won't be disappointed. ✉ *Via Accademia 7,* ☎ *081/878–4616. AE, DC, MC, V.*

$$$$ ☷ **Bellevue Syrene.** In the late 19th century, Empress Eugénie of France
★   came here for a week and wound up staying three months. You'll understand why when you become a guest at this soigné retreat, ideally
placed on a bluff high over the Bay of Naples. Inside, the hotel is a
gentle fantasia of Venetian chandeliers, Louis-Phillipe rugs, and Belle
Epoque murals, with guest rooms that are sanctums of cozy calm. If
your room doesn't have a bayside balcony, drink in the views from the
grand terrace of the hotel's Villa Pompeiana restaurant (originally
built in 1905 as part of Lord Astor's villa). No less an authority than
Hermann Schliemann, discovery of Troy, who stayed here in 1868, declared the hotel's vistas of Vesuvius the grandest in the land. A bathing
pier and beach is directly below the hotel. ⊠ *Piazza della Vittoria 5,
80067,* ☎ *081/878–1024,* ℻ *081/878–3963. 59 rooms with bath. 2
restaurants, bar, air-conditioning, beach, dock, meeting rooms, parking. AE, DC, MC, V.*

$$$$ ☷ **Excelsior Vittoria.** Overlooking the Bay of Naples, this Belle Epoque
★   dream offers gilded salons worthy of a Proust heroine, gardens and
orange groves, and an impossibly romantic terrace where musicians
lull guests with equal doses of Cole Porter and Puccini. The complex
of two mansions and two 19th-century chalets has been run by the same
family for centuries, who traded witticisms with Alexandre Dumas and
Oscar Wilde, welcomed crowned heads, and comforted a dying Caruso,
here in his final days. The public salons are virtual museums with potted palms, Victorian loveseats, and Stil Liberty ornaments. Guest
rooms are usually spacious and airy, with tile floors, minimal furnishings, and balconies and terraces over bay or gardens. If you—like
Princess Margaret, Luciano Pavarotti, and Sophia Loren—want the full
treatment, opt for the historic suites. Dine in the open-air seaside
restaurant or grand dining hall where waiters in starched white jackets don't look a bit foolish (though critics keep hoping the standards
of the kitchen will improve). When you walk out of the extensive
park, which shelters a giant pool, you are in the heart of Sorrento. ⊠
Piazza Tasso 34, 80067, ☎ *081/807–1044, 800/325–8451,* ℻ *081/
877–1206. 106 rooms with bath. 2 restaurants, bar, air-conditioning,
pool, meeting facilities, parking. AE, DC, MC, V. Closed Mar.*

$$$$ ☷ **L'Imperial Hotel Tramontano di Sorrento.** What a past. Emperor Augustus' son had his villa here, millennia before this hotel was built in
the 18th century, near the public gardens. Italian poet Torquato Tasso
was born on the site, and it still has a private 15th-century chapel from
that era. In its glory days the property hosted Shelley, Byron, and
Goethe, and royalty of many lands; today it sees mostly tour groups.
The dining room overlooks the water, the pool nestles in a lush garden, and the sight of Vesuvius remains as it was in ancient times.
Rooms are large, with antiques and small balconies. The high-tech elevator gives audio instructions like the ones in department stores, and
the lobby, with atrium ceiling, is a bit tacky and too pink. But how
can you not fall for a place upon whose terrace *Torna a Surriento* was
both written and sung for the first time? ⊠ *Via V. Veneto 1, 80067,*
☎ *081/878–2588, 081/878–1940,* ℻ *081/807–2344. 115 rooms with
bath. 2 restaurants, bar, café, air-conditioning, pool, beach access,
parking. AE, DC, V. Closed Nov.–Mar.*

$$$ ☷ **Ambasciatori.** This salmon-color stucco hotel on a cliff over the sea
is gracious inside, with marble floors, antiques, period wall sconces,
Oriental rugs, large windows—and a black cat. Rooms have bold mo-
saic tile floors and standard furnishings, but many open onto balconies
or terraces with sea views. Gardens surround the pool and a spacious
terrace-on-the-sea beckons guests to lounge, or enjoy the occasional
dances and buffet dinners organized by the Manniello family, longtime
hotel owners. ⊠ *Via A. Califano 18, 80067,* ☎ *081/878–2025,* ℻ *081/*

807–1021. *104 rooms with bath. Restaurant, bar, 2 snack bars, air-conditioning, pool, 2 tennis courts, beach, dock, meeting facilities. AE, DC, MC, V.*

$$$ ⌑ **Europa Palace.** Broad terraces overlook the Gulf of Naples and a elevator floats guests to a dock for sunning and "helio-therapeutic" bathing. High ceilings, marble floors, a grand piano, and dozens of identical pink Venetian glass chandeliers and sconces make for idiosyncratic decor. Rooms lack spark, but do have romantic views from balcony or terrace. Spacious baths have old-fashioned fixtures, and, like many villa reconversions, could use some updating. ⊠ *Via Correale 34/36, 80067,* ☎ *081/878–1501,* ℻ *081/878–1855. 80 rooms with bath. 2 restaurants, bar, dock, meeting facilities, parking. AE, DC, MC, V.*

$$$ ⌑ **Royal.** Lush, landscaped gardens surround this hotel, which features a pool with sun lounges practically leaning over the bay. An elevator descends to sea level and a private beach. Inside the hotel it's quiet and cool with a spacious lobby, lounge, and indoor or alfresco dining. Ask for a quiet room with a balcony and superb view of the pool, gardens, and bay. ⊠ *Via Correale 42, 80067,* ☎ *081/807–3434,* ℻ *081/877–2905. 96 rooms with bath. 2 restaurants, 3 bars, air-conditioning, pool, beach, meeting facilities, parking. AE, DC, MC, V. Closed Nov.–Mar.*

$$ ⌑ **Villa di Sorrento.** The best and the worst thing about this self-proclaimed "homely environment," built in 1854, is its central location—an easy walk to most attractions, but right off a noisy street, so request a room overlooking the quiet rear garden. Tile-floored rooms are meticulously clean, with Danish-modern furnishings. The lobby has wood trim, old photos, and old-fashioned touches such as embroidered antimaccars, on its many, many chairs. Rooms have either balconies or terraces, with views of the azure sea and red-clay rooftops. ⊠ *Piazza Tasso, 80067,* ☎ *081/878–1068, 081/878–5767,* ℻ *081/807–8679. 21 rooms with bath. Bar, dining room, parking. AE, DC, MC, V.*

$–$$ ⌑ **Astoria.** You may wake to pealing church bells at this clean, inexpensive little hotel on a quiet side street in the heart of the old town. The unstylish terrazzo-tile, wood-trim lobby is filled with chairs, old photos, and potted palms, and looks as if it hasn't been redecorated for decades. Rooms are basic, with art nouveau touches, and you can breakfast on the terrace. Most of your fellow guests will be Brits. ⊠ *Via S. Maria delle Grazie 24, 80067,* ☎ *081/807–6030. 37 rooms with bath. AE, DC, MC, V. Closed Dec.–Feb.*

$–$$ ⌑ **Del Corso.** This centrally located, colorful pensione is clean and basic, but with baths for all, and quirky touches such as psychedelic-patterned tablecloths and bedspreads. Fresh flowers, an occasional antique, the wooden bar in the lounge, courtyard entrances for some rooms, and rooftop dining nudge up the comfort zone. Lodgings are on the second floor (an elevator is provided from the street). Front-facing rooms are noisy and only some rooms have air-conditioning. ⊠ *Corso Italia 134, 80067,* ☎ *081/807–1016,* ℻ *081/807–3157. 19 rooms with bath. Restaurant, bar, air-conditioning. AE, DC, MC, V. Closed Nov.–Feb.*

$–$$ ⌑ **Lorelei et Londres.** Dream: sunlight on lemon trees, blazing bougainvil-
★ lea, a tiny, inexpensive inn with all the warm charm of the 19th century, suspended over the Bay of Naples. Reality: the Lorelei et Londres. This amazing relic was once favored by *Room-with-a-View* ladies from England and still looks like E.M. Forster's Miss Lavish might pull up at any moment. Out front is a magnificently beautiful terrace café, aflutter with red awnings and tablecloths. The welcoming lobby always seems to be filled with guests' laughter, so it seems that few guests mind that the rooms upstairs are tatterdemalion, with simple beds, creaking cupboards, and linoleum floors. For luxe and modernity, go elsewhere; come here to take a trip back to the 19th century. Room rates

include breakfast and dinner. ✉ *Via Califano 2, 80067,* ☎ FAX *081/ 807–3187. 23 rooms, 12 with bath. MC, V. Closed Dec.–Feb.*

CAMPING

If you wish to enjoy the great outdoors both day and night, consider **Santa Fortunata** (near Capo di Sorrento) (☎ 089/807–3579).

Nightlife and the Arts

At night, most weary sightseers will content themselves with dinner, then an evening passeggiata through the old quarter, topped off by coffee and dessert at a café. For a particularly festive *notte,* head to the Largo Dominova on Via S. Cesareo—floodlit with the 17th-century Sedile Dominova—and an inexpensive meal or nightcap at the **Caffé 2000,** with serenading musicians crooning Neapolitan favorites. Music spots and bars cluster in the side streets near Piazza Tasso, among them Tiffany, Filov and Trudy. Ask at your hotel about clubs that might interest you and to get the latest news. The main watering hole for Sorrento visitors is the **Circolo dei Forestieri** (✉ Via Luigi de Maio 35, ☎ 081/807–4033; closed early December–late February), traditionally packed with Americans, Brits, and Australians. Crowds begin to descend on this large villa (also home to the Sorrento tourist office) for an aperitif or beer at sunset, others arrive for casual dinner, while merrymakers hold out for the late-night band and karaoke.

The Tarantella Show (✉ Fauno Notte Club and La Mela Club, ☎ 081/ 878–1021, 081/878–4463) presents tarantella dances with masks, costumes, and tamborines, plus 17th-century mandolin serenades and 16th-century Neapolitan *pulcinella* (pantomime); a *passariello* (jester) is on hand.

Festas (religious festivals) include processionals through the evening on Good Friday, Christmas crèches, and celebrations on February 14—not St. Valentine's day, but St. Antony's day; he's the patron saint of Sorrento.

Estate Musicale Sorrentina (✉ cloister of the Chiesa di San Francesco) is the main cultural event of the year, offering a bevy of concerts and theatrical entertainments from the first week of July to the first week of September. Tickets usually run around 15,000 lire; check with your hotel or the Sorrento tourist office for schedules and information. Throughout the year, free municipal concerts—usually jazz or classical music—are held in several other venues. Just a three-minute bus ride away in the adjacent township of Sant'Agnello, the **Concerti di Cocumella** hosts weekend chamber-music concerts between May and September at the gorgeous 17th-century Church of Santa Maria, now part of the luxurious Hotel Cocumella (✉ Via Cocumella 7, Sant'Agnello, ☎ 081/878–2933).

Outdoor Activities and Sports

Sercomar (✉ Largo Fontana 64 in Marina Grande, ☎ 081/837–8781) is the main outfit for snorkeling, scuba diving, and inflatable motor boat rentals; 90,000 lire per dive, boat rentals from 60,000 lire per hour.

Shopping

The main shopping street is Via S. Cesario—along this pedestrian thoroughfare, lined with dozens of shops selling local and Italian crafts, the air is pungent with the perfume of fruit and vegetable stands. Corso Italia has more modern boutique offerings. Wood inlay (intarsia) is the most sought-after item, but you'll be surprised by the high quality of embroidery and metalwork. Keep your eye out for stalls that feature tiny crèche figures—tiny Punchinellos, hunchback dwarfs, and Magi figures.

Apreda (✉ Via Tasso 6, ☎ 081/878–1748) produces delicious cheeses. **A. Stinga** (✉ Piazza F.S. Gargiulo 11, ☎ 081/878–4286) is a branch of the famed family business known for marquetry and inlaid wood. Goods range from trays to furniture. **Bottega d'Arte** (✉ Via Luigi de Maio, ☎ 081/878–1162) offers a top selection of old glass, tiles, and jewelry—antique and new. **Di Maio** (✉ Via degli Archi 16, ☎ 081/878–1748) is the most celebrated name in town for inlaid wood furnishings. The store is famous for its trays, boxes, and furniture adorned with designs inspired by ancient Sorrento mosaic work. **L'Artigianato** (✉ Via S. Cesareo 45, ☎ 081/877–1583) sells attractive handicrafts in wood, ceramic, wrought iron, and other natural materials. **Laboratorio Rosbenia** (✉ Piazza Lauro 34, ☎ 081/877–2341) is renowned for traditional hand-embroidered linen and lace. **La Bottega del Gioiello** (✉ Corso Italia 179, ☎ 081/878–5419) employs master goldsmiths producing jewelry, including cameos and coral. **Limonoro** (✉ Via S. Cesareo 51, ☎ 081/807–2782) produces the lovely local lemon liqueur, limoncello. You can observe the production process in the back of this tiny white shop, and watch the owners paint designs on the pretty bottles. **Luigi Coppola** (✉ Vicolo 3 Rota 13, ☎ 081/878–4217) sits on an old stool using family tools to craft copperworks of distinctive charm. **Olga** (✉ Via Cesareo 18 on the Decumano Maggiore) sells handmade embroidered articles for children. **Stinga Tarsia** (✉ Via L. DeMaio 16, ☎ 081/878–1165) has been crafting and selling fine quality marquetry and inlaid wood, coral, and cameos since 1890.

THE SORRENTINE PENINSULA: SANT'AGNELLO TO MARINA DEL CANTONE

Grand monasteries, the finest beach along the Gulf of Positano, an Edenic botanical park, and southern Italy's finest restaurant are just a few of the discoveries that await the traveler willing to leave Sorrento's Belle Epoque splendor behind and take to the scenic-rich hills and coasts of the Sorrentine peninsula. As it turns out, many people do just that— the towns here get crowded with weekenders from Naples and Rome, and the two-lane state roads 145 and 163 are often congested. The sights here, however, are worth the bother. If you don't have a car, both blue-color SITA line and municipal orange-color buses run regularly throughout the peninsula, most routes stopping in Sorrento itself. Bus stops are frequent along the peninsula roads and you'll rarely wait more than an hour, no matter how distant the stop seems. The destinations here are mapped out in two directions: North of Sorrento, the route leads to Sant'Agnello di Sorrento, Meta, and Castellammare di Stabia; South of Sorrento, the road heads through Sant'Agata sue Due Golfi, Massa Lubrense, Punta Campanella, and Marina di Cantone.

Sant'Agnello

❾ *2 km (1 mi) south of Meta; 2 km (1 mi) north of Sorrento.*

Back in the 18th and 19th century, the tiny hamlet of Sant' Agnello was an address of choice. To escape Sorrento's crowds, Bourbon princes and exiled Russian millionaires vacationed here, some building sumptuous villas, others staying at the Hotel Cocumella, the oldest hotel on the Sorrentine peninsula. Today, some modern motels blemish its main street, but Sant'Agnello still possesses a faintly ducal air. The 15th- to 16th-century parish church, Chiesa Parrocchiale di Sant'Agnello, is as lyrical as its name: swirls of lemon-yellow and white, decorated with marble-gloss plasterwork. Nearby is a spectac-

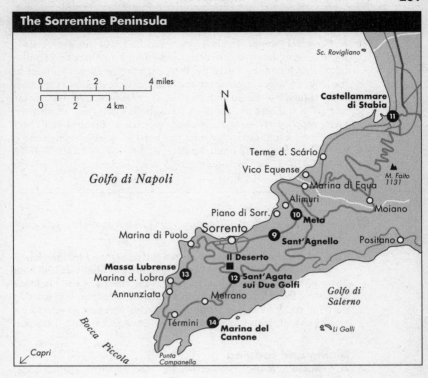

ular belvedere, the Terrazza Punta San Francesco, complete with café, which offers a hold-your-breath view of the Bay of Naples. Sant'Agnello's two most famous estates sit side by side. In the early 19th century, the Cocumella monastery was transformed into a hotel, welcoming the rich and famous. Today, only lucky guests can enjoy its gardens, but everyone can attend the chamber music concerts presented by the hotel in its 16th-century Church of Santa Maria (☞ Nightlife and the Arts *in* Sorrento, *above*). Next door is the **Parco dei Principi,** a botanical park originally laid out in 1792 by the Count of Syracusa, a cousin to the Bourbons. Traversed by a diminutive Bridge of Love, this was a favorite spot for Désireé, Napoleon's first amour, who came here often. Shaded by horticultural rarities, this park leads to the count's Villa di Poggio Siracusa, a Rococo iced-birthday cake of a house perched over the bay. Green-thumbers and other circumspect visitors can stroll through the park, now part of the Hotel Parco dei Principi.

Dining and Lodging

$$$$ ✕⊡ **Cocumella.** Cognoscenti adore this hotel, one of the most aristo-
★ cratic in Italy. With a guest list littered with names like Goethe and the Duke of Wellington, set in a cliff-top garden overlooking the Bay of Naples, the Cocumella occupies a Baroque monastery, complete with frescoed ceilings, antique reliquaries, and a marble cloister. The lobby is Italian Victorian, and 19th-century grace notes continue in grand suites offering stone fireplaces, Empire bureaux, and marble-clad bathrooms, but even smaller rooms have great charm. The del Papa family have gilded this lily with a vast pool, a beauty-farm and exercise room, one of the most cornucopic breakfasts around, the superb Scintilla restaurant, a 90-ft-long 19th-century yacht for daily excursions on the bay, and even present summer-night chamber-music recitals in the monastery's former church. Ah, the sweet life! ⊠ *Via Cocumella 7, 84067,* ☎ *081/ 878–2933,* ⅢⅩ *081/878–3712. 55 rooms with bath. Restaurant, pool,*

beauty salon, sauna, tennis court, exercise room, private beach, boating. AE, DC, MC, V.

$$$$ ▦ **Parco dei Principi.** The hotel itself may be 1960s-modern—a striking white-on-blue structure designed by noted architect Gio Ponti—but it's set within the Parco dei Principi, a fabled garden laid out by the Duke of Siracusa, cousin to the Neapolitan Bourbons, in the early 19th century. Paths lined with rare Wellingtonia palm trees and African marigolds still lead to the duke's romantic Rococo villa, set on a terrace over the bay—today, a splendiferous setting for the hotel's pool area. Long a tour-group favorite, this hotel is usually jammed and is particularly festive as a result. ⊠ *Via Rota 1 80067,* ☎ *081/878–4644,* ℻ *081/878–3786. 96 rooms with bath. Restaurant, pool, private beach. AE, DC, MC, V.*

Meta

⑩ *4 km (2½ mi) north of Sorrento; 15 km (10 mi) southwest of Castellammare di Stabia.*

Set on a steep slope hovering above the gulf on Statale 145, this charming town is lined with orange trees and its ancient buildings spill right down to the sea. Off the coastal road is the church of the Madonna del Lauro, thought to be the site of an ancient temple built to worship the goddess Minerva. Outstanding are its 16th-century wooden door, and its chapel, with frescoes and wood carvings from the 18th century.

Dining and Lodging

$$ ✕▦ **Giosue' a Mare.** Locals crowd this modern albergo (small hotel) and ristorante on the bay, and for good reason: it's the best food around these parts. Fish and seafood are pristine (try the cold combo), but you can have popular standbys such as veal marsala, too. If you care to stay on, compact rooms have balconies overlooking the water, tile floors, showers, and crisp blue-and-white decor. ⊠ *Via Caruso 2, 80062,* ☎ *081/878–6685,* ℻ *081/532–3450. 23 rooms with bath. Restaurant, air-conditioning, private beach, parking. AE, MC, V.*

Castellammare di Stabia

⑪ *23 km (14½ mi) south of Naples; 19 km (12 mi) north of Sorrento.*

Mineral springs placed this town on the map in ancient times, and sulphide, chloride, radioactive, and carbonated waters are just a few of the scary-sounding but allegedly healthy waters you can still enjoy at **Antiche Terme Stabiane** (⊠ Via Amendola, ☎ 081/871–4422), which also promotes therapeutic mud treatments. The town was built on the ruins of ancient Stabia, then buried by Vesuvius along with Pompeii and Herculaneum, in AD 79. In fact, Pliny the Elder—the eruption's most famous victim—had his villa here and was killed by the shore. Unlike Pompeii, Stabia was rebuilt almost immediately because of its magnificent setting as a country residence for the wealthy. In the **Antiquarium Stabiano** (⊠ Via Marco Mario, ☎ 081/870–7228, ⊙ Tues.–Sun. 9–6, closed Mon.), 11 rooms are filled with fragments of pre-Roman graves going as far back as 10th century BC, sarcophagi, and other artifacts of the Stabia culture, excavated in the 18th century. Ancient Roman villas, **San Marco and di Varano** (⊠ Passeggiata Archeologica [Varano], ☎ 081/871–4541, ▱ free, ⊙ 9–one hr before sunset) are two of some 30 that once adorned the hills here and, along with the thermal-bath ruins, are all worth visiting. Postwar urban development has been somewhat unkind to Castellammare, now best known for its shipyards, pasta factories, and canning industry. In the center of town, however, are the Villa Communale gardens, with grand vistas of the bay and the Arsenale, where many of Italy's most famous ships have been built, and to one side of the gardens is a complex of historic buildings, including the town hall, observatory, and the Renaissance cathedral.

OFF THE
BEATEN PATH

MONTE FAITO – For quick relief from a surfeit of Mediterranean heat at sea level, take the *funivia* (cable car) run by the local railway departing from the main Castellammare di Stabia Circumvesuviana station roughly every 20 minutes up to the top of Monte Faito, the northwesternmost mountain in the Lattari range (one of whose slopes is now defaced by an enormous steel TV-antenna tower). In only eight minutes, you will be whisked up more than 3,000 ft with some nerve-tingling vistas over the Bay of Naples. Once at the upper station (by a *piazzetta*—refreshments available—continue walking upward on Trail 36 mapped out with distinctive red and white markers by CAI, the Italian Alpine Club, which will take you into heart of the beech woods. Keep in mind that hot and humid weather can make the stratospheric vista over the bay hazy. Climb even higher along the mountain ridge to the left, and southeast past the upper cable car station, to reach the Porta dei Falto; if you're up to it (and because it's there) you can hike several hours to the summit of Monte Sant' Angelo ai Tre Pizzi, about 4,720 ft, for the best view. ⊠ *Monte Faito cable car, Stazione Circumvesuviana, Castellammare di Stabia,* ☎ *081/879–3097.* 🎫 *8,000 lire one-way, 12,000 lire round-trip.* ☉ *Apr.–Oct., with extended summer timetable.*

Sant'Agata sui Due Golfi

🔟 *7 km (4½ mi) south of Sorrento; 10 km (6 mi) east of Positano.*

Because of its spectacular vistas, Sant'Agata was an end-of-the-line pilgrimage site for beauty-lovers through the centuries, especially before the Amalfi Drive opened up the coast to the southeast. As its name suggests, this village 1,300 ft above sea level looks out over both the bays of Naples and Salerno (Sant'Agata refers to a Sicilian saint, honored here with a 16th-century chapel). The most famous point in town is, however, on the far north side of the hill, where an ancient Greek sanctuary was once dedicated to the Sirens of fable and legend. That choice

★ location became **Il Deserto,** a monastery built by the Carmel fathers in the Middle Ages. Now crumbling, its famed belvedere—with panoramic views of the blue waters all around, and of Vesuvius, Capri, and the peninsula—was a top sight for Grand Tour–era travelers. To gain entry, ring the buzzer at the gate for the attendant, who will supply you with a key to the belvedere tower (the monastery often closes for religious retreats, so you must call ahead to check that it is open). To get to the Deserto from the center of Sant'Agata, with your back to the hotel, take the road to the left of the Hotel delle Palme, pass the church of Santa Maria della Grazie, and keep walking uphill on Via Deserto. ⊠ *Via Deserto.* 🎫 *Free, but donation requested.* ☉ *Oct.–Mar. daily 8:30–12:30, 2–6:30; Apr.–Sept. daily 4–8.*

Today's travelers head to Sant'Agata less for the sublime beauties of Il Deserto than for its lodging options and to dine at Don Alfonso 1890, the finest restaurant in Campania (☞ *below*). Just across the way from Don Alfonso on the town square is the beautiful 16th-century Renaissance church of **Santa Maria delle Grazie.** The shadowy, evocative interior features an exceptional 17th-century altar brought from the Girolamini church in Naples in the 19th century. Attributed to Florentine artists, it is inlaid with lapis, malachite, mother-of-pearl, and colored marble.

Dining and Lodging

$$$$ ✕⊞ **Don Alfonso 1890.** The greatest restaurant in Campania, this is the
★   domain of Alfonso Iaccarino, who counts Prince Rainier of Monaco as
one of his many fans. *Haute*-hungry pilgrims head here to feast on culinary rarities, often centuries-old recipes given a nouvelle spin. Lobster,
for instance, is breaded with traditional Sorrentine "porri" flour, but then
is drizzled with sweet-and-sour sauce influenced by the Arabian traders
who came to Naples. The braciola of lamb with pine nuts and raisins is
a recipe that dates back to the Renaissance period, while the cannoli stuffed
with foie gras pays homage to the Neapolitan Bourbon court. Nearly
everything is home-grown, with olive oils *"de nostra produzione"* created on the family farm, vegetables so lovingly grown they have "bodyguards" not farmers, and even hand-churned butter, which finds its way
into sublime desserts such as the *pizzo di cioccolato* (white sugar "mozzarella" on a chocolate "pizza") or the *soufflé di Nirvana*. Don Alfonso
has one of the finest wine cellars in Europe, set deep in an Oscan cave—
don't be surprised if the sommelier tells you his earliest bottle is a Roman
amphora dating from 30 BC. For those who want to make a late night
of it, Alfonso and his enchanting wife, Livia, also run an inn above the
restaurant, with three apartments furnished in traditional style. ⊠ *Piazza Sant'Agata 11, 80064,* ☎ FAX *081/878–0026. 3 apartments with bath.
Parking. AE, DC, MC, V. Closed Mon., Tues. Oct. 1–May 31; Mon. June
1–Sept. 31; for vacation Jan. 10–Feb. 25.*

$$ ⊞ **Sant'Agata.** If you wish to stay in this charming rural town, this
comfortable hotel provides clean and pleasant lodging and a good bed
to fall into after a meal at Don Alfonso 1890 or a walk to the Il De-
serto belvedere. ⊠ *Via dei Campi 8/A, 80064,* ☎ *081/808–0363,* FAX
*081/808–0800. 28 rooms with bath. Air-conditioning, parking. AE,
MC, V. Closed Nov.–Easter.*

OFF THE   **MARINA DI CRAPOLLA** – Hiking from the ridge of Sant' Agata offers
BEATEN PATH   dozens of sojourns past ruins and through groves on ages-old mule
tracks and military paths. Below the hilltop town, Sorrento beckons: For
a day's excursion, a SITA bus can drop you in the center of town, or you
can opt for a two-hour walk from Sant' Agata through peaceful orchards
and vineyards to the big city. A 3½ hour hike south of Sant'Agata will
reward you with the gift of an isolated beach and the Roman ruins near
Marina di Crapolla. St. Peter, it is said, stopped at this fishing cove on
his way to Rome (you can arrange ahead in Sorrento for a reliable boat
to take you back to town). A little chapel overlooking the bay is topped
with a pedestal bell tower, its stonework having been retrieved from a
Roman abbey. The name Crapolla derives from the Greek "Akron
Apollinus"; it is believed a temple to Apollo once rose on these grounds.

Massa Lubrense

➓   *6 km (4 mi) southwest of Sorrento; 7 km (4½ mi) north of Punta Cam-
panella.*

At the far western tip of the peninsula, off Statale 145, the township
of Massa Lubrense—settled in the 10th century and now with a pop-
ulation of about 12,000—sprawls its way through farming and fish-
ing hamlets. Its name derives from the early–Middle Ages *massa* (rural
dwellings) and the Latin *delubrum* (a temple, probably dedicated to
Minerva). Faithful to the Anjou, it was made a duchy, and later de-
stroyed in 1451 by Ferrante of Aragon. When the Jesuits founded a
college here in the 17th century, the town grew into a cultural center.
Today, Massa Lubrense is a relaxation destination, close to, but so far
from, Sorrento's bustle.

Landmarking the central village, the cathedral of **Santa Maria delle Grazie,** located on the central square, Largo del Vecovado, was renovated in the late 18th century, and features a majolica pavement; in the apse is a painting of the Madonna by Andrea da Salerno. The 16th-century **Sanctuary of Santa Maria della Lobra,** on Via Marina, in the fishing village of Marina della Lobra, is on a site where pagans once worshipped. The church organ is supported by two ancient columns, perhaps from the original temple. Note also the majolica floor, the coffered ceiling, and the 18th-century wooden crucifix. The adjacent cloister was constructed in the 17th century when the complex was a Franciscan convent.

Dining and Lodging

$$-$$$ ✕ **Antico Francischiello da Peppino.** Overlooking olive groves seeming to run into the sea, this fourth-generation establishment has been welcoming hungry travelers for over 100 years. Two huge, beamed rooms with sprays of fernery, antique mirrored sideboards, hundreds of mounted plates, brick archways, old chandeliers, fresh flowers, and tangerine-hued tablecloths is quite a sight. *Farfale al salmone* (bow-tie pasta with salmon), ravioli with clams and spinach, cannelloni Sorrentini, and other bountiful country cuisine is *tutto bene.* ⊠ *Via Partenope 27, halfway between Sorrento and Massa Lubrense,* ☎ 081/807–1813. AE, DC, MC, V. Closed Wed.

$$ 🏨 **Villa Pina.** This comfortable country inn across the road from the restaurant is managed by the same family who preside over the Antico Franscischiello restaurant. Stick to the newer rooms with long decks and tile floors, and content yourself with serene views of the bay of Naples and Capri from the balconies. ⊠ *Via Partenope 40, Massa Lubrense 80061,* ☎ *081/533–9780,* 🖷 *081/807–1813. 25 rooms with bath. Air-conditioning. AE, DC, MC, V.*

Punta Campanella

7 km (4½ mi) south of Massa Lubrense; 6 km (4 mi) southwest of Marina di Cantone.

The big bell which tolled to warn the approach of pirates gave the southwesternmost tip of the Sorrentine peninsula its name. Past Termini, you'll find a lighthouse and the half-buried ruins of a Roman villa—the area was a favorite resort of the Roman imperial court.

Marina del Cantone

⓮ *5 km (3 mi) southwest of S. Agata sui due Golfi; 5 km (3 mi) southeast of Massa Lubrense.*

The largest beach on the Sorrentine peninsula attracts weekend sun-worshippers and foodies determined on great country dining at the seaside restaurants here. To get to the beach, usually dotted with dozens of festive umbrellas, a slender road winds down to the sea through through the rolling vineyards, until ending on the shore of the Gulf of Positano, near the Montaldo watchtower. To escape the jam, hire a boat to visit the islets of Li Galli—Gallo Lungo, Castelluccia, and La Rotonda—which sit on the horizon to the south of the beach. They are also called Isole Sirenuse (Isles of the Sirens), after the mythical girl-group who lured unwitting sailors onto the rocks. What goes around comes around: legend says the sirens' feet became flippers, because the Three Graces were envious of how they danced the tarantella; and, as the folkloric tale concludes, the mermaids' dancing days were really *finito* when they petrified into the isles themselves.

Dining and Lodging

$$$$ ✕ **Taverna del Capitano.** The fascinating cuisine here is based on old recipes from the various cultures—Norman, Moorish, among them—that loomed large in the history of the region. The captain and his family help cook up not-available-anywhere-else combinations: for example, chicory and prawn soup, and tagliatelle with anchovies, sardines, and fennel. For dessert, opt for the eggplant and chocolate—once an ancient Arab recipe. ⊠ *Piazza delle Sirene 10,* ☎ *081/898–1028. AE, MC, V. Closed Mon., except in summer, and Jan.–Feb.*

$$$ ✕ **Maria Grazia.** A great story lies behind this area favorite. Signora Maria was running this little waterfront trattoria between the world wars when an aristocrat came round unexpectedly to eat with the marina fishermen; she cooked up the best she had on hand—spaghetti with stuffed zucchini blossoms. Through him, the dish and the restaurant became famous. You can still enjoy it, even without a noble title, in season. ⊠ *Spiaggia di Marina,* ☎ *081/808–1011. No credit cards. Closed Wed., except in summer; except for weekends from Jan., closed Nov.–Apr.*

$–$$ ✕ **Lo Scoglio.** Dramatically set on a pier by the beach, you can hear, smell—even *taste*—the waves from here on a rough day. The cuisine, not unexpectedly, is fresh-caught seafood, but even if you only stop by for a gelato at this informal ristorante, you'll enjoy yourself immensely (especially if you're a water baby, or are accompanied by one). ⊠ *Marina del Cantone, on the pier,* ☎ *081/898–1026. AE. MC, V.*

$$$–$$$$ ✕🏨 **Quattro Passi.** "A hop, skip, and a jump" is how the name of this hotel and Italian-nouvelle restaurant translates colloquially—appropriately so, since it is located just a five-minute drive above Marina del Cantone, in the groves of the peninsula hillsides. Here, the focus is on relaxation and fine food but the comfortable environs also make it a pleasure to fall into bed. The staff can even pick up and deliver diners to and from some Positano hotels. One of the young chefs is Japanese, and his delicate touch is evident in the dollop of ham and cheese Napoléon, or a petit shrimp potpie. Dine indoors in modern white decor, on the big terrace in a lemon grove, or have a homemade limoncello in the brick-arched cantina, stocked from fine vineyards north of Salerno. Guest rooms are simple, and casually elegant, with tile floors, quilts, antiques, and some two-person whirlpool tubs. This is one of the few places with absolutely no sea view, but to make up for it, you can help harvest olives in October. This place is in Nerano, midway between Termini and Marina di Cantone. ⊠ *Via A. Vespucci 13, Nerano, 80061,* ☎ 𝙁𝘼𝙓 *081/808–1271. 10 rooms with bath. Restaurant, bar, air-conditioning, parking. AE, MC, V. Closed Nov.–Dec.*

POSITANO AND THE AMALFI COAST

Europe's unsurpassingly beautiful coastline is ". . . the only delectable part of Italy, which the inhabitants there dwelling do call the coast of Malfie, full of towns, gardens, springs and wealthy men." Thus raves Boccaccio in his 14th-century *Decameron,* writing about the Costiera Amalfitana—the Amalfi Coast. Rugged, craggy, and extending around the Bay of Salerno from Positano on the west to Vietri sul Mare on the east, this is where the Amalfi Republic once held sway in the Middle Ages, when Amalfi was one of the richest towns in Italy. Today, the coast's scenic sorcery makes this a top destination, drawing visitors who gaze longingly at the surroundings almost as much as they do each other—after all, this is a prime honeymoon location.

Statale 163—the Amalfi Drive, as we call it—was hewn from the lip of the Lattari mountains and completed in 1852, varying from 50 to 400 feet above the bay. You can thank Ferdinand, the Bourbon king of the Two Sicilies, for commissioning it, and Luigi Giordano for designing this seemingly improbable engineering feat. A thousand or so gorgeous vistas appear along these almost 40 km (29 mi) stretching from just outside Sorrento to Vietri, coursing over deep ravines and bays of turquoise-to-sapphire water, spreading past tunnels and timeless villages. This is the only coastal road in the region, and the slender two lanes hovering over the sheer drops sometimes seem impossible to maneuver by auto, let alone by buses and trucks.

Most everyone arrives from Sorrento, just to the north, connecting to the coast through Sant'Agata sui Due Golfi on the Statale 145—the Strada del Nastro Azzuro (Blue Ribbon Road), whose nickname aptly describes its width, and the color at your alternating right and left. This inland region presents rolling hills of olive, lemon, and orange groves and is dotted with rural hamlets. The white-knuckle part, or, as some call it, the Via Smeraldo (Emerald Road), begins as the road connects back to Statale 163, threading through coastal ridges at Colli di S. Pietro, and continuing to wend its way around the Vallone di Positano. From ravine to ravine, Positano beckons, appearing and disappearing like a flirtatious coquette. Just south of Positano, at Punta San Pietro, Statale 163 again winds sharply around valleys, deep ravines and precipices, affording more stunning ridge views. Just past Praiano, the Furore gorge is crossed by viaduct. From here on to Amalfi, the ridges soften just a bit.

Positano

⑮ *56 km (35 mi) southeast of Naples; 16 km (10 mi) east of Sorrento.*

Positano clings to the Monti Comune and Sant' Angelo and has been called by artist Paul Klee "the only place in the world conceived on a vertical rather than a horizontal axis." Its arcaded, cubist buildings, set in tiers up the mountainside, reflect the sky in dawn-color walls: rose, peach, purple, some tinted the ivory of sunrise's scudding clouds. The colors on these Saracen-inspired dwellings may have originally served to help returning fishermen spot their own digs in an instant. Today, these visual delights have helped make this the most photographed fishing village in the world. The four thousand or so fisherfolk and other Positanesi are joined daily by hordes arriving from Capri, Sorrento, and Amalfi, eager to celebrate the fact that Positano is, impossibly, there. When John Steinbeck lived here in 1953, he wrote that it was difficult to consider tourism an industry because "there are not enough [tourists]." Alas, there are more than enough now. What Steinbeck wrote, however, still applies: "Positano bites deep. It is a dream place that isn't quite real when you are there and becomes beckoningly real after you have gone."

It may have started with bread. Roman Emperor Tiberius, son of poison-happy Livia, sent his three-oar boat to a mill in Positano, understandably afraid that his neighbors on Capri would poison him. The (now modernized) mill still grinds healthful flour, but Positano is now more than just a grocery stop. Its name could be a corruption of the Greek "Poseidon," or derive from a man named Posides, who owned villas here during the time of Claudius; or even from Roman freedmen, called The Posdii. The most popular theory is that the name "Positano" comes from Pestano (or Pesitano), a 9th-century town by a Benedictine abbey near Montepertuso, built by refugees of Paestum to the south, whose homes had been ransacked by the Saracens.

Pisa sacked the area in 1268, but when an elaborate defensive system of watchtowers was in place, Positano once again prospered, briefly rivaling Amalfi. As a fiefdom of Neapolitan families until the end of

The Amalfi Coast

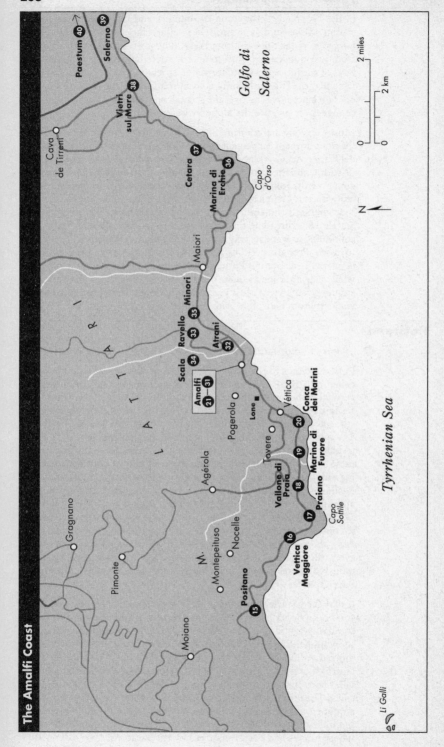

Golfo di
Salerno

Paestum 40
Salerno 39
Vietri sul Mare 38
Cava de' Tirreni
Cetara 37
Marina di Erchie 36
Capo d'Orso
Maiori
Minori 35
Ravello 33
Scala 34
Atrani 32
Amalfi 21–31
Pogerola
Lone
Véttica
Conca dei Marini
20
Agérola
Tovere
19
Marina di Furore
Praiano
18
Vallone di Praia
Capo Sottile
17
M. Montepertuso
Nocelle
16
Vettica Maggiore
Positano
15
Gragnano
Pimonte
Moiano

L A T T A R I

Tyrrhenian Sea

Li Galli

N

2 miles
2 km

the 17th century, Positano produced silk and, later, canvas goods, but decline began again in the late 18th century. With the coming of the steamship in the mid-19th century, some three-fourths of the town's 8,000 citizens emigrated to America—mostly to New York—and it eventually regressed into a backwater fishing village. That is, until artists and intellectuals, and then travelers, rediscovered its prodigious charms in the 20th century, especially after World War II; Picasso, Stravinsky, Diaghilev, Olivier, Steinbeck, Klee—even Lenin—were just an inkling of this town's talented fans. Lemons, grapes, olives, fish, resort gear, and of course, tourism keep it going, but despite its shimmery sophistication and overwrought popularity, Positano's chief export remains its most precious commodity: beauty.

Most travelers leave their wheels in one of the scarce garages near the beach if their hotel doesn't provide parking (the natives often just park on the already-too-narrow roads); The best bet for day-trippers is to get to Positano early enough so that space is still available. Even those arriving in Positano by SITA bus should get a morning start, as traffic on the Via Smeraldo grows combustible by noon. The bus has two main stops in Positano: Transita, or Upper Town—near the large church of Santa Maria della Grazie—and Sponda, or Lower Town. Those who can't wait to start the Positano triathalon should get out at the first stop and start walking down. Most, however, opt to begin their walking tour from the Sponda bus stop. From here, it's a step to Via Cristoforo Colombo, which winds down through the heart of town to the main beach.

Make sure you have some comfortable walking shoes—no heels, please!—and that your back and legs are strong enough to negotiate those picturesque, but daunting and ladderlike scalinatelli. If not, ride the municipal bus, which frequently plies along the one-and-only-one-way Via Pasitea, hairpinning from Positano's central Piazza dei Mulini to the mountains and back, making a loop through the town every half hour. Heading down from the Sponda bus stop toward the beach, you pass Le Sirenuse, the hotel John Steinbeck stayed at when he wrote his famous essay for *Harper's Bazaar* in 1953. Its stepped terraces offer vistas over the town, so you might splurge on lunch or a drink here on the pool terrace, a favorite gathering place for Modigliani-sleek jet-setters. Continue to Piazza dei Mulini, and make a left turn onto Via dei Mulini. If you want to catch your breath after a bus ride to Positano, take a quick time out for an espresso, a slice of Positanese (a chocolate cake as delectable as its namesake), or a fresh-fruit iced "granite" in the lemon-tree garden at Bar-Pasticceria La Zagara (⊠ Via Mulini 8, ☎ 089/875964). Past a bevy of resort boutiques, head to 23 Via dei Mulini to view the prettiest garden in Positano—the 18th-century courtyard of the **Palazzo Murat,** originally built by Prince Joachim Murat, whom Napolean designated as King of Naples in 1808. Murat wanted to forget the demands of power and escaped to Positano to lead the simple life. Since Murat was one of Europe's leading style setters, it couldn't be *too* simple, and he wound up building a grand abode (now a hotel) just steps from the main beach.

Just beyond the Palazzo Murat is the Chiesa Madre, or parish church of **Santa Maria Assunta,** its green and yellow majolica dome, topped by a perky cupola, visible from just about anywhere in town. Built on the site of the former Benedictine abbey of St. Vito, the 13th-century Romanesque structure was almost completely rebuilt in 1700. The last piece of the ancient mosaic floor can be seen under glass near the apse. Note the carved wooden Christ, a masterpiece of devotional religious art, with its bathetic face and bloodied knees, on view before the altar.

At the altar is a Byzantine 13th-century wooden painting of Madonna with Child, known as The Black Virgin, carried to the main beach every August 15 to celebrate the Feast of the Assumption. Legend claims that the painting was once stolen by Saracen pirates, who, fleeing in a raging storm, heard a voice from on high, *Posa, Posa*—"Put it down, put it down." When they placed the statue on the beach near the church, the storm calmed down, as did the Saracens. Positano was saved, and the town's name was established (yet again). Embedded over the doorway of the church's bell tower, set across the tiny piazza, is a medieval bas-relief of fishes, a fox, and a Pistrice, the mythical half-dragon, half-dog sea monster. This is one of the sole relics of the medieval abbey of St. Vito. ✉ *Piazza Flavio Gioia, just above the main beach.*

The walkway from the Piazza Flavio Gioia leads down to the **Spaggia Grande,** or main beach, bordered by an esplanade and some of Positano's best restaurants. Head over to the stone pier to the far right of the beach as you face the water. Here, a staircase leads to the **Via Positanesi d'America,** a lovely seaside walkway. Halfway up the path you'll find the Torre Trasìta, the most distinctive of Positano's three coastline defense towers, which define the edges of Positano in various states of repair. The Trasìta—now a residence occasionally available for summer rental—was one of the defense towers used to warn of pirate raids. Just beyond the tower is O'Guaraccino, an arbor-covered restaurant beauty spot. Continuing along the Via Positanesi d'America, you pass tiny inlets and emerald coves until the large Spaggia di Fornillo beach comes into view.

Set 3 km (2 mi) on a mountain crag directly above Positano, the tiny village of **Montepertuso** (Pierced Mountain) is where Emperor Frederick II of Sicily bred and trained hawks; some feathery descendants still nest in grottoes around the area. The dramatic hole in the arched rock—the *arco naturale*—below Monte Sant'Angelo a Tre Pizzi, is one of only three in the world where both the sun's and the moon's rays can penetrate (April–July); the other two are in India. Try to see it in the morning, when the sun shines through. Legend says the hole was created when the devil challenged the Madonna that whoever pierced the rock would own the village. In 10 attempts, the devil could only scratch the limestone, but when the Madonna touched the rock, it crumbled, the sky appeared, and she walked right through, sinking the devil into the hole. On July 2, a holy performance, games, and fireworks commemorate the Virgin's success. Another popular village festival is the Sagra del Fagiolo, held on the last Saturday in August, which celebrates the humble bean. The tiny town is set with numerous stalls full of beans and other fare, with waiters in traditional folkloric garb (but no beanies). An easy way to ride up to the Montepertuso heights is by taking the municipal Positano bus, which leaves from Piazza dei Mulini.

From Montepertuso you can hike up to the so-called lost village of **Nocelle,** pasted to a mountaintop some 1,700 ft above Positano. Cloud-riding Nocelle is a carless universe: only two stone pathways and myriad scalinatelli thread the hamlet, where a tiny piazza and picturesque church look out on a panorama. To the east of the village, the Sentiero degli Dei, or Pathway of the Gods hiking trail, begins, climbing 3,500 ft up the mountain range, crossing the Monti Lattari east to Agerola. This well-trod, steep, and scattered path was once the mountaintop route connecting settlements until the Amalfi Drive was built through the rock below; it is a true challenge, but rewards with uninterrupted views the gods seem to have personally blessed.

Beaches

Marina Grande is the main boating area, with taupe-color, semisandy Spiaggia Grande, the largest and widest beach of the 10 or so in the area. Fishermen—once the dominant workforce—now function as a cooperative group, supplying local kitchens; they can be seen cleaning their colorful, flipped-over boats and mending their torn nets throughout the day, seemingly oblivious to the surrounding throngs. To the west of town is the less crowded Spiaggia di Fornillo; to the east a string of small, pretty beaches, separated by coves—La Porta, Ciumicello, Arienzo, San Pietro, and Laurito—most of which are accessible only by boat.

Boat Excursions

From Marina Grande you can board a scheduled day boat or hire a private one, including yachts that sleep six or more—with or without a captain—for as long as you'd like, to visit Capri, the Emerald Grotto in Conca dei Marini, or coves and inlets with small beaches. Close by, in the large cave at La Porta (650 ft east of the town center), tools, utensils, and hunting weapons from the Paleolithic and Mesolithic ages have been discovered, the oldest known remains on the coast. Favorite boating destination, however, are the rocky Li Galli islets (6 km [4 mi] west), seen from any point in Positano (as they are from the beaches of the peninsula), whose name derives from their resemblance to pecking birds. Originally the site of an ancient Roman anchorage, the islands then became medieval fiefdoms of Emperor Frederick II and King Robert of Anjou. The isles remain tempting enough to lures purchasers in search of an exclusive paradise: Russian choreographer Leonide Massine in 1925, and, in 1988, dancer Rudolf Nureyev, who discovered the islands in 1984 when he came to accept the Positano Prize for the Art of Dancing, given each year in honor of Massine. The islands are still private. **L'Uomo e il Mare** (✉ Spiaggia Grande pier, ☎ 089/875211, 089/875475) is an outfit run by Gennaro Capraro and his friendly English wife, Valeria, offering boating excursions to Li Galli and five other coastal destinations. Offering all-day affairs, including luncheon stopovers, he usually fills up an excursion party with nine people (150,000 lire per person), so it's best to reserve in advance. Boating excursions can also be arranged through **Noleggio Barche Lucibello** (✉ Spiaggia Grande pier, ☎ 089/875032), which also rents motorboats and rowboats by the hour.

Dining and Lodging

$$$–$$$$ ✕ **Donna Rosa.** This minimalist little hideaway in one-street Montepertuso, the hamlet high over Positano, is truly original. Everybody gets into the act: mamma does the creative cooking, to order, pappa "makes noise," and the daughters rule out front—Rosa is the namesake nonna. Pasta has arugula *in* it, mixed with clams, mussels, porcini mushrooms, and artichokes. A dessert sampler may include orange-studded mandarin ice cream and sponge cake soaked in limoncello. Fine wine is available by the glass, live music can be anything from jazz to Australian gospel (with a daughter singing sweetly), and free car service is provided. There is a terrace, but the better view is the kitchen. ✉ *Via Montepertuso,* ☎ *089/811806. Reservations essential for dinner. AE, DC, MC, V. Closed Mon.*

$$–$$$ ✕ **Chez Black.** Nicknamed after owner Salvatore Russo's eternal tan, this nautical-looking institution has been dishing out hearty Italian fare and pouring wines since just after World War II. Sip a *grotta dello smeraldo*—gin, lemon, and crème de menthe—perhaps accompanied by *foglia di limone* (grilled mozzarella in lemon leaves). Try the renowned pizza, or signature spaghetti and crayfish, or maybe grilled *scorfano* (sea scorpion). Red-checked tablecloths, a natural stone lobster tank, a juke-

box, and fishermen who haul their catch right into the kitchen make up the scene, which grows festive at dinnertime. ⊠ *Via del Brigantino,* ☎ *089/875036. AE, DC, MC, V. Closed Nov.–Mar.*

$$ ✕ **Da Adolfo.** Several coves away from the Spiaggia Grande, on a little beach where pirates once built and launched their boats, this laid-back trattoria is a favorite Positano landmark. The pirates are long gone, but their descendents now ferry you free to the private cove, round-trip from Positano (look for the boat named for the restaurant; you can also make a steep descent from the main coastal road off the hamlet of Laurito). Sit under a straw canopy on a wooden terrace to enjoy *totani con patate* (squid and potatoes with garlic and oil), then sip white wine with peaches until sundown. Some diners even swim here—so bathing suits are just fine. ⊠ *Spiaggia di Laurito,* ☎ *089/875022. No credit cards. Closed Oct.–May.*

$$ ✕ **La Cambusa.** Two stone lions guard this "pantry" right off the Marina Grande, a safe haven for tasty local cuisine for 25-plus years. Linguine with mussels and fresh fish with new potatoes and tomato sauce are among the favorites. Owners Luigi and Baldo are well known around town for maintaining high standards even during the hectic high season. The outdoor dining terrace holds pride of place directly above the entrance to the Spiaggia Grande. ⊠ *Piazza Amerigo Vespucci 4,* ☎ *089/875432. AE, DC, MC, V. Closed Wed. except in summer.*

$$ ✕ **O' Capurale.** Positano is about easy-come elegance, and this dining
★   spot sums it all up. Graced with a coved ceiling awash with colorful Fauvist-style frescoes, the dining room is filled with happy, stylish diners, literally unwinding before your eyes, thanks to the delicious, serious food (veal cutlet in white wine and cheese crepes *al formaggio* are two favorites) and a lovely setting. Walk downstairs to wind up on a back street that has a view of the beach and tables set for alfresco dining. ⊠ *Via Regina Giovanna 12,* ☎ *089/875374. AE, DC, MC, V. Closed Nov.–mid-Feb.*

$–$$ ✕ **O' Guarracino.** This tree house overlooking the cliffs, the sea, and Torre Trasìta is an idyllic setting in which to imbibe a Positano specialty: beer sweetened with Grand Marnier. Thick, twining vines, little tables covered in cloths that match the tint of the bay, and a setting to make you fall in love, or rekindle it (be careful who you sit with) are among the big pluses; the fish is fine, as well. The pizzeria oven, adorned with an icon of Saint Pizza, only whips into action at night. ⊠ *Via Positanesi d' America, between Spiaggia Grande and Spiaggia Fornillo,* ☎ *089/875794. AE, DC, MC, V.*

$ ✕ **Il Grottino Azzurro.** High on a hill above Positano, by a church on a pretty piazza, this family-run trattoria serves delicious fresh pasta and fish to the locals as well as savvy tourists. Mamma will be happy to help you choose. The bus stops right near here on its regular runs, and if you want to burn off the meal, walk; it's downhill, all the way back. ⊠ *Via Chiesa Nuova,* ☎ *089/875466. AE, DC, MC, V. Closed Wed.*

$$$$ ✕▤ **Le Sirenuse.** As legendary as its namesake sirens, this hot-cool,
★   exquisite, in-town 18th-century palazzo vies with the Hotel San Pietro for best in show, but less flamboyantly. Venetian and Neapolitan museum-quality antiques and artwork, spacious vine-entwined terraces, a private yacht for free boating excursions, refined service, and the coast's most beautiful pool terrace—*the* place to have lunch in Positano—are only parts of the whole. A world-class operation results from the noble Sersale family's constant attentions, Swiss training, and lots and lots of cash. Rooms, each one special and many with whirlpool tubs, are accented with great art and artifacts, such as antique bedsteads or refectory tables. At night the La Sponda restaurant offers some of the best (certainly some of the priciest) food in Italy. Later, repair to the aristocratic reading room or serpentine bar, where contented patrons

swap experiences and toast their good luck at being here—and *here*. ✉ *Via Cristoforo Colombo 30, 84017,* ☎ *089/875066,* FAX *089/ 811798. 61 rooms with bath. Restaurant, 2 bars, air-conditioning, pool, spa, meeting rooms, parking. AE, DC, MC, V.*

$$$$ ✕⊡ **Palazzo Murat.** The location is perfect—in the heart of town, near
★ the beachside promenade, and within the shadow of Santa Maria Assunta. You enter through a bougainvillea-draped patio and garden that is one of the most romantic places in town, a delightful setting for dining alfresco (the restaurant has a superb chef) and the occasional summer concert. The old wing is Positano's grandest palazzo, built in the early 19th century by Joachim Murat, king of Naples, with tall windows and wrought-iron balconies; the new wing is a modern, Mediterranean building with arches and terraces. Rooms 5 and 24 have the best views of the Bay of Positano. ✉ *Via dei Mulini 23, 84017,* ☎ *089/ 875177,* FAX *089/811419. 32 rooms with bath. Restaurant, bar, air-conditioning (new wing). AE, DC, MC, V. Closed Jan.–Mar.*

$$$$ ✕⊡ **San Pietro.** Extraordinary is the word for this luxurious oasis, fa-
★ vored by the likes of Julia Roberts and Princess Caroline of Monaco, both of whom prefer this place since it's several leagues out of town (a shuttle bus whisks you back and forth), far from the crowds and any paparazzi. The place itself is more than camera-ready: Set on a cliff high over the sea, with seven levels of gardened terraces, the San Pietro has a frilly, pretty decor that mixes modern (the hotel was built in the early 1970s) with magnificent (great antiques, elegant Vietri tilework). Masses of flowers perfume the lounges, while most of the elegantly furnished rooms come with terraces and picture-window views. There's a pool on an upper level, and an elevator fit for James Bond whisks you hundreds of feet through the mountainside to the private beach and beach bar. The proprietors organize boating excursions and parties, while the restaurant's menu is ambitious and stylish. Be sure to try the hotel's incredibly delicious signature drink, called Elephant's Milk. ✉ *Via Laurito 82, 84017,* ☎ *089/875455,* FAX *089/811449. 60 rooms with bath. Restaurant, 2 bars, pool, tennis court, private beach, dock. AE, DC, MC, V. Closed Nov.–Mar.*

$$$–$$$$ ✕⊡ **Buca di Bacco.** The *Buca* in this hotel and restaurant's name is for tavern and the *Bacco* for the Greek god of wine. Originally an early 19th-century mansion that became a nightspot, its cellar boîte attracted artists and intellectuals at the turn of the last century and still maintains its party roots. Upstairs, white-on-white guest rooms have balconies and tile floors, while suites feature glass walls with sliding doors to fieldstone terraces or gardens. The restaurant acts as a town hub. Specialties include the Buca's signature *arancini* rice croquettes, along with *zuppa di cozze* (mussels), fresh *spigole* (bass), and figs and oranges in caramel, which can be enjoyed in its downstairs veranda or the upstairs loggia dining room, with its fetching geranium-bordered view of the beach. ✉ *Via Rampa Teglia 4/8, 84017,* ☎ *089/875699,* FAX *089/875731. 53 rooms with bath. Restaurant, air-conditioning. AE, DC, MC, V. Closed Nov.–Mar.*

$$$ ✕⊡ **Saraceno D'Oro.** The restaurant preceded the hotel at this beachfront spot, just in front of the fishing boats that set off in the evening. The environment is comfortable and airy, with bougainvillea covering the ceiling, windows overlooking the beach, soft lighting, and cordial service. Bass with leeks, veal with provolone, and local wines are all delicious. ✉ *Via Regina Giovanna 5, 84017,* ☎ *089/875400. AE, DC, MC, V.*

$$$–$$$$ ⊡ **Le Agavi.** Most Positano hotels are set near the sea or on the lower hillsides of town, but Le Agavi is just steps from the sky-high Belvedere di Positano and offers views of the entire town below. Organically constructed from local stone in a succession of greenery-draped terraces

(including agave, a kind of cactus), this hotel seems to be built right into the mountainside. A tiny funicular connects the levels that waterfall down (note that rooms close to the rails can be disturbed by mechanical noises). Spacious lobbies and public rooms are eclectic: modern design, wooden floors, Empire and Italianate furnishings, Oriental rugs and accessories, and important antiques. Guest-room balconies jut out over dizzying heights. For swimming you can choose between the lavish pool area, which seems to float over all Positano, or take an elevator to the private beach—a treat in a town where most share the sand, body to body. ⊠ *Via G. Marconi, 84017,* ☎ *089/875733,* FAX *089/875965. 55 rooms, 15 suites, with bath. 2 restaurants, bar, air-conditioning, pool, private beach, business services, meeting rooms, parking. AE, DC, MC, V. Closed Nov.–Mar.*

$$$ 🏨 **Covo dei Saraceni.** In Positano sea and town interact, and you see this best from the Covo dei Saraceni, perched on the main beach at the foot of Monte Comune, just steps from the main pier. Modern, charming, and increasingly luxe, this small hotel has a rooftop pool and bar set over the sea. Crisp and cool, the lobby is built around a curved staircase (with a bit too much glitzy marble for some tastes). The Bougainvillea restaurant features a pizza oven, its glass-walled dining area overhung with namesake vines. Guest-room decor is simple but stylized, with wrought-iron balconies; newer rooms and suites are ultra-deluxe and spacious, with whirlpools, larger terraces, and fanciful furnishings. The top plus here is the blissful location—you'd need to stay on a yacht to get any nearer the bay. ⊠ *Via Regina Giovanna 5, 84017,* ☎ *089/875400,* FAX *089/875878. 58 rooms with bath. 2 restaurants, bar, snack bar, air-conditioning, pool. AE, DC, MC, V. Closed Nov.–Mar.*

$$$ 🏨 **L'Ancora.** Close to everything—set back a little from the main road and just a few minutes up from the main beach, this sunny Mediterranean-style hillside hostelry commands expansive views of the deep blue—and local color, too. The lobby has a sprinkle of antiques, while the airy guest rooms are bright with local artwork and boldly patterned mosaic tiling. All rooms have balconies or terraces and sea views. ⊠ *Via Cristoforo Colombo 36, 84017,* ☎ *089/875318,* FAX *089/811784. 18 rooms with bath. Air-conditioning, parking. AE, DC, MC, V.*

$$$ 🏨 **Miramare.** Primo views, central location, and comfortable elegance are pleasing elements of this albergo converted from a 100-year-old mansion. Outdoor and indoor dining terraces are draped with bougainvillea, and antiques and comfy seating abound. Charming rooms, some with fireplace, are upgraded constantly, and offer glazed tiles, balconies or terraces, and windows overlooking the sea. Room 201 is a new suite, while Room 210 has a huge window wall opening to the balcony. ⊠ *Via Trara Genoino 27, 84017,* ☎ *089/875–0002,* FAX *089/875219. 16 rooms with bath. Restaurant, bar, air-conditioning, private beach, parking. AE, DC, MC, V. Closed Jan.–Mar.*

$$$ 🏨 **Poseidon.** One of the most popular hotels in Positano, this was built 50 years ago by the Aonzos, the same family running it today. Set in a citrus grove high up the hillside, it offers views over central Positano from its rooftop terrace with pool, sitting room with fireplace, and bar and restaurant. Public rooms have potted palms and ferns, Oriental rugs, marble or terra-cotta floors, a baby grand, and Asian and Mediterranean accents. Enjoy tea in a quiet corner or order a low-calorie specialty in the café. Most guest rooms have sea-view terraces. ⊠ *Via Pasitiea 148, 84017,* ☎ *089/811111,* FAX *089/875833. 40 rooms with bath. Restaurant, bar, air-conditioning, pool, beauty salon, exercise room, meeting facilities, parking. AE, DC, MC, V. Closed Nov.–Mar.*

$$$ 🖭 **Villa Franca.** Bay blue, lemon yellow, and cool white are the palette here, making for a stress-dissolving retreat, set halfway up the town from the beach. Tile and mosaic floors, decorative urns, and graceful archways open to sea air and views, and conversation-seating done in bold fabrics marks the public rooms and piano bar. Similarly furnished, guest rooms all have terraces over the town, while the small-ish pool enjoys a delightful view. ✉ *Viale Pasitea 318, 84017,* ☎ *089/ 875655,* 🖬 *089/875735. 28 rooms with bath. Restaurant, bar, pool, parking. AE, DC, MC, V.*

$$-$$$ 🖭 **La Fenice.** Paradise found. This tiny and unpretentious hotel on the
★   peaceful outskirts of town beckons with bougainvillea-laden vistas, cast-away cottages, and a turquoise pool, all perched over a private beach, just across a cove from Franco Zefferelli's famous villa. Thanks to the wonderful family of the owner, Constantino Mandara, you'll feel right at home in just a few minutes—that's because this *is* his home. Guest rooms, accented with coved ceilings, whitewashed walls, and native folk art, are simple havens of tranquillity. Several accommodations are in a house perched above the road, while the best are the little cottages set close to the sea. All are linked by *very* steep walkways—covered with arbors and zig-zagging their way across the hill, they tie together these little acres of heaven. ✉ *Via G. Marconi 4, 84017,* ☎ *089/ 875513,* 🖬 *089/811309. 10 rooms with bath. Pool. No credit cards.*

$$ 🖭 **Casa Albertina.** Clinging to the cliff, this little house is well loved for its Italianate charm, its homey restaurant, and its owners, the Cinque family, with Nonna Albertina herself ruling in the kitchen. Rooms have high ceilings, bright fabrics, tile flooring, and sunny terraces or balconies overlooking the sea and coastline. Car or motorboat excursions to surrounding towns and attractions can be arranged. Cars can't drive to the doorway, but porters will ferry your luggage. Note: it's 300 steps down to the main beach. ✉ *Via Tavolozza 4, 84017,* ☎ *089/875143,* 🖬 *089/811540. 21 rooms with bath. Restaurant, air-conditioning, parking. AE, DC, MC, V.*

$-$$ 🖭 **Conca d'Oro.** The name says gold, and the look sure shines at this bright, white-stucco hillside lodging. Chintz and hand-painted antique furnishings compete with boldly patterned tile flooring on the terrace. Rooms have balconies, and there are a broad, casual dining veranda and a private stretch of beach. All, of course, overlook the sea and coastline. ✉ *Via Boscariello 16, 84017,* ☎ *089/811494,* 🖬 *089/875111. 38 rooms with bath. Restaurant, air-conditioning, private beach, parking. AE, DC, MC, V.*

$ 🖭 **Casa Cosenza.** This 200-year-old lemon-yellow upscale pensione is a distant cousin to the more luxe accommodations in town. Still, it's set halfway up the hills, meaning you get a great view and can still easily walk to the beach. Breakfast is on a terrace overlooking town and sea, and rooms are clean and comfortable, many with coved ceilings. ✉ *Via Trara Genoino 18, 84017,* ☎ *089/875063,* 🖬 *089/875063. 7 rooms, 2 apartments, with bath. AE, DC, MC, V.*

Nightlife and the Arts

The night scene here is liveliest near the waterfront, where the restaurants lined up along the border of the Spiaggia Grande turn into one big open-air party on summer nights. For the latest and most complete information on all the nightspots, concerts, and special events along the Amalfi Coast, from Positano to Salerno, be sure to consult the monthly periodical, *Memo,* available at most regional newsstands. It's a day-by-day, event-filled cornucopia of information.

Music on the Rocks (☎ 089/875036) is a popular disco set in a seaside cave off the beach, favored by the likes of Sharon Stone and Luciano Pavarotti; **La Zagara** (✉ Via Mulini 8, ☎ 089/875964), a noted pastry shop by day, offers music at night; **Planet Positano** (✉ Piazza dei Mulini, ☎ 089/675433) is a local knockoff of the Planet chain; **Buca di Bacco** (✉ Via Rampa Teglia 8, ☎ 089/811461) is for grown-ups, still crazy after all these years.

CHAMBER MUSIC
The **International Chamber Music Courses and Festival** (✉ Via G. Marconi, ☎ FAX 089/812045) offers master classes, lectures, and concerts open to the public, five days a week during early July. The exquisite courtyard of the 17th-century Hotel Palazzo Murat is also a venue for concerts during the summer.

CULINARY LESSONS
In a red-washed, cliff-side villa, **Diana Folonari** (of the wine family) teaches weeklong (or daily) seminars on Italian country cooking, offered in English from May to September, with wine tastings (✉ Via del Canovaccio 10, 84017, ☎ FAX 089/875784). Bring your own apron.

FESTIVALS
Yearlong, the Positano calendar is filled with festivities and religious *festas*. Summertime plays host to the Moda Mare fashion show, in early June, when concerts are set up on the beach and in Nocelle—the sky-high village that looks down on Positano. The first week in September sees the Premio Premio Leonide Massine dance awards—officially known as the Positano Prize for the Art of Dancing—and the Vittoria da Sica Film Festival, while the last week brings the Festa del Pesce (Fish Festival); acrobats and musicians take to the streets of Montepertuso for Artisti in Strada. The star event of the year and the town's main religious festa is the **Feast of the Assumption,** held every August 15, commemorated by mock battles with the Saracens and evening fireworks on the main beach.

During Christmas, Natale wreaths are fashioned from bougainvillea, and orchestra and choir concerts pop up all over town; the Nuovo Anno (New Year) is greeted with a big town dance and fireworks on the main beach, with other folklore and caffé-concerti musical events. In neighboring Montepertuso a living crèche is enacted. Just outside Positano, heading east, is the tiny chapel of San Pietro, named in honor of St. Peter's landing here in AD 40 (and now marking the entrance to the luxurious Hotel San Pietro). Each year on New Year's Eve, the 120 villagers of San Pietro—give or take a few—greet the dawn telling stories, singing, and eating around a bonfire in the piazza in front of the town church. Visitors are always welcome; bring a blanket.

Outdoor Activities and Sports
High-flying aficionados can join an organized group of hang gliders soaring on the thermals along with the hillside swifts and gulls; check for information at the tourist board by the Chiesa Madre. Hikers often pass through Positano on their way to the region's most challenging mountainside trail, the Sentiero degli Dei (Pathway of the Gods), which can be picked up outside nearby Nocelle (☞ *below*). For less professional hikers, Ponte dei Libri (a bridge several miles west) spans a pretty valley with soaring rock pinnacles and is a moderate walk. More serious climbers can hike Mount Catiello and along the chain of Mount St. Angello a Tre Pizzi, at 4,575 ft. Mount Comune (2,950 ft) offers a less strenuous mountain climb. There is a tennis club close to the Hotel Poseidon.

Sooner or later, everyone takes to the water in Positano (for boating excursions, ☞ *above*). Divers can check out **Centro Sub Costiera Amalfitana** (✉ Via Fornillo, on the beach beneath the Pupetto and Vittoria hotels, ☎ 089/81248, FAX 089/812884) for dive classes and guided excursions, including night and archaeological dives—there's also a branch in Praiano, on Via Capriglione. Day or night trips can be organized with local fishermen, who can even cook your catch and serve it on board. Ask at your hotel or check at the beach. Waterskiing facilities are offered on the main beach, where boats and skis can be rented.

Shopping

Resort wear put Positano on the fashion map in a big way in the early 1960s; it has now taken off in more contemporary directions. Goods range from haute to kitsch, often tight tops and loose pareos in vibrant hues, with prices generally higher than in other coast towns. The fabric industry here began long ago with silk, canvas, and hand embroidery, then made headlines back in 1959 when Positano introduced Italy to the bikini (following the reasoning that less is more, boutiques now sell even more highly abbreviated ones). The most concentrated shopping area, and the least difficult to maneuver, is the souklike area near the cathedral by the beach, where the crowded pedestrian pathway literally runs through boutiques. Lining steep alleyways covered with bougainvillea, small shops display items such as local foodstuffs, wood, lace, pottery, wines and limoncello, and ceramics; you'll even find artisans who can hand-stitch a pair of stylish sandals for you while you wait.

Ceramiche Assunta (✉ Via C. Colombo 97, ☎ 875008) has a collection of the colorful and fanciful traditional ceramics of Vietri, east along the coast. **Cose Antiche** (✉ Piazza dei Mulini, ☎ 089/811811) offers antiques from minor to big deal. **Costanzo Avitabile** (✉ Piazza A. Vespucci 1, ☎ 089/875366) creates custom sandals in barely a few minutes. **La Tartana** (✉ Via della Tartana, ☎ 089/875545) is a stylish boutique that tailors and sells handmade suits. **Maria Lampo** (✉ Via Pasitea 12, ☎ 089/875021) has been creating swimsuits and beachwear in traditional fabrics for almost 50 years.

Vettica Maggiore

🔟 *3 km (2 mi) southeast of Punta San Pietro; 2 km (1 mi) northwest of Praiano.*

From afar, Vettica Maggiore looks like a landscape painting. Up close, it turns out to be just your standard-issue village along a road, but what makes it worth stopping for is the piazza, almost levitating over the water. This is a fine place to stretch your legs and view distant Positano, the coast, and the sea. Paved with an intricate, colorful pattern in majolica, the piazza is a fitting setting for the church of San Gennaro, rebuilt in the 16th century, with its notably ornate facade and a gleaming majolica-tiled dome (at night, often trimmed with festive lights). Paintings from the 16th and 17th centuries include *Martyrdom of S. Bartholomew,* by Giovanni Bernardo Lama, decorating the side chapel. Elsewhere, in this most westerly village in the township of Praiano, you'll find a pretty but hard-to-reach cliff-side beach; it's at the end of an olive grove, hidden at the bottom of the hillside, next to a tiny anchorage.

Dining and Lodging

$$ ✕ **La Taverna del Leone.** A crowd ranging from Ferrari owners to local fishermen is drawn to this rustic, convivial trattoria because of the pizza—reputedly the best around. You can choose from a variety of antipasti and creative pizza toppings, or go for a big meal topped off with a cold

beer or glass of local wine, in a lusty roadhouse setting where folks mingle happily and noisily. And if you want to stay over rather than face the drive, a few simple rooms with private baths are here as well. ⊠ *Amalfi Drive, between Positano and Vettica Maggiore,* ☎ *089/ 875474. AE, DC, MC, V. Closed Wed.*

$$-$$$ 🏨 **Tramonto d'Oro.** In the middle of Vettica Maggiore and picturesquely sited close to the town's church of San Gennaro, this hotel is a fine and popular option—modern, clean, casual-traditional in style. The real plus here is the Esposito family—who also run Conca dei Marini's Terrazze hotel—who have presided over the Tramonto d'Oro's guests for more than 40 years with true warmth and charm. The restaurant has a vast glass wall overlooking the church and piazza, while the roof has a pleasant pool. ⊠ *Via G. Capriglione 119, Praiano, 84010,* ☎ *089/874955,* 𝔽𝔸𝕏 *089/874670. 32 rooms with bath. Restaurant, air-conditioning, pool. AE, MC, V.*

Praiano

🔟 *2 km (1 mi) southeast of Vettica Maggiore; 1 km (½ mi) northwest of Marina di Praia.*

Just past Capo Sottile, the fishing village of Praiano juts to the sea at the base of the Monti Lattari. Praiano has less wealth and sophistication than its neighbors and more olive and lemon trees than tourists. The town's name comes from Plagianum, as the people who first inhabited the site were called. Back in the 13th century, King Charles I of Anjou founded a university here, the doges of Amalfi established a summer residence, and, for a while, Praiano was renowned for its silk industry. But the decline of Amalfi's 12th-century maritime republic hit hard; the charming parish Church of Santa Luca, at the top of the village, is a reminder of those headier times. A medieval lookout tower on the rocks still keeps guard over the coast, and hidden coves are for boating, bathing, and sunning off the rocks. During the summer boats leave the beach here for Capri each morning, and you can glimpse the island's Faraglioni rocks from here. If you look closely, you may be the first person in years to spot the giant *a mama de cernie* (mother of wreckfishes), the local equivalent of the Loch Ness monster.

Dining and Lodging

$$ ✕ **La Brace.** On the second floor of a simple storefront, on the inland side of the drive, you enter a little ristorante that looks disappointingly simple. Its fine reputation, however, is validated as soon as you see the fresh, homemade antipasti and when you dig into the hearty Calabrian cuisine. The friendly owner recommends the seafood, no surprise, and if you sit next to the big windows, you can see the jagged coastline and serene sea from whence it comes. ⊠ *Via G. Capriglione,* ☎ *089/874226. AE, DC, MC, V.*

$$-$$$ 🏨 **Tritone.** No other hotel on the coast has such a dizzying perch over the sea. Flagstone terraces and gardens set amid soaring rock pinnacles take full advantage of the location, while the seaside bathing area, accessed by an elevator excavated through 1,000 ft of rock, is jaw-dropping and complete with private beach, rocky tunnels, buffet, and bar. Public and guest rooms are traditional and sedate but come with to-die-for views of the sea and nearby Vettica Maggiore. A small rock chapel in a grotto is on the property should you care to give thanks for the region's natural wonders. ⊠ *Via Nazionale, Praiano, 84010,* ☎ *089/ 874333,* 𝔽𝔸𝕏 *089/874374. 58 rooms with bath. 2 restaurants, 2 bars, air-conditioning, pool, private beach, meeting rooms, parking. AE, DC, MC, V. Closed Nov.–Mar.*

$$ ☷ **Le Fioriere.** Blue-tile rooms are casually furnished, and low-key ambience is in keeping with the slow pace of the village. If requested, breakfast is served on your awning-covered balcony over the blue sea. This basic hotel offers easy access to the beach and to public transportation for trips along the coast. ⊠ *Via Nazionale 138, 84010,* ☎ *089/ 874203,* 𝐅𝐀𝐗 *089/874343. 14 rooms with bath. Bar, air-conditioning, parking. AE, DC, MC, V.*

$ ☷ **Margherita.** Basic rooms have crucifixes over the beds, French doors to terraces over a side road lined with olive groves, and partial sea views. Tile flooring, velour seating, '70s-type lighting fixtures, and potted rubber trees make up the modest surroundings. Breakfasts are minimal, as is heat. But the price is right, and Margherita and her daughter are helpful. ⊠ *Via Umberto I, 84010,* ☎ *089/874628,* 𝐅𝐀𝐗 *089/ 874628. 28 rooms with bath. Restaurant, bar, air-conditioning, parking. AE, DC, MC, V.*

$ ☷ **Open Gate.** This is a real deal, with much the same view as million-dollar-plus villas nearby. True, you're right on the main road, but the tile-floor guest rooms are white and clean, the private balconies are spacious, and the informal, vine-covered restaurant serves up tasty fare. It's 400 steps to the beach—but they'll drive you there if you didn't prep on a Stairmaster before arriving. Also, you're midway between Positano and Amalfi, and only 2 km (1 mi) from the Grotto dello Smeraldo. ⊠ *Via Nazionale, 84010,* ☎ *089/874148. 12 rooms with bath. Restaurant, bar, parking. AE, DC, MC, V.*

Marina di Praia

⑱ *1 km (½ mi) southeast of Praiano; 2 km (1 mi) west of Vallone di Furore.*

"Whoever wants to live a healthy life spends the morning in Vettica and the evening in Praiano," goes a local adage. The larger township of Praiano may not fulfill that advice, but its scenic satellite, Marina di Praia, indeed does, since it is home to a landmark eatery and famous disco. Nestling by the sea at the bottom of a dramatic chasm, this is the only anchorage along this rocky stretch where you can hire a boat and dock it and where ferries depart for points and islands along the coast. The super-picturesque hamlet comprises some parking spaces, a small sand beach tucked within cliffs, a few excellent seafood restaurants, a hotel, and a tiny church. Reached along a pretty path through the cliff rocks edging the sea is the L'Africana disco.

Dining and Lodging

$ ✕ **Alfonso a Mare.** Just steps from the Marina del Praia cove, this landmark restaurant is set in a rustic flagstone structure, once a dry haul for boats, partly open to the sea breezes on one side with an open kitchen on the other. Inside are country-style wooden tables, netting, and ceiling baskets, while outside, colorful boats, peasant dwellings, and the chasm's sheer rock walls catch the eye. In nearby Praiano, Alfonso also runs a hotel, where small rooms have tile floors, windows opening to terraces overlooking the gulf, and a few antique touches. ⊠ *Via Marina di Praia, Corso Umberto I, 84010,* ☎ *089/874091,* 𝐅𝐀𝐗 *089/ 874161. No credit cards.*

$$ ☷ **Onda Verde.** Built on a rock dramatically jutting over the tiny cove of Marina dei Praia, this fine hotel overlooks a Saracen tower and coastal ridges. Terraces overhang the sea, and common rooms and dining room feature panoramic glass walls, marble flooring, and rattan and plastic furnishings. Rooms are sparse, but some have terraces, and air-conditioning is available for a charge. You can climb down a winding path to the beach, where daily boat excursions leave for Capri and Ischia. Both a plus and a minus is the minutes-away walk to L'Africana disco. If you like to party, you can climb right into bed without having to drive; if you don't, be sure to ask for a quiet room. ⊠ *Via Terra Mare 3, 84010,* ☎ *089/874143,* 𝔽𝔸𝕏 *089/874125. 20 rooms with bath. Restaurant, bar, dock, parking. AE, DC, MC, V. Closed Nov.–Mar.*

Nightlife

Off a mile-long footpath from the Marina del Praia—or accessed via an elevator from from Statale 163—**L'Africana** (⊠ Via Torre a Mare, ☎ 089/874042) is a classic from the 1960s, a golden oldie on the coast. Even Jackie O danced on the glass-aquarium floor. With open-to-the-sea atmosphere, an indoor boat that's a buffet of antipasti, animal prints, and wildish shows with partial nudity, you can eat lightly, drink heavily, and dance away till the Gulf of Salerno sunrise. Longtime owner Luca Milano has been around the block quite a few times, lives on a cliff beneath the premises, and may even show you his parrot.

Vallone di Furore

⑲ *8 km (5 mi) southeast of Positano; 2 km (1 mi) west of Conca dei Marini.*

The ghost hamlet of Marina di Furore—perhaps three houses?—beckons as you pass over it on a towering aqueduct. This tchotchke of a fishermen's village seems sculpted out of rock walls; once former mills, these houses were abandoned when the tiny harbor here closed. After the hamlet was discovered by vacationers, the municipality moved in, restoring and painting it in pastels in 1998. Steps upstream from the viaduct reach the pebble beach. The Lilliputian settlement is at the base of a high-walled fissure in the limestone mountains—sometimes hyped as a fjord. The name is from the "furor" of stormy water that once rushed down the Torrente Schiato here, now a mere trickle, with uncleared rockslides creating a less-than-gorgeous gorge. From the beach, scalinatelli—each set with 3,000 steps (but who's counting?)—were built to portage goods from the harbor to the town of Furore above it. The hard walk up takes a couple of hours as you climb from sea to sky. To see any of this by car, you'd have to park right on the road (or at nearby Marina di Praia) and then walk a lot. Unless you're in fantastic shape, it's better to boat to the beach and just rubberneck.

Furore, the town high above the Vallone di Furore gorge, can be reached by car via a sharp turn uphill off Statale 163 just east of the gorge; look for the sign to Agerola. The landscape differs from that of the rock-ribbed coast below, containing meadows, terraced fields, dry stone walls (*macere*), chestnut forests, and wild Dolomitic mountains dotted with scrubby cactus. The local pitched-roof houses seem almost Alpine. The region is noted for dairy products, especially cheeses. You can hike all the way here from Positano, and among the villages you will pass is San Lazzaro; check out its belvedere, whose view stretches from Capri to the Monti del Cilento.

Furore is best known for its delicate, lightly tinted wine, Gran Furore Divina Costiera. Furore used to trade wine and foodstuffs for fish and foreign goods and still makes a profit being a larder for regional restaurants, as the garlands of bright red peppers and tomatoes hanging from many roof beams attest. Today Furore is becoming unexpectedly artsy; The mayor recently commissioned works from artists and sculptors, so murals of agricultural scenes, modern sculptures, and house gates patterned in fuchsia and lime enliven the scene. More ancient art can be seen at the Church of Sant'Elia Profeta, which has what some consider the most important Renaissance painting on the coast, a 15th-century triptych painted by Angelo Antonello.

Lodging

$ ☷ **Le Rocce.** Set in the agricultural zone high above the coast, this odd, stone-and-stucco edifice commands the crest of a sheer rockface overlooking the Bay of Salerno and the coastal towns. The lobby looks like an old Italian airport (and the view below seems appropriate), but some redeeming features are the wraparound windows in the restaurant, pleasant rooms with balconies, a rock grotto honoring the Virgin Mary, a nightclub in a cave, and the gentle price tag. ☒ *Via Belvedere 73, Agerola 80051,* ☎ *081/879–1182 or 081/879–1893,* 𝔽𝔸𝕏 *081/879–1893. 33 rooms with bath. Restaurant, bar, pool, nightclub, parking. AE, DC, MC, V.*

Conca dei Marini

★ ⑳ *2 km (1 mi) east of Vallone di Furore; 4 km (2½ mi) southwest of Amalfi.*

Set on the most dramatic promontory of the coast, Conca dei Marini (the name means "seafarers' basin") was originally a province of ancient Rome called Cossa and later became an important naval base of the Amalfi Republic. Much later, it became a hangout for rich and high-profile types, including John Steinbeck, Carlo Ponti, and Gianni Agnelli, who built villas along the sea. You can see why: The green of terraced gardens competes with (and loses to) the blue sea, while the town's distinctive houses flanking the ridges have thick, white walls, with cupolas, balconies, and external staircases, testimony to former Arabic, Moorish, and Greek settlements. Below, on Capo di Conca, a promontory once used as a cemetery, a 16th-century coastal tower dramatically overlooks the sea. Coral is still harvested in the waters off the coast here, while boats fish for sardines and squid through the night, their prow lanterns twinkling as if some stars above had slipped into the sea.

The **Grotta dello Smeraldo** (Emerald Grotto) is a much-touted stop for day-trippers. The rather tacky sign on the road and the squadron of tour buses may put you off, but it's definitely worth a stop. Steps and an elevator bring you almost to sea level, but more delightful is to arrive by boat, which you can hire at just about any port up and down the coast. The karstic cave was originally part of the shore, but the lowest end sank into the sea when the peninsula subsided (the coast remains active, so it may eventually sink even lower—or rise). Intense greenish light filters into the water from an arch below sea level and is reflected off the walls of the cave, quite living up to emerald expectations. You wait to board a large rowboat with about a dozen fellow passengers, and then you set off with a guide, gondolier fashion, through the smallish cavern filled with huge stalactites and stalagmites. Don't let the boatman's constant spiel detract from the half-hour experience—this is one of those tours that points out stalactites that look like Lincoln (for Americans), Napoléon (for the French), and Garibaldi (for the Italians); just tune out and enjoy the sparkles, shapes, and Harry Winston–esque color. A tourist from Amalfi raved in a hotel log in 1858 that the cave ". . . can compete with Vesuvius," but it was forgotten about for years afterward until the grotto was rediscovered by a local fisherman in the 1930s. Although the light is best at midday, arriving early or late will minimize the long wait you would have if you should be behind a group. At Christmas there's a special celebration conducted around the underwater crèche. ☒ *Beyond Punta Acquafetente by boat, or off Amalfi Drive,* ☎ *081/831516 (tourist board of Conca dei Marini).* ☷ *5,000 lire.* ☉ *Apr.–Oct., daily 9:30–5; Nov.–Mar., daily 10–6*

The main Conca dei Marini SITA bus stop is directly in front of the Hotel Belvedere. From here head west along the highway to the Saracen Tower (a private bathing beach sits within its shadow, but you might ask to dine at its café) and farther on for the Emerald Grotto. To the east, you can walk along the highway for views of Conca's harbor and lagoon (a staircase to the left of the Hotel Belvedere will take you down to the water, but unfortunately a major 1997 landslide closed off the quay and the little Chapel of Santa Maria della Neve to visitors). For Conca *in excelsis,* however, head up the mountainside to the northern reaches of the town. Your reward as you climb up the hillside roads and steep scalinatelli are three stunningly sited churches. The first is neo-Byzantine **San Pancrazio,** set in a lovely palm-tree garden. From here head up to the Scalinatella San Pancrazio to the tiny town piazza. To the east along the cliff-side road is the sky-swimming church and **Convento di Santa Rosa** (now a private home). In the 18th century the nuns of the convent created one of the great local dishes, *sfogliata Santa Rosa* (sweet cheese and ricotta pastry shaped like a nun's hood). The mother superior distributed this delicacy free to the locals back then. Today, on every Saint's Day in August, the pastries are baked, and savored, by local families and revelers in town. Heading back to the piazza from the convent, take Via Due Maggio and Via Roma to the church of **Sant' Antonio di Padova,** spectacularly cantilevered hundreds of feet over the coastline on a stone parapet. The church itself is only open for Sunday morning services, but you can always ask locals if someone can open the church with a key for a quick visit ("Dov'è la persona che ci può far visitare la chiesa?") For those who want to see churches in coastal villages, this may be the only way to gain entry.

Lodging

$$$–$$$$ ⚏ **Belvedere.** To understand this place, you must look on it not as a
   ★   hotel but as a home. This is the sort of place where guests ask for the room their great-grandparents favored. Happily, everyone, not just regulars, are treated like family here and you'll find it difficult to say goodbye to the remarkably friendly and helpful staff. Set in one of the grande dame villas of Conca dei Marini, featuring salons top-heavy with overstuffed sofas and a ravishing pool area resting by water's edge, the Belvedere is handily located for exploring Conca dei Marini, set equidistant from the town's lagoon and Saracen tower. ⊠ *Via Smeraldo, 84010,* ☎ *089/831282,* ₣Ẵ *089/831439. 36 rooms with bath. Restaurant, bar, pool, parking. AE, DC, MC, V. Closed Nov.–Mar.*

$$–$$$ ⚏ **Le Terrazze.** Just a few feet down the road from the Belvedere hotel, Le Terrazze is a more gently priced alternative. Rooms are 1970s-modern, spankingly clean, and each comes with a balcony overlooking the sea. ⊠ *Via Smeraldo, 84010,* ☎ *089/831290,* ₣Ẵ *089/831296. 26 rooms with bath. MC, V. Closed late Oct.–Mar.*

AMALFI: FIRST OF THE SEA REPUBLICS

   ★   *18 km (11 mi) southeast of Positano; 32 km (20 mi) west of Salerno.*

On Amalfi's main waterfront, a honorary statue bears this inscription: "The judgment day, when Amalfitans go to Heaven, will be a day like any other." Visitors to this charming city, set in a verdant valley of the Monti Lattari, will soon understand what it means. At first glance, it's hard to imagine that a millennium ago this resort destination, with cream-color and pastel-hue buildings tightly packing a gorge on the Bay of Salerno, was in the 11th and 12th centuries the seat of the Amalfi Maritime Republic, one of the world's great naval powers, and a sturdy rival of Genoa and Pisa for control of the Mediterranean. The harbor, which once launched the greatest fleet in Italy, now bobs with ferries

TAKE PICTURES. FURTHER.™

WITHOUT KODAK MAX
photos taken on 100 speed film

Ever see someone

waiting for the sun to come out

while trying to photograph

a charging rhino?

WITH KODAK MAX
photos taken on Kodak Max 400 film

New!
Kodak Max film:

*Now with better color,
Kodak's maximum
versatility film gives
you great pictures in
sunlight, low light,
action or still.*

It's all you need
to know about film.

www.kodak.com

Fodor's

Distinctive guides packed with up-to-date expert advice
and smart choices for every type of traveler.

Fodor's. For the world of ways you travel.

and blue-and-white fishing boats. The main street, lined with leather shops and *pasticcerias*, has replaced a raging mountain torrent, and terraced hills where *banditi* (bandits) once roamed now flaunt the green and gold of lemon groves. Bearing testimony to its great trade with Tunis, Tripoli, and Algiers, Amalfi remains honeycombed with Arab-Sicilian cloisters and covered passages that suggest Asian caravansaries. In a way Amalfi has become great again, showing off its medieval glory days with sea pageants, convents-turned-hotels, ancient paper mills, covered streets, and its mosquelike cathedral. "The sun— the moon—the stars and—Amalfi," Amalfitans used to say. Standing on the terrace of the town's Cappuccini Convento (Cappuccin Convent), you'll have to agree.

Amalfi's origin is clouded. One legend says that a general of Constantine's army, named Amalfo, settled here in 320; another tale has it that Roman noblemen from the village of Melphi (in Latin, "a Melphi"), fleeing after the fall of the empire, were first in these parts, shipwrecked in the 4th century on their way to Constantinople. Myth becomes fact by the 6th century, when Amalfi is inscribed in the archives as a Byzantine diocese, and the historical pageant really begins. Its geographic position was good defense, and the distance from Constantinople made its increasing autonomy possible. Continuously hammered by the Lombards and others, in 839 it rose against and finally sacked nearby Salerno, to which its inhabitants had been deported. In the 10th century, Amalfi constructed many churches and monasteries and was ruled by judges, later called doges—self-appointed dukes who amassed vast wealth and power.

From the 9th century until 1101, Amalfi remained linked to Byzantium but also was increasingly independent and prosperous, perhaps the major trading port in southern Italy. Its influence loomed large, thanks to its creation of the Tavola Amalfitana, a code of maritime laws taken up by most medieval-era kingdoms. It created its own gold and silver coins—or *tari,* engraved with the cross of Amalfi—and ruled a vast territory. With trade extending as far as Alexandria and Constantinople— where a large colony of Amalfitan merchants resided—it became Italy's first maritime republic, ahead of rivals Pisa, Venice, and Genoa; the population swelled to about 100,000, many of them seafarers and traders. As William of Apulia wrote in the 11th century, ". . . No other is richer in silver, cloth and gold. A great many navigators live in this city . . . famous almost throughout the world as those who travel to where there is something worth buying."

But the days of wine and doges were about to end. In the 11th century Robert Guisgard of Normandy—in the duplicitous spirit of politicos to this day—first aided, then sacked the town, and the Normans from Sicily returned, after a short Amalfitan revolt, in the 12th century. Then, when the Republic of Pisa twice conquered it, Amalfi fell into decline, hastened by a horrific storm in 1343, then by an indirect blow from Christopher Columbus's discoveries, which opened the world beyond to competing trade routes. By the 18th century, the town had sunk into gloom, looking to its lemons and handmade paper for survival. After the state road was built by Ferdinand, the Bourbon king of Naples, in the 19th century, Amalfi evolved into a tourist destination, drawing Grand Tour–era travelers like Richard Wagner, Henry Wadsworth Longfellow, and Henrik Ibsen, all of whom helped spread Amalfi's fame.

Exploring Amalfi

Amalfi's compact tourist center is split between the bustling lungomare (waterfront), with its public and private transportation hubs, and the piazza in front of the Duomo. Parking is a big problem, as the small lot in the center of town fills up fast. Traveling here via ferry and bus or staying in a hotel with a parking garage are good ideas. Once you explore the main sights near the waterfront, take off and explore the souklike center, then escape to the outskirts and the terraced hills of the Valle dei Mulini, site of Amalfi's ancient paper mills. At a little waterfall a block or so north of the Museo della Carta, look to the left for a set of scalinatelli and climb the 20-plus steps; follow a footpath to the right, where there's a bench at the edge of a lemon grove. If you buy a fresh lemon along the way—its leaves will be intact and its taste sweeter than you're accustomed to—and down it with a pinch of salt, you'll be passing time as the locals have since the age of the republic.

A Good Walk

Start on the festive waterfront, near the **Porta della Marina** ㉑, where a ceramic panel honors Amalfi's merchant seamen. Past the traffic-filled harborside Piazza Flavio Gioia, which is centered around the **Piazza Flavio Monument** ㉒—named for the Amalfitan inventor of the maritime compass—head east up the waterfront esplanade, lined with palm trees and Victorian streetlights, to the Palazzo dei Municipio (town hall) and its **Museo Civico** ㉓, devoted to civic history (a sculpted overview is on the museum's southern wall). Some may wish to continue along the waterfront up the gentle hill to the Torre di Amalfi, one of the 16th-century defensive towers along the coast, now part of the **Luna Convento** ㉔, a former Franciscan monastery–turned–hotel, where you can relax in its famous 13th-century cloister. From the museum (three minutes) or from the Luna Convento (10 minutes), look for the campanile of the Duomo di Sant' Andrea and head for the piazza in front. This is the very heart of the city, adorned with cafés and the Fontana del Popolo, graced (only in Italy, folks) by both a statue of St. Andrew and a marble female nymph whose breasts spout water. Take a deep breath and head up the monumental staircase to the **Duomo di Sant' Andrea** ㉕, with its museum and noted Paradise Cloister. Head up to the hilltop **Cappuccini Convento** ㉖, reached from Piazza Duomo by climbing Via Annuziatella—one of Amalfi's most evocative, covered passageways (or head out along the waterfront on busy Via M. Camera to the hotel's cliffside elevator). The view from this 12th-century monastery will be worth the blisters. After exploring the cloister and the hotel's frozen-in-time salons, lunch on its terrace, with all Amalfi at your feet.

Head back to Piazza Duomo and go through the medieval arch facing the piazza to the Piazza dei Dogi, also called the blacksmith area, where the Doges' Palazzo stood. The **Arsenale della Repubblica** ㉗ is just south. North, you'll cross covered passageways and little lanes such as Vico dei Pastai, and Via Herculano Marini, leading to the Contrada Campo. From here you can descend to the Via Capuano which cuts through the center of Amalfi along the riverbed of the mountain torrent. With the sound of water gurgling below the road, head up Via Lorenzo di Amalfi toward Via delle Cartiere (Paper Street), a 15- or 20- minute, slightly up-hill stroll. Here is the beginning of the **Valle dei Mulini** ㉘, where the mostly converted mills and waterfalls and the Museo della Carta are evidence of Amalfi's paper industry, still hanging on from the Middle Ages. You can picnic here if you've shopped for take-out *pannini* (sandwiches) along the Via Lorenzo d'Amalfi on the way. Back down the same road, and close to the Porta dell'Ospedale, is the marble entrance to the well-

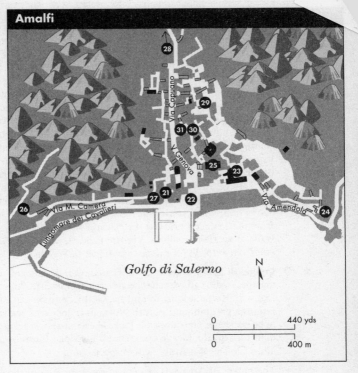

known and nearly straight **Ruga Nova Mercatorum** ㉙, also known as Via dei Mercanti, an old covered street. From here, Salita dei Curiali wends among houses with gardens, and ends at a charming square with the churches of the **Santa Maria Maggiore** ㉚ and the **Maria Santissima Addolorata** ㉛. Look for the nearby campanile of the duomo, and it's back to the piazza there, with a cathedral visit if you haven't paid your respects yet.

TIMING

You'll need at least a half day, perhaps more, depending on how long you spend in the duomo and museums, whether or not you take the optional meanderings—leading to hidden piazzas, the Valle dei Mulini, or lunch at the Cappuccini Convento. Most properties close up by 1 PM, so it's best to start early. Small churches are often open only during mass; ask at your hotel. If you leave right after breakfast and keep a blistering pace, you could finish in time for a late lunch, followed by a long beach siesta.

Sights to See

㉗ **Arsenale della Repubblica.** From the middle of the 11th century, Amalfi's center of shipbuilding, custom houses, and warehouses was the Arsenale, today the only (partially) preserved medieval shipyard in southern Italy. Ships and galleys up to 80 ft, equipped with up to 120 oars, were built at this largest arsenal of any maritime republic. The boat now used for the historical regatta (held every four years), and other ship models are kept in the two large halls accented with Gothic arches. Ten of the original 22 stone piers remain, the others destroyed by storms and changes in the sea level on this ever-active coast. ⊠ *South of Piazza dei Dogi, on corner of Via Camera, by the waterfront.* ☉ *Mon.–Sat. 10–1, 4–8.*

★ ㉖ **Cappuccini Convento.** A noted stop for Grand Tour–era travelers, this medieval monastery enjoys a magnificent hilltop perch. Long famous for its gardens, ½-km-long (¼-mi-long) terrace over Amalfi's harbor, and its Arab-Sicilian cloister, the monastery was originally founded by Cistercian monks in the 13th century as the Convento di S. Pietro della Canonica. Then abandoned, the complex was taken over by the Capuchins in 1583, only to be transformed into a hotel in the mid-19th century when the king of Naples suppressed the religious orders. Immortalized in postcards and paintings, the view of Amalfi's waterfront from the hotel terrace became one of the first travel icons of the 19th century. Henry Wadsworth Longfellow composed a poem to celebrate its beauty and Richard Wagner forsook his guest room to camp out under the stars. Stroll through the monastery and the centuries unwind: the 12th-century cloister has the intertwined Arabic columns of the Amalfi cathedral's great Paradise Cloister, the little church is a Rococo confection, while spirit-warm hallways and salons are little changed from the 19th century. Use the elevator from Via Camera if you don't want to tackle the hillside Via Annuziatella climb. ⊠ *Hotel Cappuccini Convento, Via Annuziatella 46,* ☎ *089/871877.*

★ ㉕ **Duomo di Sant' Andrea.** Complicated, grand, delicate, and dominating, the Amalfi cathedral has been remodeled since its 9th-century founding, with Romanesque, Byzantine, Gothic, and Baroque elements and retains a predominantly Arab-Norman style. Cross and crescent seem to be wed here: The campanile looks like a minaret wearing a Scheherazadian turban, the facade conjures up a striped burnoose, and its Paradise Cloister is a Arab-Sicilian spectacular.

The power of Amalfi is evident in the approach to the cathedral, set atop 62 broad steps that lead to a mosaic facade, redone in the 19th century, and framed by bands, arches, and patterned squares. The imposing bronze doors, the first in Italy, were cast in Constantinople before 1066 and signed by Simeon of Syria; they were commissioned by the leader of the large Amalfitan colony there. Silver incrustations on the doors, now difficult to see, are images of Christ, Mary, and saints. A Gothic portico connects the two basilicas: the ancient 10th-century cathedral and the larger, later Cathedral of Sant'Andrea. The 10th-century structure, called the Chapel of the Crucifix, is in Byzantine style, with a nave, two aisles, and a high, deep apse. Of special note is a 14th-century crucifixion scene by a student of Giotto. This section has now been transformed into a museum, housing sarcophagi, sculpture, Neapolitan goldsmiths' artwork, and other treasures from the cathedral complex.

The Cathedral of St. Andrew was built in the 13th century to house the saint's bones, which came from Constantinople and supposedly exuded a miraculous liquid believers call the "manna of St. Andrew." Amalfi's cathedral had always lured pilgrims—from Francis of Assisi to Pope Urban IV—but after the 14th-century manna manifestation, the pilgrim trade really picked up. The saint's remains (sans head, which is in the Vatican) are kept under the 13th-century high altar in an exceptionally beautiful crypt adorned with marble statues sculpted by Pietro Bernini, father of the famed Gianlorenzo Bernini. The cathedral's interior has elaborate polychrome marbles, and painted, coffered ceilings from its 18th-century restoration; art historians shake their head over this renovation, as the original decoration of the apse must have been one of the wonders of the Middle Ages. However, the original basilica plan has been preserved. The first chapel on the left has a red porphyry baptismal font, supposedly crafted from the ruins of ancient Paestum. Other treasures include a mother-of-pearl cross given by the people of Jerusalem in 1930, in gratitude for Amalfi's help in establishing a 2,000-bed hospital there in 1112, which later became the first military and religious order, the Knights of St. John.

The adjoining **Chiostro del Paradiso** (Paradise Cloister), built around 1266 for Bishop Augustarrico as a burial ground of Amalfi's elite, is one of the architectural treasures of southern Italy. Its flower-and-palm-filled quadrangle has a series of exceptionally delicate, intertwining arches on slender double columns in a combination of Byzantine and Arabian styles. Note the geometric patterns of colored mosaics in the walls, comprising parts of former pillars and pulpits of the earlier church. The striking 12th-century bell tower in front of the complex has a Romanesque base, and an elaborate yellow-and-green-tile top with arches in the local style, a round center surrounded by four smaller cupolas. Spiced with Saracen colors and the intricate tile work of High Barbary, Amalfi's jaunty duomo seems to bring a touch of old Istanbul to town. ⊠ *Piazza Duomo.* ⊠ *3,500 lire to Paradise Cloister and museum.* ☉ *Daily 7–1:30 and 3–8; Paradise Cloister daily 9–1:30 and 3 to 8.*

Fontana dei Popolo. Also known as the Fontana S. Andrea, this Baroque concoction was erected in 1760 in honor of the city patron saint, who legendarily raised a tempest at sea to defeat the Saracens. The cartouches on the base, loaded with cherubs and ladies whose breasts spout water, are often adorned with fresh flowers. The figure of St. Andrew gazes upward at the cathedral that honors him, oblivious to the cafés and hubbub surrounding him. ⊠ *Piazza Duomo.*

㉔ Luna Convento. Legendarily founded by none other than St. Francis of Assisi, the Luna Convento was built in the 13th century and retains a delicate cloister, with distinctive Arab-Sicilian arcaded columns and a crypt with frescoes. Transformed into the earliest hotel on the Amalfi Coast in the early 19th century, the hotel (☞ *below*) was where Henrik Ibsen wrote a large chunk of *A Doll's House.* ⊠ *Via Pantaleone Comite 19,* ☎ *089/871002.*

㉛ Maria Santissima Addolorata. This church is adjacent to the confraternity founded in 1777 to organize Amalfi's Good Friday celebrations. The entrance gate bears a late-Gothic bas-relief of the Crucifixion, once belonging to nobility from the nearby village of Scala and identified by its coat of arms at the foot of the cross. The interior is Neoclassical, with a harmonious scale and coffered ceiling; note the 16th-century marble Madonna and Child in the sacristy. ⊠ *Largo Santa Maria Maggiore.*

㉓ Museo Civico. The Municipal Museum of Amalfi contains artifacts from Amalfi's medieval period, including paintings, ancient coins, banners, and jeweled costumes. The highlight is the original 66-chapter draft of the code of the *Tavole Amalfitane,* the sea laws and customs of the ancient republic used throughout the Italian Mediterranean from the 13th to the 16th centuries. The Tavole established everything from prices for boat hires to procedures to be followed in case of shipwreck. Long one of the treasures of the Imperial Library of Vienna, the draft was returned to Amalfi after more than 500 years. Note the ceramic panel on the south outside wall of the museum, between Corso delle Repubbliche Marinare and Piazza del Municipio, created by Diodoro Cossa in the 1970s. The scenes provide an overview of local history: Roman refugees establishing themselves in nearby Scala in the 4th century; the founding of Amalfi by these same Romans; Amalfi's commercial and diplomatic role in the Mediterranean; the arrival of St. Andrew's body; the invention of the maritime compass, among other historic events. ⊠ *Piazza Municipio, entrance off Corso Roma,* ☎ *089/871066.* ⊠ *Free.* ☉ *Mon.–Sat. 9–2.*

Piazza dei Dogi. The only intact medieval piazza in Amalfi, this was once called Piazza dei Ferrari (that's as in blacksmiths, not sports cars); the city's forges were located here. Traces remain of the four churches that once stood at this spot. The focal point is the palazzo of the feudal Piccolominis, dukes of Amalfi and relatives of Pope Pius II, who held the Amalfi duchy between 1461 and 1583. Legend says that the doomed love story of the duchess of Amalfi and her steward—popularized in the famous Elizabethan-era play of Richard Webster took place in this palace. ⊠ *North of the Arsenale, just off Piazza Duomo.*

㉒ **Piazza Flavio Gioia.** A statue, set in a circular greensward in front of the harbor, honors the Amalfitan credited with inventing the maritime compass in 1302. Many say it was the Chinese who invented the compass, passing the idea along to the Arabs, who traded with Amalfi; Gioia may have adapted it for sea use (some even believe there was no such person as Gioia). ⊠ *On the waterfront.*

㉑ **Porta della Marina.** This gateway "door" to the harbor bears a ceramic panel, created by Renato Rossi in the 1950s, commemorating the trade routes of the republic during the Middle Ages. For one example, ships loaded up with timber from Italy traded it in North Africa, then used the gold obtained from those sales to buy gems, spices, and silks in Asia to trade in Italy. ⊠ *Across from Piazza Flavio Gioia, next to arsenal.*

㉙ **Ruga Nova Mercantorum.** Also known as Via dei Mercanti, evocative Ruga Nova was the main thoroughfare of medieval Amalfi, and it remains the most fascinating "street" in town. Claustrophobes, beware: It is completely covered, like a tunnel, but is especially wonderful when the light from alleys and windows plays on its white walls. Stretching from the Porta dell'Ospedale to the Salita dei Curiali, it ends at a medieval-era *contrade,* or neighborhood, filled with gardens and churches. ⊠ *Contrade S. Simone, just north of Maria Santissima Addolorata.*

㉚ **Santa Maria Maggiore.** Constructed by Duke Mansone I in 986, as inscribed on a capital at the entrance, the church has a Byzantine layout, although a 16th-century overhaul inverted the entrance and high altar, and the decoration is now mostly Baroque; the remains of San Felice and an 18th-century crèche scene are worth noting. The campanile dates from the 12th century. ⊠ *Largo Santa Maria Maggiore, near cathedral.*

㉘ **Valle dei Mulini.** The Valley of the Mills, uphill from town, was for centuries Amalfi's center for papermaking, an ancient trade learned from the Arabs (who learned it from the Chinese). Beginning in the 12th century, former macaroni mills in the town were converted to the production of paper made from cotton and linen, being among the first in Europe to do so. In 1211 Frederick II of Sicily prohibited this lighter, more readable paper for use in the preparation of official documents, favoring traditional sheepskin parchment, but by 1811 more than a dozen mills here, with more along the coast, were humming. Natural waterpower ensured that the handmade paper was cost-effective, but catastrophic flooding in 1954 closed most of the mills for good, and many of them have now been converted into private housing. The **Museo della Carta** (Museum of Paper) opened in 1971 in a 15th-century mill; paper samples, tools of the trade, old machinery, and the audiovisual presentation are all enlightening. A 20-minute stroll from the Piazza Duomo will take you to the valley via the main thoroughfare of Via Genoa, turning onto Via Capuano, at the edge of town. ⊠ *Museo della Carta,* ☎ *089/872610.* ☺ *9–1.* ☺ *Mon., Wed.–Thurs., Sat.–Sun. 9–1.*

OFF THE
BEATEN PATH

VIA MAESTRA DEI VILLAGI – West to Pogerola, with its two small churches and tower overlooking an expanse of the coast, you will have to climb about 1,000 steps through a valley—more or less; you can also take a bus or car along the upland road. A car, or a trek by foot along a path called Via Maestra dei Villagi, will bring you to Vettica, Lone, Pastena, and Tovere, a series of villages William Wadsworth Longfellow—who didn't just stay in New England writing about Hiawatha—described as "heaven beyond the sea."

Dining and Lodging

$$$$ ✕ **Da Gemma.** Cognoscenti have sung the praises of this understated landmark since 1872. Tile floors, green tablecloths, and a terrace set above the main street are soothing elements. The kitchen glistens, the menu is printed on locally handmade paper, and Amalfi foodies appreciate favorites that include *cianfotta*, a creation featuring eggplant, potatoes, onions, and peppers and *paccheri del marinaio*, or macaroni with monkfish and squid. ⊠ *Via Fra Gerardo Sasso 9, ☎ 089/871345. Reservations essential. AE, MC, V. Closed Wed. from Sept. to June; Jan. 15–Feb. 15.*

$$$$ ✕ **Eolo.** This is both one of the newest restaurants on the Amafi Coast
★ and one of the most sophisticated. The decor is suavely tranquil—white coved ceilings, Romanesque columns, mounted starfish—while the kitchen is anything but: Masterminded by a member of the Gargano family (who also own the Hotel Santa Caterina), it tosses out gastronomic delights like lobster risotto, sea bass with lemon salt and fennel leaves, zucchini flan, and a fine dessert of eggplant and chocolate. Many dishes are fetchingly adorned with blossoms and other visual allures, but nothing compares to the view of Amalfi's harbor from one of the tables in Eolo's picture-window alcove; try to get one of these. ⊠ *Via Pantaleone Comite 3, ☎ 089/874241. Reservations essential. AE, MC, V. Closed Wed.; Jan.–Feb.*

$$$–$$$$ ✕ **La Caravella.** Cobalt blue napery, antiques, tall candles, lace tablecloths, flowered curtains, marble floors, and Andrea Bocelli's golden voice on the sound system have helped to make this the most romantic restaurant in Amalfi, at least since 1959. The tasting menu is imaginative, but if you have to choose, just utter the lilting phrase *"Polpo varace affogato su letto di lentucchie"* for a masterful dish of fresh poached octopus on a bed of lentils. ⊠ *Via Matteo Camera 12, near Arsenale, ☎ 089/871029. AE, MC, V. Closed Tues. and Nov.*

$$ ✕ **Al Pesce d'Oro.** The big-hearted brothers who oversee the place, their kids who serve you, and mamma and the other family-folk who keep the kitchen hopping at this comfortable roadside restaurant just west of town will win your heart. None of them speak much English—it's a local fave, so they don't have to—but you'll have fun getting by, and you'll have a terrific meal, specializing in—what else?—pesce, fresh as the sea. Try the fusilli with mussels and clams. ⊠ *Via Giovanni Agustariccio, ☎ 089/831231. AE, DC, MC, V.*

$$ ✕ **Il Teatro.** Once a children's theater, this informal, high-ceiling, white-stucco restaurant in the medieval quarter is 50 steps above the main drag and most charming. A house pasta specialty is *scialatielli al teatro* and the pizzas are terrific. ⊠ *Via E. Marini 19, ☎ 089/872473. AE, MC, V. Closed Wed. and Jan.*

$$ ✕ **Lo Smeraldino.** Open since 1949, this airy, popular fish restaurant on Amalfi's almost-emerald waterfront dishes out reasonably priced seafood and *cucina tipica Amalfitana*, such as the tasty penne with tomatoes, cream, eggplant, peppers, basil, and cheese. You can see the boats bringing in the day's catch, along with Amalfi itself, and at night there's pizza on the terrace amid the twinkling lights of hills, sea, and sky. ⊠ *Piazzale dei Protontini 1, ☎ 089/871070. AE, MC, V.*

$$ ✕ **Trattoria da Ciccia-Cielo-Mare-Terra.** Big windows overlook the sky, sea, and land, and there is ample free parking, so this modern seafood restaurant is a good place to stop if you're driving. Young owner Francesco Cavaliere will give you a warm welcome. Spaghetti *al cartoccio,* baked in a paper bag, with clams, olives, capers, and tomatoes, is an Amalfi tradition. Finish up with a lemon profiterole, a nice adaptation for the ubiquitous citrus. ✉ *Via Giovanni Agustariccio, across from Al Pesce d'Oro,* ☎ *089/831265. AE, MC, V. Closed Nov. and Feb.*

$ ✕ **Il Tari.** Locals highly recommend this cozy little ristorante, named after the ancient coin of the Amalfi Republic and located a few minutes' walk north of the Duomo. Appealing touches include local art, red tablecloths, old photos, and tile floors—not to mention wood-oven-baked thin-crust pizza with fresh sauces, and pasta specialties including tagliatelle *alla Tari.* ✉ *Via P. Capuano,* ☎ *089/871832. AE, MC, V. Closed Nov.*

$$$$ 🏨 **Il Saraceno.** Gothic, Arabic, Oriental—and Las Vegas—influences combine to form this gorgeous extravaganza set on a chunk of cliff 3 km (2 mi) from Amalfi (its official address, but the hotel is really just outside Conca dei Marini). The evocatively exotic decor, which refers to Saracen pirates who roamed this coast centuries ago, begins in the lobby adorned with impressive 19th-century Orientalist oil paintings and antiques. Below, night-illuminated garden terraces descend the hillside to the enormous private beach, which features a saltwater pool. Dining options include a Romanesque cellar with candelabra and fireplace, a formal restaurant called Atlantis, and an alfresco terrace under a vine-covered lattice. Mosaic floors, elaborate antique lighting fixtures, a medieval warrior in full armor, and gilded murals are accents, and guest rooms have crown-molded ceilings, rich colors, antiques, and terraces with floor-to-ceiling window panoramas. The hotel also maintains a private Romanesque stone chapel. Whew. ✉ *Conca dei Marini (on the road to Amalfi), 84011,* ☎ *089/831148,* FAX *089/831595. 56 rooms with bath. 2 restaurants, 2 bars, air-conditioning, pool, private beach, meeting facilities, parking. AE, DC, MC, V. Closed Nov.–Mar.*

$$$$ 🏨 **Santa Caterina.** When Elizabeth Taylor and Richard Burton wanted
★ to escape, they headed here, and who can blame them? Owned by the Gargano family for generations, this quietly elegant, supremely comfortable hotel has long been one of the treasures of the coast. Just outside Amalfi proper, the Santa Caterina takes full advantage of its hillside location, with enormous terraced gardens and a luscious seawater-pool area, complete with a thatched-roof, open-air café. The lobby is charmingly coved, while decor is unobtrusively traditional, with Belle Epoque accents. The luckiest guests are allowed to book the hotel's 19th-century châlet, set at water's edge at the far end of the hotel's romantic orchards. ✉ *Strada Amalfitana 9, 84011,* ☎ *089/871012,* FAX *089/871351. 54 rooms with bath. Restaurant, bar, pool. AE, DC, MC, V.*

$$$ 🏨 **Cappuccini Convento.** There is more than a touch of the time ma-
★ chine to this sublimely beautiful hotel, founded as a convent in the 14th century, transformed into a hostelry in the early 19th, and whose ambience remains the most richly atmospheric of any hotel on the Amalfi Coast. Set on a sky-touching cliff above the sea, its bougainvillea-draped terrace frames a view of Amalfi's harbor so perfect it became the iconic image of the region in the 19th century. Today, the hotel seems little changed from the days when its welcomed Longfellow, Wagner, kings, and queens. Intriguing passages lined with Victorian lecterns and Savonarola chairs lead to an Arab-Sicilian cloister (now a reception center) and a Rococo-era chapel, while guest rooms are converted friar's cells and suites. Just remember: If you haven't stood on the terrace of this hotel, you really haven't been to the Amalfi Coast. ✉ *Via Annuziatella 46, 84011,* ☎ *089/871877,* FAX *089/871886. 54 rooms with bath. Restaurant, bar, parking. AE, MC, V.*

$$$ ⊞ **Luna Convento.** Founded as a convent in 1222, allegedly by no less a personage than St. Francis of Assisi, the hotel has been owned by the Barbaro family since 1822 and visited by Otto van Bismarck, Mussolini, Ingrid Bergman, and Tennessee Williams, among other noted figures. The restaurant and bar are in the 15th-century Saracen Tower, perched on a rock over the sea which provides a view that spans from Capo dei Conca to Capo d'Orso. Coved ceilings, graceful arches, and marble columns mark the architecture, along with Flemish religious artwork, church and convent artifacts, antique furnishings, and mosaic flooring, all of which mix with modern comforts. The heart of the hotel is the famed southern Romanesque cloisters and the beautiful Baroque chapel. Below the tower is a rocky beach and waterside pool. Ask for a room in the renovated wing. The food, alas, does not measure up. ⊠ *Via P. Comite 33, 84011,* ☎ *089/871002,* 🖷 *089/871333. 45 rooms with bath. Restaurant, pool, private beach, meeting rooms. AE, DC, MC, V.*

$$$ ⊞ **Miramalfi.** High above the main coastal drive, this white-stucco hotel overlooks deep blue water and coastal ridges. The hotel's elevators, or a steep hike, deposit you at the pool, with a rock ledge for sunbathing carved from the cliff. Lobbies are sleekly decorated, and the dining room serves up wraparound panoramas along with a nightly buffet; guests may also dine on the sea-air terrace. Rooms have vibrant tile flooring, brightly painted furnishings, floral fabrics, wicker, and lots of windows. All have private sea-view balconies, and some have whirlpools. ⊠ *Via Quasimodo 3, 84011,* ☎ *089/871588,* 🖷 *089/871287. 48 rooms with bath. Restaurant, bar, air-conditioning, pool, private beach, parking. AE, DC, MC, V. Closed Nov.*

$$ ⊞ **Aurora.** Regarded for its location near the beach of Spiaggia d'Sirene and the fishing harbor, this well-run little hotel is a good deal for sand potatoes who prefer absorbing rays to hiking the highlands. Amid a greenery-filled setting with three levels of arched windows, guest rooms are clean, with water views, and although just a flat and easy 10-minute walk to the town duomo, crowds rarely venture to this nook. ⊠ *Lungomare, on the harbor between Scalo d'Oriente and Lungomare dei Cavalieri, 84001,* ☎ *089/871209,* 🖷 *089/872980. 29 rooms with bath. Restaurant, breakfast room. AE, MC, V. Closed Nov.– Mar.*

$$ ⊞ **Piccolo Paradiso.** A location in the Amalfi harbor area just across from the Arsenale already makes this upscale B&B a special choice. A small elevator deposits you in the cozy house, sunny yellow with green shutters, with a casually furnished sea-air and sun-bright terrace. The atmosphere is more pleasing and elegant than that of a typical pensione. A common area has tile flooring, and rooms are smallish but comfortable, with wicker seating and wrought-iron headboards, even some private terraces. Open only a few years, everything sparkles, and you'll get to know your fellow international guests in this little paradise. ⊠ *Via M. Camera 5, 84011,* ☎ *089/873001. 8 rooms with bath. No credit cards.*

$–$$ ⊞ **La Bussola.** Originally a mill and pasta factory, this clean, well-run, moderate-price hotel is on a relatively quiet street across from the harbor. The chrome-and-wood American bar, velour seating, psychedelic tile flooring, and wall sculptures combine to create an ingenuously funk setting—the Austin Powers of decor. A big terrace features wooden shutters, wrought-iron grilles, and azure-blue tiles echoing the hue of the sea visible over the railing. The smallish guest rooms have soft lighting, warm wood furnishings, and small balconies. This is a great value for the money. ⊠ *Lungomare dei Cavalieri 16, 84011,* ☎ *089/871533,* 🖷 *089/871369. 62 rooms with bath. Restaurant, bar, parking. AE, DC, MC, V.*

$ ⊡ **Sole.** This three-story, white-stucco pensione near the municipal museum and an easy stroll to the harbor has a café and flower boxes on the balconies. The lobby is clean and airy, with a graceful staircase, archways, and wrought-iron lighting fixtures, and there's an old mahogany bar. Some simply furnished rooms have balconies or terraces. Though the place is pretty basic, choose a double room, and you will have adequate accommodations, and with half- or full-board, extra-special value. ⊠ *Largo della Zecca 2, 84011,* ☎ *089/871147 or 089/871559,* ℻ *089/871926. 22 rooms with bath. Restaurant, bar, parking. AE, DC, MC, V.*

Festivals

Amalfi's festivals best reflect the splendor of its past. The **St. Andrew Race** every June 27, dedicated to Amalfi's protector of seamen, is a joyous religious celebration commemorating the defeat of Barbarossa and the Moslem fleet in 1544. A procession of white-robed men carry a silver-gilt replica of the saint to the harbor, and fishermen at the beach run it back to the cathedral and—in one dramatic dash—straight up its 62 steps. Later, the statue gleams silver in the sunshine of the piazza, as fishermen hang tiny wooden and gilt fish amulets from the saint's left wrist as tokens of gratitude. In the evening, guitar music drifts from many boats, and candlelight flickers.

Even more of a pageant is the **Regatta Storica delle Antiche Repubbliche Marinare** (Historical Regatta; ☎ 089/871107), the mock battles in which four boats, each with eight oarsmen, represent the medieval maritime republics of Amalfi, Pisa, Genoa, and Venice. The prize, held by the winner for a year, is a scale-model gold-and-silver replica of an antique sailing ship. Each of the former republics is represented by 80 participants; Amalfi's musical contingent is adorned in jewel-encrusted costumes on loan from the town museum—doges, dogaressas, merchants, and commoners from the prosperous past come colorfully to life, with the day's festivities culminating in a show of fireworks. Held yearly on the first Sunday in June, with the four cities alternating as the urban stage sets, the pageant is scheduled to be in Amalfi in 2000.

Amalfitans love to celebrate holidays. The Good Friday candlelight procession, Easter Sunday, and Christmas pageants with crèche competitions (with cribs mounted in the city fountains) are all excuses for lavish family occasions, with special foods and church ceremonies.

Nightlife

Amalfi doesn't have many clubs for music or dancing. Check out **Torre Saracena** (⊠ Across from Luna Convento Hotel, on the water, ☎ 089/ 871064)—a historic watchtower recycled to offer music and dancing.

Shopping

The **Caritera Amatruda,** in the Amatruda Mill (⊠ Via Fiume, near museum, ☎ 089/871315) is run by descendents of an Amalfi papermaking dynasty dating from 1200; it is probably the oldest crafts paper shop in Italy and still produces and sells fine parchment-color handmade paper. The shop is a short uphill walk north of Largo Marini on Via delle Cartiere. Leather goods are popular items in small shops along the main streets; one good option is **Bazar Florio** (⊠ Via P. Capuano, ☎ 089/871980), with a fair and friendly owner. It features handbags, wallets, and backpacks. **D'Antuono** (⊠ Piazza Duomo 11, ☎ 089/ 872368) sells art books, old prints, and fine paper goods. **Mostacciuto** (⊠ Piazza Duomo 22, ☎ 089/871552) is run by a well-known and respected coral craftsmen. A must-stop for lovers of art, vintage prints, and fine books is **Andrea de Luca** (⊠ Largo Cesareo Console 8, ☎ 089/ 872976), a publisher of fine books and postcards, whose shop sells beautiful silk flowers, desk accessories, objets d'art, and art tomes.

Atrani

🔵 *1 km (½ mi) east of Amalfi; 5 km (3 mi) southwest of Ravello.*

★ Ask hotel owners and longtime residents of the Costiera Amalfitana where their favorite spot is along the coast, and they often respond "Atrani." Most actually whisper, as if it were some secret treasure— and in some respects, it is: Set atop a crag between cliffs overlooking the sea, and just a 10-minute walk from the western outskirts of Amalfi—take the seaside stairs off the drive, past the Luna Convento— this stage-set of a medieval town is centered around a small piazza. When closely linked to the republic, the town was the residential choice of Amalfi aristocracy. Now home to 1,000 or so residents, Atrani is largely overlooked by tourists, who drive right by it over the riverbed of the Torrente Dragone. But its special charms are most evident from the sea, as it appears like an amphitheater ready for a royal pageant.

Adorable Piazza Umberto I, entirely enclosed by four-storied houses, is the setting for the basics of Italian life: general store, stationery store, coffee shop, bar, fruit stand, restaurant, barber, and, of course, police station (the constable struts about as though in command of the pigeons strutting alongside him). The uncrowded square is filled with simple scenes: children giggle at hide-and-seek, *duenas* gossip, and men debate and take sips from the venerable fountain as if the world had little changed from the days of the doges. An arcade to one side offers a glimpse of beach, fishing boats, a mule or two, and the sea beyond. At Christmas the whole town congregates here at dawn to drink cappuccino and share traditional cakes.

Atrani's closely packed, dollhouse-scaled backstreets are filled with pastel and white houses and shops, fragrant gardens, arcaded lanes, and spiraling scalinatelli. But the hamlet's stellar attractions are the Baroque-style churches which dominate the skyline, and around which parish houses cluster in true medieval style. The bell of the 10th-century Church of **San Salvatore de Bireto** tolled to announce the crowning of a new doge. The coronation ceremony was restricted to those wearing a *bireto,* the cloth cap that would be ceremoniously placed on the new doge's head, and someday worn at his burial in the same church. The church was remodeled in 1810; the dome is beautifully tiled, and the paneled bronze doors cast in the 11th century came from Constantinople, as did the doors in the Amalfi Duomo. Within is a carved 12th-century marble plaque showing peacocks standing over a man and a rabbit; peacocks were considered immortal, but the symbolism of the other two in this setting is open to interpretation.

The Church of **Santa Maria Maddalena,** set on a piazza, was built in 1274 and given a Baroque facade in 1852. The dome is covered in majolica tile, and the bell tower has an octagonal belfry similar to the campanile of the Carmine church in Naples. Among the treasures here are an altar in richly colored marbles and paintings attributed to Amalfi Coast artists: *St. Magdalen between St. Sebastian and St. Andrew,* by Giovannangelo D'Amato of Maiori, and *The Incredulity of St. Thomas,* by Andrea da Salerno.

On the slopes of towering Monte Aureo, the small **Chiesa del Bando** (Church of the Banns), dedicated to the Virgin Mary, was the site of most official republic proclamations. Behind it is a cave known as the Grotto of Masaniello, named for the hero, born in Atrani, who headed the Neapolitan rebellion against Spanish domination in the 17th century; he supposedly hid out in the grotto when his public standing began to wane.

Feisty little Atrani, which produces colorful ceramics along with its charm, gained its independence from Amalfi in 1578, with whom it maintains a friendly rivalry; locals say the town holds its processions on its narrow inner streets to discourage Amalfitans from participating.

Dining and Lodging

$–$$ ✕ **A. Paranza.** In back of the piazza, on the main walkway, this fine old restaurant, graced by a mural of fishermen, is the best to be found in Atrani. Everything glistens, from the tile floors to the fresh seafood. Dine on the special tasting menu—depending on the day's catch—or you can always count on spaghetti *ai frutti di mare.* ✉ *Via Dragone,* ☎ *089/871840. AE, MC, V. Closed Tues. and Oct.*

$ ✕ **Le Arcate.** A cave is not where you'd normally expect to find good food, but this one changes the rules. The simple, dark, old restaurant tucked under the road also has a large terrace overlooking the beach. Folks dig its *Scialatielli Masaniello*—fresh pasta named after the local boy who made good—as well as its pizza and grilled fish. It's been here for 50 years, a drop in the gulf around these parts. ✉ *Via G. Di Benedetto 4, under arcades of roadway connecting Amalfi and Atrani,* ☎ *089/871367. AE, MC, V. Closed Mon. in winter; Jan.*

$ ✕ **Ristorante Masaniello.** *Cucina tipica marinara* is served informally here, between Piazza Umberto and the beach. All the best P-words are on the menu: pasta, pizza, and pesce, as well as excellent gelati. The friendly owner speaks English, and for a full-budget experience, there's a tasting menu. ✉ *Via Supportico Marinella 1,* ☎ *089/871942. AE, MC, V. Closed Tues. during winter.*

$ ▣ **A' Scalinatella.** Filippo, the Donald Trump of Atrani, runs just about the only game in the village, with hostel beds, private rooms, and apartments (some with kitchens and washing machines) spread all over the place. These are only modest digs, but if you want to wake up in Atrani, you'll deal with it. A family restaurant on the piazza offers good, inexpensive food, for guests only, and there's a special low-price menu for students. ✉ *Piazza Umberto 12, 84010,* ☎ *089/871492,* FAX *089/871930. 30 rooms, some with bath. No credit cards.*

RAVELLO TO PAESTUM

Perched atop a ridge of Monte Cerreto "closer to the sky than the sea," according to French philosopher Andre Gide, Ravello gazes down on the Bay of Salerno and the humbler towns surrounding it, including Atrani. This cloud-riding perch is just one reason why some travelers give it the laurel as the Amalfi Coast's—some say Italy's—most beautiful town. Hearty souls trek between Atrani and Ravello by a path that climbs through the Valle del Dragone, or Dragon's Valley, a name inspired by the morning mists here. Most Ravello-bound travelers, however, take the municipal bus from Amalfi's Piazza Flavio Gioia, which corkscrews its way up 1,000 ft along a road in the southern Monti Lattari. Cars follow the same route and really come in handy when driving farther south along Statale 163 to the towns rimming the Bay of Salerno, which have their off-the-beaten-track appeal.

After the Torre dello Scarpariello, Statale 163 descends into Minori, where there is a good beach. The road climbs up the cape by Torre Mezzacapo, then drops back down to sea level near the 15th-century Church of St. Francisco. Statale 163 then goes though the town of Maiori, with another good beach, and passes Capo di Baia Verde, near the 16th-century Torre Normanna. The coast here becomes dramatic again, giving grand views of the sea as you climb past the promontory topped by Torre di Badia. Capo Tummolo and then Vallone di San Nicola, with the little village of Marina di Erchie, are ahead of you. The drive then descends to the fishing village of Cetara, set along a narrow inlet, then continues along the coast, passing Torre de Fuenti and Vallone di Albori, and then faces the sea near Torre della Marina di Albori. At the junction of Raito, a lush little village, you cross the bridge over the Vallone Bonea to the town of Vietri, at which point traffic-light reality returns. Follow Statale 163 to the city of Salerno. The Autostrada A3 south connects to E45 which leads to the ancient temples of Paestum.

Ravello

★ ③ *6½ km (4 mi) northeast of Amalfi; 29 km (18 mi) west of Salerno.*

Positano may focus on pleasure, and Amalfi on history, but cool, serene Ravello revels in refinement. Thrust over Statale 163 and the Bay of Salerno on a mountain buttress, above forests of chestnut and ash, terraced lemon groves and vineyards, it early on beckoned the affluent with its island-in-the-sky views and secluded defensive positioning. Gardens out of the *Arabian Nights,* pastel palazzos, tucked-away piazzas with medieval fountains, architecture ranging from Romano-Byzantine-to-Norman-Saracen, and those sweeping blue-water, blue-sky vistas have inspired a panoply of large personalities, including Wagner and Boccaccio, princes and popes, aesthetes and hedonists, and a stream of famous authors, from Virginia Woolf to Tennessee Williams. Author and part-time resident Gore Vidal, not an easy critic, has called the town's Villa Cimbrone panorama "the most beautiful view in the world."

It was settled by Romans fleeing the sack of their dying empire, leaving behind the ruins of their once splendid villas. The town itself was founded in the 9th century, under Amalfi's rule, until residents prosperous from cotton tussled with the superpower republic and elected their own doge in the 11th century; Amalfitans dubbed them *rebelli* (rebels). In the 12th century, with the aid of the Norman king Roger, they even succeeded in resisting Pisa's army for a couple of years, though the powerful Pisans returned to wreak destruction along the coast. Even so, Ravello's skilled seafaring trade with merchants and Moors from Sicily and points east led to a burgeoning wealth, which peaked in the 13th century, when there were 13 churches, four cloisters, and dozens of sumptuous villas. Neapolitan princes built palaces; life was privileged.

But as is inevitable with all supernovas, Ravello's bright light diminished, first through Pisa's maritime rise in the 14th century, then through rivalry between its warring families in the 15th century. When the plague cast its shadow in the 17th century, the population plummeted from upwards of 30,000 to maybe a couple of thousand souls, where it remains today. When Ravello was incorporated into the diocese of Amalfi in 1804, a kind of stillness settled in. Despite the decline of its power and populace, Ravello's cultural heritage and special loveliness continued to blossom. Gardens flowered and music flowed in the ruined villas, and artists, sophisticates, and their lovers filled the crumbling palazzos. Grieg, Wagner, D. H. Lawrence, Chanel, Garbo and her companion, conductor Leopold Stokowski, and then, slowly, tourists followed in their footsteps. Today, at the Villa Rufolo, the noted Fèstival Musicale di Ravello is held in its shaded gardens. Here, special Wagnerian concerts are often held to pay homage to the great composer, who was inspired by these gardens to compose scenes of *Parsifal.*

With the exception of the Villa Rufolo concerts, however, the hush lingers, especially in off-season, when there seem to be more cats than cars. Empty, narrow streets morph into whitewashed staircases rising into a haze of azure, which could be from the sea, the sky, or a union of both. About the only places that don't seem to be in pianissimo slow motion are Piazza Vescovado, by the duomo, during the evening passeggiata, or cafés at pranzo (luncheon) or cena (dinner) time. Languor becomes Ravello's mood, a bit out of sync with the world below, and it makes this town a lovely place to catch your breath. Ravello, the slightly aloof star high above the coast, remains there for the reaching and is worth the stretch. Note that the town likes to celebrate religious festas throughout the year—one of the nicest celebrations is the blossom-strewn celebration of Pentecost (usually the first week of June), when the Piazza del Duomo is ornamented with sidewalk pictures created with flower petals.

Although cars need to park in the municipal parking lot, most arriving buses deposit their passengers at the hillside tunnel that leads to the Piazza del Duomo. On the square you'll find the tourist office, just to the left of the 11th-century duomo stairs, and the Bric-a-Brac shop, a great resource for books on Ravello. Here, pride of place is taken by the **Duomo,** or town cathedral, dedicated to patron St. Pantaleone and founded in 1086 by Orso Papiro, the first bishop of Ravello. Rebuilt in the 12th and 17th centuries, it retains traces of medieval frescoes in the transept, an original mullioned window, a marble portal, and a three-story 13th-century bell tower playfully interwoven with mullioned windows and arches. The 12th-century bronze door (1179) features 54 embossed panels depicting Christ's life, and saints, prophets, plants, and animals, all narrating biblical lore. It was crafted by Barisano da Trani, who also fashioned the doors of the cathedrals of Train and Monreale. The nave's three aisles are divided by ancient columns, and treasures include sarcophagi from Roman times and paintings by southern Renaissance artist Andrea da Salerno. Most impressive are the two 12th-century *ambos,* or pulpits: The earliest one, used for reading the Epistles, is inset with a mosaic scene of Jonah and the whale, symbolizing death and redemption. The more famous one, used for reading the Gospels, was commissioned by Nicolo Rufolo in 1272 and created by Niccolo di Bartolomeo da Foggia. It seems almost Tuscan in style, with exquisite Cosmatesque mosaic work and bas-reliefs and six twisting columns sitting on lion pedestals. An eagle grandly tops the colonnette fronting the inlaid marble lectern. Here in 1149, Adrian IV, the English pope, crowned William the Bad, king of Sicily.

A chapel is dedicated to the left of the apse to St. Pantaleone, a physician, who was beheaded in the 3rd century in Nicomedia. Every July 27 devout believers gather in hope of witnessing a miracle (similar to that of St. Gennaro in Naples), in which the saint's blood, collected in a vial and set out on an inlaid marble altar, appears to liquefy and come to a boil (it hasn't happened in recent years). In the crypt is the **Museo del Duomo**, which displays treasures from around the 13th century, during the reign of Frederick II of Sicily, in an elegant setting. You'll find gold and silver work, sculpture, and a classic Campanian marble bust of a half-smiling woman from the Rufulo dynasty, whose name was Silgigaita (try saying that one with a mouthful of *scialatelli*). ✉ *Museo del Duomo, Piazza del Duomo.* ☉ *Summer, daily 9–1 and 3–7; winter, daily 9:30–1 and 3–7.*

Hard by the duomo on the main piazza is the three-aisle 13th-century **Santa Maria a Gradillo** with its lovely dome. This was the place where the town noblemen gathered to discuss civic issues; its atrium collapsed in the 18th century. The small Sicilian-Saracenic bell tower has two light mullion windows. Next door is the **Museo dei Corallo** (Coral Museum), which shows the venerable tradition of Italian workmanship in coral, harvested for centuries from the gulfs of Salerno and Naples and crafted into jewelry, cameos, and figurines. Look in particular for a carved Christ from the 17th century and a tobacco box covered in cameos. ⊠ *Piazza del Duomo.* ⊙ *Mon.–Sat. 10–12, 3–5.*

★ Opposite the duomo is the **Villa Rufolo,** built in the 13th century by Landolfo Rufolo, whose immense fortune stemmed from trade with the Moors and the Saracens. Now the setting for the Fèstival Musicale di Ravello, its Romanesque walls contain a scene that seems from the earliest days of the Crusades. Norman and Arab architecture mingle in profusion in a welter of color-filled gardens so lush that composer Richard Wagner used them as inspiration for Klingsor's Garden, the home of the Flower Maidens, in his opera *Parsifal.* Beyond the Arab-Sicilian cloister and the Norman tower are two flower-bedded terraces that offer the prime vista of the Bay of Salerno, set off by the cupolas of the 13th-century Church of Santissima Annunziata and a dramatic umbrella pine tree. In 1851 the villa was acquired by Sir Francis Nevil Reid, a Scotsman, who hired Michele Ruggiero, head of the excavations at Pompeii, to restore the villa to its full splendor and replant the gardens with rare cyclads, cordylines, and palms. Highlights of the villa are its Moorish cloister—an Arabic-Sicilian delight with interlacing lancet arcs and polychromatic palmette decoration—and the 14th-century Torre Maggiore, the so-called Klingsor's Tower, renamed in honor of Richard Wagner's landmark 1880 visit, today a dramatic spot for chamber-music recitals (note that when weather is rainy, concerts are moved into a nearby charmless room). Beyond lie two spectacular terrace gardens, with the lower one, the "Wagner Terrace," often the site for orchestral concerts (☞ Concerts *in* Nightlife and the Arts, *below*). ⊠ *Piazza Vescovado, 84010,* ☎ *089/857866.* ⊡ *4,000 lire.* ⊙ *Daily 9–sunset.*

For a closer look at the **Santissima Annunziata** (now a center hosting conferences of the Center for Research for Villas and their Urban Environments, based at the Villa Rufolo), exit the villa and walk right to reach the Via dell'Annunziata stair path, which plummets you down the hillside past the church to the scenic Via della Repubblica. Head back up the road to the town square and take Via Richard Wagner, behind the tourist office, to Via San Giovanni a Toro, the address of Ravello's grandest palazzi (now hotels). **Villa Episcopio,** a 12th-century bishop's residence, was formerly called Villa di Sangro. Amid the gardens and ruins, Italy's King Vittorio Emanuele III abdicated in favor of his son, and Jackie Kennedy enjoyed breaks from her public obligations. Vineyards here have been cultivating grapes since 1860, and varieties of Ravello rosso and bianco, as refined as their namesake, can be purchased in town.

Farther along the Via San Giovanni a Toro, gourmands and art lovers will want to stop at the **Hotel Caruso Belvedere,** set in an historic palazzo with a Empire-era *grande salone,* adorned with dozens of 19th-century Neapolitan paintings. Picnickers can enjoy the wonderful view of the adjacent Belvedere Principessa di Piemonte. Across the tiny piazza is the 11th-century Church of **San Giovanni a Toro.** Its evocative interior has three high apses and a crypt with 14th-century frescoes of Christ and the apostles. A 12th-century ambo by Alfano da Termoli startles, with its blue Persian majolica and four columns topped with elaborate capitals. The chapel of the Coppola family in the left aisle has an exceptional 14th-century relief of St. Catherine of Alexandria. The small church's three porticos adorned with lunettes show an Arabian influence and the tripart back facade is exquisite. ⊠ *Piazza di Toro.*

To the west of the main square, a hilly 10-minute walk along Via San
★ Francesco brings you to the **Villa Cimbrone,** whose gardens and

Belvedere of Infinity perch 1,500 ft above the sea. The ultimate aerie, this medieval-style fantasy was created in 1905 by England's Lord Grimthorpe, and made world famous when Greta Garbo found sanctuary here from the world press when she holidayed in Ravello with Leopold Stokowski in 1937. The Gothic *castello-palazzo* is set in idyllic gardens, which are divided by the grand Alleé of Immensity, leading in turn to the **Belvedere of Infinity.** This grand stone parapet, adorned with amusing stone busts, overlooks the entire Bay of Salerno. Scattered among the gardens are a mock-Gothic crypt, a Temple of Bacchus folly, a tea pavilion done in the style of Florence's Pazzi Chapel, and a Grotto of Venus. Some consider this the most beautiful garden in all Italy; be sure to visit here and decide for yourself. The villa itself is now a hotel (☞ Dining and Lodging, *below*). ⊠ *Via S. Chiara 26,* ☎ *089/857459.* ☒ *5,000 lire.* ☉ *Daily 9–sunset.*

Nearly every street in Ravello has a historic church or villa. Two notable religious sites are the church and convent of **San Francesco,** founded in 1222 by St. Francis of Assisi, with a small Gothic cloister; the church was rebuilt in the 18th century (on Via S. Francesco). Majolica flooring in the 13th-century **Monastero di Santa Chiara** (on Via S. Chiara) is one special element; another is the *matronaeum,* or women's gallery, the only one left on the Amalfi Coast (not known for segregating the sexes, or anything else). Buy some gelati on the piazza by the duomo and walk east to the Piazza Fontana Moresco, below the Hotel Parsifal and above the gates of the walled perimeter, to check out the two stone lions on the fanciful 1,000-year-old fountain, still spewing water.

Dining and Lodging

$$$$ ✕ **Palazzo Della Marra.** The young chef-owners of this restaurant attempt to turn Campania classics into something more—and usually succeed. Past a fireplace that flickers in season, vaulted ceiling, and museum-size paintings and down wide stairs, you descend into a white, modernized 13th-century setting. The daily *menu turistica* may offer such dishes as *scaola ripiena* (stuffed endive), *risotto con zucca rossa e capesante dorate all salvia* (red-pumpkin risotto with seafood in sage), and *costine di agnello al rosmarino con spinaci all'uvetta* (lamb cutlets with spinach and raisins). The tasting menu is even more creative, with unexpected combinations. To match the food, the owners provide a wine list featuring the best of the region. ⊠ *Via della Marra 7,* ☎ *089/858302. AE, DC, MC, V. Closed Tues. and Jan.–Feb.*

$$ ✕ **Cumpa' Cosimo.** Lustier-looking than most Ravello spots, Cumpa' Cosimo is run devotedly by Netta Bottone, whose family has owned this *cantine* for 70 of its 300-plus years. She herself has been cooking under the arched ceiling for more than 30 of them. You can't miss here with any of the dishes featuring classic Ravellian cuisine. A favorite (share it— it's huge) is a *misto* of fettuccine, fusilli, tortellini, and whatever other homemade pasta inspires her, served with a fresh, fragrant pesto. Meats are generally excellent—after all, they are supplied by the butcher shop next door, run by Netta's father. Local wines ease it down gently, and homemade gelati is a luscious ending. ⊠ *Via Roma,* ☎ *089/857156. Reservations essential. AE, DC, V. Closed Mon. and Nov.–Mar.*

$$ ✕ **La Colonna.** Not far from the duomo, past a courtyard, you'll find this sparkling trattoria with arches, niches, marble flooring, and an appealing jumble of ceramic plates, jugs, mirrors, and whatnots, most crafted in Vietri. Even more satisfying is the food, much loved by locals—big portions of classics such as scallopini *limone* and scialatelli *ai fruitti di mare.* The warmth is genuine, and so are the vegetables from the garden. ⊠ *Via Roma 22,* ☎ *089/857876. Reservations essential. AE, DC, MC, V. Closed Wed. and Jan.–Feb.*

$ ✕ **Vittoria.** Between the duomo and the gardens of the Villa Rufulo, this is a good place for a return to reality and an informal bite. Vittoria's thin-crust pizza with loads of fresh toppings is the star attraction, and locals praise it *molto*. But also try the pasta, maybe fusilli with tomatoes, zucchini, and mozzarella. Vittoria is pretty, too, with arches and tile floors. ✉ *Via dei Rufulo 3,* ☎ *089/857947. AE, DC, MC, V.*

$ ✕🏨 **Salvatore.** Adjacent to the Hotel Graal and sharing the same glorious view, you enter by walking down into a small garden and then choosing between a large terrace or an indoor area for dining. The family creates classic Campanian cuisine, the service is friendly, and the overlook offers the best view compared to any inexpensive restaurant in the vicinity. Upstairs rooms are surprisingly upscale, with baths, TVs, air-conditioning, and balconies and with a price that makes them a great deal. ✉ *Via della Repubbliche 2,* ☎ *089/857227. 10 rooms with bath. AE, DC, MC, V. Closed Mon. in winter.*

$$$$ 🏨 **Palazzo Sasso.** In this 12th-century home of the aristocratic Sasso family, Wagner penned part of his opera *Parsifal* in the 1880s, and in the fashionable 1950s, the Sasso hosted Ingrid Bergman and Roberto Rossellini. On reopening in July 1997, after a 20-year hiatus, the hotel is still luring the glitterati—its first guests were Placido Domingo and his entourage. Ordinary mortals, too, can come to sightsee for a peek at the gleaming marble atrium, glass elevators, two rooftop hot tubs, roaring waterfall, and bar (now one of Ravello's prime watering holes). Traditionalists might look askance at all this glitzy luxury in quaint old Ravello, but no one will complain about immaculately furnished guest rooms, with the latest computer-operated lighting and air-cooling systems. The Rossellini restaurant restaurant is also not to be sniffed at. ✉ *Via San Giovanni del Toro 28, 84010,* ☎ *089/818181,* 🖷 *089/858900. 38 rooms, 5 suites, with bath. Restaurant, bar, air-conditioning, pool, outdoor hot tub. AE, DC, MC, V.*

$$$$ 🏨 **Palumbo.** Built in the 12th century as a palazzo, this famous hotel has long been a stop for visiting Someones: Wagner, who composed here; Bogart, filming *Beat the Devil*; a young Jack and Jackie. Marble columns, mosaic-tile floors, and museum-quality antiques combine to provide an elegant ambience throughout the hotel, while incredible views of the Bay of Salerno can be enjoyed from your own terrace or the lush gardens that sit below the hotel on the hillside. The classic Continental cuisine—finish off your feast with lemon soufflé and Episcopio estate wine—is grandly served in the hushed 17th-century dining hall, or you can enjoy a view as delicious as the food atop the roof belvedere. Most guest rooms display antiques and modern marble baths, except for those in the annex, which have poorer views and less charm. ✉ *Via S. Giovanni del Toro 16, 84010,* ☎ *089/857244,* 🖷 *089/858133. 27 rooms with bath. Restaurant, bar, air-conditioning, meeting rooms, parking. AE, DC, MC, V. Closed Feb.*

$$$$ 🏨 **Villa Cimbrone.** Suspended over the azure sea and set amid rose-laden
★ gardens, this magical place was once the home of Lord Grimthorpe and the holiday hideaway of Greta Garbo. Now exquisitely transformed into a hotel, the Gothic-style *castello* (castle) has guest rooms ranging from palatial to cozy (opt for the Peony Room, which has its own terrace). Tapestried armchairs, framed prints, vintage art books, and other antiques which belonged to Viscountess Frost, the lord's daughter, still grace the enchantingly elegant sitting room. Best of all, guests have the villa's famous gardens all to themselves once their gates are closed at sunset. The villa is a strenuous hike from the town center, but porters will carry your luggage and the distance helps keep this the most peaceful place on the Amalfi Coast. ✉ *Via Santa Chiara 26, 84010,* ☎ *089/857459,* 🖷 *089/857777. 19 rooms with bath. Library. AE, MC, V. Closed Nov.–Mar.*

$$$–$$$$ ⊡ **Caruso Belvedere.** This hotel inspired the likes of Virginia Woolf, Ten-
   ★   nessee Williams, and Graham Greene. What more do you need to say?
         Legendarily old-fashioned, this charming jewel, set in an 11th-century
         palazzo, overlooks an incomparable panorama of the Bay of Salerno
         and is set with gardens perfect for curling up with your favorite novel.
         Inside, the grand salon is a 19th-century set piece, complete with Neo-
         classical settees, dozens of Neapolitan paintings, and a frescoed ceiling.
         Nearby is the restaurant, open to *il mare,* where you can dine shaded
         by red-and-white striped awnings and probably feel like you're part of
         a vintage Lartique photograph. A renovation scheduled for early 2000
         will see all the guest rooms spruced up, but the unique atmosphere of
         this hotel means it has always been as much about inspiration as it has
         shelter. ⊠ *Via Toro 52, 84010,* ☎ *089/857111,* FAX *089/857372. 24 rooms
         with bath. Restaurant, parking. AE, DC, MC, V.*

$$$–$$$$ ⊡ **Rufolo.** D. H. Lawrence worked on *Lady Chatterley's Lover* dur-
         ing his 1926 visit, so it might be fun to revisit the novel's groundbreaking
         love scenes while you're here. Rooms have mosaic or terra-cotta floors,
         and some have balconies to liven up the snug quarters with gorgeous
         sea and sky vistas framed by the palm trees of the Villa Rufolo, set just
         below the hotel. But letters from readers have pointed out a drawback
         here—an unsmiling staff. ⊠ *Via San Francesco, 84010,* ☎ *089/857–
         1333,* FAX *089/857935. 30 rooms with bath. Restaurant, bar, air-con-
         ditioning, pool, meeting rooms, parking. AE, DC, MC, V. Closed Feb.*

   $$ ⊡ **Graal.** The name comes from the Holy Grail, as in Wagner's opera
         Parsifal, but this inn is more an operetta. It's much less grand that Rav-
         ello's famous hotels, with a modern decor that's a bit of a downer. Nev-
         ertheless, it reaches high-Cs for comfort, cleanliness, and contentment.
         Hovering over the water on the Via della Repubblica with a nearly un-
         obstructed view of the bay, this hotel possesses one of the friendliest
         staffs around, a pretty pool area, and facilities for whirlpools and
         fancy baths. In the dining room, meals from a family kitchen are de-
         livered to tables dressed in linen, set near large, arched windows. Most
         rooms are smallish, some are deluxe (especially No. 342, with a dou-
         ble whirlpool and a bed from which you can see the great view), but
         all offer tiled floors and balconies. ⊠ *Via della Repubblica 8, 84010,*
         ☎ *089/857222,* FAX *089/857551. 35 rooms with bath. Restaurant,
         bar, air-conditioning, pool, meeting rooms, parking. AE, DC, MC, V.
         Restaurant closed Mon. in winter.*

   $$ ⊡ **Parsifal.** In 1288 this diminutive property was a convent housing
         an order of Augustinian friars. Today the intact cloister hosts travel-
         ers simply intent on enjoying themselves mightily. Ancient, ivy-covered
         stone arches and a tiled walkway looking out over the coastline lead
         to a cozy interior that still feels a bit like a retreat. Sun lounges, a gar-
         den, a fountain with reflecting pool, and alfresco dining all overlook
         the sea. Rooms are small (monk's cells, after all), so ask for one with
         a balcony; Numbers 20, 22, 23, 24, and 26 are best. The charming
         young manager just dotes on Americans. ⊠ *Viale Gioacchino d'Anna
         5, Ravello 84010,* ☎ *089/857144,* FAX *089/857972. 50 rooms with bath.
         Restaurant, bar, parking. AE, DC, MC, V.*

   $$ ⊡ **Villa Amore.** A 10-minute walk from the main Piazza Duomo, this
         hotel is family run, with a garden and shares the same exhilarating view
         of the Bay of Salerno as Ravello's most expensive hotels. Rooms are
         small, with modest and modern furnishings. Full board is available here
         and may be required in the summer. Reserve ahead, and specify time
         of arrival if you need help with luggage from the parking lot or bus
         stop (you pay 7,000 lire per bag). ⊠ *Via Santa Chiara, 84010,* ☎ FAX
         089/857135. 12 rooms with bath. Restaurant, bar. DC, MC, V.

$–$$ ⛺ **Toro.** Right off the ladder of steps which some consider akin to a main street, this little hotel with a big garden and lots of antiques has been in the Schiavo family for three generations. Even this modest inn once boasted visiting VIPs: Composer Edvard Grieg wrote in the guest book that he was *"molto contento"* and artist E. M. Escher also stayed here (his celebrated prints of spiraling staircases were inspired by those he discovered in Ravello and Atrani). If you don't mind spare rooms and enjoy simple, good food, you, too, will be content. ✉ *Viale Wagner 3, 84010,* ☎ FAX *089/857211. 10 rooms with bath. Dining room. AE, DC. Closed Nov.–Mar.*

$–$$ ⛺ **Villa Maria.** Fronted by a vast garden terrace, terra-cotta-color Villa Maria has more sunny warmth than most formal hotels in Ravello. Public areas have tiled floors, high ceilings, lace, and antiques. All but two rooms are standard, and there's an airy suite that has a large balcony overlooking the coast. If the hotel becomes too quiet, your hosts promote fun with dancing and music out on the terrace. Note that views here look out over the Vallone del Dragone, not the bay, but are memorable all the same. Also check out Maria's next-door sibling, the Hotel Giordano, a former 18th-century manor house, which shares facilities with the villa. The rooms are less desirable here, but the pool is closer. ✉ *Via S. Chiara, 84010,* ☎ *089/857135,* FAX *089/857071. 17 rooms with bath. Restaurant, bar, air-conditioning, pool, parking. AE, DC, MC, V.*

Nightlife and the Arts

Other than the concerts offered by the Fèstival Musicale di Ravello, there is little nightlife activity, unless you count moon gazing. A few cafés and bars are scattered about, but the general peacefulness extends to evening hours. Hotels and restaurants may offer live music and can advise you about any clubs, but around these parts the sound is either soft and classical—or silence.

CONCERTS

Sublime music and views makes a nifty combo in Ravello, long host to the celebrated **Fèstival Musicale di Ravello** (Ravello Music Festival; ✉ Via Trinità 3, ☎ 089/858149, FAX 089/858249, info@rcs.amalfi-coast.it), held on the garden escarpments of the Villa Rufolo. Due to popular demand, this is no longer just a summer-only affair. In addition to the Wagner concerts held in July and the *concerti di mezzanotte* (midnight concerts, which actually begin at 11 PM) in August, many other concerts are performed from April through November and even later. The most unusual event is the *concerto all'alba* (dawn concert), when the entire town wakes up at 4:30 to watch the sun rise over the bay to the accompaniment of music from a full symphony orchestra; this event is usually scheduled for the second week of August. The Villa Rufolo concerts actually comprise a number of events through the year: the Concerti a Villa Rufolo, held in July and July; the Concerti di Mezzanotte and Genius Loci/Musicians from Campania, in August; the International Weeks of Chamber Music, in September; the Autumn Season, from October to December; and the Winter and Spring concerts, from January to May. Most evening concerts are held at 9:30, with others beginning at 6:30 or 11. Note that the 9:30 concerts begin well after the sunset hour, so come earlier if you want to catch the evening glow. Details for the concert schedule is provided in the villa's annual calendar.

Shopping

Bric-a-Brac (✉ Piazza Vescovado, ☎ 089/857153) has some 19th-century antiques, including historic crèche scenes; in the front of the store is an fine selection of books and antique prints about Ravello—

a must for history and art lovers. **Camo** (✉ Piazza Vescovado, with outlets on Via Boccaccio and Via Roma, ☎ 089/857461), a coral and cameo factory, sells jewelry from simple to overwrought, crafted from shells and coral. Hillary Rodham Clinton is among those who have dropped by. Behind the shop is the town Museo dei Corallo, with some elaborate and antique coral concoctions on exhibit. **Ceramiche d'Arte** (✉ Via dei Rufolo, ☎ 089/857303) ships its good stock of Vietri-made and other hand-painted ceramics all over the world. Bargaining may reward you with a 10% discount, maybe more if you have a talent for it. **Gruppo Petit Prince** (✉ Via San Francesco, ☎ 089/858033) has a nice selection of stationery, prints, and artworks. **Ravello Gusti & Delizie** (✉ Via Roma 28, ☎ 089/857716) is stocked to the ceiling with *prodotti tipici e naturali della costiera Amalfitana*; this is the place for foodstuffs, as well as delicacies and wines from all over Italy. Sun-dried-tomato pasta, olive oil, and other treats are available, but most intriguing are the lemon products—candles and soaps, and even lemon honey, gathered and bottled by a town police officer. **Episcopio Winery** (✉ Via Giovanni a Toro, across from Hotel Palumbo) offers selections of fine Ravello vintages.

Scala

③④ *1½ km (1 mi) northwest of Ravello; 45 km (28 mi) east of Sorrento.*

Scala is the country cousin to more sophisticated Ravello, and is a mere five-minute drive across the Vallone del Dragone. A tranquil farming center of vineyards and groves, it was once part of the Amalfi Republic, on a par with Ravello, and a few remaining traces reflect those days of grandeur. Possibly the first coastal town to be settled by the fleeing Romans, around the 4th century, the village was a bishopric until 1818 and the site of numerous convents, including the first Benedictine monasteries in southern Italy. A few churches remain from among more than 100 that were built in the tiny parishes which once threaded through its terraced hills.

The cathedral, consecrated to St. Lorenzo, dates from the 12th century, as its belfry, basilica shape, and Romanesque portal show; the interior was completely remodeled in the 17th century. The glazed-tile floor is lovely, and the pulpit is decorated with colorful tesserae (tiny mosaics). A grateful Charles I of Anjou donated an enameled miter in 1270 after repulsing a Saracen attack; other noteworthy items include 13th-century wood carvings above the altar depicting the crucifixion, and an elaborate ceiling, painted in 1748. The 13th-century crypt holds tombs of the Coppolas, a seignorial family of the town.

Among Scala's ruins is a Romanesque courtyard built by the wealthy Sasso family; Friar Gerardo da Sasso ran a hostel for pilgrims and later, in 1118, founded the Order of the Ospedalieri, an offshoot of the Knights of St. John. Scala has one distinction with which famed rival Ravello can't hope to compete: a panoramic view of Ravello.

OFF THE BEATEN PATH

SAN PIETRO AND MINUTA – The nearby hamlets of Santa Caterina and Campidoglio, both relatively easy walks from Scala, afford glimpses of peaceful rural life around the valley, far from tourists. In San Pietro, the Chapel of San Pietro in Campoleone has medieval carvings of St. Catherine and St. Michael. The Church of Our Lady of the Annunciation, in the hamlet of Minuta, was completed in the 12th century, and its crypt is faced with outstanding frescoes. The church's basilica, with a nave, two aisles, and 12 columns, was renovated in the 1930s, but original pointed arches and portals remain.

Lodging

$$$ ⊞ Marmorata. Between Ravello and Minori, set in the township of Castiglione directly below clifftop Ravello), this former paper mill has been recycled into the most stylish, unusual hotel in this east-of-Amalfi stretch of lackluster lodgings. Originality, historic vibes, stucco-coved ceilings, gulf views, Oriental rugs, and guest rooms with minibars and TVs make this a most evocative and comfy hotel overlooking the gulf. It can be reached off Statale 163. ⊠ *Marmorata, 84010,* ☎ *089/ 877777,* FAX *089/851189. 37 rooms with bath. Restaurant, bar, pool, dock, meeting rooms, parking. AE, DC, MC, V.*

$ ⊞ La Margherita. Seeming more like a New England B&B than a Campania hotel—except perhaps for the view of the Bay of Salerno below and the sounds of spoken Italian—this charming little lodging above the Valle del Dragone has a pool in which you seem to be swimming across the valley to Ravello. The parlor is especially cozy, with Oriental rugs and antiques. Compact rooms have private showers and, most important, balconies on which to laze and gaze. Breakfast and a cold lunch are served on the terrace. The delightful young signora's parents own a restaurant down the road, and her pappa sometimes comes over to play the piano in the evening. The hotel is a five-minute walk south of Scala's center. ⊠ *Via Torricello, 84010,* ☎ *089/857106,* FAX *089/857219. 9 rooms with bath. Pool, meeting rooms. MC, V.*

Minori

㉟ *6 km (3½ mi) southeast of Ravello; 2 km (1 mi) west of Maiori.*

Minori can be traced to Roman times and functioned as a garrison outpost for the forces of the Amalfi Republic. Its gray-sand beach (along with neighboring Maiori's) is the widest and longest on the coast: tree-lined, level, with a promenade, a kids' amusement park, and scads of sunning locals. These two towns are much more modern than their neighbors due to 20th-century mountain floods that wiped out many historic buildings. However, there is a Romanesque (rebuilt 19th-century) **Basilica of St. Trofimena** and, in the western part of town, a 1st-century **Roman villa.** The latter was discovered in the 1950s, and its ground-floor remains show that it incorporated a *viridarium* (garden) with a swimming-pool design—something like what an upscale vacation house would be today. The villa is two blocks from the beach. ⊠ *Strada S. Lucia,* ☎ *089/852893.* 🎫 *3000 lire.* ⊙ *9–hr before sunset.*

Dining and Lodging

$$–$$$ ✕ Capo d' Orso. The pasta with ricotta and lemon is named here to honor Roberto Rossellini, who, in 1948, directed Anna Magnani and a young Federico Fellini in a film called *Il Miracolo* (*The Miracle*), right here at this very tower on the last really gorgeous point along the Amalfi Drive. Views are to both Capri and Salerno. A buzzy restaurant with a terrace and a glass-walled main room, it's run by three of the grandsons of the nonno who opened the place in 1950—they really know how to market, cook, and serve. They even won the Gold in the Salzburg Butter Competition for their sculpture of a coach and two horses, perhaps another miracle. The restaurant is in the Toro Normana, just past Maiori, which lies beyond the township of Minori. ⊠ *Via D. Taiani 48, Maiori,* ☎ *089/877022,* FAX *089/852360. AE, DC, MC, V. Closed Nov.*

$$ ✕ Ristorante L'Arsenale. *Specialita marinare* is the focus at this little 13th-century arsenal-cum-restaurant, with stucco walls, two levels, an open kitchen, arched ceilings, and pretty plates and ceramics. It's a block from the expansive beach and a couple of blocks from the Roman villa.

The citrus risotto with shrimp and prosciutto is to live for, and for something dolce, the young, ambitious brothers who have run the place since 1992 just opened a stylish coffee bar, L'Beccio, across the street. ⊠ *Via S. G. a Mare 20,* ☎ *089/851418. AE, DC, MC, V. Closed Jan. and Mon. in winter.*

$$ 🏨 **Hotel Villa Romana.** The nearby Roman villa inspires this family-run, low-key, in-town hotel. Rooms are being upgraded (some with whirlpools) to create a more attractive ambience. A solarium looks over the picturesque coastline and up to the heights and the lights of nearby Ravello, and room balconies overlook either the street or a quieter garden courtyard. A short walk takes guests to the sea. If you like the beach, don't need sophisticated surroundings, and want to be close to Ravello, this will suit you. ⊠ *Corso Vittorio Emanuele 90, 84010,* ☎ *089/ 877237,* FAX *089/877302. 53 rooms with bath. Restaurant, bar, air-conditioning, pool, meeting rooms, parking. AE, DC, MC, V. Closed Nov.*

The Arts

Concerti di Mezza Estate (☎ 089/877135) presents music, ballet, and opera in July and August.

En Route   Passing through Maiori, look up to see the twin turrets of the perfectly preserved Abbey of Santa Maria de Olearia, founded by the Benedictines in 973, now a private dwelling. You then round the cape, going eastward, under an imposing gray cliff carved into natural spires, towers, and pinnacles—locals accord some of these fanciful shapes descriptive titles, such as the Horseback Rider. Descending from Monte Finestra to Capo d'Orso, the ridgeline runs between Valle dei Tramonti and Valle di Cava de' Tirreni; rock climbers face a challenge in this part. You may also hire a boat to take you to the Pandona Grotto, whose iridescence is similar to the Blue Grotto in Capri.

Marina di Erchie

㊱   *7 km (4½ mi) southeast of Minori; 3 km (2 mi) south of Cetera.*

With a looming Norman tower on the cliff above, the curving beachfront hamlet of Erchie is as romantic as can be, especially when it's just your party and the fishermen, who haul in their catch in the pink sun of early morning. The little village of Erchie is built around a 10th-century Benedictine abbey destroyed and abandoned in the 12th century; Salerno took over the town in the 15th century. By the 1960s the abbey was restored in neo-Renaissance style, with a portal constructed in dark tufa and stone, and the little village was discovered by city dwellers in Salerno, who now flock here to windsurf along the cove and laze the day away.

Cetara

㊲   *3 km (2 mi) north of Erchie; 4 km (2½ mi) south of Vietre.*

Tourists tend to take a pass on the village of Cetara because of the hairpin turns off the main road. A quaint and quiet fishing village set below orange groves on Monte Falerzo, it was held in subjugation to greater powers, like most of these coastal sites, throughout much of its history. From being a Saracen stronghold in the 9th century, it became the final holding of Amalfi at the eastern edge of the republic, which all through the 11th and 12th centuries tithed part of Cetara's fishing catch, *ius piscariae*—the town's claim to fame. It is rumored that the village's Latin name comes from this big catch—*cetaria* (tuna net), but the town haul is most famous for its anchovies—thousands of years ago, salted and strained, they became a spicy liquid called *garum*, used as a great delicacy by the rich of ancient Rome (it can still be purchased at local grocery stores here). After the Middle Ages, the village came under the dominion of the Benedictine abbey of neighboring Santa Maria di Erchie and then became the port of the abbey of Cava, above the coast, which traded with Africa and exchanged pilgrims with other abbeys, extracting anchorage dues. In 1534 the Turks, led by the tyrant Sinan Pasha, enslaved 300 Cetaran villagers, spiriting them away in 22 galleys, executing those who would not cooperate. A few survivors fled to Naples, which immediately ordered a watchtower to be raised in Cetara to ward off future raids. This is one of the many landmarks that remind tourists that there were coastal perils previous to the one of driving on Statale 163. Beneath the tower is a rocky little beach, and a small park overlooks the harbor, where fishermen mend their nets and paint their boats. They often are away from home for months, fishing in deep waters. Other than the scenic charm of the waterfront, there are no main sights here, other than the Church of San Pietro, near the harbor.

Dining and Lodging

$ ✕ **Acqua Pazza.** Locals along this part of the coast rave about this tiny restaurant tucked on the main street. It is a modest environment—a spare interior with a few tables—its raison d'être being remarkably fresh seafood. ⊠ *Across from church of San Pietro and a 3-min walk to the harbor. No credit cards. Closed Mon.*

$$ 🏨 **Cetus.** Cetara's leading hotel is set in a white-stucco building that seems to have grown right out of the living rock. The natural theme is continued within. A summer-light restaurant has floors of marble tile, a window-wall, and terraces. A steep walk leads to the hotel's private beach and "American" bar. Shutter doors open onto broad, stone-flagged spaces, with umbrella tables, casual seating, overflowing flower boxes, and close-up sea views. ⊠ *Right off Amalfi Drive, just outside Cetara, 84010,* ☎ *089/261388,* 𝖥𝖠𝖷 *089/261388. 46 rooms with bath. Restaurant, 2 bars, air-conditioning, meeting rooms, parking. AE, DC, MC, V. Closed Nov.–Mar.*

Vietri sul Mare

③⑧ *5 km (3 mi) northeast of Cetera; 3 km (2 mi) west of Salerno.*

Vietri sul Mare is rich in history. Founded in a river valley by the Etruscans, who called it Marcina, it was ransacked by the Samnites, became a prosperous Roman fishing outpost, and destroyed by the Vandals, all before 455. Then the Lombards made it a stronghold, the Saracens attacked regularly, and, in 1648, a French fleet pillaged the town. Perhaps to brighten their troubles, Vietrians have created renowned hand-crafted and fired faience work and majolica ceramics since the beginning of the Middle Ages, when the craft was sponsored by the abbey at Cava de' Tirreni. In 1086 there were already 50 kilns blasting away, whose ceramic output decorate buildings and churches all along the coast, including the town's own 18th-century San Giovanni Battista and Confraternita del Rosario. Dozens of shops in town, and hundreds throughout the region, feature Vietri's colorful designs. For a complete rundown on Vietri's celebrated majolica and faience work, visit the **Museo della Ceramica Vietrese** (Ceramic Museum), housed in an eye-popping tile-covered edifice built in 1922, the former home of King Victor Emmanuel during the Salerno government of World War II. Exhibits range from medieval and Renaissance urns to the German-influenced ceramics of the 1950s, along with today's modern style, all painted with the traditionally colorful and fanciful designs based on the folklore, flora, and fauna of the Amalfi Coast. ⊠ *Torretta di Villa Guariglia (Raito),* ☎ *089/211835.* ⊙ *Weekdays 9–1.*

Vietri is the end, or the beginning, of the Amalfi Coast, and drive, depending on how you look at it—a busy, bustling town, with an older section by the sea and an upper area filled with factories, shops, and that mundane sign of the encroachment of civilization: traffic lights. It may be a manufacturing center, but the residents are keenly aware of aesthetics. Recently, the town imploded a modern building, which they felt blighted the beauty of the region. "It was like a nose job," said an official.

Lodging

$$$ 🏨 **Lloyd's Baia Hotel.** A short walk from the Museo della Ceramica Vietrese, this modern hotel has a restaurant with a wraparound sea view, a candlelit piano bar, and alfresco dining on the roof overlooking the sea. An elevator delivers guests to the bottom of a cliff, where they will find one of the most beachlike swimming areas of any hotel on the coast. There are two pools, practically in the gulf, a nice strip of sandy shore, cabanas, lounge chairs, umbrellas, and a snack bar. Sea sports and boating can be arranged from the beach. Guest rooms have sea views, small writing tables, TVs, and sitting areas, and some have balconies. Owned by Tirrena Hotels, a local chain, it welcomes large groups. ✉ *Via De'Martinis, 84019,* ☎ *089/210145,* ℻ *089/210186. 120 rooms with bath. Restaurant, air-conditioning, pool, parking. AE, MC, V.*

Shopping

Dozens of shops purvey the exuberance, light, and color of the region, captured in Vietri vases, dishes, statues, wall and floor tiles, and artworks. The most famous manufacturer is **Ceramachi Solomene** (✉ Via Case Sparse at Fontana Vecchia, ☎ 089/210188), with a huge selection and established shipping. You can also visit the factory (✉ Via XXV Luglio 17).

OFF THE
BEATEN PATH

CAVA DE' TIRRENI – Set in green hills inland from the coast (✉ 3½ km/2¼ mi northwest of Vietri) is the modern town of Cava de' Tirreni—population about 50,000—reached by an easy turn off Highway A3, to or from Sorrento, Naples, or Rome. Cava was first a Roman settlement and later a major element in the Kingdom of Naples, famous for its silk tapestries. The old section has porticoed streets similar to those of Bologna, for centuries a leading importer of the local merchandise. The most picturesque area is Borgo Scacciaventi, named because its winding lanes block the winds and protect goods held beneath the porticos. The immensely rich abbey, the Abbazia della SS Trinita, was founded here in 1011 by a nobleman from Salerno and its church, monastery, cloisters, and museum hold many interesting treasures, including sarcophagi, paintings, ambos, and 15th- and 16th-century majolica tiles from Vietri.

Salerno

㊴ *3 km (2 mi) southeast of Cetera; 50 km (31 mi) east of Sorrento.*

Salerno, the provincial capital creeping along its namesake gulf, lies just east of the Amalfi Coast, below the Monti Picentini (Picentini Mountains). Founded by the Etruscans in the 6th or 5th century BC, it later became a Roman colony, and the famed Salernitan medical school was established here around the 10th century, making it perhaps the oldest in Europe. During the 11th century—Salerno's golden age—Lombards, Normans, Swabians, Aragonese, and Spaniards fought hard over the territory, as did the Allied forces during World War II.

Salerno has a plethora of ports, parks, boulevards, and great old buildings, but also masses of pollution, traffic congestion, and various kinds of urban blight—realities easily forgotten if you're coming from the idyllic Sorrentine peninsula and the Amalfi Coast. Nevertheless, Salerno is an important transportation, shopping, entertainment, and tourist-board hub, from which you can connect by bus, train, or boat to all major points in Italy. The Autostrada del Sole superhighway whisks you to Sorrento in mere minutes, a minor miracle for those who just spent hours on winding Statale 163 to cover the same distance. To get to Paestum, you just take E45 south.

If time is precious, or you simply don't want to deal with crowds and traffic, this is not a town in which to linger. But whether starting or ending your coastal drive in Salerno, try to check out the **medieval quarter,** near the grand 12th-century **duomo**, and explore **Via Mercati** for the pleasure of viewing the extant palaces and stucco work.

In addition, the **Museo Archeologico Provincale** has interesting displays of ancient artifacts from the region. ⊠ *Via San Benedetto*, ☎ *089/231135.* ⊙ *Daily 9–1.*

Dining and Lodging

$$ ✕ **Alla Brace.** Stuffed peppers, potato soufflé, ravioli, and special fish dishes are well loved at this Salerno landmark near the waterfront, an especially convenient spot if you're staying at the Jolly Hotel. ⊠ *Lungomare Trieste 13*, ☎ *089/225159. AE, DC, MC, V. Closed Sun.*

$$$ ▦ **Jolly Hotel.** Big, modern, and situated at one end of the waterfront promenade—near the major tourist sites—this lodging radiates the atmosphere of a business hotel. A member of the international Jolly chain, it is Salerno's finest: comfortable, indeed, but dull. Front-desk personnel can appear standoffish, and for those using the train, the less highly rated Hotel Plaza is a more convenient choice. ⊠ *Lungomare Trieste 1, 84100,* ☎ *089/225222, 800/221–2626, 800/247–1277,* FAX *089/237571. 100 rooms with bath. Restaurant, air-conditioning, parking. AE, DC, MC, V.*

$$ ▦ **Hotel Plaza.** Guests can easily walk to the harbor, shops, and transportation from these clean but basic lodgings, right across from the train station and tourist board. The contemporary-style lobby has scant seating plus a bar. Rooms, though small, are acceptable, with tiny baths. When booking, specify air-conditioning and a quiet room, as the street may be noisy. The rear parking lot, though packed, is a big advantage. ⊠ *Piazza Vittorio Veneto (Piazza Ferrovia), 84123,* ☎ *089/224477,* FAX *089/224477. 48 rooms with bath. Bar, breakfast room, air-conditioning. AE, DC, MC, V.*

Nightlife and the Arts

Near the train station and along main streets in the waterfront area there are many clubs. One such is **Movida** (⊠ Via Generale Clark), the place to hear the latest disco music; ask at your hotel for the most up-to-date information about other nightspots. Cultural events are scheduled throughout the year, among them the **Festival Internazionale del Cinema** (International Film Festival) (☎ 089/254404), in October; the **Salerno Festival** (☎ 089/224744), with major concerts July–September; and the municipal summer arts season, **Viva l'Estate** (☎ 089/224744), held from July to September.

Paestum

★ ⓵ *42 km (26 mi) southeast of Salerno, 99 km (62 mi) southeast of Naples.*

One of Italy's most majestic sights lies on the edge of a flat coastal plain: the remarkably well-preserved **Greek temples** of Paestum. S18 from the north passes the train station (Stazione di Paestum), which is about 800 yards from the ruins, through the perfectly preserved archway **Porta Sirena**. The ruins stand on the site of the ancient city of Poseidonia, founded by Greek colonists in the 7th century BC. When the Romans took over the colony in 273 BC and called it Paestum, they enlarged the settlement, adding an amphitheater and a forum. Much of the archaeological material found on the site is displayed in the **Museo Nazionale,** and several rooms are devoted to the unique tomb paintings discovered in the area, rare examples of Greek and pre-Roman pictorial art. About 200 yards from the museum (in front of the main entrance), framed by banks of roses and oleanders, is the **Tempio di Poseidone** (Temple of Poseidon), a magnificent Doric edifice, with 36 fluted columns and an extraordinarily well-preserved entablature (area above the capitals), which rivals the finest temples in Greece. On the left of the temple is the so-called **Basilica,** the earliest of Paestum's standing edifices; it dates from very early in the 6th century BC. The name is an 18th-century misnomer, for the structure was in fact a temple sacred to Hera, the wife of Zeus. Behind it an ancient road leads to the **Foro Romano** (Roman Forum) and the single column of the **Tempio della Pace** (Temple of Peace). Beyond is the **Tempio di Cerere** (Temple of Ceres). Try to see the temples in the late afternoon, when the light enhances the deep gold of the stone, and the air is pierced with the cries of crows that nest high on the temples. ☎ *0828/811023.* ☒ *Excavations: 8,000 lire; Museum: 8,000 lire.* ☉ *Excavations: July–Sept., daily 9 AM–10 PM; Oct.–June, daily 9–1 hr before sunset. Museum: July–Sept., daily 9 AM–10 PM; Oct.–June, daily 9–6:30; closed 1st and 3rd Mon. of each month.*

Lodging

$$ 🏨 **Helios.** Directly across the road from the Porta della Giustizia and only a few steps from the temples, the Helios has cottage-type rooms, each with a minibar, in a garden setting. Suites are also available. A pleasant restaurant serves local specialties and seafood. The home-produced ricotta and mozzarella are especially recommended. ☒ *Via Principe di Piemonte 1, Zona Archeologica, 84063,* ☎ *0828/811451,* 𝖥𝖠𝖷 *0828/721047. 30 rooms with bath. 2 restaurants, minibars. AE, DC, MC, V.*

SORRENTO AND THE AMALFI COAST A TO Z

Arriving and Departing

Running between the Sorrentine peninsula and Salerno, Statale 163 (or State Highway 163) is better known to Americans and Brits as the Amalfi Drive and to Italians as the Via Smeraldo (Emerald Road). It can be reached from Naples via the A3 Autostrada to Castellammare di Stabia, then linked from there to Sorrento via Statale 145. Most people travel from Naples, heading southeast, but other prefer to drive directly to Salerno via the A3, then return northwest using the Amalfi Drive, a concrete ribbon which rewards visitors with mountain-meets-sea views and panoramas unfolding at every turn.

By Bus

Although some travelers opt for cars when touring the Amalfi Drive, most use the convenient and inexpensive **SITA Blue Line** buses. For best views on board, sit on the sea side of the bus (on your left as you board the bus if you're starting in Sorrento, on your right if you begin in Amalfi). The trip between Sorrento and Amalfi generally takes 80 minutes. The major bus stops, in order after departing from Sorrento's bus depot (☒ Circumvesuviana railway station near Corso Italia) are: Sant'Agnello, Piano di Sorrento, Meta, Positano (the bus stops at the Chiesa

Nuovo in the upper town, then a second—and the main—stop at Sponda, in the lower town), Praiano (in the township of Vettica Maggiore), Conca dei Marini, and then Amalfi, ending at the bus hub on Piazza Flavio Gioia. The bus driver will stop anywhere on the main route as long as you inform him of your destination, be it hotel or fork in the road, when boarding.

Tickets must be purchased in advance (remember to time-stamp your ticket in the machine at the front of the bus as you board because conductors often make spot checks). You'll find ticket vendors in many cafés, bars, and newsstands area-wide; heading south, the Sorrento train station newsstand is where most people stock up, but between noon and 4, when it's closed, head for the cafés on the square two blocks to the south; heading north from Amalfi, Bar Sita, at Piazza Flavio Gioia in Amalfi, is the place to buy tickets.

SITA buses make the trip along the coast 22 times daily between 6:30 AM and 10 PM (festival, Sunday, and bank holiday schedules vary from weekday schedule). Wallet-size SITA bus schedules are available at ticket vendors, regional tourist offices, and from hotel concierges, or contact SITA in Salerno (⊠ Via Irno 2–4, ☎ 089/791660, ℻ 089/796820). If you're traveling along the coast by SITA bus, be sure to get a schedule, as it proves invaluable to planning your day. Schedules are also posted at the Sorrento train station and at the SITA bus office at Bar Sita, Piazza Flavio Gioia. One-way ticket prices range from 1,500 to 3,400 lire. An express Amalfi–Naples line runs includes stops in Sorrento, Colli S. Pietro, Positano, Praiano, with the return in reverse. This bus runs daily, except Sunday and bank holidays, usually leaves at 8 AM, and takes 2½ hours.

Amalfi: You can purchase **SITA Blue Line** bus and coach tickets prior to boarding at Bar Sita (⊠ Piazza Flavio Gioia) or any port-side bar, travel agency, or tobacco shop displaying a SITA sticker; all SITA buses leave Amalfi from Piazza Flavio Gioia. The special express bus to Naples departs many mornings at 8 AM (5,700 lire); catching this bus makes for an easy and scenic ride back to the city, allowing you to bypass a transfer from bus to the Circumvesuviana Railway in Sorrento.

Positano: Purchase **SITA Blue Line** bus and coach tickets prior to boarding at Tabaccheria (⊠ Piazza dei Mulini). The Blue Line bus stops here are at Chiesa Nuova and Sponda. SITA buses pass through Positano almost hourly on the run from Amalfi to Sorrento, 7 AM–7:30 PM (later on weekdays). From Sorrento to Amalfi, 9 (earlier on weekdays)–9:30 PM (later on weekdays). In addition to the tobacconist listed above, check around for cafés and additional tobacconists selling SITA tickets.

Ravello: ATACS (Orange Line) municipal buses make the run up and down the mountain between Ravello and Piazza Flavio Gioia in Amalfi, from where you can connect to the main Amalfi Drive run to Sorrento. You can purchase **SITA Blue Line** bus and coach tickets prior to boarding, at Bar San Domingo (⊠ Piazza Duomo, ☎ 089/857142); Bar Calce (⊠ Via Roma, 2, ☎ 089/857152); and Tabaccheria (⊠ Via dei Rufolo, 4). Buses run almost hourly.

Salerno: SITA (⊠ Via Irno 2–4, ☎ 089/791660, ℻ 089/796820) buses run hourly to Sorrento, three times per hour to Naples, and once or twice an hour to Amalfi. Purchase tickets for preboarding at the SITA office or at tobacco shops displaying the SITA sticker; ATACS (Orange Line) buses run locally through the city, while ATACS and SCAT buses (⊠ Salerno train station) run frequently to Paestum.

Sorrento: SITA Blue Line buses and coaches depart hourly from Sorrento (⊠ Circumvesuviana train station, ☎ 081/593–4644) to Amalfi; *see*

Positano and Ravello, *above,* for schedule details. Before boarding, purchase SITA tickets at the Mayflower Bar, Bar dei Fiori (⊠ Piazza Lauro), the newspaper stand in the train station, or Bar Tonino (⊠ Piazza Tasso). For trips leaving from Sorrento and heading into the coastal towns of the Sorrentine peninsula, the main run stops at Massa Lubrense, Sant'Agata, and Torca. Service usually begins at 5 AM and lasts until 10:30 PM, with varying schedule for weekends and holidays. The Sorrento-to-Nerano line (main destination: Marina di Cantone) makes stops at Priora, Sant'Agata, and Marina Lobra (⊠ Piazza Tasso, Piazza Lauro). Contact Azienda Turismo (☎ 081/807–4033, FAX 081/877–3397) for complete information. **Circumvesuviana buses** are used for local Sorrento runs (1,000 lire).

By Car
Driving the scenic and often hairpin roads of the Sorrentine peninsula and the Amalfi Drive is both a joy and a challenge. Medium-size cars are a good compromise, and turns will be easier with automatic transmission. The round reflecting mirrors set along major curves in the road intend to show if others are coming around a bend; they may help but remain ever alert. Honk before curves to let oncoming traffic know about you, and listen for honks from oncoming curves. Buses and trucks will sometimes require you to back up; if there's a standoff, take it in stride, as it goes on all the time.

By Plane
The nearest major airport is **Capodichino** in Naples (☎ 081/789–6111). You can fly directly from Rome on **Alitalia** (☎ 1478/65643). The bus from Sorrento to the **Naples airport** (⊠ Piazza Tasso, ☎ 081/801–5420, 081/801–5766, 081/801–6376, 081/801–6346), leaving and arriving in Sorrento four times daily, first leaving Sorrento for the airport at 6:30 AM, last leaving Sorrento at 6:30 PM.; first arriving in Sorrento from the airport at 10 AM, last arriving in Sorrento from airport at 10 PM. For further information contact **Naples SITA** (⊠ 80124 Via Campegna 23, ☎ 081/593–4644, FAX 081/239–5010).

By Train
The two train hubs are Salerno and Sorrento, at either end of the Amalfi Coast. You can take the train one-way, but if you take it round-trip, you'll miss the beauty of the coast.

Salerno: Train station (⊠ P. V. Vemeto, ☎ 089/888088), trains stop in Salerno on the Milan–Reggio di Calabria Line. Trains leave from Salerno for Pompeii once or twice each hour; Naples twice an hour, 5,500 lire.

Sorrento: The **Orario Train,** which departs from the S.F.S.M. Circumvesuviana train station (☎ 081/772–2144), runs approximately every half hour from Sorrento to Naples; an express line, it only make stops at S. Agnello, Vico Equense, Pompeii, Herculaneum, and Naples, returning in the reverse order. Round-trip fares are 8,400 lire; Sorrento to Naples, 6,800 lire; and Sorrento to Pompeii, 4,000 lire. In Sorrento the train stations are in Piazza Lauro and Piazza Tasso. The **Circumvesuviana Line** runs frequently between Sorrento (☎ 081/779–2144) and Naples (⊠ Stazione Centrale), 4,200 lire for entire run, 2,600 if you get off in Pompeii and Herculaneum; there are about a dozen other town stations along the way.

Getting Around

By Boat
Ferries and hydrofoils run year-round but most frequently in high season. To get to smaller towns or to take private boats, you can make ar-

rangements with private boat companies or independent fishermen. Seek out people who are recommended by the tourist office or your hotel.

Amalfi: Ferries operated by **Alilauro** (☎ 089/871483), **Cooperative Sant'Andrea** (☎ 089/873190), and **Linee Maritime Partenopee** (☎ 089/873301) sail infrequently to Positano (6,000 lire), Capri (11,000–17,000 lire), and Salerno (4,000 lire); ticket booths are on the docks and on Lungomare dei Cavalieri; hydrofoils are available in summer, but on an infrequent schedule.

Positano: The **ferry and hydrofoil ticket office** is in the Tabacchi Carpineto (✉ Via del Brigantino, ☎ 089/875092); ferries to Amalfi, Sorrento, Salerno, and Capri are available at a dock on Via Positanesi d'America, near the public beach in the center of town. Services are provided by **Linee Maritime Partenopee** (☎ 089/875092) and **F.illi Grassi** (at pier—look for logo of blue-and-white whale, ☎ 089/811620).

Salerno: Ferries to Amalfi and Positano leave from the main port at Piazza della Concordia; ferries continuing to Capri and Ischia leave from the west end of the waterfront at Molo Manfredi. A typical schedule is an early-morning departure and a late-afternoon return; the EPT office has current information, or call the **Cooperative Sant'Andrea** (☎ 089/873190). Hydrofoil service is available in summer to Amalfi, Positano, Capri, and Sorrento.

Sorrento: Ferries and Hydrofoil service is available from **Alilauro** (☎ 081/807–1430), **Caremar** (☎ 081/807–3077), **Linee Maritime Veloci** in Sorrento (☎ 081/878–1430, 081/807–3024), **Alilauro/Linee Lauro** (☎ 081/807–2009), **Linee Maritime Partenopee** (☎ 081/807–3024); services to Amalfi, Positano, Capri, Ischia, Napoli, Castellammare. There is year-round service with frequent (five times) daily trips to Capri (hydrofoil 8,000 lire), with holiday/weekend variations. Sorrento to Naples costs 12,000 lire. Service to Ischia (16,000 lire) and Amalfi (20,000 lire) is infrequent but daily; there are usually two steamers daily from Sorrento to Capri (☎ 081/807–3077).

By Bus

You can best enjoy the scenery if you leave the helm to drivers and bus power. Besides, the mighty elevation of bus seats high atop the road offers an even better perch to take in the passing show. Local **Orange Line** buses (☎ 089/811895, FAX 089/811896) regularly ply even the smallest roads and make more stops than the SITA buses. Look for the orange sign and wait there for a pickup. Taxis and boats are usually by the harbor, or ask at the tourist office, travel agency, or your hotel. Service on most Orange Line runs begins at 7:50 and ends at 9; departures are usually every half hour on the main lines. In Sorrento, the main local Orange Line bus stops are in Piazza Lauro and Piazza Tasso. You can also use **Circumvesuviana** buses (1,000 lire) for local Sorrento runs.

By Car or Taxi

Driving will be on winding two-lane roads except for the A3 highway to and from Salerno. Although (and perhaps because) driving here requires total concentration, accidents occur surprisingly infrequently. Parking is a major problem and should be factored in. Taxis are at stands by the main piazzas and harbors and can also be rented through hotels and restaurants. The following are the major taxi services in the area:

Amalfi: at pier (✉ Piazza F. Gioia, ☎ 089/872239). **Positano:** Autoservizi **Falvio Gioia** (✉ Via Cristoforo Colombo 91, ☎ 089/811895); **Rent-A-Car** (✉ Viale Pasitea, ☎ 089/811777); **Positano Car & Limo Service** (✉ Via Cristoforo Colombo 2, ☎ 089/875541), car and driver rentals, tours, excursions. **Ravello:** (✉ Piazza Duomo, ☎ 089/857917). **Salerno:**

(✉ Piazza XXIV, Maggio, ☎ 089/229171). **Sorrento:** (✉ Sorrento, Piazza Lauro, ☎ 089/878–2204; ✉ S. Agnello, ☎ 089/878–1428); **Sorrento Rent a Scooter** (✉ C. Italia 210–A, ☎ 089/878–1386).

Contacts and Resources

Car Rentals
Avis Car Rentals (☎ 064–1999, emergency 167–801180), at all major airports and towns; allows one-way rentals, including drop off in other countries.

AutoNet International Car rentals for Italy: drop-off/pickup in other countries is available (☎ 888/880–8999).

AutoEurope Car rentals: for AAA-like service (✉ 39 Commercial St., Box 7006, Portland, ME 04112, ☎ 800/223–5555, 207/842–2000, FAX 800/235–6321, 207/842–2222).

Currency Exchange
ATM machines provide the quickest currency exchange, with bank commission. Hotels have the worst exchange rate but are convenient for small change and last-minute needs.

Amalfi: Banca d'America e d'Italia (✉ Via della Rep. Marinare, 15, ☎ 089/873050); **Banco di Napoli** with cash machine (✉ Piazza Duomo, ☎ 089/871005).

Positano: Banca d'America e d'Italia (✉ Via Cristoforo Colombo 69, ☎ 089/875012, FAX 089/811045); **Ufficio Cambi** (✉ Piazza dei Mulini, ☎ 089/875864).

Ravello: Bank Banca Popolare di Salerno (✉ Via Roma, 15, ☎ 089/857872); **Bank Ufficio Cambi Spot** (✉ Via Roma, 38, ☎ 089/858086).

Salerno: Banks line Corso Vittorio Emanuele; the Salerno train station information window is open 9–7.

Sorrento: Ufficio Cambi ✉ Via Luigi de Maio, 21), open daily 9 AM–10:30 PM. The **Sorrento Post Office** (✉ C. Italia 210, ☎ 081/878–1636) has better rates than town banks.

Emergencies
Countrywide Emergency Numbers: Emergency Police Help (☎ 113); **Police** (☎ 112); **Fire Department** (☎ 115); **Road Assistance** (Italian Auto Club) (☎ 116); **International Inquiries** (☎ 176); **Phone Directory Assistance** (☎ 12); **Medical Emergencies** (☎ 118).

Amalfi: Police: (☎ 089/871633). **Ambulance:** (✉ Piazza Municipio, ☎ 089/872785).

Positano: Police: (✉ Loc. Chiesa Nuova, ☎ 089/875011). **Ambulance:** (✉ Via G. Marconi, ☎ 089/811444).

Ravello: Police: (✉ Via della Marra 4, ☎ 089/857498). **Ambulance:** (✉ Piazza Fontana 9, ☎ 089/867248).

Sorrento: Police: (☎ 081/081/807–3111 or 081/878–1010). **Ambulance:** (☎ 081/081/533–1111).

Hospitals: Infermiere Cappiello Mario, Sorrento (✉ Via Montariello 11, ☎ 081/878–1439); **Ospedale Hospital, S. Agnello** (☎ 081/533–1111), **Vico Equense** (☎ 081/801–9111).

Guided Tours
Amalfi: Divina Costiera (✉ Piazza F. Gioia 2, ☎ 089/872467).

Positano: F.illi Grassi (✉ Spiaggia Fornillo, ☎ 089/811620 or 089/811403). Private boat tours are available to the Emerald Grotto, Capri, and isolated beaches).

Ravello: Wagner Tours (✉ Via Trinita 4, ☎ 089/858416, FAX 089/858914).

Sorrento: GoldenTours International (✉ Corso Italia, 38–E, ☎ 089/878–1042, FAX 089/807–1745); excursions to Capri, Ischia, Positano, Amalfi, Ravello, Pompeii, Herculaneum, Paestum, Naples, Cassino, Rome; car rentals, limo services; package tours; train, boat, and air tickets.

Pharmacies
Amalfi: (✉ Piazza Duomo, 42, ☎ 089/871045).

Positano: (✉ Viale Pasitea 22, ☎ 089/875863).

Ravello: (✉ Piazza Duomo, 5, ☎ 089/857189).

Salerno: (✉ Via A. Mazza, ☎ 089/253965).

Sorrento: (✉ Via L. De Maio, ☎ 089/878–1349; ✉ Corso Italia, ☎ 089/878–1174).

Travel Agencies
Amalfi: Divina Costiera (✉ Piazza F. Gioia, 2–3, ☎ 089/872467 or 089/871254), also rents scooter (65,000 lire per day); **Golden Tours** (✉ Corso Reppubliche Marinare 23, ☎ 089/871301); boat tours to Grotta dello Smeraldo (Emerald Cave) from Amalfi docks.

Ravello: Ravello International (✉ Via Roma, 38, ☎ FAX 089/858086).

Positano: Positour (✉ Via Cristoforo Colombo 69, ☎ 089/875012, FAX 089/811045); **Faito Travel** (✉ Via G. Marconi 344, ☎ 089/811802); **Pasitea Travel** (✉ Via Chiesa Nuova 2, ☎ 089/811939).

Salerno: Arechi Viaggi (✉ Via Sichelmanno 17, ☎ 089/759353, FAX 089/759341).

Sorrento: The American Express representative is **Acampora Travel** (✉ Piazza Lauro 12, ☎ 081/807–2363); **Meeting Point** (✉ Piazza Lauro).

Visitor Information
Amalfi: Azienda Autonoma Soggiorno e Turismo (✉ Corso Reppubliche Marinare 29, ☎ 089/871107, FAX 089/872619), open Monday–Saturday 8–2; **Centro di Cultura e Storia Amalfitana** (✉ Via Annunziatella, ☎ 089/873143), open Tuesday, Thursday, and Saturday 9–1; Monday, Wednesday, and Friday 4 PM–8 PM.

Positano: Azienda Autonoma Soggiorno e Turismo (✉ Via del Saracino 4, ☎ 089/875067, FAX 089/875760).

Ravello: Azienda Autonoma Soggiorno e Turismo (✉ Piazza Duomo 1, ☎ 089/857096, FAX 089/877977), open Monday–Saturday 8–8 (summer); 8–7 (winter).

Salerno: EPT Office (✉ P. Vittorio Veneto 1, ☎ 089/231432), open Monday–Saturday 9–2 and 3–8.

Sorrento. Sorrento/Sant'Agnello Tourist Board (✉ Via Luigi De Maio 35, ☎ 089/807–4033, FAX 089/877–3397), open Monday–Saturday, summer 8–8, winter 8:30–2:30 and 3:20–6:30.

Surrentum: Periodico Di Informazione Turistica (11,000 lire a copy) from Tipolotografia (☎ 089/878–5988, FAX 089/807–5973).

WORDS AND PHRASES

English	Italian	Pronunciation
Basics		
Yes/no	Sí/No	see/no
Please	Per favore	pear fa-**vo**-ray
Yes, please	Sí grazie	see **grah**-tsee-ay
Thank you	Grazie	**grah**-tsee-ay
You're welcome	Prego	**pray**-go
Excuse me, sorry	Scusi	**skoo**-zee
Sorry!	Mi dispiace!	mee dis-spee-**ah**-chay
Good morning/ afternoon	Buon giorno	bwohn **jor**-no
Good evening	Buona sera	**bwoh**-na **say**-ra
Good bye	Arrivederci	a-ree-vah-**dare**-chee
Mr. (Sir)	Signore	see-**nyo**-ray
Mrs. (Ma'am)	Signora	see-**nyo**-ra
Miss	Signorina	see-nyo-**ree**-na
Pleased to meet you	Piacere	pee-ah-**chair**-ray
How are you?	Come sta?	**ko**-may **stah**
Very well, thanks	Bene, grazie	**ben**-ay **grah**-tsee-ay
And you?	E lei?	ay **lay**-ee
Hello (phone)	Pronto?	**proan**-to
Numbers		
one	uno	**oo**-no
two	due	**doo**-ay
three	tre	tray
four	quattro	**kwah**-tro
five	cinque	**cheen**-kway
six	sei	say
seven	sette	**set**-ay
eight	otto	**oh**-to
nine	nove	**no**-vay
ten	dieci	dee-**eh**-chee
eleven	undici	**oon**-dee-chee
twelve	dodici	**doe**-dee-chee
thirteen	tredici	**tray**-dee-chee
fourteen	quattordici	kwa-**tore**-dee-chee
fifteen	quindici	**kwin**-dee-chee
sixteen	sedici	**say**-dee-chee
seventeen	diciassette	dee-cha-**set**-ay
eighteen	diciotto	dee-**cho**-to

nineteen	diciannove	dee-cha-**no**-vay
twenty	venti	**vain**-tee
twenty-one	ventuno	vain-**too**-no
twenty-two	ventidue	vayn-tee-**doo**-ay
thirty	trenta	**train**-ta
forty	quaranta	kwa-**rahn**-ta
fifty	cinquanta	cheen-**kwahn**-ta
sixty	sessanta	seh-**sahn**-ta
seventy	settanta	seh-**tahn**-ta
eighty	ottanta	o-**tahn**-ta
ninety	novanta	no-**vahn**-ta
one hundred	cento	**chen**-to
ten thousand	diecimila	dee-eh-chee-**mee**-la
one hundred thousand	centomila	chen-to-**mee**-la

Useful Phrases

Do you speak English?	Parla inglese?	**par**-la een-**glay**-zay
I don't speak Italian	Non parlo italiano	non **par**-lo ee-tal-**yah**-no
I don't understand	Non capisco	non ka-**peess**-ko
Can you please repeat?	Può ripetere?	pwo ree-**pet**-ay-ray
Slowly!	Lentamente!	**len**-ta-men-tay
I don't know	Non lo so	noan lo **so**
I'm American/	Sono americano(a)	**so**-no a-may-ree-**kah**-no(a)
	Sono inglese	**so**-no een-**glay**-zay
What's your name?	Come si chiama?	**ko**-may see kee-**ah**-ma
My name is . . .	Mi chiamo . . .	mee kee-**ah**-mo
What time is it?	Che ore sono?	kay **o**-ray **so**-no
How?	Come?	**ko**-may
When?	Quando?	**kwan**-doe
Yesterday/today/ tomorrow	Ieri/oggi/domani	**yer**-ee/**o**-jee/do-**mah**-nee
This morning/ afternoon	Stamattina/Oggi pomeriggio	sta-ma-**tee**-na/**o**-jee po-mer-**ee**-jo
Tonight	Stasera	sta-**ser**-a
What?	Che cosa?	kay **ko**-za
What is it?	Che cos'è?	kay ko-**zay**
Why?	Perché?	pear-**kay**
Who?	Chi?	kee
Where is . . .	Dov'è . . .	doe-**veh**
the bus stop?	la fermata dell'autobus?	la fer-**mah**-ta del ow-toe-**booss**
the train station?	la stazione?	la sta-tsee-**oh**-nay
the subway station?	la metropolitana?	la may-tro-po-lee-**tah**-na
the terminal?	il terminal?	eel ter-mee-**nahl**
the post office?	l'ufficio postale?	loo-**fee**-cho po-**stah**-lay

Italian Vocabulary

the bank?	la banca?	la **bahn**-ka
the . . . hotel?	l'hotel . . .?	lo-**tel**
the store?	il negozio?	ell nay-**go**-tsee-o
the cashier?	la cassa?	la **kah**-sa
the . . . museum?	il museo . . .?	eel moo-**zay**-o
the hospital?	l'ospedale?	lo-spay-**dah**-lay
the first aid station?	il pronto soccorso?	eel **pron**-to so-**kor**-so
the elevator?	l'ascensore?	la-shen-**so**-ray
a telephone?	un telefono?	oon tay-**lay**-fo-no
Where are the restrooms?	Dov'è il bagno?	doe-**vay** eel **bahn**-yo
Here/there	Qui/là	kwee/la
Left/right	A sinistra/a destra	a see-**neess**-tra/a **des**-tra
Straight ahead	Avanti dritto	a-**vahn**-tee **dree**-to
Is it near/far?	È vicino/lontano?	ay vee-**chee**-no/lon-**tah**-no
I'd like . . .	Vorrei . . .	vo-**ray**
a room	una camera	**oo**-na **kah**-may-ra
the key	la chiave	la kee-**ah**-vay
a newspaper	un giornale	oon jor-**nah**-lay
a stamp	un francobollo	oon frahn-ko-**bo**-lo
I'd like to buy . . .	Vorrei comprare . . .	vo-**ray** kom-**prah**-ray
a cigar	un sigaro	oon see-**gah**-ro
cigarettes	delle sigarette	day-lay see-ga-**ret**-ay
some matches	dei fiammiferi	day-ee fee-ah-**mee**-fer-ee
some soap	una saponetta	**oo**-na sa-po-**net**-a
a city plan	una pianta della città	**oo**-na **pyahn**-ta day-la chee-**tah**
a road map of . . .	una carta stradaledi . . .	**oo**-na **cart**-a stra-**dah**-lay dee
a country map	una carta geografica	**oo**-na **cart**-a jay-o-**grah**-fee-ka
a magazine	una rivista	**oo**-na ree-**veess**-ta
envelopes	delle buste	**day**-lay **booss**-tay
writing paper	della carta da lettere	**day**-la **cart**-a da **let**-air-ay
a postcard	una cartolina	**oo**-na car-toe-**lee**-na
a guidebook	una guida turistica	**oo**-na **gwee**-da too-**reess**-tee-ka
How much is it?	Quanto costa?	**kwahn**-toe **coast**-a
It's expensive/cheap	È caro/economico	ay **car**-o/ay-ko-**no**-mee-ko
A little/a lot	Poco/tanto	**po**-ko/**tahn**-to
More/less	Più/meno	pee-**oo**/**may**-no
Enough/too (much)	Abbastanza/troppo	a-bas-**tahn**-sa/**tro**-po
I am sick	Sto male	sto **mah**-lay
Please call a doctor	Chiami un dottore	kee-**ah**-mee oon doe-**toe**-ray

Help!	Aiuto!	a-**yoo**-toe
Stop!	Alt!	ahlt
Fire!	Al fuoco!	ahl **fwo**-ko
Caution/Look out!	Attenzione!	a-ten-**syon**-ay

Dining Out

A bottle of . . .	Una bottiglia di . . .	**oo**-na bo-**tee**-lee-ah dee
A cup of . . .	Una tazza di . . .	**oo**-na **tah**-tsa dee
A glass of . . .	Un bicchiere di . . .	oon bee-key-**air**-ay dee
Bill/check	Il conto	eel **cone**-toe
Bread	Il pane	eel **pah**-nay
Breakfast	La prima colazione	la **pree**-ma ko-la-**tsee**-oh-nay
Cocktail/aperitif	L'aperitivo	la-pay-ree-**tee**-vo
Dinner	La cena	la **chen**-a
Fixed-price menu	Menù a prezzo fisso	may-**noo** a **pret**-so **fee**-so
Fork	La forchetta	la for-**ket**-a
I am diabetic	Ho il diabete	o eel dee-a-**bay**-tay
I am vegetarian	Sono vegetariano/a	**so**-no vay-jay-ta-ree-**ah**-no/a
I'd like . . .	Vorrei . . .	vo-**ray**
I'd like to order	Vorrei ordinare	vo-**ray** or-dee-**nah**-ray
Is service included?	Il servizio è incluso?	eel ser-**vee**-tzee-o ay een-**kloo**-zo
It's good/bad	È buono/cattivo	ay **bwo**-no/ka-tee-vo
It's hot/cold	È caldo/freddo	ay **kahl**-doe/**fred**-o
Knife	Il coltello	eel kol-**tel**-o
Lunch	Il pranzo	eel **prahnt**-so
Menu	Il menù	eel may-**noo**
Napkin	Il tovagliolo	eel toe-va-lee-**oh**-lo
Please give me . . .	Mi dia . . .	mee **dee**-a
Salt	Il sale	eel **sah**-lay
Spoon	Il cucchiaio	eel koo-kee-**ah**-yo
Sugar	Lo zucchero	lo **tsoo**-ker-o
Waiter/Waitress	Cameriere/cameriera	ka-mare-**yer**-ay/ka-mare-**yer**-a
Wine list	La lista dei vini	la **lee**-sta **day**-ee **vee**-nee

INDEX

NOTES

NOTES

NOTES

NOTES

NOTES

L@@king
© FOR A
great place to go?

We know just the place. In fact, it attracts more than 125,000 visitors a day, making it one of the world's most popular travel destinations. It's previewtravel.com, the Web's comprehensive resource for travelers. It gives you access to over 500 airlines, 25,000 hotels, rental cars, cruises, vacation packages and support from travel experts 24 hours a day. Plus great information from Fodor's travel guides and travelers just like you. All of which makes previewtravel.com quite a find.

Preview Travel has everything you need to plan & book your next trip.

air, car & hotel reservations

vacation packages & cruises

destination planning & travel tips

24-hour customer service

previewtravel.com

preview travel™

aol keyword: previewtravel
www.previewtravel.com